Sociology of the Body

A READER

ONE WEEK LOAN

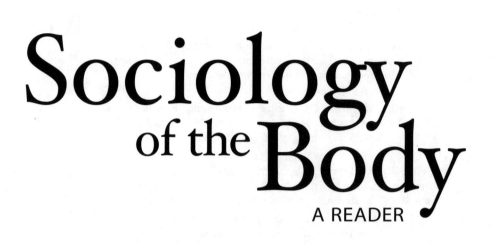

Sociology of the Body

of the

A READER

Edited by Claudia Malacrida & Jacqueline Low

OXFORD

UNIVERSITY PRESS

OXFORD
UNIVERSITY PRESS

70 Wynford Drive, Don Mills, Ontario M3C 1J9
www.oup.com/ca

Oxford University Press is a department of the University of Oxford.
It furthers the University's objective of excellence in research, scholarship,
and education by publishing worldwide in

Oxford New York

Auckland Cape Town Dar es Salaam Hong Kong Karachi
Kuala Lumpur Madrid Melbourne Mexico City Nairobi
New Delhi Shanghai Taipei Toronto

With offices in

Argentina Austria Brazil Chile Czech Republic France Greece
Guatemala Hungary Italy Japan Poland Portugal Singapore
South Korea Switzerland Thailand Turkey Ukraine Vietnam

Oxford is a trade mark of Oxford University Press
in the UK and in certain other countries

Published in Canada
by Oxford University Press

Copyright © Oxford University Press Canada 2008

The moral rights of the author have been asserted

Database right Oxford University Press (maker)

First published 2008

Library and Archives Canada Cataloguing in Publication Data

Sociology of the body : a reader / Claudia Malacrida, Jacqueline Low.

Includes index.
ISBN 978-0-19-542548-2

1. Body, Human—Social aspects. I. Malacrida, Claudia, 1953– II. Low, Jacqueline, 1964–

HM636.S62 2008   306.4   C2007-907453-7

Cover image: Juan Gris/The Bridgeman Art Library/Getty Images

1 2 3 4 - 11 10 09 08

This book is printed on permanent (acid-free) paper ∞.
Printed in Canada

Contents

Introduction ix
Acknowledgements xvi
Credits xvii

Part I Tracing the Body in Classical and Contemporary Theory 1

1 The Body in Sociology 7
   Chris Shilling
2 Bringing Bodies Back In: A Decade Review 14
   Arthur W. Frank
3 Foucault, Femininity, and the Modernization of Patriarchal Power 21
   Sandra Lee Bartky

Part II Bodies in Historical Context 28

4 From *The Civilizing Process: The History of Manners* 31
   Norbert Elias
5 Body: Tomb, Temple, Machine, and Self 38
   Anthony Synnott
6 The Hottentot and the Prostitute: Toward an Iconography of Female Sexuality 45
   Sander L. Gilman

Part III Presenting the Body 51

7 'Introduction' from *The Presentation of Self in Everyday Life* 53
   Erving Goffman
8 Big Handsome Men, Bears, and Others: Virtual Constructions of 'Fat Male Embodiment' 57
   Lee F. Monaghan
9 Nurturing and Negligence: Working on Others' Bodies in Fiji 65
   Anne E. Becker

Part IV Medical Social Control of the Body 73

10 Discipline and Dehumanization in a Total Institution: Institutional Survivors' Descriptions of Time-out Rooms 76
   Claudia Malacrida
11 The Anthropological Born Criminal 84
   Nicole Hahn Rafter
12 The Destruction of 'Lives Not Worth Living' 92
   Robert N. Proctor

Part V   Gendered Bodies   100

13 From $acred to Disembodied Motherhood: Breast-feeding with the Experts and
the State   103
Linda M. Blum

14 Anorexia Nervosa: Psychopathology as the Crystallization of Culture   110
Susan Bordo

15 Men's Bodies   116
Raewyn Connell

Part VI   Transgressive Bodies   124

16 'Introduction' from *One of Us: Conjoined Twins and the Future of Normal*   127
Alice Domurat Dreger

17 Hermaphrodites with Attitude: Mapping the Emergence of Intersex Political
Activism   133
Cheryl Chase

18 Telling Body Transgendering Stories   141
Richard Ekins and Dave King

Part VII   Risky Bodies   148

19 The Risk of Resistance: Perspectives on the Mass Childhood Immunization
Program   151
Anne Rogers and David Pilgrim

20 The Medical Model of the Body as a Site of Risk: A Case Study of
Childbirth   157
Karen Lane

21 Contemporary Hospice Care: The Sequestration of the Unbounded Body and
'Dirty Dying'   165
Julia Lawton

Part VIII   Reproductive Bodies   173

22 The Egg and the Sperm: How Science Has Constructed a Romance Based on
Stereotypical Male–Female Roles   176
Emily Martin

23 'Fetal Rights': A New Assault on Feminism   183
Katha Pollitt

24 Bodies Out of Time: Women's Reproductive Firsts   189
Elizabeth Graham and Jacqueline Low

Part IX   Children's Bodies   195

25 Children's Lived Bodies in Everyday Life   198
Berry Mayall

26 Becoming a Gendered Body: Practices of Preschools   205
Karin A. Martin

27 The Gaze of the Psychologist   212
Nikolas Rose

Part X   Working Bodies   218

28   The Contented Worker   221
     Nikolas Rose

29   Scrubbing in Maine   227
     Barbara Ehrenreich

30   Exotic Dancing and the Negotiation of Identity: The Multiple Uses of Body
     Technologies   234
     Jennifer K. Wesely

Part XI   Disabled Bodies   239

31   Somewhere a Mockingbird   242
     Deborah Kent

32   Coming to Terms: Masculinity and Physical Disability   246
     Thomas J. Gerschick and Adam S. Miller

33   (In)visibility: Accounts of Embodiment of Women with Physical Disabilities and
     Differences   252
     Hilde Zitzelsberger

Part XII   Sporting Bodies   257

34   'Holding Back': Negotiating a Glass Ceiling on Women's Muscular Strength   260
     Shari L. Dworkin

35   Looking into Masculinity: Sport, Media, and the Construction of the Male Body
     Beautiful   267
     Gay Mason

36   Sport, Genetics, and the 'Natural Athlete': The Resurgence of Racial Science   274
     Brett St Louis

Part XIII   Racialized Bodies   281

37   Feared and Revered: Media Representations of Racialized and Gendered Bodies—A
     Case Study   284
     Sarah Neal

38   The Future of Reproductive Choice for Poor Women and Women of Colour   290
     Dorothy E. Roberts

39   Gendered Racial Violence and Spatialized Justice: The Murder of Pamela George
     298
     Sherene H. Razack

Part XIV   Consumer Bodies   305

40   'Modern Primitivism': Non-mainstream Body Modification and Racialized
     Representation   308
     Christian Klesse

41   Women and Their Hair: Seeking Power through Resistance and Accommodation
     314
     Rose Weitz

42   'A Dubious Equality': Men, Women, and Cosmetic Surgery   321
     Kathy Davis

Part XV   Aging Bodies   326

43 Meno-boomers and Moral Guardians: An Exploration of the Cultural Construction
    of Menopause   329
    Joy Webster Barbre
44 Forever Functional: Sexual Fitness and the Aging Male Body   334
    Barbara L. Marshall and Stephen Katz
45 Aging, Alzheimer's, and the Uncivilized Body   342
    Chris Gilleard and Paul Higgs

Part XVI   Postmodern Bodies   350

46 A Cyborg Manifesto: Science, Technology, and Socialist-Feminism in the Late
    Twentieth Century   354
    Donna J. Haraway
47 Cyberpunk, Biomedicine, and the High-tech Body   360
    Victoria L. Pitts
48 The Sacrificial Body of Orlan   369
    Julie Clarke

Index   376

Introduction

Claudia Malacrida and Jacqueline Low

The status of the body within sociological study is a contentious issue. Some writers claim that the field has traditionally taken a **disembodied** approach to the study of the body, but that the last few decades have seen a sociological refocusing, to the extent that today one can clearly recognize a corpus of literature, research, and teaching that specifically addresses bodily issues (Frank, 1990; Shilling, 1993). At the same time, as Chris Shilling notes, sociological interest in the body has always been, at least peripherally, a part of the discipline. This book offers a collection of readings on various perspectives of the body, demonstrating how this sub-discipline has developed throughout sociological research and debate. We begin with an outline of classical approaches to a sociological understanding of the body, examining theorists such as Karl Marx and Friedrich Engels, Mary Douglas, Erving Goffman, and Norbert Elias, and introduce the recent resurgence of the body in contemporary sociology. As you read this text, you will encounter all of the authors discussed here. Finally, we offer an overview of the structure of this book, introducing the topics covered and the selected readings.

Foundational Theorists of the Body

Karl Marx (1818–1883) and Friedrich Engels (1820–1895), adopted as classical fathers of sociology but in fact political economists, are best known for their analysis of capitalist society in the late nineteenth century and as authors of the *Communist Manifesto* (1888). However, they were also among the first to provide an explicitly social analysis of the body in their work. For instance, in *The Condition of the Working Class in England*, first published in 1845, Engels provides detailed analysis of the conditions under which men and women worked at the beginning of the era of factory production, which led to the **Industrial Revolution**. Engels shows through exhaustive and detailed descriptions how the bodies of workers were quite literally shaped by this new mode of production. He writes: 'There are countless persons who have, from perpetually filing at the lathe, crooked backs and one leg crooked, "hind-leg" as they call it, so that the two legs have the form of a K' (2001: 297). While analysis of the body is less overt in Marx's writings, in *Capital*, his major work on the theory of capitalist societies, he does articulate how workers become cogs in the machinery of capitalist society. They are thus subject to the 'crippling of the body and mind' and are, in the process, literally 'worked to death' (Marx, 1967: 435, 343).

Norbert Elias (1897–1990) was a sociologist whose major contribution to the discipline is his theory of **social figuration**. For Elias (1978) individuals are bound up in series of 'figures' consisting of their relations with each other as well as with the structures and processes that make up the social contexts in which they live. His major two-volume work, *The Civilizing Process,* remained relatively unknown until it was translated and reissued at the end of the 1960s. In this work Elias analyzes etiquette books from the Medieval period to the Renaissance to show how changes in the rules surrounding body conduct, where we increasingly control bodily desires and processes, are inextricably connected to large scale changes in state structure. He argues that such changes resulted in the emergence of **self-reflexivity**, where people began to see themselves as distinct individuals rather than existing only as part of a whole. Elias also found that the civilizing process, a process concomitant with social figuration, led to the internalization of social control, a situation where people conform less to external coercion and more to internal forces such as shame or embarrassment.

Mary Douglas (1921–2007) was an eminent cultural anthropologist famous for her works on culture and symbolism. Her major contributions to the sociology of the body concern her writings on the culture of risk and the social body. In *Risk and Blame* Douglas (1992) writes of the **individualization of risk** in contemporary culture. According to Douglas, people become solely responsible for ensuring their own health and safety, and the body is conceived of as a site of risk. In her seminal text, *Purity and Danger*, first published in 1966, Douglas (2005) argues that the structure of society is quite literally reflected in the physiological arrangement of the body. To illustrate, she describes how the Hindu caste system mirrors the structure of the human body: the members of higher castes, such as administrators, are at the top of society and the part of the body concerned with intellect, the head, is likewise at the top of the body. In the same way, members of the lower castes, such as the untouchables (whose work entails dealing with waste), are reflected in bodily functions positioned in the lower portion of the body. Most often adopted by sociologists working in the area of the body is Douglas's analysis of how we construct what is clean and what is dirty, and therefore what is safe and what is risky, which she explicated through her concept of 'dirt as **matter out of place**' (Douglas, 2005: 45).

Contemporary Theory and the Body

One of the most significant scholars of early contemporary sociology was Erving Goffman (1922–1982). He developed the **dramaturgical** approach to the analysis of face-to-face interaction or what he called the 'interaction order' (1983: 1). Dramaturgy is part of the symbolic interactionist perspective and is a theoretical orientation that makes use of terminology from the theatre in conceptualizing social life as a performance, where face-to-face interaction takes place on both the front and back stages of society, and where the body plays an integral part in our performances. For Goffman the body is a '**sign vehicle**' through which social information about ourselves is both intentionally and unintentionally conveyed to others (1959: 1). Sociological theory has been open to the charge of being disembodied; however, the same cannot be said of Goffman's work, which, in contrast, is replete with reference to the **corporeal**. In his 1982 Presidential Address to the American Sociological Association Goffman argued that 'what dramaturgy is supposed to bring is flesh to bones, confronting the reader's image of a person with the lively impression created when the words come from a body not a page' (1959: 1).

In the last few decades, several threads have converged to produce a reinvigorated and theoretically sophisticated interest in the social body. From the 1960s through to the early 1980s, second wave feminism has taken the foundational position that women's bodies have been the battlegrounds upon which struggles for equality, freedom, and expression have been based (Weitz, 2003). Tackling issues as broad as abortion, the representation of women in art and the media, women's paid and unpaid labour, eating disorders, cosmetic surgery, **medicalization** and aging, second wave feminists consistently held that the female body is a public and political entity. This was a new development in the study of the social body: no longer was the focus on how bodies feel, appear, or operate within social contexts, but feminism created a comprehensive theory of power based on relations of embodiment. **Embodiment** in feminist theories thus refers specifically to the political and social relations that are acted upon and expressed within individual bodies (Witz, 2000). While in feminist studies embodiment has focused specifically on masculinity and femininity, gendered power relations, and the political consequences of bodily gendering, other social movements and intellectual groups such as Post-Colonial movements; Gay, Lesbian, Bisexual, Transsexual, Transgendered, Intersexed, and Queer movements (GLBTTIQ); and Disability movements have subsequently used the tools of feminism to unpack their own theories of embodiment (McRuer, 2006).

Poststructuralism has also contributed to current sociological thinking about the body, particularly as elucidated in the writings of Michel Foucault (1926–1984) and Pierre Bourdieu (1930–2002). In his earlier works, Foucault conceptualized the notion of **biopower**, arguing that the way that bodies are manipulated offers us a means of reading all power relations in a given society (1994, 1995). In modernity, the body is not a site of invisibility punctuated by incidents of spectacular punishment, as in Medieval and Renaissance times, but it is instead a constantly watched and painstakingly corrected site of discipline, calculation, regulation, and knowledge application. With the rise of disciplines like medicine, psychiatry, demographics, and statistics, modern bodies are counted, measured, classified, and constructed as either normal or requiring correction. The knowledge gained through these disciplines gives rise to new social institutions that exercise social control through biopower. In schools, prisons, standing armies, and clinics, citizens are taught how to discipline their bodies through proper hygiene, posture, diet, exercise, sleep, and sexual behaviour. These **docile bodies** are taught to comply with professional knowledge to vigilantly and preventatively discipline themselves to new, morally laden orders of 'normal' and 'abnormal'. In his later writings, Foucault broadened his theory of biopower into an analysis of governmentality, or the ways that the state intervenes and benefits from practices and discourses that impinge on the bodies of its citizens (1991).

Pierre Bourdieu sought to make a connection between individuals' embodied qualities and their positions in social space. Drawing on the work of Max Weber, Marx, Elias, and Marcel Mauss, Bourdieu developed the concept of **habitus**, or a set of acquired dispositions, tastes, or habits that are informed by our social status and that, in turn, inform others about our social position or class (Crossley, 2005). Our *habitus* is evidenced through acquired tastes, preferences, and competencies, such as our use of language, our postures, and our sense of style, and these permit us to negotiate our social worlds (Bourdieu, 1990). Bourdieu also expanded upon the Marxian idea of **capital**, noting that economic capital is able to offer only a partial explanation for one's social position. For Bourdieu, non-economic forms of capital, which are much more difficult to quantify, help to explain why some people are able to move up the social ladder despite lacking economic capital. In addition to traditional economic capital, Bourdieu offers us **social capital**, or the networks and social resources that an individual can lay claim to, **symbolic capital**, or the recognition and status we are accorded by others, and of most interest to sociologists of the body, **cultural capital**. Cultural capital refers to the ways that we are able to manipulate and present ourselves as a means of obtaining advantage. It includes one's knowledge about books, paintings, art, and cultural forms, but it is also available in embodied form, for example in the ways that a 'cultured' person speaks, dresses, carries himself or herself, and behaves. Thus, playing tennis well and having an upper-class British accent are forms of cultural capital that can leverage a person into an advantaged position. **Physical capital** is a subcomponent of cultural capital, and includes such things as the 'right' skin colour, body shape, age, and physical competencies such as athleticism or grace. For both Foucault and Bourdieu, then, the structure of a society—in Foucault's case, its power relations, in Bourdieu's its class relations—is literally inscribed upon and reflected by individual bodies.

A final thread to discuss is the recent work of social theorists who explicitly have engaged in developing sociology of the body over the past two decades. This includes such social theorists as Arthur W. Frank in Canada and Mike Featherstone and Bryan S. Turner in Great Britain. While these writers are not necessarily working outside of any of the above traditions, what they have done is codify and institutionalize the sociology of the body as a distinct and legitimate sociological sub-discipline through publishing numerous major works under that rubric and through establishing, in 1995, the pre-eminent journal *Body & Society*. In an earlier book (1984), Turner initiated a formal reintroduction of the body as a sociological interest. Recognizing the influence of neo-Marxists (and to a lesser extent feminists), with their focus on the body as a site of production and regulation, and poststructuralist ideas that the body is produced through multiple centres of power, Turner sought to synthesize these strains. Societies, in order to exist and thrive, must engage in four social imperatives: the regulation of populations and reproduction, the control of bodies in social spaces, the exercise of restraint of its citizens, and the organization of bodily representation. These needs, in turn, give rise to every imaginable institution within a society—schools, museums, media, medical and penal institutions, legal and regulatory practices, transportation systems, and architectural norms, etc. In other words, Turner claims that the body is more than just a reflection of social class, relations of power, or gender relations, but is instead a foundational building block of all societies. He adds that, under high capitalism, the body is more than simply productive in the Marxist sense, but that it is also a vehicle of consumption and expression, both areas worthy of sociological attention and a focus that Mike Featherstone has explored in terms of **body modifications** such as piercing, tattooing, and other subcultural forms.

All of these theoretical approaches help us to understand bodies as more than flesh and bones, but as constructs worthy of sociological examination. These theories are explored and expanded upon in the selections you will encounter in this reader. Indeed, each selection has been chosen because it illustrates a theoretical as well as a substantive focus.

The Outline of this Book

Each part of this book covers a specific topic regarding the sociology of the body and includes an introduction and overview of the three selections. You will also note that specific theoretical terms relating to the sociology of the body are in bold print and accompanied by a brief definition of the term. The index will help you to locate each occurrence of these terms.

'Tracing the Body in Classical and Contemporary Theory' (Part I) introduces major insights and debates within the sociology of the body. Chris Shilling discusses what he calls the '**absent presence**' of the body in sociological theory; Arthur W. Frank begins to draw the boundaries of what was then the newly emergent sub-discipline of the sociology of the body; and Sandra Lee Bartky applies some of Foucault's insights to demonstrate the contribution of feminist and post-structural theory to the study of the body.

In 'Bodies in Historical Context' (Part II), the works of Norbert Elias, Anthony Synnott, and Sander L. Gilman show how understandings of the body and bodily conduct have changed over the course of history. Synnott analyzes conceptions of the body from ancient Greece to the twentieth century; Elias maps the history of the impact of large-scale social change on the regulation of bodily processes and desires; and Gilman shows how **sexism** and **racism** framed Victorian-era notions of African women's bodies.

A key area in the sociological study of the body pertains to how a person's social identity is a performance accomplished largely via the body. In 'Presenting the Body' (Part III) Erving Goffman focuses on how we present and manage social information about our identities through **bodily performance**; Lee F. Monaghan addresses the social meanings of male sexuality and body size in presentations of self; and Anne E. Becker compares Fijian and American norms about ideal bodies to illustrate the impact of these norms on individual bodily presentation and performance.

In 'Medical Social Control of the Body' (Part IV) Claudia Malacrida draws on the insights of Foucault and Goffman to show how bodies are rendered docile in total institutions; Nicole Hahn Rafter discusses how a theory of body types was used to explain criminality and supported the **eugenics** movement of the late nineteenth century; and Robert N. Proctor shows how being Jewish was **pathologized** as part of the Nazis' attempts to exterminate the Jews. Each of these articles examines the ways that certain types of bodies have been controlled and even removed from the social world.

The works of Linda Blum and Susan Bordo in 'Gendered Bodies' (Part V) demonstrate the significant contribution of feminist studies to the sociology of the body. Blum presents an analysis of how the meaning of women's breasts varies from social context to social context and along class and racial lines, while Bordo argues that eating disorders and obsession with rail thin models reflects a social pathology produced by **patriarchal** social arrangements. Drawing on feminist knowledge about the body as a site of power relations, theorists of **masculinities** have recently provided another slant on gendered bodies, illustrated by Raewyn Connell's 'Men's Bodies'. Connell demonstrates that the concept of **hegemonic masculinity** is essential to understanding men's bodies in contemporary society.

In 'Transgressive Bodies' (Part VI) Alice Domurat Dreger discusses the **stigma** imposed on children born with what she calls '**non-normant** bodies', or those bodies that defy conventional normalizing practices such as using makeup; Cheryl Chase focuses on **intersexuality** and its emerging advocacy movement; and Richard Ekins and Dave King analyze narratives of the body told by individuals who identify as **transgendered**.

Anne Rogers and David Pilgrim, Karen Lane, and Julia Lawton all discuss how the body has become a site of danger in contemporary society in Part VII, 'Risky Bodies'. Rogers and Pilgrim examine the conflicting pressures parents feel about immunization as a means of protecting their children's bodies from risk; Lane discusses how the medicalization of childbirth has legitimized invasive medical practices; and Lawton's work focuses on how a particular kind of risky body, the **messy dying body**, must be controlled.

Feminist conceptualizations of the body as a political battleground are a core focus of Part VIII, 'Reproductive Bodies'. Emily Martin concentrates on how scientific representations of women's bodies have fostered gendered stereotypes and hierarchies, while Katha Pollitt draws on Marxist-feminism to argue that fetal rights discourse frames women as simple producers rather than human beings in their own rights. Finally, Elizabeth Graham and Jacqueline Low expand upon Mary Douglas's notion of dirt as matter out of place to argue that women's reproduction is regulated by social norms.

In Part IX, 'Children's Bodies', Berry Mayall and Karin A. Martin both discuss practices of children's bodily socialization in the school. Comparing school **socialization** to maternal socialization, Mayall notes that schools are neither healthy nor forgiving; children must learn to regiment themselves to the requirements of others. Martin takes a specifically gendered focus, showing us how very young children's bodies are encouraged to develop along traditional gender lines. Taking a strong Foucauldian approach, Nikolas Rose shows us how knowledge and classification are used to construct new categories of 'normal' children's development.

Rose develops a similar argument about 'Working Bodies' in Part X, drawing on Foucault's notion of biopower. Rose shows us that, as the disciplines of psychology and management studies developed knowledge about workers, employers became capable of controlling workers' bodies not through harsh punishments, but through a seemingly benevolent engagement with workers' minds. Barbara Ehrenreich and Jennifer K. Wesely both show us gendered aspects of labour. They also provide evidence that the **rationalization** of workers' bodies (in the case of house cleaners) and emotional work (in the case of sex workers) alienate workers from their bodies.

Disabled bodies are a recent addition to the sociological understanding of the body. Stemming from a **social model of disability**, which argues that social barriers, rather than bodily 'problems' are the greatest challenges to living with a disability, all three of the papers in

Part XI see the different body as a social construction and a site of regulation and marginalization. While Deborah Kent's article is autobiographical, it touches upon issues of reproductive rights, eugenics, and the 'natural' assumption that difference is undesirable. Both Thomas J. Gerschick and Adam S. Miller and Hilde Zitzelsberger provide insights on the multiplicative effects of **disability** and gender.

In Part XII, 'Sporting Bodies', we are shown how social relations such as gender and race are constructed through the body. Shari L. Dworkin's article discusses the ways that women in bodybuilding and fitness limit their strength so as to fit within gendered feminine norms, while Gay Mason evidences the pain and effort required to achieve 'natural' masculinity. Brett St Louis demonstrates how faulty scientific knowledge has been used to reinforce and **reify** existing racist assumptions about athletic bodies.

'Racialized Bodies' are the focus of Part XIII as well. Sarah Neal describes how media representations of black male bodies are used to underline common **racist** stereotypes about black male intelligence, sexuality, and dangerousness; Dorothy E. Roberts argues that American social programs operate as a covert form of eugenics while ignoring the social inequalities that structure the lives of women of colour; and Sherene H. Razack describes the case of Pamela George, whose non-white body was treated by the Canadian criminal justice system as 'naturally' **hypersexual**, immoral, and undeserving.

In Part XIV, 'Consumer Bodies', Christian Klesse draws on the work of Mike Featherstone, who argues that bodies are spaces of consumerism, play, and the transmission of identity (Featherstone, 2000). Klesse notes that Modern Primitivism, in which tattooing, binding, piercing, and burning the body are an expression of identity, is also a set of bodily practices that exploits racial, gendered, and colonial power imbalances for its pleasure. Taking an explicitly feminist stance, both Rose Weitz and Kathy Davis argue that bodily consumerism, while occasionally empowering to men and women, also operates to maintain the gendered status quo in problematic ways.

The sociological interest in 'Aging Bodies' (Part XV) reflects the reality that, with medical advances, people are continuing to live longer lives, and with demographic trends attached to the baby boom, we are experiencing a 'graying' population. Medicalization is a core concept of this area, for example in the administration of Hormone Replacement Therapy, as described by Joy Webster Barbre, and in the use of Viagra, as Barbara L. Marshall and Stephen Katz note. In these cases, despite health risks attached to medicalization, men and women's gendered roles act to keep them compliant. Drawing on Elias's ideas about the civilized body, Chris Gilleard and Paul Higgs note that very old people are regarded as '**de-civilized**'. Additionally, medicalization plays a role in aging, in the form of the '**alzheimerization**' of aging bodies.

In the last section of this book, 'Postmodern Bodies', we engage with the most recent stream of sociological theorizing on bodies. Weaving together feminism, poststructuralism, and post-Marxism, Donna J. Haraway makes an argument that our bodies need no longer keep us in thrall to gendered power relations. Instead, the cyborg—a combination of computer technology, pharmacology, body parts, and machines—offers a way to transcend the gendered body. These arguments are echoed in the section by Victoria L. Pitts. Finally, Julie Clarke provides us with the example of performance artist Orlan, whose 'bodily play' ties together feminist ideas about the representation of women's bodies and poststructural ideas about knowledge as means of **disciplining bodies**, to offer her own critique of consumerism and beauty ideals.

Today, sociological interest in the body is clearly no longer situated in the margins, but it is instead a vibrant, fascinating, and growing aspect of the discipline. In the following pages, we hope to convey a sampling of the current state of sociological theory and research on the body, and to encourage you to develop an understanding of the body—indeed, of *your* body—as a construct that is social, cultural, and political.

References

Bourdieu, P. 1990. 'Structures, Habitus, Practices', in *The Logic of Practice*. Stanford, CA: Stanford University Press, 52–79.

Crossley, N. 2005. *Key Concepts in Critical Social Theory*. Thousand Oaks, CA: Sage.

Douglas, M. 1992. *Risk and Blame: Essays in Cultural Theory*. London: Routledge.

———. 2005. *Purity and Danger: An Analysis of Concepts of Pollution and Taboo*. Oxford: Routledge Classics.

Elias, N. 1978. *The Civilizing Process: The History of Manners, Volume I*. Oxford: Basil Blackwell.

———. 1982. *The Civilizing Process: Power and Civility, Volume II*. New York: Pantheon Books.

Engels, F. 2001. *Condition of the Working Class in England*. London: ElecBook, http://site.ebrary.com/lib/unblib/Doc?id=2001797&ppg=53.

Featherstone, M. 2000. *Body Modification (Theory, Culture and Society Series)*. London: Sage.

Foucault, M. 1991. 'Governmentality', in G. Burchell, C. Gordon, and P. Miller, eds, *The Foucault Effect: Studies in Governmentality: With Two Lectures by and an Interview with Michel Foucault*. Chicago: University of Chicago Press, 87–104.

———. 1994. *The Birth of the Clinic: An Archeology of Medical Perception*. New York: Vintage Books.

———. 1995. *Discipline and Punish: The Birth of the Prison*. New York: Vintage Books.

Frank, A.W. 1990. 'Bringing Bodies Back In: A Decade Review', *Theory, Culture & Society* 7: 131–62.

Goffman, E. 1959. *The Presentation of Self in Everyday Life*. New York: Doubleday Anchor Books.

———. 1983. 'The Interaction Order', *American Sociological Review* 48, 1: 1–17.

McRuer, R. 2006. *Crip Theory: Cultural Signs of Queerness and Disability*. New York and London: New York University Press.

Marx, K. 1867. *Capital Volume I*. Moscow: Progress Publishers.

———, and F. Engels. 1988. *Manifesto of the Communist Party*, ed. and trans. L.M. Findlay, Peterborough, ON: Broadview Press.

Shilling, C. 1993. *The Body and Social Theory (Theory, Culture and Society Series)*. London: Sage.

Turner, B. 1984. *The Body and Society*. New York: Basil Blackwell.

Weitz, R., ed. 2003. *The Politics of Women's Bodies: Sexuality, Appearance and Behavior*, 2nd edn. New York: Oxford University Press.

Witz, A. 2000. 'Whose Body Matters?: Feminist Sociology and the Corporeal Turn', 'Sociology and Feminism', *Body & Society* 6, 2: 1–24.

Acknowledgements

The authors would like to thank Tiffany Boulton at the University of Lethbridge for her assistance in putting the original selections in order for editing and Tamara Larter at the University of Lethbridge and Robert McCoy at the University of New Brunswick for their work on creating the index. We are grateful to Lisa Meschino at Oxford University Press for helping to vet this project in its early stages and to Dina Theleritis and Janna Green for their excellent editorial assistance. Thank you as well to the reviewers for their helpful comments.

Credits

Sabo and D.F. Gordon, eds, *Men's Health and Illness: Gender, Power, and the Body* (Thousand Oaks, CA: Sage, 1995), 183–204. Copyright © 1995 by Sage Publications. Inc. Reprinted by permission of Sage Publications Ltd.

Chris Gilleard and Paul Higgs, 'Aging, Alzheimer's, and the Uncivilized Body', in *Cultures of Ageing: Self, Citizen and the Body* (Harlow, UK: Prentice Hall, 2000), 168–92.

Sander L. Gilman, 'The Hottentot and the Prostitute: Toward an Iconography of Female Sexuality', in *Difference and Pathology: Stereotypes of Sexuality, Race, and Madness* (Ithaca, NY, and London: Cornell University Press, 1996), 76–108. Copyright © 1985 by Cornell University. Used by permission of the publisher, Cornell University Press.

Erving Goffman, 'Introduction' from *The Presentation of Self in Everyday Life* (New York: Doubleday Anchor Books, 1959), 1–16. Copyright © 1959 by Erving Goffman. Used by permission of Doubleday, a division of Random House, Inc., and by permission of Penguin Books Ltd.

Donna J. Haraway, 'A Cyborg Manifesto', in *Symians, Cyborgs, and Women: The Reinvention of Nature* (New York: Routledge, 1993 [1991]).

Deborah Kent, 'Somewhere a Mockingbird', in Erik Parens and Adrienne Asch, eds, *Prenatal Testing and Disability Rights* (Washington, D.C.: Georgetown University Press, 2000), 57–63. Copyright © 2000 by Georgetown University Press. Reprinted with permission. www.press.georgetown.edu.

Christian Klesse, '"Modern Primitivism": Non-mainstream Body Modification and Racialized Representation', *Body & Society* 5 (1999): 15–38. Copyright © 1999 Sage Publications Ltd. Reproduced by permission of the publisher.

Karen Lane, 'The Medical Model of the Body as a Site of Risk: A Case Study of Childbirth', in Jonathan Gabe, ed, *Medicine Health and Risk: Sociological Approaches* (London: Blackwell Publishers, 1995), 53–72.

Julia Lawton, 'Contemporary Hospice Care: The Sequestration of the Unbounded Body and "Dirty Dying"', *Sociology of Health and Illness* 20, 2 (1998): 121–43.

Claudia Malacrida, 'Discipline and Dehumanization in a Total Institution: Institutional Survivors' Descriptions of Time-out Rooms', *Disability & Society* 20, 5 (2005): 523–37. Reprinted by permission of Taylor & Francis Ltd, http://www.informaworld.com.

Barbara L. Marshall and Stephen Katz, 'Forever Functional: Sexual Fitness and the Aging Male Body', *Body & Society* 8, 4 (2002): 43–70. Copyright © 2002 Sage Publications Ltd. Reproduced by permission of the publisher.

Emily Martin, 'The Egg and the Sperm: How Science Has Constructed a Romance Based on Stereotypical Male–Female Roles', *Signs: Journal of Women in Culture and Society* 16, 31 (1991): 485–502. Copyright © 1991, The University of Chicago Press.

Karin A. Martin, 'Becoming a Gendered Body: Practices of Preschools', *American Sociological Review* 63, 4 (1998): 494–511.

Gay Mason, 'Looking into Masculinity: Sport, Media, and the Construction of the Male Body Beautiful', *Social Alternatives* 11, 1 (1992): 27–35. Reprinted by permission of the publisher.

Berry Mayall, 'Children's Lived Bodies in Everyday Life', in *Children, Health and the Social Order* (Buckingham and Philadelphia: Open University Press, 1996), 85–112. Reprinted by permission of the author.

Lee F. Monaghan, 'Big Handsome Men, Bears, and Others: Virtual Constructions of "Fat Male Embodiment"', *Body & Society* 11, 2 (2005): 81–111. Copyright © 2005 Sage Publications Ltd. Reproduced by permission of the publisher.

Sarah Neal, 'Feared and Revered: Media Representations of Racialized and Gendered Bodies—A Case Study', in L. McKie and N. Watson, eds, *Organizing Bodies: Policy, Institutions, and Work* (New York: Palgrave, 2000), 102–116. Reproduced with permission of Palgrave Macmillan.

Victoria L. Pitts, 'Cyberpunk, Biomedicine, and the High-tech Body', in *In the Flesh: The Cultural Politics of Body Modification* (London: Palgrave MacMillan, 2003), 151–185. Reproduced with permission of Palgrave Macmillan.

Katha Pollitt, '"Fetal Rights": A New Assault on Feminism', *The Nation* 26 March 1990. Reprinted by permission of the author.

Robert N. Proctor, 'The Destruction of "Lives not Worth Living"', in *Racial Hygiene: Medicine Under the Nazis*. (Cambridge, MA: Harvard University Press, 1988),

Part I

Tracing the Body in Classical and Contemporary Theory

Claudia Malacrida and Jacqueline Low

Before we can begin to examine specific aspects of social bodies, it is important to understand the theories that sociologists have used to understand the body. Chris Shilling's 'The Body in Sociology' (1993) provides us with a nuanced argument about the role of the body in sociological thinking. On the one hand, sociology followed the **mind/body dualism** of the Enlightenment, which positioned body and mind as distinct from each other and privileged the mind because it separated humans from animals. Seeking to enhance its reputation as a fledgling discipline, sociology chose the exalted half of this dualism as its focus. Concentrating on the cognitive and collective aspects of human experience, sociology's analysis has primarily been on collective actions rather than on the 'physical, fleshy body' (17). Arguing for another type of dualism in addition to the mind/body split, founding fathers of sociology Emile Durkheim and Max Weber posited that emotional responses to and embodied relationships with the field of sociological study were impure and biased. They argued in favour of a separation of mind from emotion in the form of 'higher' methods that relied on abstract cognitive inquiry, based on ideals of objectivity and emotional distance. Shilling speculates that, in part, this valuing of rationality, objectivity, and cognition over nature, embodiment, and emotionality reflects another dualism—that of **masculinity/femininity**. He obliquely implies that, had there been some 'founding mothers' of sociology, the body might have found its way into sociological thinking much sooner (1991).

The omission of the body in sociology has not been universal, however. Later European sociologists studied the bodily implications of civility, education, and other social institutions. For example, eminent French sociologist Pierre Bourdieu has been recognized as a foundational figure in defining a sociology of the body (Shilling, 1991). Bourdieu expanded Marx's notion of economic capital to give us a model of four other kinds of capital, all of which can be manipulated and leveraged to achieve economic capital: **social capital** (networks of friends, family, and mentors who can help us to transcend our class position); **symbolic capital** (our ability to manipulate symbols such as language or clothing to our advantage); **cultural capital** (cultural competencies such as gestures, dispositions, tastes, and abilities); and **physical capital** (originally conceived as a subsystem of cultural capital, meaning the uses of the body to convey one's social position and to display culturally valued physical attributes) (Shilling, 1991: 654). Unfortunately, Bourdieu's theories and their implications for a sociology of the body have only recently found their way into North American and British sociological thinking (Shilling, 1993: 21).

Shilling (1993) characterizes the body as an 'absent presence' that has implicitly underpinned sociological thinking. Thus, while classical sociology may not have developed a direct analysis of the body, 'facets of human embodiment' such as language, consciousness, manners, or emotions have driven the sociological study of race, sex, class, health, illness, and demography. Likewise, classical sociological theories, despite their grand historical narratives and macro-level analyses, relied on human bodies to shore up their theories. For example, Marx's theories of capitalism and **historical materialism** rely on the relationship of human labour and working bodies to economic forms and industrialization; the alienated worker's body and the tyranny of the machine form the base of Marx's analysis. Weber's analysis of the development of capitalism and a Protestant work ethic describes the increasing **rationalization** of workers' bodies with the advent of bureaucratization. In Weber's view, modernity heralded an increasingly impersonal, fragmented, and regulated relationship between workers and their bodies. Thus, the body, although not forming a highly visible presence, does operate as an important hidden element in classical sociology.

Shilling (1993) describes four main developments that served to 'bring the body back in' to sociological thinking. These are the rise of consumerism, which has provided new avenues for human expression; demographic changes in population, which has increased our focus on health and the body; the development of feminist critiques; and the double-edged sword of modern bodily technologies, such as implants, cybernetics, and artificial/virtual reality, which prolong and enhance life while subjecting our bodies to increasing surveillance and raising questions of where bodies begin and machines end.

In 'Bringing Bodies Back In' Arthur W. Frank (1990) reviews 10 years of sociological study of the body, highlighting what he considers to be its major influences. He argues that, first and foremost, feminist scholarship has informed the sociological analysis of the body. Feminist researchers were the first to explicitly demonstrate, for instance in studies of violence against women, how structural forces, such as the politics of gender, affect bodies. Second, he credits the work of Foucault (1978) with a fundamental role in shaping the sociology of the body, noting in particular Foucault's work on sexuality, bodily disciplines, and the political repression of the body. Third, he points to the socio-historical context of modernity as both a mainspring of and a major theme within the sociology of the body literature. He writes that there is a contradiction in modern culture between **material objectivism**, where the social world is real and knowable, and **constructionist relativism**, where what we take for reality is understood as informed by subjective interpretation. This contradiction makes the study of the body inevitable—we believe the body to have a concrete and unchanging reality, yet disease, disability, and our increasing ability to modify the body all remind us that it is not.

The central question Frank raises in this critical review is whether the sociology of the body is more rightly a sub-discipline within sociology or if attention to the body needs to be woven through sociological theory itself. He notes that only two theorists, Bryan S. Turner (1996) and John O'Neill (1985), have moved anywhere towards the latter. For example, in his macro theory, Turner argues that there are four regulatory tasks all societies must accomplish with regards to the body: the regulation of reproduction, representation, restraint, and movement of bodies in society. However, an excess of regulation in any of these areas will result in social pathology in the form of diseases specific to particular socio-cultural and historical contexts. For instance, an excess of regulation of women's bodies in the Victorian era, when women were restricted to the domestic sphere (the home), resulted in the emergence of **the disease of agoraphobia** (literally meaning fear of the market place but more commonly understood as fear of public spaces). Likewise, O'Neill takes a structural perspective on the body. In his book *Five Bodies* (1985), O'Neill discusses the world body, social body, body politic, consumer body, and medical body, showing how each plays a role in maintaining aspects of social structure, such as the institution of religion or the political and economic structure of society.

Frank next reviews key texts in four major areas within the sociology of the body by dividing the relevant literature into four types of bodies: medicalized, sexual, disciplined, and talking. In doing so he refers to several key concepts that you will encounter in this book. For instance, in discussing the medicalized body, where **medicalization** is the process by which social phenomena come to be understood as medical problems, Frank refers to Talcott Parsons's **sick role**, a social role that allows people to relinquish other social obligations while they recover from illness. According to Parsons (1951), people may adopt this role only temporarily; they must also comply with doctors' orders and make an effort to get well. Another important issue relating to the medicalized body that

Frank examines is **stigma**, which, according to Goffman (1963), is a characteristic of identity that reduces the social value of a person.

Turning to the sexual body, Frank highlights how sexuality and gender are both key defining elements of the body and 'organizing features' of society (145). To illustrate his argument, he discusses gang rape in the Mehinaku tribe (146). He addresses these issues again in his discussion of the disciplined body, a body that is subject to regimes where bodily desires, such as hunger and fatigue, are denied. Here he reviews Bell's (1985) study of medieval nuns' aesthetic practices, where these women **mortified** or subjugated their bodies by, among other things, engaging in excessive fasting. They did this not only in an effort to become closer to God but also in an attempt to be free and independent in a **patriarchal**, or male-dominated, society. Frank adds that in contemporary consumer culture, we are obsessed with **body maintenance** and **body disciplines** through such practices as diet, exercise, and cosmetic surgery.

Finally, Frank discusses the paradox of modern society through what he refers to as the **talking body**, arguing that it resolves the modernist subjectivist/objectivist contradiction. By the talking body, Frank means an understanding of communication as quite literally embodied—human cognition and communication are grounded in **corporeal** (physiological) experience. Thus, Frank concludes that, while our experience of society is subjectively perceived, we all share common bodily experiences that are grounded in the objective reality of physiology. For Frank, such common corporeal experience makes possible a mutual understanding of the social world.

The reading by Sandra Lee Bartky (1988) provides an application of ideas presented in Foucault's famous book *Discipline and Punish: The Birth of the Prison* (1995). Foucault argued that the Enlightenment shift from a model of social control characterized by spectacles of punishment and raw power in public spaces to a modern, 'benign' model of social control characterized by the routinized, private discipline of the new prison systems was in fact a shift towards an increasingly invasive means of regulating the social body. This shift was characterized by new forms of bodily regimentation that penetrated every aspect of the prisoner's life. For example, the architecture of the ideal prison was epitomized by the **panopticon**, a central tower around which open cells were ranged, permitting the constant surveillance of prisoner's bodies. In Foucault's theory, power is implemented through the use of a **disciplinary gaze**; seeing and judging are vehicles of power, and the gaze is a ubiquitous mechanism of social control in modern societies. Ultimately, between the painstaking daily discipline of institutional routines and the constant possibility of surveillance, Foucault argued that prisoners began to engage in their own preventative self-policing. His term for these kinds of operations, in which the social relations of power are literally written upon the body, is **biopowe.** ultimate product of this kind of pervasive power is a **docile body**, which will comply with social regimens readily and willingly.

Foucault's model extended beyond prison life to include students, soldiers, hospital patients, and factory workers, and ultimately this model of social control extended its network of power relations to all citizens in modern societies. Bartky takes up these ideas and applies a feminist lens to her analysis, extending it to the ways that all modern women experience patriarchal power. Beginning with the shape, size, and space appropriation of women's bodies, she notes that the 'tyranny of slenderness' and the constraints of feminine comportment demand constant self-vigilance from women. Additionally, beauty norms place demands on women's time and self-mastery—unwanted hairs must be removed, skin must be kept baby-smooth, makeup must be applied within narrow constraints of what is deemed 'attractive', and hair must be groomed. Ultimately, the standards of proper femininity are so high as to be unattainable. As a result, women constantly judge each other through a disciplining gaze and engage in their own preventative self-policing to ensure that they do not transgress the multiple rules attached to the feminine body. This gendered discipline, written on the bodies of women, does not require an enforcer or an identifiable disciplinarian (although patriarchal power does imply that men benefit from this set of relations), but is instead enforced through a network of informal sanctions that 'circulate through progressively finer channels, gaining access to individuals themselves, to their bodies, their gestures, and all their daily actions' (Foucault, 1995). As Bartky notes, for women, this increasingly exhaustive list of feminine 'musts' comes at tremendous costs, in terms of time and money and in keeping women burdened and less competitive than their male counterparts. Finally, in true Foucauldian style, Bartky argues that resistance to this self-disciplining network is unlikely because of the seeming naturalness and inevitability of the beauty imperative.

References

Bartky, S.L. 1988. 'Foucault, Femininity, and the Modernization of Patriarchal Power', in I. Diamond and L. Quinby, eds, *Feminism & Foucault: Reflections on Resistance*. Boston: Northeastern University Press.

Bell, R.M., with an epilogue by W. C. Davis. 1985. *Holy Anorexia*. Chicago: University of Chicago Press.

Foucault, M. 1995. *Discipline and Punish: The Birth of the Prison*. New York: Vintage Books.

Frank, A.W. 1990. 'Bringing Bodies Back In: A Decade Review', *Theory, Culture and Society* 7, 1: 131–62.

Goffman, E. 1963. *Stigma: Notes on the Management of Spoiled Identity*. New Jersey: Prentice Hall Inc.

O'Neill, J. 1985. *Five Bodies: The Shape of Modern Society*. Ithaca, NY: Cornell University Press.

Parsons, T. 1951. *The Social System*. Glenco, IL: The Free Press.

Shilling, C. 1991. 'Educating the Body: Physical Capital and the Production of Social Inequalities' *Sociology* 25, 4: 653–72.

———. 1993. 'The Body in Sociology', in *The Body and Social Theory (Theory, Culture and Society Series)*. London: Sage, 17–36.

Turner, B. 1996. *The Body and Society*, 2nd edn. London: Sage.

Chapter 1

The Body in Sociology

Chris Shilling

Throughout its establishment and development, sociology has adopted a disembodied approach towards its subject matter. At least, that is the picture that is usually constructed from the writings of those social theorists who have grown accustomed to regarding the body variously as the province of another discipline, an uninteresting prerequisite of human action, or simply a target of social control. It would probably be more accurate, though, to portray the body as having a dual status in sociology. Instead of being missing entirely from the discipline, the body has historically been something of an 'absent presence' in sociology.

It has been absent in the sense that sociology has rarely focused on the embodied human as an object of importance in its own right. . . . However, it is also possible to argue that the body had been present at the very heart of the sociological imagination. . . .

The dual status of the body in sociology is illustrated by the briefest of glances at some of the core areas of the discipline. . . . In the study of health and illness, for example, inequalities in morbidity and mortality rates have prompted sociologists to ask what it is about the social existence of people that affects their bodies in such dramatic ways. Clearly bodies matter, and they matter enough to form the 'hidden' base of many sociological studies.

Despite this, though, sociologists have shied away from specific analyses of the body. Rather, they have tended in the examples above to concentrate on questions concerned with the social structure of particular nation-states, prejudice and discrimination, attachment to work and family, access to services, and the interlocking of local and global processes in the spheres of culture, economics, and politics. . . .

Our experience of life is inevitably mediated through our bodies. As Goffman has clearly demonstrated, our very ability to intervene in social life—to make a difference to the flow of daily affairs—is dependent on the management of our bodies through time and space. . . . The embodiment of humans is central to the intricate techniques involved in the formation and maintenance of families and friendships (Allan, 1989), and societies depend for their very existence on the reproduction of existing and new bodies.

Bodies, then, have occupied a place in the sociological imagination as our experience and management of them form part of the general material out of which social life and social theory is forged. Our experiences of embodiment provide a basis for theorizing social commonality, social inequalities, and the construction of difference. We all have bodies and this constitutes part of what makes us human beings possessed of the ability to communicate with each other, and experience common needs, desires, satisfactions, and frustrations (Doyal and Gough, 1991).

While human embodiment provides at least the potential for communication and shared experiences, however, bodies are inhabited and treated differently both within and between social systems. As Marcel Mauss pointed out in 1934, cultures have specific 'techniques of the body' that provide their members with identities, govern infancy and adolescence and old age, and inform such activities as resting, talking, and walking (1973 [1934]). Furthermore, as the work of Norbert Elias demonstrates, bodily differences vary historically as well as cross-culturally. For example, in the Western world our sensitivity to bodily waste has increased enormously in recent centuries, as has the tendency to perceive the surface of our bodies as an immovable barrier between ourselves and the outside world (Corbin, 1986; Elisa, 1978b). Bodies also vary on an individual basis. We all have bodies but we are not all able to see, hear, feel, speak, and move about independently. Having a body is constraining as well as enabling, and people who are old or disabled often feel more constrained by their bodies than do those who are young and able bodied (Campling, 1981). . . .

The Body in Classical Sociology

The dual status of the body in sociology is clearly apparent in the concerns and work of the 'founding fathers' of the discipline. On the one hand, Karl Marx, Max Weber, Emile Durkheim, and other classical sociologists such as Georg Simmel, Ferdinand Toddies, and Karl Mannheim rarely focused on the body in its entirety as a subject of investigation. . . . On the other hand, though, the body was just too important to be excluded completely from the writings of these sociologists. As well as being concerned with aspects of embodiment, such as language and consciousness, the body as a physical component of social control had a habit of appearing in some of their most important writings on methodology and modernity. This is particularly evident in Marx's analysis of how the development of capitalist technology linked and subordinated working class bodies to machinery, and Weber's writings on the rationalization of the body within bureaucracy. . . .

. . . Sociologists such as Durkheim were concerned with identifying and establishing a disciplinary field that was distinct from and irreducible to the natural sciences. In proclaiming sociology as an independent science, Durkheim (1938: xlix) also defined its interests and methods as opposed to those of psychology. Psychology was concerned with the individual as opposed to the social, and psychological explanation was seen by Durkheim to be based on what he called 'organico-psychic' factors. These are the supposedly pre-social features of the individual organism that are given at birth and are independent of social influences (Lukes, 1973: 17). Humans, then, were marked by a nature/society dualism, and the biological body for Durkheim was placed firmly in the sphere of nature.

This view had an enduring effect on sociology and meant that the natural and biological were frequently ruled outside of, and unimportant to, the sociologist's legitimate sphere of investigation (Newby, 1991). . . .

Bryan Turner (1991) has identified four specific reasons for the failure of classical sociology to generate an overt sociology of the body, and these can all be related to the disciplinary project undertaken by the 'founding fathers'. First, sociologists such as Durkheim, Weber, Simmel, and Mannheim were generally . . . attempting to make sense of the industrial, political, and ideological revolutions occurring in Europe during the late eighteenth and early nineteenth centuries. . . . The very scale of these changes appeared to necessitate explanations based on changes in such societal factors as the social division of labour (Durkheim), class struggle and the forces of production (Marx), or processes of rationalization (Weber).

Second, sociology has tended to concentrate on the conditions required for order and control or social change in society. The complexity of industrial capitalism generated an interest in its functioning that focused on society as a social system. As Weber's work demonstrated this did not rule out a concern with individuals. However, it did encompass a commitment to the construction of theories based on interrelationships with a social rather than biological basis. . . .

Third, the capabilities required for human agency became equated with consciousness and the mind, rather than with the management of the body as a whole. Bodies came to be seen, at best, as an uninteresting condition of social action. The body was usually considered as a passive container that acted as a shell to the active mind (that was identified as distinguishing humans from animals). . . . .

Fourth, a theoretical consequence of these epistemological and ontological commitments was that sociology did not show much interest in the anthropological view of the body as a classification system. It was the mind, rather than the body, which served as the receptor and organizer of images concerned with, and deriving from, social stratification. As Turner (1991) notes, in its most enduring form, this approach is evident in the Marxist tradition's focus on ideology, false consciousness, and reification.

Two further points should, perhaps, be added to Turner's list of reasons why the 'founding fathers' failed to develop a sociology of the body. The first concerns the methodological approaches promoted by the discipline. These laid great emphasis on abstract cognitive inquiry that was somehow meant to operate as if it was located outside of, and was entirely separate from, the body. For example, Durkheim argued that it was the open and empty mind of the professional sociologist, rid of bodily impurities such as emotional prejudices, which was able to apprehend the reality of social facts. . . .

Finally, perhaps one of the major reasons why the 'founding fathers' failed to develop a sociology of the body concerns their embodiment as men. . . . The risks women faced during pregnancy, the high numbers who died during childbirth, and the rates of infant mortality that characterized the Industrial Revolution may possibly have been reflected through a greater consideration of the body if Marx, Weber, and Durkheim had been women. . . .

It would be inaccurate, though, to argue that classical sociology completely ignored the body. . . . For example, Marx and Engels were concerned with the corporeal conditions surrounding consciousness, the condition of the English working class, and the detrimental consequences of the division of labour under capitalism, which deformed the bodies of workers and made them fit only for limited and repetitive activities in the workplace. . . .

Weber was also concerned with the body. . . . According to Weber, the Calvinist view of predestination produced in people a deep insecurity that manifested itself in a motivation to lead a wholly disciplined and dedicated life on earth. This especially directed puritans into business, in which endless hours could be dedicated to the accumulation of money. Central to this 'spirit of modern economic life' was the voluntary subjugation of the body to strict routine. Hard work and effort in the sphere of production was coupled with frugality and denial of the sensuous in the sphere of consumption. . . .

The Rise of the Body in Sociology

Despite the limited concerns of classical sociology, the importance of the body has been highlighted by a growing number of sociologists since the 1980s. . . .

More specifically, the social and academic changes that have formed the context for the current concern with the body involve the rise of 'second wave' feminism; demographic changes that have focused attention on the needs of the elderly in Western societies; the rise of consumer culture linked to the changing structure of modern capitalism; and the previously mentioned 'crisis' in our certainty about what bodies are.

First, the rise of 'second wave' feminism in the 1960s and its subsequent development placed on the political agenda issues related to the control of fertility and abortion rights. They also formed the context for a more general project among women to 'reclaim' their bodies from male control and abuse. As Gill Kirkup and Laurie Smith Keller (1992) note, self-help groups were important parts of the women's movement in this respect, and they incorporated attempts to further women's knowledge and control over their bodies (e.g., Boston Women's Health Collective, 1971). This is linked to a strong tradition in which women have placed their bodies at risk during political struggles, for example, in the suffragette and nuclear peace movements. Such methods of protest, though not entirely novel, have also been drawn on by new social movements; members of Greenpeace, for example, have put themselves at considerable physical risk in order to increase public awareness of the bodily dangers of pollution.

As well as using the body as a vehicle of political action and protest, feminist analyses of women's oppression brought the body into academic conceptualizations of patriarchy. In contrast to those theories that identify the family as the basis of women's position in society, a number of feminists gave primacy to the biological body as the source of patriarchy. . . . For example, McDonough and Harrison (1978) viewed patriarchy in terms of the control of fertility together with the sexual division of labour; Heidi Hartmann (1979) sought to define patriarchy by considering men's control of women's sexuality and their access to economically productive services; while Sylvia Walby's model of patriarchy (1989) as six partially independent structures explored the importance of human embodiment in her discussions of male violence and sexuality. Radical feminists have also placed great importance on the body as a basis of female oppression through, for example, its location as a site for the construction of 'compulsory heterosexuality' (Rich, 1980).

In addition to the appearance of the body in general discussions of patriarchy, feminists also undertook more specific studies of the commodification of women's bodies in pornography, prostitution, and surrogate motherhood (Singer, 1989). They have also done much to highlight both the differential socialization to which girls' and boys' bodies are subject (Lees, 1984), and the male orientated knowledge that has informed the development of the medical services and the treatment of women's bodies during pregnancy and childbirth (Greer, 1971; Martin, 1989 [1987]; Miles, 1991; Oakley, 1984). Debates about the role of reproduction and housework in the economy also highlighted the position of women as the prime servicers of men's and children's bodies (Oakley, 1974). . . .

In sum, feminist work highlighted the fact that women frequently have to learn to live with what can be termed 'over burdened bodies'. . . .

This feminist focus on the embodied existence of women did more than simply highlight the multiple ways in which bodies were implicated in social relations of inequality and oppression. Analysis of the sex/gender, nature/culture, and biology/society divisions began to break down, or at least reduce the strength of, some of the corporeal boundaries that popular and academic thought had posited between 'women' and 'men' (e.g., Oakley, 1972). Indeed, feminist scholarship has helped to problematize the very nature of the terms 'woman' and 'man', 'female' and 'male', and 'femininity' and 'masculinity', by questioning the ontological bases of sexual difference.

This touches on a further important point that is worth emphasizing here. Feminist thought did not concentrate on women's bodies to the exclusion of men's bodies. These subjects were inextricably related, as it was the power and force exercised by male bodies that was instrumental in controlling the bodies of women. Furthermore, the development of 'men's studies' in North America and the United Kingdom gave an added impetus to the study of the embodiment of masculinity. . . . This tradition has also included important works on the social construction of the 'male homosexual' (Bray, 1982; Weeks, 1977). As Jeff Hearn and David Morgan (1990) point out, the focus on sexuality within men's studies did not automatically entail an examination of the body. In practice, however, the two subjects have become related. This situation has been reinforced by recent studies on men, sexuality, and the transmission of HIV that include a concern with the cultural meanings given to specific sexual acts involving penetration and the exchange of sexual fluids (Connell and Kippax, 1990).

One aspect of men's studies that is particularly relevant to this discussion is the examination of male body images that has been undertaken by several writers. For example, Mishkind argues that men have become increasingly preoccupied with male body images and maintain an idealized image of the perfect body type to which they aspire: the 'muscular mesomorph'. In summarizing Mishkind's work, Kimmel (1987) identifies three social trends that have led to this preoccupation. First, the decreasing stigmatization of gay men as 'failed men'—the replacement of the old stereotype of the limp-wristed 'sissy' with the new stereotype of the gay macho bodybuilder—has increased men's overall concerns with body image and also legitimized these concerns. Second, women's increased participation in the public sphere has led to a kind of 'muscular backlash' given that cognitive, occupational, and lifestyle differences between men and women are decreasing. In this context, body image emerges as one of the few areas in which men can differentiate themselves from women. The third related trend concerns the decreasing importance that the 'breadwinning' role assumes in the formation of men's self-identity. In its place, there has been an increasing emphasis on consumption and self-identity that has at its centre a concern with the surface territories of the body (Bourdieu, 1984; Ehrenreich, 1983; Featherstone, 1987). . . . .

If the rise of feminism was the first factor to highlight the importance of the body, the second factor concerns the growth in the number of aged in Western societies. This has become a matter of international concern largely because of the economic implications of this demographic trend. Increasing elderly populations have serious implications for social policy and state expenditure in the areas of pensions, medical provision, caring services, and accommodation (Turner, 1991). An increased focus on human bodies has come about both as a cause and a consequence of these changes. Medical advances have helped create much greater life expectancy rates in comparison with the last century. At the same time, the medical services have been faced with more problems concerning the health and well-being of the elderly. In a very real sense, they have become victims of their own success. This situation has been made more visible with the rise to power of governments in both the United States and the United Kingdom during the 1970s and 1980s that were influenced by the ideas of the 'new right' and were concerned not to increase but to reduce public expenditure commitments. . . . .

The third factor that has increased the focus on the body in contemporary society concerns a shift in the structure of advanced capitalist societies in the second half of the twentieth century. Broadly speaking, there has been a shift in emphasis from a focus on hard work in the sphere of production coupled with frugality and denial in the sphere of consumption. . . . Related to this, the body in consumer culture has become increasingly central and has helped promote the 'performing self', which treats the body as a machine to be finely tuned, cared for, reconstructed, and carefully presented through such measures as regular physical exercise, personal health programs, high-fibre diets, and colour-coded dressing. As Featherstone (1982: 22) argues, within consumer culture the body ceases to be a vessel of sin and presents itself instead as an object for display both inside and outside of the bedroom.

Placed in a broader historical context, these events can also be seen to be outgrowths of changes initiated in the nineteenth century when clothes and the presentation of the body shifted from being instant signs of social place to become manifestations of personality (Sennett, 1974). Whereas flamboyant clothes, hats, makeup, and wigs were once seen as objects of interest in their own right, inextricably bound to and expressive of social position, the 'presentation of self' (Goffman, 1969) is now seen as signifying the real character of individuals. In contemporary consumer culture this has helped promote among people the experience of both *becoming* their bodies, in the sense of identifying themselves either negatively or positively with the 'exterior' of the body, and of being regularly *anxious* about the possibility that their body will let them down or 'fall apart' if they withdraw from its constant work and scrutiny. This notion of body anxiety is central to the way many people perceive their bodies as projects and is also linked to the experience of the environment as dangerous and out of control, and the fear of aging, illness, and death. . . . .

The fourth factor behind the rise of interest in the body is concerned with the tendency mentioned in the introduction for an increase in the potential to control our bodies to be accompanied by a crisis in their meaning. In discussing the increased control that modernity exerted over the body, Turner (1992) has pointed out that diet was central to the early rationalization of the body. Whereas early dietary schemes were connected to religious values, the nineteenth century saw an increasing scientific literature of diet emerge with the establishment of nutritional sciences. These knowledges were first applied in the realm of social policy to measure the food required by various populations such as prisoners and army recruits, and were applied by the social reformers Charles Booth and Seebohm Kowntree as measurements of poverty levels in the larger British cities. Furthermore, the rationalization of the body was intimately connected to the 'sciences of man' that sought in such places as prisons, armies, and workplaces to 're-educate the mind via the discipline and organization of bodies in a regime that sought to maximize efficiency and surveillance' (Turner, 1992: 123, 126).

Our ability to control the body has continued apace as a result of advances in transplant surgery, artificial insemination, in vitro fertilization, and plastic surgery. As John O'Neill (1985) demonstrates, there are now few parts of our body which technology cannot restructure in some way or other. . . .

One of the images that is frequently employed in describing such developments is the 'body as machine', and it is pertinent to this discussion to note the increasing appearance of this metaphor in lay perceptions of health and illness (Rogers, 1991). . . .

The 'body as machine' is not merely a medical image, however; one of the areas in which the body is most commonly perceived and treated in this way is in the sphere of sport. Radical critics of sport have noted that the vocabulary of the machine dominates the language of sport and have argued that it is through the practice of sport that the body has come to be understood as 'a technical means to an end, a reified factor of output and production . . . as a machine with the job

of producing the maximum work and energy' (Brohm, 1978). In sport, the body is seen as a complex machine whose performance can be enhanced, and that can break down and be repaired, just like any other machine. . . .

In discussing the rationalization of the body, it is important to recognize that this is a deeply gendered phenomenon. One of the ways in which the body has been subjected to increased discipline and control is through bureaucratic regimes that specify when particular quantities and qualities of work must be carried out irrespective of the bodily needs of workers. Productivity schemes sometimes fall into this category and, by failing to allow for adequate rest and relaxation during the working day, can lead to stress-related illness among both women and men (Hochschild, 1983). However, as Emily Martin (1989 [1987]) and Sophie Laws (1990) argue, bureaucratic regimes frequently subject women's bodies to more control than men's bodies. This is because women are expected to manage and conceal menstruation, pregnancy, and menopause 'in institutions whose organization of time and space takes little cognizance of them' (Martin, 1989 [1987]: 94).

So far I have concentrated on the vast increase in control over the body that has accompanied processes of rationalization in modernity. However, while rationalization may have provided us with the potential to control our bodies more than ever before, and have them controlled by others, its double-edged nature has also reduced our certainty over what constitutes a body, and where one body finishes and another starts. . . .

Four major social factors, then, have formed the context for the relatively recent rise of the body in sociology. These are the growth of 'second wave' feminism; demographic changes that have focused attention on the needs of the elderly in Western societies; the rise of consumer culture linked to the changing structure of modern capitalism; and a growing crisis in our knowledge of what the body is. . . .

References

Allan, G. 1989. *Friendship, Developing a Sociological Perspective.* New York: Harvester Wheatsheaf.

Berger, P., and T. Luckmann. 1967. *The Social Construction of Reality.* London: Allen Lane.

Bourdieu, P. 1984. *Distinction: A Social Critique of the Judgement of Taste.* London: Routledge.

Bray, A. 1982. *Homosexuality in Renaissance England.* London: Gay Men's Press.

Brohm, J.-M. 1978. *Sport: A Prison of Measured Time.* London: Ink Books.

Corbin, A. 1986. *The Foul and the Fragrant, Odor and the French Social Imagination.* Cambridge, MA: Harvard University Press.

Cornell, R., and S. Kippax. 1990. 'Sexuality in the AIDS Crisis: Patterns of Sexual Practice and Pleasure in a Sample of Australian Gay and Bisexual Men', *Journal of Sex Research* 27, 2: 167–98.

Durkheim, E. 1938. *The Rules of the Sociological Method.* New York: Free Press.

Ehrenreich, B. 1983. *The Hearts of Men: American Dreams and Their Flight from Commitment.* London: Pluto.

Elias, N. 1978. 'The Civilizing Process Revisited', *Theory and Society* 5: 243–53.

Featherstone, M. 1982. 'The Body in Consumer Culture', *Theory, Culture and Society* 1: 18–33.

———. 1987. 'Leisure, Symbolic Power, and the Life Course', in J. Horne, D. Jary, and A. Tomlinson, eds, *Sport, Leisure and Social Relations.* London: RKP.

Goffman, E. 1969. *The Presentation of Self in Everyday Life.* Harmondsworth, UK: Penguin.

Green, H. 1986. *Fit for America: Health, Fitness, Sport and American Society.* New York: Pantheon.

Greer, G. 1971. *The Female Eunuch.* London: Paladin.

Hearn, J., and O. Morgan, eds. 1990. *Men, Masculinities and Social Theory.* London: Unwin Hyman.

Hochschild, A. 1983. *The Managed Heart: Commercialization of Human Feeling.* Berkeley, CA: University of California Press.

Jeffords, S. 1989. *The Remasculinization of America: Gender and the Vietnam War.* Bloomington, IN: Indiana University Press.

Kimmel, M, ed. 1987. *Changing Men. New Directions in Research on Men and Masculinity.* Newbury Park, CA: Sage.

Kirkup, G., and L.S. Keller. 1992. *Inventing Women: Science, Technology and Gender.* Cambridge: Polity Press.

Laws, S. 1990. *Issues of Blood: The Politics of Menstruation.* Houndmills: Macmillan.

Martin, E. 1989 [1987]. *The Woman in the Body.* Milton Keynes: Open University Press.

Mauss, M. 1973 [1934]. 'Techniques of the Body', *Economy and Society* 2: 70–88.

Miles, A. 1991. *Women, Health and Medicine.* Milton Keynes: Open University Press.

O'Neill, J. 1985. *Five Bodies. The Human Shape of Modern Society.* Ithaca, NY: Cornell University Press.

Oakley, A. 1974. *The Sociology of Housework.* London: Martin Robertson.

———. 1984. *The Captured Womb: A History of the Medical Care of Pregnant Women.* Oxford: Basil Blackwell.

Rogers, W. 1991. *Explaining Health and Illness.* New York: Harvester Wheatsheaf.

Schwartz, H. 1986. *Never Satisfied: A Cultural History of Diets, Fantasies and Fats.* New York: Free Press.

Sennett, R. 1974. *The Fall of Public Man.* New York: W. W. Norton and Co.

Singer, L. 1989. 'Bodies, Pleasures, Powers', *Differences* 1: 45–65.

Turner, B.S. 1991. 'Recent Developments in the Theory of the Body', in M. Featherstone, M. Hepworth, and B. Turner, eds, *The Body: Social Process and Cultural Theory.* London: Sage.

———. 1992. *Max Weber: From History to Modernity.* London: Routledge.

Weber, M. 1985 [1904–5]. *The Protestant Ethic and the Spirit of Capitalism.* London: Counterpoint.

Weeks, J. 1977. *Coming Out: Homosexual Politics in Britain from the Nineteenth Century to the Present.* London: Quartet.

Chapter 2

Bringing Bodies Back In: A Decade Review

Arthur W. Frank

The Body as Topic

. . . Can we have a sociological theory of the body, or alternatively, a theoretical sociology that takes full account of the body? Of course the body had not escaped the notice of earlier social theorists (see, e.g., discussions of Marx, Durkheim, and Weber in Turner, 1984, 1987; and Bologh, 1987 on Weber; and Scarry, 1985 on Marx). But what it means for social theory to account for the body has recently taken on added dimensions. Three incitements to interest in the body deserve mention, as these will recur as explicit and implicit motifs in the discussions that follow.

The first influence on body interest is feminism, which affects most of what will be reviewed later, though the variation of these influences reflects what can only properly be called feminisms. . . . An implication of the collective authorship is that whatever is done to bodies is political. Feminism . . . has taught us to look first for the effects of politics in what is done to bodies. Scarry (1985: 243 ff.) is clearest about how we could have learned this from Marx, but it took a woman academic fully to embody his argument. . . . In establishing the self/body/politics/violence nexus, feminism has set an agenda for the sociology of the body.

A second aspect of this agenda derives from the pervasive influence of Michel Foucault. . . .

What Foucault contributes to the study of the body—beyond his studies of the body as a site of political violence—is an enhanced self-reflectiveness about the project of body study itself. . . . The enduring belief that the body can provide us with a grounded truth suggests why interest in it should flourish within cultural modernity.

The contradictory impulses of modernity are the third and most complicating influence on interest in the body. One aspect of modernity is the positivistic spirit, the will to knowledge, the Enlightenment quest for transcendental reason. . . . These extremes of discourse both direct our attention to the body and then muddle thinking about it. The body first presents itself as that which will remain solid, but then it does melt into air. There is a desire to use the physical reality of body as final arbiter of what is just and unjust, humane and inhumane, progressive and retrogressive. But often in the same texts, the cultural and historical range of body practices is used to attest the truth of a radical constructionism. Constructionist relativism alternates and combines with materialist objectivism.

If modernity, feminism, and Foucault are three sources of, and dominant motifs within, the literature on the body, the most coherent sociological theory of the body is provided by Bryan Turner (1984). . . . Turner describes four tasks with which bodies confront any social organization: '[1] the *reproduction* of populations in time, [2] the *regulation* of bodies in space, [3] the *restraint* of the "interior" body through disciplines, and [4] the *representation* of the "exterior" body in social space' (1984: 2; emphasis added; see also: 41, 90 ff.). . . . Turner can then theorize how both critical Marxisms and feminisms have underestimated the functional requirement of commodification. The need for workers not only to produce, but also to consume . . .

An alternative conceptualization for a sociology of the body is found in John O'Neill's *Five Bodies* (1985), which are the world's body, social bodies, the body politic, consumer bodies, and medical bodies. These categories . . . each represent . . . how the body has been used as a resource for instantiating and legitimating an institutional practice (political thought, the state, capitalism, medicine). . . .

To organize the material at hand, I suggest four bodies: (1) the medicalized body, (2) the sexual body, (3) the disciplined body, and (4) the talking body. . . .

The Medicalized Body

How are our bodies 'medicalized' in the sense of our experience of them being conditioned by parametres that institutionalized medicine has set in place? Crimp (1988: 3) begins his discussion of AIDS by quoting Francois Delaporte's *Disease and Civilization: The Cholera in Paris, 1832*: 'I assert, to begin with, that "disease" does not exist. It is therefore illusory to think that one can "develop beliefs" about it to "respond" to it. What does exist is not diseases but practices.' If we could say in the same way that bodies do not exist, but only practices, then the practices of organized medicine are among the most crucial. In seeking the proper verb to express the relation of medicine to bodies we are tempted towards 'create' or 'generate', but is this taking the constructionist perspective too far?

Crimp suggests a more balanced view that while the 'ravages . . . in the body' are not social constructions, AIDS 'does not exist apart from the practices that conceptualize it, represent it, and respond to it', and that AIDS can only be known through these practices. Generalizing this argument beyond the issue of AIDS, we must recognize that medicine does not create the body, though it may recreate it in some respects. Medicine does, however, occupy a paramount place among those institutional practices by which the body is conceptualized, represented, and responded to. At present, our capacity to experience the body directly, or theorize it indirectly, is inextricably medicalized.

Crimp's distinction of bodily ravages versus social practices finds its analogue in the distinction of disease and illness, in which disease refers to physiological processes and illness to social constructions. This distinction unhappily reflects the nature/culture bifurcation that pervades the body literature. As Delaporte might object, our capacity to reflect on 'nature' already presupposes and is mediated by 'culture', but as Crimp acknowledges, the body's nature has a stubborn reality that is not reducible to cultural practices. The social history of these practices, however rich, can only tell part of the story.

James Patterson's *The Dread Disease* is social history at its best: a meticulously researched and well-plotted narrative of a distinctly American obsession with cancer. Among the book's lessons is that popular attitudes cannot be separated from institutional responses. Nor can the cultural be separated from the economic . . .

. . . Medicine continues to want to keep the understanding of cancer with a 'scientific' rather than public health perspective; more research has been directed to the level of the cell than toward stress, pollution, and habits such as smoking. Politicians, for their part, needed to be perceived as at least fighting, if not winning, a 'war on cancer', and funding institutionalized research displayed their commitment. Both medical and political interests articulated well with a corporate capitalism interested in finding a cause with the body itself rather than in the body's interaction with the environment. Thus, cure could take the form of a marketable technological intervention rather than a social reform. On the other side is a history of popular theories of aetiology and cure, many of them dismissible as con games and quackery, others expressing a grassroots resistance to professional imperialism of health.

But as always in the sociology of the body, this rather neat construction of cancer as practices then has to respond to certain realities that may not be constructed. Virus theories may well prove correct and cures may be developed through a medical technology, without social reform. Whatever political and economic interests may have conspired to define cancer this way, their 'practices' may be, in some very real, embodied sense, true. . . .

The recurring theme is that if illness occurs within a culture of social practices, these practices are heavily affected by an autonomous physiology of disease. The plague victim died within a few hours; the term 'victim' seems to fit. A change in the dominant disease prevalence brings a change in the trajectory of dying. Ill persons are no longer just victims; they have choices, since they now have time to experience their illness. 'One died individually and rather slowly of tuberculosis, so that the victim was in a position to perceive his condition, to form a self-image, and to discern the way in which others saw him.' . . .

The dilemma of the ill in this century is that they are constructed as responsible for their health and thus feel guilty, and simultaneously understand themselves as having less and less control over their bodies. 'As for the sufferers, though they were no longer sinners, they had failed; not, as in the past, in their souls, but in their bodies. They were now "damaged"' (1987: 153). . . .

But while patients feel responsible, professional medicine places the cause of illness beyond their control. . . .

For [Sue] Fisher control is patriarchal in the sense of being gender based: male physicians make decisions about women's bodies based on a set of normal life trajectory expectations. What counts (1986: 143, 159–62) is to protect a woman's fertility during child-bearing years, to regard birth itself as dangerous and requiring professional intervention, and finally to view an older woman's sexual organs as disease producing and best removed. . . .

'Limitation' is perhaps the key word for [Irving] Zola (1982). The disabled, and by extension all the ill, exist within the limitations imposed by bodies experienced as failures of self. They live their lives with a self-consciousness of experiencing only a subset of what a healthist society defines as a full life. . . .

. . . [Robert F.] Murphy theorizes his position as one of 'liminality . . . literally, at the threshold— a kind of a social limbo in which he [the ill person] is left standing outside the formal social system' (1987: 131). The concept of liminality suggests an expansion of Parsons's 'sick role' on the one hand and Goffman's formulation of stigma on the other. More people are becoming liminal. Murphy points out that antibiotics have provided for what he calls 'an explosion' (1987: 137) of the wheelchair population over the past 40 years. The problem is that social priorities have yet to catch up with medical technology: 'the same society that sustains the body beyond its normal limits shies away from the results' (1987: 138).

Murphy's situation represents the extreme, which is the value of his narrative. But even those who can deny their own risk of such illness cannot deny that they will grow old. Age may be the last area of medicalization. . . .

The Sexual Body

In style and content, two books could hardly be more disparate than Thomas Gregor's traditional ethnography of the Mehinaku and [Arthur and Marilouise] Kroker's (1987) collection of postmodernist interpretations of sexuality in contemporary America. . . .

. . . In many aspects of their culture, the Mehinaku present an almost idyllic society. Families show affection, initiations involve minimal brutality, tribal rivalries are resolved through wrestling matches rather than war. Gender is an essential organizing feature of public life, with men estimated to spend three and a half hours a day in productive labour, compared to women's seven to nine hours ([Gregor,]1986: 24). But this division of labour is accepted by women, whose work is communal and even eroticized (1986: 83–4). Most idyllic of all, the Mehinaku seem to have a playfully libertine attitude toward extramarital sexuality. . . .

Paradise, however, is only an apparent condition. The sexual division of social order is sustained not only by the ideology of tradition, but more explicitly by gang rape. In the men's house, which women cannot enter, there are kept the sacred flutes, which women are not allowed to see. On certain occasions, the flutes are taken out into the main square of the village and played; women are to hide in their huts. Should a woman happen into the village and see the flutes, she is dragged into the bush and gang raped. . . .

. . . The latter issue most clearly suggests the theme with which the Krokers introduce the collection, the capacity of modern technology to move sexuality outside the body and thus generate 'panic bodies'. In vitro fertilization was, as recently as a decade ago, a feminist dream of liberating the body from reproduction; the artificial womb now foreshadows the loss of the feminine ('panic ovaries'). Nor is the male body any less endangered, as its reproductive function is similarly severed ('panic penis') from sexuality as interaction. And all this at a time when AIDS makes sexuality a danger . . .

Phallic aggression in an age of AIDS brings new fears, though the legalities are still being sorted out (see Johnson and Murray, 1988). . . . The key to reproductive technologies is that they are dominated by males. Women have three basic fears: that 'contractual conception', as [Eileen] Manion argues it should be called, will create an underclass of women as 'rental wombs', that amniocentesis will be used to select female fetuses for abortion, and that in vitro fertilization will render women dispensable. . . .

The Disciplined Body

. . . Foucault came to use the term 'discipline' . . . [to mean] a technology of the self, that is, a set of systematic techniques that society makes available, or requires, for the self to discipline itself into a higher form of being. . . .

Foucault, who was perpetually redefining the nature of what his project had always been, understood himself in 1982 as investigating the interface 'between the technologies of domination of others and those of self' (1988: 19). . . .

[His] theories of the body function . . . as 'a kind of currency through which power . . . is defined and extended'. . . .

Rudolph Bell sets himself the difficult task not just of describing the fasting and self-mortification

practices of medieval women, but of understanding these as 'one aspect of the struggle by females striving for autonomy in a patriarchal culture' (1985: 86) and in this context to relate medieval religious fasting to contemporary psychiatrically defined anorexia. Bell is clear that these are 'not the same thing' (1985: 86), but he is provocative on their similarities. Bell's description of the life of Catherine of Siena has all the paradoxical nuance of a contemporary systemic family therapy case history. When her parents try to marry her off against her will, 'Catherine not only forgave them but contracted to save them as well.' . . .

Although the church exalted individual holy anorexics as saints, its general attitude towards fasting women was negative. The motivation for fasting was subject to constant interrogation, much of this taking the form of diaries and journals . . . [w]omen and their confessors were required to keep. . . . Bell writes 'even as they extol an individual who was in God's grace [these writings] serve to remind confessors of all the false steps and errors that women fall into'. . . . 'Unless she is inspired purely by the divine, and only male clerics seem able to ascertain this, her piety is not only useless but dangerous.' As the Middle Ages become the Renaissance, 'the inspired wisdom of female mystics . . . comes to be replaced with charges of heresy' (1985: 152). In calling holy anorexia heresy, the Church seemed to imply that its quality of resistance outweighed that of submissive self-mortification. In their extraordinary discipline over themselves, holy anorexics showed themselves impervious to temporal power—having already done worse to themselves than others could imagine doing—and thus became dangerous, but never very dangerous.

. . . And so it is with contemporary anorexics, whose resistance affirms a male medical establishment's patriarchy. . . .

Historical investigation . . . leads one to a certain relativism: immersion in the multiplicity of what were once received truths makes any contemporary attempt at truth seem just another game. . . . Even if there is a physiological link between weight, diet, and such diseases as heart attack and cancer, how we choose to incorporate this knowledge—how we take it into our bodies and the corporate structure that mediates our doing so—is by no means self-evident. . . .

Diet is of course only one aspect of the social obsession with the body's surface. The curious twist of the contemporary construction of bodies is expressed by Featherstone (1983: 18): 'Discipline and hedonism are no longer seen as incompatible, indeed the subjugation of the body through body maintenance routines is presented within consumer culture as a precondition for the achievement of an acceptable appearance and the release of the body's expressive capacity.' *Surviving Middle Age* is an ethnography of the rhetoric and practices of body maintenance routines from exercise to cosmetic surgery. As the authors have written more recently, 'a new breed of body main-tenance experts optimistically prescribe health foods, vitamins, dieting, fitness techniques, and other regimens to control *biological* age' (Feather-stone and Hepworth, 1989: 146). . . .

. . . At the foundation of these tastes is the body. Taste 'is *embodied* being inscribed onto the body and made apparent in body size, volume, demeanour, ways of eating, drinking, walking, sitting, speaking, making gestures, etc.' ([Feather-stone,] 1987: 123). Empirical investigation can then proceed in a number of directions, for exam-ple sport: 'Whereas the working-class men may engage in gymnastics to develop a *strong* body, the new middle class seek to produce a *healthy* or slim body' (1987: 129). What remains at issue in these choices is power, since the body is also a form of capital, this time 'physical capital' (Bourdieu, 1978: 832). . . .

Talking Bodies

. . . Objectivism presupposes the possibility of a 'God's-Eye-View' of the world. Reason, which cul-minates in formal propositional logic, employs abstract symbols to describe a reality that exists independently of the act of description. Such rea-son is disembodied ('transcendental') and univo-cal; since there is only one reality, there will ultimately be only one adequate description of it.

In the Objectivist version, abstract symbols can be mapped on to the single reality. 'The classical Objectivist view of knowledge assumes that "sci-ence" produces successive theories that progress ever and ever closer to *the* correct description of reality' (Johnson, 1987: xiii). . . .

[In contrast, w]hat the program is, is the embodiment of reason. . . . Thought begins at a pre-verbal level, in a primary experience of embod-iment. Through our bodies we first experience bal-ance, containment, force, cycles, and other basic metaphors. These experiences of embodiment then become what Johnson calls 'image schemata', which 'function somewhat like the abstract struc-ture of an image, and thereby connect up a vast range of different experiences that manifest this same recurring structure' (1987: 2). . . .

What is produced is not a new Objectivism based on compelling the truth of the body, but rather a resolution of the Objectivist/relativist dichotomy. If understanding and knowledge are projections of embodied image schemata, then they are clearly multivocal, not univocal. But because bodily experience is shared—we all experience balance, force, containment, and many, but not infinitely many, other bases of metaphor—there is a basis for mutual under-standing. The demise of Objectivism need not be rootless, anarchic, nihilistic relativism. . . . the body is not just 'practices', but neither is thinking unconstrained. Bodily metaphors may be multi-vocal, but they are not random. Multivocal embodiment suggests both the need and the grounding for what Habermas would call consen-sus about validity claims; claims will differ, but these differences admit commonalities of under-standing. What counts about validity claims is that they no longer can afford to exclude the body. We need to understand 'validity' as a cate-gory of shared experience that is both imagina-tive and embodied. . . .

For a Sociology of the Body

. . . Schwartz (1986: 109) . . . having constructed an elegantly simple model of the cultural bases of dietary practices, admits that when we turn from ideal types to empirical actions, 'The truth was a mess.' Between uncertainty as to what the body is, and the explanatory mess which its empirical study presents, can we have a sociology of the body?

Returning to Turner's theoretical matrix, we can certainly fit the materials surveyed here into it. We found patriarchy in the medieval families that produced holy anorexics and in contemporary medical clinics; panopticism takes on a new intensity in emotional labour; the asceticism of the modern dieter may be less intense than that of the holy anorexic, but it is more pervasive as a cultural phenomenon; and finally it is the commodification of the body that generates such problems for Zola's handicapped, since in its terms of representation their bodies can only be considered as deficient commodities. But as we consider any of these studies, the truth remains a mess. The holy anorexic responds to familial patriarchy, but only exchanges this for confessional panopticism; her asceticism turns her representational body into a commodity that she exchanges for warranted sanctity. In all of this the body itself slips away, lost in the social practices that constitute our dispositions and understandings of it. . . .

The body may be too slippery as substance for us to have a sociology *of*, but sociology is no less inevitably embodied. Thus, the value of Turner's theory, or any other, is not that it discloses some truth of bodies, but that it is an embodied conceptualization of society. 'Bringing bodies back in' is no rallying call to a sociology of the body; we do not need another 'theory group'. What we need is the reframing of the traditional concerns of social theory—order, function, contingency, rationality, and conflict could be mentioned—to understand these as categorical projections of embodiment. . . .

Note

My thanks to Mike Featherstone, Stephen O. Murray, Bryan S. Turner, and Kevin Young for their comments and suggested readings.

References

Bell, Rudolph M., with an epilogue by William N. Davis. 1985. *Holy Anorexia*. Chicago: University of Chicago Press.

Bologh, Rosalyn Wallace. 1987. 'Max Weber on Erotic Love', in Sam Whimster and Scott Lash, eds, *Max Weber, Rationality and Modernity*. London: Allen and Unwin.

Bourdieu, Pierre. 1978. 'Sport and Social Class', *Social Science Information* 17, 6: 819–40.

Crimp, Donald. 1988. 'AIDS: Cultural Analysis/Cultural Activism', *October* 43: 3–16.

Featherstone, Mike. 1983. 'The Body in Consumer Culture', *Theory, Culture & Society* 1, 2: 18–33.

———. 1987. 'Leisure, Symbolic Power, and the Life Course', in J. Horne et al., eds, *Leisure, Sport, and Social Relations*, Sociological Review Monograph 33. London: Routledge.

———, and Mike Hepworth. 1989. 'Aging and Old Age: Reflections on the Postmodern Life Course', in B. Bytheway et al., *Being and Becoming Old*. London: Sage.

Fisher, Sue. 1986. *In the Patient's Best Interest*. New Brunswick, NJ: Rutgers University Press.

Gregor, Thomas. 1986. *Anxious Pleasures: The Sexual Lives of an Amazonian People*. Chicago: University of Chicago Press.

Johnson, Diane, and John F. Murray. 1988. 'AIDS Without End', *New York Review of Books* 35, 13: 57–63.

Johnson, Mark. 1987. *The Body in the Mind: The Bodily Basis of Meaning, Imagination, and Reason*. Chicago: University of Chicago Press.

Kroker, Arthur, and Marilouise Kroker, eds. 1987. *Body Invaders: Panic Sex in America*. Don Mills, ON: Oxford University Press.

Murphy, Robert F. 1987. *The Body Silent*. New York: Henry Holt.

O'Neill, John. 1985. *Five Bodies*. Ithaca, NY: Cornell University Press.

Patterson, James T. 1987. *The Dread Disease: Cancer and Modern American Culture*. Cambridge, MA: Harvard University Press.

Scarry, Elaine. 1985. *The Body in Pain*. New York: Oxford University Press.

Schwartz, Hillel. 1986. *Never Satisfied: A Cultural History of Diets, Fantasies, and Fat*. New York: Free Press.

Turner, Bryan S. 1984. *The Body and Society*. Oxford: Blackwell.

———. 1987. 'The Rationalization of the Body: Reflections on Modernity and Discipline', in Sam Whimster and Scott Lash, eds, *Max Weber, Rationality and Modernity*. London: Allen and Unwin.

Zola, Irving Kenneth. 1982. *Missing Pieces*. Philadelphia: Temple University Press.

Additional References

Featherstone, Mike. 1989. 'Postmodernism, Cultural Change, and Social Practice', in D. Kellner, ed, *Postmodernism/Jameson/Critique*. Washington: Maisonneuve Press.

Foucault, Michel. 1978. *The History of Sexuality, Volume 1*. New York: Pantheon.

Lakoff, George, and Mark Johnson. 1980. *Metaphors We Live By*. Chicago: University of Chicago Press.

Roche, Maurice. 1988. 'On the Political Economy of the Lifeworld: A Review of John O'Neill's *Five Bodies*', *Philosophy of the Social Sciences* 18, 2: 259–63.

Chapter 3

Foucault, Femininity, and the Modernization of Patriarchal Power

Sandra Lee Bartky

I

In a striking critique of modern society, Michel Foucault has argued that the rise of parliamentary institutions and of new conceptions of political liberty was accompanied by a darker counter-movement, by the emergence of a new and unprecedented discipline directed against the body. More is required of the body now than mere political allegiance or the appropriation of the products of its labour: the new discipline invades the body and seeks to regulate its very forces and operations, the economy and efficiency of its movements.

The disciplinary practices Foucault describes are tied to peculiarly modern forms of the army, the school, the hospital, the prison, and the manufactory; the aim of these disciplines is to increase the utility of the body, to augment its forces . . .

The production of 'docile bodies' requires that an uninterrupted coercion be directed to the very processes of bodily activity, not just their result; this 'micro-physics of power' fragments and partitions the body's time, its space, and its movements.[1]

The student, then, is enclosed within a classroom and assigned to a desk he cannot leave; his ranking in the class can be read off the position of his desk in the serially ordered and segmented space of the classroom itself. Foucault tells us that 'Jean-Baptiste de la Salle dreamt of a classroom in which the spatial distribution might provide a whole series of distinctions at once, according to the pupil's progress, worth, character, application, cleanliness, and parents' fortune.'[2] The student

must sit upright, feet upon the floor, head erect; he may not slouch or fidget; his animate body is brought into a fixed correlation with the inanimate desk. . . .

The body's time, in these regimes of power, is as rigidly controlled as its space: the factory whistle and the school bell mark a division of time into discrete and segmented units that regulate the various activities of the day. . . . Control this rigid and precise cannot be maintained without a minute and relentless surveillance.

Jeremy Bentham's design for the panopticon, a model prison, captures for Foucault the essence of the disciplinary society. At the periphery of the panopticon, a circular structure; at the centre, a tower with wide windows that opens onto the inner side of the ring. The structure on the periphery is divided into cells, each with two windows, one facing the windows of the tower, the other facing the outside, allowing an effect of backlighting to make any figure visible within the cell. 'All that is needed, then, is to place a supervisor in a central tower and to shut up in each cell a madman, a patient, a condemned man, a worker, or a schoolboy.'[3] Each inmate is alone, shut off from effective communication with his fellows, but constantly visible from the tower. The effect of this is 'to induce in the inmate a state of conscious and permanent visibility that assures the automatic functioning of power'; each becomes to himself his own jailer.[4] This 'state of conscious and permanent visibility' is a sign that the tight, disciplinary control of the body has gotten a hold on the mind as well. In the perpetual self-surveillance of the inmate lies the genesis of the celebrated 'individualism' and heightened self-consciousness that are hallmarks of modern times. . . .

Foucault's account in *Discipline and Punish* of the disciplinary practices that produce the 'docile bodies' of modernity is a genuine tour de force, incorporating a rich theoretical account of the ways in which instrumental reason takes hold of the body with a mass of historical detail. But Foucault treats the body throughout as if it were one, as if the bodily experiences of men and women did not differ and as if men and women bore the same relationship to the characteristic institutions of modern life. Where is the account of the disciplinary practices that engender the 'docile bodies' of women, bodies more docile than the bodies of men? . . .

II

Styles of the female figure vary over time and across cultures: they reflect cultural obsessions and preoccupations in ways that are still poorly understood. Today, massiveness, power, or abundance in a woman's body is met with distaste. The current body of fashion is taut, small-breasted, narrow-hipped, and of a slimness bordering on emaciation; it is a silhouette that seems more appropriate to an adolescent boy or a newly pubescent girl than to an adult woman. Since ordinary women have normally quite different dimensions, they must of course diet. . . .

Dieting disciplines the body's hungers: appetite must be monitored at all times and governed by an iron will. Since the innocent need of the organism for food will not be denied, the body becomes one's enemy, an alien being bent on thwarting the disciplinary project. Anorexia nervosa, which has now assumed epidemic proportions, is to women of the late twentieth century what hysteria was to women of an earlier day: the crystallization in a pathological mode of a widespread cultural obsession.[5] . . .

It is not only her natural appetite or unreconstructed contours that pose a danger to woman: the very expressions of her face can subvert the disciplinary project of bodily perfection. An expressive face lines and creases more readily than an inexpressive one. Hence, if women are unable to suppress strong emotions, they can at least learn to inhibit the tendency of the face to register them. Sophia Loren recommends a unique solution to this problem: a piece of tape applied to the forehead or between the brows will tug at the skin when one frowns and act as a reminder to relax the face.[6] The tape is to be worn whenever a woman is home alone.

III

There are significant gender differences in gesture, posture, movement, and general bodily comportment: women are far more restricted than men in their manner of movement and in their spatiality. In her classic paper on the subject, Iris Young observes that a space seems to surround women in imagination that they are hesitant to move beyond: this manifests itself both in a reluctance to reach, stretch, and extend the body to meet resistances of matter in motion—as in sport or in the performance of physical tasks—and in a typically constricted posture and general style of movement. Woman's space is not a field in which her bodily intentionality can be freely realized but an enclosure in which she feels herself positioned and by which she is confined.[7] The 'loose woman' violates these norms: her looseness is manifest not only in her morals, but [also] in her manner of speech and quite literally in the free and easy way she moves.

In an extraordinary series of over two thousand photographs, many candid shots taken in the street, the German photographer Marianne Wex has documented differences in typical masculine and feminine body posture. Women sit waiting for trains with arms close to the body, hands folded together in their laps, toes pointing straight ahead or turned inward, and legs pressed together.[8] The women in these photographs make themselves small and narrow, harmless; they seem tense; they take up little space. Men, on the other hand, expand into the available space; they sit with legs far apart and arms flung out at some distance from the body. Most common in these sitting male figures is what Wex calls the 'proffering position': the men sit with legs thrown wide apart, crotch visible, feet pointing outward, often with an arm and a casually dangling hand resting comfortably on an open, spread thigh. . . .

. . . Women are trained to smile more than men, too. In the economy of smiles, as elsewhere, there is evidence that women are exploited, for they give more than they receive in return; in a smile elicitation study, one researcher found that the rate of smile return by women was 93 per cent, by men only 67 per cent.[9] In many typical women's jobs, graciousness, deference, and the readiness to serve are part of the work; this requires the worker to fix a smile on her face for a good part of the working day, whatever her inner state.[10] The economy of touching is out of balance, too: men touch women more often and on more parts of the body than women touch men: female secretaries, factory workers, and waitresses report that such liberties are taken routinely with their bodies.[11] . . .

IV

We have examined some of the disciplinary practices a woman must master in pursuit of a body of the right size and shape that also displays the proper styles of feminine motility. But woman's body is an ornamented surface too, and there is much discipline involved in this production as well. Here, especially in the application of makeup and the selection of clothes, art and discipline converge, though, as I shall argue, there is less art involved than one might suppose.

A woman's skin must be soft, supple, hairless, and smooth; ideally, it should betray no sign of wear, experience, age, or deep thought. Hair must be removed not only from the face but from large surfaces of the body as well, from legs and thighs, an operation accomplished by shaving, buffing with fine sandpaper, or applying foul-smelling depilatories. With the new high-leg bathing suits and leotards, a substantial amount of pubic hair must be removed too.[12] The removal of facial hair can be more specialized. Eyebrows are plucked out by the roots with a tweezer. Hot wax is sometimes poured onto the mustache and cheeks and then ripped away when it cools. The woman who wants a more permanent result may try electroly-

sis: this involves the killing of a hair root by the passage of an electric current down a needle that has been inserted into its base. The procedure is painful and expensive.

The development of what one 'beauty expert' calls 'good skincare habits' requires not only attention to health, the avoidance of strong facial expressions, and the performance of facial exercises, but also the regular use of skincare preparations, many to be applied more often than once a day: cleansing lotions (ordinary soap and water 'upsets the skin's acid and alkaline balance'), wash-off cleansers (milder than cleansing lotions), astringents, toners, makeup removers, night creams, nourishing creams, eye creams, moisturizers, skin balancers, body lotions, hand creams, lip pomades, suntan lotions, sunscreens, and facial masks. . . .

The normalizing discourse of modern medicine is enlisted by the cosmetics industry to gain credibility for its claims. . . . The Clinique computer at any Clinique counter will select a combination of preparations just right for you. Ultima II contains 'procollagen' in its anti-aging eye cream that 'provides hydration' to 'demoralizing lines'. 'Biotherm' eye cream dramatically improves the 'biomechanical properties of the skin'.[13] . . .

. . . A woman must learn the proper manipulation of a large number of devices—the blow dryer, styling brush, curling iron, hot curlers, wire curlers, eyeliner, lipliner, lipstick brush, eyelash curler, and mascara brush. And she must learn to apply a wide variety of products—foundation, toner, covering stick, mascara, eyeshadow, eyegloss, blusher, lipstick, rouge, lip gloss, hair dye, hair rinse, hair lightener, hair 'relaxer', and so on.

In the language of fashion magazines and cosmetic ads, making-up is typically portrayed as an aesthetic activity in which a woman can express her individuality. In reality, while cosmetic styles change every decade or so, and while some variation in makeup is permitted depending on the occasion, making-up the face is, in fact, a highly stylized activity that gives little rein to self-expression. Painting the face is not like painting a picture; at best, it might be described as painting the same picture over and over again with minor variations. Little latitude is permitted in what is considered appropriate makeup for the office and for most social occasions; indeed, the woman who uses cosmetics in a genuinely novel and imaginative way is liable to be seen not as an artist but as an eccentric. . . .

V

. . . To succeed in the provision of a beautiful or sexy body gains a woman attention and some admiration but little real respect and rarely any social power. A woman's effort to master feminine body discipline will lack importance just because she does it: her activity partakes of the general depreciation of everything female. In spite of unrelenting pressure to 'make the most of what she has', women are ridiculed and dismissed for their interest in such 'trivial' things as clothes and makeup. . . .

VI

If what we have described is a genuine discipline—a system of 'micro-power' that is 'essentially non-egalitarian and asymmetrical'—who then are the disciplinarians?[14] Who is the top sergeant in the disciplinary regime of femininity? Historically, the law has had some responsibility for enforcement: in times gone by, for example, individuals who appeared in public in the clothes of the other sex could be arrested. While crossdressers are still liable to some harassment, the kind of discipline we are considering is not the business of the police or the courts. Parents and teachers, of course, have extensive influence, admonishing girls to be demure and ladylike, to 'smile pretty', to sit with their legs together. The influence of the media is pervasive, too, constructing as it does an image of the female body as spectacle . . .

. . . The disciplinary power that inscribes femininity in the female body is everywhere and it is nowhere; the disciplinarian is everyone and yet no one in particular. . . .

Now the transformation of oneself into a properly feminine body may be any or all of the following: a rite of passage into adulthood, the

adoption and celebration of a particular aesthetic, a way of announcing one's economic level and social status, a way to triumph over other women in the competition for men or jobs, or an opportunity for massive narcissistic indulgence.[15] The social construction of the feminine body is all these things, but at its base it is discipline, too, and discipline of the inegalitarian sort. The absence of formally identifiable disciplinarians and of a public schedule of sanctions only disguises the extent to which the imperative to be 'feminine' serves the interest of domination. This is a lie in which all concur: making-up is merely artful play; one's first pair of high-heeled shoes is an innocent part of growing up, not the modern equivalent of foot-binding. . . .

VII

The lack of formal public sanctions does not mean that a woman who is unable or unwilling to submit herself to the appropriate body discipline will face no sanctions at all. On the contrary, she faces a very severe sanction indeed in a world dominated by men: the refusal of male patronage. For the heterosexual woman, this may mean the loss of a badly needed intimacy; for both heterosexual women and lesbians, it may well mean the refusal of a decent livelihood. . . .

. . . Women, then, like other skilled individuals, have a stake in the perpetuation of their skills, whatever it may have cost to acquire them and quite apart from the question whether, as a gender, they would have been better off had they never had to acquire them in the first place. . . .

Resistance from this source may be joined by a reluctance to part with the rewards of compliance; further, many women will resist the abandonment of an aesthetic that defines what they take to be beautiful. But there is still another source of resistance, one more subtle, perhaps, but tied once again to questions of identity and internalization. To have a body felt to be 'feminine'—a body socially constructed through the appropriate practices—is in most cases crucial to a woman's sense of herself as female and, since persons currently can *be* only as male or female, to her sense of herself as an existing individual. To possess such a body may also be essential to her sense of herself as a sexually desiring and desirable subject. Hence, any political project that aims to dismantle the machinery that turns a female body into a feminine one may well be apprehended by a woman as something that threatens her with de-sexualization, if not outright annihilation. . . .

. . . [M]odern society has seen the emergence of increasingly invasive apparatuses of power: these exercise a far more restrictive social and psychological control than was heretofore possible. In modern societies, effects of power 'circulate through progressively finer channels, gaining access to individuals themselves, to their bodies, their gestures, and all their daily actions.'[16] Power now seeks to transform the minds of those individuals who might be tempted to resist it, not merely to punish or imprison their bodies. This requires two things: a finer control of the body's time and of its movements—a control that cannot be achieved without ceaseless surveillance and a better understanding of the specific person, of the genesis and nature of his 'case'. The power these new apparatuses seek to exercise requires a new knowledge of the individual: modern psychology and sociology are born. Whether the new modes of control have charge of correction, production, education, or the provision of welfare, they resemble one another; they exercise power in a bureaucratic mode—faceless, centralized, and pervasive. A reversal has occurred: power has now become anonymous, while the project of control has brought into being a new individuality. In fact, Foucault believes that the operation of power constitutes the very subjectivity of the subject. Here, the image of the panopticon returns: knowing that he may be observed from the tower at any time, the inmate takes over the job of policing himself. The gaze that is inscribed in the very structure of the disciplinary institution is internalized by the inmate: modern technologies of behaviour are thus oriented toward the production of isolated and self-policing subjects.[17]

Women have their own experience of the modernization of power, one that begins later but follows in many respects the course outlined by Foucault. In important ways, a woman's behaviour is less regulated now than it was in the past. She has more mobility and is less confined to domestic space. She enjoys what to previous generations would have been an unimaginable sexual liberty. Divorce, access to paid work outside the home, and the increasing secularization of modern life have loosened the hold over her of the traditional family and, in spite of the current fundamentalist revival, of the church. Power in these institutions was wielded by individuals known to her. Husbands and fathers enforced patriarchal authority in the family. As in the *ancien régime*, a woman's body was subject to sanctions if she disobeyed. Not Foucault's royal individual but the Divine Individual decreed that her desire be always 'unto her husband', while the person of the priest made known to her God's more specific intentions concerning her place and duties. In the days when civil and ecclesiastical authority were still conjoined, individuals formally invested with power were charged with the correction of recalcitrant women whom the family had somehow failed to constrain. . . .

As modern industrial societies change and as women themselves offer resistance to patriarchy, older forms of domination are eroded. But new forms arise, spread, and become consolidated. Women are no longer required to be chaste or modest, to restrict their sphere of activity to the home, or even to realize their properly feminine destiny in maternity: normative femininity is coming more and more to be centred on woman's body—not its duties and obligations or even its capacity to bear children, but its sexuality, more precisely, its presumed heterosexuality and its appearance. . . .

To subject oneself to the new disciplinary power is to be up-to-date, to be 'with-it'; as I have argued, it is presented to us in ways that are regularly disguised. It is fully compatible with the current need for women's wage labour, the cult of youth and fitness, and the need of advanced capitalism to maintain high levels of consumption. Further, it represents a saving in the economy of enforcement: since it is women themselves who practise this discipline on and against their own bodies, men get off scot-free.

The woman who checks her makeup half a dozen times a day to see if her foundation has caked or her mascara has run, who worries that the wind or the rain may spoil her hairdo, who looks frequently to see if her stockings have bagged at the ankle or who, feeling fat, monitors everything she eats, has become, just as surely as the inmate of the panopticon, a self-policing subject, a self committed to a relentless self-suveillance. This self-surveillance is a form of obedience to patriarchy. It is also the reflection in woman's consciousness of the fact that *she* is under surveillance in ways that *he* is not, that whatever else she may become, she is important-ly a body designed to please or to excite. There has been induced in many women, then, in Foucault's words, 'a state of conscious and perma-nent visibility that assures the automatic func-tioning of power'.[18] Since the standards of female bodily acceptability are impossible fully to realize, requiring as they do a virtual transcendence of nature, a woman may live much of her life with a pervasive feeling of bodily deficiency. Hence a tighter control of the body has gained a new kind of hold over the mind. . . .

In the current political climate, there is no rea-son to anticipate either widespread resistance to currently fashionable modes of feminine embodi-ment or joyous experimentation with new 'styles of the flesh'; moreover, such novelties would face profound opposition from material and psycho-logical sources identified earlier in this essay (see section VII). In spite of this, a number of opposi-tional discourses and practices have appeared in recent years. An increasing number of women are 'pumping iron', a few with little concern for the limits of body development imposed by current canons of femininity. Women in radical lesbian communities have also rejected hegemonic images of femininity and are struggling to devel-op a new female aesthetic. A striking feature of such communities is the extent to which they have overcome the oppressive identification of female beauty and desirability with youth; here, the physical features of aging—'character' lines and graying hair—not only do not diminish a woman's attractiveness, they may even enhance it. A popular literature of resistance is growing, some of it analytical and reflective, like Kim Chernin's *The Obsession*, some oriented toward practical self-help, like Marcia Hutchinson's recent *Transforming Body Image, Learning to Love the Body You Have*. This literature reflects a mood akin in some ways to that other and earlier mood of quiet desperation to which Betty Friedan gave voice in *The Feminine Mystique*. . . .

Notes

1. Michel Foucault, *Discipline and Punish: The Birth of the Prison*, trans. Alan Sheridan (New York: Vintage Books, 1979): 28.

2. Ibid., 147.

3. Ibid., 200.

4. Ibid., 201.

5. Susan Bordo, 'Anorexia Nervosa: Psychopathology as the Crystallization of Culture', *Philosophical Forum* 17, 2 (Winter 1985–86): 73–104.

6. Sophia Loren, *Women and Beauty* (New York: William Morrow, 1984): 57.

7. Iris Young, 'Throwing Like a Girl: A Phenomen-ology of Feminine Body Comportment, Motility, and Spatiality', *Human Studies* 3 (1980): 137–56.

8. Marianne Wex, *Let's Take Back Our Space: "Female" and "Male" Body Language as a Result of Patriarchal Structures* (Berlin: Frauenliterarurverlag Hermine Fees, 1979). Wex claims (23) that Japanese women are still taught to position their feet so that the toes point inward, a traditional sign of submissiveness.

9. Nancy Henley, *Body Politics* (Englewood Cliffs, NJ: Prentice Hall, 1977): 176.

10. For an account of the sometimes devastating effects on workers, like flight attendants, whose conditions of employment require the display of a perpetual friendliness, see Arlie Hochschild, *The Managed Heart: The Commercialization of Human Feeling* (Berkeley: University of California Press, 1983).

11. Henley, *Body Politics*, 108.

12. Clairol has just introduced a small electric shaver, the 'Bikini', apparently intended for just such use.

13. *Chicago Magazine* (March 1986): 43, 10, 18, and 62.

14. Foucault, *Discipline and Punish*, 222: 'The general juridical form that guaranteed a system of rights that were egalitarian in principle was supported by these tiny, everyday, physical mechanisms, by all those systems of micro-power that are essentially non-egalitarian and asymmetrical that we call disciplines.'

15. See my paper 'Narcissism, Femininity, and Aliena-tion', in *Social Theory and Practice* 8, 2 (Summer 1982): 127–43.

16. Michel Foucault, *Power/Knowledge: Selected Interviews and Other Writings, 1972–1977*, ed. Colin Gordon (Brighton, UK: 1980): 151. Quoted in Peter Dews, 'Power and Subjectivity in Foucault', *New Left Review*, no. 144 (March–April 1987): 17.

17. Dews, 'Power and Subjectivity in Foucault', 77.

18. Ibid., 201.

Part II

Bodies in Historical Context

Jacqueline Low and Claudia Malacrida

In *The Civilizing Process* Norbert Elias (1978) explains his theory of **social figuration**, by which he means the process of large-scale socio-cultural change over time, from the Medieval period to the beginnings of modern society during the Renaissance (fourteenth–seventeenth centuries). He argues that, in the West, social figuration has led to the process of **individuation**, the emergence of a private person with individual motives, desires, and modes of action, rather than a public person existing only as part of a larger society that imposes its will on him or her. He supports his claims by analyzing the history of manners, in particular how they relate to body conduct, and demonstrates how the **civilized body** is one that is more often subject to internal rather than external forms of social control. For instance, in childhood we internalize table manners so deeply that we no longer need any person or thing external to ourselves to tell us to chew with our mouths closed.

Beginning in ancient Greece, Anthony Synnott (1993) critically discusses the various types of body that have existed throughout history. He explains how in ancient Rome and Greece public discourses of the body emphasized a separation of the mind from the body, as well as a higher valuing of the mind over the body. Among early Christians a division was also made between the soul and the body, where the body was understood to be merely a temple or container for the soul. It is here that we see the emergence of the **aesthetic body**, where the devout **mortify their flesh** by such bodily practices as fasting or flagellation (whipping themselves) in order to show that the physical body is of little importance and that it is the soul that matters. These dualistic bodies culminate in the Renaissance with Descartes' concept of **Cartesian dualism**, where the body is understood to be separate from the mind and emotions. Descartes also gives us the machine metaphor for the body, where the body, like a clock, is understood as an entity made up of parts. Such a **mechanistic** view of the body remains with us today as part of the **biomedical model** of health, illness, and the workings of the body. Under this model the body is reduced to a machine comprised of parts. Moreover, under the biomedical model, the victim of ill health is blamed for disease by locating the sources and solutions to health problems solely within the parts of the individual body rather than being located in the environment or being explained through social forces.

Sander L. Gilman's article (1996) provides an overview of historical sociological treatments of race and sexuality, and along the way shows us that some Victorian-era (1840–1900) sociologists and criminologists were obsessed with the study of bodies, indirectly contradicting Shilling's claim that sociology traditionally had little direct interest in the body (see Part I). He begins with the story of Sarah Bartmann, an African woman who was exhibited across Europe as 'proof' of the physical and moral differences between Europeans and Africans. This treatment of Bartmann can be seen as an example of **biodeterminism**, wherein biological, bodily characteristics are presumed to be the immutable and natural cause of traits that are in fact cultural or social. In Bartmann's case, the Europeans' exploitation of her buttocks, labia, and other sexual attributes provided the basis for an argument that Africans, and African women particularly, were hypersexual and foundationally immoral. In light of the slave trade and the colonial ambitions of Europeans at the time, these ideas formed a basis for the argument that Africa *needed* Europeans to bring moral propriety and a 'civilizing touch' to the 'dark continent'. Thus, the sociological use of Sarah Bartmann's body was political, manipulated to provide evidence of and justification for European ambitions. Students interested in learning more about Sarah Bartmann and in seeing some of the imagery Gilman describes are advised to explore the following website: http://www.southafrica.info/ess_info/sa_glance/history/saartjie.htm.

Another Victorian-era sociological focus on the body is exemplified in early criminology. Stemming from moral panics concerning the rise of prostitution and street crime during the early stages of **urbanization**, where large numbers of people moved from rural to urban areas, and the **Industrial Revolution**, where the means of production turned from home-based subsistence labour to factory-based wage labour, criminologists such as Cesare Lombroso were intensely focused on certain kinds of unruly or criminal bodies. Their work was also **biodeterminist**, based on the assumption that these bodily 'types' represented mirrors onto the soul and moral properties of their owners. From attempting to determine the physical properties of women 'prone to prostitution' to outlining the facial features of the thief, an entire field of study was formed. With the advent of technologies such as photography and statistics, these researchers were able to draw on large samples of people in order to formulate their tables and typologies. The ability to identify potentially dangerous types would permit reformers to rid society of this threat and would provide them with a biological argument to justify their **racist** (tying of negative behavioural traits to physical characteristics) and **misogynist** (negative attitudes towards women) beliefs. Thus, Victorian-era sociological thinking about race and about female sexuality can be seen as a form of scientific **'othering'**, in which the 'other' is characterized as dangerous or abnormal, unlike the 'one' (in this case, white, 'moral', European males). The 'other' becomes a site for social control and also acts 'because of its difference' to highlight the 'natural' goodness of the 'one'.

References

Elias, N. 1978. *The Civilizing Process: The History of Manners* trans. E. Jephcott. Oxford: Basil Blackwell Publishers.

Gilman, S.L. 1996. 'The Hottentot and the Prostitute: Toward an Iconography of Female Sexuality', in *Difference and Pathology: Stereotypes of Sexuality, Race, and Madness*. Ithaca, NY, and London: Cornell University Press, 76–108.

Rafter, N.H. 1997. *Creating Born Criminals*. Urbana and Chicago: Illinois University Press.

Synnott, A. 1993. 'Body: Tomb, Temple, Machine, and Self', in A. Synnott, *The Body Social: Symbolism, Self and Society*. London and New York: Routledge, 7–37.

Chapter 4

From *The Civilizing Process: The History of Manners*

Norbert Elias

Changes in Attitude Toward the Natural Functions

From *S'ensuivent les contenances de la table*:
Before you sit down, make sure your seat has not been fouled.

From *Ein spruch der ze tische kêrt*:[1]
329 Do not touch yourself under your clothes with your bare hands.
. . .

Some Remarks on the Examples and on these Changes in General

Erasmus's treatise marks, for these areas too, a point on the curve of civilization that represents, on the one hand, a notable rise of the shame threshold, compared to the preceding epoch; and on the other, compared to more recent times, a freedom in speaking of natural functions, a 'lack of shame', which to most people adhering to the present-day standard may at first appear incomprehensible and often 'embarrassing'.

But at the same time, it is quite clear that this treatise has precisely the function of cultivating feelings of shame. . . .

The different standard of society at Erasmus's time becomes clear if one reads how commonplace it is to meet someone 'qui urinam reddit aut alvum exonerat' (urinating or defecating). [It indicates] . . . greater freedom with which people were able at this time to perform and speak about their bodily functions before others. . .

The different standard is also visible when Erasmus says it is not civil to require that the young man 'ventris flatum retineat' (hold back his wind), for in doing so he might, under the appearance of urbanity, contract an illness; and Erasmus comments similarly on sneezing and related acts.

Medical arguments are not found very frequently in this treatise. When they occur it is almost always, as here, to oppose demands for the restraint of natural functions; whereas later, above all in the nineteenth century, they nearly always serve as instruments to compel restraint and renunciation of instinctual gratification. It is only in the twentieth century that a slight relaxation appears. . . .

. . . However, if one takes a comprehensive view, a pattern emerges that is typical of the civilizing process. . . .

Stricter control of impulses and emotions is first imposed by those of high social rank on their social inferiors or, at most, their social equals. It is only comparatively late, when bourgeois classes comprising a large number of social equals have become the upper, ruling class, that the family becomes the only—or, more exactly, the primary and dominant—institution with the function of installing drive control. Only then does the social dependence of the child on its parents become particularly important as leverage for the socially required regulation and moulding of impulses and emotions.

In the stage of the feudal courts, and still more in that of the absolute courts, the courts themselves largely fulfilled this function for the upper class. In the latter stage, much of what has been made 'second nature' to us has not yet been inculcated in this form, as an automatic self-restraint, a habit that, within certain limits, also functions when a person is alone. Rather, restraint on the instincts is at first imposed only in the company of others, i.e., more consciously for social reasons. And both the kind and the degree of restraint correspond to the social position of the person imposing them, relative to the position of those in whose company he is. This slowly changes as people move closer together socially and as the hierarchical character of society becomes less rigid. As the interdependence of men increases with the increasing division of labour, everyone becomes increasingly dependent on everyone else, those of high social rank on those socially inferior and weaker. The latter become so much the equals of the former that they, the socially superior, feel shame even before their inferiors. It is only now that the armour of restraints is fastened to the degree that is gradually taken for granted by people in democratic industrial societies. . . .

But this isolation of the natural functions from public life, and the corresponding regulation or moulding of instinctual urges, was only possible because, together with growing sensitivity, a technical apparatus was developed that solved fairly satisfactorily the problem of eliminating these functions from social life and displacing them behind the scenes. The situation was not unlike that regarding table manners. The process of social change, the advance in the frontiers of shame and the threshold of repugnance, cannot be explained by any one thing, and certainly not by the development of technology or by scientific discoveries. . . .

After a reshaping of human needs had once been set in motion with the general transformation of human relations, the development of a technical apparatus corresponding to the changed standard consolidated the changed habits to an extraordinary degree. This apparatus served both the constant reproduction of the standard and its dissemination. . . .

The individual inclinations and tendencies that medieval writings on etiquette were con-

cerned to control were often the same as can be frequently observed in children today. However, they are now dealt with so early that certain kinds of 'misbehaviour' that were quite commonplace in the medieval world scarcely manifest themselves in present-day social life. . . .

The standard of delicacy represented by *Galateo* also demands a detachment from these instinctual tendencies. But the pressure to transform such inclinations exerted on the individual by society is minimal compared to that of today. The feeling of revulsion, distaste, or disgust aroused by such behaviour is, in keeping with the earlier standard, incomparably weaker than ours. Consequently, the social prohibition on the expression of such feelings is much less grave. This behaviour is not regarded as a 'pathological anomaly' or 'perversion', but rather as an offense against tact, politeness, or good form. . . .

Nevertheless, in one way this example marks a turning point. It may be supposed that the expression of these feelings was not lacking in the preceding period. But only now does it begin to attract attention. Society is gradually beginning to suppress the positive pleasure component in certain functions more and more strongly by the arousal of anxiety; or, more exactly, it is rendering this pleasure 'private' and 'secret' (i.e., suppressing it within the individual), while fostering the negatively charged affects—displeasure, revulsion, distaste—as the only feelings customary in society. But precisely by this increased social proscription of many impulses, by their 'repression' from the surface both of social life and of consciousness, the distance between the personality structure and behaviour of adults and children is necessarily increased.

On Blowing One's Nose

. . . In medieval society people generally blew their noses into their hands, just as they ate with their hands. That necessitated special precepts for nose-cleaning at table. Politeness, *courtoisie*, required that one blow one's nose with the left hand if one took meat with the right. But this precept was in fact restricted to the table. It arose solely out of consideration for others. The distasteful feeling frequently aroused today by the mere thought of soiling the fingers in this way was at first entirely absent.

Again . . . examples show very clearly how slowly the seemingly simplest instruments of civilization have developed. They also illustrate to a certain degree the particular social and psychological preconditions that were required to make the need for and use of so simple an instrument general. The use of the handkerchief—like that of the fork—first established itself in Italy, and was diffused on account of its prestige value. . . . And since it is precious and relatively expensive, at first there are not many of them even among the upper class. Henri IV, at the end of the sixteenth century, possessed . . . five handkerchiefs. And it is generally taken as a sign of wealth not to blow one's nose into one's hand or sleeve but into a handkerchief. Louis XIV is the first to have an abundant supply of handkerchiefs, and under him the use of them becomes general, at least in courtly circles.

Here, as so often, the transitional situation is clearly visible in Erasmus. It is proper to use a handkerchief, he says, and if people of a higher social position are present, turn away when blowing your nose. But he also says: If you blow your nose with two fingers and something falls to the ground, tread on it. The use of the handkerchief is known but not yet widely disseminated, even in the upper class for which Erasmus primarily writes.

Two centuries later, the situation is almost reversed. The use of the handkerchief has become general, at least among people who lay claim to 'good behaviour'. But the use of the hands has by no means disappeared. Seen from above, it has become 'ill-mannered', or at any rate common and vulgar. One reads with amusement La Salle's gradations between *vilain*, for certain very coarse ways of blowing the nose with the hand, and *très contraire à la bienséance*, for the better manner of doing so with two fingers. . . .

Once the handkerchief begins to come into use, there constantly recurs a prohibition on a new form of 'bad manners' that emerges at the same time as the new practice—the prohibition on looking into one's handkerchief when one has used it. . . . It almost seems as if inclinations that have been subjected to a certain control and restraint by the introduction of the handkerchief are seeking a new outlet in this way. . . .

. . . The difference between what is expected of knights and lords, on the one hand, and of the *donizelli*, pages, or servants, on the other, calls to mind a much-documented social phenomenon. The masters find the sight of the bodily functions of their servants distasteful; they compel them, the social inferiors in their immediate surroundings, to control and restrain these functions in a way that they do not at first impose on themselves. The verse addressed to the masters says simply: If you blow your nose, turn round so that nothing falls on the table. There is no mention of using a cloth. Should we believe that the use of cloths for cleaning the nose was already taken so much for granted in this society that it was no longer thought necessary to mention it in a book on manners? That is highly improbable. The servants, on the other hand, are expressly instructed to use not their fingers but their foot bandages if they have to blow their noses. To be sure, this interpretation of the two verses cannot be considered absolutely certain. But the fact can be frequently demonstrated that functions are found distasteful and disrespectful in inferiors that superiors are not ashamed of in themselves. This fact takes on special significance with the transformation of society under absolutism, and therefore at absolutist courts, when the upper class, the aristocracy as a whole, has become, with degrees of hierarchy, a subservient and socially dependent class. This at first sight highly paradoxical phenomenon of an upper class that is socially extremely dependent will be discussed later in another context. Here we can only point out that this social dependence and its structure have decisive importance for the structure and pattern of affect restrictions. The example [of blowing the nose] contain[s] numerous indications of how these restrictions are intensified with the growing dependence of the upper class. It is no accident that the first 'peak of refinement' or 'delicacy' in the manner of blowing the nose—and not only here—comes in the phase when the dependence and subservience of the aristocratic upper class is at its height, the period of Louis XIV. . . .

The dependence of the upper class also explains the dual aspect that the behaviour patterns and instruments of civilization have at least in this formative stage. They express a certain measure of compulsion and renunciation, but they also immediately become a weapon against social inferiors, a means of distinction. Handkerchief, fork, plates, and all their related implements are at first luxury articles with a particular social prestige value. . . .

The social dependence in which the succeeding upper class, the bourgeoisie, lives, is of a different kind, to be sure, from that of the court aristocracy, but tends to be greater and more compelling.

In general, we scarcely realize today what a unique and astonishing phenomenon a 'working' upper class is. Why does it work? Why submit itself to this compulsion even though it is the 'ruling' class and is therefore not commanded to do so? The question demands a more detailed answer than is possible in this context. What is clear, however, is the parallel to what has been said on the change in the instruments and forms of conditioning. During the stage of the court aristocracy, the restraint imposed on inclinations and emotions is based primarily on consideration and respect due to others and above all to social superiors. In the subsequent stage, renunciation and restraint of impulses is compelled far less by particular persons; expressed provisionally and approximately, it is now, more directly than before, the less visible and more impersonal compulsions of social interdependence, the division of labour, the market, and competition that impose restraint and control on the impulses and emotions. It is these pressures, and the corresponding manner of explanation and conditioning mentioned above, which make it appear that socially desirable behaviour is voluntarily produced by the individual himself, on his own

initiative. This applies to the regulation and restraint of drives necessary for 'work'; it also applies to the whole pattern according to which drives are modelled in bourgeois industrial societies. . . .

On Behaviour in the Bedroom

. . . The bedroom has become one of the most 'private' and 'intimate' areas of human life. Like most other bodily functions, sleeping has been increasingly shifted behind the scenes of social life. The nuclear family remains as the only legitimate, socially sanctioned enclave for this and many other human functions. Its visible and invisible walls withdraw the most 'private', 'intimate', irrepressibly 'animal' aspects of human existence from the sight of others.

In medieval society this function had not been thus privatized and separated from the rest of social life. It was quite normal to receive visitors in rooms with beds, and the beds themselves had a prestige value related to their opulence. It was very common for many people to spend the night in one room: in the upper class, the master with his servants, the mistress with her maid or maids; in other classes, even men and women in the same room,[2] and often guests staying overnight.[3]

Those who did not sleep in their clothes undressed completely. In general, people slept naked in lay society, and in monastic orders either fully dressed or fully undressed according to the strictness of the rules. . . .

This unconcern in showing the naked body, and the position of the shame frontier represented by it, are seen particularly clearly in bathing manners. It has been noted with surprise in later ages that knights were waited on in their baths by women; likewise, their night drink was often brought to their beds by women. It seems to have been common practice, at least in the towns, to undress at home before going to the bathhouse. 'How often', says an observer, 'the father, wearing nothing but his breeches, with his naked wife and children, runs through the streets from his house to the baths. . . . How many times have I seen girls of 10, 12, 14, 16, and 18 years entirely naked except for a short smock, often torn, and a ragged bathing gown at front and back! With this open at the feet and with their hands held decorously behind them, running from their houses through the long streets at midday to the baths. How many completely naked boys of 10, 12, 14, and 16 run beside them.' . . .[4]

This unconcern disappears slowly in the sixteenth and more rapidly in the seventeenth, eighteenth, and nineteenth centuries, first in the upper classes and much more slowly in the lower. Up to then, the whole mode of life, with its greater closeness of individuals, made the sight of the naked body, at least in the proper place, incomparably more commonplace than in the first stages of the modern age. 'We reach the surprising conclusion', it has been said with reference to Germany, 'that . . . the sight of total nakedness was the everyday rule up to the sixteenth century. Everyone undressed completely each evening before going to bed, and likewise no clothing was worn in the steambaths.'[5] And this certainly applies not only to Germany. People had a less inhibited—one might say a more childish—attitude toward the body, and to many of its functions. Sleeping customs show this no less than bathing habits.

A special nightdress slowly came into use at roughly the same time as the fork and handkerchief. Like the other 'implements of civilization', it made its way through Europe quite gradually. And like them it is a symbol of the decisive change taking place at this time in human beings. Sensitivity toward everything that came into contact with the body increased. Shame became attached to behaviour that had previously been free of such feelings. . . . [A]n advance of the shame frontier, a thrust toward greater restraint—is repeated here, as so often in the course of history. The unconcern in showing oneself naked disappears, as does that in performing bodily functions before others. And as this sight becomes less commonplace in social life, the depiction of the naked body in art takes on a new significance. More than hitherto it becomes a dream image, an emblem of wish-fulfillment. To use Schiller's terms it becomes 'sentimental', as

against the 'naïve' form of earlier phases.

In the courtly society of France—where getting up and going to bed, at least in the case of great lords and ladies, is incorporated directly into social life—nightdress, like every other form of clothing appearing in the communal life of man, takes on representational functions as it develops. This changes when, with the rise of broader classes, getting up and going to bed become intimate and are displaced from social life into the interior of the nuclear family. . . .

The examples [above] give a rough idea of how sleep, becoming slowly more intimate and private, is separated from most other social relations, and how the precepts given to young people take on a specific moralistic undertone with the advance of feelings of shame. In the medieval quotation . . . the restraint demanded of young people is explained by consideration due to others, respect for social superiors. It says, in effect, 'If you share your bed with a better man, ask him which side he prefers, and do not go to bed before he invites you, for that is not courteous.' . . . In Erasmus we begin to hear a moral demand, which requires certain behaviour not out of consideration for others but for its own sake: 'When you undress, when you get up, be mindful• of modesty.' But the idea of social custom, of consideration for others, is still predominant. The contrast to the later period is particularly clear if we remember that these precepts . . . were clearly directed to people who went to bed undressed. That strangers should sleep in the same bed appears, to judge by the manner in which the question is discussed, neither unusual nor in any way improper even at the time of Erasmus.

In . . . quotations from the eighteenth century this tendency is not continued in a straight line, partly because it is no longer confined predominantly to the upper class. But in the meantime, even in other classes, it has clearly become less commonplace for a young person to share his bed with another: 'If you are forced by unavoidable necessity to share a bed with another person . . . on a journey, it is not proper to lie so near him that you disturb or even touch him', La Salle writes. . . . 'You ought neither to undress nor go to bed in the presence of any other person.'

In the 1774 edition, details are again avoided wherever possible. And the tone is appreciably stronger. 'If you are forced to share a bed with a person of the same sex, which seldom happens, you should maintain a strict and vigilant modesty'. . . This is the tone of moral injunction. Even to give a reason has become distasteful to the adult. The child is made by the threatening tone to associate this situation with danger. The more 'natural' the standard of delicacy and shame appears to adults and the more the civilized restraint of instinctual urges is taken for granted, the more incomprehensible it becomes to adults that children do not have this delicacy and shame by 'nature'. . . .

The line followed by this development scarcely needs further elucidation. Here, too, in much the same way as with eating, the wall between people, the reserve, the emotional barrier erected by conditioning between one body and another, grows continuously. To share a bed with people outside the family circle, with strangers, is made more and more embarrassing. Unless necessity dictates otherwise, it becomes usual even within the family for each person to have his own bed and finally—in the middle and upper classes—his own bedroom. Children are trained early in this isolation from others, with all the habits and experiences that this brings with it. Only if we see how natural it seemed in the Middle Ages for strangers and for children and adults to share a bed can we appreciate what a fundamental change in interpersonal relationships and behaviour is expressed in our manner of living. . . .

. . . The transition from the intensified self-perception of the individual as an entirely self-sufficient entity independent and cut off from other people and things—these and many other phenomena of the time bear the structural characteristics of the same civilizational shift. They all show marks of the transition to a further stage of self-consciousness at which the inbuilt self-control . . . grows stronger . . .

The image of man as a 'closed personality' is here replaced by the image of man as an 'open personality' who possesses a greater or lesser degree of relative (but never absolute and total) autonomy vis-à-vis other people and who is, in fact, fundamentally oriented toward and dependent on other people throughout his life. The network of interdependencies among human beings is what binds them together. Such interdependencies are the nexus of what is here called the figuration, a structure of mutually oriented and dependent people. Since people are more or less dependent on each other first by nature and then through social learning, through education, socialization, and socially generated reciprocal needs, they exist, one might venture to say, only as pluralities, only in figurations. That is why, as was stated earlier, it is not particularly fruitful to conceive of men in the image of the individual man. It is more appropriate to envisage an image of numerous interdependent people forming figurations (i.e., groups or societies of different kinds) with each other. Seen from this basic standpoint, the rift in the traditional image of man disappears. The concept of the figuration has been introduced precisely because it expresses what we call 'society' more clearly and unambiguously than the existing conceptual tools of sociology, as neither an abstraction of attributes of individuals existing without a society, nor a 'system' or 'totality' beyond individuals, but the network of interdependencies formed by individuals. It is certainly quite possible to speak of a social system formed of individuals. But the undertones associated with the concept of the social system in contemporary sociology make such an expression seem forced. Furthermore, the concept of the system is prejudiced by the associated notion of immutability. . . .

Notes

1. F. Zarncke, *Der deutsche Cato* (Leipzig, 1852): 138.
2. W. Rudeck, *Geschichte der öffentlichen Sittlichkeit in Deutschland* (Jena, 1897): 397.
3. T. Wright, *The Home of Other Days* (London, 1871): 269.
4. Quoted in M. Bauer, *Das Liebesleben in der deutschen Vergangenheit* (Berlin, 1924): 208.
5. Rudeck, *Geschichte der öffentlichen Sittlichkeit*: 399.

Chapter 5

Body: Tomb, Temple, Machine, and Self

Anthony Synnott

. . . What is the body? . . . The body has been regarded as a tomb of the soul, a temple, a machine, and the self, and much more . . . Ideas about what the body is, what it means, its moral value and the values of its constituent parts, the limits of the body, its social utility and symbolic value, in sum, how the body is defined both physically and socially, vary widely from person to person, and have changed dramatically over time. . . .

Greek Philosophy: The Body as Pleasure or Tomb?

The Greeks glorified the body. Their sculptors, painters, and potters celebrated the beauty of the naked human form in stone and paint and clay. The Olympic Games, which were held every four years from 776 BC to AD 394, celebrated the poser and strength of the male body. . .

Although Greek culture was body-centred, there was no philosophical consensus on the body. Several theories prevailed. Hedonism was asserted by Aristippus (*c.* 435–366 BC), the founder of the Cyrenaic school, and a friend of Socrates, who insisted that 'bodily pleasures are far better than mental pleasures' . . . (in Laertius, vol. 1, 1972: 219).

Countervailing this philosophy were the Epicureans. Epicurus (341–270 BC), the founder of this school, stated clearly: 'we call pleasure the alpha and omega of a blessed life. Pleasure is our first and kindred good' (in Laertius, vol. 2, 1972:

655). But they believed mental pleasures were superior to those of the body. . . .

The third stream of Greek thought, Orphism, . . . was said to have been founded by Orpheus, one of the Greek heroes and an Argonaut. According to Orphic belief, Dionysus, the son of Zeus, was killed and eaten by the Titans, the wicked sons of Earth. Zeus destroyed them, but from their ashes rose the human race with a dual nature, part earthly (the Titans) and part heavenly (Dionysus, the son of Zeus). The Orphic life consisted of the cultivation of the divine nature by asceticism: abstention from meat, wine, and sexual intercourse. The body was regarded as the tomb of the soul. . . .

Socrates (466–399 BC) described the soul as a 'helpless prisoner, chained hand and foot in the body' . . . (Plato). Indeed the body is 'the grave [tomb] of the soul' (1963: 437). Body and soul are not only separate but opposed and unequal. Plato (*c.* 427–348 BC) maintained this dualism in his last work, stating that 'soul is utterly superior to body . . . the body is no more than a shadow which keeps us company' (1963: 1503). Only in death is 'the soul . . . liberated from the desires and *evils* of the body' (1963: 441; emphasis added).

The conflict between body and soul is therefore built-in, permanent and total. . . .

Aristotle (384–322 BC), a former student of Plato's, and a keen naturalist, was enormously interested in the body; he also promptly rejected Plato's dualism and his body-negativism. . . . In his treatise *On the Soul*, he states: 'we can dismiss as unnecessary the question whether the soul and body are one: it is as though we were to ask whether the wax and its shape are one' (1984: 657). . . . None the less he did agree with Plato that the soul is superior to, and rules, the body . . .

The Romans: The Body as Clay, Corruption, and Corpse

Stoicism was the dominant philosophy in the Roman Empire . . . and exerted a strong influence over Christian thought during its formative years. Seneca (d. 65 BC) was very clear: 'a high-minded and sensible man divorces soul from body, and dwells much with the better or divine part, and only as far as he must with this complaining and frail portion' . . . (1953, Vol. 2: 187, 455). The dualism and the superiority of the soul reflect Plato, although Seneca is not so body-negative: a cloak is not a tomb or a prison, indeed it protects from the elements; but nor is it as important as the wearer of the cloak. . . . Epictetus (first century) was more emphatic: both more dualistic and more negative. He says of humanity: 'There are two elements mingled in our birth, the body which we share with the animals, and the reason and mind which we share with the gods' (1968: 11, 182, 221). . . . [I]n an epigrammatic comment he states that 'Man is a poor soul burdened with a corpse' (Aurelius, 1964: 73). Marcus Aurelius spoke in similar terms in his *Meditations*, describing the body as 'but clay and corruption'. He described death as 'a release from impressions of sense, from twitchings of appetite, from excursions of thought and from service to the flesh' (1964: 55, 97). . . .

The Christians: The Body as Temple or Enemy?

The early Christians entertained several different paradigms of the body. They distinguished between the body as physical, as spiritual, and as mystical . . . At the same time, the body was a per-

vasive allegory of the hierarchies of society: church and family, and then state (cf. O'Neill, 1985). . . .

> Jesus took a piece of bread, gave a prayer of thanks, broke it, and gave it to his disciples. 'Take and eat it', he said, 'this is my body.'. . . (Matthew 26: 26–7)

. . . For the believer, therefore, the body participates in an order other than the purely corporeal: holy, sacramental, and mystical, and also personal, loved, and loving. . . . Saint Paul . . . insisted: 'You know that your bodies are parts of the body of Christ . . . Don't you know that your body is the temple of the Holy Spirit, who lives in you and was given to you by God? . . . So use your bodies for God's glory' (I Corinthians 6: 15, 19–20). This view of the body as a temple, and as part of Christ, is a far cry from the Orphic view of the body as a 'tomb' or the Stoic belief in the body as a 'corpse', an 'ass', or 'clay and corruption'. . . .

In Christ's teaching, the care of the physical body figures prominently. . . . None the less, there is a balance. The body is important, but it is not everything. Christ's teaching is uncompromising on this point:

> If your hand or your foot makes you lose your faith, cut it off and throw it away. It is better for you to enter life without a hand or a foot than to keep both hands and both feet and be thrown into the eternal fire. . . . (Matthew 18: 8–9)

. . . [T]hroughout his ministry Christ emphasized the necessity of self-denial, fasting, watchfulness, renunciation, poverty, and even chastity. . . .

. . . This 'double message' in the teachings of Christ and Paul caused a split in the early church between the ascetics and the moderates: a split that has continued through the centuries, and is strikingly evident in the deep ambivalence towards the body in general and sexuality in particular.

In the first centuries of the church, asceticism was expressed particularly in the ideals of martyrdom, virginity, and celibacy, regarded as the total dedication of the self to God. . . . [B]ut many Christians 'left the world', i.e., society, either to live in the new monastic communities or as hermits and stylites (pillar ascetics). Simeon Stylites (*c*. 390–459) was one of the first of the pillar ascetics, living on the top of a pillar for years. . . . They were perhaps not typical; certainly only a minority of Christians were martyrs, monks, celibates, or stylites. But dualism was widely assumed.

John Chrysostom (*c*. 347–407), Archbishop of Constantinople, distinguished clearly between body and soul: 'There is soul and body: they are two substances' . . . The body is relatively unimportant: 'The man ought to be praised and admired, . . . not . . . for his bodily form, but for his soul.' . . . On the other hand, Chrysostom also praised the body, 'leading us on by its beauty to admiration of Him who framed it' (1956: 264–5, 466, 104, 413). . . .

In the second millennium of Christianity, asceticism took new directions again. First, there was the founding of the great monastic orders of the West. . . . All the members of these orders took vows of poverty, chastity, and obedience, and some, in the contemplative orders, took vows of silence. In this sense asceticism was institutionalized. The second change in asceticism . . . was a new type of practice: the deliberate infliction of pain. Hitherto asceticism had involved, generally, the acceptance of physical sufferings imposed by others (e.g., the persecutions) or asceticism by omission (e.g., denying the physical needs of the body, for sleep, sex, talk, etc.); the new asceticism demanded self-denial and pain by commission. The reasons, however, remained the same: the expiation of sin, self-conquest, the intercession for divine graces and favours, and the imitation of Christ. All these are logical consequences of the belief in . . . the evils of the body in a dualistic philosophy . . .

Francis of Assisi (*c*. 1182–1226) was very straightforward in one of his letters: 'We must hate our bodies with [their] vices and sins.' . . .

. . . After various outbreaks of the plague in the twelfth century arose the Flagellants: groups of Christians who practised public flagellation as a penance. . . .

. . . Not all the medievals lived such ascetic lives, however, nor held such ascetic views. . . . Similarly the stories of . . . Chaucer (*c*. 1340–1400) in *The Canterbury Tales* show men and women thoroughly enjoying each other's bodies. This frank admission of sensuality ran counter to the Christian tradition. . . . The body was more lusted after than distrusted. Attitudes towards the body varied considerably during the Middle Ages, and so did the treatment of the body, but the ascetics were presumably a minority. Indeed, popular attitudes towards the body may well have been precisely the opposite of what the ascetics and religious described.

The Renaissance: The Body as Secular and Private

The Renaissance, beginning in Italy in the fourteenth century, re-discovered the body, and transformed attitudes towards it. Artists like Botticelli, Leonardo da Vinci, Michelangelo, Raphael, and Titian painted the body as beautiful and in glowing colours. . . . Philosophers like Castiglione (1517 [1983]: 330–2) praised beauty as a 'sacred thing' and 'a true sign of inner goodness'; 'the good and the beautiful are identical, especially in the human body'. . . .

The secularization of the body is indicated by Erasmus's (1530 [1985]) treatise *De civilitate morum puerilium*. He discussed the social control of such bodily functions as eating and drinking, spitting, blowing the nose, and so on far more frankly than they are discussed in contemporary etiquette books. . . . New notions of civility began to *privatize* the body. Increasingly people distanced themselves from bodily functions and indeed from the body itself, both their own and other people's, not only ideologically but also with implements of various sorts: table cutlery, handkerchiefs, commodes, nightwear, spittoons, etc. . . .

The Renaissance therefore witnessed the beginning of the end of the ascetic idea of the body as *enemy*, and the strengthening of the idea of the body as beautiful, good, personal, and *private*. This movement should not be over-emphasized, however. For the leper—and leprosy was endemic in Europe in the early Middle Ages—the disfigured body was a *public* symbol of sin, and was a visitation from God. Thus, the body remained an instrument of God's will, public or private, beautiful or leprous, friend or enemy.

The Renaissance did not displace traditional ascetic ideas totally. . . . Angela of Fuligno described how she drank the dirty water with which she had just been washing the hands and feet of lepers:

> The beverage flooded us with such sweetness that the joy followed us home. Never had I drunk with such pleasure. In my throat was lodged a piece of scaly skin from the lepers' sores. Instead of getting rid of it, I made a great effort to swallow it and I succeeded. I shall never be able to express the delight that inundated me (In de Beauvoir, 1953: 676). . . .

Ignatius Loyola (1491–1536), the founder of the Society of Jesus, . . . gave clear instructions on penance, . . . 'chastise the body by inflicting actual pain on it. This is done by wearing hairshirts or cords or iron chains, by scourging or beating ourselves, and by other kinds of harsh treatments' (1963: 22, 39–40). . . .

Loyola's contemporary, Martin Luther (1483–1546), had a very different attitude towards the body. He enjoyed his food and drink and once remarked: 'If our Lord is permitted to create nice, large pike and good Rhine wine, presumably I may be allowed to eat and drink' (Friedenthal, 1970: 445). . . .

The Christian body of the Renaissance and the Reformation is therefore fluid and multiple. Since Vatican II, however, modern Christians have constructed a gentler and friendlier body. A Franciscan work on spirituality advises that:

> The modern mortification is to start taking care of our health once more out of reverence for who we are: temples of the Spirit of God . . . Our mortification . . . does not involve punish-

ing the body, or depriving ourselves of food and drink. It involves the dull task of eating and drinking what is healthy and lifegiving . . . (Bodo, 1984: 133–4)

Modern theologians increasingly stress that the body is not an 'enemy', nor a 'poor ass'. Thomas Merton states: 'What is important is not liberation from the body but liberation from the mind. We are not entangled in our own body but entangled in our own mind' (1973: 90). This seems, on the face of it, to be a complete reversal of the attitudes of some of the Desert Fathers and Doctors of the Church. . . . None the less, asceticism is not dead. Warriors, athletes, dancers, weightlifters and others still train; and their slogan, 'No pain, no gain', expresses a secular asceticism. . . .

Descartes to the Moderns: The Body as Machine

René Descartes (1596–1650) . . . formulated the first principle of his philosophy: '*Cogito, ergo sum*'—I think, therefore I am; and he went on to say that 'this "I", that is to say, the mind, by which I am what I am, is entirely distinct from the body' (1968: 53–4). And what was this body? Descartes replied: 'I considered myself, firstly, as having a face, hands, arms, and the whole *machine* made up of flesh and bones, such as it appears in a corpse and which I designated by the name of body'. . . .

Descartes' division of *homo sapiens* into soul and body effectively allocated the soul to the church and the body to science in a clear 'separation of powers'. The division within the self coincided with and reflected the division within society. . . .

During the nineteenth century, the philosophy and science of the body were in a ferment . . . Marx, [and Engels] . . . both researched the destruction, mechanization, and animalization of the bodies of the workers. Not only are human and animal labour interchangeable, . . . the worker 'becomes an appendage of the machine' in a sense never intended by Descartes (Marx and Engels, 1967: 87). . . .

Meanwhile Sigmund Freud demonstrated in his *Studies on Hysteria* (1895), with Breuer, that psychological phenomena can be converted into physical phenomena, and that hysterical symptoms are psychogenic. Thus, body and mind are one. In his first case history 'Dora' (1905), he asserted that the symptoms of hysteria are both psychical and somatic in origin. Once the psychic material is analyzed, the somatic symptoms disappear (1977: 73). Freud's theory . . . seemed to call into question traditional Cartesian dualism, and the separation of mind and body. . . .

The year 1853 therefore marks a turning-point in the political anatomy of the body in England . . . During the previous decades the state had slowly expanded its authority and powers over more and more sectors of the population. . . .

The body was . . . the last bastion to fall before the new, modern, intrusive government. There were precedents for this conquest, however. The state had always exercised the right to take away life, to inflict pain, to remove parts of the body, to tattoo or brand the body; to quarantine individuals, houses, ships, and even towns in times of plague; to imprison people or banish them; and both church and state had traditionally forbidden many physical activities, as in matters of sexual intercourse, masturbation, self-mutilation, abortion, and suicide. . . . The body had never been entirely private or autonomous; it had always been under some surveillance and some control; but such control had been individual, specific, and localized in time and space.

The 1853 legislation was qualitatively and quantitatively different precisely because it had universal and compulsory applicability and was prescriptive for the future. Furthermore, it was legitimized by the Utilitarian doctrine of 'the greatest good'. . . .

The Twentieth Century: The Mechanical Body

. . . Co-existing with the new body-positive constructions of the body, mechanism remained the dominant paradigm in biomedicine. . . . The principal killers of the eighteenth and nineteenth centuries—smallpox, typhoid, and cholera—had been largely eliminated by social reforms, and improved standards of living. . . . The development of vaccines, anaesthetics, sterilization, the sulfa drugs, and antibiotics contributed also to further lowering the death-rates. The body, therefore, became not 'something' to be feared, potentially dangerous, to be watched all the time, but something to be enjoyed; it can even be abused, and then 'cured' by a 'magic bullet'. . . .

Cartesian mechanism persisted in psychology as in biology. John B. Watson, the founder of Behaviourism in 1924, asserted that 'the human body . . . is not a treasure house of mystery but a very commonsense kind of *organic* machine' (1966: 49). . . . Thus, by the early twentieth century, biology, medicine, psychology, and philosophy were largely agreed in their materialism: the body is all.

This mechanistic construction of the body was congruent with the mechanization of society. The first Model T Fords were produced in 1908; and the automobile transformed thinking about the body. Watson indeed referred to the individual as a body, the body as a machine, and the machine as a car:

> Let us try to think of man as an assembled organic machine ready to run. We mean nothing very difficult by this. Take four wheels with tires, axles, differentials, gas engine, body; put them together and we have an automobile of a sort. (1966: 269) . . .

Mechanism became so powerful a philosophy that it was applied not only to the body but also to children and industrial workers. A popular work on child care published in the United States in 1921 advised:

> It is quite possible to train the baby to be an *efficient little machine*, and the more nearly perfect we make *the running of this machine*, the more wonderful will be the results achieved and the less trouble it will be for the mother. (In Synnott, 1983: 87; emphasis added)

This was entirely congruent with the view of the worker as machine developed by Frederick Taylor, founder of the 'scientific management' school and of the time-and-motion study. Workers become part of the machinery of production, cogs in the wheel, numbers and units of production, scientifically studied and managed. . . .

Existentialism: The Body as Self

Tombs and temples, clocks and cars—all these metaphors imply a distance between the body and the self. In *Being and Nothingness* (1943), however, Sartre insisted that the body is the self, and that the self is the body: 'I *live* my body . . . The body is what I immediately am . . . I *am* my body to the extent that I *am*' (Sartre, 1966: 428–60). Sartre's monism contrasts sharply with Descartes's dualism. . .

. . . Mind and body have changed places in the popular scale of values. None the less traditional Christian values still do persist; and not everyone subscribes to the new materialist existentialism. Furthermore, those with stigmatized bodies, to borrow Goffman's phrase, are fully aware that the body is political, central to personal identity and life chances. People judged by their bodies do not take them for granted, and may love or hate their bodies—not for philosophical but for political and very practical reasons, whether they are judged by their physical handicaps, age, colour, gender, or aesthetics (Goffman, 1963; Murphy, 1987). Malcolm X explained: '[The whites] very skillfully make you and me hate our African identity, our African characteristics . . . (1966: 169). . . .

Attitudes to the body, individual and collective, persist even after death; and indicate how powerful these attitudes are. In every culture, the dead body is treated with respect and with ceremony; and the body remains the symbol of the self. . . . Medical students are particularly traumatized when they first have to dissect cadavers: this becomes a rite of passage into the profession (Lella and Pawluch, 1988). . . .

Recent Paradigms: The Body as Plastic, Bionic, Holistic . . .

. . . Reconstructive Surgery is one of the fastest growing specialties in medicine in the United States, with over two million operations performed annually. . . . The body is not only plastic, it is also *bionic*, with cardiac pacemakers, valves, titanium hips, polymer blood vessels, electronic eye and ear implants, collagen fibre and silicon rubber skins, and even polyurethane hearts. Furthermore, we are increasingly dependent upon machines: diagnostic machines of various sorts, CAT scans, heart monitors, ultra-sound; and even for our lives: incubators soon after birth, dialysis machines and iron lungs, and respirators and life-support systems towards the end. Finally, the humans/machines may be 'unplugged' or 'switched off'. The line between human and machine is blurred, so is the fine line between life and death. The brain-dead can be kept 'alive'.

The body is also *communal* and interchangeable in its parts. Hearts, livers, pancreas, kidneys, corneas, and bone marrows are all transplanted, alone or in various combinations. . . . The mechanistic implications are clear: just as cars are cannibalized for spare parts, so now humans and animals are also being 'cannibalized'. . . .

The body may also be *chosen*, selected from a wide range of possibilities in sperm and ovum bank catalogues. The new reproductive technologies, including in vitro fertilization, artificial insemination, surrogate motherhood, embryo freezing, the research into artificial wombs, and embryo implantation in men are raising a host of ethical problems about the body, and humanity. . . .

Holistic thinkers . . . have expressed concern that in Western societies mind and body are so compartmentalized as to be treated by different disciplines: psychology and psychiatry for the mind, medicine for the body. Furthermore, the American Medical Association now recognizes 24 distinct specializations within the profession. Thus, the illness is increasingly 'removed', first by dualism and then by specialization, from the individuals who are ill, and from the physical, psychological, social, and environmental contexts in which they become ill. . . .

Conclusion

Despite centuries of debate about the meaning of the body, there are no signs of universal agree-

ment. Each new age seems to create and reconstruct the body in its own image and likeness; yet at any given time there are likely to be many paradigms of the body; competing, complementary, or contradictory. And no doubt the redefinitions of corporeality will continue in the twenty-first century. . . .

References

Aristotle. 1884. *The Complete Works of Aristotle*, Jonathan Barnes, ed. Bollingen Series. Princeton, NJ: Princeton University Press.

Aurelius, Marcus. 1964. *Meditations*, trans. M. Staniforth. Harmondsworth, UK: Penguin Books.

Bodo, Murray, OFM. 1984. *The Way of Saint Francis*. Garden City, NY: Doubleday.

Castiglione, Baldesar. 1983 [1517]. *The Book of the Courtier.* Harmondsworth, UK: Penguin Books.

Chrysostom, Saint John. 1956 [387]. *Works. The Nicene and Post-Nicene Fathers. Vol. IX*, trans. Rev. W.R. Stephen, ed. Philip Schaff. Grand Rapids, MI: Eerdman's.

de Beauvoir, Simone. 1953. *The Second Sex*, trans. H.M. Parshley. New York: Knopf.

Descartes, René. 1968 [1637]. *Discourse on Method and the Meditations*, trans. F. E. Sutcliffe. Harmondsworth, UK: Penguin Books.

Epictetus. 1968. *The Discourses*, trans. P.E. Matheson. New York: Heritage Press.

Erasmus, Desiderius. 1985. *Collected Works*, trans, Brian McGregor, ed. J.F. Sowards. Toronto: University Press.

Freud, Sigmund. 1977. *Case Histories 1: 'Dora' and 'Little Hans'*, trans. James Strachy, ed. Audrey Richards. The Pelican Freud Library, Vol. 8. Harmondsworth, UK: Penguin Books.

Friedenthal, Richard. 1970. *Luther: His Life and Times.* New York: Harcourt, Brace, Jovanovich.

Goffman, Erving. 1963. *Stigma*. Englewoood Cliffs, NJ: Prentice Hall.

Laertius, Diogenes. 1972. *Lives of Eminent Philosophers,* 2 vols., trans. R.D. Hicks. Cambridge, MA: Harvard University Press.

Lella, Joseph W., and Dorothy Pawluch. 1988. 'Medical Students and the Cadaver in Social and Cultural Perspective', in Margaret Lock and Deborah Gordon, eds, *Biomedicine Examined*. Dordrecht: Kluwer Academic Publishers.

Loyola, Ignatius. 1963 [1548]. *The Spiritual Exercises,* trans. Thomas Corbishley, SJ. London: Burns & Oates.

Marx, Karl, and Friedrich Engels. 1967. *The Communist Manifesto*. Introduction by A.J.P. Taylor. Harmondsworth, UK: Penguin Books.

Merton, Thomas. 1973. *The Asian Journal*. New York: New Directions.

Murphy, Robert F. 1987. *The Body Silent*. New York: Henry Holt.

O'Neill, John. 1985. *Five Bodies*. Ithaca, NY: Cornell University Press.

Plato. 1963. *The Collected Dialogues*, eds. Edith Hamilton and Huntington Cairns, Bollingen Series. Princeton, NJ: Princeton University Press.

Sartre, Jean-Paul. 1966 [1943]. *Being and Nothingness,* trans. H. Barnes. New York: Washington Square Press.

Seneca. 1953. *Ad Lucilium*. 2 vols., trans. Richard M. Gunmere. London: Heinemann.

Synnott, Anthony. 1983. 'Little Angels, Little Devils: A Sociology of Children', *Canadian Review of Sociology and Anthropology* 20, 1: 79–95.

Watson, John B. 1966. *Behaviorism*. Chicago: University of Chicago Press.

Chapter 6

The Hottentot and the Prostitute: Toward an Iconography of Female Sexuality

Sander L. Gilman

. . . J.J. Virey . . . was the author of the standard study of race published in the early nineteenth century, *Histoire naturelle du genre humain*. He also contributed a major essay (the only one on a specific racial group) to the widely cited *Dictionary of Medical Sciences* (1819).[1] In this essay Virey summarized his and many of his contemporaries' views on the sexual nature of black females in terms of accepted medical discourse. Their 'voluptuousness' is 'developed to a degree of lascivity unknown in our climate, for their sexual organs are much more developed than those of whites'. Virey elsewhere cites the Hottentot woman as the epitome of this sexual lasciviousness and stresses the consonance between her physiology and her physiognomy (her 'hideous form' and her 'horribly flattened nose'). His central proof is a discussion of the unique structure of the Hottentot female's sexual parts, the description of which he takes from the anatomical studies of his contemporary Georges Cuvier. . . .[2]

The black female looks different. Her physiognomy, her skin colour, the form of her genitalia mark her as inherently different. The nineteenth century perceived the black female as possessing not only a 'primitive' sexual appetite, but also the external signs of this temperament, 'primitive' genitalia. Eighteenth-century travellers to southern Africa, such as Francois Levaillant and John Barrow, had described the so-called 'Hottentot apron', a hypertrophy of the labia and nymphae caused by manipulation of the genitalia and considered beautiful by the Hottentots and Bushman as well as tribes in Basutoland and Dahomey.[3] In

1815 Saartje Baartman, also called Sarah Bartmann, or Saat-Jee, a 25-year-old Hottentot female who had been exhibited in Europe for over five years as the 'Hottentot Venus', died in Paris. . . . An autopsy that was performed on her was first written up by Henri Ducrotay de Blainville in 1816 and then, in its most famous version, by Georges Cuvier in 1817.[4] Reprinted at least twice during the next decade, Cuvier's description reflected de Blainville's two intentions: the likening of a female of the 'lowest' human species with the highest ape, the orangutan, and the description of the anomalies of the Hottentot's 'organ of generation'.

Sarah Bartmann had been exhibited not to show her genitalia, but rather to present to the European audience a different anomaly, one that they (and pathologists such as de Blainville and Cuvier) found riveting: her steatopygia, or protruding buttocks, a physical characteristic of Hottentot females that had captured the eye of early travellers. For most Europeans who viewed her, Sarah Bartmann existed only as a collection of sexual parts. . .

The audience that had paid to see Sarah Bartmann's buttocks and fantasized about her genitalia could, after her death and dissection, examine both, for Cuvier presented 'the Academy the genital organs of this woman prepared in a way so as to allow one to see the nature of the labia'.[5] And indeed Sarah Bartmann's sexual parts serve as the central image for the black female throughout the nineteenth century; and the model of de Blainville's and Cuvier's descriptions, which centre on the detailed presentation of the sexual parts of the black, dominates medical description of the black during the nineteenth century. To an extent, this reflects the general nineteenth-century understanding of female sexuality as pathological. The female genitalia were of interest in examining the various pathologies that could befall them, but they were also of interest because they came to define the sum of the female for the nineteenth century. When a specimen was to be preserved for an anatomical museum, more often than not the specimen was seen as a pathological summary of the entire individual. Thus, the skeleton of a giant or a dwarf represented 'giantism' or 'dwarfism', the head of a criminal, the act of execution that labelled him as 'criminal'.[6] Sarah Bartmann's genitalia and buttocks summarized her essence for the nineteenth-century observer, as indeed they continue to do for twentieth-century observers, since they are still on display at the Musée de l' Homme in Paris. . . .

How is it that both the genitalia, a primary sexual characteristic, and the buttocks, a secondary sexual characteristic, function as the semantic signs of 'primitive' sexual appetite and activity? A good point of departure for addressing this question is the fourth volume of Havelock Ellis's *Studies in the Psychology of Sex* (1905), which contains a detailed example of the great chain of being as applied to the perception of the sexualized Other.[7] Ellis believed that there is an absolute, totally objective scale of beauty that ranges from the European to the black. Thus, men of the lower races, according to Ellis, admire European women more than their own, and women of lower races attempt to whiten themselves with face powder. . . . His discussion of the buttocks ranks the races by size of the female pelvis, a view that began with Willem Vrolik's 1826 claim that a wide pelvis is a sign of racial superiority and was echoed by R. Verneau's 1875 study of the form of the pelvis among the various races.[8] . . . Darwin himself, who held similar views as to the objective nature of human beauty, saw the pelvis as a 'primary rather than as a secondary character' and the buttocks of the Hottentot as a somewhat comic sign of the black female's primitive, grotesque nature.[9] . . .

The influence of this vocabulary on nineteenth-century perception of the sexualized woman can be seen in Edwin Long's 1882 painting, *The Babylonian Marriage Market*. This painting claimed a higher price than any other contemporary work of art sold in nineteenth-century London. It also has a special place in documenting the perception of the sexualized female in terms of the great chain of aesthetic beauty presented by Ellis. For Long's painting is based on a specific text from Herodotus, who described the marriage auction in Babylon in which maidens were sold in order of comeliness. In the painting they are arranged in order of their attractiveness according to Victorian aesthetics. Their physiognomies are clearly portrayed. Their features run from the most European and white (a fact emphasized by the light reflected from the mirror onto the figure at the far left) to the Negroid features (thick lips, broad nose, dark but not black skin) of the figure farthest to the observer's right. . . . The only black female present is the servant-slave shown on the auction block, positioned so as to present her buttocks to the viewer. . . .

The Iconography of Prostitution

The prostitute is the essential sexualized female in the perception of the nineteenth century. She is perceived as the embodiment of sexuality and of all that is associated with sexuality, disease as well as passion.[10] Within the large and detailed literature concerning prostitution written during the nineteenth century, most of which is devoted to documenting the need for legal controls and draws on the medical model as perceived by public health officials, there is a detailed analysis of the physiognomy and physiology of the prostitute. We can begin with the most widely read early nineteenth-century work on prostitution, the 1836 anthropological study of prostitution in Paris by A.J.B. Parent-Duchatelet.[11] . . . Parent-Duchatelet believes himself to be providing objective description as he presents his readers with a statistical profile of the physical types of the prostitutes, the nature of their voices, the colour of their hair and eyes, their physical anomalies, their characteristics in childbearing, and their sexually transmitted disease. . . . Prostitutes have a 'peculiar plumpness' owing to 'the great number of hot baths that the major part of these women take'. Or perhaps to their lassitude, rising at 10 or 11 in the morning, 'leading an animal life'. They are fat as prisoners are fat, from simple confinement. As an English commentator noted, 'the grossest and stoutest of these women are to be found amongst the lowest and most disgusting classes of prostitutes.'[12] . . .

From Parent-Duchatelet's description of the physical appearance of the prostitute—a catalogue that reappears in most nineteenth-century studies of prostitutes, such as Josef Schrank's study of the prostitutes of Vienna . . .—it is but a small step to the use of such catalogues of stigmata to identify those women who have, as Freud states, 'an aptitude for prostitution'.[13] The major work of nineteenth-century physical anthropology, public health, and pathology to undertake this was written by Pauline Tarnowsky. Tarnowsky, one of a number of St Petersburg female physicians in the late nineteenth century, wrote in the tradition of her eponymous colleague V.M. Tarnowsky, who was the author of the standard study of Russian prostitution, a study that appeared in both Russian and German and assumed a central role in late nineteenth-century discussions of the nature of the prostitute.[14] She followed his more general study with a detailed investigation of the physiognomy of the prostitute.[15] Her categories remain those of Parent-Duchatelet. She describes the excessive weight of prostitutes and their hair and eye colour, provides measurements of skull size and a catalogue of their family background (as with Parent-Duchatelet, most are the children of alcoholics), and discusses their fecundity (extremely low), as well as the signs of their degeneration. These signs are facial abnormalities: asymmetry of the face, misshapen noses, overdevelopment of the parietal region of the skull, and the so-called 'Darwin's ear'. All of these signs belong to the lower end of the scale of beauty, the end dominated by the Hottentot. All of the signs point to the 'primitive' nature of the prostitute's physiognomy; stigmata such as Darwin's ear (the simplification of the convolutions of the ear shell and the absence of a lobe) are a sign of atavism.

In a later paper, Tarnowsky provided a scale of the appearance of the prostitute in an analysis of the 'physiognomy of the Russian prostitute'. . . .[16] The upper end of the scale is the 'Russian Helen'. Here, classical aesthetics are introduced as the measure of the appearance of the sexualized female. A bit further on is one who is 'very handsome in spite of her hard expression'. Indeed, the first 15 on her scale 'might pass on the street for beauties'. But hidden even within these seeming beauties are the stigmata of criminal degeneration: black, thick hair; a strong jaw; a hard, spent glance. Some show the 'wild eyes and perturbed countenance along with facial asymmetry' of the insane. Only the scientific observer can see the hidden faults, and thus identify the true prostitute, for the prostitute uses superficial beauty as the bait for her clients. But when they age, their 'strong jaws and cheek-bones, and their masculine aspect . . ., hidden by adipose tissue, emerge, salient angles stand out, and the face grows virile, uglier than a man's; wrinkles deepen into the likeness of scars, and the countenance, once attractive, exhibits the full degenerate type which early grace had concealed'. . . . For Pauline Tarnowsky, the appearance of the prostitute and her sexual identity are pre-established in her heredity. What is most striking is that as she ages, the prostitute begins to appear more and more mannish. Billroth's *Handbook of Gynecological Diseases* links the Hottentot with the lesbian; here the link is between two other models of sexual deviancy, the prostitute and the lesbian. Both are seen as possessing physical signs that set them apart from the normal.

The paper in which Pauline Tarnowsky undertook her documentation of the appearance of the prostitute is repeated word for word in the major late nineteenth-century study of prostitution and female criminality, *La donna deliquente*, written by Cesare Lombroso together with his son-in-law,

Guglielmo Ferrero, and published in 1893.[17] Lombroso accepts all of Tarnowsky's perceptions of the prostitute and articulates one further subtext of central importance, a subtext made apparent by the plates in his book. For two of the plates illustrate the Hottentot's 'apron' and steatopygia. . . . Lombroso accepts Parent-Duchatelet's image of the fat prostitute, and sees her as being similar to Hottentots and women living in asylums. The prostitute's labia are throwbacks to the Hottentot, if not the chimpanzee; the prostitute, in short, is an atavistic subclass of woman. . . .

. . . The primitive is the black, and the qualities of blackness, or at least of the black female, are those of the prostitute. The strong currency of this equation is grotesquely evident in a series of case studies on steatopygia in prostitutes by a student of Lombroso's, Abele De Blasio, in which the prostitute is quite literally perceived as the Hottentot.[18]

The late nineteenth-century perception of the prostitute merged with that of the black. Aside from the fact that prostitutes and blacks were both seen as outsiders, what does this amalgamation imply? It is a commonplace that the primitive was associated with unbridled sexuality. This hypersex-

uality was either condemned, as in Jefferson's discussions of the nature of the black in Virginia, or praised, as in the fictional supplement written by Diderot to Bougainville's voyages.[19] Historians such as J.J. Bachofen postulated it as the sign of the 'Swamp', the earliest stage of human history.[20] Blacks, if both Hegel and Schopenhauer are to be believed, remained at this most primitive stage, and their presence in the contemporary world served as an indicator of how far humanity had come in establishing control over the world and itself. The loss of control was marked by a regression into this dark past, a degeneracy into the primitive expression of emotions, in the form of either madness or unbridled sexuality. Such a loss of control was, of course, viewed as pathological and thus fell into the domain of the medical model. . . .

. . . It is . . . the innate fear of the Other's different anatomy that lies behind the synthesis of images. The Other's pathology is revealed in her anatomy, and the black and the prostitute are both bearers of the stigmata of sexual difference and thus pathology. . . . The 'white man's burden', his sexuality and its control, is displaced into the need to control the sexuality of the Other, the Other as sexualized female. . . .

Notes

1. *Dictionnaire des sciences médicales* (Paris, C.L.F. Panckoucke, 1819), 35, 398–403.
2. J.J. Virey, *Histoire naturelle du genre humain* (Paris: Crochard, 1824), 2, 151. My translation.
3. George M. Gould and Walter L. Pyle, *Anomalies and Curiosities of Medicine* (Philadelphia: W. B. Saunders, 1901), 307; and Eugen Holländer, *Äskulap und Venus: Eline Kultur- und Sittengeschichte in Spiegel des Arztes* (Berlin: Propyläen, 1928). Much material on the indebtedness of the early pathologists to the reports of travellers to Africa can be found in the accounts of the autopsies presented below. One indication of the power the image of the Hottentot still possessed in the late nineteenth century is to be found in George Eliot's *Daniel Deronda* (1876). On its surface the novel is a hymn to racial harmony and an attack on British middle-class bigotry. Eliot's liberal agenda is

nowhere better articulated than in the ironic debate concerning the nature of the black in which the eponymous hero of the novel defends black sexuality (376). This position is attributed to the hero not a half-dozen pages after the authorial voice of the narrator introduced the description of this very figure with the comparison: 'And one man differs from another, as we all differ from the Bosjesman' (370). Eliot's comment is quite in keeping with the underlying understanding of race in the novel. For just as Deronda is fated to marry a Jewess and thus avoid the taint of race mixing, so too is the Bushman, a Hottentot equivalent in the nineteenth century, isolated from the rest of humanity. That a polygenetic view of race and liberal ideology can be held simultaneously is evident as far back as Voltaire. But the Jew is here contrasted to the Hottentot, and, as has been seen, it is the Hottentot who serves as the icon of pathologically corrupted sexuality. Can Eliot be drawing a line between outsiders such as the Jew and the sexualized female in Western society and the Hottentot? The Hottentot comes to serve as the sexualized Other onto whom Eliot projects the opprobrium with which she herself was labelled. For Eliot the Hottentot remains beyond the pale, showing that even in the most Whiggish text the Hottentot remains the essential Other. (George Eliot, *Daniel Deronda*, ed Barbara Hardy. [Harmondsworth, UK: Penguin, 1967.])

4. de Blainville, 'Sur une femme de la race hottentote', *Bulletin des Sciences par la société philomatique de Paris* (1816): 183–90. This early version of the autopsy seems to be unknown to William B. Cohen, *The French Encounter with Africans: White Response to Blacks, 1530–1880* (Bloomington: Indiana University Press, 1980) (see esp. pp. 239–45, for his discussion of Cuvier). See also Stephen Jay Gould, 'The Hottentot Venus', *Natural History* 91 (1982): 20–7.

5. Georges Cuvier, 'Extraits d'observations faites sur le cadavre d'une femme connue à Paris et à Londres sous le nom de Vénus Hottentote', *Memoires du Musée d'histoire naturelle* 3 (1817): 259–74. Reprinted with plates by Geoffrey Saint-Hilaire and Frédéric Cuvier, *Histoire naturelle des mammifères avec des figures originales* (Paris: A. Belin, 1824), 1:1 ff. The substance of the autopsy is reprinted again by Flourens in the *Journal complémentaire du dictionnaire des sciences médicales* 4 (1819): 145–9, and by Jules Cloquet, *Manuel d'anatomie de l'homme descriptive du corps humain* (Paris: Béchet jeune, 1825), plate 278. Cuvier's presentation of the 'Hottentot Venus' forms the major signifier for the image of the Hottentot as sexual primitive in the nineteenth century. This view seems never really to disappear from the discussion of difference. See the discussion of the 'bushmen' among French anthropologists of the 1970s, especially Claude Rousseau, as presented by Patrick Moreau, 'Die neue Religion der Rasse', in Iring Fetscher, ed., *Neokonservative und 'Neue Rechte'* (Munich: C.H. Beck, 1983), 139–41.

6. See for example Walker D. Greer, 'John Hunter: Order out of Variety', *Annals of the Royal College of Surgeons of England* 28 (1961): 238–51. See also Barbara J. Babiger, 'The *Kunst- und Wunderkammern*: A catalogue raisonné of Collecting in Germany, France, and England, 1565–1750' (diss., University of Pittsburgh, 1970).

7. Havelock Ellis, *Studies in the Psychology of Sex, Vol. 4, Sexual Selection in Man* (Philadelphia: F.A. Davis, 1920), 152–85.

8. Willem Vrolik, *Considérations sur la diversité du bassin des diffirentes races humaines* (Amsterdam: Van der Post, 1826); R. Verneau, *Le bassin dans les sexes et dans les races* (Paris: Bailliere, 1876), 126–9.

9. Charles Darwin, *The Desent of Man and Selection in Relation to Sex* (Princeton: Princeton University Press, 1981 [1871]), 2: 317 on the pelvis, and 2: 345–6 on the Hottentot.

10. The best study of the image of the prostitute is Alain Corbin, *Les filles de noce: Misère sexuelle et prostitution aux 19ᵉ et 20ᵉ siecles* (Paris: Aubier, 1978). On black prostitute see Khalid Kistainy, *The Prostitute in Progressive Literature* (New York: Schocken, 1982), 74–84. On the iconography associated with pictorial representation of the prostitute in nineteenth-century art see Hess Nochlin, eds., *Woman as Sex Object*, as well as Linda Nochlin, 'Lost and Found: Once More the Fallen Woman', *Art Bulletin* 60 (1978): 139–53, and Lynda Nead, 'Seduction, Prostitution, Suicide: *On the Brink* by Alfred Elmore', *Art History* 5 (1982): 310–22. On the special status of medical representations of female sexuality see the eighteenth-century wax models of female anatomy in the Museo della Specola (Florence), reproductions of which are in Mario Bucci, *Anatomia come arte* (Firenze: Edizione d'arte il Fiorino, 1969), esp. plate 8.

11. A.J.B. Parent-Duchatelet, *De la prostitution dans la ville de Paris* (Paris: J.B. Baillière, 1836), 1, 193–244.

12. *On Prostitution in the City of Paris* (London: T. Burgess, 1840), 38. It is of interest that it is exactly the passages on the physiognomy and appearance of the prostitute that this anonymous translator presents to an English audience as the essence of Parent-Duchatelet's work.

13. Sigmund Freud, *Standard Edition*, 7: 191.

14. V.M. Tarnowsky, *Prostitutsija i abolitsioniszm* (St Petersburg: n.p., 1888); *Prostitution und Abolitionismus* (Hamburg: Voss, 1890).

15. Pauline Tarnowsky, *Etude anthropométrique sur les prostituées et les voleuses* (Paris: E. Lecrosnier et Bebé, 1889).

16. Pauline Tarnowsky, 'Fisiomie di prostitute russe', *Archivio di Psichiatria, scienze penali ed antropologia criminale* 14 (1893): 141–2.

17. Cesare Lombroso and Guglielmo Ferrero, *La donna deliquente* (Turin: Roux, 1893). On the photographs of the Russian prostitutes, 349–50; on the fat of the prostitute, 361–2; and on the labia of the Hottentots, 38.

18. Abele De Blasio, 'Steatopia in prostitute', *Archivio dipsichiatria* 26 (1905): 257–64.

19. Jefferson commented on the heightened sensuality of the black in slavery in his *Notes from Virginia* (1782); Diderot, in his posthumously published fictional *Supplément au voyage de Bougainville* (1796), represented the heightened sexuality of the inhabitants of Tahiti as examples of the nature of sexuality freed from civilization. See the general discussion of this theme in Alexander Thomas and Samuel Sillen, *Racism and Psychiatry* (New York: Brunner/Mazel, 1972), 101ff.

20. On Bachofen's view of primitive sexuality see the Introduction, Chapter 9, and selections by Joseph Campbell to J.J. Bachofen, *Myth, Religion & Mother Right*, trans. Ralph Manheim (Princeton, NJ: Princeton University Press, 1973).

Part III

Presenting the Body

Jacqueline Low

Erving Goffman opens *The Presentation of Self in Everyday Life* with his famous statement: 'When a person enters the presence of others, they commonly seek to acquire information about him [or her]' (1959: 1). In particular, we look for social information such as the person's level of education, marital status, social class, gender, sexual identity, and even religious affiliation, among much more. An important '**sign vehicle**', or carrier of this information, is the body (Goffman, 1959: 1). How people present and adorn their bodies, how they stand, and how they move all impart information about themselves to others. Information about the person is communicated by the body in two forms: '**expressions given**', that information the person wishes to convey to others, and '**expressions given off**', information that is 'presumably unintentionally' conveyed (Goffman, 1959: 4). How people present their bodies is always, in part, an attempt to influence the '**definition of the situation**', that shared sense of social reality that develops within social groups. They do this in part by managing the '**impressions**' others have of them (Goffman, 1959: 2–4). For instance, you may try to impress upon your peer group that you are cool by wearing the latest fashions (expression given); however, that impression is compromised if you return from the bathroom with your fly open or trailing toilet paper from your shoe (expression given off).

Depending on the signs they give or give off, bodies are vulnerable to being stigmatized. Lee F. Monaghan discusses this process in 'Big Handsome Men, Bears, and Others' (2005). '**Stigma**' is a social attribute that devalues the person in the eyes of others (Monaghan, 2005: 82). The person that possesses a body bearing stigma is correspondingly less valued and is subject to the negative, often punitive, reactions of others in society. This is most likely the case with bodies that carry '**discrediting stigma**', which is stigma that the individual is not able to hide from others, in contrast to '**discreditable stigma**', which is stigma not 'immediately evident' to others (82). For example, in contemporary Western capitalism bodies labelled overweight are stigmatized. In fact, such is our valuing of thinness that we can speak about our antipathy towards those labelled overweight as 'bodyism' in the same way that we refer to differential treatment based on sex as sexism (83).

Individuals whose bodies are stigmatized cope with their 'spoiled identities' by making use of an infinite range of stigma management techniques (Monaghan, 2005: 82). For instance, in Monaghan's article you will read how some men labelled overweight manage stigma by participating in the accepting subcultures they find within specialized Internet chat rooms. There, 'big handsome men, bears, and others' engage in 'face work', the construction of positive self images, through depictions of their 'personal fronts', the descriptions and images of their 'fat male' bodies that are for public, not private, display (Monaghan, 2005: 81, 89).

All the readings in this section show that analysis from a sociology of the body perspective not only entails taking account of how the body is presented, but also how it is experienced and how it is shaped by socio-cultural forces. Moreover, how the body is experienced necessarily includes the 'corporeal' (Monaghan, 2005: 83), the actual fleshiness related to 'somatic sensation' or one's perception of physiological processes (Becker, 1994: 109). The intersection between these processes is what many sociologists mean when they refer to the concept of embodiment (Becker, 1994: 100; Monaghan, 2005: 83). Finally, these articles highlight that 'cultural values' shape aesthetic preferences about the body, meaning that what is considered beautiful varies across cultures and throughout history (Becker, 1994: 100, 103; Donohoe, 2006: 5). However, what is common to all cultures is that 'body morphology' (Becker, 1994: 106–07), the physical appearance of the body, its shape and size, is in fact 'bodily capital' (Monaghan, 2005: 82). Bodily capital, more often referred to as physical capital, means that the body, just like money, status, and time, is a valuable resource in society.

References

Becker, A.E. 1994. 'Nurturing and Negligence: Working on Others' Bodies in Fiji', in T. J. Csordas, ed, *Embodiment and Experience: The Existential Ground of Culture and Self*. Cambridge, MA: Cambridge University Press.

Donahoe, M. 2006. 'Beauty and Body Modification', *Medscape Ob/Gyn & Women's Health* 11, 1: 1–6.

Goffman, E. 1959. *The Presentation of Self in Everyday Life*. New York: Doubleday Anchor Books.

Monaghan, L.F. 2005. 'Big Handsome Men, Bears, and Others: Virtual Constructions of 'Fat Male Embodiment', *Body & Society* 11, 2: 81–111.

Chapter 7

'Introduction' from *The Presentation of Self in Everyday Life*

Erving Goffman

When an individual enters the presence of others, they commonly seek to acquire information about him . . . They will be interested in his general socio-economic status, his conception of self, his attitude toward them, his competence, his trustworthiness, etc. Although some of this information seems to be sought almost as an end in itself, there are usually quite practical reasons for acquiring it. Information about the individual helps to define the situation, enabling others to know in advance what he will expect of them and what they may expect of him. Informed in these ways, the others will know how best to act in order to call forth a desired response from him.

For those present, many sources of information become accessible and many carriers (or 'sign-vehicles') become available for conveying this information. If unacquainted with the individual, observers can glean clues from his conduct and appearance that allow them to apply their previous experience with individuals roughly similar to the one before them or, more important, to apply untested stereotypes to him. . . .

However, during the period in which the individual is in the immediate presence of the others, few events may occur that directly provide the others with the conclusive information they will need if they are to direct wisely their own activity. Many crucial facts lie beyond the time and place of interaction or lie concealed within it. For example, the 'true' or 'real' attitudes, beliefs, and emotions of the individual can be ascertained only indirectly, through his avowals or through what appears to be involuntary expressive behav-

iour. Similarly, if the individual offers the others a product or service, they will often find that during the interaction there will be no time and place immediately available for eating the pudding that the proof can be found in. They will be forced to accept some events as conventional or natural signs of something not directly available to the senses. In Ichheiser's terms,[1] the individual will have to act so that he intentionally or unintentionally *expresses* himself, and the others will in turn have to be *impressed* in some way by him.

The expressiveness of the individual (and therefore his capacity to give impressions) appears to involve two radically different kinds of sign activity: the expression that he *gives*, and the expression that he *gives off*. The first involves verbal symbols or their substitutes that he uses admittedly and solely to convey the information that he and the others are known to attach to these symbols. This is communication in the traditional and narrow sense. The second involves a wide range of action that others can treat as symptomatic of the actor, the expectation being that the action was performed for reasons other than the information conveyed in this way. As we shall have to see, this distinction has an only initial validity. The individual does of course intentionally convey misinformation by means of both of these types of communication, the first involving deceit, the second feigning.

Taking communication in both its narrow and broad sense, one finds that when the individual is in the immediate presence of others, his activity will have a promissory character. The others are likely to find that they must accept the individual on faith, offering him a just return while he is present before them in exchange for something whose true value will not be established until after he has left their presence. (Of course, the others also live by inference in their dealings with the physical world, but it is only in the world of social interaction that the objects about which they make inferences will purposely facilitate and hinder this inferential process.) The security that they justifiably feel in making inferences about the individual will vary, of course, depending on such factors as the amount of information they already possess about him, but no amount of such past evidence can entirely obviate the necessity of acting on the basis of inferences. As William I. Thomas suggested:

> It is also highly important for us to realize that we do not as a matter of fact lead our lives, make our decisions, and reach our goals in everyday life either statistically or scientifically. We live by inference. I am, let us say, your guest. You do not know, you cannot determine scientifically, that I will not steal your money or your spoons. But inferentially I will not, and inferentially you have me as a guest.[2] . . .

Let us now turn from the others to the point of view of the individual who presents himself before them. He may wish them to think highly of him, or to think that he thinks highly of them, or to perceive how in fact he feels toward them, or to obtain no clear-cut impression; he may wish to ensure sufficient harmony so that the interaction can be sustained, or to defraud, get rid of, confuse, mislead, antagonize, or insult them. Regardless of the particular objective that the individual has in mind and of his motive for having this objective, it will be in his interests to control the conduct of the others, especially their responsive treatment of him.[3] This control is achieved largely by influencing the definition of the situation that the others come to formulate, and he can influence this definition by expressing himself in such a way as to give them the kind of impression that will lead them to act voluntarily

in accordance with his own plan. Thus, when an individual appears in the presence of others, there will usually be some reason for him to mobilize his activity so that it will convey an impression to others that it is in his interests to convey. Since a girl's dormitory mates will glean evidence of her popularity from the calls she receives on the phone, we can suspect that some girls will arrange for calls to be made, and Willard Waller's finding can be anticipated:

> It has been reported by many observers that a girl who is called to the telephone in the dormitories will often allow herself to be called several times, in order to give all the other girls ample opportunity to hear her paged.[4]

Of the two kinds of communication—expressions given and expressions given off—this report will be primarily concerned with the latter, with the more theatrical and contextual kind, the nonverbal, presumably unintentional kind, whether this communication be purposely engineered or not. As an example of what we must try to examine, I would like to cite at length a novelistic incident in which Preedy, a vacationing Englishman, makes his first appearance on the beach of his summer hotel in Spain:

> But in any case he took care to avoid catching anyone's eye. First of all, he had to make it clear to those potential companions of his holiday that they were of no concern to him whatsoever. He stared through them, round them, over them—eyes lost in space. The beach might have been empty. If by chance a ball was thrown his way, he looked surprised; then let a smile of amusement lighten his face (Kindly Preedy), looked round dazed to see that there *were* people on the beach, tossed it back with a smile to himself and not a smile *at* the people, and then resumed carelessly his nonchalant survey of space.
>
> But it was time to institute a little parade, the parade of the Ideal Preedy. By devious handlings he gave any who wanted to look a chance to see the title of his book—a Spanish

translation of Homer, classic thus, but not daring, cosmopolitan too—and then gathered together his beach-wrap and bag into a neat sand-resistant pile (Methodical and Sensible Preedy), rose slowly to stretch at ease his huge frame (Big-Cat Preedy), and tossed aside his sandals (Carefree Preedy, after all).

The marriage of Preedy and the sea! There were alternative rituals. The first involved the stroll that turns into a run and a dive straight into the water, thereafter smoothing into a strong splashless crawl towards the horizon. But of course not really to the horizon. Quite suddenly he would turn on to his back and thrash great white splashes with his legs, somehow thus showing that he could have swum further had he wanted to, and then would stand up a quarter out of water for all to see who it was.

The alternative course was simpler, it avoided the cold-water shock and it avoided the risk of appearing too high spirited. The point was to appear to be so used to the sea, the Mediterranean, and this particular beach, that one might as well be in the sea as out of it. It involved a slow stroll down and into the edge of the water—not even noticing his toes were wet, land and water all the same to *him!*—with his eyes up at the sky gravely surveying portents, invisible to others, of the weather (Local Fisherman Preedy).[5]

The novelist means us to see that Preedy is improperly concerned with the extensive impressions he feels his sheer bodily action is giving off to those around him. We can malign Preedy further by assuming that he has acted merely in order to give a particular impression, that this is a false impression, and that the others present receive either no impression at all, or, worse still, the impression that Preedy is affectedly trying to cause them to receive this particular impression. But the important point for us here is that the kind of impression Preedy thinks he is making is in fact the kind of impression that others correctly and incorrectly glean from someone in their midst.

I have said that when an individual appears before others his actions will influence the definition of the situation that they come to have. Sometimes the individual will act in a thoroughly calculating manner, expressing himself in a given way solely in order to give the kind of impression to others that is likely to evoke from them a specific response he is concerned to obtain. Sometimes the individual will be calculating in his activity but be relatively unaware that this is the case. Sometimes he will intentionally and consciously express himself in a particular way, but chiefly because the tradition of his group or social status require this kind of expression and not because of any particular response (other than vague acceptance or approval) that is likely to be evoked from those impressed by the expression. Sometimes the traditions of an individual's role will lead him to give a well-designed impression of a particular kind and yet he may be neither consciously nor unconsciously disposed to create such an impression. The others, in their turn, may be suitably impressed by the individual's efforts to convey something, or may misunderstand the situation and come to conclusions that are warranted neither by the individual's intent nor by the facts. In any case, in so far as the others act *as if* the individual had conveyed a particular impression, we may take a functional or pragmatic view and say that the individual has 'effectively' projected a given definition of the situation and 'effectively' fostered the understanding that a given state of affairs obtains. . . .

When we allow that the individual projects a definition of the situation when he appears before others, we must also see that the others, however passive their role may seem to be, will themselves effectively project a definition of the situation by virtue of their response to the individual and by virtue of any lines of action they initiate to him. Ordinarily the definitions of the situation projected by the several different participants are sufficiently attuned to one another so that open contradiction will not occur. I do not mean that there will be the kind of consensus that arises when each individual present candidly expresses what he really feels and honestly agrees with the expressed feelings of the others present. This kind of harmony is an optimistic ideal and in any case not necessary for the smooth working of society. Rather, each participant is expected to suppress his immediate heartfelt feelings, conveying a view of the situation that he feels the others will be able to find at least temporarily acceptable. The maintenance of this surface of agreement, this veneer of consensus, is facilitated by each participant concealing his own wants behind statements that assert values to which everyone present feels obliged to give lip service. Further, there is usually a kind of division of definitional labour. Each participant is allowed to establish the tentative official ruling regarding matters that are vital to him but not immediately important to others, e.g., the rationalizations and justifications by which he accounts for his past activity. In exchange for this courtesy he remains silent or noncommittal on matters important to others but not immediately important to him. . . . Together the participants contribute to a single overall definition of the situation, which involves not so much a real agreement as to what exists but rather a real agreement as to whose claims concerning what issues will be temporarily honoured. Real agreement will also exist concerning the desirability of avoiding an open conflict of definitions of the situation. . . . I will refer to this level of agreement as a 'working consensus'. It is to be understood that the working consensus established in one interaction setting will be quite different in content from the working consensus established in a different type of setting. Thus, between two friends at lunch, a reciprocal show of affection, respect, and concern for the other is maintained. In service occupations, on the other hand, the specialist often maintains an image of disinterested involvement in the problem of the client, while the client responds with a show of respect for the competence and integrity of the specialist. Regardless of such differences in content, however, the general form of these working arrangements is the same. . . .

Notes

1. Gustav Ichheiser, 'Misunderstandings in Human Relations', Supplement to *The American Journal of Sociology*, LV (September 1949), 6–7.
2. Quoted in E.H. Volkart, ed, *Social Behaviour and Personality*, Contributions of W.I. Thomas to Theory and Social Research (New York: Social Science Research Council, 1951), 5.
3. Here I owe much to an unpublished paper by Tom Burns of the University of Edinburgh. He presents the argument that in all interaction a basic underlying theme is the desire of each participant to guide and control the responses made by the others present. A similar argument has been advanced by Jay Haley in a recent unpublished paper, but in regard to a special kind of control, that having to do with defining the nature of the relationship of those involved in the interaction.
4. Willard Waller, 'The Rating and Dating Complex', *American Sociological Review* II, 730.
5. William Sansom, *A Contest of Ladies* (London: Hogarth, 1956), 230–32. Copyright © William Sansom, 1956. Reproduced by permission of Greene & Heaton Ltd.

Chapter 8

Big Handsome Men, Bears, and Others: Virtual Constructions of 'Fat Male Embodiment'

Lee F. Monaghan

. . .

Fatness and the Management of Spoiled Masculine Identities

The appropriateness of fatness has long been bounded and regulated in Western culture, even when fat bodies are sexed as male. Note, for instance, William Banting's 1863 *A Letter on Corpulence* (cf. Huff, 2001), Falstaff's proclaimed frailty, Shakespeare's *Henry IV* and cultural commentary on the medical category 'morbid [sic] obesity' since Hippocrates (Gilman, 2004: 11). Of course, this does not translate to a naturalized and universal condemnation of fatness. Forms of fat embodiment have long had historical and cross-cultural currency. Mennell (1991: 147), for example, notes that 'healthy stoutness' and 'the magnificent amplitude of the human frame' constituted the cultural model in medieval and early modern Europe. The anthropology of the body tells a similar story, especially in relation to female fecundity (Brain, 1979). However, in contemporary Anglophone culture, such bodily capital is often 'discredited', that is, it is a stigma that, unlike 'discreditable' stigma, is immediately evident during face-to-face interaction (Goffman, 1968: 14).

Once good, fat bodies putatively belong to the bad and/or the ugly according to the definitional workings of . . . society . . . This degradation, which is currently being extended to Asia and Pacific regions (where body mass, in contrast to the United Kingdom and the United States, is positively correlated with socio-economic status),

is certified and accentuated by the Western disease-focused biomedical model (International Diabetes Institute, 2000). According to the World Health Organization (WHO, 1998), 'overweight' and 'obesity' are reaching 'epidemic' proportions in both developed and developing nations. Compounding the stigma of fatness, such pathologizing typifications are increasingly taken for granted in the English-speaking world. Even so, alternative definitions exist in various communicative contexts. Using qualitative data generated in Anglophone cyberspace, this article explores more positive typifications of fat male embodiment—social constructions that could be described as 'virtual' given their digital expression and 'connotation[s] of "not quite", adequate for practical purposes even if not strictly the real thing' (Hine, 2000: 65). Extending Goffman's (1968) arguments about stigma, such typifications are also 'virtual' in another sense, representing expectations that may figure in the management of spoiled identities. . . . Embodiment is a social process, and . . . one that is often gendered in classic social thought, with men typically being accorded the capacity to transcend their immediate corporeal selves. Finally, I use the word 'fat', but such usage is reflexive and qualified. This is a potentially problematic label if imposed from without as a bodily descriptor and identity: fat is not a four-letter word, but it is often intended, and received, as a term of abuse. This is compounded by what I call bodyism—the cultural belief that the whole body, perhaps more so than the face (Synnott, 1989), reflects individual

character. The 'f' word is therefore less than ideal.
. . .

In Western culture, coercive ideals of slenderness and 'the body beautiful' (or, more accurately, the body acceptable) have long been a pernicious dimension of female corporeality (Bordo, 1993). However, while male bodies are not generally objects-for-others in the same way female bodies typically are, men and boys are increasingly being subjected to normalizing body discourses and practices (Grogan and Richards, 2002). Recent critical commentary on 'obesity' immediately stresses the problems faced by women, but adds that men are also increasingly showing signs of damage in the war against fat (Campos, 2004: xvii–xviii; also, note the rise in eating disorders among boys at the same time that obesity is rising). There are many overlapping reasons for this convergence between the sexes. The greater prevalence of 'excess' weight among men compared to women (NAO, 2001; WHO, 1998) is important, but this is not simply a matter of numbers and epidemiology. For example, Campos (2004) underscores the immense power and profitability of the US obesity industry, which has fabricated an 'obesity myth' that reproduces typically white, middle-class cultural anxieties.

. . . [T]his article focuses upon on-line co-constituted meanings that could figure in the management of spoiled masculine identities. Drawing from a 'virtual ethnography' (Hine, 2000) of size-accepting or -admiring (SA) groups primarily based in the United States, I explore cyberspace as a possible domain for constructing positive masculinities. These constructions overwhelmingly relate to men (often in sexualized contexts), though boyhood and adolescence are sometimes topical. Data were obtained over a 10-month period (December 2003 to September 2004), incorporating observations of websites (N = 15) and on-line group interactions. I also actively generated data in chat rooms (Internet Relay Chat or IRC) and through e-mail exchanges with key informants (N = 7). As with off-line ethnography, research participants and sites are rendered anonymous through the use of pseudonyms. Textual data were regularly imported into, and systematically analyzed using *Atlas.ti* (Muhr, 1997). . . .

Typifying 'Fat' Male Body-subjects and Their Cybersociates

Many types of 'fat' male body-subject (forms of embodiment) are identifiable in SA cyberspace . . . In contrast to the physicality of fatness, these virtual bodies are clearly 'reduced versions of the primordial real thing' (Goffman, 1983: 2). They may even be radically different from their off-line correlates: the Internet, in contrast to bodily co-presence (Goffman, 1967), provides limited opportunity for sharing corporeal signs and visual clues. Yet, . . . [r]eported age, height, weight, ethnicity, and other physical markers of selfhood may also be relevant. . . .

Table 8.1 presents a typology of 'fat' male body-subjects and cybersociates who may act as supportive others. In defining terms, cybersociates are 'imagined' types (dissembling is certainly acknowledged on-line) who may never meet face to face but who nonetheless have the potential to influence and/or interact with others via the Internet. The traffic of communication and influence between cybersociates is variable. Communication may be unidirectional or reciprocal, depending upon the features and temporal dimensions of different communicative channels. For example, notices may be posted on discussion boards, and remain for some time, without any further dialogue between the originator and successive readers. . . .

Generic modalities of fat male embodiment, which, in this paper, largely refer to adult males, include: Big Handsome Men (BHM), 'Cuddly' Bears, and other corpulent males. . . . In biomedicine, 'big' bodies are negatively typified as 'overweight' or 'obese' depending upon Body Mass Index, calculated using a simple weight-for-height formula (WHO, 1998: 9). SA typifications are more ambiguous and complex. Even so, when observing modalities-of-embodiment-in-action, points of identification, convergence, and divergence emerge. It is therefore possible to concisely define types of fat male body-subject.

BHM, in association with supportive cybersociates, typically engage in processes of accepting and promoting (rather than simply measuring)

Table 8.1 A Typology of 'Fat' Male Body-subjects and Their Cybersociates

Generic types of fat male body	Subtypes	Supportive cybersociates
Big Handsome Men (BHM)	Super Size BHM (SSBHM)	Female Fat Admirers (FFA), including but not limited to Big Beautiful Women (BBW)
	Teen BHM	
	Big Handsome Black Men (BHBM)	Size Acceptance community more generally
'Cuddly' Bears	Daddy or Polar Bear	Other Bears and thinner subtypes (e.g., the Otter and Wolf)
	Cub	Gay Bear Lovers or Admirers more generally
	Hybrids and other subtypes (e.g., Chubby or Grizzly Bear, Big Teddy Bear, Black Bear)	STR8 women who admire 'bear-like' men
	Other large hirsute men identified as heterosexual (STR8) Bears	
Other Big/Fat Males	Chubbies	Chubby Chasers, Encouragers or Gay Fat Admirers
	Gainers	Feeders
	Belly Builders	Various others, including those supporting or admiring BHM and Bears
	Feedees	
	Foodees	
	Gluttons	

their already sizeable bodies in heterosexual space. A romantic or sexual focus is common, alongside other concerns that render direct reference to off-line bodily dimensions (e.g., weight, height, and waist measurement) more or less relevant. Bears engage in similar processes in gay male space. . . . Bears have a distinct symbolic style. Their body schema incorporates full facial hair, an assured sense of masculinity, and a level of body-mass typically equated with the aging male body. Other types include gay male Chubbies. Typically more expansive than Bears (visible on-line from digital photographs, though body weight may be cited), their expressions of self-acceptance are less assured. Others promote feeding and/or fattening processes, possibly with a sexual focus. Foodees or Gluttons are primarily food-oriented. . . .

Big Handsome Men: Putting On(-line) a Desirable Body and Face

This typification is relatively inclusive. One of my contacts wrote: 'Any fat guy is a BHM, be he gay, teenager, African American, Asian, or if he comes from Jupiter' (AdorableFFA, e-mail: 11 May 2004). However, in practice, this universality is highly circumscribed. If reference is made to sexuality, the BHM label is largely constructed within heterosexual SA groups (some meet off- as well as on-line). Although primarily catering to Big Beautiful Women (BBW), and their typically slim male Fat Admirers (FAS), these (cyber-)groups also offer acceptance, support, and heterosexual validation for fat men. On-line, self-typifying BHM (or, more modestly, 'big men') often seek corporeal connections and off-line dating opportunities with Female Fat Admirers (FFAS). This is illustrated below. Here 'nice and thick' refers to the author's off-line body, rather than intellect, amidst similar postings where geographically locatable BHM described their eye and hair colour, as well as weight and height:

> Any FFA's in California? Hi, I'm a big man in Santa Barbara, I would just love to meet a woman who appreciates someone nice and thick. If you're a FFA who is hungry for a date, e-mail me! (Posting on a BHM/FFA discussion board)

In contrast to gay male typifications (discussed below), the genus BHM is relatively homogeneous. When differentiation was observed, this often coincided with the heavy off-line stigma associated with particular categories of fat male. These include adolescents (Teen BHM), who are often considered 'body conscious' (WHO, 1998: 61), and those clinically defined as 'morbidly [sic] obese' (Super Size BHM). The typification Big Handsome Black Men (BHBM) was unusual, despite AdorableFFA's ethnically inclusive defini-

tion. Following Mosher (2001: 176), this could be due to a more accommodating attitude to fat among African Americans. However, I did observe one self-typifying BHBM (reportedly weighing 260 pounds at 5 feet 10 inches) admonish African American women for ignoring or insulting their fat 'brothers' off-line. However, while all BHM may be vulnerable to off-line stigma, or 'non-person treatment' (Goffman, 1959), the Internet allows fleshy bodies to become more durable and valued cyborgs. For Haraway (1991: 175), cyborgs embrace technology in order to exercise 'the power to survive . . . to mark the world that marked them as other, [to] reverse and displace hierarchical dualisms' such as ugly and handsome. Following Wernick (1991), this also meshes with a promotional culture where men, like women, are increasingly being constructed as fleshy advertisements for the self.

The BHM label is a 'personal front' (Goffman, 1959) in the theatre of life. As part of the on-line presentation or promotion of self, BHM seek acceptance and heterosexual matching through 'face work' (Goffman, 1967), which could more appropriately be termed 'screen work'. This work, sometimes manifest in lighthearted sociability, draws positive meanings from the symbolism of the desirable (handsome) male face . . . Here the Internet provides a stage upon which 'real' fat males may (virtually) construct a self . . . [C]ybersociates are instrumental in manufacturing favourable (recognizably human) versions of fat male embodiment. Through collaborative efforts, participants promote a 'line' (Goffman, 1967), which, in the words of AdorableFFA, 'is designed to make both the person of size and the public aware that fatness does not imply ugliness' (e-mail: 11 May 2004). . . .

Bears: 'Cuddly' Hirsute Types in Gay Culture

This typification 'includes many big men deemed fat and denigrated by the mainstream of gay male social and community networks' (Textor, 1999: 223). . . . Similar to BHM, Bears also engage in processes of self-acceptance and promotion. . . .

Gay culture, more so than heterosexual culture, objectifies a standard image of male beauty: 'the young, blond, smooth-skinned, gym-buffed' model type or 'twink' (Wright, 1997: 2). Bears seek to transcend this body ideal through their symbolic style . . . :

> The most common definition of a 'bear' is a man who is hairy, has facial hair, and a cuddly body. However, the word 'bear' means many things to different people, even within the bear movement. Many men who do not have one or all of these characteristics define themselves as bears, making the term a very loose one. . . . (Bear Information Website) . . .

Other Fat-friendly Typifications

There are other typifications and associated relevances. For example, eating 'excessively' is a primary concern among Gluttons while the gay eroticization of corpulence is thematic among Chubbies and Chubby Chasers. Inseparable from the history of Christian asceticism, where eating and sex have long been considered 'gross activities of the body' (Turner, 1996: 49), other recalcitrant types embody an amalgam of corporeal concerns. In pursuing greater pleasures from eating and growing, Gainers or Feedees seek eroticized relations with Encouragers or Feeders. . . .

However, while 'most chubbies want to weigh less' (Harry, e-mail: 12 June 2004), their corpulence is eroticized. The Internet and off-line convergences, organized by 'fat-friendly' European and US gay clubs, offer spaces for sexual expression and matching. Websites for and by Chubbies and Chubby Chasers (who may not necessarily be 'big' themselves) are often sexually explicit. . . .

Virtually Constructing Acceptable, Admirable, or Resistant Masculinities

The above gendered typifications figure within on-line schemes of orientation and interpretation and have implications for positive subjectivity. At a time when the obesity industry is actively constructing overweight as a serious problem, the Internet provides space for alternative definitions of fat male embodiment. Some common ways of managing spoiled masculine identities on-line are outlined below under four headings: (1) appeals to 'real' or 'natural' masculinity; (2) the admiration and eroticization of fat men's bodies; (3) transgression, fun, and the carnivalesque; and (4) the pragmatics and politics of fat male embodiment.

Appeals to 'Real' or 'Natural' Masculinity

. . . [I]n the context of bodyism, fatness may be used to emasculate male bodies or render them subordinate on masculine hierarchies. In contemporary Anglophone culture, fatness symbolizes lack of self-discipline and adherence to masculinist imperatives such as being active and in control. Participants in various SA groups challenge this effacement. Whether focusing upon heterosexual or gay male groups, the competing rhetoric is clear: fat men have 'real' or 'natural' bodies.

Similar to Watson's male interviewees, cyber-persona criticized media images of 'ideal' men's bodies on the basis that such bodies are unrepresentative of the 'normal bloke's everyday body' (Watson, 2000: 80). . . . The symbolism of body and facial hair, physical bulk, and male-coded activity are also relevant. Bears self-present as having the 'correct attitude' towards their 'natural' aging male bodies, hair on the body and face differentiates men from women (baldness is acceptable for the same reason), 'the battle of the bulge' is rejected (it is typically associated with the feminine), and being camp is replaced by a sense of being an 'everyday guy' who also happens to be gay. Comfort with other men's bodies is also framed in terms of 'real' masculinity—Bears are not 'afraid' to touch others, for example.

Other types also engage on-line in masculine validating processes. For example, Belly Builders assert control and licence over their 'body territory' (Lyman and Scott, 1970: 106) in response to a society that dispraises the 'obese' for their putative lack of control. Gluttons emphasize 'man-size' appetites, the capacity for sheer quantitative stuffing, and the enjoyment of food without fear of calories (also, see Bordo, 1993: 132–4). . . .

Admiring and Eroticizing Fat Men's Bodies
. . . As noted, BHM seek to efface the perceived ugliness of fatness by putting on(-line) a desirable body and face. Such 'screen work' may be tentative (real-life rejection may be mentioned, for example), but some cybersociates are highly supportive. Those reporting off-line relationships with fat men, including women who have struggled to reinterpret their own fat, sometimes offer encouragement. As expressed within a heterosexual Gainer group:

> Subject: Yeah, she's gaining!! Once I accepted the fact that fat does not make me a bad person, it was easy to give in to my natural tendency to be fat as well as my feelings that fat is erotic and desirable. I not only like being fat, I like Fred [partner] to be fat too. So I rub his belly and encourage him. What about you? Would you like to be fat? Would she like it if you were fat too? (Sugar Plum Fairy, Weight-Watching group e-mail). . . .

The range of acceptable or desirable male body types is reportedly much narrower in gay culture, rendering many gay men insecure about their looks (Locke, 1997). One response is to reject the objectification (symbolic feminization) of gay men's bodies where the emphasis upon beauty is recast as an impediment to intimacy (Wright, 1997: 9). However, many SA spaces promote the gay eroticization of expansive male bodies. Textor's (1999) work on representations of fat men and homosexual desire within the big men's magazine media is extendable to cyberspace. Similar to magazines, 'an erotic lexicon is in place' forming 'a discourse of desire' that reflects and produces an imagined community wherein fat men have sexual currency (Textor, 1999: 218). . . .

Transgression, Fun, and the Carnivalesque
The stigma of fatness is often challenged in a convivial atmosphere, characterized by fun and

enjoyment rather than illness and disease. Again, sexual desire is relevant. However, in exploring other (interrelated) themes, I will briefly consider on-line representations of feeding and fattening processes. For Gainers, Belly Builders, Gluttons, and Feedees, the vicarious pleasures of gluttony and/or body modification are central. . . . The following supportive interchange in a mixed-sex Gainer group humorously refers to measurable off-line bodies and seasonal celebrations. . . .

> Subject: Have gained, how do I know? Kevin wrote:

> I went out today and I think I have gained, my fly on my jeans would not stay up, the pressure of that extra belly was not going to give in. :), [symbol signifies a smiling face]. Just as well it is winter and I had a large loose jumper so you could not tell anyway, blush. I am now a good 173 cm in girth, when I was 168 cm I was 172 kg so I estimate that I am now 176–78 kg or about 390 lbs, I am aiming for 180 cm by Xmas. . . .

. . . Here monstrous appetites and bellies (a typical grotesque hyperbola) acquire an extreme and fantastic character. A series of morphed photographs depicting a Belly Builder's fattening career (with dates and accumulating poundage written next to a massively expanding torso), or images of forced feeding among Fatties (e.g., a funnel and tube for administering liquidized calories) mock common proprieties. . . .

. . . Extolling the virtues of periodically permitting oneself the sensual experience of gluttony ('the beastlike satisfaction of a bloated belly'), Klein (1996: 60) writes: 'You need once in a while to transgress the barrier between eating well and eating like a pig, in order to understand what eating well might mean.' Interestingly, this idea of 'eating like a pig'—painfully implicated in forms of public harassment against fat people (Joanisse and Synnott, 1999: 58–9)—figures within premodern carnivalesque imagery where participants subvert high/low distinctions between humans and (dirty) animals. . . .

The Pragmatics and Politics of Fat Male Embodiment

Common difficulties and common solutions to fat embodiment are discussed on-line. The keyword here is support for those encountering (and perhaps hoping successfully to challenge) an unaccommodating 'real' world. Importantly, prominent SA groups do not officially support mainstream efforts to neutralize fat bodies through restrictive dieting and other techniques of contraction. (After all, that would reinforce the acceptability of slimness among those who are unwilling and/or unable to become and remain slim.) Rather, the everyday practicalities and experiences of being fat are discussed, alongside what might be done to redress social discrimination and promote wider tolerance. . . .

Regarding pragmatics, communication and advice abound on tackling the routine, everyday difficulties of being large. Themes include finding suitable clothes suppliers; ensuring good health regardless of size; dealing with prejudiced clinicians; travelling comfortably (cramped aircraft seating is particularly problematic); buying reinforced furniture and other everyday items. . . .

Such talk reproduces a supportive context where fat men are not condemned for their 'excessive' weight. It also reinforces a resistant position against those who would urge the 'obese' to embark upon a difficult-to-sustain and reportedly risky weight-loss regime (cf. Campos, 2004).

Pragmatics are also intertwined with gendered body politics. The politicization of women's bodies is well documented and is clearly articulated with second-wave feminism (e.g., Boston Women's Health Collective, 1971). There the female body is claimed to be a political, material subject constituted by and through 'anti-fat' cultural representations (Textor, 1999: 223). Following feminism's impact upon female body consciousness, many fat women in the United States have organized and mobilized their efforts in order to protest against size discrimination in the real world. Men (who may also, but not necessarily, be fat) are also supportive. . . .

References

Bordo, S. 1993. *Unbearable Weight: Feminism, Western Culture and the Body*. Berkeley: University of California Press.

Brain, R. 1979. *The Decorated Body*. New York: Harper and Row.

Campos, P. 2004. *The Obesity Myth: Why America's Obsession with Weight is Hazardous to your Health*. New York: Gotham Books.

Garfinkel, H. 1967. *Studies in Ethnomethodology*. Englewood Cliffs, NJ: Prentice Hall.

Gilman, S. 2004. *Fat Boys: A Slim Book*. Lincoln: University of Nebraska Press.

Goffman, E. 1959. *The Presentation of Self in Everyday Life*. New York: Doubleday Anchor.

———. 1967. *Interaction Ritual: Essays on Face-to-face Behavior*. New York: Doubleday Anchor.

———. 1968. *Stigma: Notes on the Management of Spoiled Identity*. Middlesex: Penguin Books.

———. 1983. 'The Interaction Order', *American Sociological Review* 48: 1–17.

Grogan, S., and H. Richards. 2002. 'Body Image: Focus Groups with Boys and Men', *Men and Masculinities* 4, 3: 219–32.

Haraway, D. 1991. *Simians, Cyborgs, and Women*. London: Routledge.

Hine, C. 2000. *Virtual Ethnography*. London: Sage.

Huff, J. 2001. 'A "Horror of Corpulence": Interrogating Bantingism and Mid-nineteenth-century Fat-phobia', in J.E. Braziel and K. LeBesco, eds, *Bodies out of Bounds: Fatness and Transgression*. Berkeley and Los Angeles: University of California Press.

Joanisse, L., and A. Synnott. 1999. 'Fighting Back: Reactions and Resistance to the Stigma of Obesity', in J. Sobal and D. Maurer, eds, *Interpreting Weight: The Social Management of Fatness and Thinness*. New York: Aldine De Gruyter.

Klein, R. 1996. *Eat Fat*. New York: Pantheon Books.

Locke, P. 1997. 'Male Images in the Gay Mass Media and Bear-oriented Magazines: Analysis and Contrast', in L. Wright, ed, *The Bear Book: Readings in the History and Evolution of a Gay Male Subculture*. New York: Hawthorne Press.

Lyman, S., and M. Scott. 1970. *A Sociology of the Absurd*. New York: Appleton.

Mennell, S. 1991. 'On the Civilizing of Appetite', in M. Featherstone, M. Hepworth, and B. Turner, eds, *The Body: Social Process and Cultural Theory*. London: Sage.

NAO. 2001. *National Audit Office: Tackling Obesity in England*. London: Stationery Office.

Synnott, A. 1989. 'Truth and Goodness, Mirrors and Masks—Part I: A Sociology of Beauty and the Face', *British Journal of Sociology* 40, 4: 607–36.

Textor, A. 1999. 'Organization, Specialization, and Desires in the Big Men's Movement: Preliminary Research in the Study of Subculture-Formation', *Journal of Gay, Lesbian, and Bisexual Identity* 4, 3: 217–39.

Turner, B. 1996. *The Body and Society*, 2nd edn. London: Sage.

Watson, J. 2000. *Male Bodies: Health, Culture and Identity*. Buckingham: Open University Press.

WHO. 1998. *Obesity: Preventing and Managing the Global Epidemic*. Geneva: World Health Organization.

Wright, L., ed. 1997. *The Bear Book: Readings in the History and Evolution of a Gay Male Subculture*. New York: Hawthorne Press.

Chapter 9

Nurturing and Negligence: Working on Others' Bodies in Fiji

Anne E. Becker

This chapter examines the impact of culturally specific notions of personhood on the experience of embodiment. More specifically, it explores how the representational uses of the body unfold in the context of the relationship between the person, the community, and the body. I will first comment on the intensive cultivation of the body's surfaces and contours in some sectors of contemporary American society in order to contrast it with a relative disinterest in personal cultivation among Fiji Islanders . . . This difference is best understood as stemming from the disparity in the experience of personhood of these two cultures.

My argument begins with the premise that core cultural values are encoded in—among other things—aesthetic or moral ideals of body shape (see Ritenbaugh, 1982). . . . [T]here is widespread participation in the ethos of bodily cultivation in American popular culture directed at approximating the recognized ideals of bodily perfection. Ethnographic data suggest that there is a parallel consensus regarding the aesthetics of bodily form in Fijian society. . . . What differentiates the Fijian from the American participant in popular culture, however, is . . . the relative lack of interest and investment in attaining the ideal by cultivating, nurturing, and disciplining the body.

In the last several decades, the disciplined body has emerged as a popular culture ideal in American society. Social success is contingent on the belaboured construction of a particular image, which, in turn, hinges on the cultivation of 'successful bodies, which have been trained, disciplined, and orchestrated to enhance our personal value' (Turner, 1984: 111). . . . [B]ody shape and weight are ultimately seen as the residue of indulgence (obesity), restraint (thinness), or discipline (toned musculature). The culture validates this ethic of intensive investment in the body as a key to the projected self-image, suggesting that the goal is not necessarily to attain a particular physical feature, but rather to signal participation in the process of body work and image-making.

Bodily cultivation has arguably reached its extreme in the restrictive dieting and obsessive exercise regimens that verge toward eating-disordered behaviour. Indeed the epidemiology of anorexia and bulimia nervosa reveals that behaviours associated with these syndromes are quite culturally grounded. While it is a stretch to prove that these syndromes are created by their cultural context, a conservative view at least allows that they flourish in a milieu that sanctions a dedicated concern with self-image, most notably when it seeks to emulate culturally identified aesthetic (and moral) ideals. . . .

The Semantics of Body Shape

The use of the body as a malleable . . . medium for signalling participation in or deviation from cultural norms is well known. The virtually limitless parameters of manipulation include adornment with cosmetics and jewellry, . . . scarification, and reshaping of the body. . . .

Aesthetic preferences for body shape and size are informed by core societal values. . . . In a well-known study in the eating disorder literature, Garner et al. (1980) argued that the shifting measurement and weight norms of *Playboy* centrefolds and beauty pageant finalists demonstrate a trend toward valuation of more slender and tubular female bodies in the 1960s and 1970s, if we accept their premise that these media figures constitute meaningful cultural icons. In a follow-up study, Wiseman et al. (1992) concluded that this trend of valuing thinness has continued up through the 1980s and created incentives to diet, presumably to emulate the ideal. . . . [T]here is no shortage of evidence that bodies are starved, stretched, exercised, and even surgically reconstructed for the purpose of portraying the ideal self through their surfaces and contours. In short, bodies are cultivated to effect the attributes imbued with culturally relevant values that the self wishes to display.

Given the historical flux of American preferences for body shape, it seems logical that there will also be cross-cultural variability in these preferences. A study comparing female Kenyan with British subjects found that the former group perceived heavier female shapes in a significantly more positive way than did the British subjects. The positive valuation of obese female figures by the Kenyans was attributed to their association of body fat with sufficient access to food in a land of scarce resources (Furnham and Alibhai, 1983). In the South Pacific, ethnographers have noted the association of social status with physical stature. For instance, Mackenzie (1985) has noted that the perceived ideal body shape in Tonga or Samoa is influenced by the relative vulnerability to food shortage, making it unlikely that prestige would be symbolized in dietary restraint.

Like Americans, Fijians express admiration for certain ideal features represented in body shapes. These ideal features, such as sturdy calves (*bodi la*), or a body that is well-formed and filled out (*jubu vina*), are also associated with particular cultural virtues—in this case, the ability to work hard and the evidence that a person has been cared for well. Moreover, the language of insults

reveals a relative distaste for overly obese or thin persons and there is a clear preference for a robust form (sometimes corresponding to overweight by American standards). Although these relative differences are intriguing, the most striking difference between the Fijian and the American attitude toward ideal body shapes is the Fijian's absence of interest in attaining the ideal shape as a personal goal. In contrast with the American, the Fijian does not personally cultivate his or her body to project a public image.

What remains puzzling is that despite this relatively passive stance toward their bodies, commentary on body shape—the form of one's body, whether one has lost or gained weight—is absolutely central to everyday discourse in the Fijian village. Remarks drawing attention to size and changes in others' bodies are virtually unremitting, and the language of greeting, teasing, and insults is riddled with references to weight loss or gain or unusual body size.

Although this initially appears paradoxical, it can be best understood in the context of the Fijian experience of personhood and embodiment. The fundamental orientation of the Fijian is to the community. . . . [T]he Fijian certainly experiences his or her body, but his or her self-awareness is substantially defined by his or her membership and participation in a community.

What is encoded, read, and no doubt experienced in the changes and form of the Fijian body, therefore, is not the individual's finesse in tapping into core symbols of prestige, but rather, the social positioning of the person—how he or she has been nurtured or neglected in his or her social milieu. . . . While by comparison, the American cultivation of the body is motivated by its potential to represent personal prestige and accomplishments, the cultivation of the Fijian body records the collectivity's achievement in crafting its form.

The following discussion will illustrate the attention to individual bodies in an attempt to gauge the community's success in nurturing its members. The quality of this nurturance is measured by the enactment of duties that relate to caring for others according to complex social protocols. Specifically, the concept of care comprises several types of service that are rendered within the context of various social roles. These include *viqwaravi*, i.e., looking after the needs and comforts of another, especially with regard to serving and attending meals; *vikawaitaki*, i.e., showing interest in and attentiveness to another's well-being; and *vilomani*, i.e., having general interest and empathy for another's problems, growth, successes, and so forth. The modes of behaviour encompassed by the concept of care are most frequently and visibly evident in the procuring and sharing of food resources. Finally, the cumulative effects of care are manifest in the body morphologies of the receivers. So in essence, a body is the responsibility of the feeding and caring microcommunity and consequently, its form shows the work of the community rather than of the self. What differentiates the Fijian from the American modes of cultivation of the body is other-centredness. . . .

Body shape not only suggests personal abilities, but also marks connection to the social network and reflects its powers to nourish. Children and guests (*vulagi*) are often targeted for extraordinary efforts in care, since their weight gain or robust forms will be credited to the caretaker's social prowess. Similarly, the collective devotion to cultivating the chief's body reflects his or her representation of the community (see Leenhardt, 1979: 108). . . .

Kana valevu and Going Thin: The Rhetoric of Care and Negligence

Caregiving is central to social life in the Fijian village; it is practically expressed through the moral imperative to share food resources and materializes in the bodies that are fed. Care is also symbolically enacted in continuous rhetorical commentary guaranteeing the commitment to share food resources.

The primary cultural preoccupation with hunger and the distribution of food throughout Melanesia and Polynesia is reflected in the language of insults that has been elaborated to lambaste both those who are hungry and those who do not share food. Malinowski reported that in

the Trobriand Islands, the most deg_ ment to make about another is to call him _ gry' (Young, 1979). Commentary that condemns those who do not share food runs parallel to this discourse. For example, Kahn (1986) describes how character judgment in Papua New Guinea directly relates to the generosity with which people share food.

Since feeding and food-sharing in the household and the community are the chief means through which social relations are conceived and maintained, Fijians are loath to be considered *kanakana lo* (i.e., one who eats secretly) and are explicit in their desire to share food. References to hunger and generosity with food can be contextualized as a commentary on care and being cared for in the social milieu. Moreover, the disparagement of hunger is a moral indictment of someone who can neither provide food nor obtain it through affiliation with a community that feeds its members. Inferences based on the appearance of the body are made explicit in the associations between thinness and deprivation (material and social) or thinness and laziness.

. . . [W]hen a household serves food, its members are obliged to throw open their doors and windows, so that the meal is, in essence, publicly displayed and accessible. Moreover, persons who are eating or serving a meal maintain watchful eyes toward the doorway for passersby—whether kinsmen or strangers—in order to invite them in to partake of the meal. The standard greetings, 'Come and eat', 'There is cassava here', or 'Have your noonday meal here', issue forth from every household at mealtimes. Although the invitations are compulsory, they are also rhetorical. That is, while people are genuinely welcome to enter the household and eat, they usually continue on to their expected mealtime destination.

To accommodate potential guests, Fijians prepare large quantities of food—especially root crops—to allow wide margins of excess so they may confidently extend invitations to their meals. They routinely affirm that to have inadequate food supplies to feed guests or to contribute to ceremonial exchange confers disgrace. One woman explained:

[If there] is not enough for us, the members of the household are going to be ashamed that there is too little food . . . we should eat, we should be well-sated (*bori vina*), never mind if there are leftovers . . . if only because it should never happen that we eat just a little . . . that we still feel hungry—yet the food is finished . . . that would make us ashamed.

Whether the potential guest is a friend or relative stranger is immaterial. In fact, if a guest is known to be staying in the village, households will carry a food offering (*kabekabe*) to the household in which he or she is staying in order to pay their respects to the stranger.

Another central feature to the *viqwaravi* of a meal is the running verbal encouragement by hosts and servers to their guests to consume as much as possible. This rhetorical commentary during the meal complements the requisite invitations cast outside the cookhouse to passersby. The women tending to the serving keep a vigilant watch on each plate. They urge, '*kana valevu*' ('Eat a lot'), '*kana tale*' ('Eat some more'), or '*e hi vo na cawa*' ('There's still more food'); alternatively, they express disappointment with the allegedly meagre amount the guest has eaten, saying, '*o iko tasi kana valevu*' ('You haven't eaten much'). Oftentimes, a particularly assiduous host or hostess will insist '*kana valevu, mo urouro!*' ('Eat a great deal, so that you may become fat!'). Although this is a matter of politesse, these enjoinders are often meant quite literally.

Fijians hope that their efforts to nurture their guests will be rewarded with the recognition of their *vikawaitaki* and *viqwaravi*, or care. It is assumed that these efforts are ultimately manifest in body morphology. To this end, there is extraordinary attention paid to changes in the face and body indicative of a weight gain or loss; moreover, their recurrent commentary on changes to body shape make their assessments explicit. Hosts routinely direct their guests to eat well to avoid any possibility that their care be deemed negligent. For example, a rural village woman stated,

They'll be very, very proud if you put on weight and really look healthy before you go back to your parents; and if you go back to your parents skinny, you know, there are a lot of reasons behind it. And maybe they'll think that your parents won't want to send you back to them, and then maybe they'll think that they'll never feed you properly.

Given its explicit reference to nurturance and *vikawaitaki*, the mealtime commentary indicates concern for well-being by invoking a complex set of symbols that refer to food exchange and body morphology. The idiom is pressed to its limits in formulating the ultimate goal of the intensive care of an individual: that he or she should become fat. It is important to recall, however, that Fijians do not find obesity particularly appealing. Nurturing, rather than the actual cultivation of body shape, is the ostensible mandate.

Fijians monitor changes in body morphology within their network of care with great vigilance. The consequences of material and emotional deprivation or loss are thought to be manifest in bodily thinness, and use of the idiomatic 'gone thin' (*a luju hara ga e lala*) evokes a certain social disconnectedness. Any evidence of weight loss is assumed to reflect a disruption in the cohesiveness of the social milieu or gross negligence on the part of the caretakers. In this respect, the effective and social positions of the individual are condensed in bodily form.

The Preoccupation with *Macake*: The Defence against an Appetite Disorder

. . . Fijians scrutinize the appetites of their charges to prevent a decline that might result in weight loss. Indeed, appetite is negotiated as the key variable in health. The loss of appetite is not only considered a herald of serious illness, but it is also the . . . symptom for the culturally elaborated syndrome, *macake*. *Macake* is a syndrome characterized by a variety of symptoms—a whitish coating on the tongue, sores in the mouth, a change in urine colour, inflamed gums, a running nose, and fever—but its *sine qua non* is appetite disturbance. This illness is endemic in young children and quite prevalent in the adult population as well.

Descriptions of the experience most often focus on the absence of interest in eating, for example, the sensation that 'One's inside doesn't want to eat' or 'One just doesn't feel like eating'. This lapse in appetite leads to the most worrisome feature of *macake*: its manifestation in weight loss. While bracketing the issue of whether *macake* has a correlate in Western biomedical nosology (see Good and Good, 1982: 141–5), the concern to identify and treat it can be understood as an elaboration of the Fijian interest in body morphology. The tandem concerns with *hunger per se*, and its opposite category, *macake*, or *lack of hunger*, underscore the ultimate interest in maintaining the body's strength and weight.

. . . [M]*acake* generates the requirement that careful attention be directed to changes in appetite and body shape as possible indicators of distress in the body or distress in the social world. The practice of guarding and monitoring appetite is fundamentally integrating, since treatment of *macake* both practically and symbolically enmeshes the afflicted individual (or individual at risk) in a network of care. Hence, Fijians have not only elaborated a variety of idiomatic expressions to stimulate the appetite socially, but have also institutionalized social vigilance over the appetite by means of detection and treatment of *macake*.

Body Surveillance through Somatic Experience

Attention to hunger is central to the Fijian ethos of care. The constant watchfulness during mealtimes to identify persons with whom to share food, the surveillance of those in the community who may be materially or emotionally deprived, and the vigilance directed toward appetite integrate individual persons into communities that can bestow care on them. However, any situation that may potentially alienate an individual is attended to by virtue of its concrete manifestations, which are not necessarily confined to the space of the body. Bodily states are not only accessible to the beholder by their visual presentation, but by their patency in additional perceptual modalities, including somatic sensation. Monitoring of bodily states is particularly intense when the integrity of the community is threatened in some way by the social isolation of an individual, such as in the case of having an illness or keeping a secret. In these situations, it is notable that what the American may think of as personal experience is not encapsulated by the individual body in Fiji, but rather reverberates in other bodies and events.

Perhaps the most striking illustration of bodily experience transcending the individual occurs in the case of an undisclosed pregnancy. Within the context of the extended family, or *mataqali*, the productive and reproductive capacities of the body are theoretically appropriated toward community ends, with only tenuous individual control over allocation of bodily resources. Given this imperative, the knowledge of a pregnancy must be conveyed immediately to a community. If it should be retained as a secret of the body, this embezzlement of community property will be experienced as socially disruptive.

Anecdotal accounts of undisclosed pregnancies and the havoc they bring to their communities comprise the most compelling testimony by Fijians legitimizing the social claim to individual bodies. Mishaps are often interpreted as indications of a possible violation of the moral obligation to notify a community of a pregnancy, which thereby obstruct the integration of the new member into the group. For this reason there is an inspired watchfulness for signs of pregnancy, both as bodily changes and unexplained environmental occurrences.

Women in particular are informed of and attentive to the early signs and symptoms that herald the more obvious stages of pregnancy. A young woman explained,

> For Fijians, oh, the old ladies, they're smart . . . they can tell when a woman is one month pregnant, or two months pregnant . . . by the look of the lady, eh? the pregnant woman, eh? they can

tell. They said . . . in the early pregnancy, first month of pregnancy, second month, eh? they can tell by the look of the pregnant lady, she'll lose a lot of weight, eh? . . . They used to say that they automatically lose weight . . . they said when it comes . . . when the baby inside is getting, you know, more matured or bigger, fully formed, eh, they say that that's the time when she'll gain weight again . . . four months time, five months pregnant . . . they'll uh, regain their weight again . . . they'll get fatter that time. And also . . . another sign the old ladies can really tell that she's pregnant, by you know, they'll eat a lot of unripe fruits . . . like mangoes . . . they won't eat the ripe one, they prefer the unripe one . . . that's a sign of pregnancy.

Again, there is emphasis on weight and appetite as key variables to be monitored. Other women explained the changes as an initial weight loss noticeable in the face and prominent clavicles (*domo bale*); another woman observed that the legs, especially the calves, become thin along with the neck, and in general, 'the bones will show'. Later the hips and the breasts enlarge as the pregnancy develops. The complexion is also thought to become fairer.

While detected in subtleties of body shape, pregnancy manifests itself extracorporally as well in certain cases. Generally this occurs when there is a breach in the obligation promptly to inform (verbally and ceremonially) the community of a pregnancy. This non-disclosure constitutes a major moral transgression that results in a variety of untoward environmental epiphenomena. Not only is the secrecy an intolerable anti-social offense, but in many ways, the implied autonomy is unfathomable. Experience is neither private, nor individual; it is fundamentally social and diffuse. . . . [A] Fijian woman has no choice but to reveal her pregnancy simply because her body is unable to contain the experience as a personal event. Her body divulges the pregnancy in token catastrophes: cakes not rising, chairs falling flat, and boats encountering rough seas in her presence. More threatening are the effects of her undisclosed pregnancy that manifest in other bodies.

The hair she cuts may fall out, her glance may dry up the milk of a lactating mother, or her very touch may contaminate food, making it toxic to children and the frail elderly for whom she cooks. The food she prepares for a young child may even cause the child to lose weight or to 'go thin'.

The explanation of one woman who had not yet properly shared the news of her pregnancy illustrates her concern that she needed to ask someone else to cook for her toddler because of the danger her state posed to his health. She reasoned:

> Because if I give him the food . . . he is eating a lot, but he is thin now, he won't grow . . . his weight will go down, even if he [eats a lot] he will just stay tiny.

In retrospect, she recalled that continuing to cook for her child had been at great risk:

> [My son] went thin! You can notice it in the photo . . . he looks terrible . . . because I was hiding [my pregnancy] and taking care of him . . . children can go thin . . . or an elderly person can die.

Given the intensive concern with weight and body morphology, an undisclosed pregnancy is morally irresponsible. The guarantee of disclosure, however, is often the revelation of the secret in another's body. A Fijian woman described her mother's experience of an 'itching breast' whenever a member of the family was pregnant. The evidence was considered compelling enough to address formally the possibility of a hidden pregnancy:

> She'll say, 'Oh, someone's pregnant' . . . There'll be signs too, in the family . . . And then usually, if the signs are there, the father will call all the girls and ask, 'One of you is, uh, you know, you better say it before something really bad happens.'

Again, the anticipation of danger reflects a concern that the secret is toxic to the community. Its most dreaded effects are always around the interruption of nurturing activities, as illustrated in the following account by a woman of the effects of a secret pregnancy on her mother.

> If [a] pregnant woman sees the breast of the lactating mother, one [breast] can become shorter, or else, she might, uh . . . the milk just dries up . . . It happened to me when I was a kid . . . One woman . . . she was pregnant . . . and she saw my mother's breast, and as a result, my mother's breast dried up . . . my mother had to resort to powdered milk to feed me.

In other words, intimate social knowledge of another's body is made explicit by means of its embodiment elsewhere. Verbal disclosure may be a matter of moral deliberation as an individual weighs the risk of containing private knowledge in the body, yet the information is readily available to the community since the body inevitably releases its secrets—directly or indirectly—through a second body.

. . . When the locus of identity is simultaneously fixed in bodies and relationships, both the information conveyed by body weight and shape and embodied experiences are indicative not only of a person's situation within the flesh of a body, but his or her situation within a social plexus as well.

Since the Fijian body cannot hide its secrets nor circumscribe the person, an undisclosed pregnancy threatens the community with its powers to capsize boats, contaminate food, and spoil group endeavours. In so far as it condenses multiple symbols of disruption of group integrity, the real threat it poses is of self-community alienation. This alienation is circumvented, in part, by monitoring bodies—just as body weight, shape, and appetites are watched —for the evidence of social connectedness manifest in their forms.

Conclusions

In conclusion, I have compared the cultivation of bodily space by Fijians and Americans. While there is evidence that Americans labour on their bodies to exploit their representational capacities in conveying personal qualities of the self, Fijians are relatively complacent with respect to cultivating the body's space as a marker of personal attributes. Initially, this complacency seemed paradoxical. If Fijians are not concerned with manipulating self-image through the body, why did they invent and invest in rhetorical instructions to nourish—even to fatten—one's family and guests? Why, moreover, had their commentaries on the body proliferated into parallel discourses on nurturing and negligence?

Capitalist-derived values in contemporary American society encourage competitive working on the self to promote it above other selves. Post-industrial cultures invent the body by means of a calculated social representation of the self, exploiting symbols of prestige. Given what we witness in contemporary popular culture in America, we might conjecture that there is a universal aesthetic valuation of pleasing bodily forms. So, for instance, we might guess that in the Fiji Islands, where abundance of food is valued, it would be a well-fed shape that might be the operant ideal of beauty. We might further expect that Fijians are personally motivated to effect the morphologic analogues of prestige in bodily space. This is not the case, however, because in Fiji it is the capacity to be nurturant—to use food and care to potentiate social relations—that confers prestige, not the individual's achievement of any bodily aesthetic ideal. Therefore it is not the cultivation of bodies that is legitimated in Fiji, but rather the cultivation of social relationships. The success of the community in this endeavour is relative to a multiplicity of symbols that refer to the core value of *vikawaitaki* and are condensed and represented in body morphology. . . .

References

Furnham, Adrian, and Naznin Alibhai. 1983. 'Cross-cultural Differences in the Perception of Female Body Shapes', *Psychological Medicine* 12: 829–37.

Garner, David, Paul E. Garfinkel, Donald Schwartz, and Michael Thompson. 1980. 'Cultural Expectations of Thinness in Women', *Psychological Reports* 47: 483–91.

Good, Byron, and Mary-Jo DelVecchio Good. 1982. 'Toward a Meaning-centred Analysis of Popular Illness Categories: "Fright Illness" and "Heart Distress" in Iran', in A.J. Marsella and G.M. White, eds, *Cultural Conceptions of Mental Health and Therapy*. Dordrecht, Holland: D. Reidel Publishing Company.

Kahn, Miriam. 1986. *Always Hungry, Never Greedy*. Cambridge: Cambridge University Press.

Leenhardt, Maurice. 1979. *Do Kamo*. Chicago: University of Chicago Press.

Mackenzie, Margaret. 1985. 'The Pursuit of Slenderness and Addiction to Self-control', in Jean Weininger and George M. Briggs, eds, *Nutrition Update, Volume II*. John Wiley and Sons. HSC. QU 145 N9758

Ritenbaugh, Cheryl. 1982. 'Obesity as a Culture Bound Syndrome', *Culture, Medicine, and Psychiatry* 6, 4 (December): 287–94.

Turner, Bryan. 1984. *The Body and Society*. Oxford: Basil Blackwell.

Wiseman, Clare V., James J. Gray, James E. Mosimann, and Anthony H. Ahrens. 1992. *International Journal of Eating Disorders* 11, 1: 85–9.

Young, Michael. 1979. *Ethnography of Malinowski*. London: Routledge and Kegan Paul.

Part IV

Medical Social Control of the Body

Claudia Malacrida and Jacqueline Low

The construction of deviance and illness is one way that social institutions manage populations and control citizens. In this section, we are shown how science, medicine, and the helping professions have used knowledge and authority to control sections of the population that are deemed 'undesirable'. Claudia Malacrida's (2005) article on survivors of a total institution for 'mental defectives' draws both on the work of Michel Foucault (1995) and Erving Goffman (1961, 1963). In particular, she uses Foucault's concept of the panopticon, an architectural technique of surveillance and social control. For Foucault, although the modern prison system seemed like a more benign form of enforcement than in previous times, in actuality these prison reforms ushered in a new, preventative, and more invasive type of discipline, which he called biopower. **Biopower** is that form of power that is not enacted through formal laws and punishments, but it is the everyday, constant, and omnipresent enactment of power enacted through knowledge as applied to individual bodies. For Foucault, the architectural panopticon of the prison becomes a metaphor for modern-day biopower. Bodies under the modern gaze of professionals, agents of social control, and modern institutions such as the workplace, army, school, or clinic ultimately become docile bodies, not only because they are being watched, but also because they are under threat of being watched. Thus, the modern-day student, patient, worker, client, or citizen engages in **self-policing**, or self-discipline *just in case* they may be observed by the disciplining gaze. Malacrida's informants describe numerous ways that the gaze operated to create docile bodies within the institution. They also provide illustrations of concepts that Goffman (1961) developed in his study on asylums and stigmatization.

Goffman saw asylums as **total institutions**, worlds unto themselves for the segregation and control of people who were removed from society; these included prisons and asylums, but also monasteries and retreats. The point, for Goffman, was that these total institutions provided a regimented, isolated, and complete environment in which the inmate's former self was stripped away, to be replaced by a new identity (1961). Power, in Goffman's

(1963) model, is not enacted through the gaze, but through stigma, which are marks on the body of an individual that signal a discredited status. In Malacrida's study, the inmates who describe being left unclothed and without sanitation are also describing practices that both stigmatized and disempowered them.

Nicole Hahn Rafter (1997) takes a historical approach to show how early criminologists constructed 'scientific' information about criminals and their bodies both to attempt the prevention of criminal behaviour and to legitimize the fledgling discipline of criminology. Using the newly developed technology of photography and phrenology, Italian criminal anthropologist Cesare Lombroso developed **biodeterminist typologies** of bodily and facial traits which, he argued, could predict criminal 'types' on the basis of their physical features. This biodeterminist argument meant that the social causes of crime, such as poverty and marginalization, were ignored in favour of biological causes of criminality. It also meant that social prejudices such as racism, nationalism, and classism became enshrined in criminological thinking. Lombroso's ideas were taken up with great enthusiasm by American intellectuals worried about the increasing crime and poverty they saw in their newly industrializing cities. Prominent reformers and leaders expressed concerns about '**race degeneration**', where the 'Progressive Classes' (composed of white, upper- and middle-classed citizens) were failing to reproduce themselves, while the 'Stationary or Retrogressive classes' (comprised of immigrants, non-whites, and poor or working-class citizens) were breeding rampantly and were responsible for the deterioration of society. Combining Lombroso's biodeterminist scientism with Darwin's genetic theories allowed criminologists to develop theories of social control that tied race, gender, and class *biologically* to crime and disorder. Ultimately, this paved the way for **eugenic** efforts (literally meaning 'well-born') that attempted to 'weed out' people who were deemed to be 'unfit' long before they committed anti-social or criminal acts.

In his study of the eugenics movement in Nazi Germany, Robert N. Proctor (1988) provides a meticulous historical analysis of how the legitimizing stamp of 'medical science' was used by the Nazis in their eugenics campaign against the Jews and other social groups they constructed as 'sub-human', such as Gypsies, people with disabilities, and patients in psychiatric hospitals. As Proctor (1988: 170) writes, 'Nazi physicians sought to rid the nation of its "lives not worth living" in the years leading up to and throughout World War II (1939–1945)'.

The eugenics movement flourished between the late 1800s and the 1950s in North America as well as Europe. Francis Galton, a natural scientist as well as a cousin of Charles Darwin, coined the term **eugenics**, which refers to the belief that a host of social problems, including delinquency, poverty, and crime, are genetically inherited in the same way as eye colour or height. By 'selective breeding' (controlled human reproduction), all social problems could be eliminated, resulting in a utopian, or perfect, society (McLaren, 1990).

In North America such attempts at 'selective breeding' were most often carried out by court-ordered sterilizations, largely without people's knowledge or consent. In contrast, in Nazi Germany the method quickly adopted was **euthanasia**, which commonly means to put to death humanely. However, in the hands of the Nazis, these practices later culminated in the mass murder in Nazi concentration camps' gas chambers of those they dubbed subhuman. The Nazis sought to justify their attempt to create a master race via the **medicalization** of Jewish bodies, where medicalization refers to the process by which social phenomena (such as racial tensions) become defined as medical problems. More specifically, they aimed to medicalize **anti-Semitism** (hatred of Jews), whereby Nazi physicians were able to construct the Jews as a 'diseased race' whose sub-humanness was carried in their blood (Proctor, 1988: 132). Their efforts to eliminate the Jews constitute an attempt at **genocide**, which is 'the deliberate killing off of an entire people' (Chalk and Jonassohn, 1990).

References

Chalk, F., and K. Jonassohn. 1990. *The History and Sociology of Genocide: Analyses and Case Studies.* New Haven, CT: Yale University Press.

Foucault, M. 1995. *Discipline and Punish: The Birth of the Prison.* New York: Vintage Books

Goffman, E. 1961. *Asylums: Essay on the Social Situation of Mental Patients and Other Inmates.* Garden City, NY: Doubleday Books.

———. 1963. *Stigma: Notes on the Management of Spoiled Identity.* New Jersey: Prentice Hall.

Malacrida, C. 2005. 'Discipline and Dehumanization in a Total Institution: Institutional Survivors' Descriptions of Time-Out Rooms', *Disability & Society* 20: 523–38.

McLaren, A. 1990. *Our Own Master Race: Eugenics in Canada, 1885–1945.* Toronto: McClelland and Stewart.

Proctor, R.N. 1988. *Racial Hygiene: Medicine Under the Nazis.* Cambridge, MA: Harvard University Press.

Rafter, N.H. 1997. *Creating Born Criminals.* Urbana and Chicago: University of Illinois Press.

Chapter 10

Discipline and Dehumanization in a Total Institution: Institutional Survivors' Descriptions of Time-out Rooms

Claudia Malacrida

. . . This article examines the narratives of 12 women and nine men who are survivors of the Michener Centre, a total institution for 'mental defectives'[1] that has operated in . . . Alberta . . . from 1923 to the present day. Although these survivor narratives are specific to one institution, Michener Centre's practices of institutionalization and segregation reflected broader discourses and practices relating to science, eugenics, and fitness in the West during the twentieth century. In this paper, survivor narratives covering experiences that occurred well into the 1980s are examined, with a focus on 'Time-out Rooms', which were used to discipline misbehaving and runaway inmates.

Since the mid-1980s, historical, sociological, and disability studies researchers have begun to expose the systematic institutionalization, degradation, and eugenicization of disabled individuals in general, and developmentally disabled[2] people in particular, that occurred in the West during much of the twentieth century (McLaren, 1986; McLaren, 1990; Kuhl, 1994; Dowbiggin, 1995; Kevles, 1995; Proctor, 1995; Jones, 1999). Most of these histories exclude accounts from those who, having survived these practices, can tell us about the intimate mechanisms of disability oppression at its most profound level. . . .

[Michener Centre's] mandate was to engage in the work of 'academic, vocational, and personal development of retarded children and young adults' (Alberta Government Publications, 1985: 3), indicating that 'trainees' would receive an education with the ultimate goal of a productive rein-

tegration to society. Rhetoric concerning the training mandate of the institution and community reintegration persisted throughout Michener's[3] history: in the 1950s, the involvement of parent advisory groups resulted in 'emphasis on increasing the trainee's independence' (13), and in the 1960s 'program development produced a growing emphasis on resident training' (14). Institutional rhetoric about training for 'real' life aside, however, population figures for the institution indicate that residents remained in the institution for long periods, rarely returned to their communities, and their numbers grew steadily over the years. The institutional population peaked in 1969 with almost 2400 residents. In the 1970s and 1980s, through community and parent-driven advocacy efforts, deinstitutionalization began in earnest: by 1983 there were approximately 1600 residents, and in the year 1999, approximately 400 individuals remained (Alberta Government Publications, 1985; Michener Centre Communications Officer, 1999). Most of the participants in this study left the institution between the mid-1970s [and] late-1980s as part of that deinstitutionalization movement. . . .

Eugenics and the Michener Centre

While training and education were the given reasons for the institution's existence, eugenics concerns played an important role in establishing and sustaining the institution. During the first half of the twentieth century, a belief that 'feeble-mindedness' could be attributed to poor genetic material prevailed in the minds of social reformers, government officials, and medical and scientific practitioners (Smith, 1985; McLaren, 1986, 1990). At Michener Centre, institutionalization, segregation, and eugenics were intimately linked. The housing of 'mental defectives' in a virtual fortress set at a distance from a small rural town, and the reportedly almost obsessive arrangements for sexual segregation within the Michener Centre institution functioned as a covert form of eugenics; 'defective' individuals segregated in these ways posed little risk of 'polluting' the social body with their genetic material. More overt eugenics programs also operated within the Michener Centre; in 1928, just five years after the opening of the PTS, the Province of Alberta implemented the Sexual Sterilization Act and established the Alberta Eugenics Board. The Board regularly convened meetings at the Michener Centre, and although things started slowly with 'only' 16 sterilizations performed in 1930, by the time of the Board's closing in 1973, it was approving between 30 and 40 involuntary sterilizations per year, most of them on Michener Residents (Alberta Government Publications, 1985; Park and Radford, 1998). . . .

Time-out Rooms

Time-out Rooms were an omnipresent means of exercising both reactive and precautionary control within the institution. From survivor narratives, it seems each unit in Michener Centre had at least one of these rooms; rather than being hidden away, the rooms were a part of the wards, within the sightlines of warders and other residents in each residential unit. Each room had a heavy, locked door with a small aperture through which instructions or food could be passed, and the inside of the room was fitted out with a drain . . . in the middle of the floor and little else. A mattress would be dragged in at night for inmates to sleep on, to be removed in the morning to facilitate cleaning the cell. Inmates who were housed in the Time-out Rooms were typically

naked, because staff feared that inn harm themselves by chewing at torn (perhaps by trying to hang themselv ..., 2004). Furthermore, these rooms had a one-way mirror through which warders (and other inmates) could observe the individual being given a 'Time-out', and in which the individuals inside could, no doubt, see themselves reflected.

All of the individuals interviewed for this project knew about the Time-out Rooms, speaking consistently about their uses and practices. According to participants, inmates were housed in Time-out Rooms as a result of resistance to daily institutional practices; acts of resistance included refusing to eat the food they were given, refusing to go to bed or wake up at the times they were told to, aggressive behaviour towards staff or towards other residents, or refusing to perform work duties as instructed. Above all, however, survivors noted that people were sent to the Time-out Rooms because of escape attempts. The detection of escape was a public event; its discovery would be heralded at any time of the day or night by wailing sirens and the hustle and bustle of ward searches and intra-institutional communications relating to the attempt. The combination of the sirens, the hubbub, and the knowledge that those who attempted escape would inevitably end up in the Time-out Rooms comprised a powerful presence in survivor narratives about institutional life. Hence, Time-out Rooms were a central form of physical and psychological, reactive and proactive social control.

Michel Foucault, Bodily Discipline and the Gaze

Michel Foucault provides disability scholars with important tools for understanding institutional and embodied practices of social control in general, and the disciplinary practices attached to Time-out Rooms in particular. His theories permit us to see how bodily practices and visual power are implicated in institutional routines and undertakings. In Foucault's analysis of institutions, the physical layout of such places is never innocent or arbitrary; instead, vantage points, lines of surveillance, and the omnipresence of physical spaces like the Time-out Room are constructed in ways that can be read as discursive practices, the means through which a society's underlying ideas and values circulate and are made material (Foucault, 1995). Thus, the Time-out Room's interior layout and its positioning within the institution give expression to institutional and societal norms about acceptable treatment for individuals in Michener Centre and, more broadly, for all individuals who are considered to be 'less-than' normal. The rooms, with their vault-like qualities, express societal fears of those who are different; in this architecture, the unruly 'defective' must 'naturally' be contained, isolated, and broken, and any acknowledgement of their human needs for comfort, safety, or dignity is denaturalized.

For Foucault, the body is the critical site upon which discursive formations are practised. Societal values and knowledge, administered through discursive practices such as institutional routines, are written on the surfaces of individual bodies, in what Foucault termed biopower (Foucault, 1988a, 1990). In Time-out Room practices, the inmate's naked body, placed in the room for all to view, is both a reflection and an expression of the kind of society in which such a body is positioned. In Foucault's model, the body, and particularly the body that is different or 'less-than', has not been responded to uniformly across time and space; a careful observation of the ways that such bodies are handled or treated can provide us with insight into the workings of power and knowledge in a particular society. Thus, the Time-out Room, and its use on 'less-than' bodies, reflects societal understandings about who is entitled to a minimum standard of decency and humane treatment, despite scientific or institutional rhetoric to the contrary. In other words, understanding the bodily practices of the Time-out Room can help us to understand the construction of non-humanness embedded in these institutional routines. . . .

A final, important contribution of Foucauldian theory to understanding the Time-out Rooms rests in the metaphor of the gaze. In the clinic, the physician whose power is drawn from his disciplinary knowledge is the observer whose gaze penetrates even beneath the surface of the patient's body, exposing not only the patient's disease or difference, but also providing evidence of the need for increased surveillance and expert intervention on the unruly body (Foucault, 1994). Foucault shows us that this gaze replaced brutality, as exemplified by the metaphor of the panopticon, an ideal prison designed by Jeremy Bentham that promised a means of exercising power through the simple use of the gaze. From the panopticon's central guard tower, the warder's gaze, which can be neither detected nor deflected by the prisoner, is the means through which bodily discipline is enforced. The effectiveness of the gaze as disciplinary force occurs to such extent that prisoners, engaging in 'technologies of the self', preemptively discipline their own bodies, simply because at any time the warder *could* be watching (Foucault, 1988b, 1995). . . .

Erving Goffman has also provided us with an analysis of 'total institutions' that is fruitful to understanding the daily regimes of Michener Centre. Total institutions, to Goffman, are 'a place of residence and work where a large number of like-situated individuals, cut off from the wider society for an appreciable period of time, together lead an enclosed, formally administered round of life' (1961: xv). He noted that life in such places is permeated with formal and informal practices designed to humiliate, degrade, and deface the identity of the institutionalized person (20–1). The Michener Centre was a total institution, serving a purportedly homogeneous 'population' of 'mental defectives', located on a large, self-contained farm outside of a small farming town in Alberta. 'Residents' were often admitted to Michener Centre in childhood and literally spent decades there before having even a hope of discharge. In this setting, as Goffman might predict, processes of stigmatization operated as more than simple mechanisms of social control. Instead, institutionalized practices of humiliation and degradation operated to construct residents not only as individuals stripped of their former identity, but also as individuals who were stripped of their humanity. . . .

Dehumanization can be an end in itself, by making the daily work of cleaning, bathing, feeding, housing, and 'training' inmates simpler for staff, who are no longer compelled to observe the decencies demanded by *human* inmates. When the daily chores attendant with 'care' are constructed in such a way as to be aimed toward 'non-humans', the niceties of privacy, respect, and tenderness come to be seen as superfluous. While this effect of dehumanization—the facilitation of impersonal and unthinking care—undoubtedly occurred in the Michener Centre, for many residents, the dehumanization process made possible abuse beyond the routinized brutality of total institutional life. In the narratives of Michener survivors, it becomes possible to imagine how the processes of dehumanization opened the way not only for careless and cruel daily practices, but also facilitated Michener's eugenics routines.

The Time-out Room: View From Outside, View From Within

. . . Stan and Roy provide us with descriptions of the procedures for 'admitting' a misbehaving resident into the Time-out Rooms that introduce us to contradictions between discipline-based modes of engendering social control and punishment-based methods in the practices of the Michener Centre. Stan told me, 'They would put you down on the floor in a "sleeper." It's like a headlock, and they put you to sleep and throw you in the Time-out Room. . . . It was scary, not nice. Had a window and glass, and a mat on the floor, and a drain in the middle.' Roy concurred, saying, 'They would put you in there in this room. You had no bed. You slept on the floor. They had windows . . . people could see you walking back and forth. Some of them, they would put straitjackets on.'

Stan and Roy's descriptions remind us of Foucault's panopticon, with its deployment of the gaze as a disciplining arm of those in power. Like the panopticon, the one-way mirror of the Time-

out Room acted as a window to those who observed from outside, and it operated as the means through which warders could exercise constant and easy surveillance upon miscreants. Conversely, because Time-out Room inmates could not tell when they were being observed nor see who was outside, the one-way mirror acted as a visual reminder to inmates of the constant possibility of being observed. From these comments, it seems the Time-out Room did operate to create compliance and control through what Foucault would term 'disciplinary' means—through observations of the self by others and through pre-emptive self-observations. However, Stan and Roy's comments allow us to see that in Michener Centre, there was more to social control than the disciplinary gaze. Instead, these comments convey that brute power, in the form of the straitjacket and the stranglehold, was a common and publicly-displayed accompaniment to the behaviourist disciplinary control of the Time-out Room. Thus, rather than the smooth, rational, and impersonal surveillance-based power that Foucault imagined would take place in modern institutional orders, the stories these survivors tell us about the public violence and brute force of routine discipline at Michener Centre show us a more terrifying and chaotic picture of social control in action. Indeed, we can hear that both discipline-based or 'modern' practices and punishment-based or 'pre-modern' practices operated in concert within the institution.

Foucault also offers us the concept of biopower with which to understand the circulation of power. Recall that, for Foucault, the body is the site upon which societal values and knowledge are inscribed through the practices of institutions and professions. In the Time-out Room, the rationality of science meets the unruly bodies of inmates who refuse to comply. From inmate descriptions, we can see that the Time-out Room, despite its veneer of science, was also a means of displaying and reinforcing the 'non-person' status of Time-out Room residents in particular, and perhaps of Michener inmates more generally. Glen, for example, described his experiences inside the Time-out Room as follows:

The staff could look in from a window in the door but I couldn't see out of it. There was no toilet, and when I had to go, I had to bang on the door with my feet. But most of the time, no one would come, so I wet myself. I had to sit like that sometimes for hours until staff would come. That hurt my feelings.

This gentleman—naked, wet, and ignored—is not simply being treated with operant conditioning's sensory deprivation as a means of extinguishing undesirable behaviours. Instead, what Glen describes is systematic humiliation, enacted through bodily practices that would not be deemed fitting for someone 'deserving' or fully human. The message of this kind of biopower is that people like Glen are not part of the general social body, and hence have no claim to human rights or human dignity. Of course, Glen's descriptions also remind us of Goffman's claim that dehumanization is a central object of the daily routines and practices of total institutions (1961). This dehumanization, while making it 'simple' for workers to handle inmates in unthinking and humiliating ways, also conceivably made it easier for the institution itself to treat inmates in ways that denied their human rights. In this way, the interactions relating to the Time-out Room can be imagined to extend beyond the walls of the immediate ward, connecting to broader practices within the Michener Centre and its work with the Eugenics Board. In an institution where inmates were routinely conceived of as being less than human, and where this view was systemically upheld through institutional practices like the Quiet Rooms, it is possible to understand how other routinized violence such as involuntary sterilizations came to be seen not only as acceptable, but even as necessary accoutrements to institutional life.

Glen's description also draws on Foucauldian notions of the gaze as a form of power and the use of spectacle as a disciplining force. Glen's comments build on Foucault's ideas, however, by reminding us that the added visual plane of the one-way mirror operates not only as a window through which outsiders view the humiliation of

the inmate, but that the mirror also can provide the inmate with a view of himself that is both sombre and humiliating. Thus, the views and perspectives represented in the actual construction [of] Time-out Rooms offer support and development of Foucauldian notions of the power of the gaze. . . .

The Time-out Room: Spectacle, Prevention, and Division

When discussing the Time-out Rooms, survivors noted that there was little secrecy or mystery surrounding the use of the space or the ways that individuals came to be incarcerated in them. The highly visible positioning of the rooms themselves, with one on each ward, typically part of the 'regular' hallway of resident rooms and within the sightlines of both the nursing stations and the public day-rooms of each ward, meant that residents of the institution could not avoid knowing about and seeing the Time-out Rooms. Furthermore, the sirens, and flashlight searches that accompanied the internment of runaway residents into Time-out Rooms, and the struggles and straitjacketing that accompanied the internment of inmates with 'bad' behaviour, meant that other residents could hardly ignore the violence attached to these spaces.

The public aspect of the Time-out Rooms' spatial designs is reminiscent of Foucault's punishment-type means of social control. Foucault tells us that, in pre-modern societies, punishments were enacted in highly visible public spectacles, to warn the general public about what would happen to transgressors. While the Time-out Rooms, with their locked doors and windowed walls at first glance seem to reflect a more private, disciplinary means of social control, the public positioning of the space, and the often violent and noisy means by which inmates were admitted to the space in fact offered a spectacle of punishment to other inmates that let them know who was a 'bad' inmate and the institutional response to inmates who resist. The spectacle of admission and the public positioning of the space offered all residents a visual performance of institutional might, evidenced by swift, brutal, and unforgiving punishment for those who failed to comply with institutional regimes.

Survivors themselves acknowledged the cautionary or preventative qualities of Time-out Rooms. John, for example, noted that, 'Some of the kids got put away on the side in this little place. In this dark room with a big window on the door. Sometimes they were there for two to three days.' When I asked him whether that had ever happened to him, he emphatically noted, 'No, I made sure I stayed out of trouble.' For John, as for others, the architectural, spatial, and physical aspects of the Time-out Rooms engendered preventative self-discipline and self-technologies, exercised in efforts to avoid trouble.

Recall Foucault's argument that technologies of the self are engaged in by individuals not only so that they can avoid social sanctions, but also so that they can come to think of themselves as good, deserving, and worthy citizens (Foucault, 1988b). Drawing on Foucault, it is possible to understand that in John's description of himself as a person who 'made sure [he] stayed out of trouble', there was more at stake than simply avoiding punishment. In addition, we can understand that compliance and avoiding punishment are ways that John can see himself as good, smart, and unlike those who failed to avoid the stigma and brutality of the Time-out Rooms. . . . Like John, most participants in this study were loathe to admit to actually doing time in a Time-out Room, and they were remarkably unsympathetic towards those who did end up in them. . . .

Humiliation and the Gaze

. . . When we recall Glen's description of being left unattended and incontinent, we can understand the Quiet Room as more than discipline or punishment, or a vehicle to create divisions amongst inmates. Instead, Glen allows us to understand that the Time-out Rooms had another, central function, which was to humiliate and dehumanize its inmates. This perhaps explains why few

survivors were willing to admit that they had ever experienced such humiliations, and why they spoke so harshly about individuals who had been in them.

Finally, Glen's description reminds us that the added visual plane of the one-way mirror operated not only to provide outsiders with a view on the inmate and her/his disgrace, but [also] offered a view of the individual her/himself that was both sombre and shaming. . . .

Discussion

Survivors' descriptions of Quiet Rooms provide us with both confirmations of and contradictions to Foucauldian concepts. Foucauldian ideas about punishment and discipline-based societies offer fruitful constructs for analyzing the Quiet Room practices. Nonetheless, these ideas fall short of explaining the unruly, non-routinized brutality of the Michener Centre when juxtaposed against the actual experiences described by those who lived in the institution. In addition to the use of science, routinization, and the gaze in engendering institutional control, survivors describe both quotidian and extraordinary violence occurring in Time-out Room practices, and such brutality is more reminiscent of Foucault's pre-Enlightenment punishment model of social control than the disciplinary practices he theorized as the hallmarks of modernity. Foucault's concept of a historical transition from punishment-based social practices to discipline-based control is complicated in the survivor narratives, where both types of control are exercised simultaneously.

Furthermore, Foucauldian notions of technologies of the self can help us to understand why individuals might want to comply in the institution, why individuals in the institution distanced themselves from their fellow inmates, and how hierarchies and divisions were maintained within the institution. Drawing on survivor narratives sheds light on the personal power that can be gained when such hierarchies exist, and what gains can be had by individuals who seek to distance themselves from those who are suffering most from the order of things. Survivor narratives enable us to understand the terror and lack of control that prevailed in places such as Michener Centre, in turn making it possible to see how personal power could be obtained by individuals who told themselves that, given the right behaviours, they could remain safe and exercise some control over their lives.

Finally, Foucault's ideas provide tools for understanding the power of the spatial designs of the Rooms, their locations within the institution, and the ways that vision and visibility were organized to sustain power relations within the institution. Thus, the mirrored door, the viewing window, and the hallways vista with the Time-out Room at its centre can be understood as means of exercising discipline through biopower. These spectacles and views provided staff, fellow patients, and inmates themselves with specific and strategic perspectives, wherein the incarcerated individual can be seen and can become objectified and degraded. However, survivors' narratives move us beyond understanding the simple mechanics of space, vistas, and the gaze. These survivor accounts provide us an added layer that permits an understanding of how such technologies of power can feel when one is at the receiving end of such visions, and they allow us to see that humiliation and dehumanization,

rather than benign behaviourism in the form of operant conditioning, lie at the core of Time-out Room practices.

By drawing on Erving Goffman's work on stigma and institutionalization, it becomes possible to understand, if not why, then at least *how* dehumanization occurs. Goffman has provided us with an analysis of 'total institutions' that can be used fruitfully in understanding the daily regimes of Michener Centre. Recall that for Goffman, total institutions are permeated with practices of humiliation, degradation, and identity erasure (Goffman, 1961: 20–1). In the Michener Centre, and particularly in the Time-out Rooms, as Goffman might predict, institutional processes operated as more than means of discipline and control. Instead, institutionalized practices of humiliation and degradation operated to erase the very humanity of the institution's residents. . . .

Acknowledgements

Thank you to Alberta Association for Community Living (Bruce Uditsky and Anne Hughson in particular), Alberta Historical Resources Foundation, and the University of Lethbridge (Chinook Student Summer Research Award) for supporting this project.

Notes

1. I wish to make clear that this term is not my own, but reflects official language concerning the mandate of the Michener Centre at the time of its opening in 1923, and for several decades thereafter.
2. In Canada, the term 'developmentally disabled' is used to describe individuals with intellectual challenges; in the United Kingdom 'learning disabled' is more typical.
3. In 1973, in the midst of the shift away from institutionalization and the development of a community-living movement, a new swimming-pool complex was built on the premises, and the institution was renamed the Michener Centre in celebration of Red Deer's most famous citizen, Roland Michener, a former athlete who became the Governor-General of Canada.

References

Alberta Government Publications. 1985. *Michener Centre: A History 1923–1983*. Edmonton, AB.

Anon. 2004. Interview with ex-worker from Michener Centre.

Dowbiggin, I. 1995. 'Keeping This Young Country Sane: C.K. Clarke, Immigration Restriction, and Canadian Psychiatry, 1890–1925', *The Canadian Historical Review* 76, 4: 598–627.

Foucault, M. 1988a. 'The Political Technology of Individuals', in L.H. Martin, H. Gutman, and P. H. Hutton, eds, *Technologies of the Self: A Seminar with Michel Foucault*. Amherst, MA: University of Massachusetts Press.

———. 1988b. 'Technologies of the Self', in L.H. Martin, et al., *Technologies of the Self: A Seminar with Michel Foucault*.

———. 1990. *The History of Sexuality. Volume I: An Introduction*. New York: Vintage Books.

———. 1994. *The Birth of the Clinic: An Archeology of Medical Perception*. New York: Vintage Books.

———. 1995. *Discipline and Punish: The Birth of the Prison*. New York: Vintage Books.

Goffman, E. 1961. *Asylums: Essays on the Social Situation of Mental Patients and Other Inmates*. Garden City, NY: Doubleday Books.

Jones, R.L. 1999. 'The Master Potter and the Rejected Pots: Eugenic Legislation in Victoria, 1918–1939, *Australian Historical Studies* 113: 319–43.

Kevles, D.J. 1995. *In the Name of Eugenics: Genetics and the Uses of Human Heredity*. Cambridge, MA: Harvard University Press.

Kuhl, S. 1994. *The Nazi Connection: Eugenics, American Racism, and German National Socialism*. New York: Oxford University Press.

McLaren, A. 1986. 'The Creation of a Haven for "Human Thoroughbreds": The Sterilization of the Feeble-minded and the Mentally Ill in British Columbia', *Canadian Historical Review* LXVII, 2: 127–50.

———. 1990. *Our Own Master Race: Eugenics in Canada, 1885–1945*. Toronto: McClelland and Stewart.

Michener Centre Communications Officer. 1999. Private conversation concerning resident statistics.

Park, D.C., and J.P. Radford. 1998. 'From the Case Files: Reconstructing a History of Involuntary Sterilization', *Disability & Society* 13, 3: 317–42.

Proctor, R.N. 1995. 'The Destruction of "Lives Not Worth Living"', in J. Terry and J. Urla, eds, *Deviant Bodies: Critical Perspectives on Difference in Science and Popular Culture*. Bloomington, IN: Indiana University Press.

Smith, J.D. 1985. *Minds Made Feeble: The Myth and Legacy of the Kallkas*. Rockville, MD: Aspen Publications.

Chapter 11

The Anthropological Born Criminal

Nicole Hahn Rafter

Ladies and gentlemen, herein lies the source of failure of the old methods of study and reform of the criminal class—their bodies were forgotten.

G. Frank Lydston, 'Some General Considerations of Criminology'

Essentialism *is* cultural construction.

Marjorie Garber, *Vested Interests*

The first biological theory of crime to attract widespread attention was that which Cesare Lombroso, its best-known proponent, named 'criminal anthropology'. According to Lombroso and his followers, incorrigible offenders are 'born criminals', apelike throwbacks to a more primitive evolutionary stage. Born criminals differ so radically from lawful people that scientists can identify them by their physical and mental abnormalities, just as physical anthropologists can identify members of different races by their physical characteristics. . . .

A New Science

. . . American criminal anthropologists, like Lombroso himself, insisted that their work was a 'new science', one that carried the study of crime causation across the great divide between idle speculation and hard fact.[1] . . .

. . . [C]riminal anthropologists drew a firm line between themselves and earlier commentators on crime who had unscientifically included God and free will in the causational picture.

Unlike their predecessors, they would examine only phenomena rooted in the natural world of matter. When they described their school as 'materialist' or 'positivist', they invoked a philosophical position according to which all phenomena can be explained in terms of physical laws. Like other scientists, they would investigate the laws of matter, ignoring such foolishness as free will.

Lombroso's American followers did not always refer to their new science as 'criminology'. Because the field was just beginning to take shape, they sometimes folded the study of criminals into other fields—'scientific sociology', 'the science of penology', or the 'scientific' study of degeneracy.[2] They all considered their work to be 'scientific', however, a term they used to express their commitment to empirical methods and dispassionate analyses.[3] . . . They would measure criminals' bodies with scientific equipment such as calipers, the dynamometre, and the aesthesiometre, objectively recording facts. And they would use induction and quantitative methods to formulate causal laws. Like other true scientists they would work up to whatever theory the facts indicated.

Their materialist premises led criminal anthropologists to their central assumption that the body must mirror moral capacity. Lombrosians took for granted a one-to-one correspondence between the criminal's physical being and unethical behaviour. Criminals, wrote the American criminal anthropologist Henry Boies, are 'the imperfect, knotty, knurly, worm-eaten, half-rotten fruit of the human race', their bodies illustrating 'the truth of the reverse Latin adage, "*insana mens insano corpore*"'.[4] Nature had made the expert's task relatively simple: to detect born criminals, one needed only the appropriate apparatus. Degree of criminality could be determined by measuring the number and extent of the offender's 'stigmata', or physical deformities.

The assumption that offenders literally embody their criminality led criminal anthropologists to present not just graphs and statistical tables but also drawings and photographs, pictures that claim a direct access to reality and purport to present the criminal's essence. The illustrations of criminal anthropology in effect deny that they are representations and hence constructions. . . . Charts and photographs become a rhetorical gesture, a means of signifying science and objectivity. Reducing the social problem of crime to a biological problem, the visual and verbal languages of criminal anthropology also reduce themselves to thin air, claiming to be media through which perception flies, unobstructed, straight to the essence of the criminal body. . . .

Criminal Anthropology in the United States

. . .

Originators

The first book on criminal anthropology published in the United States, Moriz Benedikt's *Anatomical Studies upon Brains of Criminals,* appeared in 1881, well in advance of any work by Lombroso. A Hungarian who taught in Vienna, Benedikt was inspired to study criminals' craniums and brains by the work of Franz Joseph Gall, the founder of phrenology.[5] Dissections led Benedikt to conclude that 'the brains of criminals exhibit a deviation from the normal type, and criminals are to be viewed as an anthropological variety of their species, at least amongst the cultured races'.[6] . . .

The other originator, Cesare Lombroso,[7] exercised far greater influence, but for years Americans knew his work mainly through secondary sources. . . . Portions of one of his major studies also appeared in English in 1895 as *The Female Offender,* just two years after its initial Italian publication, and this work was reprinted six times before 1911. Nonetheless, Americans who knew only English had to wait another 16 years before they could read even a digest of Lombroso's key work, *L' uomo delinquente,* the first Italian edition of which had appeared in 1876. This summary, compiled by Lombroso's daughter with his assistance and carrying yet another of his introductions, was published in 1911 as *Criminal Man.* His *Crime: Its Causes and Remedies* appeared in the same year.[8]

Channellers

Among the channellers who provided access to the originators' work, translators played an important role by determining, through their initiatives, which European works would reach American audiences. . . .

European criminal anthropology further flowed to the United States through writers who, by summarizing the originators' work in English, first alerted Americans to it. Of these, far and away the most influential was Havelock Ellis, author of *The Criminal* (1890). The multilingual Ellis, an English eugenicist, wrote on an enormous range of subjects, from art to sexology. Although *The Criminal* was his only foray into criminal anthropology, it proved to be an extended one: by 1911 the book was in its fourth edition and had gone through nine printings. . . . *The Criminal's* main message is that Ellis is a learned scientist and the criminal is an anthropological freak. This book became the well into which many Americans dipped for data on born criminals.[9] . . .

American Criminal Anthropologists

As news of Lombroso's theory spread, many Americans began writing about it; thus the third group of producers, American elaborators of criminal anthropology, greatly outnumbers the other two. We can identify its key members, however, by defining them as authors of book-length works that to some degree endorsed the concept of the criminal as a physically distinct, atavistic human being and that are frequently cited in both the primary and secondary literature on criminal anthropology.[10] . . .

The authors of these books were all well-educated, male professionals. Those common denominators aside, however, the group was characterized by occupational diversity: its members included social welfare workers (Boies, Drähms, and Henderson), educators (Henderson, Lydston, MacDonald, Parsons, and Talbot), physicians (Lydston, McKim, and Talbot), and ministers (Drähms and Henderson; MacDonald, too, had studied theology). . . .

The Substance of American Criminal Anthropology

A Criminal Class

American criminal anthropologists used their texts to demonstrate that there exists a criminal class, physically and psychologically different from normal citizens. They devoted their treatises to describing the abnormalities of that class, but by implication they were also establishing criteria for the normality of noncriminal classes. . . .

In his *Introduction to the Study of the Dependent, Defective and Delinquent Classes,* Charles R. Henderson divides 'all the members of society' into two groups. The 'Progressive Class' consists of those who are 'self-supporting, self-respecting, law-abiding, industrious, and under the educational influences of schools, churches, newspapers, and the public sentiment of Christian civilization'. The 'Stationary or Retrogressive Class', on the other hand, is made up of dependents, defectives, and delinquents, degenerate types linked by 'a very close and organic connection'.[11] With such statements Henderson and other American criminal anthropologists established themselves and their sort as normal while relegating their inferiors to a common pool, the biologically dangerous, criminalistic underclass.

According to these criminal anthropologists, members of the criminal class are bestial, childish, drunken, and drawn to urban squalor. Including disproportionate numbers of foreigners, Catholics, and Negroes, the criminal class breeds more rapidly than upright citizens, producing ever more paupers, imbeciles, and criminals. . . .

When criminal anthropologists referred to 'the criminal class', they meant sometimes only criminals and sometimes all members of the lower classes. . . . [T]he terminology was imprecise because it was a way of indicating a universe through a particular, of discussing all social problems by speaking of one. In the same way criminal anthropologists defined *the born criminal* as but one of several criminal types while often equating that term with all criminals. Again, imprecision was crucial to their meaning.

The *Criminal*

According to American criminal anthropologists, of all offender types, the born (or instinctive, or incorrigible) criminal departs most profoundly from normality. Covered by the stigmata of crime, he[12] is most obviously atavistic in origin. Lawbreakers of this sort, Talbot writes in a typical passage, 'form a variety of the human family quite distinct from law-abiding men. A low type of physique indicating a deteriorated character gives a family likeness due to the fact that they form a community which retrogrades from generation to generation.'[13] American criminal anthropologists gleefully repeat Lobroso's litany of the born criminal's physical anomalies—his heavy jaw, receding brow, scanty beard, long arms, and so on. They also closely follow Lobroso by enumerating the criminal's 'psychical' anomalies—his laziness and frivolity, his use of argot, his tendency to inscribe his cell with hieroglyphs and his body with tattoos, and his moral insensibility and emotional instability.

The Americans augment Lombroso's picture of the born criminal, however, by placing greater emphasis on the criminal's weak intelligence. . . . This American concern with the criminal's poor intelligence reflects the growing body of literature on moral imbecility.

The American authors, realizing that degeneracy could explain the criminal's bad heredity, thoroughly integrate criminal anthropology with degeneration theory. . . . [T]he born criminal comes (in McKim's words) 'of a degenerate line', like Lombroso in his later work, they picture the born criminal as a product of not freakish heredity but continuous devolution.[14] Stressing the close connections among socially problematic groups, American criminal anthropologists argue that poverty, disease, and crime are interchangeable and almost indistinguishable.

Other Criminal Types

Just as Lombroso eventually distinguished between the born criminal and higher offender types, so did most of his American followers create typologies that located incorrigibles at the bottom of the criminal class and ranked other offenders by the degree to which they approached normality. . . .

. . . On the one hand are the 'born' or 'incorrigible' offenders who have 'inherited criminality' and constitute 40 per cent of the 'criminal class'; the remaining 60 per cent are 'the victims of heteronomy [various other factors], the subjects of evil associations, and environment'. Only the latter can be reformed. . . .

Identifying even more criminal types, Parsons's *Responsibility for Crime*, the last work in the series, begins with the most abnormal type, the *insane criminal*, thereafter describing the *born criminal* ('His normal condition is abnormal . . . he is born to crime. It is his natural function.'), the *habitual criminal* ('He is capable of something else, at least in one period of his life. The born criminal never is.'), and the *professional criminal* ('frequently of a high order of intelligence,—often a college graduate. His profession becomes an art in which he sometimes becomes a master.'). Of the next type on his list, the *occasional criminal*, Parsons informs us that 'here, for the first time, environment plays an important part in the nature of the crime committed'. The occasional criminal, moreover, 'frequently possesses a keen sense of remorse' and is 'frequently a useful citizen'. Parsons's typology is topped by the *criminal by passion or accident*, characterized by a high 'sense of duty' and 'precise motive', unmarred by

anomalies, and requiring neither cure nor punishment.[15]

. . . At the bottom of the scale is the born criminal, rough in appearance and manners, uneducated, and poor. At the summit stands, the gentlemanly normal offender, anomaly-free, produced by not heredity but environment, intelligent and skilled, conscience-stricken and reformable, capable of self-determination, and requiring no state intervention. . . .

Criminal Anthropology and Eugenics

Urging that punishments be tailored to fit the offender types they had identified, criminal anthropologists hoped to make justice, as well as criminology, a 'science' based on the lawbreaker's biology.[16] Much as some Americans had gone beyond Lombroso in developing aspects of criminal anthropology, so too some outdid the master in deriving eugenic conclusions from his doctrine.

In *Criminal Man* and *Crime: Its Causes and Remedies*, Lombroso argues merely for individualization of consequences: 'Punishments should vary according to the type of criminal.' . . .

Like Lombroso, four of the eight American criminal anthropologists show little or no interest in eugenic solutions.[17] The other four champion them, however. Two—Boies and Parsons—support life sentences on the grounds that these would prevent criminals from breeding. . . . Heteronomic offenders can be placed on probation; after a first or second conviction, criminals should receive completely indefinite sentences; but for those who are convicted a third time, thus revealing themselves to be born criminals, life incarceration is the solution. 'The gangrened member must be cut off from the body politic.'[18]

In addition to urging prophylactic life sentences, the Americans propose other eugenic measures. Several recommend marriage restrictions. 'The marriages of all criminals should be prohibited', Boies explains, 'but the utmost vigilance should be exercised to prevent the marriage of the instinctive.'[19] Some American criminal anthropologists promote sterilization. . . .

The most extreme eugenic solution came from W. Duncan McKim. For 'the *very* weak and the *very* vicious who fall into the hands of the State', McKim proposes 'a *gentle, painless death*' by 'carbonic acid gas'. This is the 'surest, the simplest, the kindest, and most humane means for preventing reproduction among those whom we deem unworthy of this high privilege.'[20] . . .

. . . [F]ew Americans abandoned themselves completely to criminal anthropology, however, many found the doctrine to be appealing and persuasive. Of the factors that nurtured American receptivity, three were particularly influential: the buildup of positivist research on criminal biology, developments in the natural sciences, and perceptions of social deterioration.

The Positivist Tradition

Although Lombrosians liked to contrast their empiricism and determinism with the free-will assumptions of earlier discussions of crime, the distinction between 'new' and 'old' was far less pronounced than they claimed. Their work merely made explicit a tendency to associate crime with biological defects that had been evolving throughout the nineteenth century. . . . Moreover, they were determinists in that they portrayed moral imbeciles and incorrigibles as helpless, irresponsible victims of a mental ailment. Owing to the persistence of positivist methods and the theme of moral incorrigibility in US work on crime causation, Americans easily digested Lombroso's scientism and his lesson that born criminals lack the 'moral sense'.[21]

Criminal anthropology also had much in common with phrenology, another contributor to the development of positivism. . . . They extended phrenology's equation of inner with outer—its belief that skull shape reflects the faculties within—from the head to the entire body, so that not only cranial protuberances but also the arm's length, the nipple's colouration, and the foot's prehensility became signs of criminality. For both groups, moreover, mind was inherited and morality based in biology. . . .

Developments in the Natural Sciences

Criminal anthropology flourished at a time when science enjoyed an admiration verging on awe. The doctrine's particularly close fit with physical anthropology and evolutionary biology—sciences that promised to unlock the secrets of human history and human nature—made it inherently attractive and conferred on its advocates prima facie respectability. Criminal anthropology, like physical anthropology, focused on comparative anatomy and physiology. It, too, aimed at classifying humankind into types through the study of skulls. For a public familiar with research on American Indian tribes and the extensive anthropological collections at the Smithsonian and other museums, it was but a short step to the classification of the criminal, a type as exotic as any Inca or Hottentot.

Speculation about evolution and humans' relationship to less complex organisms ran strong from the early years of the nineteenth century, nourished by work in the natural sciences and by the English sociologist Herbert Spencer, who coined the phrase 'survival of the fittest'.[22] Such speculation intensified with the 1859 publication of *The Origin of Species*, in which Darwin argues that 'the innumerable species, genera, and families of organic beings, with which this world is peopled, have all descended . . . from common parents.'[23] Commonly misunderstood as a 'monkey theory' of evolution, Darwin's ideas seemed to be congruent with the notion of the criminal as an animalistic holdover from the primitive past.[24] Passages in which Darwin remarks on 'rudimentary, atrophied, or aborted organs', moreover, could easily be read as confirmations of Lombroso's reports of the criminal's snakelike teeth and other animalistic anomalies.[25]

Many natural science findings suggested that evolution is purposeful, its goal an ever-higher civilization. If this is true, then it follows that the criminal must be primitive, a holdover from an earlier evolutionary stage. Some of Darwin's own statements appear to equate adaptation with progress. In the final pages of *The Origin of Species* he rhapsodizes that 'from the war of nature, . . . the most exalted object which we are capable of conceiving namely, the production of the higher animals, directly follows'. *The Descent of Man* (1871), in which Darwin applies his theory of evolution specifically to humans, argues that man's 'intellectual and moral faculties' are 'inherited' and 'perfected or advanced through natural selection'.[26] With nature itself apparently striving to advance civilization, surely progressive nations should help by getting rid of born criminals.

America's Deterioration

As the nineteenth century drew to a close, middle-class Americans increasingly perceived a deterioration in the nation's health. One source of weakness seemed to be the hordes of 'new immigrants' from southern and eastern Europe. As the photographs in Boies's *Prisoners and Paupers* graphically demonstrated, Syrians, Sicilians, and Russian Jews came from decaying stock. In neither body, mind, nor morals did they measure up to earlier, Anglo-Saxon immigrants. Pouring into American cities, the new immigrants were creating a host of sanitary, educational, and political problems that further drained the nation's energies.

A close look, moreover, revealed that even native-born Americans were less sturdy than in former years and that the sickliest among them had begun to contaminate rural areas, those cradles of American tradition and values. . . . Sapped by immigrants on the one hand and native-born

paupers on the other, the nation's health was in alarming decline.

Henry Boies perceived 'a general degeneracy' everywhere: the 'lower tenth' of the population was multiplying rapidly while all ranks were being depleted by 'constitutional defects' and by imbecility, suicide, and insanity. 'Stature is decreasing', Boies warned, 'the proportion of normal perfectly healthy people diminishing, the general average of physical endurance and vitality becoming lowered . . .; hair, the common indication of vigour, is disappearing, and bald heads becoming numerous early in life; weak nerves, weak stomachs, weak hearts, weak heads are ordinary ailments. All these are indicative of a general deterioration, which must be due to faulty breeding.'[27] W. Duncan McKim similarly warned of an 'ever-strengthening torrent of defective and criminal humanity'.[28]

Not only individuals but the body politic was deteriorating. Many Americans now perceived their nation as a vast organism, its parts interconnected by the hidden currents of blood and heredity. If one part grew ill, its poisons might secretly infect the whole. The crime problem, then, included not only criminals but also criminality, the biological taint that flowed from criminals into the body of society. It seemed obvious that the crucial need was to increase control over the bodies of those who, like the anthropological born criminal, propagated the diseases of society.

Notes

1. On Lombroso's own attitudes, see Lombroso-Ferrero [1911] 1972: 5.
2. MacDonald, 1893: 173; Boies, 1901; Talbot, 1898: viii.
3. MacDonald, 1893: 17.
4. Boies, 1893: 266, 265.
5. Benedikt, 1881: vii; he was also aware of Lombroso's investigations.
6. Ibid., 157 (original entirely capitalized for emphasis).
7. I do not deal here with the work of Lombroso's colleagues, Enrico Ferri and Raffaele Garofalo, partly because they were so closely associated with him and partly because I could not confidently

gauge their impact on US criminal anthropology. Some American criminal anthropologists cite Ferri; as a group they were poor footnoters, however, and it is sometimes tempting to conclude from internal evidence that they were using secondary sources instead of the Italian and French originals that they cite.
8. Lombroso, 1893, [1900] 1971, 1895; Lombroso and Ferrero, [1895] 1915; Lombroso-Ferrero [1911] 1972; Lombroso, [1911] 1918. Neither *The Female Offender* nor *L' uomo delinquente* has been completely translated into English. A French edition of *L'uomo delinquente*, *L' Homme criminel*,

became available considerably earlier (1887, 1895) than the English translation; several American criminal anthropologists cite it as their source on Lambroso's work.

9. In addition to writing *The Criminal*, Ellis wrote on criminal anthropology in his preface to Winter's *New York State Reformatory at Elmira* (Ellis, 1891). On how he came to write *The Criminal*, see Grosskurth, 1985: 115–16.

10. After formulating this definition of 'leading American criminal anthropologists', I listed all books mentioned in the relevant chapters of three secondary sources on US criminal anthropology: Fink's *Causes of Crime: Biological Theories in the United States, 1800–1915* ([1938] 1962); Haller's *Eugenics: Hereditarian Attitudes in American Thought* (1963); and Zeman's dissertation on the American criminological tradition (1981). When I excluded books on juvenile crime and general sociology from these lists and reduced Arthur MacDonald's many criminal anthropological works to one, *Criminology* (his major study), I ended up with nine books by eight authors. I then read the nine books to discover whether they frequently cited other works that fit my definition. I found that, writings by the originators and channellers aside, they primarily referred to previously published books already on my list. This made me confident that my nine books were indeed influential and that their authors did constitute a core group that included the major American writers on criminal anthropology.

11. Henderson, 1893: 13–14.

12. Lombroso's *Female Offender* (1895) had little influence on the American criminal anthropologists discussed here; with the partial exception of Lydston ([1904] 1905), they pay almost no attention to female born criminals. Because my main interest here lies in the substance of writings by American criminal anthropologists, I follow their lead by focusing on male born criminals and using masculine pronouns in this chapter. On nineteenth-century female criminals, see Gibson, 1982, 1990; and, more generally, Fee, 1979.

13. Talbot, 1898: 18.

14. McKim, 1900: 23.

15. Parsons, 1909: 35–44.

16. E.g., Parsons, 1909: 194.

17. Talbot (1898: 347–8) explicitly rejects eugenics, while MacDonald (1893) and Drähms ([1900] 1971) recommend life imprisonment to incapacitate born criminals physically but not reproductively. Henderson (1893: 229) proposes 'a life sentence for recidivists' for mildly eugenical reasons ('to reduce the supply of morally deformed offspring'), but merely in passing.

18. Boies, 1893: 181, 175–6, 178–90, 267.

19. Boies, 1901: 239.

20. McKim, 1900: 188 (emphases in original), 193, 188, 192, 255. Boies and Parsons praised McKim's proposal while reluctantly rejecting it, Boies because he feared that 'public sentiment does not yet support the purely scientific plan of Dr McKim, and Parsons (1909: 90) because it was too violent.

21. Lombroso-Ferrero, [1911] 1972: 28

22. On pre-Darwinism evolutionary theory and Spencer, see Burrow, 1985 and Hofstadter, 1955.

23. Darwin, [1859] 1985: 434.

24. P. Becker (1994) argues that Lombroso derived his theory of the Criminal as atavism not from Darwin but from other evolutionists who stressed recapitulation, the idea that every human starts at step one in the evolutionary process. Criminals differ from the lawful in that they do not evolve as far.

25. Darwin, [1859] 1985: 428; Lombroso-Ferrero, [1911] 1972: 7.

26. Darwin, [1859] 1985: 459, [1871] 1986: 496.

27. Boies, 1893: 278–9.

28. McKim, 1900: iii.

References

Becker, Peter. 1994. 'Controversy over Meanings: The Debate Between Cesare Lombroso and His Critics about the Signs and the Habit of Criminals'. Paper delivered at the 1994 annual meeting of the American Society of Criminology, Miami.

Benedikt, Moriz. 1881. *Anatomical Studies upon Brains of Criminals*. New York: William Wood.

Boies, Henry M. 1893. *Prisoners and Paupers*. New York: Putnam's.

———. 1901. *The Science of Penology*. New York: Putnam's.

Burrow, John W. 1985. Editor's Introduction, in Charles Darwin, *The Origin of Species by Means of Natural Selection*. London: Penguin Classics, 11–48.

Darwin, Charles. [1859] 1985. *The Origin of Species by Means of Natural Selection*. London: Penguin Classics.

———. [1871] 1986. *The Descent of Man and Selection in Relation to Sex*. Repr. n.p.: Telegraph.

Drähms, August. [1900] 1971. *The Criminal: His Personnel and Environment—A Scientific Study*. Repr. Montclair, NJ: Patterson Smith.

Ellis, Havelock. 1891. Preface, in Alexander Winter, *The New York State Reformatory at Elmira*. London: Swan Sonnenschein, iii–viii.

Fee, Elizabeth. 1979. 'Nineteenth-Century Craniology: The Study of the Female Skull', *Bulletin of the History of Medicine* 53: 415–33.

Fink, Arthur E. [1938] 1962. *Causes of Crime: Biological Theories in the United States, 1800–1915*. Repr. New York: A.S. Barnes.

Gibson, Mary. 1982. 'The "Female Offender" and the Italian School of Criminal Anthropology', *Journal of European Studies* 12: 155–65.

———. 1990. 'On the Insensitivity of Women: Science and the Woman Question in Liberal Italy, 1890–1910', *Journal of Women's History* 2: 11–41.

Grosskurth, Phyllis. 1985. *Havelock Ellis: A Biography*. New York: New York University Press.

Haller, Mark H. 1963. *Eugenics: Hereditarian Attitudes in American Thought*. New Brunswick, NJ: Rutgers University Press.

Henderson, Charles R. 1893. *An Introduction to the Study of the Dependent, Defective and Delinquent Classes*. Boston: D.C. Heath.

Hofstader, Richard. 1955. *Social Darwinism in American Thought*. Rev. ed. Boston: Beacon.

Lombroso, Cesare. 1893. Introduction, in Arthur MacDonald, *Criminology*. New York: Funk and Wagnalls, vii–x.

———. 1895. 'Criminal Anthropology: Its Origin and Application', *Forum* 20: 33–49.

———. [1900] 1971. 'Introductory', in August Drähms, *The Criminal*. Repr. Montclair, NJ: Patterson Smith, xxvii–xxviii.

———. [1911] 1918. *Crime: Its Causes and Remedies*. Boston: Little, Brown.

———. 1912. 'Crime and Insanity in the Twenty-first Century', *JCLC* 3: 57–61.

———, and William Ferrero. [1895] 1915. *The Female Offender*. New York: D. Appleton.

Lombroso-Ferrero, Gina. [1911] 1972. *Criminal Man According to the Classification of Cesare Lombroso*. Repr. Montclair, NJ: Patterson Smith.

Lydston, G. Frank. [1904] 1905. *The Diseases of Society*. Philadelphia: J.B. Lippincott.

MacDonald, Arthur. 1893. *Criminology*, 2nd edn. Intro. Dr Cesare Lombroso. New York: Funk and Wagnalls.

McKim, W. Duncan. 1900. *Heredity and Human Progress*. New York: Putnam's/Knickerbocker.

Parsons, Philip A. 1909. *Responsibility for Crime*. New York: Columbia University/Longmans, Green.

Talbot, Eugene S. 1898. *Degeneracy: Its Causes, Signs, and Results*. London: Walter Scott.

Zeman, Thomas Edward. 1981. 'Order, Crime, and Punishment: The American Criminological Tradition'. Ph.D. diss., University of California, Santa Cruz.

Chapter 12

The Destruction of 'Lives Not Worth Living'

Robert N. Proctor

In early October of 1939, designated by the government as the year of 'the duty to be healthy', Hitler authored a secret memo certifying that 'Reichsleiter Bouhler and Dr Brandt are hereby commissioned to allow certain specified doctors to grant a mercy death (*Gnadentod*) to patients judged to be incurably sick, by critical medical examination.[1] By 24 August 1941, when the first phase of this 'adult operation' was brought to an end, over 70,000 patients from more than 100 German hospitals had been killed, in an operation that provided the stage rehearsal for the subsequent destruction of Jews, homosexuals, communists, Gypsies, Slavs, and prisoners of war.[2]

The Medicalization of Anti-Semitism

Historians exploring origins of the Nazi destruction of 'lives not worth living' have only in recent years begun to stress the ties between the destruction of the mentally ill and handicapped, on the one hand, and the Jews on the other. And yet the two programs were closely linked in both theory and practice. One of the key ideological elements was the 'medicalization of anti-Semitism'—the view developed by Nazi physicians that the Jews were 'a diseased race' and that the Jewish question might be solved by 'medical means.'[3]

According to Walter Gross, head of the Office of Racial Policy and one of the period's foremost racial activists, it was first with the Nuremberg Laws of 1935 (especially the Blood Protection

Law) that the explicit link was made between the 'genetically healthy' (*Erbgesunden*) and the 'German-blooded' (*Deutschblütigen*). . . . [I]t was not until the Nuremberg Laws banned marriage and sexual relations between Jews and non-Jews that legislation for the protection of Germans against the Jews was put on a biological basis. All subsequent legislation in the sphere of race and population policy, Gross claimed, was based upon this distinction between 'healthy' and 'diseased' races.[4]

The Nazi concept of healthy and diseased races was at one level expressed in medical metaphors of the Jew as 'parasite' or 'cancer' in the body of the German Volk. One physician phrased this in the following terms: 'There is a resemblance between Jews and tubercle bacilli: nearly everyone harbours tubercle bacilli, and nearly every people of the earth harbours the Jews; furthermore, an infection can only be cured with difficulty.'[5] . . . Wagner concluded that Jews were a 'diseased race' [and] Judaism was 'disease incarnate.'[6]

Alexander Pilcz . . . had reported . . . that Jews suffer disproportionately from acute psychosis and insanity, and are especially susceptible to psychoses of a 'hereditary-degenerate nature.'[7]

. . . Gerhard Wagner cited these and other articles as evidence for his claim that Jews suffer many diseases that non-Jews do not and concluded from this that the interbreeding of Jews and non-Jews posed grave risks to German public health: . . . if Germans continued to allow the mixing of 'Jewish and non-Jewish blood', this would result in the spread of the 'diseased genes' . . . of the 'already bastardized' Jewish race into the 'relatively pure' European stocks.[8] . . .

The study of racial specificity of disease was to become one of the chief priorities of biomedical science under the Nazis. Otmar Freiherr van Verschuer, director of the Frankfurt Institute for Racial Hygiene was one of the leaders in this effort. In his 1937 book on genetic pathology, Verschuer identified more than 50 different ailments suspected of being genetic in origin. He also classified diseases according to how common they were among particular racial groupings. . . .

Nazi physicians sometimes speculated that Jewish racial degeneracy might be explained in terms of the supposedly hybrid origins of the Jewish race. In 1935, for example, Dr Edgar Schulz of the Office of Racial Policy published an article demonstrating higher rates of insanity (manic depression and dementia praecox), feeble-mindedness, hysteria, and suicide among Jews than among non-Jews.[9] Schulz claimed that these and other disorders arose from the fact that Jews were not, strictly speaking, a single race, but rather an amalgam of Negro and Oriental blood. As a result of this impure racial constitution, Jews suffered 'tensions and contradictions' that became manifest as disease. This was a phenomenon supposedly observed not just among the Jews, but among any population that had suffered racial mixing.[10] . . .

There is evidence that some Nazis did recognize that differences in racial susceptibility to disease might be due to social rather than 'racial' causes. In 1940, for example, Martin Stämmler and Edeltraut Bieneck analyzed demographic shifts among Jewish and non-Jewish inhabitants of Breslau in the period 1928–37. Stämmler and Bieneck noted that Jewish birthrates had declined considerably over this period, and that consequently there was a higher proportion of elderly among Jews than non-Jews. This fact helped account for the higher rates of mortality Jews suffered from disorders such as cancer, diabetes, and circulatory failure; it also helped explain the lower death rates for tuberculosis and infectious diseases, ailments that commonly strike the young.[11] They also noted the rise in Jewish mortality rates over this period: from 14/1000 in 1928 to more than 21/1000 in 1937. As the *British Medical Journal* . . . pointed out, however, nowhere in their analysis did Stämmler and Bieneck discuss the role of state violence . . . in producing these statistics.[12]

The interpretation of the 'Jewish problem' as a 'medical' problem was to prove useful in Nazi attempts to find a 'final solution to the Jewish question in Europe'. In the early months after the invasion of Poland in 1939, Nazi police officials were able to turn to medicine to justify the 'concentration' and extermination of the Jews. Just how this was done illustrates not only something about the role of medical ideology in the persecution of Germany's minorities, but also how the concept of the Jew as 'disease incarnate' began to take on the character of a self-fulfilling prophecy.

Genocide in the Guise of 'Quarantine'

On 1 September 1939, Hitler's armies invaded Poland on the pretext of retaliation for an attack on a German border station by Polish troops—an attack that we now know to have been staged by SS guards disguised as Polish officers. Shortly after the occupation of Poland, SS officers were ordered to confine all of Poland's Jews into certain ghettos, including, first and foremost, the traditional Jewish ghetto of Warsaw.

In territories occupied by the German army, Nazi medical authorities used the pretext of danger of disease to justify a series of repressive measures against the Jewish population. In Warsaw, when the Nazis established a separate section for Germans on the city's streetcars, the Nazi-controlled *Krakauer Zeitung* explained: 'The separation of the Germans from the Poles— and particularly from the Jews—is not merely a question of principle; it is also, at least as far as Warsaw is concerned, a hygienic necessity.'[13] When the Nazis banned Jews from unauthorized railway travel in occupied Poland, Nazi newspapers printed headlines announcing: 'Germ-carriers

Banned from the Railways'.[14] . . . One of the most brutal forms of persecution for which hygiene was used as a pretext was the confinement of Jews to the ghettos. In February 1940, for example, more than 160,000 Jews from the areas surrounding the industrial town of Lodz . . . were rounded up and forced into one small part of the town. The original intention was to remove all Poles and Jews thereby leaving the town entirely German; when this proved impractical, Nazi authorities decided to confine the Jews to the northern part of the town and to regulate all trade or interchange of any kind between the Jewish and non-Jewish sectors. On 30 April, the Jewish quarter was sealed off and surrounded by a wall . . . German newspapers reported that the ghetto in Lodz was the 'most perfect' of all the settlements established by the Germans in occupied Poland; one author called it the 'purest temporary solution to the Jewish question anywhere in Europe'.[15] . . .

In each of these cases, hygiene was preferred as one of the leading grounds for concentration. The establishment of the Jewish ghetto at Lodz, for example, was justified on the grounds that this was necessary to protect against the dangers of epidemic disease.[16] And soon after confinement, of course, the people in these ghettos did begin to suffer from higher rates of infectious disease. These outbreaks of disease allowed Nazi medical philosophers to justify the continued concentration of the Jews in terms of a medical quarantine. Medical police powers were often invoked for such actions: on 1 December 1938, the German government had granted health authorities broad powers to confine anyone suspected of being a carrier of infectious disease. This allowed officials to confine individuals to a certain area or to transport them to hospitals or to other 'appropriate' areas.[17] This measure was most commonly used for tuberculosis victims, but it was also used for racial deportations.

It was in the Warsaw Ghetto, however, that the Nazis were able to realize to the fullest their prophecies of 'Jewish disease'. Shortly after the invasion of Poland, German radio stations carried a report of an associate of Goebbels who had recently returned from a visit to Warsaw and Lodz. The author of this report described the Jews of the ghettos as 'ulcers which must be cut away from the body of the European nations'; he claimed that if the Jews of the ghettos were not completely isolated, the 'whole of Europe would be poisoned'.[18]

. . . When Nazi occupation forces began forcibly concentrating Poland's rural Jews into the ghetto, one effect was to create a breeding ground for disease. The crowded living conditions were exacerbated by shortages of food and clean water. In 1940 and 1941, as the number of Jews arriving in the ghetto grew from 500 per day to over 1000 per day, diseases began to break out, soon reaching epidemic proportions. The world medical press was not unaware of these conditions. The 6 July 1940, issue of the *British Medical Journal* reported that 'typhoid fever is still raging in Warsaw, where there are from 200 to 300 cases every day'. Fully 90 percent of the victims were Jews.[19] . . .

The situation was to become much worse. Before the war, mortality in the ghetto due to all causes had been about 400 deaths per month. By January 1941 nearly 900 people were dying every month, and death rates were increasing week by week. By March, the number of deaths had grown to 1608 per month, and, in the single month of June 1941, 4100 people died from infection and disease, compounded by starvation, physical abuse, and lack of adequate medical supplies.[20] According to Wilhelm Hagen, the German commissioner of the ghetto (a Dr Auersbach) sabotaged efforts on the part of well-meaning German doctors to alleviate the situation by his order to block shipment of food and medical supplies to the city. By the end of 1941 official rations had been reduced to bread worth about 2000 calories per person per day, and many were receiving even less than this. Hunger and epidemic disease reinforced each other as mortality rates for tuberculosis alone rose from 14/100,000 in 1938 to more than 400/100,000 in the first quarter of 1941. The case was even more dramatic with typhus. In the single month of October 1941, health authorities responsible for the Warsaw ghetto recorded

300 deaths from typhus—nearly as many as from all causes combined before German occupation.[21]

Epidemics that raged inside the Warsaw ghetto in 1941 and 1942 provided Nazi occupation forces with a medical rationale for the isolation and extermination of the Jewish population. On 29 October 1940, the *Hamburger Fremdenblatt* noted that 98 per cent of all cases of typhoid and spotted fever in Warsaw were to be found in the ghetto. In the spring of 1940, non-Jewish doctors were barred from treating Jewish patients; on 12 March, the *Krakauer Zeitung* explained this ban as follows:

> This decree is based on the fact that infectious diseases, particularly spotted fever and typhoid, are widespread especially among the Jewish population. When Jews suffering from those diseases are treated by non-Jewish doctors— doctors who are at the same time treating the sick of other races—there is a danger of their transmitting diseases from the Jews to the non-Jewish population.[22]

In the first months of the German occupation of Poland, traffic between Jews and non-Jews in and outside the Warsaw ghetto was not restricted. Germans and non-Jewish Poles were allowed to enter the ghetto. After 1940, however, contact with Jews was declared a 'threat to public health'. Jews trying to escape from the ghetto were shot on the grounds that they were violating the 'quarantine' imposed by the Nazis . . .[23]

Criminal Biology

Criminal biology was to forge a further link in the medical solution to the Jewish question. According to the psychiatrist Robert Ritter, the urgent task of criminal biology was 'to discover whether or not certain signs can be found among men which would allow the early detection of criminal behaviour; signs which, in other words, would allow the recognition of criminal tendencies *before* the actual onset of the criminal career'.[24] Such efforts were not, of course, an invention of the Nazis. Criminal biologists had tried, since Cesare Lombroso's *L' uomo delinquente* in the late nineteenth century, to construct a medical-forensic system linking moral, criminal, and racial degeneracy. Crime, in this view, was a disease; criminality was linked with certain physical manifestations such as facial shape or body hair. . . .

In the twentieth century, spurred by advances in genetics and hopes for eugenics, criminal biology became an important research priority in the German scientific community. Concerns on the part of criminal biologists were in many ways close to those of the racial hygienists. Criminal biologists argued that crime was both genetically determined and racially specific; they worried that criminals were reproducing at a faster rate than noncriminal elements of the population. . . . In the Nazi period, government statistical offices tried to determine what proportion of murderers were 'genetically defective': in 1938, government statisticians provided data to show that, whereas in 1928–30, only 14.5 per cent of all murderers were genetic defectives (*erblich belastet*), by 1931–33, this proportion had supposedly grown to 20.1 per cent.[25] [Citing] twin studies . . . racial theorists argued time and again that studies of identical and non-identical twins proved that crime was the product of hereditary disposition and not . . . social environment.[26] . . .

Interest in criminal biology accelerated with the rise of the Nazis. By 1935, legal and medical journals were regularly reporting that crime and other 'anti-social behaviour' were genetically determined racial characteristics. . . . By the end of the mid-1930s most German universities offered instruction in this area—often in conjunction with courses on racial hygiene.[27] . . . In October of 1936, Justice Minister Franz Gürtner ordered the establishment of 50 Examination Stations throughout Germany to explore the genetics and racial specificity of crime. . . . In addition, larger Criminal Biology Research Stations . . . were established at Munich, Freiburg-Breslau, Cologne, Münster, Berlin, Königsberg, Leipzig, Halle, and Hamburg to evaluate the effects of various measures on the incidence of crime—especially the 1935 castration law.[28] In 1939, the Deutsches Arzteblatt reported Himmler's orders that henceforth, examination of the genetics and genealogy of criminal suspects would become a routine part of criminal investigations.[29]

Criminal biologists also addressed the 'Jewish question'. The conceptual link here, as one might imagine, was the idea that Jews were racially disposed to certain forms of crime, just as they were racially disposed to certain kinds of disease. One should recall that disease for the Nazis was often broadly construed to cover not just physical disorders, but also behavioural and cultural maladies.[30] . . .

Science thus conspired in the solution to the Jewish question: Jews were racially disposed to commit crime, as they were racially disposed to suffer from a host of other diseases. By the late 1930s, German medical science had constructed an elaborate world view equating mental infirmity, moral depravity, criminality, and racial impurity. This complex of identifications was then used to justify the destruction of the Jews on medical, moral, criminological, and anthropological grounds. To be Jewish was to be both sick and criminal; Nazi medical science and policy united to help 'solve' this problem.

The Final Solution

. . . Germany's medical journals made it clear that Jews had no place in the New German Order. Dr W. Bormann, for example, writing in the *Ärzteblatt für den Reichsgau Wartheland,* declared that the 'retrieved' German territories of the occupied east were to be settled 'exclusively with German men'.[31] On 23 November 1939, when laws were passed requiring Jews in occupied Poland to wear the yellow star, Germany's foremost medical journal justified this as necessary 'to create an externally visible separation between the Jewish and Aryan population'. The journal argued further that in order to establish a geographical separation between the races, there were two possible solutions: the creation of a separate Jewish state, and confinement to a ghetto. The latter solution was preferable, because 'it could be implemented more rapidly and with greater effect'.[32] The *Deutsches Ärzteblatt* reported with satisfaction that, as a result of Nazi policies, areas of mixed Polish–Jewish population had already begun to disappear, and Jewish businesses were gone. . . .

. . . In post-war testimony at Nuremberg, [Dr Victor] Brack recounted the alternatives pondered by Nazi authorities:

In 1941, it was an 'open secret' in higher Party circles that those in power intended to exterminate the entire Jewish population in Germany and occupied territories. I and my co-workers, especially Drs Hefelmann and Blankenburg, were of the opinion that this was unworthy of Party leaders and humanity more generally. We therefore decided to find another solution to the Jewish problem, less radical than the complete extermination of the entire race. We developed the idea of deporting Jews to a distant land, and I can recall that Dr Hefelmann suggested for this purpose the island of Madagascar. We drew up a plan along these lines and presented it to Bouhler. This was apparently not acceptable, however, and so we came up with the idea that sterilization might provide the solution to the Jewish question. Given that sterilization is a rather complicated business, we hit upon the idea of sterilization by X-rays. In 1941 I suggested to Bouhler the sterilization of Jews by X-rays; this idea was also rejected, however. Bauhler said that sterilization by X-rays was not an option, because Hitler was against it. . . . [33]

. . . Sterilization was ultimately rejected as a solution to the Jewish question. The decision to destroy Europe's Jews by gassing them in concentration camps emerged from the fact that the technical apparatus already existed for the destruction of the mentally ill. In the early phases, both the children's and the adult 'euthanasia' operations were administered at first only to non-Jews[34]: . . . But the operations were eventually extended to Jews, and in mass fashion. . . . In fact, Jewish psychiatric patients from the hospital at Berlin-Buch had begun to be rounded up and sent to gas chambers at Brandenburg since earlier that summer (June 1940).[35] In early September 1940, 160 Jewish patients held at Eglfing-Haar were filmed as part of the propaganda film *Scum of Humanity* (*Abschaum der Menschheit*). Later that month, on 20 September, these patients were sent to Brandenburg, where they were gassed on 22 September 1940.

In early 1941, the Reich Ministry of the Interior ordered that all Jews in German hospitals be killed—not because they met the criteria required for euthanasia, but because they were Jews.[36] The Jews were not the first group to be singled out for extraordinary euthanasia. Criminals in Germany's hospitals had already been disposed of by this time; and, in the course of the year 1941, a number of other groups would fall within the shadow of the program. On 8 March 1941, Dr Werner Blankenburg wrote to local *Gauleiter*, asking that all 'asocials' and 'anti-socials' in Germany's workhouses be registered with euthanasia officials. In April, Germany's concentration camps began a new program designed to destroy camp inmates no longer capable of or willing to work. This project, within which Jews were also to be included, was code named '14 f 13'.

Operation 14 f 13 represents the transition under way at this time from the systematic destruction of the handicapped and the psychologically ill to the systematic destruction of the ethnically and culturally marginal. In 1941 Buchenwald Commandant Koch announced to SS officers of his camp that he had received secret orders from Himmler that all feeble-minded and crippled inmates of Germany's concentration camps were to be killed. Koch also announced at this time that all Jewish prisoners were to be included in this operation 14 f 13. In December of 1941, SS Leiutenant Colonel Liebehenschel notified the concentration camps at Sachsenbuch, Gross-Rosen, Neuengamme, Mauthausen, Auschwitz, Flossenbürg, Niedernhagen, Sachsenhausen, and Dachau that a medical commission

would soon arrive to select prisoners for 'special treatment'. Camp officials were instructed to prepare the necessary paperwork; forms were to be filled out indicating the diagnosis of the inmates, including information on race, and whether the individuals were suffering from incurable physical ailments. SS Lieutenant Colonel Friedrich Mennecke, head of the Eichberg State Medical Hospital, arrived in Gross-Rosen in mid-January 1942, to begin selecting prisoners for destruction. By this time, selection had moved some distance from what we today would consider criteria for health. Psychopaths, criminals, asocials, antisocials, and individuals 'foreign to the community' (*Gemeinschaftsfremde*) were now all included; people were being taken from tuberculosis hospitals and from workhouses. . . .[37]

. . . The selection of the Jews alongside the mentally ill began first either in Buchenwald or in Dachau.[38] Throughout the remaining years of the war, co-operation continued between concentration camps and psychiatric hospitals administering euthanasia. From July 1944 through the spring of 1945, for example, 400 Russians and Poles were gassed in the psychiatric hospital at Hadmar—now with years of experience in execution by gas chamber.[39]

It is important to realize today that for the Nazi physicians, there was no sharp line dividing the destruction of the racially inferior and the mentally or physically defective. The physicians responsible for administering the euthanasia operation in German hospitals were also responsible for formulating criteria and administering the first phases of the destruction of the Jews and handicapped in Germany's concentration camps (14 f 13). When cross-examined after the war at the Nuremberg Trials, physicians pointed out that they often did not distinguish whether certain exterminations were for racial, political, or medical reasons.[40] . . .

. . . Walter Gross [head of the Office of Racial Policy] reviewed the shortcomings of previous attempts to [address the Jewish question] . . . (emancipation, persecution, partial annihilation, and so forth) and claimed that a 'final could come only with the "removal of Jews from Europe"'.[41]

Racial hygienists appreciated Nazi efforts to solve the Jewish question. In 1944, not long after he accepted Josef Mengele as his scientific assistant, Verschuer proudly claimed that the dangers posed by Jews and Gypsies to the German people had been 'eliminated through the racial-political measures of recent years'. He also noted in this context that the purification of Germany from 'foreign racial elements' required a larger effort extending across the entirety of Europe.[42]

In November 1942, the *Informationsdienst des Hauptamtes für Volksgesundheit der NSDAP,* a journal published by the Reich Health Publishing House, noted that in the 'Confidential Information of the Party Chancellery' there had appeared a paper (no. 881) titled 'Preparatory Measures for the Final Solution of the European Jewish Question'.[43] . . .

Sexual and Racial Pathologies

It was not just the Jews or the mentally or physically handicapped, but other groups as well that were stigmatized as 'sick' and 'degenerate' by Germany's racial scientists. Jews, Gypsies, communists, homosexuals, the feeble-minded, the tubercular, and a wide class of 'anti-socials' (alcoholics, prostitutes, drug addicts, the homeless, and other groups) were also marked for destruction. . . .

Part of our revulsion for Nazi medical experiments stems from the fact that they violated a relationship of supposedly unique confidence and trust. In the Nazi period, the doctor–patient relationship was exploited to achieve goals that would have been difficult to attain by other means. At Buchenwald for example, 8000 Russian prisoners of war were executed in the course of supposed medical exams; unsuspecting prisoners were taken to an examination room, where they were told to stand in front of a device apparently designed to measure their height. Prisoners were then shot in the head from a secret cavity built into the device. . . . The traditional doctor–patient relationship was exploited in other ways as well. SS troops suspected of disloyalty were executed under the guise of medical treatment—through intravenous injections of phenol or gasoline.[44]

It is possible of course, in hindsight, to separate analytically the sterilization program (eugenics), the destruction of the mentally ill (euthanasia), and the destruction of Germany's racial minorities (the final solution). The fact is, however, that each of these programs was seen as part of a larger program of racial purification. Medical journals used the term 'life not worth living' to refer to those sterilized under the 1933 Sterilization Law[45], to those killed in psychiatric hospitals, and to those killed in concentration camps. . . .

. . . Physicians played an active role in both the theory and the practice of each phase of the Nazi program of racial hygiene and racial destruction. . . .

Notes

1. *Der prozess gegen die Hauptkriegsverbrecher vor dem internationalen Militargerichtshof,* vol. 26 (Nuremberg, 1947), 169. . . .

2. For background on the killings, see the comprehensive study by Ernst Klee *'Euthansie' im NS-Staat* (Frankfurt, 1983). . . .

3. See, for example, Theobald Lang, 'Die Belastung des Judentums mit Geistig-Auffalligen,' *Nationalsozialistische Monatshefte,* 3 (1932): 23–30.

4. Walter Gross, 'Die Familie', *Informationsdienst,* 20 September 1938. Peltret, 'Der Arzt als Führer and Erzieher', *Deutsches Ärzteblatt* 65 (1935): 565–6.

5. Peltret, 'Der Arzt als Fuhrer und Erzieher,' DA, 65 (1935): 565–6.

6. Wagner, 'Die periodischen Geistesstorungen,' *Wiener Klinische Rundschau,* 16 (1902): 490.

7. See A. Pilcz, 'Die periodischen Geistesstörungen', *Wiener Klinische Rundschau* 16 (1902): 490.

8. Wagner, '*Unser Reichsärzteführer Spricht*', 432.

9. Edgar Schultz, 'Judentum und Degeneration,' *Ziel und Weg,* 5 (1935): 349–55.

10. Interestingly, a number of racial hygienists rejected

the notion that inbreeding produces a decline in racial fitness. Fritz Lenz, for example, supported marriage between cousins and even siblings, arguing that such inbreeding was dangerous only where deleterious recessive allies were present. See his *Menschlinche Auslese*, 506.

11. M. Stämmler and E. Bieneck, 'Statistische Untersuchungen über die Todesursachen der deutschen and jüdischen Bevölkerung von Breslau', *Münchener medizinische Wochenschrift* 87 (1940): 447–50.

12. 'German Medicine, Race, and Religion', *British Medical Journal* 17 August 1940, 230.

13. *Krakauer Zeitung*, 14–15 January, 1940.

14. *Krakauer Zeitung* of 8 February 1940. See also the German New Order in Poland, published for the Polish Ministry of Information in London, 1942, 218.

15. *Kölnische Zeitung*, 5 April 1941. See also *The German New Order*, 241

16. Wilhelm Hagen, *Auftrag and Wirklichkeity, Sozialarzt im 20. Jahrhundert* (Munich-Gräfelfing, 1978), 166.

17. *Informationsdienst des Hauptamtes fur Volksgesundheit der NSDAP*, October/December 1943, 110.

18. *Manchester Guardian*, 3 November 1939.

19. *British Medical Journal*, 6 July 1940, 36.

20. Hagen, *Auftrag and Wirklichkeit,* 179, 171. . . .

21. Hagen, *Auftrag and Wirklichkeit,* 171–81.

22. *Krakauer Zeitung*, 12 March 1940.

23. On Hamburg attorney Jürgen Rieger's 1978 defense of Arpad Wigand, see 'SS und Polizeifuher van Warschau verureilt,' *Frankfurter Allgemeine Zeitung*, 8 December 1981

24. Robert Ritter, 'Kriminalität and Primitivität', *Monatsschrift für Kriminalbiologie* 31 (1940): 197–210. . . .

25. *Informationsdienst*, 10 October 1938.

26. See, for example, Johannes Lange, *Verbrechen als Schicksal Studien and kriminellel Zwillingen* (Leipzig, 1928).

27. For a comprehensive listing of course offerings in criminal biology at German universities, see the *Monatsschrift für Kriminalbiologie und Strafrechtsreform* 32 (1941): 53–73.

28. *Reichs-Gesundheitsblatt* 12 (1937): 118. See also 'Kriminalbiologische Sammelstelle in Berlin', *Ärzteblatt für Berlin* 42 (1937): 623. . . .

29. *Deutsches Ärzteblatt* 68 (1938): 858.

30. Johannes Schottky, ed., *Rasse und Krankheit* (Munich 1937).

31. W. Bormann, 'Grundsätze der deutschen Ostraumpolitik', *Ärzteblatt für den Reichsgau Wartheland* 2 (1941): 168.

32. 'Die Juden im Generalgouvernement,' DA, 70 (1940): 430–1.

33. Mitscherlich and Mielke, *Medizin ohne Menschlichkeit*, 240–1.

34. Kaul, *Nazimordaktion T-4*, 90–5.

35. Kaul, *Nazimordaktion*, 97–9; also Klee Euthanasie, 258–9.

36. Aly, 'Medzin gegen Unbrauchbare', 28. . . .

37. Aly, 'Medzin gegen Unbrauchbare', 30–9.

38. The first gassing of Jews who had not been in hospitals took place at the concentration camp at Chelmo on 9 December 1941. (Jews were singled out for destruction among psychiatric patients as early as June 1940.)

39. Mitscherlich and Mielke, *Medizan ohne Mensschlichkeit*, 219–20.

40. Mitscherlich and Mielke, *Medizan ohne Mensschlichkeit*, 216.

41. Gross, 'Rassenpolitische Voraussetzungen', 1–6. . . .

42. Otmar von Verschuer, 'Bevöolkerungs un Rassefragen in Europa', *Europäischer Wissenschaftsdienst* 1 (1944): 3.

43. 'Vorbereitende Massnahmen zur Endlösung der europäischen Judenfragen', listed as paper no. 881 in the 'Vertrauliche Informationen' der Parteikanzlei, cited in the *Informationsdienst des Hauptamtes für Volksgesundheit der NSDAP,* November 1942: 69.

44. Alexander, 'Medicine under Dictatorship', 41.

45. See Kulenkampf, 'Die technik der Tubensterilisation zyr Verhutung lebensunwerten Lebens', *Deutsche Medizinische Wochenschrift* 59 (1933): 1294–5.

Part V

Gendered Bodies

Claudia Malacrida and Jacqueline Low

Feminist studies have made a major contribution to reintroducing the body into social research and theory, most notably by developing an analysis of the politics of women's bodies and women's reproductive labour. Linda M. Blum's chapter introduces us to the feminist concept of women's **bodily representation**, in which it is understood women's bodies have been represented in art, literature, and scientific and popular discourse in ways that shore up patriarchal power relations (1993). Blum provides us with a concrete example of **embodiment**, a term describing the ways that attitudes and practices relating to bodies reflect political, economic, and moral trends in societies (Witz, 2000). She shows that varying historical representations of women's breasts have served specific classed, raced, and gendered interests. For example, wealthy white women in the eighteenth and nineteenth centuries typically did not breast-feed their children because the 'unused' breast better suited their roles as socialites and status symbols to their husbands. Conversely, poor and non-white women breast-fed not only their own children, but also those of wealthy women, in return for payment. The breast thus acted as an embodied unit of exchange, reflecting Bourdieu's ideas about physical capital, where normatively valued bodily qualities can be used in exchange for economic advantage. It is useful to note that physical capital worked advantageously, although differently, for both poor and wealthy women. Blum goes on to note that **exclusive motherhood** (childrearing practices that require a full-time, stay-at-home mother, rather than a communal approach) was a white, middle-class project that not only positioned children's needs above all else, but also had moral effects on poor, non-white women. This discourse was used to **pathologize** poor and middle-class working women by constructing them as deficient or harmful.

With increased knowledge about bacteria and sterilization, adequate techniques for artificial breast-feeding developed so that, in theory, breast-feeding was not necessary to good mothering. However, psychoanalytic discourse, particularly in the form of attachment theory, was deployed to fuel a 'bonding' craze that constructed breast-feeding and full-time, intensive mothering as necessary to children's psychological development.

Ironically, feminists and the 'back-to-the land' movements of the 1960s and 1970s also contributed to this notion. Nevertheless, the economic and normative realities of the late twentieth century mean that mothers must often work full-time for wages.

Although modern women may not be able to engage in full-time mothering, they are encouraged to offer a metaphorical presence to their children by providing breastmilk, even while away from the child. In an ironic turn that Blum terms **disembodied mothering**, the breast and its milk become stand-ins for mothers' full-time care. On the surface this leaves women 'free' to pursue both paid employment and motherhood, but in the end it has resulted in a heightened set of expectations of women, who are exhorted to be super-careerists and super-moms at the same time.

Susan Bordo's (1988) essay offers another example of problems associated with the representation of women's bodies. Bordo argues that young women's starving bodies are a predictable response to a culture in which women are continuously represented as and encouraged to be small, frail, and childlike. Bordo also argues that young women experience **alienation** from their own bodies; their bodies are experienced as separate from themselves, reminiscent of Descartes' dualism, or mind–body split.

Indirectly, Bordo's article also provides insight into processes of medicalization. In the case of anorexia, young women's 'natural' (or at least predictable) responses to the excesses of culture have been treated as individual medical problems. In this way, the societal pressures aimed at young women are not addressed, but young women are treated as pathological. Bordo attempts to unmask this medicalization, instead finding pathology in cultural practices like modernity's rail-thin fashion models and the historical binding of Chinese women's feet. She sees these practices as part of the **gender/power axis** of patriarchy, where women's bodies act as battlegrounds upon which male power is played out.

Theories of masculinity address various forms of the question of what it means to be a man. Answering this question involves attention not only to male physiology but also to the social, cultural, historical, and political processes that shape the male body. In 'Men's Bodies' Raewyn Connell (1995) critiques two dominant discourses of men's bodies: the socio-biological and the social constructionist. According to the former perspective there is a 'natural' male body that is grounded in the biological differences between it and the female body. As such, this male body is characterized by bodily attributes such as strength and aggression. These same features are among those that make up the construct of **hegemonic masculinity**, the dominant socio-cultural construct of what it means to be masculine in Western society. From the latter perspective (social constructionism), the male body emerges as a disembodied performance that has lost its **corporeality** (its actual physical existence).

In contrast to these discourses, Connell (1995: 59) argues for an understanding of gendered bodies accomplished through the frame of '**body-reflexive practices**', which includes understanding bodies as both **objects** (acted upon by social forces) and **agents of practice** (bodies capable of action). She asserts that we can understand the social forces that play upon bodies without disembodying them in the process. To illustrate, she gives the example of a male informant who, when throwing a ball, was taunted by his father for throwing 'like a girl'. For Connell this demonstrates the inextricability of the physical action (throwing the ball) from the social meanings attached to that action, meanings that are shaped by hegemonic masculinity.

References

Blum, L.M. 1993. 'Mothers, Babies, and Breast-feeding in Late Capitalist America: The Shifting Contexts of Feminist Theory', *Feminist Studies*, 19, 2: 291–311.

Bordo, S. 1988. 'Anorexia Nervosa: Psychopathology as the Crystallization of Culture', in I. Diamond and L. Quinby, eds, *Feminism and Foucault: Reflections on Resistance*. Boston: Northeastern University Press, 87–117.

Butler, J. 1990. *Gender Trouble*. New York and London: Routledge.

Connell, R.W. 1995. *Masculinities*. Cambridge: Polity Press.

Conrad, P. 1992. 'Medicalization and Social Control', *Annual Review of Sociology* 18: 209–32.

Holt, N.L. 2003. 'Representation, Legitimation, and Autoethnography: An Autoethnographic Writing Story', *International Journal of Qualitative Methods* 2, 1: Article 2. Available at http://www.ualberta.ca/~iiqm/backissues/2_final/html/holt.html. Accessed 9 December 2006.

Witz, A. 2000. 'Whose Body Matters? Feminist Sociology and the Corporeal Turn', *Sociology and Feminism, Body & Society* 6, 2: 1–24.

Chapter 13

From $acred to Disembodied Motherhood: Breast-feeding with the Experts and the State

Linda M. Blum

In the United States, maternal breast-feeding has long been advocated as a key to good mothering, womanly honour, and even to women's citizenship. Such prescriptive advice has been expressed in differing vocabularies, but the notion of breast-feeding as a mother's obligation to both her child and the larger social body extends from the colonial days, when nursing was a mother's sacred duty, through the eighteenth and nineteenth centuries, when it was considered a mother's civic duty to the growing republic, and finally, to twentieth-century public health campaigns that portray nursing as her contribution to US global dominance. The mid-twentieth century break in which artificial feeding predominated, in fact, was only a brief hiatus, and, on scrutiny, it was more rather than less continuous with this history at the breast. . . .

A Quick Backward Glance: The Eighteenth and Nineteenth Centuries

Infant-feeding decisions directly affected infant mortality rates, and, through this, the demographic structure and long-run viability of societies; such 'private' decisions were, therefore, thoroughly public (Golden, 1996: 2).[1] Infants, furthermore, could only be fed at the breast of the mother, at the breast of another lactating woman (wet-nursing), or by 'hand-feeding' or 'dry nursing' with an 'artificial' food, usually diluted animal milk or a 'pap' of flour, sugar, milk, water, or

tea. . . . High-born mothers were sometimes condemned for placing their babies out to nurse, but twentieth-century analysts suggest important reasons why many may have done so: proscriptions against sexual relations during lactation interfered with husbands' conjugal rights; the contraceptive effect of lactation interfered with pressures to produce male heirs; and notions of beauty prized the 'unused' bosom.[2] . . .

In the United States, however, with little such wealth, Puritan ministers like Cotton Mather harshly criticized mothers who did not nurse their young (Treckel, 1989). . . . Along with such exhortations, the lack of an established aristocracy made the use of wet-nurses less common than in Europe, and church and state were little involved in such arrangements. . . . Maternal breast-feeding, moreover, became almost an emblem of new democratic ideals, as images of 'nature' were linked with equality, the rejection of decadent, aristocratic 'culture', and the rising health and wealth of the middle class of the young nation.[3] . . .

The Early Twentieth Century: Maternalists and Baby-saving

In the United States in the early twentieth century, the state became more explicitly involved in infant care and feeding and the control of maternal bodies. As elite groups strove to make the country a world power, they saw domestic power relations and social order threatened by mass immigration. Concerns with population 'quality' flared up over high infant mortality rates, the declining predominance of the Anglo-Saxon 'race', and the physical 'degeneration' bemoaned during World War I.[4] . . .

State policies of 'race betterment' and public health promotion emerged in this nation-building climate. . . . Educated, middle-class women became centrally involved in these social welfare efforts. Historians have labelled such women-reformers 'maternalists'. . .

Most US maternalist reformers believed that mothers should be full-time homemakers to fully dependent children; the baby-saving campaign worked to discourage mothers' wage-earning as well as to prohibit child labour (Ladd-Taylor, 1994). . . .

Many low-income mothers early in the century brought in family income, either by working in factories or sweatshops, or by taking in boarders, laundry, or piecework. Some black mothers worked as fieldhands and by taking in work, but many were domestics in the homes of affluent whites.[5] . . . US maternalists, however, argued for the need to 'educate, educate, educate' mothers to stop their waged-work (cited in Mink, 1995: 68–9). . . .

Along with this aversion to wage-earning, maternalist 'baby savers' condemned artificial feeding and irregular breast-feeding as causes of infant death and disease, and, linked closely with this, the consumption of 'unAmerican' foods (Mink, 1995: 58–9). . . .

. . . [B]y the 1930s, discoveries in bacteriology, physiology, and nutrition had made it possible for medical researchers to improve their simulation of human milk substantially.[6]

Physicians, however, drew a primarily middle-class clientele; once they began to supervise infant-feeding, it became a large and lucrative part of family practice and pediatric medicine. . . .

Of course, middle-class mothers' advantages made it easier to adhere to breast-feeding advice and to 'regulate' their babies' and their own bodies. They rarely faced financial pressures to seek paid work and usually lived in more comfortable, cleaner neighbourhoods. Many middle-class mothers, however, were influenced to turn to bot-

tles and formula by the prestige and authoritative weight of modern science, the growing confidence in artificial products, and the declining confidence in breastmilk. Confidence in breast-feeding had been shaken by the discovery of such 'problems' as newborn weight loss and the variability of mother's milk in quantity and quality. . . .

. . . As artificial infant-feeding became safer, the bottle was similarly an emblem of modernity, progress, and enhanced autonomy for affluent women in their maternal bodies. . . .

Middle-class mothers, reformers, and pediatricians were also influenced or 'medicalized' by another related science, the emerging field of child psychology. . . .

Mid-Twentieth-Century Motherhood: Science and Its Discontents

. . . Breast-feeding became a low priority to the majority of physicians, child development experts, and state authorities in the post-war era. Yet, those influenced by British psychoanalysis and by post-war Christian familialism revived a sentimental view of this 'natural' mother–child tie.

British psychoanalytic thought on mothering emerged from war-time work with orphan and refugee children,[7] but the notion that *any* separation of the young child from its mother would result in psychic damage was codified by psychiatrist John Bowlby. . . .

Although Bowlby primarily used breast-feeding as a metaphor for good mothering (Carter, 1995: 57), many practitioners, like registered maternity-ward nurses, used his attachment theory to enforce it according to the rigid medical/behaviourist model. Of course, adding the imperative 'to attach' to one's newborn to the fears of insufficient milk and 'excessive' cuddling could hardly make mothers feel more nurturing (Eyer, 1992: 41–2, 159; Apple, 1887). In the late 1970s and 1980s, Bowlby's work would fuel a similar 'bonding craze', which made the first skin-to-skin, breast-to-mouth contact so critical that mothers feared disastrous consequences if they missed it (due to complications) or were not instantly enthralled (Eyer, 1992: 13, 43). . . .

. . . Maternal nursing hit an all-time low by 1970, with only some 20 per cent of mothers nursing in-hospital, and very few, perhaps only 5 per cent, continuing for several months (Hendershot, 1984: 599–600, *Newsweek*, 1970). In this 'baby boom' era, more mothers were at home with more children, so fewer would have felt a conflict between breast-feeding and wage-earning. Bottles, however, meant that they could *get out*. It was easier to leave the baby, but also to be *out* in public with her, for with bottles, mothers could keep their breasts *out* of sight (see Carter, 1995).

Nursing was doubly dangerous in this era, when breasts were singled out and increasingly sexualized (Carter, 1995: 124, 128). Breast-feeding threatened to expose the breasts to the heterosexual gaze, but also to compromise the object of that gaze, the stiff, uplifted breasts of Barbie, the fashion doll who so epitomized the era (Young, 1990: 190; also NPR, 1992b). Even Dr Spock admitted, 'Some women are hesitant to breast-feed because of the fear of what it may do to the shapeliness of their breasts, which is understandable in an age when this is considered so important' (1964: 18).[8] . . .

The Late Twentieth Century: A Machiavellian Plot?

In the late twentieth century two seemingly contradictory trends have reshaped mothering: the dramatic increase in mothers' wage-earning *and* the revival of breast-feeding prescriptions. These two trends 'work' through (and on) maternal bodies— bodies that have to get out into the public sphere to seek autonomy, but also to engage in a most interdependent, private, and time-consuming act. . . .

. . . It is true that at the height of the 'baby boom' only 12 per cent of mothers of preschool children were out earning wages (1950 figure); but by the 1970s a changing economy and feminist goals had pushed, pulled, and inspired mothers, and over 30 per cent of those with preschoolers were employed (cited in Eyer, 1992:

122). . . . This rose dramatically in the next decade and has remained high; in the 1990s slightly over half of mothers of infants were earning wages, many on a full-time basis. . .

The feminist health movement shared the 'back to nature' ethos of the 'counterculture' and the many social movements of the period (anti-Vietnam war, liberation movements of people of colour and of gays and lesbians, environmentalism). Breast-feeding, in particular, was viewed through this social movement lens, as a 1970 *Newsweek* article announced: 'the *hippies* seem to be in the forefront of a back-to-the-breast movement' (my emphasis). Breast-feeding also became politicized on a world scale through church and social movement activism pressing for corporate responsibility. In the 1970s church and university-based coalitions uncovered the corrupt practices of infant-formula producers selling to the Third World. The coalitions pressed corporations to change their policies and led the highly publicized boycott against Nestlé, the Swiss-based multinational that dominated the two-billion dollar world market.[9] . . .

. . . The medical community, meanwhile, could not help but be influenced by this politicized consciousness. . . Finally, in late 1978 the American Academy of Pediatrics (AAP) changed its official position to state that 'human milk is superior to infant formulas', they advised that, 'newly discovered advantages' mean that '[i]deally, breast milk should be the only source of nutrients for the first four to six months' (Clark, 1978).

This represented a switch from the mid-century advice that bottle-fed babies could be just as happy and well nourished. Beginning in the late 1970s, advice questioned the interchangeability of breast and bottle, emphasized the term 'superior', and went to new lengths to paint the bottle-fed baby as 'an immunologic orphan, forced to fend for himself' (Marano, 1979: 60, 56). . . .

But What *Does* Breast-feeding Do?

The American Academy of Pediatrics (AAP) now recommends breast-feeding more strongly than ever (1997), though the cautions from their detailed 1984 Task Force Assessment still concern scientists. In the earlier report, the AAP emphasized the difficulties of isolating breast-feeding from the confounding social factors within which it is embedded, and concluded that infant-health benefits in advanced societies were likely modest (AAP, 1984: 580). . . .

The latest claims for breast-feeding's benefits are even less scientifically established: breast-feeding may slightly heighten IQ and visual acuity (Horwood and Fergusson, 1998; Glick, 1997; NPR, 1992a): it may condition the body to better process fats and cholesterol and prevent obesity (deMauro, 1991; LLLI, 1987: 154), or even teach the baby to enjoy a more varied, healthful diet (Shapiro, 1997); and finally, it may enhance facial, dental, and speech development (Eiger and Olds, 1987: 25; LLLI, 1987: 370–2). These most recent claims speak to less serious health issues than earlier concerns about infectious and chronic disease. Furthermore, researchers are again concerned that claims could be spurious, for example, mothers in New Zealand, whose breast-fed children scored slightly higher on IQ tests, were older, better educated, and wealthier (*New York Times*, 1998b). The exhortation that 'breast is best', in light of such small, unverified claims, may represent new kinds of middle-class anxieties about children as much as rational health-enhancing advice. . . . In terms of breast-feeding, the new cultural imperatives imply that certainly no good mother would deny her child optimal health and longevity, and that the best mothers will do all they can to maximize their children's intelligence and beauty. Even one advocate wrote: '[I]n reality much of this [increased breast-feeding] has occurred among well-educated . . . women seeking optimal outcome of the few well-planned and carefully-engineered pregnancies they will experience' (Lawrence, 1988: 267). . . .

But What about Mom?

Research and advice literature each pay less attention to maternal health and breast-feeding.

Assumptions of maternal altruism run high, and mothers particularly curious about the effects of breast-feeding on their bodies are likely to meet with frustration. . . .

Advice to mothers typically mentions a few ostensible health benefits, but also instructs that youthful, slim bodies are culturally required. One popular manual features under the bold subtitle 'Good for Your Figure' that breast-feeding speeds the contraction of the uterus back to prepregnancy size (something never achieved fully by bottle-feeding mothers) and burns extra calories so that mothers can enjoy gradual weight loss without dieting (Eiger and Olds, 1987: 29). Dr Spock devotes most of his discussion of maternal health to 'the mother's figure'. . .

Many women, in my experience, want to know if breast-feeding helps prevent breast cancer, an important question, as the disease now touches one of eight women (Love, 1995). Unfortunately, there has been less research than we would like and little conclusive evidence (Love, 1995: 37). This may be because women's health research has been a low funding priority (though recent political activism had helped to change this), or because breast-feeding is seen as a mother's duty to her child rather than something she should pursue in self-interest . . .

At Last, the Disembodied Mother

Although combining wage-earning with mothering and breast-feeding was a concern early in the century, the question loomed large again in the 1980s and 1990s as the majority of mothers, even mothers of infants, even middle-class mothers, began returning to the workplace. . .

Many in the medical community express concern that the modern workplace is hardly 'baby-friendly' (NPR, 1992a; AAP, 1997); however, they use their authority to recommend little in the way of workplace or public policy reforms. Instead, the medical profession solves the wage-earning/breast-feeding dilemma by glibly advising mothers to use breast pumps.[10] An employed mother, in other words, can feed her baby at the breast at home, but she should collect her milk and keep up her supply by using a pump (or expressing milk by hand) during worktime. In fact, the AAP's recent statement prioritizing longer breast-feeding mentions only the need for employers to provide space and time for breast-pumping (1997: 1037). . . .

Popular advice is now pervaded by the medical model and its reliance on the breast pump at work. Authors and experts proclaim 'it's easy' (Pars, 1993) or even that it's a 'modern woman's dream' (Foreman, 1998). . . . Mothers are urged to practise pumping during their maternity leave; to bring pictures and baby clothes, even play soft music and sip wine, to stimulate let-down at work; all during their 'uninterrupted' 30-minute breaks, even if they must use the 'ladies' lounge' (Mauk, 1984). Other heroic suggestions are to nurse frequently through the night to keep up the milk supply and satisfy the baby (e.g., Barr, 1900; Meda Johnson, 1990: 8), to pump on airplanes while on business trips (cabin pressure makes it 'easy') (Katz, 1980), or even, when your schedule gets hectic, to pump while stuck in traffic (Paterno, 1992; also Slade, 1997).

The ads and advice tend to skirt the issue of the workplace environment itself. Although some acknowledge that limited maternity leaves and inhospitable workplaces make breast-feeding seem 'unmanageable', good mothers know that 'with careful planning' these apparent barriers can be overcome (Mauk, 1984). . . .

Instead, expert advice along the medical model presents a new Supermom. In the popularized feminist rhetoric of 'juggling multiple roles', she chooses to meet her baby's needs and keep her 'freedom'; she can 'balance' work and breast-feeding (e.g., Mason and Ingersoll, 1986: 94–5). She can pump in a parking lot, a supply closet, a bathroom stall, or on the freeway. Although compromising the century-long emphasis on exclusive mothering as the mother's full-time physical presence, this breast-feeding Supermom testifies: 'I have a lot less guilt leaving this baby *that I'm nursing* than I did leaving my other baby, who was bottle-fed' (Ross Labs, 1984: 13, my emphasis). This Supermom, of course, also keeps herself attractive and slim: she won't fill up on 'empty calories' (Ross Labs, 1984: 11), and perhaps breast-feeding is part of her 'postpartum weight-loss plan' (*Parents*, 1992). . . .

Even from this rather limited history, we see that 'breast-feeding', like 'children's needs', has been and can be organized in varied ways, with differing compatibilities and incompatibilities with mothers' waged-work, as well as with dominant discourses of sexuality. . . .

Notes

1. This section draws heavily from historian Janet Golden (1996).
2. According to historian Valerie Fildes, the proscription against sexual activity was stronger in Catholic than in Protestant countries, leading to larger, more institutionalized systems of wet-nursing (1986: 105, 121, 152–67; on husbands' claims and beauty ideals, see Yalom, 1997: 107, 105).
3. Maternal breast-feeding and 'natural' childrearing became a part of democratic ideals by the mid-eighteenth century. The importance of virtuous mothers for the raising of democratic citizens was promulgated by Rousseau in his popular novel *Emile* (1762) (although it was later revealed that he was raised by a wet-nurse and abandoned his five children to a founding hospital), and by physician William Cadogan in the widely read *An Essay Upon Nursing, and the Management of Children from Their Birth to Three Years of Age* (1748) (Golden, 1996: 13–15; also Carter, 1995: 35–6, 40; Yalom, 1997: 105–23).
4. Infant mortality rates were much higher for non-whites than whites, but all mothers shared the fear of death. In 1915, 99 white babies per every 1000 live births died in their first year; but fully 181 out of 1000 non-white babies died. Stated differently, about 10 per cent of white babies and nearly 20 per cent of babies of colour died (Ladd-Taylor, 1994: 18–19, 35, n.5).

   At the same time, large numbers of young men failed their army physicals, and this was attributed to race and ethnicity rather than poverty (Ladd-Taylor, 1994: 89; Mink, 1995: 58).

5. Ladd-Taylor cites a number of studies showing, for example, that in Philadelphia 44 per cent of black mothers and 19 per cent of white mothers went out to work, and that, in another city, some 67 per cent of Italian immigrant mothers with infants took in boarders (1994: 29–30).

6. Furthermore, physicians' overall confidence in artificial feeding grew. By the 1920s, studies began to show that medically supervised infant-feeding, whether by breast or bottle, had comparable results, with hygiene and medical care the most decisive factors in infants' health. (Of course, this begged the question of who could obtain medical care and decent hygienic conditions.) With 'discoveries' that breastmilk seemed to lack vitamins C and D (begging the question of the mothers' nutritional status), physicians became even quicker to recommend artificial feeding and supplements to breastmilk in the 1930s, and artificial feeding came to appear as good or better—and more reliable than—human milk.

7. This work, begun by Anna Freud, complemented her father's theory of the 'normal', mature woman's fulfillment in motherhood (she desires babies to compensate for the lack of a penis), and of the baby's primary love for the mother; but it extends this to stress the child's need for her full-time, exclusive love, and it de-emphasizes Freud's focus on later Oedipal conflicts with the father. The significant work of Melaine Klein also fits in this tradition, focusing on the pre-Oedipal mother–baby relationship (see Chodorow, 1978, 1994).

8. Another typical advice article, aptly entitled 'Why Women May Fail in Breast-feeding', listed both the fear that the breasts will become pendulous and the inconvenience of needing so much privacy (*Good Housekeeping*, 1963: 140).

9. In the 1990s, the figure was higher and was estimated to reach $4 billion per year (Palmer, 1988: 6). By the 1960s, the US market was dominated by two corporations: Bristol-Meyers (makers of Enfamil), and Abbot Laboratories (owners of Ross Labs' Similac and Isomil) (Miller, 1983: 4). Carnation, which has a small market share in the United States, is owned by Nestle.

10. The formula companies that distribute educational pamphlets are also happy to sell you breast pumps: 'the Ross/Faultless Deluxe Breast Pump System is widely recommended' (Ross Labs, 1985: 7). And of course, 'If you find that you can't express enough breast milk to feed your baby', they are happy to sell you their formula products (Mead Johnson, 1990: 23). 'Breast milk is the best milk for feeding throughout the first year of life. The next best choice is infant formula, such as Similac' (Ross Labs, 1987: 26).

References

AAP. 1984. American Academy of Pediatrics, Report of the Task Force on the Assessment of the Scientific Evidence Relating to Infant-Feeding Practices and Infant Health. Supplement to *Pediatrics* 74.

———. 1997. Amercian Academy of Pediatrics, Work Group on Breastfeeding. 'Breast-feeding and the Use of Human Milk', *Pediatrics* 100: 1035–9.

Barr, Amy Biber. 1990. 'Breast-feeding Can Work for Working Mothers', *Working Mother* July: 62–6.

Carter, Pam. 1995. *Feminism, Breasts and Breast-feeding*. New York: St. Martin's Press.

Chodorow, Nancy. 1978. *The Reproduction of Mothering*. Berkeley: University of California Press.

———. 1994. *Femininities, Masculinities, Sexualities*. Lexington, KY: University of Kentucky Press.

Clark, M. 1978. 'Back to the Breast', *Newsweek* 6 November: 92.

deMauro, Lisa. 1991. 'Beating the Bottle', *New York Times* 21 September: A13.

Eiger, Marvin S., and Sally Wendkos Olds. [1972] 1987. *The Complete Book of Breastfeeding*. New York: Workman.

Eyer, Diane E. 1992. *Mother-Infant Bonding: A Scientific Fiction*. New Haven: Yale University Press.

Fildes, Valerie. 1986. *Breasts, Bottles, and Babies: A History of Infant Feeding*. Edinburgh: Edinburgh University Press.

Foreman, Judy. 1998. 'Space for Working Mothers: Health Sense', *Boston Globe* 5 January: C1.

Glick, Daniel. 1997. 'Rooting for Intelligence,' *Newsweek* special issue Spring/Summer: 32.

Golden, Janet. 1996. *A Social History of Wet Nursing in America: From Breast to Bottle.* Cambridge: Cambridge University Press.

Good Housekeeping. 1963. 'Why Women Fail in Breastfeeding'. August: 140.

Hendershot, Gerry E. 1984. 'Domestic Review: Trends in Breast-feeding', *Pediatrics* 74: 591–602.

Horwood, L. John, and David M. Fergusson. 1998. 'Breast-feeding and Later Cognitive and Academic Outcomes', *Pediatrics* 101, 1: E91–E97.

Katz, S. 1980. 'Yes, You Can Keep on Nursing Your Child After You Go to Work', *Glamour* November: 170.

Ladd-Taylor, Molly. 1994. *Mother-Work: Women, Child Welfare, and the State, 1890–1930.* Urbana: University of Illinois Press.

Lawrence, Ruth A. 1988. 'Major Influences in Promoting Breast-feeding: US Perspectives', in D.B. Jelliffe and E.F.P. Jelliffe, eds, *Programmes to Promote Breastfeeding.* Oxford: Oxford University Press.

Love, Susan M., with Karen Lindsey. 1995. *Dr. Susan Love's Breast Book.* Reading, MA: Addison-Wesley.

Marano, H. 1979. 'Breast or Bottle: New Evidence in an Old Debate', *New York* 29 October: 56–60.

Mason, Diane, and Diane Ingersoll. 1986. *Breastfeeding and the Working Mother.* New York: St. Martin's.

Mauk, S. 1984. 'Breast-feeding and Work', *Working Woman* April: 43–4.

Mead Johnson. [1990] 1986. *The Breastfeeding Guide for Working Mothers.* Evansville, IN.

Miller, Fred D., Jr. 1983. *Out of the Mouths of Babes: The Infant Formula Controversy.* Bowling Green, OH: Social Philosophy and Policy Centre, Bowling Green State University.

Mink, Gwendolyn. 1995. *The Wages of Motherhood: Inequality in the Welfare State, 1917–1942.* Ithaca, NY: Cornell University Press.

NPR (National Public Radio). 1992a. Interview with James Grant, Executive Director of the United Nations Children's Fund. *Morning Edition* 9 March.

———. 1992b. Report on silicone breast implants. *Morning Edition.* 17 April.

New York Times. 1998. 'Breast-Feeding is Tied to Brain Power'. 6 January: C-4.

Palmer, Gabrielle. 1988. *The Politics of Breastfeeding.* London: Pandora Press.

Parents. 1992. 'Breast-feeding and Weight Loss'. February: 126.

Parks, P. L. 1993. 'How to Breast-feed—and Work'. *Essence* February: 110.

Paterno, Susan. 1992. 'Nursing at Work: Secrets for Breast-feeding Away from Home, Express Yourself', *Parenting* February: 43.

Ross Labs. 1984. *The Best of Both Worlds: A Guide for the Working, Breast-feeding Mother.* Columbus, OH: Division of Abbott Laboratories.

———. 1985. *Supplemental Feeding: What Breastfeeding Mothers Ask.* Columbus, OH: Division of Abbott Laboratories.

———. 1987. *Breastfeeding: Feeding Your Baby 'The Natural Way'.* Columbus, OH: Division of Abbott Laboratories.

Shapiro, Laura. 1997. 'Beyond an Apple a Day', *Newsweek* Special Issue. Spring/Summer: 52–6.

Slade, Margot. 1997. 'Have Pump, Will Travel: Combining Breast-feeding and a Career', *New York Times* December 27: BU-12.

Spock, Benjamin. [1957] 1985. *Baby and Child Care.* New York: Pocket Books.

Treckel, Paula A. 1989. 'Breast-feeding and Maternal Sexuality in Colonial America', *Journal of Interdisciplinary History* 20: 25–51.

Yalom, Marilyn. 1997. *A History of the Breast.* New York: Knopf.

Young, Iris Marion. 1990. *Throwing Like a Girl and Other Essays in Feminist Philosophy and Social Theory.* Bloomington, IN: Indiana University Press.

Chapter 14

Anorexia Nervosa: Psychopathology as the Crystallization of Culture

Susan Bordo

. . . Psychopathology, as Jules Henry has said, 'is the final outcome of all that is wrong with a culture'.[1] In no case is this more strikingly true than in the case of anorexia nervosa and bulimia, barely known a century ago yet reaching epidemic proportions today. Far from being the result of a superficial fashion phenomenon, these disorders reflect and call our attention to some of the central ills of our culture—from our historical heritage of disdain for the body, to our modern fear of loss of control over our futures, to the disquieting meaning of contemporary beauty ideals in an era of female presence and power. . . .

What we need to ask is *why* our culture is so obsessed with keeping our bodies slim, tight, and young that when 500 people were asked in a recent poll what they feared most in the world, 190 replied 'getting fat'.[2] So, too, do we need to explore the fact that it is women who are most oppressed by what Kim Chernin calls 'the tyranny of slenderness',[3] and that this particular oppression is a post-1960s, post-feminist phenomenon. . . .

The Dualist Axis

I will begin with . . . our dualistic heritage: the view that human existence is bifurcated into two realms or substances—the bodily or material on the one hand, and the mental or spiritual on the other. . . .

Dualism here appears as the offspring, the by-product, of the identification of the self with control, an identification that Watts sees as lying at the centre of Christianity's ethic of antisexuality. The attempt to subdue the spontaneities of the body in the interests of control only succeeds in constituting them as more alien, and more powerful, and thus more needful of control. The only way to win this no-win game is to go beyond control, is to kill off the body's spontaneities entirely. That is: to cease to *experience* our hungers and desires.

This is what many anorexics describe as their ultimate goal. '[I want] to reach the point', as one put it, 'when I don't need to eat at all' (*ED*, 84). Kim Chernin recalls her surprise when, after fasting, her hunger returned: 'I realized [then] that my secret goal in dieting must have been the intention to kill off my appetite completely' (*TS*, 8). . . .

While the body is experienced as alien and outside, the soul or will is described as being trapped or confined in an alien 'jail', as one woman puts it.[4] A typical fantasy, as it is for Plato, is of total liberation from the bodily prison: 'I wish I could get out of my body entirely and fly!'[5] 'Please dear God, help me . . . I want to get out of my body, I want to get out!'[6] . . .

In this battle, thinness represents a triumph of the will over the body, and the thin body (that is, the nonbody) is associated with 'absolute purity, hyperintellectuality, and transcendence of the flesh. My soul seemed to grow as my body waned; I felt like one of those early Christian saints who starved themselves in the desert sun. I felt invulnerable, clean, and hard as the bones etched into my silhouette.'[7] Fat (i.e., becoming *all* body) is associated with the 'taint' of matter and flesh, 'wantonness' (*Solitaire*, 109), mental stupor, and mental decay.[8] One woman describes how after eating sugar she felt 'polluted, disgusting, sticky through the arms, as if something bad had gotten inside'.[9] Very often, sexuality is brought into this scheme of associations, and hunger and sexuality are psychically connected. . . .

. . . Sexuality, similarly, is 'an abominable business' to Aimée Liu; for her, staying reed-thin is seen as a way of avoiding sexuality, by becoming 'androgynous', as she puts it (*Solitaire*, 101). In the same way, Sarah, a patient of Levenkron's, connects her dread of gaining weight with 'not wanting to be a "temptation" to men' (*TO*, 122). In Aimée Liu's case, and in Sarah's, the desire to appear unattractive to men is connected to anxiety and guilt over earlier sexual abuse. Whether or not such episodes are common to many cases of anorexia,[10] 'the avoidance of any sexual encounter, a shrinking from all bodily contact', according to Bruch, is characteristic.[11]

The Control Axis

. . . Looking now at contemporary American life, a second axis of continuity emerges on which to locate anorexia. I will call it the *control axis*.

The anorexic, typically, experiences her life as well as her hungers as being out of control. She is torn by conflicting and contradictory expectations and demands, wanting to shine in all areas of student life, confused about where to place most of her energies, what to focus on, as she develops into an adult. Characteristically, her parents expect a great deal of her in the way of individual achievement (as well as physical appearance, particularly her father), yet have made most important decisions for her (*GC*, 33). Usually, the anorexic syndrome emerges, *not* as a conscious decision to get as thin as possible, but as the result of her having begun a diet fairly casually, often at the suggestion of a parent, having succeeded splendidly in taking off five or 10 pounds, and then having gotten *hooked* on the intoxicating feeling of accomplishment and control. . . .

The frustrations of starvation, the rigors of the constant exercise and physical activity in which anorexics engage, and the pain of the numerous physical complications of anorexia do not trouble the anorexic; indeed, her ability to ignore them is further proof to her of her mastery of her body. . . .

Surely we must recognize in this . . . a central modus operandi for the control of contemporary bourgeois anxiety. Consider compulsive jogging and marathon running, often despite shin-splints and other painful injuries, with intense agitation over missed days or not meeting goals for particular runs. Consider the increasing popularity of triathlon events like the 'Iron Man', which appear to have no other purpose than to allow people to find out how far they can push their bodies before collapsing. . . .

None of this is to dispute that the contemporary concern with fitness has nonpathological, nondualist dimensions as well. Particularly for women, . . . the cultivation of strength, agility, and confidence has a clearly positive dimension. Nor are the objective benefits of daily exercise and concern for nutrition in question here. My focus, rather, is on a subjective stance, increasingly more prominent over the last five years, which, although preoccupied with the body and deriving narcissistic enjoyment from its appearance, takes little pleasure in the *experience* of embodiment. Rather, the fundamental identification is with the mind (or will), ideals of spiritual perfection, fantasies of absolute control. . . .

. . . 'Nowadays', says Michael Sacks, associate professor of psychiatry at Cornell Medical College, 'people no longer feel they can control events outside themselves—how well they do in their jobs or in their personal relationships, for example—but they can control the food they eat and how far they can run. Abstinence, tests of endurance, are ways of proving their self-sufficiency.'[12] . . .

Our contemporary body fetishism, however, expresses more than a fantasy of self-mastery in an increasingly unmanageable culture. It also reflects our alliance *with* culture against all reminders of the inevitable decay and death of the body. . . . And it is striking that although the anorexic may come very close to death (and 15 per cent do indeed die), the dominant experience throughout the illness is of *invulnerability*. . . .

Finally, it may be that in cultures characterized by gross excesses in consumption, the 'will to conquer and subdue the body' (as Chernin calls it—*TS,* 47) expresses an aesthetic or moral rebellion. Anorexics initially came from affluent families, and the current craze for long-distance running and fasting is largely a phenomenon of young, upwardly mobile professional[s] (Dinitia Smith calls it 'Deprivation Chic'). . . .

The Gender/Power Axis

Ninety per cent of all anorexics are women. We do not need, of course, to know that particular statistic to realize that the contemporary 'tyranny of slenderness' is far from gender neutral. Women are more obsessed with their bodies than men, less satisfied with them,[13] and permitted less latitude with them by themselves, by men, and by the culture. In a recent *Glamour* poll of 33,000 women, 75 per cent said that they were 'too fat'. Yet by Metropolitan Life Insurance tables—themselves notoriously affected by cultural standards—only 25 per cent of these women were heavier than the specified standards, and a full 30 per cent were *below*.[14] The anorexic's distorted image of her body—her inability to see it as anything but 'too fat'—while more extreme, is not radically discontinuous from fairly common female misperceptions. . . .

. . . Over and over, extremely slender women students complain of hating their thighs or their stomachs (the anorexic's most dreaded danger spot); often, they express concern and anger over frequent teasing by their boyfriends: Janey, a former student, is 5'10" and weighs 132 pounds. Yet her boyfriend calls her 'Fatso' and 'Big Butt' and insists she should be 110 pounds. . . . He calls this 'constructive criticism', and seems to experience extreme anxiety over the possibility of her gaining any weight . . .

What is the meaning of these gender associations in the anorexic? I propose that there are two levels of meaning. One has to do with fear and disdain for traditional female *roles* and social limitations. The other has to do more profoundly with a deep fear of 'The Female', with all its more nightmarish archetypal associations: voracious hungers and sexual insatiability. Let us examine each of these levels in turn.

Adolescent anorexics express characteristic fears about growing up to be mature, sexually developed, potentially reproductive women. 'I have a deep fear', says one, 'of having a womanly body, round and fully developed. I want to be tight and muscular and thin.'[15] If only she could stay thin, says another, 'I would never have to deal with having a woman's body; like Peter Pan I could stay a child forever.'[16] The choice of Peter Pan is telling here—what she means is, stay a *boy* forever. And indeed, as Bruch reports, many anorexics, when children, dreamt and fantasized about growing up to be boys.[17] Some are quite conscious of playing out this fantasy through their anorexia: Adrienne, one of Levenkron's patients, was extremely proud of the growth of facial and body hair that often accompanies anorexia, and especially proud of her 'skinny, hairy arms' (*TO,* 82). . . .

In a characteristic scenario, anorexia will develop just at the beginning of puberty. Normal body changes are experienced by the anorexic, not surprisingly, as the takeover of the body by disgusting, womanish fat. 'I grab my breasts', says Aimée Liu, 'pinching them until they hurt. If only I could eliminate them, cut them off if need be, to become as flat-chested as a child again' (*Solitaire,* 79). She is exultant when her periods stop (as they do in *all* cases of anorexia) (*GG,* 65). The disgust with menstruation is typical . . .

Many anorexics appear to experience anxiety over falling into the lifestyle they associate with their mothers. It is a prominent theme in Aimée Liu's *Solitaire.* One woman describes her feeling that she is 'full of my mother . . . she is in me even if she isn't there' in nearly the same breath as she complains of her continuous fear of being 'not human . . . of ceasing to exist' (*GG,* 12). . . .

. . . It is indeed essential to recognize in this illness a dimension of protest against the limitations of the ideal of female domesticity . . .

But we must recognize that the anorexic's 'protest', . . . written on the bodies of anorexic women, and *not* embraced as a conscious politics, nor, indeed, does it reflect any social or political understanding at all. Moreover, the symptoms themselves function to preclude the emergence of such an understanding: the *idée fixe*—staying thin—becomes at its farthest extreme so powerful as to render any other ideas or life projects meaningless. Liu describes it as 'all-encompassing' (*Solitaire*, 141). West writes that 'I felt all inner development was ceasing, that all becoming and growing were being choked, because a single idea was filling my entire soul' (*EW*, 257).

Paradoxically—and often tragically—these pathologies of female 'protest' (and we must include agoraphobia here, as well as hysteria, and anorexia)[18] actually function as if in collusion with the cultural conditions that produced them. The same is true for more moderate expressions of the contemporary female obsession with slenderness. Women may feel themselves deeply attracted by the aura of freedom and independence suggested by the boyish body ideal of today. Yet, each hour, each minute that is spent in anxious pursuit of that ideal (for it does not come 'naturally' to most mature women) is *in fact* time and energy diverted from inner development and social achievement. . . .

It is important to recognize, too, that the anorexic is terrified and repelled, not only by the traditional female domestic role—which she associates with mental lassitude and weakness—but by a certain archetypal image of the female: as hungering, voracious, all-needing, and all-wanting. It is this image that shapes and permeates her experience of her own hunger for food as insatiable and out-of-control, which makes her feel

that if she takes just one bite, she won't be able to stop.

Let's explore this image. Let's break the tie with food and look at the metaphor: Hungering. Voracious. Extravagantly and excessively needful. Without restraint. Always wanting. Always wanting too much affection, reassurance, emotional and sexual contact, and attention. This is how many women frequently experience themselves, and, indeed, how many men experience women. . . .

Anxiety over women's uncontrollable hungers appears to peak, as well, during periods when women are becoming independent and asserting themselves politically and socially. The second half of the nineteenth century saw a virtual 'flood' (as Peter Gay calls it) of artistic and literary images of the dark, dangerous, and evil female . . . 'No century', claims Gay, 'depicted woman as vampire, as castrator, as killer, so consistently, so programmatically, and so nakedly as the nineteeth.'[19] No century, too, was as obsessed with female sexuality, and its medical control. Treatment for excessive 'sexual excitement' and masturbation included placing leeches on the womb (*TS*, 38), clitoridectomy, and removing of the ovaries (also recommended for 'troublesomeness, eating like a ploughman, erotic tendencies, persecution mania, and simple "cussedness"').[20]

It is in the second half of the nineteenth century, too, despite a flurry of efforts by feminists and health reformers, that the stylized 'S-curve', which required a tighter corset than ever before, comes into fashion.[21] . . .

On the gender/power axis the female body appears, then, as the unknowing medium of the historical ebbs and flows of the fear of woman-as-too-much. . . .

Notes

1. Jules Henry, *Culture Against Man* (New York: Knopf, 1963).

2. Kim Chernin, *The Obsession: Reflections on the Tyranny of Slenderness* (New York: Harper and Row, 1981), 36–7 (cited parenthetically in the text

as *TS*). My use of the term 'our culture' may seem overly homogenizing here, disrespectful of differences among ethnic groups, socio-economic groups, subcultures within American society, etc. It must be stressed here that I am discussing ideology and images whose power is precisely the power to homogenize culture. Even in pre-mass media cultures, we see this phenomenon: the fifteenth-century ideal of the 'perfect lady' tyrannized even those classes who couldn't afford to realize it. With television, of course, a massive deployment of images becomes possible, and there is no escape from the mass shaping of our fantasy lives. Although they may start among the wealthy and elite ('A woman can never be too rich or too thin'), media-promoted ideals of femininity and masculinity quickly and perniciously 'trickle down' to everyone who owns a TV or can afford a junk magazine or is aware of billboards. Recent changes in the incidence of anorexia among lower-income groups (see note 11) bear this out.

3. Until very recently, this dimension was largely ignored or underemphasized, with a very few notable exceptions. Kim Chernin and Susie Ohrbach (*Fat is a Feminist Issue*) were ground-breakers in exploring the connections between eating disorders and images and ideals of femininity. Robert Seidenberg and Karen DeCrow (*Women Who Marry Houses: Panic and Protest in Agoraphobia*) provide a very brief, interesting discussion, the value of which is marred, however, by some fundamental errors concerning the typical pattern of the disorder. Hilde Bruch touches these issues, but only barely, in her otherwise excellent work on eating disorders. Lately, however, there has been a veritable explosion of creative work, both theoretical and therapeutic, confronting the connections between eating disorders and the situation of women. Shortly after this paper was completed, I attended the Third Annual Conference of the Center for the Study of Anorexia and Bulimia (New York, 17–18 November 1984), which was devoted entirely to the theme of 'The Psychology of Women and the Psychotherapy of Eating Disorders'. Institutes such as The Women's Therapy Institute in New York have developed techniques of treatment that are specifically grounded in a feminist reconstruction of object-relations theory (see Luise Eichenbaum and Susie Ohrbach, *Understanding Women: A Feminist Psychoanalytic Approach* [New York: Basic Books, 1983]). And new perspectives are emerging all the time, from

ideological quarters as diverse as experimental psychology and Jungian analysis (see, for example, Angelyn Spignesi, *Starving Women* [Dallas, TX: Spring Publications, 1983]).

4. Entry in student journal, 1984.

5. Aimée Liu, *Solitaire* (New York: Harper and Row, 1979), 141 (cited parenthetically in the text as *Solitaire*).

6. Jennifer Woods, 'I Was Starving Myself to Death', *Mademoiselle*, May 1981: 200.

7. Ibid., 242.

8. 'I equated gaining weight with happiness, contentment, then slothfulness, then atrophy, then death.' (From case notes of Binnie Klein, MSW, to whom I am grateful for having provided parts of a transcript of her work with an anorexic patient.) See also Binswanger, 'The Case of Ellen West', 343.

9. Binnie Klein, case notes.

10. A Minnesota study of high-school students determined that one in every 10 anorexics was a victim of sexual abuse. Comments by and informal discussion with therapists at the Third Annual Conference for the Study of Anorexia and Bulimia bear these findings out; therapist after therapist remarked on the high incidence of early sexual violence and incest in anorexic patients.

11. Hilde Bruch, *The Golden Cage: The Enigma of Anorexia Nervosa* (New York: Vintage, 1979), 73. The same is not true of bulimic anorexics, who tend to be sexually active (Paul Garfinkel and David Garner, *Anorexia Nervosa: A Multidimensional Perspective* [New York: Brunner/Mazel, 1982], 41). Bulimic anorexics, as seems symbolized by the binge/purge cycle itself, stand in a somewhat more ambivalent relationship to their hungers than do abstinent anorexics.

12. Dinita Smith, 'The New Puritans', *New York* 11 June 1984: 29.

13. Sidney Journard and Paul Secord, 'Body Cathexis and the Female Figure', *Journal of Abnormal and Social Psychology* 50: 243–6; Orland Wooley, Susan Wooley, and Sue Dyrenforth, 'Obesity and Women—A Neglected Feminist Topic', *Women's Studies Institute Quarterly* 2 (1979): 81–92. Student journals and informal conversations with women students certainly have borne this out. See also Garfinkel and Garner, *Anorexia Nervosa*, 110–15.

14. 'Feeling Fat in a Thin Society', *Glamour*, February 1984: 198.
15. Entry in student journal, 1983.
16. Ibid.
17. Bruch, *The Golden Cage*, 72; Bruch, *Eating Disorders*, 277. Others have fantasies of androgyny: 'I want to go to a party and for everyone to look at me and for no one to know whether I was the most beautiful slender woman or handsome young man' (as reported by therapist April Benson, panel discussion, 'New Perspectives on Female Development', Third Annual Conference of the Center for the Study of Anorexia and Bulimia, New York, 1984).
18. On the protest dimension in anorexia, see Chernin, *The Obsession*, 102–3; Robert Seidenberg and Karen DeCrow, *Women Who Marry Houses: Panic and Protest in Agoraphobia*, 88–97; Bruch, *The Golden Cage*, 58; Ohrbach, *Hunger Strike*, 97–115. For an examination of the connections between hysteria, agoraphobia, and anorexia, see Susan Bordo, 'The Body and the Reproduction of Femininity', in Alison Jaggar and Susan Bordo, eds, *Gender/Body/Knowledge: Feminist Reconstruction of Being and Knowing* (New Brunswick, NJ: Rutgers University Press, 1988).
19. Peter Gay, *The Bourgeois Experience, Vol. 1, Education of the Senses* (New York: Oxford University Press, 1984), 197–201, 207.
20. Barbara Ehrenreich and Deirdre English, *For Her Own Good* (Garden City, NJ: Doubleday, 1979), 124.
21. Lois Banner, *American Beauty* (Chicago, University of Chicago Press, 1983), 86–105, 149–50. It is significant that these efforts failed, in large part, because of their association with the woman's rights movement. Trousers, such as those proposed by Amelia Bloomer, were considered a particular badge of depravity and aggressiveness, the *New York Herald* predicting that bloomer women would end up in 'lunatic asylums or perchance in the state prison (96).

Chapter 15

Men's Bodies

Raewyn Connell

True Masculinity

. . . Mass culture generally assumes there is a fixed, true masculinity beneath the ebb and flow of daily life. We hear of 'real men', 'natural man', the 'deep masculine'. . . .

True masculinity is almost always thought to proceed from men's bodies—to be inherent in a male body or to express something about a male body. Either the body drives and directs action (e.g., men are naturally more aggressive than women; rape results from uncontrollable lust or an innate urge to violence), or the body sets limits to action (e.g., men naturally do not take care of infants; homosexuality is unnatural and therefore confined to a perverse minority).

These beliefs are a strategic part of modern gender ideology, in the English-speaking world at least. . . .

Two opposing conceptions of the body have dominated discussion of this issue in recent decades. In one, which basically translates the dominant ideology into the language of biological science, the body is a natural machine that produces gender difference—through genetic programming, hormonal difference, or the different role of the sexes in reproduction. In the other approach, which has swept the humanities and social sciences, the body is a more or less neutral surface or landscape on which a social symbolism is imprinted. Reading these arguments as a new version of the old 'nature vs. nurture' controversy, other voices have proposed a common-sense compromise: both biology and social influence combine to produce gender differences in behaviour.

. . . I . . . argue that all three views are mistaken. We can arrive at a better understanding of the relation between men's bodies and masculinity. . . .

Machine, Landscape, and Compromise

Since religion's capacity to justify gender ideology collapsed, biology has been called in to fill the gap. The need may be gauged from the enormous appetite of the conservative mass media for stories of scientific discoveries about supposed sex differences. . . .

Speculation about masculinity and femininity is a mainstay of sociobiology, the revived attempt at an evolutionary explanation of human society that became fashionable in the 1970s. . . .

According to these theorists, men's bodies are the bearers of a natural masculinity produced by the evolutionary pressures that have borne down upon the human stock. We inherit with our masculine genes tendencies to aggression, family life, competitiveness, political power, hierarchy, territoriality, promiscuity, and forming men's clubs. The list varies somewhat from theorist to theorist, but the flavour remains the same. . . .

The account of natural masculinity that has been built up in sociobiology is almost entirely fictional. It presupposes broad differences in the character traits and behaviours of women and men. . . . [A] great deal of research has now been done on this issue. The usual finding, on intellect, temperament, and other personal traits, is that there are no measurable differences at all. Where differences appear, they are small compared to variation within either sex, and very small compared to differences in the social positioning of women and men. . . . And the evidence of cross-cultural and historical diversity in gender is overwhelming. For instance, there are cultures and historical situations where rape is absent, or extremely rare; where homosexual behaviour is majority practice (at a given point in the life-cycle); where mothers do not predominate in child care (e.g., this work is done by old people, other children, or servants); and where men are not normally aggressive.

The power of biological determination is not in its appeal to evidence. Careful examinations of the evidence . . . show that nothing like one-way determination of the social by the biological can be sustained; the situation is far more complex. . . .

Rather, the power of this perspective lies in its *metaphor* of the body as machine. The body 'functions' and 'operates'. Researchers discover biological 'mechanisms' in behaviour. Brains are 'hardwired' to produce masculinity; men are genetically 'programmed' for dominance; aggression is in our 'biogram'. Both academic and journalistic texts are rich in these metaphors. . . .

When a metaphor becomes established it pre-empts discussion and shapes the way evidence is read. This has certainly happened with the metaphor of biological mechanism, and it affects even careful and well-documented research (which most sociobiology is not). A good example is a widely discussed study by Julianne Imperato-McGinley and others. A rare enzyme deficiency, of which 18 cases were found in two villages in the Dominican Republic, led to genetic-male infants having genitals that looked female, so they were raised as girls. . . . But in the Dominican Republic cases, the situation changed at puberty. At this point, normal testosterone levels masculinized the adolescents physically. The authors reported that 17 of the 18 then shifted to a male 'gender identity' and 16 to a male 'gender role'. The researchers saw this as proof that phys-

iological mechanisms could override social conditioning.[1]

Closely examined, the paper shows something very different. McGinley and her colleagues describe a village society with a strong gender division of labour and a marked cultural opposition between masculine and feminine—both of which are social facts. The authors trace a gradual recognition by the children and their parents that a social error had been made; the children had been wrongly assigned. This error was socially corrected. The bodily changes of puberty clearly triggered a powerful *social* process of re-evaluation and reassignment. What the study refutes is not a social account of gender, but the particular thesis that core gender identity formed in early childhood always pre-empts later social development.

The Dominican Republic study inadvertently shows something more. The authors observe that, since the medical researchers arrived in the community, 5-alpha-reductase deficiency is now identified at birth, and the children are mostly raised as boys. Medicine thus has stepped in to normalize gender: to make sure that adult men will have masculine childhoods, and a consistent gender dichotomy will be preserved. . . . The medical practice pulls bodies into line with a social ideology of dichotomous gender. . . .

These practices can be institutionally elaborated on a very large scale. This is demonstrated, and connected to the production of gender, in recent work on the sociology of sport. Nancy Theberge's 'Reflections on the Body in the Sociology of Sport' convincingly shows how the different regimes of exercise for women and men, the disciplinary practices that both teach and constitute sport, are designed to produce gendered bodies. And if social discipline cannot produce adequately gendered bodies, surgery can. Cosmetic surgery now offers the affluent an extraordinary range of ways of producing a more socially desirable body, from the old 'facelifts' and breast implants to the newer surgical slimming, height alterations, and so on. . . .

Social constructionist approaches to gender and sexuality underpinned by a semiotic approach to the body provide an almost complete antithesis to sociobiology. Rather than social arrangements being the effects of the body-machine, the body is a field on which social determination runs riot. This approach too has its leading metaphors, which tend to be metaphors of art rather than engineering: the body is a canvas to be painted, a surface to be imprinted, a landscape to be marked out.

This approach also—though it has been wonderfully productive—runs into difficulty. . . .

The problem is particularly striking for that unavoidable bodily activity, sex. . . . Gender is hardly in better case, when it becomes just a subject-position in discourse, the place from which one speaks; when gender is seen as, above all, a performance; or when the rending contradictions within gendered lives become 'an instatement of metaphor'. . . .

Bodies, in their own right as bodies, do matter. They age, get sick, enjoy, engender, give birth. There is an irreducible bodily dimension in experience and practice; the sweat cannot be excluded. On this point we can learn even from the sex role literature. One of the few compelling things the male role literature and Books About Men did was to catalogue Problems with Male Bodies, from impotence and aging to occupational health hazards, violent injury, loss of sporting prowess, and early death. Warning: the male sex role may be dangerous to your health.[2]

Can we, then, settle for a common-sense compromise, asserting both biology and culture in a composite model of gender? This is, essentially, the formula of sex role theory, which . . . adds a social script to a biological dichotomy. Moderate statements of sociobiology often acknowledge a cultural elaboration of the biological imperative. A similar position was argued in the 1980s by Alice Rossi, who had been one of the feminist pioneers in sociology:

> Gender differentiation is not simply a function of socialization, capitalist production, or patriarchy. It is grounded in a sex dimorphism that serves the fundamental purpose of reproducing the species.[3]

Masculinity, it would follow, is the social elaboration of the biological function of fatherhood.

If biological determinism is wrong, and social determinism is wrong, then it is unlikely that a combination of the two will be right. . . .

. . . Yet we cannot ignore either the radically cultural character of gender or the bodily presence. It seems that we need other ways of thinking about the matter.

The Body Inescapable

A rethinking may start by acknowledging that, in our culture at least, the physical sense of maleness and femaleness is central to the cultural interpretation of gender. Masculine gender is (among other things) a certain feel to the skin, certain muscular shapes and tensions, certain postures and ways of moving, certain possibilities in sex. Bodily experience is often central in memories of our own lives, and thus in our understanding of who and what we are. . . .

***

Hugh Trelawney is a heterosexual journalist aged about 30, who remembers his earliest sexual experience at age 14. . . . The well-crafted memory is set in a magical week with perfect waves, Hugh's first drink in a hotel, and 'the beginning of my life':

> The girl was an 18-year-old Maroubra beach chick. What the hell she wanted to have anything to do with me I don't know. She must have been slightly retarded, emotionally if not intellectually. I suppose she just went to it for the image, you know, I was already the long-haired surfie rat. I recall getting on top of her and not knowing where to put it and thinking, gee, it's a long way down . . . and when I sort of finally got it in, it only went in a little way, and I thought this isn't much. Then she must have moved her leg a little way, and then it went further and I thought oh! gee, that's all right. And then I must have come in about five or six

strokes, and I thought the feeling was outrageous because I thought I was going to die. . . And then during that week I had a whole new sense of myself. I expected—I don't know what I expected, to start growing more pubic hair, or expected my dick to get bigger. But it was that sort of week, you know. Then after that I was on my way.

***

This is a tale of a familiar kind, recounting a sexual coming-of-age. In almost every detail it shows the intricate interplay of the body with social process. Choice and arousal, as Hugh reconstructs it, are social (the 'beach chick', the 'surfie rat'). The required performance is physical, 'getting it in'. The young Hugh lacks the knowledge and skill required. But his skill is improved interactively, by his partner's bodily response ('she must have moved her leg a little bit'). The *physical* feeling of climax is immediately an interpretation ('I thought I was going to die'). It triggers off a familiar symbolic sequence—death, rebirth, new growth. Conversely the *social* transition Hugh has accomplished, entering into sexual adulthood, immediately translates as bodily fantasy ('more pubic hair', 'dick to get bigger').

Hugh jokingly invokes the metonymy by which the penis stands for masculinity— . . . but his memory also points beyond it. The first fuck is set in a context of sport: the week of perfect waves and the culture of surfing. In historically recent times, sport has come to be the leading definer of masculinity in mass culture. Sport provides a continuous display of men's bodies in motion. Elaborate and carefully monitored rules bring these bodies into stylized contests with each other. In these contests a combination of superior force (provided by size, fitness, teamwork) and superior skill (provided by planning, practice, and intuition) will enable one side to win.[4]

The embodiment of masculinity in sport involves a whole pattern of body development and use, not just one organ. Highly specific skills are of course involved. . . . But players who can do only one thing are regarded as freaks. . . .

The institutional organization of sport embeds definite social relations: competition and hierarchy among men, exclusion or domination of women. These social relations of gender are both realized and symbolized in the bodily performances. . . .

. . . The performance is symbolic and kinetic, social and bodily, at one and the same time, *and these aspects depend on each other.*

The constitution of masculinity through bodily performance means that gender is vulnerable when the performance cannot be sustained —for instance, as a result of physical disability. . . .

Nor can the manual workers whose vulnerability comes from the very situation that allows them to define masculinity through labour. Heavy manual work calls for strength, endurance, a degree of insensitivity and toughness, and group solidarity. Emphasizing the masculinity of industrial labour has been both a means of survival, in exploitative class relations, and a means of asserting superiority over women.

This emphasis reflects an economic reality. . . . [W]orking men's bodily capacities *are* their economic asset, are what they put on the labour market. But this asset changes. Industrial labour under the regime of profit uses up the workers' bodies, through fatigue, injury, and mechanical wear and tear. The decline of strength, threatening loss of income or the job itself, can be offset by the growth of skill—up to a point. 'It is at that point, unless he is very lucky, that a man's labouring days are over.'

The combination of force and skill is thus open to change. Where work is altered by deskilling and casualization, working-class men are increasingly defined as possessing force alone. The process is virulent where class exclusion combines with racism, as in South Africa under apartheid. (The apartheid economy literally 'reserved' skilled jobs for white men, and casualized black labour on a massive scale.) Middle-class men, conversely, are increasingly defined as the bearers of skill. This definition is supported by a powerful historical change in labour markets, the growth of credentialism, linked to a higher education system that selects and promotes along class lines.[5]

This class process alters the familiar connection between masculinity and machinery. The new information technology requires much sedentary keyboard work, which was initially classified as women's work (key-punch operators). The marketing of personal computers, however, has redefined some of this work as an arena of competition and power—masculine, technical, but not working class. These revised meanings are promoted in the text and graphics of computer magazines, in manufacturers' advertising that emphasizes 'power' (Apple Computer named its laptop the 'PowerBook'), and in the booming industry of violent computer games. Middle-class male bodies, separated by an old class division from physical force, now find their powers spectacularly amplified in the man/machine systems (the gendered language is entirely appropriate) of modern cybernetics.

The body, I would conclude, is inescapable in the construction of masculinity; but what is inescapable is not fixed. The bodily process, entering into the social process, becomes part of history (both personal and collective) and a possible object of politics. Yet this does not return us to the idea of bodies as landscape. . . .

Complexities of Mire or Blood

. . . Not only are men's bodies diverse and changing, they can be positively recalcitrant. Ways are proposed for bodies to participate in social life, and the bodies often refuse. . . .

***

Tip Southern, starting from a position of greater class advantage, partied even harder [than others]. His private-school peer group called itself the 'Sick Patrol', dressed outlandishly, crashed parties and took them over, smoked lots of dope. . . .

Off to university, things got heavier again: 'really heavy wild parties', punch made with industrial alcohol, hash, and hallucinogens. In due course both Tip's family and his body stopped coming through. . . .

> . . . I don't think I looked like the most respect—I mean, I was very undernourished in a general way, I was taking a lot of drugs, a lot of acid, drinking a lot. I have got this picture of me in my room, hidden away, of myself in the worst state that you can imagine: big stoned swollen red eyes, a huge stye in this eye, and just the most pallid face. . . .

***

Crisis stories such as these show bodies under pressure reaching limits. Michael Messner, interviewing former athletes in the United States, heard parallel stories. The pressure of high-level competitive sport obliges professional players to treat their bodies as instruments, even as weapons. . . . Playing hurt, accidents, drug use, and constant stress wear down even the fittest and strongest. . . . The body is virtually assaulted in the name of masculinity and achievement. Ex-athletes often live with damaged bodies and chronic pain, and die early.[6]

These are extreme cases; but the principle applies in much more routine situations, such as the industrial workplaces discussed above. Bodies cannot be understood as a neutral medium of social practice. Their materiality matters. They will do certain things and not others. Bodies are *substantively* in play in social practices such as sport, labour, and sex. . . .

. . . Body-reflexive Practices

How can we understand the situation when bodies . . . refuse to stay outdoors in the realm of nature and reappear uninvited in the realm of the social? Mainstream social science gives little help. . . .

To break out of this universe it is not enough to assert the significance of bodily difference, important as this has been in recent feminist theory. We need to assert the activity, literally the *agency*, of bodies in social processes. . . .

. . . Jogging, for instance, is certainly a socially disciplined activity. I tell myself this every second morning while struggling out of bed and tying on the running shoes. Yet each August in Sydney, 40,000 pairs of feet *willingly* set off down William Street towards Bondi in the 'City to Surf' run. A crowd run is a striking illustration of the pleasure of sociability through shared bodily performance. . . .

With bodies both objects and agents of practice, and the practice itself forming the structures within which bodies are appropriated and defined, we face a pattern beyond the formulae of current social theory. This pattern might be termed body-reflexive practice. . . .

***

Adam Singer recalled a moment of trauma with his father:

> He bought my brother a cricket bat for Christmas and he wouldn't buy me one. He'd say I couldn't play cricket. And things like throwing a ball. How a man throws a ball is different to how a woman throws a ball. I didn't want to throw a ball in front of my Dad because I knew it wouldn't look right, it wouldn't be like the way a good strong boy should throw it. And once, I remember, I was brave enough to throw it. And he made fun of me and said I threw it like a girl.

***

Here the circuit is condensed in time. The public gender meanings are instantaneously fused with the bodily activity and the emotions of the relationship. Even so, there is a split perception. Adam has learned how to be both in his body (throwing), and outside his body watching its gendered performance ('I knew it wouldn't look right').

In Adam's story the body-reflexive practice of sport called out a declaration of difference ('he made fun of me and said . . .'), with all the emotional charge of the father–son relationship behind it. . . .

***

Steve Donoghue . . . was a national champion in surf sport, making a rich living from prizes, sponsorships, and commercials. He had a superb physique, cultivated with four to five hours' training every day. Steve's body was capable of astonishing feats of precision as well as endurance:

> . . . When I swam, I used to do 200 metres, which is four 50-metre laps. I can start off, and any 50 is pretty well to the tenth of a second the same time each lap, and I wouldn't even be looking at a watch . . .

***

The body-reflexive practice here is familiar; its gender consequences perhaps less so. Steve Donoghue, young-man-about-beach, was trapped in the practices required to sustain Steve Donoghue, famous-exemplar-of-masculinity. He could not drink-drive, nor get into fights when pushed around (for fear of bad publicity). He could not go boozing (because of training), nor have much of a sex life (his coach was against it, and women had to fit in with his training schedule). In other words, much of what was defined in his peer culture as masculine was forbidden him.

Indeed, the body-reflexive practice that constructed Steve's hegemonic masculinity also undermined hegemonic masculinity. . . . Though encouraged by the coach to hate his competitors, Steve did not. Rather, he talked of 'mental toughness' and his ability to 'control the pain', to 'make my body believe that I am not hurting as much as I am'.

In short, Steve was driven towards narcissism—while the hegemonic construction of masculinity in contemporary Australian culture is outward-turned and plays down all private emotion. Yet the narcissism could not rest in self-admiration and bodily pleasure. This would have destroyed the performance on which Steve's life trajectory depended.

In his version of competition, the decisive triumph was over one's body. Steve's magnificent physique had meaning only when deployed in winning. The will to win did not arise from personal 'drive', a familiar word in sports talk that Steve did not use at all. It was given to him by the social structure of sporting competition; it was his meaning, as a champion.

The circuit of Steve's body-reflexive practice was thus a complex one, moving through the institutionalized system of commercialized sport, beach product manufacturing and advertising, and mass media, to the personal practices of training and competition. This system is far from coherent. Indeed it contains substantial contradictions, betrayed by the contradictory masculinity produced in Steve's life. . . .

Body-reflexive practices, as we see in all these instances, are not internal to the individual. They involve social relations and symbolism; they may well involve large-scale social institutions. Particular versions of masculinity are constituted in their circuits as meaningful bodies and embodied meanings. Through body-reflexive practices, more than individual lives are formed: a social world is formed.

Forming the World

Through body-reflexive practices, bodies are addressed by social process and drawn into history, without ceasing to be bodies. They do not turn into symbols, signs, or positions in discourse. Their materiality (including material capacities to engender, to give birth, to give milk, to menstruate, to open, to penetrate, to ejaculate) is not erased; it continues to matter. The *social* process of gender includes childbirth and child care, youth and aging, the pleasures of sport and sex, labour, injury, death from AIDS. . . .

Practice never occurs in a vacuum. It always responds to a situation, and situations are structured in ways that admit certain possibilities and not others. Practice does not proceed into a vacuum either. Practice makes a world. In acting, we convert initial situations into new situations. . . .

Notes

1. Imperato-McGinley et al., 1979.
2. Harrison, 1978. For the latest example of this preoccupation in Books About Men, see Farrell, 1993, chs 4–7.
3. Rossi, 1985, 161.
4. It is specifically men's bodies that form the mass spectacle of sport, women's sports being marginalized by the media: Duncan et al., 1990. My argument here draws on the research collected in Messner and Sabo, 1990.
5. Donaldson, 1991, 18. On South Africa, see Nattrass, 1992: on 'new class' and education, Gouldner, 1979.
6. Messner, 1992; Curry, 1992.

References

Curry, Timothy John. 1992. 'A Little Pain Never Hurt Anyone: Athletic Career Socialization and the Normalization of Sport Injury', *Gregory Stone Symposium*, Las Vegas, 9 February.

Donaldson, Mike. 1991. *Time of our Lives: Labour and Love in the Working Class*. Sydney: Allen & Unwin.

———. 1993. 'What is Hegemonic Masculinity?' *Theory and Society* 22: 643–57.

Duncan, Margaret Carlisle, Michael A. Messner, Linda Williams, and Kerry Jensen. 1990. *Gender Stereotyping in Televised Sports*. Los Angeles: Amateur Athletic Foundation Los Angeles.

Farrell, Warren. 1993. *The Myth of Male Power: Why Men are the Disposable Sex*. New York: Simon & Schuster.

Gouldner, Alvin W. 1979. *The Future of Intellectuals and the Rise of the New Class*. New York: Continuum.

Harrison, James. 1978. 'Warning: The Male Sex Role

May Be Dangerous to Your Health', *Journal of Social Issues* 34: 65–86.

Imperato-McGinley, Julianne, Ralph E. Peterson, Teofilo Gautier and Erasmo Sturla. 1979. 'Androgens and the Evolution of Male-Gender Identity Among Male Pseudohermaphrodites with 5-alpha-reductase Deficiency', *New England Journal of Medicine* 300: 1233–7.

Messner, Michael A. 1992. *Power at Play: Sports and the Problem of Masculinity.* Boston: Beacon Press.

———, and Don Sabo, eds. 1990. *Sport, Men and the Gender Order: Critical Feminist Perspectives.* Champaign, IL: Human Kinetics Books.

Nattrass, Nicoli. 1992. *Profits and Wages: The South African Economic Challenge.* Harmondsworth, UK: Penguin.

Part VI

Transgressive Bodies

Claudia Malacrida and Jacqueline Low

Sociologists of the body do more than discuss the body's relation to social norms. They also recognize the ways that many bodies fail to fit these socially prescribed categories, and examine the roles of various institutions in attempting to enforce those norms. Alice Domurat Dreger (2004) introduces the idea of **anatomically based rules** that are unspoken but nonetheless normative ideas of what a body 'should be', noting that such restrictions have been formally and informally sanctioned across eras and cultures. These rules, while ostensibly helping to maintain order and protect those who are vulnerable, also exclude some people while providing privilege to (most) others. Perhaps this explains why such rules persist, and why all of us comply with them to greater or lesser degrees. Dreger describes the daily attempts that all people make to fit into a societally-constructed 'normal', such as wearing glasses, working out, using a wheelchair, and grooming, as **normalizations**. When children are born with '**non-normate bodies**' that defy such normalizing efforts, such as children who are conjoined twins, achondoplastic dwarfs, or children with ambiguous sexual characteristics, the adults in their lives (parents, medical professionals, family members, and others) recognize the potential for stigmatization and feel compelled to go to extraordinary lengths to 'assist' their children to comply to normative bodily ideals. For example, parents and medical and helping professionals push for life-threatening separation surgeries on conjoined twins, often in direct opposition to the experiences and wishes of the twins themselves. Finally, Dreger draws comparisons between the stigmatizations and normalizations experienced by 'non-normate bodies' and those of women and people of colour. In her view, the 'non-normate' body represents something of a 'final frontier' for embodied social control and for social activism to fight against that control.

Cheryl Chase's (1998) article, 'Hermaphrodites with Attitude', provides an overview of one social movement that has arisen in response to the normalizing efforts of pediatric physicians and psychiatrists to eradicate **intersexuality** (her discussion centres on the medical response to sexually ambiguous genitalia, although intersexuality can be related to hormones as well, often manifesting itself only at puberty). Chase notes that pediatric practitioners respond to intersex births as though they were a 'psychosocial emergency', despite the reality that this is seldom the case; the children's health is not at risk, nor is there clear evidence that 'leaving things be' necessarily causes emotional or social problems for intersexed individuals. Further, because medical technology is limited, children are more routinely assigned a female sex than a male one, regardless of which sex seems more 'real' for the individual. According to Chase, it is possible to understand that the insistence on one sex or another is motivated more by medical technology and societal anxieties than by any physical or psychological benefits to intersexed individuals themselves. Further, it is clear that these medical efforts operate not only to erase difference, but they also shore up a **binary system of sexes** where being either male or female—at least on the surface— is both naturalized and normalized. In short, the medical response to intersexuality has been to engage in the **social construction** of maleness and femaleness as opposite and exclusive to one another.

In past decades, a social movement of intersexed people has grown, making their situations more public and taking their protests to the medical establishment. This movement has met with significant resistance from the medical establishment, which on the one hand appears to operate from a sincere desire to 'fix' what it perceives as a significant social problem, and on the other hand enjoys significant prestige from its 'own power to change sex and its drive to rescue parents' (203).

In 'Telling Body Transgendering Stories', Richard Ekins and Dave King (2001) analyze discourses of, or ways of thinking and speaking about, the transgendered body. By **transgender** they mean gender identities that not only move, 'either temporarily or permanently' from one side to the other of the binary model of gender, but may also eclipse it (2001: 180). The **binary model of gender** is a dominant cultural construct that allows for only two genders, the masculine and the feminine (Hird, 2002). Ekins and King argue that people who identify as transgendered embody, at differing times, feminine or masculine traits and/or gender characteristics that are neither precisely feminine nor precisely masculine. They present four types of transgendering stories: 'migrating, oscillating, erasing, and transcending' stories (2001: 181). **Migrating body stories** are those that describe a permanent movement from one side of the binary model of gender to the other. **Oscillating body stories** are those that illustrate gender identity as alternating between the two sides of the binary model of gender. **Erasing body stories** depict instances where female and male bodies 'seek to expunge their [femaleness] or maleness and eliminate in themselves the existence of a binary divide' (191). They use the example of Christine Elan-Cane who had per breasts and uterus removed to erase per femaleness. **Per** is not a typographical error, rather it is the pronoun Christine uses to refer to perself without buying into the binary model of gender. Finally, Ekins and King use the concept of transcending body stories to refer to accounts of a third gender identity that transcends the binary model of gender.

References

Chase, C. 1998. 'Hermaphrodites with Attitude: Mapping the Emergence of Intersex Political Activism', *A Journal of Lesbian and Gay Studies: The Transgender Issue* 4, 2: 189–212.

Dreger, A.D. 2004. 'Introduction' from *One of Us: Conjoined Twins and the Future of Normal*. Cambridge, MA: Harvard University Press, 1–16.

Ekins, R., and D. King. 2001. 'Telling Body Transgendering Stories', in K. Backett-Milburn and L. McKie, eds, *Constructing Gendered Bodies*. New York: Palgrave, 179–203.

Hird, M. 2002. 'For a Sociology of Transsexualism', *Sociology* 36, 3: 577–95.

Chapter 16

'Introduction' from *One of Us: Conjoined Twins and the Future of Normal*

Alice Domurat Dreger

A pair of conjoined twins walks into a bar. One of them orders a drink from the bartender, who looks the twin over and asks for proof of her age. Hearing the bartender's request, the other twin turns around so that she's the one facing the bartender. Because the second twin appears older, the bartender reconsiders and decides to serve the drink without seeing proof of age.

Another true story: An unrelated man and woman, Americans visiting Japan, try to enter a bar together. But they can't find one that will allow them in. Both are gay and they're in Ni-chome, the 'queer' district of Tokyo. The bouncers at the lesbian bars won't let him in, because he's obviously a man. The bouncers at the gay bars won't let her in, because she's obviously a woman.

Another: Three teenagers with dwarfism go into a bar and order drinks. The bartender, too embarrassed to ask for their IDs, goes ahead and serves them. He's afraid to risk offending them by asking them to prove they're legal adults.

And one more: A young woman walks into a bar with a group of friends. Within a few minutes, she thinks she may be going deaf. Everyone around her is communicating as usual, but she can't hear what they're saying above the background noise. Soon she figures it out: it's not that she's going deaf—it's that she's legally blind. She can't read lips and gestures the way others are doing, to 'hear' above the noise.

The first story was told to me by Lori Schappell, who is conjoined at one side of her forehead to her sister Reba.[1] The second story was told to me by Cheryl Chase, who was born with a condition known as true hermaphroditism, characterized by mixed sex anatomy (both ovarian and testicular tissue)—not that bar bouncers can tell this sort of thing.[2] The third story was told to me by Danny Black, the owner of ShortDwarf.com, a talent agency and distributor of specialized products for people with small stature.[3] The fourth story came from a medical student named Ruta Sharangpani, who told it to me after I'd said to her, 'Hold on a minute. Let me put on my glasses so I can hear you better.'[4]

Anatomy matters a lot, and not just in bars. It matters because the senses we possess, the muscles we can control, the resources we require to keep our bodies alive limit and affect what we can experience in any given context: a bar, a school, a house, a courtroom, a subway, a mountaintop, the deep sea, or outer space. But anatomy also matters because it influences the assumptions people make on the basis of our anatomies: that we are too young-looking to drink, too male-looking to be in a lesbian bar, conjoined and therefore incapable of a meaningful, individual life.

Anatomical restrictions have long been explicitly written into the rules governing human life. When kings and queens reigned, their power derived from society's robust notion of how much anatomy mattered: certain people had the birthright. Thousands of years ago, the book of Leviticus stipulated that only men with perfect bodies were worthy of becoming priests: 'And the Lord said to Moses, "Say to Aaron, None of your descendents throughout their generations who has a blemish may approach to offer the bread of his God. For no one who has a blemish shall draw near, a man blind or lame, or one who has a mutilated face or a limb too long, or a man who has an injured foot or an injured hand, or a hunchback, or a dwarf, or a man with a defect in his sight or an itching disease or scabs or crushed testicles'" (21: 16–24). It went without saying that no woman should draw near. The liberal progression started by the Enlightenment has loosened many of these sorts of anatomical rules, at least in the United States. The radical theory that 'All men are created equal'—in itself an anatomical claim, though a relatively generous one—eventually gave rise to the practice of allowing people to vote regardless of whether they are men or women, black or white or brown. The legislation known as Title IX (1972 amendments to the Civil Rights Act of 1964) enforced the idea that girls should be as involved in sports as boys. In Vermont, a man can now enter into a civil union with another man.

Because anatomically based rules help to maintain order and protect those perceived as vulnerable, and because restriction brings privilege and privilege is pleasurable, we still have many regulations that dictate who can do what based on anatomy: who can drink alcohol, who can marry whom, who can vote, who can play golf as a member at the Augusta National Club, who may be afforded special legal protections or be promised equity. Beyond the written anatomical rules are the unwritten ones that do the same sort of work of maintaining order, protecting the vulnerable, and restricting privilege. These are the rules—or norms, or standards, call them what you will depending on how stringent they seem at any given moment—that tell us what to expect of a dark-skinned old woman who wears glasses and walks upright, what to expect of a tall light-skinned man with a shaved head and lots of tattoos. We learn and relearn these from our parents, from our peers, from our own bodily experiences, from advertisements, from almost every human encounter.[5] We learn these rules well enough to manipulate our bodies, sometimes slightly and

sometimes drastically, to shape the assumptions made about them.

The truth is, most of us go through minor anatomical 'normalization' procedures every day, changing our bodies ever so slightly to fit the identity we wish to present socially. We brush the plaque off our teeth, in part to keep them healthy but also so that they won't disgust others with a smell or appearance that would signal we are unclean (and therefore, by the rules of anatomy and identity, slovenly or poor or ill). We wash and style our hair and put on clothes meant to signal who we are underneath (man, woman, corporate team player, professor, artist, rebel). We add a wristwatch to enhance our imperfect internal clocks, to keep our bodily movements well timed in relation to others'. We shave various parts of our bodies depending on what kind of sexuality we wish to signal. We put on eyeglasses or slide into a wheelchair to compensate for the anatomical deficits that might otherwise keep us out of the stream of human life, which largely requires sight and autonomous movement. We worry about getting too fat, knowing that fat is widely equated with weak will and ill health, and so we step on the scale, choose the diet soda, go to the gym for a workout.

Participation in these little normalizations helps us to construct an architecture of certainty in what would otherwise be a very unpredictable social world. Thanks to the regularity of these sorts of normalizing rules and acts, we can be fairly certain that the person who dresses, looks, and smells like a man will have male anatomy under his clothes; that the charming professional colleague we have met only by phone will be, when encountered in person, wearing clothes and smelling good; that a newly discovered female model, when she appears in a swimsuit calendar, will have conventionally sexy legs—thin, smooth, hairless, without a sign of manliness.

Nevertheless, some people are born with anatomies that don't fit the social rules so far as anatomy and identity are concerned and that cannot be 'normalized' through any simple procedure like shaving or the donning of eyeglasses. These people are born with anatomies that complicate efforts to easily categorize them. Cheryl Chase, for example, was born with mixed sex anatomy, internally and externally, which made it hard for people to figure out whether to expect her to become a boy or a girl. Lori and Reba Schappell were born conjoined at the head, an anatomy that can make a new acquaintance unsure whether they are to be approached as one person or two. Ruta Sharangpani is profoundly nearsighted but can see just enough to manage without an obvious aid like a cane or dog; she also has an eye that can't quite meet yours because it shakes and wavers. Danny Black has achondroplasia, a form of dwarfism, and though he is middle-aged he inhabits a body whose proportions are supposed to characterize only the immature.

Despite the fact that these people did not choose to have these bodies—at least not in any simple sense of choice—they are often treated as if they have intentionally violated a social norm, which in a way they have.[6] People avoid meeting their eyes, whisper about them, and act in a way that signals shame.[7] I find myself doing this. When, without warning, I encounter someone whose legs are bent so that he walks very strangely, or someone who is an unusual size for her age, I find myself feeling very awkward, making apologies for them or for me, struggling to get beyond my discomposure yet chewing on the image for a long time afterward. Most of us are so used to dealing with people who fit invisibly into the standard categories of anatomy and identity that it is jarring when we meet someone who doesn't. And it is the recognition of this awkwardness, the recognition of how comfortable it can be to be considered normal, how uncomfortable it can be to be considered abnormal, that motivates adults to want to surgically normalize children born with unusual anatomies, to separate the Loris and Rebas, to make the Cheryls look like 'real' girls, to stretch the limbs of the Dannys, to make the Rutas look fully sighted.

Often the adults who impose such a normalization understand it as a charitable manifestation of pity. And no doubt it is. But 'pity' is defined as sorrow for another's suffering or misfortune, and that's exactly why it is experienced by many people born with unusual anatomies as not only unsupportive but [also] actively oppressive; for pity implies that the subject must be suffering and unfortunate. When I asked Lori Schappell how she felt when people treated her with pity, she bristled, saying that as soon as she saw such a 'pity conversation' starting, she would end it or leave it.[8] Trying to fight the degradation of pity, Ruta Sharangpani told me once, is 'like trying to climb a glass wall. There are no handholds, no way to talk to a pitying person, because she or he does not see the disabled person as a competent individual.'[9] So, however unintentionally, pity silences the person who might otherwise speak to defend the value of her person and her life. That's why parents of children born with unusual anatomies often also insist they don't want or need anyone's pity. Patty Hensel, mother of the conjoined girls Abigail and Brittany, told *Life* Magazine in 1996: 'People say, "We pray for you and the girls." . . . But we don't need anyone to feel sorry for us.'[10]

Yet at least until quite recently, sorrow and pity formed the narrative backbone of the usual story told about children born with unusual anatomies. The story went like this: These innocent, pitiful children are born cursed with tragic deformities; but through the miracle of modern medicine, doctors can remove the curse, changing them into normal little kids and saving them from a life of shame and mockery. Delivered into the happy realm of those who were created normal, they are henceforth free to live a full life otherwise unavailable to them.

 . . . By considering conjoined twinning, arguably the most extraordinary form of human anatomy, in relation to other anatomical states that challenge cultural norms of identity—intersex, dwarfism, giantism, cleft lip (once known as harelip)—. . . [I explore] the extent to which anatomies do or must limit political and social identity, the extent to which a 'deformed' or 'malformed' anatomy must be pitiful. By considering conjoined twinning and other 'deformities' within the larger historical context of anatomical politics, . . . [I argue] for a more radical understanding of 'abnormal' bodies. . . . [I seek] to change assumptions made about people born with unusual anatomies, and by doing so . . . seek to change the context built around those people. The typical story told about such individuals is one in which the child's anatomy is changed to fit the social context. . . . I seek instead to change the social context by exposing the breadth and depth of that context. . . . [I] endeavour to show what something as rare as conjoinment could have to do with the rest of us.

To what extent are people who are conjoined abnormal? . . . There's no question that statistically they are extremely rare, accounting for perhaps as few as one in 200,000 births and no more than one in 50,000. But the reason they are treated so differently from others is not simply that they are rare; it is that people in general expect, quite reasonably, that any individual they meet will be the only person inhabiting his or her skin. Because most singletons—by which I mean people born with no anatomical bond to anyone but their mothers—understand psychosocial individuality as *requiring* anatomical individuality, they tend to assume that conjoined twins are trapped in such a way that makes a happy, normal life impossible. Only surgical separation could truly make them free.

New York Magazine vividly exemplified this assumption when it printed a photograph of infant twins Carmen and Rosa Taveras in November 1993—several months after they'd been surgically separated—under the headline 'FREE AT LAST'.[11] But . . . such a headline would make little sense to people who are conjoined, because most people who are conjoined do not feel physically entrapped. They do not wish they had been born into singleton bodies. Indeed, Laleh and Ladan Bijani, who chose to be separated in 2003 at the age of 29, were the first conjoined twins in history to consent to separation surgery. Though it may seem shocking, in none of the hundreds of previous separation operations performed were surgeons given permission by the patients themselves to do the surgery.[12] This is not simply because most conjoined twins fear the risks of separation. It is because . . . people who are con-

joined typically feel that their bodies and lives are perfectly normal and acceptable—sometimes even preferable. They don't think there is anything fundamentally wrong with being conjoined. Thus, one of the ways in which conjoined twins are like almost everyone else is that they tend to readily accept, and even prefer, the anatomy with which they were born. So in light of what such people themselves have said, we might well understand conjoinment as an integral part of their individuality, paradoxical as that sounds.

Why, then, do doctors ever separate conjoined twins? . . . Of course there are many other ways in which we seek to normalize children (for example, through formal and informal education), often with beneficent intentions. But one must ask whether normalization surgeries really work in the sense of providing otherwise unavailable psychosocial health, whether they are the best route to psychosocial health and social justice, and what basic criteria ought to be fulfilled by any normalizing surgical procedure. While by no means arguing against all normalizing surgeries, I would like to problematize a process that is too often portrayed as a technological fairytale in which everyone but the dragon called Deformity ends up happily ever after.

. . . [An] extraordinary form of separation surgery [is one] in which doctors intentionally 'sacrifice' one conjoined twin in an attempt to save the other's life. Increasingly common and increasingly controversial, these surgeries represent the only case in which surgeons are given explicit permission to separate a brain-live person (or at least her mind) from the organs keeping her alive, so that someone else may survive. Because such surgeries are motivated by the belief that both children will die imminently unless there is an intervention, and because surgeons are forced to terminate the life of one child to try to save the other, sacrifice surgeries are ethical hornets' nests and wrenching affairs for all involved. . . .

. . . [Moving] this story out of the surgical theatre and back to the social theatre, . . . [we can] consider the cultural context in which parents and doctors make decisions about normalizing surgeries. . . . I look at the way people with unusual anatomies have been presented, displayed, and exhibited over the centuries, by themselves and others, particularly in the medical sphere. Again departing from the usual story ('These poor people used to be stuck in freak shows, and now they're saved by medicine'), I pose three questions: What, exactly, was wrong with freak shows? Are we really past them, or have they just been shifted into legitimate forms by being medicalized? And finally, shouldn't we wonder why it is socially acceptable for some people—models, anchormen, basketball stars—and not others to make money from their unusual bodily differences? . . .

The great theorist of racism W. E.B. DuBois asserted that the problem of the twentieth century was the problem of the colour line.[13] I argue . . . that we are far from having solved this problem, and that the problem of the twenty-first century will be the great fault on which the colour line falls: the anatomy identity line. It's true that we've come a long way since the days when power and wealth were viewed as a birth right, men were considered inherently superior to women, and whites were seen as inherently superior to all other races. Scientists are continually revealing cracks and holes in anatomical borders once thought to be seamless: female/male, black/white, human/animal, even living/non-living/dead. The progress of science and of democracy continues to decouple social and political identity from anatomy. And an underground 'freak chic' combined with an aboveground disability rights movement is slowly eroding the hegemony of the normate. Yet all the while we see attempts to re-establish clear categories, norms, and authorities—attempts that include the FDA's approval of Botox as a medically administered antiwrinkle treatment, the Supreme Court's efforts to narrowly construe the category of 'disabled', the scientific search for the 'violence gene', and a bouncer's decision to keep a man out of a lesbian bar. . . . [I] look at the ideals of Enlightenment progress, the tools of medicine and technology, and the knowledge of how anatomies become pleasurable or painful, and see whether these can be used to construct a rational, democratic civilization that grants full membership to people born with socially challenging anatomies—recognizing that human civilization as we know it cannot exist without anatomical norms. How is the social context of conjoinment and other unusual forms of anatomy likely to change in the coming years? Who, in the future, will count as one of us? And how will we indicate that belonging? Through a politically correct labelling process? A protected right? A guaranteed genetic endowment? An ensured normality? . . .

. . . [T]here are clear similarities among the conditions of being black in a white world, a woman in a man's world, and conjoined in a singleton's world. In all of them, anatomical difference is assumed to be some sort of determiner of one's future: different body, different person, different life. These assumptions then become self-fulfilling prophecies. In all of these cases, difference tends to be seen as a cause of suffering, and only suffering—something to be pitied. Most normates assume that everyone, given the choice, would choose a 'normal' body. But many of the 'fixed' say they feel damaged by being 'fixed'; and many of the 'unfixed' claim that they feel normal, that the people who know them well—as individuals, not simply as examples of various conditions—see them as normal. All this is true of people who were born missing limbs, people who were born blind, people who were born black or female or with an intersex condition. It surely isn't a coincidence that historically there have been some close ties between the civil rights movement and the disability rights movement.[14] So why, I wondered, do we try to change the children in some of these cases and change the world in others? Why not change minds instead of bodies?

Let me make clear that I am not interested in romanticizing conjoinment or dwarfism or intersex, or any other anatomical condition. What I am attempting to do here, with stories, history, and analysis, is to suggest that there is another way to think about 'deformity' other than as a medical tragedy that needs fixing. In fact, most atypical anatomies—conjoinment, intersex, cleft lip, and so on—are, by this point in history, fairly well documented human experiences. And in that documentation we discover that they are remarkably like many other human experiences, such as motherhood, marriage, 'racial' differences, and radical size variations—similar enough that we ought to reconsider our views of people with unusual anatomies. We should take seriously the possibility that they are entitled to what the rest of us are, including a validated sense of normality and a reasonably wide degree of self-determination. Right now, they don't have that. I'm thinking: enough pity already.

Notes

1. Lori Schappell, personal communication, 9 December 2002. The scene described took place in a liquor store when Reba, Lori's sister, tried to make a purchase.
2. Cheryl Chase, personal communication, 25 November 2002.
3. Danny Black, personal communication, 13 December 2002.
4. Ruta Sharangpani, personal communication, 13 November 2002.
5. The classic discussion of stigma and shame is Erving Goffman's *Stigma: Notes on the Management of Spoiled Identity* (New York: Touchstone, 1963). Goffman's sociological insights remain quite persuasive, though the book is more than 40 years old and though his tone occasionally betrays a problematic contempt for his subjects. For an analysis of *Stigma* from a disability studies perspective, see Rosemarie Garland Thomson, *Extraordinary Bodies: Figuring Physical Disability in American Culture and Literature* (New York: Columbia University Press, 1997), 30–2.
6. See Susan Wendell, *The Rejected Body: Feminist Philosophical Reflections on Disability* (New York: Routledge, 1996), ch. 4; see also Thomson's use of the work of anthropologist Mary Douglas (*Extraordinary Bodies*, 33–8).
7. On the attribution of shame, see Goffman, *Stigma*, 7–10.
8. Lori Schappell, personal communication, 9 December 2002.
9. Ruta Sharangpani, 'Pity and Other Green Monsters'; unpublished essay, quoted with permission.
10. Quoted in Kenneth Miller, 'Together Forever', *Life* April 1996: 56.
11. Janice Hopkins Tanne, 'Free at Last', *New York Magazine* 15 November 1993: 54–62.
12. Keep in mind that . . . most separations are done before patients are old enough to give their consent.
13. W.E.B. DuBois, *The Souls of Black Folk* (New York: Dover, 1994 [1903]), v.
14. See Joseph P. Shapiro, *No Pity: People with Disabilities Forging a New Civil Rights Movement* (New York: Three Rivers Press, 1993), 54, 109. For a comparison of slavery and institutionalization, see ibid., 159–60.

Chapter 17

Hermaphrodites with Attitude: Mapping the Emergence of Intersex Political Activism

Cheryl Chase

. . .

Hermaphrodites: Medical Authority and Cultural Invisibility

. . . Though the male/female binary is constructed as natural and presumed to be immutable, the phenomenon of intersexuality offers clear evidence to the contrary and furnishes an opportunity to deploy 'nature' strategically to disrupt heteronormative systems of sex, gender, and sexuality. The concept of bodily sex, in popular usage, refers to multiple components including karyotype (organization of sex chromosomes), gonadal differentiation (e.g., ovarian or testicular), genital morphology, configuration of internal reproductive organs, and pubertal sex characteristics such as breasts and facial hair. Because these characteristics are expected to be concordant in each individual—either all male or all female—an observer, once having attributed male or female sex to a particular individual, assumes the values of other unobserved characteristics.[1]

Because medicine intervenes quickly in intersex births to change the infant's body, the phenomenon of intersexuality is today largely unknown outside specialized medical practices. General public awareness of intersex bodies slowly vanished in modern Western European societies as medicine gradually appropriated to itself the authority to interpret—and eventually manage—the category that had previously been widely known as 'hermaphroditism'. Victorian medical taxonomy began to efface hermaphroditism as a legitimated status by establishing mixed gonadal histology as a necessary criterion for 'true' hermaphroditism. By this criterion, both ovarian and testicular tissue types had to be present. Given the limitations of Victorian surgery and anesthesia, such confirmation was impossible in a living patient. All other anomalies were reclassified as 'pseudo-hermaphroditisms' masking a 'true sex' determined by the gonads.[2]

With advances in anesthesia, surgery, embryology, and endocrinology, however, twentieth-century medicine moved from merely labelling intersexed bodies to the far more invasive practice of 'fixing' them to conform with a diagnosed true sex. The techniques and protocols for physically transforming intersexed bodies were developed primarily at Johns Hopkins University in Baltimore during the 1920s and 1930s under the guidance of urologist Hugh Hampton Young. 'Only during the last few years', Young enthused in the preface to his pioneering textbook, *Genital Abnormalities*, 'have we begun to get somewhere near the explanation of the marvels of anatomic abnormality that may be portrayed by these amazing individuals. But the surgery of the hermaphrodite has remained a *terra incognita*.' The 'sad state of these unfortunates' prompted Young to devise 'a great variety of surgical procedures' by which he attempted to normalize their bodily appearances to the greatest extents possible.[3]

Quite a few of Young's patients resisted his efforts. One, a '"snappy" young Negro woman with a good figure' and a large clitoris, had married a man but found her passion only with women. She refused 'to be made into a man' because removal of her vagina would mean the loss of her 'meal ticket', namely, her husband.[4] By the 1950s, the principle of rapid postnatal detection and intervention for intersex infants had been developed at Johns Hopkins with the stated goal of completing surgery early enough so that the child would have no memory of it.[5] One wonders whether the insistence on early intervention was not at least partly motivated by the resistance offered by adult intersexuals to normalization through surgery. Frightened parents of ambiguously sexed infants were much more open to suggestions of normalizing surgery, while the infants themselves could of course offer no resistance whatever. Most of the theoretical foundations justifying these interventions are attributable to psychologist John Money, a sex researcher invited to Johns Hopkins by Lawson Wilkins, the founder of pediatric endocrinology.[6] Wilkins's numerous students subsequently carried these protocols to hospitals throughout the United States and abroad.[7] Suzanne Kessler notes that today Wilkins and Money's protocols enjoy a 'consensus of approval rarely encountered in science'.[8]

In keeping with the Johns Hopkins model, the birth of an intersex infant today is deemed a 'psychosocial emergency' that propels a multidisciplinary team of intersex specialists into action. Significantly, they are surgeons and endocrinologists rather than psychologists, bioethicists, representatives from intersex peer support organizations, or parents of intersex children. The team examines the infant and chooses either male or female as a 'sex of assignment', then informs the parents that this is the child's 'true sex'. Medical technology, including surgery and hormones, is then used to make the child's body conform as closely as possible to that sex.

The sort of deviation from sex norms exhibited by intersexuals is so highly stigmatized that the likely prospect of emotional harm due to social rejection of the intersexual provides physicians with their most compelling argument to justify medically unnecessary surgical interventions. Intersex status is considered to be so incompatible with emotional health that misrepresentation, concealment of facts, and outright lying (both to parents and later to the intersex person) are unabashedly advocated in professional medical literature.[9] Rather, the systematic hushing up of the fact of intersex births and the use of violent techniques to normalize intersex bodies have caused profound emotional and physical harm to intersexuals and their families. The harm begins when the birth is treated as a medical crisis, and the consequences of that initial treatment ripple out ever afterward. The impact of this treatment is so devastating that until just a few years ago, people whose lives have been touched by intersexuality maintained silence about their ordeal. As recently as 1993, no one publicly disputed surgeon Milton Edgerton when he wrote that in 40 years of clitoral surgery on intersexuals, 'not one has complained of loss of sensation, *even when the entire clitoris was removed*'.[10]

The tragic irony is that, while intersexual anatomy occasionally indicates an underlying medical problem such as adrenal malfunction, ambiguous genitals are in and of themselves neither painful nor harmful to health. Surgery is essentially a destructive process. It can remove and to a limited extent relocate tissue, but it cannot create new structures. This technical limitation, taken together with the framing of the feminine as a condition of lack, leads physicians to assign 90 per cent of anatomically ambiguous infants as female by excising genital tissue. Members of the Johns Hopkins intersex team have justified female assignment by saying, 'You can make a hole, but you can't build a pole.'[11] Positively heroic efforts shore up a tenuous masculine status for the remaining 10 per cent assigned male, who are subjected to multiple operations—22 in one case[12]—with the goal of straightening the penis and constructing a urethra to enable standing urinary posture. For some, the surgeries end only when the child grows old enough to resist.[13]

Children assigned to the female sex are subjected to surgery that removes the troubling hypertrophic clitoris (the same tissue that would have been a troubling micropenis if the child had been assigned male). Through the 1960s, feminizing pediatric genital surgery was openly labelled 'clitorectomy' and was compared favourably to the African practices that have been the recent focus of such intense scrutiny. As three Harvard surgeons noted, 'Evidence that the clitoris is not essential for normal coitus may be gained from certain sociological data. For instance, it is the custom of a number of African tribes to excise the clitoris and other parts of the external genitals. Yet normal sexual function is observed in these females.'[14] A modified operation that removes most of the clitoris and relocates a bit of the tip is variously (and euphemistically) called clitoroplasty, clitoral reduction, or clitoral recession and is described as a 'simple cosmetic procedure' to differentiate it from the now infamous clitorectomy. However, the operation is far from benign. Here is a slightly simplified summary (in my own words) of the surgical technique—recommended by Johns Hopkins Surgeons Oesterling, Gearhart, and Jeffs—that is representative of the operation:

> They make an incision around the phallus, at the corona, then dissect the skin away from its underside. Next they dissect the skin away from the dorsal side and remove as much of the corpora, or erectile bodies, as necessary to create an 'appropriate size clitoris'. Next, stitches are placed from the pubic area along both sides of the entire length of what remains of the phallus; when these stitches are tightened, it folds up like pleats in a skirt, and recesses into a concealed position behind the mons pubis. If the result is still 'too large', the glans is further reduced by cutting away a pie-shaped wedge.[15]

For most intersexuals, this sort of arcane, dehumanized medical description, illustrated with close-ups of genital surgery and naked children with blacked-out eyes, is the only available version of *Our Bodies, Ourselves*. We as a culture have relinquished to medicine the authority to police the boundaries of male and female, leaving intersexuals to recover as best they can, alone and silent, from violent normalization.

My Career as a Hermaphrodite: Renegotiating Cultural Meanings

I was born with ambiguous genitals. A doctor specializing in intersexuality deliberated for three days—sedating my mother each time she asked what was wrong with her baby—before concluding that I was male, with a micropenis, complete hypospadias, undescended testes, and a strange extra opening behind the urethra. A male birth certificate was completed for me, and my parents began raising me as a boy. When I was a year and a half old my parents consulted a different set of experts, who admitted me to a hospital for 'sex determination'. 'Determine' is a remarkably apt word in this context, meaning both 'to ascertain by investigation' and 'to cause to come to a resolution'. It perfectly describes the two-stage process whereby science produces through a series of masked operations what it claims merely to observe. Doctors told my parents that a thorough medical investigation would be necessary to determine (in the first sense of that word) what my 'true sex' was. They judged my genital appendage to be inadequate as a penis, too short to mark masculine status effectively or to penetrate females. As a female, however, I would be penetrable and potentially fertile. My anatomy having been relabelled as vagina, urethra, labia, and outsized clitoris, my sex was determined (in the second sense) by amputating my genital appendage. Following doctors' orders, my parents then changed my name, combed their house to eliminate all traces of my existence as a boy (photographs, birthday cards, etc.), changed my birth certificate, moved to a different town, instructed extended family members no longer to refer to me as a boy, and never told anyone else—including me—just what had happened. My intersexuality and change of sex were the family's dirty little secrets.

At age eight, I was returned to the hospital for abdominal surgery that trimmed away the testicular portion of my gonads, each of which was partly ovarian and partly testicular in character. No explanation was given to me then for the long hospital stay or the abdominal surgery, nor for the regular hospital visits afterward, in which doctors photographed my genitals and inserted fingers and instruments into my vagina and anus. These visits ceased as soon as I began to menstruate. At the time of the sex change, doctors had assured my parents that their once son/now daughter would grow into a woman who could have a normal sex life and babies. With the confirmation of menstruation, my parents apparently concluded that that prediction had been borne out and their ordeal was behind them. For me, the worst part of the nightmare was just beginning.

As an adolescent, I became aware that I had no clitoris or inner labia and was unable to orgasm. By the end of my teens, I began to do research in medical libraries, trying to discover what might have happened to me. When I finally determined to obtain my medical records, it took me three years to overcome the obstruction of the doctors whom I asked for help. When I did obtain them, a scant three pages, I first learned that I was a 'true hermaphrodite' who had been my parents' son for a year and a half and who bore a name unfamiliar to me. The records also documented my clitorectomy. This was the middle 1970s, when I was in my early twenties. I had come to identify myself as lesbian, at a time when lesbianism and a biologically based gender essentialism were virtually synonymous: men were rapists who caused war and environmental destruction; women were good and would heal the earth; lesbians were a superior form of being uncontaminated by 'men's energy'. In such a world, how could I tell anyone that I had actually possessed the dreaded 'phallus'? I was no longer a woman in my own eyes but rather a monstrous and mythical creature. Because my hermaphroditism and long-buried boyhood were the history behind the clitorectomy, I could never speak openly about that or my consequent inability to orgasm. I was so traumatized by discovering the circumstances that produced my embodiment that I could not speak of these matters with anyone.

Nearly 15 years later, I suffered an emotional meltdown. In the eyes of the world, I was a highly successful businesswoman, a principal in an international high-tech company. To myself, I was a freak, incapable of loving or being loved, filled with shame about my status as a hermaphrodite and about my sexual dysfunction. Unable to make peace with myself, I finally sought help from a psychotherapist, who reacted to each revelation about my history and predicament with some version of 'no, it's not' or 'so what?' I would say, 'I'm not really a woman', and she would say, 'Of course you are. You look female.' I would say, 'My complete withdrawal from sexuality has destroyed every relationship I've ever entered.' She would say, 'Everybody has their ups and downs.' I tried another therapist and met with a similar response. Increasingly desperate, I confided my story to several friends, who shrank away in embarrassed silence. I was in emotional agony, feeling utterly alone, seeing no possible way out. I decided to kill myself.

Confronting suicide as a real possibility proved to be my personal epiphany. . . .

I slowly developed a newly politicized and critically aware form of self-understanding. . . . I felt almost completely isolated from gay politics, feminism, and queer and gender theory. I did possess the rudimentary knowledge that the gay rights movement had gathered momentum only when it could effectively deny that homosexuality was sick or inferior and assert to the contrary that 'gay is good'. As impossible as it then seemed, I pledged similarly to affirm that 'intersex is good', that the body I was born with was not diseased, only different. I vowed to embrace the sense of being 'not a woman' that I initially had been so terrified to discover. . . .

Birth of an Intersex Movement: Opposition and Allies

Upon moving to San Francisco, I started telling my story indiscriminately to everyone I met. Over the course of a year, simply by speaking openly within my own social circles, I learned of six other intersexuals—including two who had been fortunate enough to escape medical attention. I realized that intersexuality, rather than being extremely rare, must be relatively common. I decided to create a support network. In the summer of 1993, I produced some pamphlets, obtained a post office box, and began to publicize the Intersex Society of North America (ISNA) through small notices in the media. Before long, I was receiving several letters per week from intersexuals throughout the United States and Canada and occasionally some from Europe. . . .

ISNA's most immediate goal has been to create a community of intersex people who could provide peer support to deal with shame, stigma, grief, and rage as well as with practical issues such as how to obtain old medical records or locate a sympathetic psychotherapist or endocrinologist. . . .

ISNA's longer-term and more fundamental goal, however, is to change the way intersex infants are treated. We advocate that surgery not be performed on ambiguous genitals unless there is a medical reason (such as blocked or painful urination), and that parents be given the conceptual tools and emotional support to accept their children's physical differences. While it is fascinating to think about the potential development of new genders or subject positions grounded in forms of embodiment that fall outside the familiar male/female dichotomy, we recognize that the two-sex/gender model is currently hegemonic and therefore advocate that children be raised either as boys or girls, according to which designation seems most likely to offer the child the greatest future sense of comfort. Advocating gender assignment without resorting to normalizing surgery is a radical position given that it requires the willful disruption of the assumed concordance between body shape and gender category. However, this is the only position that prevents irreversible physical damage to the intersex person's body, that respects the intersex person's agency regarding his or her own flesh, and that recognizes genital sensation and erotic functioning to be at least as important as reproductive capacity. If an intersex child or adult decides to change gender or to undergo surgical or hormonal alteration of his or her body, that decision should also be fully respected and facilitated. The key point is that

intersex subjects should not be violated for the comfort and convenience of others.

One part of reaching ISNA's long-term goal has been to document the emotional and physical carnage resulting from medical interventions. As a rapidly growing literature makes abundantly clear (see the bibliography on our website, http://www.isna.org/bigbib.html), the medical management of intersexuality has changed little in the 40 years since my first surgery. Kessler expresses surprise that 'in spite of the thousands of genital operations performed every year, there are no meta-analyses from within the medical community on levels of success'.[16] They do not know whether postsurgical intersexuals are 'silent and happy or silent and unhappy'.[17] . . .

Since ISNA has been on the scene, other groups with a more resistant stance vis-à-vis the medical establishment have begun to appear. In 1995, a mother who refused medical pressure for female assignment for her intersex child formed the Ambiguous Genitalia Support Network, which introduces parents of intersexuals to each other and encourages the development of pen-pal support relationships. In 1996, another mother who had rejected medical pressure to assign her intersex infant as a female by removing his penis formed the Hermaphrodite Education and Listening Post (HELP) to provide peer support and medical information. Neither of these parent-oriented groups, however, frames its work in overtly political terms. Still, political analysis and action of the sort advocated by ISNA has not been without effect on the more narrowly defined service-oriented or parent-dominated groups. . . .

Outside the rather small community of intersex organizations, ISNA's work has generated a complex patchwork of alliances and oppositions. . . . Transgender and lesbian/gay groups have been supportive of intersex political activism largely because they see similarities in the medicalization of these various identities as a form of social control and (especially for transsexuals) empathize with our struggle to assert agency within a medical discourse that works to efface the ability to exercise informed consent about what happens to one's own body. . . .

ISNA has deliberately cultivated a network of nonintersexed advocates who command a measure of social legitimacy and can speak in contexts where uninterpreted intersex voices will not be heard. Because there is a strong impulse to discount what intersexuals have to say about intersexuality, sympathetic representation has been welcome—especially in helping intersexuals reframe intersexuality in nonmedical terms. Some gender theory scholars, feminist critics of science, medical historians, and anthropologists have been quick to understand and support intersex activism. Years before ISNA came into existence, feminist biologist and science studies scholar Anne Fausto-Sterling had written about intersexuality in relation to intellectually suspect scientific practices that perpetuate masculinist constucts of gender, and she became an early ISNA ally.[18] Likewise, social psychologist Suzanne Kessler had written a brilliant ethnography of surgeons who specialize in treating intersexuals. After speaking with several 'products' of their practice, she, too, became a strong supporter of intersex activism.[19] Historian of science Alice Dreger, whose work focuses not only on hermaphroditism but on other forms of potentially benign atypical embodiment that become subject to destructively normalizing medical interventions (conjoined twins, for example), has been especially supportive. . . .

Allies who help contest the medicalization of intersexuality are especially important because ISNA has found it almost entirely fruitless to attempt direct, nonconfrontational interactions with the medical specialists who themselves determine policy on the treatment of intersex infants and who actually carry out the surgeries. Joycelyn Elders, the Clinton administration's first surgeon general, is a pediatric endocrinologist with many years of experience managing intersex infants but, in spite of a generally feminist approach to health care and frequent overtures from ISNA, she has been dismissive of the concerns of intersexuals themselves.[20] Another pediatrician remarked in an Internet discussion on intersexuality: 'I think this whole issue is preposterous. . . . To suggest that [medical decisions about the treatment of intersex conditions] are

somehow cruel or arbitrary is insulting, ignorant, and misguided. . . . To spread the claims that [ISNA] is making is just plain wrong, and I hope that this [on-line group of doctors and scientists] will not blindly accept them.' Yet another participant in that same chat asked what was for him obviously a rhetorical question: 'Who is the enemy? I really don't think it's the medical establishment. Since when did we establish the male/female hegemony?' While a surgeon quoted in a *New York Times* article on ISNA summarily dismissed us as 'zealots',[21] there is considerable anecdotal information supplied by ISNA sympathizers that professional meetings in the fields of pediatrics, urology, genital plastic surgery, and endocrinology are buzzing with anxious and defensive discussions of intersex activism. In response to the Hermaphrodites with Attitude protests at the American Academy of Pediatrics meeting, that organization felt compelled to issue the following statement to the press: 'The Academy is deeply concerned about the emotional, cognitive, and body image development of intersexuals, and believes that successful early genital surgery minimizes these issues.' Further protests were planned for 1997.

The roots of resistance to the truth claims of intersexuals run deep in the medical establishment. Not only does ISNA critique the normativist biases couched within most scientific practice, it advocates a treatment protocol for intersex infants that disrupts conventional understandings of the relationship between bodies and genders. But on a level more personally threatening to medical practitioners, ISNA's position implies that they have—unwittingly at best, through willful denial at worst—spent their careers inflicting a profound harm from which their patients will never fully recover. ISNA's position threatens to destroy the assumptions motivating an entire medical subspecialty, thus jeopardizing the ability to perform what many surgeons find to be technically difficult and fascinating work. Melissa Hendricks notes that Dr Gearhart is known to colleagues as a surgical 'artist' who can 'carve a large phallus down into a clitoris' with consummate skill.[22] More than one ISNA member has discovered that surgeons actually operated on their genitals at no charge. The medical establishment's fascination with its own power to change sex and its drive to rescue parents from their intersex children are so strong that heroic interventions are delivered without regard to the capitalist model that ordinarily governs medical services.

Given such deep and mutually reinforcing reasons for opposing ISNA's position, it is hardly surprising that medical intersex specialists have, for the most part, turned a deaf ear toward us. The lone exception as of April 1997 is urologist Justine Schober. After watching a videotape of the 1996 ISNA retreat and receiving other input from HELP and the AIS Support Group, she suggests in a new textbook on pediatric surgery that while technology has advanced to the point that 'our needs [as surgeons] and the needs of parents to have a presentable child can be satisfied', it is time to acknowledge that problems exist that 'we as surgeons . . . cannot address. Success in psychosocial adjustment is the true goal of sexual assignment

and genitoplasty. . . . Surgery makes parents and doctors comfortable, but counselling makes people comfortable too, and is not irreversible.'[23]

While ISNA will continue to approach the medical establishment for dialogue (and continue supporting protests outside the closed doors when doctors refuse to talk), perhaps the most important aspect of our current activities is the struggle to change public perceptions. By using the mass media, the Internet, and our growing network of allies and sympathizers to make the general public aware of the frequency of intersexuality and of the intense suffering that medical treatment has caused, we seek to create an environment in which many parents of intersex children will have already heard about the intersex movement when their child is born. Such informed parents we hope will be better able to resist medical pressure for unnecessary genital surgery and secrecy and to find their way to a peer-support group and counselling rather than to a surgical theatre. . . .

Acknowledgements

My appreciation goes to Susan Stryker for her extensive contributions to the structure and substance of this essay.

Notes

1. Suzanne Kessler and Wendy McKenna, *Gender: An Ethnomethodological Approach* (New York: John Wiley and Sons, 1978).

2. Alice Domurat Dreger, 'Doubtful Sex: Cases and Concepts of Hermaphroditism in France and Britain, 1868–1915' (Ph.D. diss., Indiana University, 1995); Alice Domurat Dreger, 'Doubtful Sex: The Fate of the Hermaphrodite in Victorian Medicine', *Victorian Studies* (Spring 1995): 336–70; Alice Domurat Dreger, 'Hermaphrodites in Love: The Truth of the Gonads', *Science and Homosexualities*, Vernon Rosario, ed. (New York: Routledge, 1997), 46–66; Alice Domurat Dreger, 'Doctors Containing Hermaphrodites: The Victorian Legacy', *Chrysalis: The Journal of Transgressive Gender Identities* (Fall 1997): 15–22.

3. Hugh Hampton Young, *Genital Abnormalities,*

Hermaphroditism, and Related Adrenal Diseases (Baltimore: Williams and Wilkins, 1937), xxxix–xl.

4. Ibid., 139–42.

5. Howard W. Jones Jr. and William Wallace Scott, *Hermaphroditism, Genital Anomalies, and Related Endocrine Disorders* (Baltimore: Williams and Wilkins, 1958), 269.

6. John Money, Joan G. Hampson, and John L. Hampson, 'An Examination of Some Basic Sexual Concepts: The Evidence of Human Hermaphroditism', *Bulletin of the Johns Hopkins Hospital* 97 (1955): 301–19; John Money, Joan G. Hampson, and John L. Hampson, 'Hermaphroditism: Recommendations Concerning Assignment of Sex, Change of Sex, and Psychologic Management', *Bulletin of Johns Hopkins Hospital* 97 (1955): 284–300; John Money, *Venuses Penuses* (Buffalo: Prometheus, 1986).

7. Robert M. Blizzard, 'Lawson Wilkins', in Kappy et al., *Wilkins*, xi–xiv.

8. Suzanne Kessler, 'The Medical Construction of Gender: Case Management of Intersexual Infants', *Signs: Journal of Women in Culture and Society* 16 (1990): 3–26.

9. J. Dewhurst and D. B. Grant, 'Intersex Problems', *Archives of Disease in Childhood* 59 (1984): 1191–4; Anita Natarajan, 'Medical Ethics and Truth-Telling in the Case of Androgen Insensitivity Syndrome', *Canadian Medical Association Journal* 154 (1996): 568–70; Tom Mazur, 'Ambiguous Genitalia: Detection and Counselling', *Pediatric Nursing* (1983): 417–22; F. M.E. Slijper et al., 'Neonates with Abnormal Genital Development Assigned the Female Sex: Parent Counselling', *Journal of Sex Education and Therapy* 20 (1994): 9–17.

10. Milton T. Edgerton, 'Discussion: Clitoroplasty for Clitoromegaly due to Adrenogenital Syndrome without Loss of Sensitivity (by Nobuyuki Sagehashi)', *Plastic and Reconstructive Surgery* 91 (1993): 956.

11. Melissa Hendricks, 'Is It a Boy or a Girl?', *Johns Hopkins Magazine*, November 1993, 10–16.

12. John F. Stecker et al., 'Hypospadias Cripples', *Urologic Clinics of North America: Symposium on Hypospadias* 8 (1981): 539–44.

13. Jeff McClintock, 'Growing Up in the Surgical Maelstrom', *Chrysalis: The Journal of Transgressive Gender Identities* (Fall 1997): 53–4.

14. Robert E. Gross, Judson Randolph, and John F. Crigler, 'Clitorectomy for Sexual Abnormalities: Indications and Technique', *Surgery* 59 (1966): 300–08.

15. Joseph E. Oesterling, John P. Gearhart, and Robert D. Jeffs, 'A Unified Approach to Early Reconstructive Surgery of the Child with Ambiguous Genitalia', *Journal of Urology* 138 (1987): 1079–84.

16. Suzanne Kessler, *Lessons from the Intersexed* (New Brunswick, NJ: Rutgers University Press, forthcoming).

17. Robert Jeffs, quoted in Ellen Barry, 'United States of Ambiguity', Boston *Phoenix*, 22 November 1996: 6–8, quotation on 6.

18. Anne Fausto-Sterling, 'The Five Sexes: Why Male and Female Are Not Enough', *The Sciences* 33, 2 (March/April 1993): 20–25; Anne Fausto-Sterling, *Myths of Gender: Biological Theories about Women and Men*, 2nd edn. (New York: Basic Books, 1985), 134–41.

19. Kessler, 'The Medical Construction of Gender'; Suzanne Kessler, 'Meanings of Genital Variability', *Chrysalis: The Journal of Transgressive Gender Identities* (Fall 1997): 33–8.

20. 'Dr Elders' Medical History', *New Yorker* 26 September 1994: 45–6; Joycelyn Elders and David Chanoff, *From Sharecropper's Daughter to Surgeon General of the United States of America* (New York: William Morrow, 1996).

21. Natalie Angier, 'Intersexual Healing: An Anomaly Finds a Group', *New York Times* 4 February 1996: E14.

22. Hendricks, 'Is It a Boy or a Girl?': 10.

23. Justine M. Schober, 'Long Term Outcomes of Feminizing Genitoplasty for Intersex', in Pierre Mouriquant, ed, *Pediatric Surgery and Urology: Long Term Outcomes* (Philadelphia: W. B. Saunders, forthcoming).

Chapter 18

Telling Body Transgendering Stories

Richard Ekins and Dave King

Introduction

. . . The term 'transgender' has been used in four rather different senses. Virginia Prince pioneered the terms 'transgenderist' and 'transgenderal' to refer to people who lived full-time in the gender opposite to their biological sex, but did not seek sex/gender reassignment surgery (1976: 145). Richard Ekins established the Trans-Gender Archive in 1986. The term was chosen to provide an umbrella concept that avoided such medical categories as transsexual and transvestite; that included the widest possible range of transgender phenomena; and that took the sociological view that aspects of sex, sexuality, and gender (not just gender), including the binary divide, all have socially constructed components. Not long afterwards, the 'transgender community' came to be used as an umbrella term to include transsexuals, transvestites, transgenderists, drag queens, and so on, as well as (in some uses) to include their partners and friends and professional service providers.

. . . Mindful of transgender diversities yet to be explored, we find Thom and More's (1998: 3) embracive and futuristic usage of 'transgender' particularly useful:

> 'Transgender' is used as a broad and inclusive term to describe the community of all self identified cross gender people whether intersex, transsexual men and women, cross dressers, drag kings and drag queens, transgenderists, androgynous, bi-gendered, third gendered, or as yet unnamed gender gifted people.

Modes and Processes of Transgendering the Body

. . . [W]e focus in this paper on the various stories that are told of transgendering and particularly the role of the body in that process. . . . A number of conceptually distinct contemporary transgendering body stories have emerged from our research. Here we group them into four main modes of body transgendering stories depending on their relationship to the male/female binary divide. In particular, we have categorized four types of body stories in terms of four modes of transgendering: 'migrating', 'oscillating', 'erasing' and 'transcending'—terms that reflect the core characteristics of each mode. Migrating body stories involve moving the body from one side of the binary divide to the other on a permanent basis (see also, Hirschauer, 1997). Oscillating body stories are stories of moving backwards and forwards over the gender 'border', only temporarily resting on one side or the other. Erasing body stories are those in which the gender of the person erasing is expunged. Transcending body stories tell of moving beyond gender into a third space. . . .

. . . The person who is transgendering their body (with or without outside help) replaces the body parts (or the characteristics of those parts) that are associated with one gender, with those associated with the other. Thus, a penis is replaced with a vagina; a flat chest is replaced with breasts; smooth skin replaces rough skin; no body hair replaces body hair; a short hair style is replaced with a long hair style and so on. The degree of substitution will depend on a number of factors such as the particular personal project of the individual, the personal circumstances, the availability and development of any technology and aids that may be used, and (where not covered by a relevant health-care scheme) the financial resources to afford them. Where substituting is controlled in some way (that is, subject to medical or legal regulation), the question of a person's entitlement to the substitution may arise. . . .

'Concealing', as the second sub-process, refers to the concealing or hiding or parts of the body that are seen to conflict with the intended gender display. It may involve hiding the Adam's apple; tucking the penis; binding the breasts. But this will depend on the actual bodily features; a male femaler with a prominent Adam's apple and heavy dark beard growth will have more concealing to do than a male femaler without these recognizably male characteristics. However, even male femalers with ideal body characteristics for their projects and who have undergone as much substitution as possible will remain chromosomally male and in some settings (for example, some sporting contests) this will require concealing. . . . In addition to concealing and displaying, body transgendering may involve 'implying' certain body parts. Because the body is usually apprehended in social interaction in its clothed form, it is possible to imply the gendered form of the body beneath. So, for example, males can wear breast forms inside a bra, or hip pads inside a panty girdle; females may place something in their underpants to imply the possession of a penis. Implying may be the only sub-process involved in the case of what Turkle (1997) calls 'virtual gender swapping' on Internet discussion lists or, indeed, in any situation where interaction is not face to face such as that involving the telephone or written communication.

The fourth sub-process is 'redefining'. . . . The male to female transsexual may redefine her beard growth as facial hair. The penis may be redefined as a 'growth between the legs'. . . (Spry, 1997: 152). More subtly, the self may be redefined, and insofar as the self is an embodied self, body transgendering will be coterminous with this self redefining. Finally, these kinds of self and body redefinitions may involve redefining the classificatory systems of gender. The transcending body story, for instance, seeks to subvert and/or move beyond the binary divide. In the process of this redefining, the selves, bodies, and body parts within the redefined system of classification will take on new meanings.

We turn now to develop our mapping of contemporary transgender diversity in terms of the four major body transgendering stories, and their attendant sub-process.

Migrating Body Stories

. . . Many body migrants speak of starting a new life or of being reborn. While return may be possible, at its inception the journey is seen as one way; it is not expected that there will be any turning back. . . .

In migrating body stories, the prominent sub-process of body transgendering is that of substituting, which may be variously progressive, problematic, rapid, and extensive. Complete substitution (transformation), however, is not possible except in fantasy. Modern medical interventions can accomplish a great deal especially if administered early in the life of the body. Even so, chromosomal and gonadal substitutions are not possible and after puberty certain aspects of the body such as height or skeletal shape may be beyond substitution. Therefore, transgendering the body will always involve other sub-processes. . . . Stella finds the effect of hormones on her developing bust to be unremarkable, until she stops taking them. Following her genital surgery, her body substituting proceeds more swiftly. As Stella puts it:

> I thought my bust wasn't developing very much until I was due to go into hospital and had to stop taking the hormones. And then I noticed that the reverse on my bust was very quick. I noticed that it did not disappear and that, I suppose, was the first time I realized just how much it had developed. I've been back on the hormones now for three weeks and it's amazing how my bust has developed as much in those three weeks as it had in the three years before. . . .

Body substituting is altogether more speedy and dramatic, however, in the following account (written by Mark Rees for Ekins and King, 1996a):

> The action of the hormones was almost immediate. A couple of weeks later I had my last period and within a month or so people began to notice a change in my voice. . . . Although the growth of my facial hair took much longer, I was surprised by the rapidity of the changes generally. . . . My superficial veins especially in the forearms became more obvious as the subcutaneous fat decreased. The decrease was most obvious around the breasts, hips and thighs. There was an increase in muscle development with a corresponding weight increase, redistribution and increase in body hair and clitoral enlargement. After six months I was able to live as a man. . . .

We can discern three major variations of the migrating body story depending on the nature of the relationship between the 'gendered body' and the 'gendered mind': 'simple-matching migrating', where the migrator seeks to acquire a new body to fit his or her mind, which is thought of as being located in the 'wrong body'; 'coterminous migrating' where, to varying degrees, a new mind and new body emerge simultaneously; and, finally, 'mix-matching migrating', where the new body is sought, but the mind remains of the opposite sex to the new body. The 'classic' transsexual story is a good example of the 'simple-matching' variation. Following is a recent example from the autobiography of Raymond Thompson (1995):

> The first time I was born, it was in a body which was other than male. By some cosmic mistake, as a budding human being I had somehow chosen the wrong body, or the wrong body had chosen me. . . .

Coterminous migrating may have the same end result, but here the mind migrates with the body. An interview excerpt from Ekins (1997: 21–2) is illustrative:

Maria: There are two sorts of transsexual. There are those like Helen, who see their appendage as an accident. They see themselves as women, who have some mistake as regards their bodies. And then there are the other sort, who know they are men, but still want to be women.
Researcher: Isn't that a bid odd? Going through the change, but still thinking you're male?
Maria: Well, I don't know. As I keep on with this, I find that I'm like stripping away what I have learned in being male. It's like peeling away the layers of an onion.
Researcher: So, what is underneath?
Maria: I don't know, but I'm finding out. All I can say is that whenever I act the female role, I feel more like myself. It might be that underneath all the layers is a female identity.

A final, and so far little discussed, variant, is where the body migrates from one sex to another, but the mind remains in its original sex (mix-matching migrating). Ronnie did not like living as a man. He underwent electrolysis on his facial and body hair. He ingested female hormones and had breast implant surgery. He adopted feminine intonation in his voice. After such body and gender transgendering he became 'Carole' and was able to 'pass' as a woman in most settings. Indeed, providing he 'tucked' his penis, he was able to share a bed with 'other' females without them suspecting he was other than the female he appeared. He did, however, retain his penis, and notwithstanding his extensive use of female hormones was able to maintain an erection and experience male orgasm. He made attachments to a number of lesbian women and once he felt that they would not be put off by his disclosure, he told them of what he referred to as his 'she-male' identity. By no means were all the self-identified lesbian women put off sexual relations with him by his disclosure. A number of Ronnie's lesbian partners engaged in penetrative intercourse with him, with Ronnie taking the 'masculine' active and aggressive role. In his/her identification as a 'she male', Ronnie/Carole did not regard him/herself as either a woman with a penis (a phallic woman), or a male to female transsexual. Rather he/she perceived of him/herself as 'a man in a woman's body'. (Research interview)

There is no necessary congruity between sex, sexuality, and gender in body migrating stories. Many body migrators identify as gay or lesbian. Some do not display in the clothes of their new 'sex'. However, where maximum substituting takes place sexuality and gender substituting will variously precede, accompany, or follow the body migrating, and the migrating will be permanent. . . .

Oscillating Body Stories

While migrating body stories for the most part entail a one-way journey, oscillating body stories, in contrast, entail moving to and fro between male and female polarities, across and between the binary divide. . . . Some may spend a few hours every week on the other side of the divide; others may only manage the journey every few months but they might be able to stay for a week or more; still others may spend their working day as male and the rest of the time as female. There are oscillators who oscillate (largely in fantasy) minute to minute, even second to second. Some may, like the couples who retire to their favourite holiday destination, eventually decide to buy a one-way ticket and migrate. . . . As with migrating stories the binary divide is accepted. Medical help is not enlisted, although other people may play a part in facilitating the excursions.

The main sub-processes involved in oscillating body stories are implying, concealing, and redefining. . . . Oscillating body stories will typically involve much implying: the wearing of wigs, the use of padded bras and padded girdles; the wearing of false moustaches and beards and something in the underpants to imply the possession of a penis.

One common oscillating story is that of the male transvestite. . . .

Pauline is 41, divorced and living alone. She has a well-paid job and lives in a very private, moderately expensive flat. She never cross-dresses in public, so Pauline spends as much time as she can in her flat, dressed as a woman, only leaving it for necessary work or shopping trips.

She buys her large collection of women's clothes through mail-order catalogues, and buys her wigs, padded girdles, and silicone breasts from a specialist mail-order transvestite supplier. Her body is kept free of hair by depilating, shaving, or plucking. She was clean shaven at the time of interview, and was keenly experimenting with her new electrolysis machine.

Whereas Pauline's body transgendering is known only to herself, Brenda's wife knows and tolerates her husband's cross-dressing. Brenda (38) initiated her wife into her activities early in their marriage and was free to buy women's clothes or to borrow her wife's. . . .

Helena, on the other hand, participates in a number of social worlds within which she wishes to present different aspects of her body femaling, while presenting a male body in other settings. Helena is 35, single, and living alone. She advertises her services as a transvestite prostitute in contact magazines and for these engagements presents as a look-alike of 1940s movie stars. She maintains an hourglass figure with the use of a corset and a padded bra placed over her chest carefully taped to create cleavage. Helena is also a member of a transvestite group that meets to cross-dress, principally in leather fetish gear. For this group, she adopts a punk image and redefines her slim male body as an anorexic girl's body. As a male, Helena works as a teacher in a boys' secondary school, involving herself in cricket coaching in the summer months. The extent of her body substituting is limited, primarily by her need to avoid possible detection in this work setting. . . .

In the above examples, substituting is limited by the need to return to the male side of the divide at some point. . . . Where this is not the case, substituting is likely to be more extensive and visible, as, for instance, where the oscillator is known to be a drag queen prominent in gay and transvestite settings. . . .

Erasing Body Stories

. . . Those with male bodies seek to expunge their maleness and eliminate in themselves the existence of a binary divide. Similarly, but conversely, with female erasers. . . . There are two principal variants of the erasing story depending on the position of the eraser in relation to the traditional version of the binary male/female divide. In one variant, erasing self-consciously buttresses the traditional version of the binary male/female divide for all males and females who are not erasing/being erased. In the other variant, the eraser considers the binary divide a source of oppression and seeks a modification of the binary gender system that will enable those 'without gender' to live 'gender-free' lives.

Illustrative of the first variant are the writings of Debra Rose (1993a, 1993b, 1994, 1995). Rose's writings are a blend of fact and fiction. They do, however, provide a particularly systematic account of one major sissy maid lifestyle and a lifestyle that has a considerable following. Many of our sissy informants tell us that her journal *Sissy Maid Quarterly* (SMQ: 1994–1996) 'plugs into' their innermost thoughts, fantasies, and wishes with astonishing insight and accuracy. . . .

While the details of the trainings vary, the *sine qua non* of all of them is systematic erasing. There is much concealing (of attributes of masculinity). There is much redefining (sissies dress in effeminate and feminine attire *not* in order to cross the binary divide, but to further their emasculating). Such substituting and implying as there is, is co-opted in the service of erasing. . . .

In marked contrast to Rose's vision of erasing is that of writer and activist Christie Elan-Cane. Christie is the first to pioneer publicly 'per'[1] particular 'third gender' body erasing. Christie, a biological female, felt 'in the wrong body' from per earliest days. With the onset of puberty, per development of breasts and menstruation was particularly distressing. As Christie (1997: 1) puts it: 'I was never able to come to terms with "womanhood". I had the body of a woman and therefore I was considered by everyone to be a woman and I was repelled. I was disgusted by the physical changes to my body when I started to develop at puberty.' Never identifying as transsexual, Christie eventually found a surgeon who would remove per breasts and, some years later, per

womb. Now at ease with per body, Christie began to identify as 'neither male, nor female': 'a third gender person'. Although open to the possibility of further body erasing—having per ovaries removed, for instance—for Christie, 'everything fell into place' once surgery was completed. Whereas Christie had flirted with a lesbian identity prior to surgery, now Christie found perself attracted to men, provided they saw per as being a third gender person. Per sexual partner is now a male who relates to per as third gender—neither male, nor female. Christie wears androgynous 'gender-free' clothes—mostly black 'neither male, nor female' 'shirts'; black trouser suits—a sort of contemporary Chairman Mao suit, and keeps per head meticulously shaven—all appropriate to per 'third gender' identification, following per body erasing. . . .

Secure in per personal erasing, Christie has increasingly turned per attention to publicizing per position, with the intention of enabling a space to be provided within a bi-polarized gender system, for 'third genders' like perself. Initial steps include campaigning for the use of a non-gender specific form of address ('per'—derived from person; Pr as a title to replace Mr or Mrs), and the inclusion of the gender-free in equal rights legislation (Elan-Cane, 1997; 1998). In Christie's view: 'there is no reason why there should be two diametrically opposed genders nor is there any reason why gender should exist at all' (Elan-Cane, 1998: 7) and, in these senses, per position might be seen as a subversive one. However, it is not per present intention to seek to undermine the binary divide, an approach that Christie regards as both unrealistic and impracticable. Rather, Christie seeks social legitimacy for perself and others like per (Personal communication, 1998).

Transcending Body Stories

In recent years there have emerged a number of body stories that we focus on here under the general title of 'transcending body stories'. Despite her chapter title 'Transcending and Transgendering: Male-to-Female Transsexuals, Dichotomy and

Diversity', Bolin (1994) does not discuss the meaning of the word 'transcending'. We have chosen the term because of its idea of 'going beyond'. In these stories, while the body may be transgendered by means of substituting, concealing, and implying, as in the other modes, the meaning of this is fundamentally redefined. They are, in Stone's (1991: 295) words, 'disruptive to the accepted discourses of gender'. In these stories, the whole process of transgendering is radically redefined by rendering problematic the binary gender divide. Further, these stories go beyond the framing of transgendering within the medical categories of transvestism and transsexualism. . . .

In contrast to migrating stories . . . these transcending stories tell bold tales of 'transgender warriors' fighting a war against an enemy and for a people. The enemy is seen as our cultural rules concerning gender . . . The people who are being fought for are the members of a broadly defined transgender community. . . .

In migrating body stories, a 'pathological state' (gender dysphoria) is dealt with by means of a medically assisted and controlled migration across the gender divide. Transcending body stories question the idea of pathology in a manner analogous to the way in which gays challenged the disease status of homosexuality. If there is no disease, then genital surgery and other body gender alterations may be a matter of personal choice. As Califia (1997: 224) puts it: 'transsexuals are becoming informed consumers of medical service'. . . . A new sort of transgendered person has emerged, one who approaches sex reassignment with the same mindset that they would obtaining a piercing or a tattoo.'

That some doctors may be prepared to see themselves as providing a service for their transgendered clients rather than diagnosing and treating them is evident in the work by Bockting and Coleman (1992). They use the term 'gender dysphoric client' rather than patient throughout. Such clients, they claim, often have a more ambiguous gender identity and are more ambivalent about a gender role transition than they initially admit' (1992: 143). Their treatment program, they say, allows their clients to 'discover and express their unique identity' (1992: 143) and 'allows for individuals to identify as neither man nor woman, but as someone whose identity transcends the culturally sanctioned dichotomy' (1992: 144).

The idea of the 'gender outlaw' shifts our attention to another way in which transcending stories go beyond our conventional understandings. This idea points to the position of trans people as located somewhere outside the spaces customarily offered to men and women, as people who are beyond the laws of gender. So the assumption that there are only two (opposite) genders is opened up to scrutiny. Instead, it is suggested that there is the possibility of a 'third' space outside the gender dichotomy.

A recent variant of the transcending story is being told by those people born with intersexed bodies. As Fausto-Sterling (1993) states, 'Hermaphrodites have unruly bodies. They do not fall naturally into a binary classification; only a surgical shoehorn can put them there.' And this is exactly what has happened: during this century, intersexed bodies have been surgically and hormonally fitted into one or the other gender category. Now, some people with intersexed bodies who were neither aware nor able to control such surgical and hormonal intervention, are questioning those practices and demanding the right to determine if, when, and how their bodies should be altered. These intersex stories contain many of the elements of those transcending stories considered above: the emphasis on personal choice, the challenging of medical authority, the acceptance of bodies that are not unambiguously male or female. . . .

Note

1. For Christie Elan-Cane: 'To gain validity and social legitimacy it is imperative that the Third Gender has a proper title that is non-gender specific and a correct form of address.' Christie's own preference rejects 'his' or 'her' for 'per', derived from 'person' (Elan-Cane, 1998: 3–4).

References

Bocting, W. O., and E. Coleman. 1992. 'A Comprehensive Approach to the Treatment of Gender Dysphoria', in W. O. Bockting and E. Coleman, eds, *Gender Dysphoria: Interdisciplinary Approaches in Clinical Management*. New York: Haworth Press.

Bolin, A. 1994. 'Transcending and Transgendering: Male-to-Female Transsexuals, Dichtomy and Diversity', in G. Herdt, ed, *Third Sex, Third Gender: Beyond Dimorphism in Culture and History*. New York: Zone Books.

Califia, P. 1997. *Sex Changes: The Politics of Transgenderism*. San Francisco: Cleis Press.

Ekins, R. 1997. *Male Femaling: A Grounded Theory Approach to Cross-Dressing and Sex-Changing*. London: Routledge.

Elan-Cane, C. 1997. 'Prepared Speech for Cybergender Discussion', Transgender Film and Video Festival, London.

———. 1998. 'A World Without Gender', talk for the Third International Congress on Sex and Gender, Exeter College, Oxford.

Fausto-Sterling, A. 1993. 'The Five Sexes: Why Male and Female Are Not Enough', *Sciences* 33, 2: 20–5.

Hirschauer, S. 1997. 'The Medicalization of Gender Migration', *International Journal of Transgenderism* 1, 1. Available at http://www.symposion.com/ijt/ijtc0104.htm.

Prince, V. 1976. *Understanding Cross Dressing*. Los Angeles: Chevalier Publications.

Rees, M. 1996. 'Becoming a Man: The Personal Account of a Female-to-Male Transsexual', in R. Ekins and D. King, eds, *Blending Genders: Social Aspects of Cross-Dressing and Sex-Changing*. London: Routledge.

Rose, D.R. 1993a. *Maid in Form 'A', 'B', and 'C'*. Capistrano Beach, CA: Sandy Thomas Adv.

———. 1993b. *The Sissy Maid Academy, Vols 1 & 2*. Capistrano Beach, CA: Sandy Thomas Adv.

———. 1994. 'Top Drawer', *Sissy Maid Quarterly* 1: 36–7.

———. 1995. *Where the Sissies Come From*. Capistrano Beach, CA: Sandy Thomas Adv.

Sissy Maid Quarterly, 1994–96. 1–5. Capistrano Beach, CA: A Sandy Thomas Publication, produced in conjunction with Rose Productions.

Spry, J. 1997. *Orlando's Step—An Autobiography of Gender*. Norwich, VT: New Victoria Publishers.

Stone, S. 1991. 'The Empire Strikes Back: A Posttranssexual Manifesto', in J. Epstein and K. Straub, eds, *Bodyguards*. London: Routledge.

Thom B., and K. More. 1998. 'Welcome to the Festival', in *The Second International Transgender Film and Video Festival*. London: Alchemy.

Thompson, R., and K. Sewell. 1995. *What Took You So Long: A Girl's Journey to Manhood*. London: Penguin.

Turkle, S. 1997. 'Tinysex and Gender Trouble', in S. Kemp and J. Squires, eds, *Feminisms*. Oxford: Oxford University Press.

Part VII

Risky Bodies

Jacqueline Low and Claudia Malacrida

Social theorist Anthony Giddens (1990, 1994) describes modern Western societies as **risk cultures**. Such societies are characterized by increasing knowledge about the risks associated with progress (1990). He argues that modern industrial societies produce **reflexive modernity**, in which individuals must constantly assess their risks reflexively and make choices based on these risk assessments. Unfortunately, as people access increasingly contradictory expert knowledge concerning risks, such assessments become increasingly difficult to make (1994). Anne Rogers and David Pilgrim's (1996) article on Mass Childhood Immunization (MCI) provides an example of the tensions attached to 'choosing' the level of risk one should expose children to, in light of several competing bodies of knowledge relating to health, immunity, and risk. In this case, knowledge produced by medical scientists and health promoters often contradicts the experiential knowledge of primary health practitioners and parents, complicating parents' 'choices' about whether or not to immunize their children.

Rogers and Pilgrim's article also indicates the underlying power relations embedded in these knowledge conflicts. These contradictions can be explained by Foucault's (1991) ideas about **biopower**, the modern approach to social regulation in which bodies are controlled through professional 'truth' claims about health and citizenship (Foucault, 1991; Lupton, 1999). According to Rogers and Pilgrim, the constructed 'truth' about MCI makes actions like 'choosing' immunization seem rational and sensible, and opting out seem emotional and problematic. This situation is an example of Foucault's concept that the body, constructed by knowledge production, is a political field.

In 'The Medical Model of the Body as a Site of Risk: A Case Study of Childbirth' Karen Lane (1995) situates her study within the literature on the **risk society**. As noted above, a fundamental characteristic of the risk society is the **individualization of risk** where, increasingly, we are held responsible for the risks we face in daily life (Beck, 1992). For example, problems of ill health are not understood to be caused by environmental, political, or other social processes, but are said to be the result of individual lifestyle choices and behaviours. Consistent with this individualization of risk is the **biomedical model**, a model of health, illness, and workings of the body that locates 'the sources and solutions to health problems solely within the individual' (Low, 2004: 79). From this vantage point, Lane argues that biomedicine equates 'risky' pregnancies with individual women's bodies, despite the fact that 'the major risks [of childbirth] are associated with factors that exist socially and historically' rather than individually (1995: 66). The individualization of risk has consequences for women, and Lane (1995: 55) reports how the biomedical model has legitimated a number of invasive techniques, including amniocentesis, where a large needle is inserted into the uterus in order to extract amniotic fluid. Such tests are regularly used to check for birth defects and are ostensibly meant to guard against risk; it is ironic, however, that these invasive medical procedures are themselves dangerous and put women's health at risk.

Another example of the individualization of risk can be found in prenatal testing, where prospective parents are offered fetal assessments in a routine manner. While this may seem to offer parents 'choices', it also leaves parents who refuse testing or who continue what are deemed high-risk pregnancies in a position of responsibility for that child's health and care. Finally, similar to the immunization discourse, the ability of prenatal testing to predict or prevent ill health or disability in children is often overstated, meaning parents' decisions occur in unclear knowledge contexts.

From children's health we turn to the other end of the life cycle. In her sociological study of palliative care, Julia Lawton (1998) grounds her analysis in Mary Douglas's (2005) insights about the socio-cultural construction of risk. Douglas argues that, in all societies, classificatory systems exist that allow members to distinguish between that which is pure and therefore safe, and that which is dangerous and therefore risky. What is significant about Douglas's insight is that purity and danger are not fixed states of things but rather are socially constructed and their meaning entirely dependant on social context. In Douglas's classic words, 'dirt [is] matter out of place' (2005: 44). For instance, there is nothing inherently dangerous about a pair of dirty socks lying in a laundry hamper, but place them on the counter where you are cutting up raw chicken and the same socks become items infused with risk—they are 'dirt'. Douglas conceptualizes 'dirt' and any other phenomena that does not fit our societal classifications as **cultural 'anomalies'**, arguing that we react to them with **pollution behaviour**, rituals and activities aimed at containing and neutralizing the risk anomalies present (2005: 48).

For Lawton, a certain type of dying body, the 'dirty dying', is one such anomaly, and palliative care is an institutionalized form of pollution behaviour that deals with the risks the dirty dying present. She uses the concept of **dirty dying** to refer to those dying bodies that exhibit 'bodily deterioration, demise, and decay' (Lawton, 1998: 123). Such bodies are 'dirty' in Douglas's sense because they have become 'unbounded' (Lawton, 1998: 127). For Lawton, **unbounded bodies** are those bodies where the barrier between what is proper to the inside of the body and the outside of the body begins to breakdown. For example, Lawton describes how one of the patients in the hospice she studied had uncontrollable and unrestrained nosebleeds. These nosebleeds were so severe that the blood from them would soak the bedclothes surrounding the patient. What this example illustrates is that while there is nothing dangerous about blood when it flows through our veins, when it or other matter proper to the inside of the body is no longer contained by the body it becomes dangerous. We react to it with disgust, necessitating the neutralization of the risk it poses via the rituals of palliative care.

References

Beck, U. 1992. *Risk Society: Towards a New Modernity*. London: Sage.

Douglas, M. 2005. *Purity and Danger: An Analysis of Concepts of Pollution and Taboo*. London: Routledge.

Foucault, M. 1991. 'Governmentality', in G. Burchell, C. Gordon, and P. Miller, eds, *The Foucault Effect: Studies in Governmentality: With Two Lectures By and an Interview With Michel Foucault*. Chicago: The University of Chicago Press, 87–104.

Giddens, A. 1990. *The Consequences of Modernity*. Cambridge: Polity Press.

———. 1994. 'Living in a Post-Traditional Society', in U. Beck, A. Giddens, and S. Lasch, eds, *Reflexive Modernization: Politics, Tradition and Aesthetics in the Modern Social Order*. Cambridge: Polity Press, 56–109.

Lane, K. 1995. 'The Medical Model of the Body as a Site of Risk: A Case Study of Childbirth', in J. Gabe, ed, *Medicine, Health and Risk: Sociological Approaches*. London: Blackwell Publishers, 53–72.

Lawton, J. 1998. 'Contemporary Hospice Care: The Sequestration of the Unbounded Body and "Dirty Dying"' *Sociology of Health and Illness* 20, 2: 121–43.

Low, J. 2004. *Using Alternative Therapies: A Qualitative Analysis*. Toronto: Canadian Scholar's Press.

Lupton, D. 1999. *Risk*. London and New York: Routledge.

Rogers, A., and D. Pilgrim. 1996. 'The Risk of Resistance: Perspectives on the Mass Immunization Program', in J. Gabe, ed, *Medicine, Health and Risk: Sociological Approaches*. Oxford: Blackwell Publishers, 73–90.

Chapter 19

The Risk of Resistance: Perspectives on the Mass Childhood Immunization Program

Anne Rogers and David Pilgrim

Introduction

The policy of mass childhood immunization (MCI) enjoys the support of medical professionals and government health agencies worldwide. In 1977, the World Health Organization and UNICEF proposed that there should be a 90 per cent immunization coverage of children in all countries (Egan et al., 1994). This aim had been met already in Britain and The Health of the Nation (DOH, 1992) sets a higher target of 95 per cent coverage for 1995. MCI is deemed to be an effective health promotion strategy for two reasons: it has a direct impact on individuals immunized, by stimulating resistance to infectious disease; and an indirect impact, by reducing the circulation of pathogenic micro-organisms within a population. The latter effect is technically called 'herd immunity'.

In Britain, since 1990, when a new general practitioner (GP) contact was introduced, a cash payment of £1800 has been given to each doctor reaching the 90 per cent target for their infant patients. The introduction of this financial inducement signalled that spontaneous parental compliance was not considered sufficient, in itself, to ensure targets being met. . . .

Using documentary and interview data, this chapter will examine the views of four communities about MCI: health promoters; medical scientists; primary health-care workers; and dissenting parents. . . .

Health Promoters

The Department of Health (DOH) produces an annual guidance book to health workers in Britain, entitled Immunization Against Infectious Disease. This book, known in the trade as the 'green book', contains information about schedules, the individual vaccines and their contraindications. Sometimes this is augmented by pointed advice or directives from the government's Chief Medical Officer. These letters or memoranda are circulated to all medical practitioners and health personnel responsible for encouraging and monitoring uptake.

In addition to this dissemination of guidance to local agencies, there is a mass circulation of DOH and [Health Education Authority] (HEA) leaflets to parents through libraries, surgeries, and health centres. One DOH leaflet points out, under the heading 'Vaccination of infants—the facts' that:

> Vaccines are amongst the safest and most effective medicines there are. Every year they prevent countless serious illnesses and many deaths . . . Vaccines like other medicines can cause reactions. These are usually middle and brief. Very rarely, they are serious. For this reason, vaccines should be given only by doctors, or nurses, who are qualified to give them and who are in a position to advise where there is any indication against their use . . . (1990: 1). . . .

The official promotional literature emphasizes the scarcity of iatrogenic risk; effectiveness of vaccines in protecting individuals and in reducing infection outbreaks; rarity of vaccine failure; reliability and authority of primary health-care workers as sources of risk assessment on behalf of parents; and the irrationality of parental doubts about immunization.

Together these points reflect the strong affective and moral character of promotional literature. Despite the recurrent use of the term 'facts' (which implies the transmission of neutral information), the literature clearly sets out to induce anxiety and guilt in those parents responsible for children who are not immunized. A formula to immediately reverse this induced distress is then prescribed—'immunize your child'. . . . For instance, when the (Haemophilus influenzae type B) Hib vaccine was introduced, the HEA commissioned television and magazine advertisements that showed a nursery in which a toy box was transformed into a coffin.

The literature also has its relevant silences about the factors that determine risk of infection and its possible lasting consequences. There is nothing on the role of poverty, low social class, poor diet, or inadequate sanitation—even though these determinants of risk are well known within public health (McKeown, 1979). Nothing is mentioned about the uncertainty surrounding the natural history of the virulence of microorganisms. Scarlet fever, syphilitic psychosis, and rheumatic fever all increased then declined in incidence in the absence of vaccine use. This was officially recognized by the DHSS in the 1970s (DHSS, 1976) but health promoters today do not put this knowledge into the public domain. State payments to vaccine damaged children, which between 1987 and 1993 amounted to £780,000 (Hansard, 1994), are not mentioned, nor is the GP contract, with its financial inducement.

In the health promoters' campaign is a righteous commitment to the view that MCI is safe and effective. Parents are there to be persuaded. Their views of contraindications are reported in studies by public health doctors as being 'mythical' (Klein et al., 1981), 'parentally' perceived, or 'false' (Bar-low and Walker, 1990). Essentially, the defaulting parent is either neglectful or neurotically wrong-headed. For health promoters the problem of MCI is only the problem of parental non-compliance. . . .

Medical Scientists

The views of epidemiologists studying the relationship between MCI and disease transmission are not as clear cut as the above position, but more cautious. Risk is viewed as the probability of an event, combined with the extent of the gains and losses it will entail, and risk assessment is an all round estimation of probable outcomes. For example, in relation to the notion of herd immunity, some epidemiologists have expressed doubts about the simple mathematical rule of 90 per cent coverage . . .

Researchers studying the impact of MCI have drawn attention to three perverse or contradictory features of the policy. First, the higher the immunization coverage the higher is the average age of those who do become infected. This has particularly threatening consequences for females in relation to rubella, who are pushed nearer to child-bearing age. With mumps and measles, later ages of infection bring with them more serious symptoms and complications. Second, the greater the coverage, the higher the risk ratio becomes between the iatrogenic effects from vaccines and complications from contracting the disease, as the proportion of those infected becomes smaller and the number immunized becomes higher. Third, certain vaccine types may be high on efficacy but low on safety. This can lead to the contradiction that the greatest benefit at the population level is associated with the greatest risk at the individual level:

> Ultimately if an infectious disease had been nearly eradicated, the risks associated with the vaccination are expected to exceed those of infection. Hence there is a conflict of interest between the individual (risk associated with the vaccine) and the group (benefits of herd immunity) (Nokes and Anderson, 1991: 1312). . . .

Despite the identification of vaccine risk, the cost-benefit analysis leads to the conclusion that MCI remains a sound policy. Support for MCI is based on an assessment of its population level benefit; it is not denied, indeed the evidence is supplied, that some individuals may be iatrogenic casualties of the policy. However, what is left unacknowledged in the 'neutral' calculations of risk and subsequent support for MCI are the underlying interests of medical practitioners as a group working in the field of epidemiology or public health. Epidemiologists have access to knowledge that suggests that 90 per cent of the decline in infectious disease levels occurred before the introduction of MCI (McKeown, 1979). . . .

Primary Health-care Workers

GPs and health visitors are the recipients, mediators, and executors of advice and directives from health promoters and the DOH. By deploying a variety of strategies they are in a position to alter compliance levels. In addition to passing on DOH and HEA literature, they can use computer records to trigger follow-up letters and uncooperative parents. When faced with parents and their infants in the surgery, they can remind them about immunization and then offer the vaccination on the spot.

In the study conducted by the authors (Rogers and Pilgrim, ibid) the 10 primary health-care workers interviewed (seven GPs and three health visitors selected via a local medical committee of GPs in South East London) varied in their negotiating position with doubting parents. At one extreme there was the GP who told defaulters that they were being selfish in putting their child and other children at risk by not complying with immunization. At the other extreme was a health visitor who set up meetings between groups of parents and a local homeopath to discuss an alternative viewpoint about MCI. She saw defaulting as a civil right and complained that dissenting parents were regularly harassed by GPs and health visitors. She was also concerned that a preoccu-

pation with increasing uptake in high-risk groups might lead to the selective surveillance and targeting of those who were already vulnerable and oppressed (like poor Asian families in inner-city areas).

In between were those who enacted the paternalistic role set for them by health promoters as an authoritative advisor. They gave time to parents to air their anxieties and then offered them advice about potential risks and benefits. However, GPs did not always share the same assumptions about vaccine risk. For example, two doctors in different practices only a few miles apart spoke of the potential danger of arthritic problems linked to the rubella component of the Mumps, Measles, and Rubella Vaccine (MMR). . . .

Thus, the dilemma for primary health-care workers about MCI is how to negotiate a population level driven policy with individual parents. The dilemma also illuminates something of the ambiguity of self-identity that primary health-care workers face. They identify both with being parents *and* the 'rational' scientific knowledge that forms the core of their secondary socialization as primary health-care workers. Doubt is reinforced by the position that primary health workers occupy at the interface between official, state endorsed, immunization policy and the immediacy of the reactions of the dissenting recipients of such a policy.

Dissenting Parents

The study by the authors also included interviews with 19 mothers who had refused immunization for their children. . . .

These parents articulated a complex rationale that was derived from a mixture of world views held about the environment, healing, holism, and the roles and responsibilities of parenting, and a critical reading of the scientific and alternative literature discussed above. The balance between these varied across accounts. For example, one mother, who was a research psychologist, focused her comments almost exclusively around methodological problems and uncertainties of research reports and the lack of knowledge she perceived her GP to have both about infectious diseases and vaccine side effects. Another parent (a choreographer and artist) described her reasons for becoming a non-complier in relation to her views about fate. When faced with the rationalistic argument put forward by some health professionals that the risk of damage from vaccine was far less than crossing the road—she responded by saying that if her child was killed or injured by a car she could accept this as an inevitability—something that she had no control over. She felt she could not 'forgive herself' if something happened to her child as the result of her decision to introduce deliberately something she viewed as toxic into her child's body. Generally, however, the doubts about immunization were initiated by a maternal 'instinct', or intuition, which were confirmed and solidified into a coherent anti-immunization position by finding out more from the medical and alternative literature.

The question of risk assessment for these parents was essentially in conflict with the types of knowledge claim common in the health promotion literature outlined earlier. The data elicited suggest that this risk assessment involves a combination of some of the following: medical opinion on vaccine risk is misleading; host health status, not immunization status, is the best predictor of healthy recovery from naturally contracted infections (in those committed to homeopathy); immunization debilitates a child's immune system, making him or her prone in later life to auto-immune disorders; naturally acquired immunity is permanent, whereas vaccine induced immunity may wear off or even fail to provoke antibody activity at all; and vaccines provoke a far greater level of serious iatrogenic effects than are officially conceded and recorded.

Some of these ideas were arrived at intuitively, but often they were shaped and reinforced by access to anti-immunization arguments in their social network, or by reading critiques of MCI from alternative medicine and social medicine literature. One of the paradoxes about this group of mothers, in their challenge to the official health promotion position, is that they were paragons of

virtue, if not zealots, about reducing potential risks to their children's health in every respect apart from their opposition to immunization. They adhered slavishly to long periods of breast-feeding. They also emphasized healthy eating, mental, and physical well-being.

In rejecting the passive acceptance of expert interventions, like immunization, they were acting consistently with the overarching rationale of modern health promotion—that health is maintained by attending to personal responsibility, action, and lifestyle duties. Immunization represented an anomaly within this rationale. It is vaccination that is at odds with the general policy of health promotion, not those who refuse it. . . .

Discussion

The difference in understanding between the positions taken up highlight two central questions: are unvaccinated children a health risk to themselves and others and are vaccines a health risk to individual children? From the data and literature examined here the health promoters and dissenting parents have expressed diametrically opposed positions in answering these questions, and the primary health-care workers have given a variety of answers. . . .

. . . Whereas the medical researchers have tended to ally themselves to the position taken by health promoters (swayed perhaps by the lure of the 'technical fix'), primary health-care workers do not have a fixed self-identity in relation to MCI. They are at the interface between the state-endorsed position on MCI and that of doubting or dissenting parents. Often they are parents themselves and they have to maintain workable personal relationships with their patients. Faced with apparently contradictory evidence and pressures in the face of uncertainty, they employ a variety of risk communication strategies ranging from authoritarianism to libertarianism. . . .

. . . In advanced Western capitalist societies, increasing expectations of consumer rights in service transactions have led to the need for greater availability of information and the citizen's right to accept or reject a product. The MCI program fits poorly with these expectations, leading to a conflict of values and interests between state/medical paternalism and citizen consumerism. . . .

. . . The willingness of the media to give voice to parental concerns about vaccine risk is likely to reinforce rather than detract from concerns about risk. Short (1984) notes that public awareness of risk is heavily influenced by media coverage. The increasing tendency for various social groups to consult with what Giddens (1991) terms 'guides to living' (manuals, guides, books on self-help) may mean that the knowledge accumulated at the moment by a small group of dissenting parents about vaccine versus infection risk may become more widespread at the expense of more orthodox literature.

The tendency for late modernity to engender the creation of 'new' social movements concerned with challenging expert risk assessments may also present a problem for the traditional public health view of MCI. The traditional pattern of authority and deference between expert and non expert is breaking down. Traditional authority enjoys less deference from non experts than in the past. The lay person is now faced with a range of experts who disagree with one another on a topic like vaccination. Doctors, alternative therapists, lawyers, campaigning journalists, public health specialists, and primary care workers may all offer authoritative advice to be assessed by lay people. As Giddens (1991) points out, this range of expert views leads to lay people now consulting other sources of information such as self-help manuals. . . .

Thus, the inherited tension between the medical rationale of the early twentieth century and the tradition of questioning state interference is now amplified by consumerism and the loss of trust in expert systems (Giddens, 1991). Consequently, it is not surprising that MCI is surfacing as a controversial policy. This controversy is made more likely by other emerging cultural emphases about health, such as self-responsibility and holism and the emergence of new social movements. . . .

Acknowledgements

We are grateful to the respondents who took part in the Health Education Authority funded study for their time and interest in the project. We would also like to thank Jonathan Gabe, Maggie Pearson, and the two anonymous reviewers for their helpful and constructive comments on an earlier draft of this chapter.

References

Barlow, H., and D. Walker. 1990. 'Immunization in Fife Part II—Failure to Immunize Against Whooping Cough—Reasons Given By Parents', *Health Education Journal* 49, 103–5.

DHSS. 1976. *Prevention and Health: Everybody's Business.* London: HMSO.

DOH. 1990. *Vaccination Protects.* London: HMSO.

———. 1992. *Health of the Nation.* London: HMSO.

Egan, S., G. Logan, and H. Bedford. 1994. *Low Uptake of Immunization. Associated Factors and the Role of Health Education Initiatives in Uptake of Immunization. Issues for Health Educators.* London: Health Education Authority.

Giddens, A. 1991. *Modernity and Self-Identity.* London: Polity.

Hansard. 1994. *Vaccine Damage Payment Scheme.* Written answer to Mr Ian McCartney MP, Monday 27 June, PQ2080.

Klein, N., K. Morgan, and M.H. Washborough-Jones. 1981. 'Parents' Beliefs About Vaccination—The Continuing Propagation of False Contraindications', *British Medical Journal* 283: 1231–3.

McKeown, T. 1979. *The Role of Medicine.* Oxford: Blackwell.

Nokes, D.J., and R.M. Anderson. 1991. 'Vaccine Safety Versus Vaccine Efficacy in Mass Immunization Programs', *The Lancet* 338, 1309–12.

Roger, A., and D. Pilgrim. 1994. 'Rational Non-Compliance with Childhood Immunization: Personal Accounts of Parents and Primary Health-Care

Professionals', in Health Education Authority, eds, *Uptake of Immunization: Issues for Health Education*. London: Health Education Authority.

Short, J. 1984. 'The Social Fabric of Risk: Toward the Social Transformation of Risk Analysis', *American Sociological Review* 49: 711–25.

Chapter 20

The Medical Model of the Body as a Site of Risk: A Case Study of Childbirth

Karen Lane

. . .

Medical Science and Childbirth

. . . It is the case that under the medical model of childbirth, risk has been assigned to individuals rather than structural and social conditions. The individualization of risk has, therefore, legitimated the routine use of interventions such as amniotomy (artificial breaking of fetal membranes); pharmacological induction of labour; . . . drugs for pain relief and epidural; routine intrapartum electronic fetal monitoring; and episiotomy (Marsden, 1994). Consumer dissatisfaction with antenatal care has always existed. However, organized protest by women's lobby groups, by concerned doctors and academics, and other consumer groups generally, of medical practice relating to women's health began mainly in the United Kingdom and the United States in the 1960s and 1970s. Medical and state responses to the 'vocal minority', as they were labelled, have included co-option of dissent, a more rationalized approach to antenatal care, an acceleration towards more technical controls of the kind mentioned above and even greater specialization within obstetrics (Oakley, 1986). These responses at the same time both increased state and medical surveillance over women and individualized the blame for adverse outcomes. Beck's (1992) argument is that it is only in recent years that medical practices and interventions have received systematic scrutiny by state agencies. Previously, as Oakley (1986) has shown, the state and medical science formed an unholy alliance. The state exercised indirect control over medicine through the construction

of social and economic policy, but left the profession to control technological development and assessment. Beck has been correct to argue, in one sense, that medical science has proceeded largely undeterred by widespread democratic evaluation.

Critics of the medical model have not denied the utility of risk assessment. That is, an alternative, social model of childbirth, would not dispense with risk criteria in evaluating level of risk, although the kinds of criteria and measuring devices may well be challenged. For example, the value of electronic fetal monitoring and ultrasound scanning as early screening devices have come under attack for their unreliable predictive properties and possible harmful effects (Marsden, 1994). Extra-medical criteria such as emotional equilibrium may also be used to supplement obstetric factors in the designation of risk status. However, the assessment of risk will continue to organize the delivery of maternity services. Beck would appear to be correct, therefore, at least at the more general level of his framework about late modernity. . . .

. . . Medical science has not remained immune from internal and external critique. However, Beck has identified a characteristic feature of late modernity—the prominent nature of debates about risk. It is the case that debates about childbirth will most likely continue to pivot around the notion of risk despite the low rates of mortality and morbidity relative to pre-war figures in advanced Western economies. What is at issue in childbirth, therefore, is not the question of risk or no risk, but i) the iatrogenic risk of medical interventions; ii) the realization of social control over women by the use of a risk vocabulary to describe maternity; iii) what additional criteria should be used to assess risk (such as women's perception of their physical and social environment); and iv) whether risk has monopolized the debates about childbirth to the exclusion of other factors such as emotional satisfaction and control over the events and procedures surrounding birth. This chapter will consider these issues.

Bodies at Risk

Interventions

I am not concerned here with the intention of doctors, but with the central assumptions of the medical model. The medical model assumes that the body is always ready to fail, even in ostensibly low-risk cases. As Douglas (1990) has argued, risk is not a neutral term. Doctors do not talk about a 'good' risk. The term is used negatively—and with negative consequences for women. For example, the following table (Table 23.1) is indicative of the higher rates of intervention experienced by

women in Victorian hospitals compared with women who delivered in a midwifery-run birth centre (Health Department, Victoria, 1990; Monash Medical Centre, 1993). . . .

Mortality: Home Versus Hospital

. . . [L]arge studies . . . all conclude that midwifery care (sometimes in collaboration with a GP) achieves comparable or better perinatal mortality rates (PNMR's) than obstetric care. . . .

It is unlikely that the debate about safety relative to setting and location will be resolved satisfactorily because the definition of risk, or what criteria should be employed to determine level of risk, is a contested terrain. There are different discourses of risk around differing views of the body, women, and the nature of childbirth. . . .

The Attribution of Risk as a Form of Social Control

In the case of childbirth, it is argued that the imposition of a risk category on all women acts as

Table 23.1   Comparative Rates of Interventions—Hospital and Birth Centre

	Rep. study of 100 women in Vic hospitals[1] %	Birth Centre (Moorabin)[2] %
Spon. Labour	62.0	89.0
Induction	27.0	4.7
Augmentation	11.0	5.4
Forceps	6.0	4.7
Caesarean	14.0	5.1
Episiotomy	14.0	0.0
Tears, stitches	16.0	33.0 (11.5% 1st degree)
No intervention	11.0	44.7

1. Health Dept., Victoria, 1990
2. Monash Med. Centre, 1993

form of micro-social regulation bringing about quiescence to medical intervention. It is true that the majority of women are deemed medically low-risk cases, but the very term 'risk' implies a probability of mischance. Douglas (1990) is correct to point out that the term 'risk' has a temporal dimension. It is employed retrospectively to explain a mishap and it is used to forewarn of imminent disaster should the action be repeated. The rhetoric of risk is further augmented within maternity discourse. Adverse events are not only regarded as inevitable, but their timing is seen to be capricious and unpredictable. By deduction, therefore, all women are subject to obstetric control and surveillance because all women are regarded as 'at risk'. For example, the obstetric team at the Royal Women's Hospital, Melbourne believes that:

> Despite careful selection of a low-risk population there remains a persistent incidence of potential serious complications and a continuing need for obstetric intervention (Permezel et al., 1987: 22). . . .

Risk Communities

The imposition of a risk category also involves a moral dimension (Douglas, 1990). Women may be categorized into those who are voluntarily risk-inducing because of their 'irresponsible' actions, as opposed to those who are voluntarily risk-avoiding because of their adherence to medical norms. Women who report to a doctor that they intend to birth at home, for example, may find themselves admonished for irresponsible behaviour. The following is a typical account from an Australian woman:

> *Caroline*: My sister was also planning a home-birth . . . so we both fronted up together [at the public hospital] to book as public patients, just in case. I spoke to the sister in charge . . . who said 'Well don't worry about booking, we won't refuse you care but just don't mention the home birth or just come in—come into the clinic and just go through the motions and make your

booking and it's best if you just don't mention the homebirth.'

British women have reported similar responses from their GPs in the 1980s, although not all GPs in Britain have been antipathetic to homebirth. More recently the Winterton recommendations (Department of Health, 1992) demanded that GPs respect women's choices to birth at home. . . .

Women's Perceptions of the Social and Physical Environment

It is argued here that women's interpretations of their social and physical environment are determining factors in the progress of the labour. Affective states should therefore be included in risk assessment. Yet women's emotional and subjective responses are regarded as either secondary or insignificant by obstetric staff. This suppression of women's emotional responses follows from a medical theory that embraces a reductionist and mechanistic view of the birthing process. In the medical model, birthing is conceptualized as a set of discrete internal, muscular, and chemical reactions unrelated to external (social, historical, and personal) factors. When the body fails, it is logical under this philosophy for an external agent to correct the internal malfunction. Immediate contextual factors, including positive and negative social exchanges and emotional responses to physical surroundings, are rarely examined or considered in the causal framework of the medical model. However, these contextual factors are the primary social determinants of risk precipitating medical intervention. . . .

. . . [O]ver one third of hospital deliveries in Victorian hospitals in Australia cited 'lack of progress in labour' as the reason for transfer (Health Department, Victoria, 1990: 93). This umbrella term incorporates uterine inertia, lack of dilatation of the cervix, and maternal exhaustion. It is argued here that these terms merely describe an already existing state. They are not reasons, but states of being. These states of being may seem legitimate reasons for medical intervention, but they do not provide a causal explanation. It is suggested here that the social context is a crucial determining influence, among others, in the progress of labour. . . .

Women's negative perceptions of hospitalized birthing are also demonstrated dramatically in the sequence that is called the 'cascade of intervention' (Health Department, Victoria, 1990: 90; World Health Organization, 1985: 98). It is common for women to enter hospital in 'good' labour but to find that their progress deteriorates over time. The following account from a woman who delivered in a British hospital in 1991 describes such a case:

Mona: By that time [on entry to the maternity ward at 1 p.m.], I was already 3 cm dilated, it was very quick . . . The room itself was very stark and not particularly comfortable, and they did offer me the option of a bean bag, but I ended up finding that lying on my side was comfortable. Then there was all this panic over not being able to find the baby's heartbeat that started fairly early on in the first stage. They kept making me lie down to find the baby's heartbeat. I asked for Pethidine an hour before the end of the first stage, when things were getting really tense and the contractions were very painful. . . . And then they wouldn't let me get into that position where I was upright. [Because she was asked to lie down the urge to push receded]. Once or twice I actually persuaded them to let me come up and they put the back of the bed into a sitting position. I lent forward over it and that was really comfortable but they were fumbling around with this monitor around my stomach. At this stage the urge was beginning to come back and then they said, 'No, no, we can't trace the baby's heart, this is no good, you'll have to lie down.' So I did. . . . Really I didn't have the urge . . . so I was having to really work and that was up here in my head. It was such hard work and I can remember towards the last few hours I was really, every time I pushed I was shouting out. I remember the midwife saying, 'If you put more energy into

the pushing and not through your vocal cords you'd get there a lot quicker.' They said that to me and I thought that was miserable. . . . They wouldn't let me do what I wanted, which was to sit up. They seemed to be overly panicky tracing the baby's heartbeat and they wouldn't actually let me sit up. . . . Then because I just got so tired and his head was coming and going, coming and going, they gave me whatever the drug is that helps you to push. And then they gave me an episiotomy, because I just couldn't push him out and I was tearing and I tore all the way to the anal canal. I needed 26 stitches and what was worse was my GP went and left it to the sister, who didn't realize how deep the tear was. The next day the whole lot broke down and I had to have it all done again. Despite the anaesthetic I could feel every stitch and they were giving me gas and air and I was just sobbing as every stitch went in. I can just remember feeling uncontrolled, I just had no pride any more, I just sobbed and sobbed.

It is not claimed here that there is a direct, causal effect between entering hospital and intervention. What follows is a 'cascade of intervention'—a situation where a minor, initial intervention is followed by a further intervention and where the accumulative effect is a catalogue of treatments that deny autonomy, choice, and satisfaction for most women. . . .

Hospital rules are designed to rationalize the birthing process in the interests of medical and hospital planning, to guard against any unforeseen adversity, and to protect doctors against litigation procedures on the grounds of neglect or mismanagement (Katz-Rothman, 1982). In many cases, intervention occurs precipitously and defensively 'just in case something goes wrong'. It is now conventional for medical staff to state that a safe birth can only be judged in retrospect. . . . The effect of the medicalization of birth is to incite varying degrees of anxiety, irritation, humiliation, pain, and fear, rather than comfort, confidence, and security.[1] Yet confidence in her body is probably the greatest asset to the mother during labour and delivery. Conversely, fear is the most decisive element in the erosion of safety and ease of delivery.

Has the Risk Vocabulary Colonized the Debate?

Debates about childbirth have been colonized around the notion of 'risk'. My argument is that obstetricians have pursued the issue of mortality rather than the quality of the woman's experience. For obstetricians, a birth has been successful if both the mother and the baby remain alive after the birth. . . . As one obstetrician reported:

> It was what we were all trained to always go after—the perfect baby. That's what we were trained to produce. The quality of the mother's experience—we rarely thought about that. (Davis-Floyd, 1990: 277) . . .

A joint study by women's health units in Monash and Melbourne universities found that women experienced a greater degree of dissatisfaction and an increased risk of being depressed after major obstetric intervention during birth (Brown et al., 1992). A randomized controlled trial conducted by Giles et al. (1992) at the antenatal clinic at Westmead Hospital, University of Sydney, indicated that the group cared for by midwives showed significantly greater appreciation of the continuity of care and information given than the group cared for by obstetricians. . . .

Chamberlain et al. (1991) found from a survey of 1109 Canadian women that those who had experienced a homebirth would make the same choice again. . . .

Conclusion

Oakley (1986) and Tew (1990) have argued that, although childbirth involves a risk to life and health for a minority of women and babies, the major risks are associated with factors that exist socially and historically. Risk is, therefore, both general and systemic. Major risks to women include i) medical interventions; ii) generalized historical factors that produce poor health including low income, poor diet, and smoking, and factors that are associated with the manual social class; and iii) women's negative perceptions of the social and physical environment (Lane, 1993, 1994).

Studies of comparative models of care show that midwifery care has been associated with higher consumer participation in decision-making; a greater degree of control experienced by women over conditions and procedures; and higher levels of emotional satisfaction, which in turn contribute to the ease, efficiency, and safety of labour and delivery. These conditions in turn discourage intervention. The conclusion is that the moral high-ground traditionally occupied by orthodox obstetrics has no rational or scientific basis. It is evidence of their political power that, until recent years, little pressure has been exerted by governments to exhort obstetricians to explain the inordinate and unjustifiably high intervention rates and depressed levels of maternal satisfaction associated with hospital birth. Further, since hospitals are said to be safer because of rapid access to high-technology and superior medical knowledge, it is logical to assume that hospital PNMRs should be lower than homebirth mortality levels. Tew (1990) and Campbell and Macfarlane (1987) have shown that this has not been the case in Britain, especially for the vast majority of low-risk cases, but also for high-risk infants.

Beck (1992) is partially correct to argue that the self-referential nature of medical science discourages autocritique, even in the face of mounting evidence to show its narrow and mechanistic fallibility. However, his thesis asserts a hermetically-sealed professional closure. This is why he calls it 'the extreme case of sub-politics'.

Some qualification needs to be made. It is not the case that obstetric power is impregnable from consumer criticism. Medical litigation in Australia in relation to obstetrics represented 30 per cent of the total sum that was awarded for all payments between 1984–7 and obstetricians feel themselves to be increasingly under attack (Sweet,

1989). Forde found that 'there is a degree of paranoia among some doctors that their patients and/or lawyers are out to get them' (1989: 6). In addition, Bastian (1990) has argued that for those obstetricians who feel the outcome of birth is their total responsibility, a damaged baby may be seen as a personal failure as well as grounds by consumers for financial compensation. Policymakers have identified one solution in the expansion of birth centres staffed by midwifes, who will care for women in all stages of maternity—antenatal, delivery, and postnatal phases. It is also worth noting that governments have favoured alternative models of midwifery care partly because of the cost savings associated with lower intervention levels—lower wages, lower theatre costs, lower pharmaceutical costs, and reduction in days spent in hospital proceeding the birth (Health Department, Victoria, 1990).

In cases where a woman-centred model of care is adopted as birth-centre policy (and this may not always be the case), the problem of litigation may be alleviated. Women will be encouraged to exercise agency at all stages of labour, and a policy of non-intervention may be institutionalized except in extraordinary cases. Women will maintain control over procedures and they will experience continuity of care—two of the most important criteria identified in the study reported elsewhere in this chapter as germane to positive birthing. The other criteria are peace and security of the birth place. In terms of risk discourse, the criteria of risk assessment will be expanded from purely medical and obstetric criteria to include social and environmental factors. These changes could be a progressive step for women giving birth so long as the new model is not used repressively. That is, so long as the new model does not set a specific standard that must be reached in order to avoid being labelled a failure. For example, it would be repressive for childbirth reformers to suggest that women should only birth at home, in a birth centre, or without any medical or obstetric intervention (such as analgesia, or caesarean section). Such a proposition would only introduce a new set of social controls. Women may perceive themselves to have exercised full control where they participated in the decision to have an epidural or a caesarean section, or where they agreed to transfer from home to hospital for whatever reason. The issue is to what extent women are consulted and informed of possible options and outcomes.

It is unlikely that the expansion of birth centres will be recognized in terms of expanding the set of risk criteria, or as an arrangement that recognizes the equal importance of women's experiences in the assessment of a 'good' outcome. Obstetricians are not trained to address the emotional and affective determinants of physiological efficiency. However, they may reasonably accept that 'patients' in hospitals feel resentment at perceiving themselves simply 'as numbers in the system' (Sweet, 1989). The social outcome of medical changes may be the same—to facilitate greater participation by women in the events surrounding their delivery. Increased participation may well induce a greater responsibility on the part of women where there is an unexpected and adverse outcome and less consumer resentment towards medical professionals. Studies cited above show that an alternative model may render childbirth a more satisfactory event for women and their families. The more general point to be made is that consumer resistance is growing. This is in response to individual experience of unsatisfactory treatment and because the popular literature offering women alternative views of birthing is expanding significantly. As I argued earlier, government policies in Britain and Australia are also changing, although at a much slower pace in Australia.

'Risk society' is an insightful description of one of the negative legacies of the Enlightenment. However, whereas Habermas (1992) pessimistically sought the apogee of the Enlightenment in a perfection yet to come with an illuminated form of communicative rationality, Beck has characterized the risk society as perfection realized. Science and industry are now held accountable for the production of risk. Beck's (1992) only reservation is applied to medical science because medicine's self-referentiality has historically protected it from democratic intervention and consumer criticism. In addition, the insatiable appetite for medicine in the risk society means that medicine creates a permanently expanding market for itself.

Beck used in vitro fertilization to argue his case for medical science as an extreme case of sub-politics, that is, one that was substantially immune from external criticism. In the case of obstetrics, Beck's thesis is substantially supported. For example, until more recently, obstetricians have successfully colonized the debate on childbirth by directing attention specifically and narrowly to the question of mortality, despite an expanded range of criteria applied by women to assess a successful birth. However, obstetrics is not immune from general and growing consumer criticism, which is itself substantially reflexive. Most consumer lobbying groups systematically carry out their own research and amass critical literature regarding the long-term risks to infants associated with a range of 'routine' medical procedures. This critical literature has not escaped the notice of governments, committees of inquiry, and policymakers. The case of obstetrics shows that the power of the medical lobby is immense, but that it is not impenetrable. Beck's thesis regarding medical sub-politics refers to a very broad and largely undifferentiated range of medical institutions and industries. Beck does not investigate a range of specific medical activities and/or interactions between practitioners and patients. It is at this level that his thesis cannot be supported. Many studies have been cited in this paper that show a sustained critique of medical science. Governments have more recently been persuaded by these critiques and subsequent policy changes indicate that medical power has been challenged.

Note

1. Women who gave birth in hospitals almost universally reported some negative assessments of procedures and relations. Women who gave birth at home in this study reported no negative experiences. This finding is supported by a study conducted by Bastian (1992) of 552 women who planned to give birth at home. In that study, 98.9 per cent of women said they would choose homebirth in the future.

References

Bastian, H. 1992. *Who Gives Birth at Home and Why? A Survey of 552 Australian Women Who Planned to Give Birth at Home.* Canberra: Homebirth Australia Inc.

Beck, U. 1992. *Risk Society: Towards a New Modernity.* London: Sage.

Brown, S., J. Lumley, R. Small, and J. Astbury. 1992. 'The Social Costs of Intervention in Childbirth'. Paper presented at Public Health Association 24th Annual Conference: 'Choice and Change: Ethics, Politics and Economics of Public Health', 27–30 September.

Campbell, R., and A. Macfarlane. 1987. *Where to be Born: The Debate and the Evidence.* Oxford: National Perinatal Epidemiology Unit.

Chamberlain, M., B. Soderstrom, C. Kaitell, and P. Stewart. 1991. 'Consumer Interest in Alternatives to Physician-Centred Hospital Birth in Ottawa', *Midwifery* 7: 74–81.

Davis-Floyd, R.E. 1990. 'Ritual in the Hospital: Giving Birth the American Way', in D.E.K. Hunter and P. Whitten, eds, *Anthropology: Contemporary Perspectives,* 6th edn. Glenview: Scott Foreman.

Department of Health (Great Britain). 1992. *Maternity Services: Government Response to the Second Report from the Health Committee,* Session 1991–2. London: HMSO.

Douglas, M. 1990. 'Risk as a Forensic Resource', *Daedalus* 119: 16.

Forde, K. 1989. 'Reducing the Risk of Being Sued', *Australian Practical Management* 1: 6–11.

Giles, W., J. Collins, G. Ong, and R. MacDonald. 1992. 'Antenatal Care of Low-Risk Obstetric Patients by Midwives. A Randomized Controlled Trial', *Medical Journal of Australia* 156: 158–61.

Habermas, J. 1992. *The Structural Transformation of the Public Sphere: An Inquiry into a Category of Bourgeois Society*. Cambridge: Polity Press.

Health Department, Victoria. 1990. *Final Report of the Ministerial Review of Birthing Services in Victoria: Having a Baby in Victoria*. Victoria: Health Department (referred to as the Birthing Services Review).

Katz-Rothman, B. 1982. *In Labour: Women and Power in the Birthplace*. London: Junction Books.

Lane, K. 1993. 'The Politics of Homebirth', in M. Mills, ed, *Prevention, Health and British Politics*. Avebury: Aldershot.

———. 1994. 'Birth as Euphoria: The Social Meaning of Birth', in D. Colquohoun and A. Kellehear, eds, *Health Research in Practice, Volume Two—Recent Changes and Ongoing Issues*. London: Chapman and Hall.

Marsden, W. 1994. *Pursuing the Birth Machine: The Search for Appropriate Birth Technology*. New South Wales: ACE Graphics.

Monash Medical Centre. 1993. *Midwives Community Birth Centre 1993 Statistics*. Monash: Monash Medical Centre.

Oakley, A. 1986. *The Captured Womb: A History of the Medical Care of Pregnant Women*. Oxford: Basil Blackwell.

Permezel, J.M.H., R.J. Pepperel, and M. Kloss. 1987. 'Unexpected Problems in Patients Selected for Birthing Unit Delivery', *Australian and New Zealand Journal of Obstetrics and Gynacology* 27: 21–3.

Sweet, R. 1989. 'The Obstetrician's Dilemma', *The Medical Journal of Australia* 150: 545–6.

Tew, M. 1990. *Safer Childbirth? A Critical History of Maternity Care*. London: Chapman and Hall.

World Health Organization. 1985. *Having a Baby in Europe: Report on a Study, Public Health in Europe No. 26*. Copenhagen: World Health Organization.

Chapter 21

Contemporary Hospice Care: The Sequestration of the Unbounded Body and 'Dirty Dying'

Julia Lawton

. . . [A] significant proportion of patients are now cared for, and do die, at home. Certainly, in the part of England where I conducted my fieldwork, approximately one-third of all cancer deaths occurred at home, with the remaining two-thirds being divided roughly equally between the hospice and the hospital. Hence, it will be my contention in this paper that, within the developing climate of community care, hospices are progressively able only to cater to those patients who cannot be looked after within the community, because the community cannot accommodate them either practically or symbolically. Consequently, it is not dying as such but, rather, certain kinds of deaths that are to be found within contemporary hospices. As the following ethnography and analysis will highlight, it is important to focus upon the body of the patient, and the disease processes taking place within it and upon its surfaces, in order to understand why some patients are now contained within the bounded spaces of hospices, whereas others are not. I will argue that contemporary hospices set a particular type of bodily deterioration, demise, and decay apart from mainstream society. . . .

Methodology

The data presented in this paper were collected by means of participant observation. I worked directly alongside the nursing staff and in-house volunteers, as this allowed me to make sustained and repeated observations on patients, their families, and the staff in the wards, side rooms, and other communal areas in the hospice, without the internal dynamics taking place there being affected. The patients were allowed to control the content of any conversations they had with me; this allowed original and unanticipated material to emerge, and avoided the possibility of the patient being drawn into discussing a topic that they might find distressing. I was also able to obtain data by sitting in on staff-handovers and multidisciplinary meetings. In accordance with the wishes of the Local Research Ethics Committee, the patients were, whenever possible, informed of the research and given the choice of 'opting out' of any observations made. Only one patient asked to be excluded from the study. Consequently, with the exception of this one person, the observations and themes developed in this paper are drawn from the entire population of this hospice. During the 10-month period of study, I was able to make observations on approximately 280 different patients in total. . . .

I begin with an extended case study of a patient named 'Annie'. In some respects the following example is remarkable because her death was considered by the staff to be one of the most distressing that occurred within the hospice during the period of my fieldwork. Nevertheless, it provides a useful starting point because Annie's experience encompasses a number of features shared entirely, or in part, by the majority of patients receiving care within the hospice.

Case Study: Annie

Annie was 67 when she was first admitted to the hospice on 12 April 1995. Prior to her admission she was living at home with her retired husband and recently divorced son. She also had a married daughter living locally.

Annie had been diagnosed as having cancer of the cervix in April 1994. Following surgery and post-operative radiotherapy it was believed that she had made a full recovery. However, in February 1995 a smear test revealed a large recurrence that was subsequently found to have spread to her pelvic wall. Annie was informed by her doctor that there was little further that could be done for her because her cancer was too far advanced. She was referred to a Macmillan nurse for palliative care in March.

Initially, Annie managed at home with regular medical and emotional support from her District and Macmillan nurses. At this stage, her greatest problem stemmed from the development of severe edema in both of her legs, which had caused her to become bed-bound. She found it difficult to relinquish her 'housewife' duties to her husband and son, and was still trying to manage the household from her bed. . . .

At the beginning of April, Annie's condition began to deteriorate. She developed a recto-vaginal fistula, which meant that her urine and feces started coming out through the same passageway. Problems of fecal leakage precipitated her admission to the hospice for symptom control.

Originally, Annie had been very anxious about the possibility of being admitted to the hospice. As she explained about one week into her stay: 'Initially I didn't want to come in here because I didn't think I'd get out again.' In fact, when recurrence of cancer was first diagnosed, Annie made her family promise they would do everything possible to enable her to stay at home. It is highly relevant, therefore, that it was Annie herself who finally requested admission to the hospice. Her rationale was twofold. First, she was concerned about how exhausted her husband had become: 'I could see him crumbling in front of me.' Second, she felt she could not get enough privacy at home to attend to her personal hygiene. Annie had become semi-incontinent and was also suffering from periodic bouts of diarrhea, which she found deeply distressing and embarrassing. She did not want her family to witness her bodily degradation first hand. . . .

About 10 days into her admission, Annie deteriorated further. Her fistula enlarged substantially and, as a result, every time she attempted to get out of bed and stand up, diarrhea would pour straight out of her body. Consequently, Annie had to start using a commode on the ward rather than walking to the toilet. She also started passing blood. In addition, she contracted a bladder infection that caused her urine to develop a 'very offensive' smell.

It was around this time that Annie's bodily degradation began to have a significant impact upon the hospice as a whole. Whenever she used the commode on the ward, the smell would penetrate right through the building to the main entrance. The staff burnt aromatherapy oils around her bed, but, generally, these did little to mask the odour. The other patients complained that sometimes the smell made them want to vomit.

Annie became increasingly anxious about the possibility of being discharged home. She felt that she had lost all her dignity. She also stressed that there would be insufficient privacy at home to mask the smell and her degradation from her family. At the multidisciplinary team meeting to discuss her case, the Senior Consultant argued that it would be 'cruel and futile' to press for discharge. None of the other staff members challenged his decision in spite of the economic pressures to free Annie's bed. There was no further talk of discharge and Annie and her family were promised that she could remain in the hospice until she died.

Throughout April, Annie continued to deteriorate. She 'rotted away below' (as the nurses put it) and lost all control over her bowel and bladder functions. As a consequence, she suffered from continuous bouts of incontinence. It proved impossible to keep her clean and her sheets fresh.

On several occasions when the nurses came to attend to her they found her covered to her shoulders in her own urine and excreta. . . .

. . . Annie became increasingly agitated and afraid. Her diarrhea escalated, and at lunch time she asked to be sedated. The staff fulfilled her request after she repeated it several further times. This was the last time I spoke to Annie; she remained heavily sedated and unconscious until she died approximately two weeks later. . . .

Outside: Inside :: Boundedness: Unboundedness: Hospice Care and the Unbounded Body

Annie's case will be referred to at various points in this paper because of the rich and complex issues it brings to the fore. However, the one theme I want to focus upon at this stage concerns the way in which the development and spread of her cervical cancer affected the boundedness of her body. One of the main factors that precipitated Annie's admission to the hospice for symptom control was the development of a fistula that resulted in fecal leakage. As the fistula enlarged, Annie ceased to have any control over her bowel and bladder functions. . . .

In this respect, Annie's case is far from atypical. During the course of my fieldwork, the most common reason for a patient to be admitted to the hospice was for the control of symptoms . . . In a study conducted to identify the factors influencing the admission of patients to St Christopher's hospice in London, Woodhall similarly found that 'the major cause of admission is either "poor symptom control" or "good to fairly good symptom control" that subsequently fails' (1986: 32). . . . [W]hat most of the symptoms requiring control shared in common was that they caused the surfaces of the patient's body to rupture and break down. As a consequence, fluids and matter normally contained within the patient's body were leaked and emitted to the outside, often in an uncontrolled and *ad hoc* fashion. Staff often employed metaphors such as 'falling apart at the seams' when referring to such patients

who were 'rotting inside' and 'being eaten away by their cancer'. Patients requiring symptom control thus had bodies that I will term here as 'unbounded'.

Symptom control encompassed a wide range of bodily ailments and their side effects. Amongst the most common were incontinence of urine and feces, uncontrolled vomiting (including fecal vomit), fungating tumours (the rotting away of a tumour site on the surface of the skin), and weeping limbs that resulted from the development of gross edema in the patient's legs and/or arms. As a result, the patient's limbs would swell to such an extent that the skin burst and lymph fluid continuously seeped out.

Other symptoms, though less common, were equally pertinent. For example, . . . Tony was admitted after he developed a facial tumour. Apart from causing a gross distortion of his features (Tony's left eye was gradually being pushed sideways and out of its socket), the expanding tumour was also causing the arteries in his nasal area to break down. As a result, Tony suffered from continuous nosebleeds. He had to have a bolus of cloth permanently attached beneath his nose to absorb the frequent outpourings of blood and mucus. The doctors predicted that Tony's death could be caused at any time by a 'catastrophic nosebleed'. . . .

On a number of occasions patients' symptoms could be successfully treated or controlled by the medical staff, and the boundedness of their bodies could thus be reinstated. For example, several patients were admitted with incontinence of urine, and were able to return home once they had been catheterized. . . . In this respect, the hospice could be understood as a mediator between the unbounded and the bounded body, with patients being moved into the hospice when the surfaces of their bodies ruptured and broke down, and moved out again when their bodily boundedness and integrity were subsequently restored.

A number of patients, however, like Annie, had symptoms that escalated following their admission to the hospice and, as a consequence, their deterioration was such that the boundedness of their bodies was impossible to reinstate.

. . . What was striking about this sub-group of patients was that they all exhibited behaviour that suggested a total loss of self and social identity once their bodies became severely and irreversibly unbounded.

Annie was one of several patients admitted with recto-vaginal fistulas during my fieldwork. Another woman, Deborah, experienced a similar trajectory of deterioration and decline. She was originally admitted for a blood transfusion with a view to being discharged within a couple of days, but a developing fistula, coupled with periodic bouts of confusion (possibly caused by the spread of cancer to her brain), kept her in the hospice until she died. . . .

When Deborah's bodily deterioration escalated, I observed that she had suddenly become a lot more withdrawn. After she had been on the ward for a couple of days she started asking for the curtains to be drawn around her bed to give her more privacy. A day or so later she stopped talking altogether, unless it was really necessary (to ask for the commode, for example), even when her family and other visitors were present. Deborah spent the remaining 10 days of her life either sleeping or staring blankly into space. She refused all food and drink. The staff also noticed this 'strange' behaviour. One of the hospice doctors concluded that 'for all intents and purposes she [had] shut herself off in a frustrated and irreversible silence'. Deborah was moved back into a side room and died there a couple of days later.
. . .

What Deborah appears to have done was to 'disengage' and 'switch herself off' before her physical cessation. This type of withdrawal was common amongst unbounded patients. . . .

This type of 'switching off' has been identified in other settings such as the Holocaust. Pines points to instances in which women 'overwhelmed by physical and emotional helplessness and despair, almost reached a state of psychic death' (1993: 185; see also Langer, 1996). . . . [T]he self appears to have 'gone' altogether, leaving little, if anything, but the 'empty' body. . . .

Other patients, like Annie, attempted to 'switch themselves off' by requesting heavy sedation. Kath, for example, requested that she [be] moved to a side room and given a large dose of analgesics after commenting, on repeated occasions, that 'you wouldn't put a dog through this'. Her message was clear and simple: it would be much more compassionate if the staff put her out of her misery. Some patients, like Deborah, refused to eat or drink, thereby accelerating their own demise; others, like Dolly, made more explicit requests for euthanasia. . . .

What all these examples serve to highlight is that once a patient's body fell severely and irreversibly apart, she or he exhibited behaviour that suggests a loss of sense of self. . . .

. . . My findings suggest that the identity and selfhood of the contemporary Western person is fundamentally dependent upon the possession of a physically bounded body . . . Thus, it could be argued that hospices served on one level as 'fringe'/'liminal' spaces within which these 'non-persons', wavering 'between two worlds', remain buffered (Van Gennep, 1972: 18).

The 'Special Status' Accorded to Patients with Advanced Cancer

Within medical and social science literatures, concern has been expressed about the fact that cancer patients are accorded a special social status in relation to other persons (particularly older people) suffering from chronic degenerative diseases. Contemporary hospices are principally geared to care for patients with advanced cancer, whereas elderly and other patients with degenerative diseases—'the disadvantaged dying' (Harris, 1990)—are rarely included in planning services for continuing and terminal care (Clark, 1993: 172; Cohen, 1996). 'The disproportionate concentration of care on those dying of cancer', as Harris suggests, 'has created an underclass of dying people' (1990: 28). Seale, likewise, observes that it is much easier to raise money for cancer services (e.g., for building a hospice) than for older people (1989). However, no wholly satisfactory explanation has as yet been offered as to why this should be the case.

The special status accorded to cancer patients can perhaps be explained in part by the fact that the cancer death is commonly associated with the 'untimely' and hence 'tragic' death (Hockey, 1990: 78). In addition, . . . life expectancy can be predicted with a fair degree of accuracy (Standing Medical Advisory Committee, 1993; see also Sudnow, 1967: 67). Consequently, as Field has observed, it is much easier to see patients with advanced malignant disease as 'dying' in both lay and medical perceptions (1996: 263).

My findings, however, suggest that another reason why institutionalized hospice care caters now more or less exclusively for cancer patients may be because of the way in which cancer, in its late stages, can severely affect the boundedness of the patient's body. . . .

The Sequestration of the Unbounded Body: An Ethnographic and Theoretical Discussion

One obvious question clearly remains to be addressed: namely, why the sequestration of the unbounded body is deemed both appropriate, and necessary, within the contemporary Western context. This section will be used to demonstrate that contemporary marginalizing practices should be understood as a culturally and historically specific response to bodily unboundedness.

When carers discussed their reasons for wanting a patient to come into the hospice, their comments highlighted a common theme. Carers were not explicitly concerned about the fact that the patient was dying, rather, the primary reason they suggested for wanting the patient to be admitted was because they felt repelled by the patient being incontinent, vomiting, and/or emitting other bodily fluids within their own homes. As the wife of one patient put it:

> He started having a lot of problems with vomiting. You just never knew when it was going to happen. All of a sudden it would just come pouring out. It went everywhere . . . all over his bed, all over the carpet. It was disgusting. . . .

Carers' perceptions were also shared by the patients themselves. As Annie's case study serves to highlight, patients often felt that home did not afford an appropriate space in which their bodily disintegration should occur.

The breakdown of the body's boundedness, furthermore, was often accompanied by the emission of smells. It quickly came to my attention that the odours released from patients' disintegrating bodies not only precipitated their admission to the hospice, but, in addition, often brought about a further marginalization within the building itself. I observed that smell created a boundary around the patient, shunting others away. On several occasions, patients were driven out of the wards after another patient had been heavily incontinent in bed. . . .

Sometimes, staff attempted to manage problems of smell by transferring a patient to a side room, thereby enabling the odours emitted from their body to be contained within a more bounded space. . . .

The negative reaction that carers and other participants within the hospice exhibited towards unbounded patients can perhaps be understood in terms of the capacity of the unbounded body to breach and percolate their own body boundaries. The smells, and other fluids and matter emitted from the unbounded body, extended the boundaries of the patient's corporeality, such that the patient's body 'seeped' into the boundaries and spaces of other persons and other places. Hence, strategies such as avoidance and/or the removal of a patient to a side room were employed in cases where the *effects* of the patient's unboundedness could not be contained or controlled. In effect, the other participants in the hospice were trying to maintain the integrity of their own selves, by avoiding having their body boundaries breached by the corrosive effects of the sick person's bodily disintegration.

Douglas, in her analysis of pollution concepts and taboos, argues for a symbolic classificatory approach to culturally embedded ideas of defilement and disorder. Concepts of 'dirt', she suggests, emerge in situations where a set of ordered relations and classificatory schema are directly contravened. Hence, pollution behaviour 'is the reaction that condemns any object or idea likely to confuse or contradict cherished classifications' (1984: 35). Douglas's approach, I suggest, can be usefully applied to provide insights into why intolerance of bodily emissions and smells has become such a marked feature of the contemporary 'deodorized' West. Whilst the carers observed in my study expressed revulsion towards unbounded patients, both Classen et al. (1994) and Corbin (1986) have provided rich accounts that demonstrate that historically (especially in the Medieval period) mainstream European social life was pervaded by the smells of bodies, bodily emissions, and other pungent odours. As Classen has argued, 'odours cannot easily be contained, they escape and cross boundaries, blending different olfactory wholes' (1994: 4). Because of their boundary-transgressing nature, smells are thus opposed to 'our modern linear world view, with its emphasis on privacy, discrete divisions, and superficial interactions' (1994: 5). Such a perspective helps to explain why unbounded patients were sequestered within the hospice. The hospice, I suggest, served to impose order upon disorder through enclosing and containing the odours emitted from patients' disintegrating bodies within a bounded space. It requires little further imagination to argue that the walls of the hospice served as the boundaries of the patient's body in situations where the patient lacked the corporal capacity for self-containment.

Yet, as the following discussion will serve to make evident, the current Western intolerance of bodily disintegration and bodily emissions can also be related to contemporary individualistic constructions of the person as a stable, bounded, and autonomous entity. . . .

. . . Elias . . . [argues] that contemporary Western constructions of the body as a 'peculiarly intimate and private thing' are neither natural nor innate, but rather the product of a long, gradual, and historically specific 'civilizing process' (1994). This process, which extended over many centuries, involved the gradual elaboration and internalization—in the form of self controls—of a whole series of taboos and precepts regulating such things

as bodily functions and bodily exposure. . . . As Elias further suggests, the privatization of bodily functions did not occur uniformly across society. Bodily taboos and effect controls first became commonplace amongst the upper classes in Western Europe, and slowly filtered down to, and became established amongst, the bourgeoisie, followed later by the lower social classes.

Elias thus traces a gradual historical transition from an 'open', 'incomplete body', to a body with clearly defined boundaries, isolated, alone, and fenced off from other bodies (1994: 56; Fontaine, 1978: 245). What is particularly pertinent in Elias's historical account is the relationship that can be drawn between the emergence of the bounded body as central to contemporary Western concepts of the person and the rise of individualism. . . .

. . . [I]n cultural contexts where persons are not thought of as having a singular authentic identity mapped onto a singular body, substances emitted from the body—whether they are attributed a positive or negative value—are not thought of as 'waste' or 'dirt' in the same way as in contemporary Western paradigms (Meigs, 1984: 112; Douglas, 1984: 121). . . . Elias . . . suggests that the closure of the body, achieved through the isolation of natural functions from public life, was originally grounded in 'moral' concerns, and only later came to be understood as necessary for 'hygienic' reasons (1994: 123). In other words, advances in science and medicine cannot be accorded a deterministic role in the development of modern Western 'hygiene sensibilities'; instead we should understand these sensibilities as being essentially symbolic in nature, stemming, in the first instance, from the construction of the person, and the body, as self-contained, bounded entities.

It is now possible to understand why unbounded patients were sequestered within the hospice. As the above analysis serves to demonstrate, within the context of contemporary Western paradigms, the unbounded body is perceived symbolically both as a locus and a source of 'dirt'; as 'matter out of place' (Douglas, 1984: 35). . . .

The Unbounded Body and the Loss of the Person

The above discussions also throw light upon why the severely unbounded patients I observed within the hospice evinced, and experienced, a total loss of selfhood. As I have demonstrated, the bounded, sealed, isolated body has become central to constructions of selfhood and identity within the contemporary Western context. Hence, it could be argued that unbounded patients fall out of the category of personhood by virtue of their lacking the corporeal capacity for self-containment. It has, indeed, been recognized within the social scientific literature that bodily closure—achieved through continence—is one of the key criteria upon which entry into 'full person' status is now gained and sustained within contemporary Western society. Hockey and James, for instance, have noted that one of the central markers of a child's progress from infancy to maturity is the ability to control bowel and bladder functions (1993: 85). In a similar vein, Mitteness and Barker have observed that incontinence amongst elderly people is frequently thought to symbolize 'that the elder is no longer an adult person but is on the road to the ultimate in disorderliness and decrepitude, to becoming a non-person' (1995: 206).

Discussion

. . . [H]ospices do not veil the dying process per se; rather they have come to sequester a particular type of dying and a particular category of patient; namely, one who is disintegrating and has a body that is unbounded.

The above observations thus lead me to suggest that contemporary hospices in fact employ one set of taboos, namely their stereotype as 'houses of death' (Kastenbaum and Aisenberg, 1974) or 'little pockets in which our culture hides the terminally ill and muffles the voice of death' (Scott, 1994) to veil a second more pertinent set of taboos, namely those associated with the way in which a number of patients admitted to hospices actually deteriorate and die. Issues of dirt, decay, disintegration, and smell are rarely, if ever, written about by hospice professionals or covered in media representations of hospice care. Rather they are 'glossed over' as 'symptoms' requiring 'control'. Hospices practise a type of care now termed palliative. Palliative care is formally defined as:

> active total care offered to a patient with a progressive disease and their family when it is recognized that the illness is no longer curable, in order to concentrate on the quality of life and the alleviation of distressing symptoms within the framework of a co-ordinated service. (Standing Medical Advisory Committee, 1992)

As Scott points out, however, the actual word 'palliative' is derived from the Latin noun pallium, meaning 'cloak'. Palliate means, quite literally, 'to cover with or as with a cloak . . . to hide, conceal, disguise' (1994: 37). My fieldwork experience suggests that the latter understanding and use of the term is much more salient in understanding the contemporary role of hospices. . . .

References

Clark, D. 1993. 'Whither the Hospices?', in D. Clark, ed, *The Future for Palliative Care: Issues of Policy and Practise.* Milton Keynes: Open University Press.

Classen, C., D. Howes, and A. Synnott. 1994. *Aroma: The Cultural History of Smell.* London: Routledge.

Cohen, P. 1996. 'Death Duties', *Community Care* January: 19.

Corbin, A. 1986. *The Foul and the Fragrant: Odor and the French Social Imagination.* New York: Berg.

Douglas, M. 1984. *Purity and Danger: An Analysis of the Concepts of Pollution and Taboo.* London: Ark.

Elias, N. 1994. *The Civilising Process: The History of Manners and State Formation and Civilisation*, trans. E. Jephcott. Oxford: Blackwell.

Fontaine, N. 1978. 'The Civilizing Process Revisited: Interview with Norbert Elias', *Theory and Society* 5: 243–53.

Harris, L. 1990. 'The Disadvantaged Dying', *Nursing Times* 86: 26–8.

Hockey, J. 1990. *Experiences of Death: An Anthropological Account.* Edinburgh: Edinburgh University Press.

———, and A. James. 1993. *Growing Up and Growing Old: Ageing and Dependency During the Life Course.* London: Sage.

Kastenbaum, R., and R. Aisenberg. 1974. *The Psychology of Death.* London: Duckworth.

Langer, L. 1996. 'The Alarmed Vision: Social Suffering and the Holocaust Atrocity', *Daedalus: Journal of the American Academy of Arts and Sciences, Social Suffering.* Issued as Vol. 125.

Meigs, A. 1984. *Food, Sex, and Pollution: A New Guinea Religion.* New Brunswick, NJ: Rutgers University Press.

Mitteness, L.S., and J.C. Barker. 1995. 'Stigmatizing a "Normal" Condition: Urinary Incontinence in Late Life', *Medical Anthropology Quarterly* 9: 188–210.

Pines, D. 1993. *A Woman's Unconscious Use of Her Body: A Pschoanalytical Perspective.* London: Virago Press.

Scott, J. 1994. 'More Money for Palliative Care? The Economics of Denial', *Journal of Palliative Care* 10: 35–8.

Seale, C. 1989. 'What Happens in Hospices: A Review of Research Evidence', *Social Science and Medicine* 28: 551–9.

Standing Medical Advisory Committee and Standing Nursing and Midwifery Advisory Committee. 1993. *The Principles and Provision of Palliative Care.* Joint report of the Standing Medical Advisory Committee and Standing Nursing and Midwifery Committee 1992. London: HMSO.

Sudnow, D. 1967. *Passing On: The Social Organisation of Dying.* Upper Saddle River, NJ: Prentice Hall.

Van Gennep, A. 1972. *The Rites of Passage.* Chicago: University of Chicago Press.

Woodhall, C. 1986. 'Care of the Dying: A Family Concern', *Nursing Times* 22 October: 31–3.

Part VIII

Reproductive Bodies

Jacqueline Low and Claudia Malacrida

According to feminist sociologists, biomedical assumptions about female reproduction have greatly determined perceptions of women's bodies. Societal responses and expectations concerning reproduction also influence women's view of themselves, especially when their personal experience does not reflect or measure up to the dictates of society. In 'The Egg and the Sperm: How Science Has Constructed a Romance Based on Stereotypical Male–Female Roles' (1991), Emily Martin concludes that even biological theories of human reproduction are shaped by cultural stereotypes of masculine and feminine romantic roles. She argues that despite biological evidence to the contrary, medical discourse is heavily influenced by **hegemonic masculinity** and **hegemonic femininity**, the dominant constructs of what it means to be feminine or masculine in Western culture (Connell, 1995; Krane et al., 2004). **Discourse** refers to ways of thinking and speaking about things, and, in this case, includes the contents of medical textbooks. For instance, in medical discourse, the 'feminine' egg is portrayed as passive and waiting to be 'courted' by 'aggressive' and 'competitive', 'masculine' sperm.

Katha Pollitt's '"Fetal Rights": A New Assault on Feminism' (1998) addresses the question of the womb as a **social space** within which struggles relating to inequality, racism, and gendered power relations are played out. As we learned from Lane's (1995) article in Part VII, all women's reproductive capacities are potentially sites of medicalization and subsequent intervention. However, Pollitt indicates that women who are poor, racialized, and marginalized are at heightened risk of professional surveillance and judgment. Women who are deemed to be 'at risk' of harming their unborn children as a result of their use of drugs, their inadequate prenatal care, and their use of alcohol are particularly subject to surveillance, moral regulation, and social control. The surveillance that pregnant women experience is reminiscent of Foucault's (1995) panopticon (see the introduction to Part IV), wherein a **gaze** of surveillance exercises power on citizens' bodies. Ultimately, this constant possibility of surveillance results in individuals **internalizing** the gaze and engaging in their own **self-policing**. This represents a new means of social control that is no longer reactive, but that is instead **preventative discipline**. In Pollitt's article, we see that the preventative policing of 'troublesome' pregnant bodies acts as a cautionary tale for all pregnant women.

Many mothers face **structural** problems relating to their pregnancies that operate at institutional, macro levels. These include discrimination, poverty, barriers in accessing adequate and affordable health care, lack of abortion services, and inadequate social programs (Armstrong, 2003). As well, women who are dealing with addictions are hard-pressed to find rehabilitation services, particularly when they are pregnant (Armstrong, 2003; Boyd, 1999). This lack of support for pregnant women is, according to Pollitt, rarely the target of social reformers. Instead, authorities engage in **individualization**, where social problems such as poverty or lack of services are seen to be the responsibility of individuals, who are then exhorted to correct these problems through their own efforts. Thus, women whose pregnancies are unplanned or unwanted, or who become pregnant while impoverished, addicted, or otherwise marginalized, are held liable for problems that the state has in fact strongly contributed to.

Elizabeth Graham and Jacqueline Low (2008) offer the final article in this section. Like Julia Lawton (1998) in Part VII, Graham and Low make use of Douglas's (1985: 35) concept of 'matter out of place' in order to understand the experiences of women as they undergo the **reproductive firsts** of menarche (first menstruation), pregnancy, and menopause. By conceptualizing bodies that do not correspond to societal expectations as a form of 'matter out of place' (Douglas, 1985: 35), and by adding a temporal element, they argue that when women's reproductive bodies do not coincide with the chronological expectations of the social audience, they become '**bodies out of time**' (Graham and Low, 2008: 189). For example, the woman who experiences menopause by what is considered 'too early' by the social audience is treated as a '**cultural anomaly**' and is reacted to with '**pollution behaviour**' in the form of biomedical intervention (Douglas, 1985: 94–7).

References

Armstrong, E. 2003. *Conceiving Risk, Bearing Responsibility: Fetal Alcohol Syndrome and the Diagnosis of Moral Disorder*. Baltimore: The Johns Hopkins University Press.

Boyd, S.C. 1999. *Mothers and Illicit Drugs: Transcending the Myths*. Toronto: University of Toronto Press.

Connell, R.W. 1995. *Masculinities*. Cambridge: Polity Press.

Douglas, M. 1985. *Purity and Danger: An Analysis of the Concepts of Pollution and Taboo*. London: Routledge and Kegan Paul.

Foucault, M. 1995. *Discipline and Punish: The Birth of the Prison*. New York: Vintage Books.

Graham, E., and J. Low. 2008. 'Bodies Out of Time: Women's Reproductive Firsts', in C. Malacrida and J. Low, eds, *Sociology of the Body: A Reader*. Don Mills, ON: Oxford University Press, 189–194.

Krane, V., P. Y.L. Choi, S. Baird, C.M. Aimar, and K. Kauer. 2004. 'Living the Paradox: Female Athletes Negotiate Femininity and Masculinity', *Sex Roles: A Journal of Research* March: 315–29.

Lane, K. 1995. 'The Medical Model of the Body as a Site of Risk: A Case Study of Childbirth', in J. Gabe, ed, *Medicine, Health and Risk: Sociological Approaches*. London: Blackwell Publishers, 53–72.

Lawton, J. 1998. 'Contemporary Hospice Care: The Sequestration of the Unbounded Body and "Dirty Dying"', *Sociology of Health and Illness* 20, 2: 121–43.

Martin, E. 1991. 'The Egg and the Sperm: How Science Has Constructed a Romance Based on Stereotypical Male–Female Roles', *Signs: Journal of Women in Culture and Society* 16, 31: 485–502.

Pollitt, K. 1998. '"Fetal Rights": A New Assault on Feminism', in M. Ladd-Taylor and L. Umanski, eds, *Bad Mothers: The Politics of Blame in Twentieth-Century America*. New York: New York University Press, 286–98.

Chapter 22

The Egg and the Sperm: How Science Has Constructed a Romance Based on Stereotypical Male–Female Roles

Emily Martin

. . . As an anthropologist, I am intrigued by the possibility that culture shapes how biological scientists describe what they discover about the natural world. . . . In the course of my research I realized that the picture of egg and sperm drawn in popular as well as scientific accounts of reproductive biology relies on stereotypes central to our cultural definitions of male and female. The stereotypes imply not only that female biological processes are less worthy than their male counterparts but also that women are less worthy than men. Part of my goal in writing this article is to shine a bright light on the gender stereotypes hidden within the scientific language of biology. Exposed in such a light, I hope they will lose much of their power to harm us.

Egg and Sperm: A Scientific Fairy Tale

At a fundamental level, all major scientific textbooks depict male and female reproductive organs as systems for the production of valuable substances, such as eggs and sperm.[1] In the case of women, the monthly cycle is described as being designed to produce eggs and prepare a suitable place for them to be fertilized and grown—all to the end of making babies. But the enthusiasm ends there. By extolling the female cycle as a productive enterprise, menstruation must necessarily be viewed as a failure. Medical texts describe menstruation as the 'debris' of the uterine lining, the result of necrosis, or death of tissue. The descriptions imply that a system has

gone awry, making products of no use, not to specification, unsalable, wasted, scrap. . . .

Male reproductive physiology is evaluated quite differently. One of the texts that sees menstruation as failed production employs a sort of breathless prose when it describes the maturation of sperm . . . In the classic text *Medical Physiology*, edited by Vernon Mountcastle, the male/female, productive/destructive comparison is more explicit: 'Whereas the female *sheds* only a single gamete each month, the seminiferous tubules *produce* hundreds of millions of sperm each day' (emphasis mine).[2] . . .

One could argue that menstruation and spermatogenesis are not analogous processes and, therefore, should not be expected to elicit the same kind of response. The proper female analogy to spermatogenesis, biologically, is ovulation. Yet ovulation does not merit enthusiasm in these texts either. Textbook descriptions stress that all of the ovarian follicles containing ova are already present at birth. Far from being produced, as sperm are, they merely sit on the shelf, slowly degenerating and aging like overstocked inventory: 'At birth, normal human ovaries contain an estimated one million follicles [each], and no new ones appear after birth. Thus, in marked contrast to the male, the newborn female already has all the germ cells she will ever have. Only a few, perhaps 400, are destined to reach full maturity during her active productive life. All the others degenerate at some point in their development so that few, if any, remain by the time she reaches menopause at approximately 50 years of age.'[3] . . .

Nor are the female organs spared such vivid descriptions. One scientist writes in a newspaper article that a woman's ovaries become old and worn out from ripening eggs every month, even though the woman herself is still relatively young: 'When you look through a laparoscope . . . at an ovary that has been through hundreds of cycles, even in a superbly healthy American female, you see a scarred, battered organ.'[4]

To avoid the negative connotations that some people associate with the female reproductive system, scientists could begin to describe male and female processes as homologous. . . .

. . . 'During the 40 or so years of a woman's reproductive life, only 400 to 500 eggs will have been released', [Alberts et al.] write. 'All the rest will have degenerated. It is still a mystery why so many eggs are formed only to die in the ovaries.'[5]

The real mystery is why the male's vast production of sperm is not seen as wasteful.[6] Assuming that a man 'produces' 100 million (10^8) sperm per day (a conservative estimate) during an average reproductive life of 60 years, he would produce well over two trillion sperm in his lifetime. Assuming that a woman 'ripens' one egg per lunar month, or 13 per year, over the course of her 40-year reproductive life, she would total 500 eggs in her lifetime. But the word 'waste' implies an excess, too much produced. Assuming two or three offspring, for every baby a woman produces, she wastes only around 200 eggs. For every baby a man produces, he wastes more than one trillion (10^{12}) sperm.

How is it that positive images are denied to the bodies of women? A look at language—in this case, scientific language—provides the first clue. Take the egg and the sperm. It is remarkable how 'femininely' the egg behaves and how 'masculinely' the sperm. The egg is seen as large and passive. It does not *move* or *journey*, but passively 'is transported', 'is swept'[7] or even 'drifts'[8] along the fallopian tube. In utter contrast, sperm are small, 'streamlined',[9] and invariably active. They 'deliver' their genes to the egg, 'activate the developmental program of the egg',[10] and have a 'velocity' that is often remarked upon.[11] Their tails are 'strong' and efficiently powered.[12] Together with the forces of ejaculation, they can 'propel the semen into the deepest recesses of the vagina'.[13] For this they need 'energy', 'fuel',[14] so that with a 'whiplash like motion and strong lurches'[15] they can 'burrow through the egg coat'[16] and 'penetrate' it.[17]

At its extreme, the age-old relationship of the egg and the sperm takes on a royal or religious patina. The egg coat, its protective barrier, is sometimes called its 'vestments', a term usually reserved for sacred, religious dress. The egg is said to have a 'corona',[18] a crown, and to be accompanied by 'attendant cells'.[19] It is holy, set apart and above, the queen to the sperm's king. The egg is also passive, which means it must depend on sperm for rescue. Gerald Schatten and Helen Schatten liken the egg's role to that of Sleeping Beauty: 'a dormant bride awaiting her mate's magic kiss, which instills the spirit that brings her to life'.[20] Sperm, by contrast, have a 'mission',[21] which is to 'move through the female genital tract in quest of the ovum'.[22] One popular account has it that the sperm carry out a 'perilous journey' into the 'warm darkness', where some fall away 'exhausted'. 'Survivors' 'assault' the egg, the successful candidates 'surrounding the prize'.[23] Part of the urgency of this journey, in more scientific terms, is that 'once released from the supportive environment of the ovary, an egg will die within hours unless rescued by a sperm'.[24] The wording stresses the fragility and dependency of the egg, even though the same text acknowledges elsewhere that sperm also live for only a few hours.[25] . . .

Bringing out another aspect of the sperm's autonomy, an article in the journal *Cell* has the sperm making an 'existential decision' to penetrate the egg: 'Sperm are cells with a limited behavioural repertoire, one that is directed toward fertilizing eggs. To execute the decision to abandon the haploid state, sperm swim to an egg and there acquire the ability to effect membrane fusion.'[26] . . .

There is another way that sperm, despite their small size, can be made to loom in importance over the egg. In a collection of scientific papers, an electron micrograph of an enormous egg and tiny sperm is titled 'A Portrait of the Sperm'.[27]

This is a little like showing a photo of a dog and calling it a picture of the fleas. . . .

The . . . common picture—egg as damsel in distress, shielded only by her sacred garments; sperm as heroic warrior to the rescue—cannot be proved to be dictated by the biology of these events. While the 'facts' of biology may not *always* be constructed in cultural terms, I would argue that in this case they are. The degree of metaphorical content in these descriptions, the extent to which differences between egg and sperm are emphasized, and the parallels between cultural stereotypes of male and female behaviour, and the character of egg and sperm all point to this conclusion.

New Research, Old Imagery

As new understandings of egg and sperm emerge, textbook gender imagery is being revised. But the new research, far from escaping the stereotypical representations of egg and sperm, simply replicates elements of textbook gender imagery in a different form. . . .

In all of the texts quoted above, sperm are described as penetrating the egg, and specific substances on a sperm's head are described as binding to the egg. Recently, this description of events was rewritten in a biophysics lab at Johns Hopkins University—transforming the egg from the passive to the active party.[28]

Prior to this research, it was thought that the zona, the inner vestments of the egg, formed an impenetrable barrier. Sperm overcame the barrier by mechanically burrowing through, thrashing their tails, and slowly working their way along. Later research showed that the sperm released digestive enzymes that chemically broke down the zona; thus, scientists presumed that the sperm used mechanical *and* chemical means to get through to the egg.

In this recent investigation, the researchers began to ask questions about the mechanical force of the sperm's tail. (The lab's goal was to develop a contraceptive that worked topically on sperm.) They discovered, to their great surprise,

that the forward thrust of sperm is extremely weak, which contradicts the assumption that sperm are forceful penetrators. Rather than thrusting forward, the sperm's head was now seen to move mostly back and forth. The sideways motion of the sperm's tail makes the head move sideways with a force that is 10 times stronger than its forward movement. So even if the overall force of the sperm were strong enough to mechanically break the zona, most of its force would be directed sideways rather than forward. In fact, its strongest tendency, by tenfold, is to escape by attempting to pry itself off the egg. Sperm, then, must be exceptionally efficient at *escaping* from any cell surface they contact. And the surface of the egg must be designed to trap the sperm and prevent their escape. Otherwise, few if any sperm would reach the egg.

The researchers at Johns Hopkins concluded that the sperm and egg stick together because of adhesive molecules on the surface of each. The egg traps the sperm and adheres to it so tightly that the sperm's head is forced to lie flat against the surface of the zona . . . The trapped sperm continues to wiggle ineffectually side to side. The mechanical force of its tail is so weak that a sperm cannot break even one chemical bond. This is where the digestive enzymes released by the sperm come in. If they start to soften the zona just at the tip of the sperm and the sides remain stuck, then the weak, flailing sperm can get oriented in the right direction and make it through the zona—provided that its bonds to the zona dissolve as it moves in.

Although this new version of the saga of the egg and the sperm broke through cultural expectations, the researchers who made the discovery continued to write papers and abstracts as if the sperm were the active party who attacks, binds, penetrates, and enters the egg. The only difference was that sperm were now seen as performing these actions weakly.[29] Not until August 1987, more than three years after the findings described above, did these researchers reconceptualize the process to give the egg a more active role. They began to describe the zona as an aggressive sperm catcher, covered with adhesive molecules that can capture a sperm with a single bond and clasp it to the zona's surface.[30] In the words of their published account: 'The innermost vestment, the *zona pellucida*, is a glyco-protein shell, which captures and tethers the sperm before they penetrate it. . . . The sperm is captured at the initial contact between the sperm tip and the *zona*. . . . Since the thrust [of the sperm] is much smaller than the force needed to break a single affinity bond, the first bond made upon the tip-first meeting of the sperm and *zona* can result in the capture of the sperm.'[31] . . .

Like . . . the biophysicists at Johns Hopkins, another researcher has recently made discoveries that seem to point to a more interactive view of the relationship of egg and sperm. This work, which Paul Wassarman conducted on the sperm and eggs of mice, focuses on identifying the specific molecules in the egg coat (the zona pellucida) that are involved in egg–sperm interaction. At first glance, his descriptions seem to fit the model of an egalitarian relationship. Male and female gametes 'recognize one another', and 'interactions . . . take place between sperm and egg'.[32] But the article in *Scientific American* in which those descriptions appear begins with a vignette that presages the dominant motif of their presentation: 'It has been more than a century since Hermann Fol, a Swiss zoologist, peered into his microscope and became the first person to see a sperm penetrate an egg, fertilize it, and form the first cell of a new embryo.'[33] This portrayal of the sperm as the active party—the one that *penetrates* and *fertilizes* the egg and *produces* the embryo—is not cited as an example of an earlier, now outmoded view. In fact, the author reiterates the point later in the article: 'Many sperm can bind to and penetrate the zona pellucida, or outer coat, of an unfertilized mouse egg, but only one sperm will eventually fuse with the thin plasma membrane surrounding the egg proper (*inner sphere*), fertilizing the egg and giving rise to a new embryo.'[34]

The imagery of sperm as aggressor is particularly startling in this case: the main discovery being reported is isolation of a particular molecule *on the egg coat* that plays an important role in

fertilization! Wassarman's choice of language sustains the picture. He calls the molecule that has been isolated, ZP3, a 'sperm receptor'. By allocating the passive, waiting role to the egg, Wassarman can continue to describe the sperm as the actor, the one that makes it all happen . . .

Social Implications: Thinking Beyond

All . . . of these revisionist accounts of egg and sperm cannot seem to escape the hierarchical imagery of older accounts. Even though each new account gives the egg a larger and more active role, taken together they bring into play another cultural stereotype: woman as a dangerous and aggressive threat. In the Johns Hopkins lab's revised model, the egg ends up as the female aggressor who 'captures and tethers' the sperm with her sticky zona, rather like a spider lying in wait in her web.[35] The Schatten lab has the egg's nucleus 'interrupt' the sperm's dive with a 'sudden and swift' rush by which she 'clasps the sperm and guides its nucleus to the centre'.[36] Wassarman's description of the surface of the egg 'covered with thousands of plasma membrane-bound projections, called microvilli' that reach out and clasp the sperm adds to the spiderlike imagery.[37]

These images grant the egg an active role but at the cost of appearing disturbingly aggressive. Images of woman as dangerous and aggressive, the femme fatale who victimizes men, are widespread in Western literature and culture.[38] More specific is the connection of spider imagery with the idea of all engulfing, devouring mother.[39] New data did not lead scientists to eliminate gender stereotypes in their descriptions of egg and sperm. Instead, scientists simply began to describe egg and sperm in different, but no less damaging, terms.

Can we envision a less stereotypical view? Biology itself provides another model that could be applied to the egg and the sperm. The cybernetic model—with its feedback loops, flexible adaptation to change, coordination of the parts within a whole, evolution over time, and changing response to the environment—is common in genetics, endocrinology, and ecology and has a growing influence in medicine in general.[40] This model has the potential to shift our imagery from the negative, in which the female reproductive system is castigated both for not producing eggs after birth and for producing (and thus wasting) too many eggs overall, to something more positive. The female reproductive system could be seen as responding to the environment (pregnancy or menopause), adjusting to monthly changes (menstruation), and flexibly changing from reproductivity after puberty to nonreproductivity later in life. The sperm and egg's interaction could also be described in cybernetic terms. J.F. Hartman's research in reproductive biology demonstrated 15 years ago that if an egg is killed by being pricked with a needle, live sperm cannot get through the zona.[41] Clearly, this evidence shows that the egg and sperm *do* interact on more mutual terms, making biology's refusal to portray them that way all the more disturbing.

We would do well to be aware, however, that cybernetic imagery is hardly neutral. In the past, cybernetic models have played an important part in the imposition of social control. These models inherently provide a way of thinking about a 'field' of interacting components. Once the field can be seen, it can become the object of new forms of knowledge, which in turn can allow new forms of social control to be exerted over the components of the field. During the 1950s, for example, medicine began to recognize the psychosocial *environment* of the patient: the patient's family and its psychodynamics. Professions such as social work began to focus on this new environment, and the resulting knowledge became one way to further control the patient. Patients began to be seen not as isolated, individual bodies, but as psychosocial entities located in an 'ecological' system: management of 'the patient's psychology was a new entrée to patient control'.[42]

The models that biologists use to describe their data can have important social effects. During the nineteenth century, the social and natural sciences strongly influenced each other: the social ideas of Malthus about how to avoid the natural increase of the poor inspired Darwin's *Origin of Species*.[43] Once the *Origin* stood as a description of the natural world, complete with competition and market struggles, it could be reimported into social science as social Darwinism, in order to justify the social order of the time. What we are seeing now is similar: the importation of cultural ideas about passive females and heroic males into the 'personalities' of gametes. This amounts to the 'implanting of social imagery on representations of nature so as to lay a firm basis for reimporting exactly that same imagery as natural explanations of social phenomena'.[44]

Further research would show us exactly what social effects are being wrought from the biological imagery of egg and sperm. At the very least, the imagery keeps alive some of the hoariest old stereotypes about weak damsels in distress and their strong male rescuers. That these stereotypes are now being written in at the level of the *cell* constitutes a powerful move to make them seem so natural as to be beyond alteration.

The stereotypical imagery might also encourage people to imagine that what results from the interaction of egg and sperm—a fertilized egg—is the result of deliberate 'human' action at the cellular level. Whatever the intentions of the human couple, in this microscopic 'culture' a cellular 'bride' (or femme fatale) and a cellular 'groom' (her victim) make a cellular baby. Rosalind Petchesky points out that through visual representations such as sonograms, we are given 'images of younger and younger, and tinier and tinier, fetuses being "saved"'. This leads to 'the point of visibility being "pushed back" *indefinitely*'.[45] Endowing egg and sperm with intentional action, a key aspect of personhood in our culture, lays the foundation for the point of viability being pushed back to the moment of fertilization. This will likely lead to greater acceptance of technological developments and new forms of scrutiny and manipulation, for the benefit of these inner 'persons': court-ordered restrictions on a pregnant woman's activities in order to protect her fetus, fetal surgery, amniocentesis, and rescinding of abortion rights, to name but a few examples.[46]

Notes

1. The textbooks I consulted are the main ones used in classes for undergraduate premedical students or medical students (or those held on reserve in the library for these classes) during the past few years at Johns Hopkins University. These texts are widely used at other universities in the country as well.

2. Vernon B. Mountcastle, *Medical Physiology*, 14th edn. (London: Mosby, 1980): 2, 1624.

3. Arthur J. Vander, James H. Sherman, and Dorothy S. Luciano, *Human Physiology: The Mechanisms of Body Function*, 3rd edn. (New York: McGraw Hill, 1980), 568.

4. Melvin Konner, 'Childbearing and Age', *New York Times Magazine* 27 December 1987, 22–3, esp. 22.

5. Bruce Alberts et al., *Molecular Biology of the Cell* (New York: Garland, 1983), 795.

6. In her essay 'Have Only Men Evolved?' (in Sandra Harding and Merrill B. Hintikka, eds, *Discovering Reality: Feminist Perspectives on Epistemology, Metaphysics, Methodology, and Philosophy of Science* [Dordrecht: Reidel, 1983], 45–69, esp. 60–1), Ruth Hubbard points out that sociobiologists have said the female invests more energy than the male in the production of her large gametes, claiming that this explains why the female provides parental care. Hubbard questions whether it 'really takes more "energy" to generate the one or relatively few eggs than the large excess of sperms required to achieve fertilization'. For further critique of how the greater size of eggs is interpreted in sociobiology, see Donna Haraway, 'Investement Strategies for the Evolving Portfolio of Primate Females', in Mary Jacobus, Evelyn Fox Keller, and Sally Shuttleworth, eds, *Body/Politics* (New York: Routledge, 1990): 155–6.

7. Arthur C. Guyton, *Physiology of the Human Body*, 6th edn. (Philadelphia: Saunders College Publishing, 1984), 619; and Mountcastle, 1609.

8. Jonathan Miller and David Pelham, *The Facts of Life* (New York: Viking Penguin, 1984), 5.

9. Alberts et al., 796.

10. Ibid., 796.

11. See, e.g., William F. Ganong, *Review of Medical Physiology*, 7th edn. (Los Altos, CA: Lange Medical Publications, 1975), 322.

12. Alberts et al., 796.

13. Guyton, 615.

14. Eldra Pearl Solomon, *Human Anatomy and Physiology* (New York: CBS College Publishing, 1983), 683.

15. Vander, Sherman, and Luciano (no. 3 above), 4th edn. (1985), 580.

16. Alberts et al., 796.

17. All biology texts quoted above use the word 'penetrate'.

18. Solomon, 700.

19. A. Beldecos et al., 'The Importance of Feminist Critique for Contemporary Cell Biology', *Hypatia* 3, 1 (Spring 1988): 61–76.

20. Gerald Schatten and Helen Schatten, 'The Energetic Egg', *Medical World News* 23 (23 January 1984): 51–3, esp. 51.

21. Alberts et al., 796.

22. Guyton, 613.

23. Miller and Pelham, 7.

24. Alberts et al., 804.

25. Ibid., 801.

26. Bennet M. Shapiro, 'The Existential Decision of a Sperm', *Cell* 49, 3 (May 1987): 293–4, esp. 293.

27. Lennart Nilsson, 'A Portrait of the Sperm', in Bjorn A. Afzelius, ed., *The Functional Anatomy of the Spermatozoan* (New York: Pergamon, 1975), 79–82.

28. Jay M. Baltz carried out the research I describe when he was a graduate student in the Thomas C. Jenkins Department of Biophysics at Johns Hopkins University.

29. Jay Baltz and Richard A. Cone, 'What Force Is Needed to Tether a Sperm?' (abstract for Society for the Study of Reproduction, 1985), and 'Flagellar Torque on the Head Determines the Force Needed to Tether a Sperm' (abstract for Biophysical Society, 1986).

30. Jay M. Baltz, David F. Katz, and Richard A. Cone, 'The Mechanics of the Sperm–Egg Interaction at the Zona Pellucida', *Biophysical Journal* 54, 4 (October 1988): 643–54. . . .

31. Ibid., 643, 650.

32. Paul M. Wassarman, 'Fertilization in Mammals',

Scientific American 259, 6 (December 1988): 78–84, esp. 78, 84.

33. Ibid., 78.

34. Ibid., 79.

35. Baltz, Katz, and Cone, 643, 650.

36. Schatten and Schatten, 53.

37. Wassarman, 'The Biology and Chemistry of Fertilization', *Science* 235, 4788 (30 January 198): 557.

38. Mary Ellman, *Thinking about Women* (New York: Harcourt Brace Jovanovich, 1968), 140; Nina Auerbach, *Woman and the Demon* (Cambridge, MA: Harvard University Press, 1982), esp, 186.

39. Kenneth Alan Adams, 'Arachnophobia: Love American Style', *Journal of Psychoanalytic Anthropology* 4, 2 (1981): 157–97.

40. William Ray Arney and Bernard Bergen, *Medicine and the Management of Living* (Chicago: University of Chicago Press, 1984).

41. J.F. Hartman, R.B. Gwatkin, and C.F. Hutchison, 'Early Contract Interactions between Mammalian

Gametes In Vitro', *Proceedings of the National Academy of Sciences (US)* 69, 10 (1972): 2767–9.

42. Arney and Bergen, 68.

43. Ruth Hubbard, 'Have Only Men Evolved?', 51–2.

44. David Harvey, personal communication, November 1989.

45. Rosalind Petchesky, 'Fetal Images: The Power of Visual Culture in the Politics of Reproduction', *Feminist Studies* 13, 2 (Summer 1987): 263–92, esp. 272.

46. Rita Arditti, Renate Klein, and Shelley Minden, *Test-Tube Women* (London: Pandora, 1984); Ellen Goodman, 'Whose Right to Life?' *Baltimore Sun* (17 November 1987); Tamar Lewin, 'Courts Acting to Force Care of the Unborn', *New York Times* (23 November 1987), Al and B10; Susan Irwin and Brigette Jordan, 'Knowledge, Practice, and Power: Court Ordered Cesarean Sections', *Medical Anthropology Quarterly* 1, 3 (September 1987): 319–34.

Chapter 23

'Fetal Rights': A New Assault on Feminism

Katha Pollitt

Some scenes from the way we live now:

- In New York City, a pregnant woman orders a glass of wine with her restaurant meal. A stranger comes over to her table. 'Don't you know you're poisoning your baby?', he says angrily, pointing to a city-mandated sign warning women that drinking during pregnancy causes birth defects.
- In California, Pamela Rae Stewart is advised by her obstetrician to stay off her feet, to eschew sex, and 'street drugs', and to go to the hospital immediately if she starts to bleed. She fails to follow this advice and delivers a brain-damaged baby who soon dies. She is charged with failing to deliver support to a child under an old criminal statute that was intended to force men to provide for women they have made pregnant.
- In Washington, DC, a hospital administration asks a court whether it should intervene and perform a caesarean section on Angela Carder, seriously ill with cancer, against her wishes and those of her husband, her parents, and her doctors. Acknowledging that the operation would probably shorten her life without necessarily saving the life of her 25-week-old fetus, the judge nonetheless provides the order. The caesarean is performed immediately, before her lawyers can appeal. Angela Carder dies; so does her unviable fetus. That incident is subsequently dramatized on *LA Law*, with post-feminist softy Ann Kelsey arguing for the hospital; on TV the baby lives.
- In the Midwest, the US Court of Appeals for

the Seventh Circuit, ruling in *UAW v. Johnson Controls*, upholds an automotive battery plant's seven-year-old 'fetal protection policy' barring fertile women (in effect, all women) from jobs that would expose them to lead (see Carolyn Marshall, 'An Excuse for Workplace Hazard', 25 April 1987). The court discounts testimony about the individual reproductive lives and plans of female employees (many in their late forties, celibate, and/or with completed families), testimony showing that no child born to female employees had shown ill effects traceable to lead exposure and testimony showing that lead poses a comparable danger to male reproductive health. The court accepts testimony that says making the workplace safe would be too expensive.

All over the country, pregnant women who use illegal drugs and/or alcohol are targeted by the criminal justice system. They are 'preventively detained' by judges who mete out jail sentences for minor crime that would ordinarily result in probation or a fine; charged with child abuse or neglect (although by law the fetus is not a child) and threatened with manslaughter charges should they miscarry; and placed under court orders not to drink, although drinking is not a crime and does not invariably (or even usually) result in birth defects. While state legislatures ponder bills that would authorize these questionable practices by criminalizing drug use or 'excessive' alcohol use during pregnancy (California senator Pete Wilson is pushing a similar bill at the federal level), mothers are arrested in their hospital beds when their newborns test positive for drugs. Social workers increasingly remove positive-testing babies into foster care on the presumption that even a single use of drugs during pregnancy renders a mother ipso facto an unfit parent.

What's going on here? Right now the hot area in the developing issue of 'fetal rights' is the use of drugs and alcohol during pregnancy. We've all seen the nightly news reports of inner-city intensive care units overflowing with crack babies, of Indian reservations where one in four children are said to be born physically and mentally stunted by fetal alcohol syndrome (FAS) or the milder, but still serious, fetal alcohol effect. We've read the front-page stories reporting studies that suggest staggering rates of drug use during pregnancy (11 per cent, according to the *New York Times*, or 375,000 women per year) and the dangers of even moderate drinking during pregnancy.

But drugs and alcohol are only the latest focus of a preoccupation with the fetus and its 'rights' that has been wandering around the zeitgeist for the past decade. A few years ago, the big issue was forced caesareans. . . . The 'save the babies' mentality may look like a necessary, if troubling, approach when it's a matter of keeping a drug addict away from a substance that is, after all, illegal. What happens if the same mentality is applied to some 15 million to 20 million highly paid unionized jobs in heavy industry to 'protect' fetuses that do not even exist? Or if the list of things women are put on legal notice to avoid expands to match medical findings on the dangers to the fetus posed by junk food, salt, Aspirin, air travel, and cigarettes?

Critics of the punitive approach to pregnant drug and alcohol users point out the ironies inherent in treating a public-health concern as a matter for the criminal justice system: the contradiction, for instance, of punishing addicted women when most drug treatment programs refuse to accept pregnant women. Indeed, Jennifer Johnson, a Florida woman who was the first person convicted after giving birth to a baby who tested positive for cocaine, had sought treatment and been turned away. (In her case the charge was delivering drugs to a minor.) The crit-

ics point out that threats of jail or the loss of their kids may drive women away from prenatal care and hospital deliveries, and that almost all the women affected so far have been poor and black or Latino, without private doctors to protect them (in Florida, non-white women are 10 times as likely to be reported for substance abuse as white women, although rates of drug use are actually higher for whites).

These are all important points. But they leave unchallenged the notion of fetal rights itself. What we really ought to be asking is, How have we come to see women as the major threat to the health of their newborns, and the womb as the most dangerous place a child will ever inhabit? Why is our basic model 'innocent' fetuses that would be fine if only presumably 'guilty' women refrained from indulging their 'whims'? The list of dangers to the fetus is, after all, very long; the list of dangers to children longer. Why does maternal behaviour, a relatively small piece of the picture, seem such an urgent matter, while much more important factors—that one in five pregnant women receive no prenatal care at all, for instance—attract so little attention? Here are some of the strands that make up the current tangle that is fetal rights.

The Assault on the Poor

It would be pleasant to report that the aura of crisis surrounding crack and FAS babies—the urge to do something, however unconstitutional or cruel, that suddenly pervades society, from judge's bench to chic dinner party to seven o'clock news—was part of a massive national campaign to help women have healthy, wanted pregnancies and healthy babies. But significantly, the current wave of concern is not occurring in that context. Judges order pregnant addicts to jail, but they don't order drug treatment programs to accept them, or Medicaid, which pays for heroin treatment, to cover crack addiction—let alone order landlords not to evict them, or obstetricians to take uninsured women as patients, or the federal government to fund fully the Women, Infants, and Children supplemental feeding program, which reaches only two-thirds of those who are eligible. . . .

The focus on maternal behaviour allows the government to appear to be concerned about babies without having to spend any money, change any priorities, or challenge any vested interests. As with crime, as with poverty, a complicated, multi-faceted problem is construed as a matter of freely chosen individual behaviour. We have crime because we have lots of bad people, poverty because we have lots of lazy people (Republican version) or lots of pathological people (Democratic version), and tiny, sickly, impaired babies because we have lots of women who just don't give a damn.

Once the problem has been defined as original sin, coercion and punishment start to look like hardheaded and commonsensical answers. . . .

The New Temperance

While rightly sounding the alarm about the health risks and social costs of drugs, alcohol, and nicotine, the various 'just say no' crusades have so upped the moral ante across the board that it is now difficult to distinguish between levels and kinds of substance use and abuse and even rather suspect to try. A joint on the weekend is the moral equivalent of a 24-hour-a-day crack habit; wine with meals is next door to a daily quart of rotgut. The stigmatizing of addicts, casual users, alcoholics, social drinkers, and smokers makes punitive measures against them palatable. It also helps us avoid uncomfortable questions about why we are having all these 'substance abuse' epidemics in the first place. Finally, it lets us assume, not always correctly, that drugs and alcohol, all by themselves, cause harm during pregnancy, and ignore the role of malnutrition, violence, chaotic lives, serious maternal health problems, and lack of medical care.

Science Marches On

We know a lot more about fetal development than we did 20 years ago. But how much of what we know will we continue to know in 10 years? As recently as the early 1970s, pregnant women were harassed by their doctors to keep their weight down. They were urged to take tranquilizers and other prescription drugs, to drink in moderation (liquor was routinely used to stop premature labour), to deliver under anesthesia, and not bother to breast-feed. Then too, studies examined contemporary wisdom and found it good. Today, those precepts seem the obvious expression of social forces: the wish of doctors to control pregnancy and delivery, a lack of respect for women, and a distaste for science that outmoded these practices. It was another set of social forces: the women's movement, the prepared-childbirth movement, and the natural-health movement.

What about today's precepts? At the very least, the history of scientific research into pregnancy and childbirth ought to make us skeptical. Instead, we leap to embrace tentative findings and outright bad science because they fit current social prejudices. Those who argue for total abstinence during pregnancy have made much, for example, of a recent study in the *New England Journal of Medicine* that claimed women are more vulnerable than men to alcohol because they have less of a stomach enzyme that neutralizes it before it enters the bloodstream. Universally unreported, however, was the fact that the study included alcoholics and patients with gastrointestinal disease. It is a basic rule of medical research that results cannot be generalized from the sick to the healthy.

In a 1989 article in *The Lancet*, 'Bias against the Null Hypothesis: The Reproductive Hazards of Cocaine', Canadian researchers reported that studies that found a connection between cocaine use and a poor pregnancy outcome had a better than even chance of being accepted for presentation at the annual meeting of the Society for Pediatric Research, while studies that found no connection had a negligible chance—although the latter were better designed. While it's hard to imagine that anyone will ever show that heavy drug use or alcohol consumption is good for fetal development, studies like this one suggest that when the dust settles . . . the current scientific wisdom will look alarmist.

Media Bias

The assumptions that shape the way researchers frame their studies and the questions they choose to investigate are magnified by bias in the news media. Studies that show the bad effects of maternal behaviour make the headlines, studies that show no bad effects don't get reported, and studies that show the bad effects of paternal behaviour (alcoholic males, and males who drink at conception, have been linked to lower IQ and a propensity to alcoholism in offspring) get two paragraphs in the science section. So did the study, briefly mentioned in a recent issue of the *New York Times*, suggesting that housewives run a higher risk than working women of having premature babies, stillbirths, underweight babies, and babies who die in the first week of life. Imagine the publicity had it come out the other way around! . . .

The 'Pro-life' Movement

Anti-choicers have not succeeded in criminalizing abortion, but they have made it inaccessible to millions of women (only 16 states pay for poor women's abortions, and only 18 per cent of countries have even one abortion provider) and made it a badge of sin and failure for millions more. In Sweden, where heavy drinking is common, relatively few FAS babies are born, because alcoholic women have ready access to abortion and it is not a stigmatized choice. In America anti-choice sentiment makes it impossible to suggest to a homeless, malnourished, venereally diseased crack addict that her first priority ought to be getting well: Get help, then have a baby. . . .

As lobbyists, anti-choicers have sought to bolster their cause by interjecting the fetus-as-person argument into a wide variety of situations that would seem to have nothing to do with abortion. They have fought to exclude pregnant women from proposed legislation recognizing the validity of 'living wills' that reject the use of life support systems (coma baby lives!), and have campaigned to classify as homicides assaults on pregnant women that result in fetal death or miscarriage. Arcane as such proposals may seem, they have the effect of broadening little by little the areas of the law in which the fetus is regarded as a person, and in which the woman is regarded as its container.

At a deeper level, the 'pro-life' movement has polluted the way we think about pregnancy. It has promoted a model of pregnancy as a condition that by its very nature pits women and fetuses against each other, with the fetus invariably taking precedence, and a model of women as selfish, confused, potentially violent, and incapable of making responsible choices. . . .

The Privileged Status of the Fetus

. . . Although concern for the fetus may look like a way of helping children, it is actually, in a funny way, a substitute for it. It is an illusion to think that by 'protecting' the fetus from its mother's behaviour we have insured a healthy birth, a healthy infancy, or a healthy childhood, and that the only insurmountable obstacle for crack babies is prenatal exposure to crack.

It is no coincidence that we are obsessed with pregnant women's behaviour at the same time that children's health is declining, by virtually any yardstick one chooses. Take general well-being: in constant dollars, welfare payments are now about two-thirds the 1965 level. Take housing: thousands of children are now growing up in homeless shelters and welfare hotels. Even desperately alcoholic women bear healthy babies two-thirds of the time. Will two-thirds of today's homeless kids emerge unscathed from their dangerous and lead-permeated environments? Take access to medical care: inner-city hospitals are closing all over the country, millions of kids have no health insurance, and most doctors refuse uninsured or Medicaid patients. Even immunization rates are down: whooping cough and measles are on the rise.

The 'Duty of Care'

Not everyone who favours legal intervention to protect the fetus is anti-choice. Some pro-choicers support the coercion and punishment of addicts and alcoholics . . . For some years now bioethicists have been fascinated by the doctrine of 'duty of care', expounded most rigorously by Margery Shaw and John Robertson. In this view, a woman can abort, but once she has decided to bear a child she has a moral, and should have a legal, responsibility to insure a healthy birth. It's an attractive notion because it seems to combine an acceptance of abortion with intuitive feelings shared by just about everyone, including this writer, that pregnancy is a serious undertaking, that society has an interest in the health of babies, that the fetus, although not a person, is also not property.

Whatever its merits as a sentiment, though, the duty of care is a legal disaster. Exactly when, for instance, does the decision to keep a pregnancy take place? For the most desperately addicted—the crack addicts who live on the subway or prostitute themselves for drugs—one may ask if they ever form any idea ordinary people would call a decision, or indeed know they are pregnant until they are practically in labour. Certainly the inaccessibility of abortion denies millions of women the ability to decide. . . .

It is also, even as an abstraction, a false picture. Try as she might, a woman cannot insure a healthy newborn; nor can statistical studies of probability (even well-designed ones) be related in an airtight way to individual cases. We know that cigarettes cause lung cancer, but try proving in a court of law that cigarettes and not air pollution, your job, your genes, or causes unknown caused *your* lung cancer.

Yet far from shrinking from the slippery slope, duty of care theorists positively hurl themselves down it. Margery Shaw, for instance, believes that the production of an imperfect newborn should make a woman liable to criminal charges and 'wrongful life' suits if she knows, or should have known, the risk involved in her behaviour, whether it's drinking when her period is late (she has a duty to keep track of her cycle), delivering at home when her doctor advises her not to (what doctor doesn't?), or failing to abort a genetically damaged fetus (which she has a duty to find out about). So much for that 'decision' to bear a child—a woman can't qualify it in her own interests, but the state can revoke it for her on eugenic grounds.

As these examples show, there is no way to limit the duty of care to cases of flagrant or illegal misbehaviour—duty is duty, and risk is risk. . . . For there is no way to define the limits of what a pregnant woman must sacrifice for fetal benefit, or what she 'should have known', or at what point a trivial risk becomes significant. . . .

Although duty of care theorists would impose upon women a virtually limitless obligation to put the fetus first, they impose that responsibility *only* on women. . . . But what about Dad? It's his kid too, after all. His drug and alcohol use, his prescription medications, his workplace exposure, and general habits of health not only play a part in determining the quality of his sperm but affect the course of pregnancy as well. Cocaine dust and smoke from crack, marijuana, and tobacco present dangers to others who breathe them; his alcoholism often bolsters hers. Does he have a duty of care to make it possible for his pregnant partner to obey those judge's orders and that doctor's advice that now has the force of law? To quit his job to mind the children so that she can get the bed rest without which her fetus may be harmed? Apparently not. . . .

It is interesting to note in this regard that approximately 1 in 12 women are beaten during pregnancy, a time when many previously non-violent men become brutal. We do not know how many miscarriages, stillbirths, and damaged newborns are due, or partly due, to male violence—this is itself a comment on the skewed nature of supposedly objective scientific research. But if it ever does come to be an officially recognized factor in fetal health, the duty of care would probably take yet another ironic twist and hold battered pregnant women liable for their partner's assaults. . . .

Looked at in this light, the inconsistent and fitful nature of our concern about the health of babies forms a pattern. The threat to newborns is interesting when and only when it can, accurately or fancifully, be laid at women's doorstep. Babies 'possibly' impaired by maternal drinking? Front-page stories, a national wave of alarm. A *New England Journal of Medicine* report that 16 per cent of American children have been mentally and neurologically damaged because of exposure to lead, mostly from flaking lead paint in substandard housing? Peter Jennings looks mournful and suggests that 'all parents can do' is to have their children tested frequently. If the mother isn't to blame, no one is to blame. . . .

There are lots of things wrong with the concept of fetal rights. It posits a world in which women will be held accountable, on sketchy or no evidence, for birth defects; in which all fertile women will be treated as potentially pregnant all the time; in which courts, employers, social workers, and doctors—not to mention nosy neighbours and vengeful male partners—will monitor women's behaviour. It imposes responsibilities, without giving women the wherewithal to fulfill them, and places upon women alone duties that belong to both parents and to the community. . . .

Chapter 24

Bodies Out of Time: Women's Reproductive Firsts

Elizabeth Graham and Jacqueline Low

Introduction

There are few biological functions that have been researched as much as women's reproductive experiences (Walters, 1994). From a medical sciences perspective female reproductive processes remain conceptualized largely as potential health problems (Boddy, 1998; Hays, 1996; Oakley, 1993). In contrast, feminist scholars and others have argued that in most contexts, these reproductive functions are normal biological events and should be conceptualized as such (Graham and Oakley, 1981). In the end, whether one conceives of women's reproductive lives as medical concerns or matters of everyday life, it is clear that within contemporary Western culture there are distinct time expectations for women in relation to each reproductive function. Below, using data collected via face-to-face and focus group interviews conducted with women from the Cape Breton Regional Municipality of Nova Scotia[1], we present analysis of these expectations and their influence on women's experiences of their reproductive lives. In doing so we develop our concept of *bodies out of time* by extending Mary Douglas's (1985: 35) understanding of dirt as 'matter out of place'.

From Matter Out of Place to Bodies Out of Time

In her classic text, *Purity and Danger: An Analysis of the Concepts of Pollution and Taboo*, Douglas concludes that dirt should be understood in relativist

rather than absolute terms as 'matter out of place' (Douglas, 1985: 35). What this means is that things are not dirt in and of themselves, rather, they are considered dirt when they appear in inappropriate contexts or places. In her words:

> Shoes are not dirty in themselves, but it is dirty to place them on the dining-table; food is not dirty in itself, but it is dirty to leave cooking utensils in the bedroom, or food bespattered on clothing; similarly, bathroom equipment in the drawing room; clothing lying on chairs; outdoor things indoors; upstairs things downstairs; underclothing appearing where over-clothing should be, and so on. (Douglas, 1985: 35–6)

Matter out of place are by definition socio-cultural anomalies making them, in Douglas's (1985: 94–7) terms, instances of cultural pollution that are dangerous to the social collectivity.

In the same way as the shoes Douglas (1985: 35–6) discusses above, bodies can be conceptualized as 'matter out of place' and can be reacted to as 'pollution' depending on the socio-cultural contexts in which they are found. For instance, homeless bodies found sleeping on the streets are in most cases seen as problematic and are regularly subject to the social control efforts of the police and social welfare agencies. Similarly, naked bodies found almost anywhere other than in private spaces or within the bounds of specialized subcultures are likewise seen as dangerous and are subject to social control in contemporary Western society. Such social control efforts are instances of 'the reaction that condemns any object or idea likely to confuse or contradict cherished classifications', such as the examples above of the distinction made between the public and private spheres of socio-cultural life (Douglas, 1985: 35–6).

Thus our concept of bodies out of time shares much with Douglas's (1985: 35) notion of 'matter out of place' as both foreground the underlying issue of socio-cultural reactions to pollution or disorder. What we add to Douglas's (1985) understanding in conceptualizing bodies out of time is a temporal dimension. In applying bodies out of time to the corporeality of the female reproductive body we can gain a deeper understanding of the relationship between socio-cultural expectations of female reproductive functions and chronological time, as well as the implications these have for women's experiences of their reproductive lives.

Reproductive Bodies Out of Time

Cultural expectations concerning the timing of a woman's reproductive life in contemporary Western society are largely informed by medical discourse of women's bodies and reproductive processes (Crook, 1995; Williams and Calnan, 1996). It is medical professionals who publish research on such processes as menstruation, pregnancy, and menopause and it is their views concerning these topics that are often foregrounded in discussions in public fora such as the media. In this way medical discourses of women's reproductive bodies are a significant socio-cultural factor in the shaping of women's experiences of their reproductive lives.

According to medical science, which reproductive experience a woman has had is largely determined by her age and medical professionals have identified 'appropriate' or average ages for each reproductive experience. For instance, they tell us that a woman can expect to begin menstruation at age 13; that she will typically experience pregnancy for the first time in her early twenties; and that while menopause is a gradual process,

she can expect identifiable bodily changes around the age of 45. In addition to a biological event, these reproductive processes represent instances of status passages in a woman's life, such as the status change from child to young woman and from young woman to mother.

A woman's experience of these status passages are framed by the lay rituals of the mother to daughter and/or female friend to female friend passing of information to address the occurrence of a reproductive function and to aid the woman in her transition to a new status. For example, Marie stated that during childbirth women need other women. She said, 'Women become like a women's network, womanly network. You can really understand one another . . . How can a man really understand because they have never had the opportunity to experience it.' Indicating a similar reliance on other women, Carla, whose mother had died when she was quite young, explained, 'You do miss a lot when you don't have a mother . . . Sometimes you feel too stupid to ask some things that you'd get from your mother.'

The significance of socio-cultural expectations concerning the timing of women's reproductive processes are most obvious when we examine a woman's first experience with menstruation, childbirth, and menopause. When we do we find that when a woman experiences a reproductive function too early or too late, she is having a bodily experience that does not correspond to socio-cultural expectations—she is experiencing a *reproductive body out of time*. A consequence of possessing a reproductive body out of time is that the woman is more often than not labelled as abnormal. She, therefore, experiences complications making the transition to her new status as it is only when the timing of a woman's reproductive experience, and the secular ritual of females passing on information come together, that the transition runs smoothly. Only when these two events coincide is a woman able to easily adopt the new status associated with the particular reproductive function. In contrast, when her reproductive body is out of time there is a lack of lay ritual to guide the women through status transitions such as that from child to young woman or from potential mother to mother. Her body becomes a cultural anomaly and it is as 'if . . . [she] has no place in the social system and is therefore a marginal being' (Douglas, 1985: 97).

Menarche Out of Time

The first reproductive function a woman can expect to experience is menstruation or, more specifically, menarche, a woman's first menstrual period. The general socio-cultural expectation is that a young woman will experience menarche at approximately age 13. Women who experience menarche earlier than that, however, are less likely to know what is happening to them or what is expected of them as many mothers, as well as representatives of relevant social institutions and other individuals, wait until the socially designated time to prepare young women for menarche. Moreover, others may continue to treat her as a child rather than as a 'young woman'. Correspondingly, while the woman who experiences menarche late in life may be very well informed about menstruation prior to her first experience with it, she is likely to think that there is something wrong because of the delay in menarche. In either case, the woman experiences difficulty in adopting the new status that is expected of her as only those who experience menarche at the expected time are able to easily transition into the new status of 'young woman' and 'potential mother' in line with socio-cultural expectations about the temporal nature of their reproductive bodies.

To illustrate, all the women who participated in this study experienced menarche between the ages of 11 and 16. The women who began menstruating at age 11 were rarely informed about menstruation because the socio-cultural expectation is that they were not yet ready to occupy the status of 'young woman' or 'potential mother'. Consequently, they had not learned what would happen to their bodies or what was expected of them in this new status. Many of the women in this age category felt traumatized by the experience of menarche out of time. According to Nina:

The first . . . period, that was scary. Nothing was ever said to me. I had no idea such a thing was going to happen to me. And the day that I started I was terrified 'cause, well I thought I cut myself, I really did and I kept searching to see where I had cut myself.

Finally, she told her mother that evening and her mom just said: 'This is something that you are going to have the rest of your life. She didn't tell me that I needed this to have children or anything. That was it' (Nina).

Unlike those in the younger age ranges, the woman experiencing menarche at age 16 has been exposed to considerable information regarding the status of 'young woman' and 'potential mother' as well as social expectations regarding the personal hygiene practices associated with menstruation in Western culture. She is also likely to have experienced the lay ritual of the mother/daughter or female friend talk about menarche but has yet to experience the biological event that is supposed to coincide with the ritual. This left Tina feeling that she was abnormal because the onset of menstruation was so late for her. For example, she said: 'I thought for a while that one day I'd find out I was really a boy. That was scary. I was so relieved when I finally started.' Also problematic is that when menarche is delayed others often assume, incorrectly, that the woman has had the experience and has moved onto her new status. In attempting to manage this anomalous status some women behave as if they have begun menstruation when they have not. Carla put it this way: 'They'd all be talking about theirs [their periods], saying how much they hated it 'cause of the cramps and stuff. So I just went along and said: "Oh yeah, it's a pain".'

Pregnancy and Childbirth Out of Time

Socio-cultural time expectations are more elastic for first-time pregnancy than they are for menarche. Consequently, the timing of first pregnancy has to deviate more widely from these expectations for the woman's reproductive process to be out of time for her to be considered a socio-cultural anomaly or for her not to have engaged in at least some of the lay rituals that frame the experience of first pregnancy. For instance, women who had their first child 'later in life', but not 'too late', were well informed about pregnancy and childbirth as they had deliberately sought out information about these reproductive processes. For example, Liz, who was 34 at the time she became pregnant said:

> Once I got pregnant I talked a lot with my mother-in-law, I talked to my friend in the States who took the medical sociology course with me, . . . I spent a lot of energy and time trying to find a midwife, . . . I found a labour coach instead. So I talked a lot with my labour coach and we also took Lamaze class. So . . . I guess that's quite a wide support group. And then . . . as I got bigger and it became more of a thing of conversation local friends as well got in on the support network. Go along with that and to discuss things and answer questions.

One reason for this is that unlike first pregnancy in 'too early' age categories, these women were more likely to become pregnant because they planned to.

In contrast, women considered to be too young to move from potential mother to mother status were typically not well prepared for pregnancy or childbirth. For instance, Sue, who was 18 and unmarried when she experienced an unplanned pregnancy, explained that she had not participated in any of the lay rituals of childbirth and pregnancy described by Liz above. She didn't attend childbirth classes and she did not talk to family or friends about her pregnancy, saying that she 'didn't feel connected with them'.

Menopause Out of Time

There is even less consensus in society as to when a woman 'should' begin menopause as the socio-cultural expectations for the timing of menopause

are by far the least precise of the reproductive processes we discuss in this chapter. Medically defined normal menopause can begin at any point between the early forties and mid-fifties, a time span of 10 to 15 years. The imprecision of socio-cultural expectations here also has to do with the more gradual onset of the menopausal experience compared to menarche and pregnancy. For example, many women are uncertain about whether they have even begun menopause. Donna put it this way: 'The only thing I know is that sometimes I wake up in the night really, really hot and someone told me that's part of it [menopause], but I don't know.' Nonetheless, the impact of socio-cultural expectations of time are still an issue in relation to menopausal experiences as extreme deviations from the socially expected age range results in circumstances similar to those identified in relation to menarche and pregnancy. To illustrate, Karen began to experience changes associated with menopause in her early thirties. In her words:

> It's only when I came off the birth control pill that I noticed that I had a big problem because the minute I stopped taking the birth control pill, no more periods. And I figured that it was just an adjustment. Four months later, still nothing and I thought well I should probably go in and have this checked and the first question [the doctor] asked me was: 'how old are you?' and at the time I was 33 and [she said] 'Oh, well, I'm sure it's nothing because you're too young.'

She found herself to be completely unprepared for what was happening to her saying: 'So I've just gone through the hot flashes and the whole menopause experience only I didn't know that's what was happening.' That she was having a reproductive experience out of time, and that this makes her body culturally anomalous, was made plain to her when she engaged with the medical profession. According to Karen:

> If you go see a gynecologist or a doctor, if you start menopause before a certain age they give it

a different name. It is the exact same thing only they call it premature ovarian failure so that really makes you feel like . . . a big failure . . . It's not normal.

Discussion

When a woman experiences reproductive processes in sync with socio-cultural expectation of time within the lifespan, we have lay rituals that frame her first experience of a reproductive function and aid her in the concomitant status passage that the biological processes of menarche, pregnancy and childbirth, and menopause entail. Such lay rituals also serve to control the potential dangers inherent in status passage by disengaging the woman from her prior status, temporarily separating her out from the rest of society, and then publicly declaring her entry into her new status (Douglas, 1985). According to Douglas (1985: 96) 'danger lies in the transitional states, simply because transition is neither one state nor the next'. However, women who are 'early birds' or 'late bloomers' where their reproductive processes are concerned will spend much longer in such status limbo as we lack lay rituals to guide their socio-culturally anomalous status passage. Indeed, it is only in the extreme cases of deviation from socio-culturally expected timing of menarche, pregnancy, childbirth, and menopause that we have any ritual at all and these particular types of reproductive bodies out of time become subject to ritual purification almost exclusively via medical diagnosis and intervention. For example, when Karen began missing her period, she went to the doctor, who sent her for a hormone level test.

The test came back and she said 'it's full-blown menopause' and she referred me to a gynecologist right away and he said 'I'm really interested in your case because' he said 'it's very unusual and I might treat two or three women in my whole career who will have the condition that you have.

While this ritual provided Karen with information about the biological implications of 'too early' menopause, the ritual of medical intervention did little to prepare her for the more wide-ranging implications of this status passage.

So, he was really good and really explained a lot. But even when they explain it to you, they deal with the physical things, what's happening to your body, you have to take this medicine because at your age you desperately need estrogen and there are going to be some major complications if you don't take this medicine. But they don't really prepare you for the, when they tell you that you are never going to have any children and this is it, like you have to deal with this and it's a bit of an adjustment.

In the case of other reproductive bodies out of time, the ritual of medical intervention took on a decidedly punitive quality. For example, Joan described an incident she observed one day in the hospital where a very young woman had arrived at the hospital in the late stages of labour. Joan said that the attending physician treated this young woman terribly and refused to offer the young woman any emotional support or pain relief, asserting that she deserved the pain she was experiencing. Joan was horrified. In other cases of reproductive bodies out of time women had procedures *done to* them. This was the case for Marie's sister-in-law. Marie stated, 'They didn't even ask her if it was okay to do an episiotomy or to use forceps. . . . They did not ask her. I was there. They did not ask her.' The physician simply performed the episiotomy. As Marie said, there was 'no informed consent'. Finally, in many cases these women were left to fashion their own rituals to manage the status passage of their reproductive bodies out of time. In Karen's words:

Well, when I walked out of the doctor's office the first day I felt like a total idiot 'cause, . . . when I went to the gynecologist, you know they start asking you questions about your cycle and your estrogen and progesterone you know and I'm, and he was saying: 'You're following me, right?' and . . . I'm thinking, 'I don't have a clue what you're talking about, when I get out of here I'm going to find out, I'm gonna be informed for my next visit.' . . . When I walked out of there I thought 'Geez, gotta go out and buy books, I'm gonna read on this.' . . . And I called a couple of friends who were my age . . .

and that's when we discovered we knew very little about a lot of women's reproductive system 'cause you know when things are going right you don't ask, you know you basically know what's goin' on and it's when something goes wrong that you start thinkin', 'Oh my god'.

Note

1. Forty-seven women participated in focus groups and/or individual semi-structured interviews. They were all white and their ages ranged from 20 to 64. All of these women had had experience with menstruation; 43 had experienced at least one pregnancy and birth; 29 women were experiencing or had experienced menopause at the time of data collection; and 15 women were experiencing the post-menopausal phase of their lives (Graham, 2003).

References

Boddy, J. 1998. 'Remembering Amal: On Birth and the British in Northern Sudan', in M. Lock and P.A. Kaufert, eds, *Pragmatic Women and Body Politics*. Cambridge: Cambridge University Press, 28–57.

Crook, M. 2005. *My Body: Women Speak Out About Their Health Care*. New York: Insight Books.

Douglas, M. 1985. *Purity and Danger: An Analysis of the Concepts of Pollution and Taboo*. London: Routledge and Kegan Paul.

Graham, E. 2003. *An Intensified Pragmatism in Response to Reproductive Experiences and Medicalization: A Case Study of Cape Breton Women*. Unpublished Doctoral Dissertation, McMaster University, Hamilton, ON.

Graham, H., and A. Oakley. 1981. 'Competing Ideologies of Reproduction: Medical and Maternal Perspectives on Pregnancy', in C. Currer and M. Stacey, eds, *Concepts of Health, Illness and Disease*. Leamington Spa: Berg, 99–115.

Hays, B. 1996. 'Authority and Authoritative Knowledge in American Birth', *Medical Anthropology Quarterly* 10, 2: 291–98.

Oakley, A. 1993. *Essays on Women, Medicine and Health*. Edinburgh: Edinburgh University Press.

Walters, V. 1994. 'Women's Perceptions Regarding Health and Illness', in S.B. Bolaria and H. D. Dickinson, eds, *Health, Illness and Health Care in Canada*, 2nd edn. Toronto: Harcourt Brace, 307–25.

Williams, B., and S. Calnan. 1996. 'The Limits of Medicalization? Modern Medicine and the Lay Populace in "Late" Modernity', *Social Science and Medicine* 42, 12: 1609–20.

Part IX

Children's Bodies

Claudia Malacrida and Jacqueline Low

The socialization of children is often accomplished through bodily practices. The classroom presents a micro-society, in which individualization, gender roles, and discipline of bodily needs and desires are taught. Berry Mayall (1996) examines differences in children's bodily socialization in school and at home. Children's bodies in both arenas are **socialized**, or shaped and encouraged through social interaction, to evidence culturally valued traits such as control over bodily functions, emotional control, 'good' manners, and good physical health and hygiene. In Mayall's view, however, the bodily socialization that occurs between mothers and children is significantly different from that which occurs between teachers and students. Drawing on interviews with mothers and children, Mayall found that mothers, whose socialization of their children is based in relations of care and intimacy, have a deep understanding of the nuances of their children's bodies and know the linkages between their children's physical, social, and emotional lives. Thus, the bodily socialization that mothers engage in is accompanied by emotional support. The net result is that children describe their home-based achievement of bodily norms, such as hygiene, self-care, and self-control, positively and with pride of accomplishment. Further, the bodily socialization children learned at home provides benefits beyond self-mastery, including responsibility to and for others, and a sense of contributing to the social world.

At school, however, bodily socialization permitted children to engage in considerably less negotiation and self-mastery. Children's bodily needs—to use the toilet, to obtain a drink, to eat, and to move—were regulated by the routine of the classroom and the teacher's need to create and maintain order. Thus, individual bodily socialization became subordinated to collective **bodily regulation**. At school, children described feeling that they had little control over the collective day, and hence they felt no sense either of self-mastery or of contributing to the 'construction of the school as a social order' (Mayall, 1996). In the end, Mayall intimates that, reminiscent of Michel Foucault's (1995) theories, schools **discipline** children's bodies through regulation, surveillance, and control. Conversely, reflecting Norbert Elias's (1994) ideas, mothers **civilize** children's bodies through socialization enacted in relations of interdependency and interaction.

Karin A. Martin (1998) discusses how the hidden curriculum operates in preschools to teach students to discipline their bodies and to embody appropriate gender behaviour. Used by conflict theorists, the **hidden curriculum** refers to those things we learn in school that are not part of the academic curriculum (Russell, 1999). For example, we learn conformity and deference to authority when we are made to raise our hands before speaking, stand in lines, and refrain from speaking until a teacher gives us permission. Martin provides evidence that a hidden gender curriculum operates in schools to replicate gendered power relations in society. In analyzing how young children play out a **gender hierarchy**—a vertical ranking of men and women that mirrors male/female inequality in the larger society—Martin uses Goffman's (1959) concepts of front and back stage performances. In **front stage performances** the individual's embodied behaviour conforms to what the social audience considers appropriate to the role he or she is playing, whereas **back stage performances** involve embodied behaviour that most often contradicts those societal expectations. For instance, Martin describes how boys would perform gender by dressing up as monsters (front stage behaviour) but would contradict expectations of male embodied behaviour by wearing women's high-heeled shoes and carrying a purse (back stage behaviour).

Drawing on the work of Foucault, Nikolas Rose (1999) notes that children's bodies were core targets of nineteenth- and twentieth-century **individualization**, a cultural shift in which the individual rose up from the masses of previously ignored citizens to become a focus of study and of regulation. Individualization was facilitated through the rise of institutions like schools, which permitted the detailed collection and maintenance of documentation on the individuals they housed. This new knowledge led to new **moral panics** (social concerns over issues perceived to threaten social order). Early schools' congregated populations produced a plethora of individual records that identified **feeble-minded** children as not only 'hard-to-educate', but also as threats to productive society. The IQ test arose in response to these concerns, and came to be an accepted measure of 'normal' and 'abnormal' intelligence. Rose makes the point that the repeated application of this test and the collection of its scores resulted in the **normalization** of intelligence through assigning it a mathematical score.

Rose's argument is based on the mathematic principle of **central tendency**, where in any frequency distribution there is a tendency for scores or values to congregate at a central average and produce a normal distribution curve, particularly as the size of the sample increases. Because the IQ test has been so widely used and recorded, its distribution of scores is normal, and as Rose notes, 'The psychological test takes the powers of individuals and turns them into writing as numbers, quotients, scores . . .' (1999: 143).

From these beginnings, and aided by technologies such as photography and the standardized checklist, the discipline of child psychology has developed a broad array of scales and models of childhood behaviour, embodiment, and milestones. All of these construct an increasingly detailed differentiation between 'normal' and 'abnormal' children, resulting in new, rigid ways of responding to and engaging with children.

References

Elias, N. 1994. *The Civilizing Process*. Oxford and Cambridge, MA: Blackwell.

Foucault, M. 1995. *Discipline and Punish: The Birth of the Prison*. New York: Vintage Books.

Goffman, E. 1959. *The Presentation of Self in Everyday Life*. New York: Doubleday Anchor Books.

Martin, K.A. 1998. 'Becoming A Gendered Body: Practices of Preschools', *American Sociological Review* 63, 4: 494–511.

Mayall, B. 1996. 'Children's Lived Bodies in Everyday Life', in *Children, Health and the Social Order*. Milton Keynes: Open University Press, 85–112.

Rose, N. 1999. 'The Gaze of the Psychologist', in *Governing the Soul: The Shaping of the Private Self*. London: Free Association Books, 123–34.

Russell, S. 1999. 'The Hidden Curriculum of School: Reproducing Gender and Class Hierarchies', in R.J. Brym, ed, *Society in Question: Sociology for the 21ˢᵗ Century*, 2nd edn. Toronto: Harcourt Brace, 444–57.

Chapter 25

Children's Lived Bodies in Everyday Life

Berry Mayall

Introduction

. . .

The incorporation of children into sociology should reinforce the centrality of embodied experience in everyday life, since children's learning is a basis for life-long knowledge. Children learn that their social value depends partly on the evaluation of their embodied activity. Broadly, at both home and school children are required to submit their bodies to adult control and restriction, but home offers emotional and moral approval of bodily achievement as an end in itself, whereas school sees bodily control as a means to an end. Children's body works at home—working to take control of bodily functions—provides them with knowledge of how bodily behaviour links into the social order. In the first two years of life, children find that their achievements in skills such as walking, eating with fingers, spoons, and cups, excreting in socially acceptable times and places receive social approval. Their own intimate knowledge of links between their bodies, feeling[s], and minds is constructed and reconstructed through parental recognition, that is, their perception of their social value is embodied perception. Older children bring their bodies with them into the public world of school, and endeavour to maintain some control over them in a social context that both devalues and regulates the body. But, once they get to school children find little scope for the enactment and development of their bodily achievements, nor do they meet delighted adult recognition of them. . . .

In particular, children are conscious both positively and negatively of their bodies, in daily encounters during their early years. Their bodies are present to them through the behaviour of adults. Not only are they routinely and affectionately handled by adults (dressing, toileting, hugs, lifting), but they are also encouraged to think about their bodies, as mothers urge them to eat, take them through the processes of toilet-training, praise their physical achievements. Establishing the normalcy of one's child includes discussion between mothers, above the listening ears of their children, on the minutiae of growth and development. And adults comment on children's rapid growth, size, and beauty. More negatively, children's bodies are subject to regulation: not to hit out at others, to confine excretion to certain places and times, to accept confinement in buggies and car seats. Increasing age brings bodily responsibilities: not to hit your younger sib, to sit still at meal times, to hold hands across the road. Children themselves, as Allison James (1993: ch. 4) describes, consider their physical growth as a marker of status—when I'm big, I'm going to big school. She also notes how children (aged four years) show their ancient scars, not so much, she argues, to get adult sympathy, but as part of their thinking about their embodied social identities, developed over time, through bodily encounters.

Women's relationships with their children are constructed and reconstructed through the care of children's bodily and emotional well-being. Typically mothers can describe in detail changes they observe in their young children, and will consider what balance of physical and emotional factors may account for these changes. . . .

. . . [The data] indicate mothers' knowledge of the range of their child's normal behaviours and moods. They show how mothers assume that the physical, social, and the emotional are inter-linked. Interpretation may include both physical and social factors: thus, a child going off his food may be reacting to toilet-training. The examples indicate knowledge of minor adjustments that will restore well-being or alleviate distress. They also show how mothers manipulate children's bodies and emotions as a linked enterprise to restore their children's well-being.

Children at Home—Constructing and Reconstructing Bodies and Minds

Children's control over their health maintenance is the topic under discussion here. This implies consideration of how, and how effectively, they manage their bodies, their minds, and their emotions to preserve a sense of well-being. Children's social positioning, how they interact with, negotiate with, and resist adult approaches and practices will be considered, taking in turn children's daily experiences at home and school. . . Firstly, child–adult relationships are structured by the specifics of adult understandings of children; and parents and teachers differ here. Secondly, experiential learning at home contrasts with abstracted learning at school. Thirdly, the degree of 'fit' between moral precepts and practices differs in the two settings. Finally, the home and school provide differing understandings and implementations of body–emotion links.

Here data from five- and nine-year-olds is explored to consider their understandings of their social position at home.[1] . . .

Self-care

Broadly, at five, Greenstreet children's accounts indicate that they had both the relevant knowledge of and competence to carry out self-care activities under the overall care of their mothers, while at nine they were fully competent, although in most cases their mothers supervised them. Two five-year-olds speak first, about their early morning activities. Both five- and nine-year-olds assumed that they controlled self-care, in the sense that they had the means and the encouragement to do it.

John: I got up and I had Ready Brek. You can put sugar on it to make it tasty. You mix it with milk. I got dressed, and I got my bag and my apple and brought it to school.

A second example:

Dan: I wash me first.
I: Yourself? [skeptical adult]
Dan: Yes, my face, my hands. I get dressed, I put my shoes on, on my own. I get ready for school, I get my book. I remember it, to bring it back.
I: Do you have breakfast?
Dan: Yes, I have my breakfast. Toast, banana, Piedmont.
I: What's that?
Dan: It's apple juice, it's sparkling. Then we go to school with my daddy or my mummy. I cross the street by the lollipop lady.

These boys had just started in the reception class, and their accounts of what they did at home indicated pleasure, pride, and confidence in their achievements there. One of these is to slot together the worlds of home and school: remembering to take back the book borrowed overnight and put an apple in your school-bag. . . .

Contributions to Home Maintenance

Both mothers and children referred to contributions children made to the social order of the home. With under-twos, mothers' accounts suggest that children were taking the initiative in engaging in the work of home maintenance (Mayall and Foster, 1989: 25). With five-year-olds, most mothers report asking children to help in order to accustom them to the idea of responsible participation. Children, however, suggest that at five they regarded the contribution they made as real in response to the moral code of the home. In this respect one can see a development over the years of childhood, as described in other studies, for instance, Fortes's study of Tale children (1970). For those children by the age of nine, as for the children studied here, jobs were for real in the eyes of mothers too.

The interactive character of the establishment and reconstruction of the social order is indicated at the conversational level in the following extracts from an interview with a mother, with her five-year-old son, Bill, contributing:

Mother: He's much more mature now, more responsible, dresses himself in the morning.
Bill: My teeth.
Mother: Sometimes brushing your teeth. And he's willing to take his share. For instance, we were out shopping and size for size he did, he carried some bags. He started saying, 'I'm only little', but in the end he did, and he was running home at the end, so he could carry them.
I: What do you think are the most important ways of keeping him healthy?
Mother: He did have trouble going to the loo. I found when he was with his Dad [who lives elsewhere] he wasn't eating fibre. So now he has bananas.
Bill: I do eat bananas. . .
Mother: I wish he'd eat more green veg. He won't eat anything hot.
Bill: I will eat cucumber.
Mother: Yes, you do eat cucumber. Yes, you do eat cucumber and tomatoes. But he won't eat any hot vegetables. I know it's not sensible [i.e., of mother to think that], but I think he should.
Bill: I do eat eggs and cheese!
I: Do you have any rules?
Mother: Oh, dear, it's mainly don't hurt each other . . . I don't like it if they keep punching each other.
Bill: Not break the furniture up!
Mother: Yes! What else, Bill?
Bill: No chocolate—
Mother: —unless they've eaten something decent beforehand.
Bill: No smashing the windows!

And so on. This five-year-old and his mother suggest a shared understanding both of what is

expected, and of how behaviour is negotiable within the overall limits set by the mother. . . .

Similarly, a mother talked about her five-year-old son's participation and helpfulness.

I: Does he look after himself more, or less, nowadays?
Mother: He gets dressed himself. He makes his own bed, and he makes [his two younger sibs'] beds. He wants to go across the road to the shop, because he wants to help with the shopping. But I've told him, we're waiting for a year till he's six.
I: Have things changed recently?
Mother: He's found out that he's got more responsibility. In the playground—he knows what he can do and can't do, and what he can and can't take to school. He told me, I have to take indoor shoes to school—I have to take off my outdoor shoes when I get there. He tries to be teacher at home, he teaches the others [sibs] how to do things, and he acts the teacher, copying Miss X. He does housework, he washes up, makes beds, polishes, not very well. He'll tidy up my bedroom for me. He's great.

Children were thus engaging in household routines and taking aboard parental edicts about what was good and bad. In . . . the above quotation as in the second in this section, an important new responsibility children took on was linking the worlds of home and school. They knew the minutiae of school requirements: to return the book borrowed overnight, to make sure mothers provided dinner money on the right day, to remind mothers that indoor shoes should be provided and taken to school. . . .

Children's Contributions to Relationships at Home

. . . The children's accounts suggest that by the age of nine they felt a sense of responsibility of other people, in that they knew their own behaviour impacted on that of others in the family, and other's behaviour affected them. They were thus constructing themselves as people who build relationships. This finding links with the points made by

Judy Dunn (1984: ch. 4): children of five or six tend to use concrete terms ('He hits me when he gets mad') to describe their sibs, whereas older children will use more abstract terms—'she's kind', 'she's mean'—and will comment on a wider range of aspects of the sib's personality. In the Greenstreet study nine-year-old children noted tensions between the competitive and hostile behaviour of both themselves and their sibs to each other, and also the pleasures of playing harmoniously together. Hostility and affection had to be negotiated and managed. As one boy wrote: 'I like my brother—sometimes we play rugby together, but sometimes I don't because he can be a pain. And then I don't like him because he can pull my hair really tight.'

The character of living at home was described by both girls and boys in terms of whether or not it provided opportunities for social interaction (school scored higher here: it provided the company of other children). But, as above, interactions with family were a source of both difficulty and pleasure. . . .

Children at School—Constructing and Reconstructing Bodies and Minds

In this section the order of events is as for life at home: how the children see self-care; contributions to school maintenance; and relationships. The issues of concern are children's sense of control, their desire to do things and achieve things, and how they understand adult ordering of the social environment.

Self-care

Data from five-year-olds indicate that their self-care practices at home were not current at school. The social order of the school assumed that children's health maintenance was ordered through school practices and determined by the demands of the formal curriculum. Such important matters as getting a drink or going to the lavatory were not within their control, but conditioned by school agendas. Control over food consumption was a major issue . . .

Children's physical activity was limited through the implementation of school routines. The reception-class day included many occasions demanding strict physical conformity. The day began with the class sitting on the carpet with the teacher, again before morning break, dinner break, and afternoon break and finally at the end of the day for last discussion of the day, the next day, and story-time. Lining up was also a frequent ritual of the day—for each of the three breaks and for expeditions to assembly, the school library, and gym.

The demand made by the school regime for control over the body and legs, folded arms, no touching of other children, eyes front (towards the teacher). Lining up was also a strictly defined social event: movement was to take place only on the word Go! Requisite behaviours included due but not undue speed towards the line, lining up in single file, not jostling or pushing in, keeping your arms to yourself, not shouting. Infringements were quickly identified and reprimanded. A boy's enthusiasm to get to the playground and a girl's slow movement both called up comment. As the teacher explained, it was not just that 20 or more children had to be regulated, in the interests of preventing chaos, but that half her job was to get the children used to the 'way we do things here'. . .

Margaret sums up what for many reception-class children were the main pros and cons of school. Playtime and exercise, including imaginative play were the good points. Having to do things and being told off were the bad points:

I: What are the best things about school?
Margaret: One of them is having playtime, one of them is doing apparatus and one of them is drawing, and playing teachers.
I: Do you like playing teachers then?
Margaret: Yes.
I: Are there bad things?
Margaret: Having to always, just, being told off.
I: What are the best things about being at home?
Margaret: That I don't have to do anything I don't wanna and I don't have to write anything

I don't want to when I'm writing. I don't have to play anything I don't wanna.

During my days with the reception class, I quickly formed the impression through observation that the newest children felt very much on their own. It was up to them to make out, through learning the social norms quickly. An important aide was a companion, someone to play with and help defend you against other groups of children. This impression was substantiated by some of the children's comments. In the case of illness or accident, children did not always go direct and alone to an adult; a common sight was a child leading her companion to the teacher or helper, or reporting that her friend needed help. Thus, it seemed that children were subject to a highly structured regime, and also felt responsible for their own health care and, to an extent, for that of others. . . .

Some further points about health maintenance emerge from nine-year-olds' conversations and writing. After over four years at school, these children were indeed socialized into the social norms of the school. They did not complain about sitting on the carpet, lining up, getting a drink, going to the lavatory. They had grown accustomed to the regime and had learned how to manage it—notably by bringing packed lunches, and by judging when it was acceptable to chat and move about in class, or ask leave to go to the toilet. But they were vociferous on physical and psychological adult constraint.

Both girls and boys emphasized their enjoyment of enterprise and of achievement, and valued both mental and physical activities. School, particularly in its upper classes, did not offer enough opportunity for these. Children reported that school was highly controlling, work was repetitive (copying out 'in best', doing countless maths examples). . . .

It was notable that children valued 'silent reading' (half an hour after dinner): the children chose their own book and got on at their own pace; thus, they had some control over time use. Certainly they looked contented—they sat quietly and absorbed in their reading. Even here, though, the teacher sometimes intervened:

June: My best part of the day is silent reading, because you feel like a character in it. My best series is Sweet Valley—they are brilliant books because they are true to life . . . It gets on my nerves when Miss X just hints for us to read other books. . . .

As was indicated above, children's control over self-care as regards getting a drink was subject to teachers' understandings of their motives, in the context of work requirements. Dinner-time is conditioned by organizational considerations and by staff job remits. Ensuring that a whole school is fed in the space of about an hour requires pushing children through the system. Opportunities for choosing the food on offer, and for leisurely, pleasant food consumption are constrained by time demands. Some children experience the social occasion as unpleasant. . . . All in all, children are likely to experience dinner-time as a low status occasion, which is poorly valued by the adults who organize their day.

The value of play, for educationalists, is sited within developmental discourses. Play is regarded as valuable—as a means of learning—for the infants, but not for the juniors; the regime in the two stages of school life correspondingly differs. The youngest Greenstreet children almost all made positive mention of opportunities for play with class-time; the balance between play and work seemed to work well for them. For the juniors, play was not so legitimated, and children reported that the balance of play and work was experienced as uncomfortable. Timetabled exercise—swimming, gym, and playground games—was not enough to redress the discomfort of hours of work in the classroom. . . .

Thus, the school constructs ideas about what matters: children's cognitive achievement is valued above their physical welfare and above their social well-being. The school also delivers messages about what sort of body matters: it is a disciplined body, rather than an active one. Further, school suggests to children that what they hear in health education sessions does not matter, since the social environment of the school does not carry through the points on nutrition and exercise. . . .

Contributions to School Maintenance

The quotations above indicate that, compared to the home, Greenstreet children found that the school offers little opportunity for children to contribute to the construction of the school as a social order. It will be a rare school where children contribute to planning and organizing the school day, and in particular to rethinking food and exercise—key topics for children's well-being. The social order was experienced as firmly in place; it was their task to conform to it.

Three main points emerge from children's own accounts. Firstly, they did not identify school as a health-maintenance environment. . . .

Secondly, children regarded school as detrimental to health, particularly as regards food and exercise. . . .

Thirdly, children did not perceive the teacher as a health-care worker. They found that sickness bids were often met with devaluation or dismissal, or with referral to the helpers, or to the secretary—who somewhat resented the assumption that she had health-care skills and willingness. . . .

Constructing Relationships

Certain points arising from the children's accounts may be flagged here. It was essential to have friends; at five these provided protection and companionship; they helped you to make sense of school. When children arrive at school they are thrown on their own resources . . .

For all the children one of the principal advantages of school was the pool of other children with whom to form friendships and engage in play. School provided space to play, almost certainly a larger space than they could find elsewhere locally, with adult sanction.

In this study, children were not asked targeted questions—for instance, for their views on their teacher. Instead they were asked to talk about their day, their likes and dislikes, what interested them. Under these circumstances, it is notable that the reception-class children did not mention their teachers at all. They talked about food, play, friends, and aspects of the formal curriculum. This point reinforces the earlier suggestion that children feel very much on their own when they start school; it is as if, lacking their mother, they do not seek a teacher. The older children, at nine, in both writing and conversation about their days at school, did refer to teachers as an important influence for better or worse on the quality of the day. . . .

Children identify mothers rather than school staff as their main caregivers and save up their hurts and problems for the end of the school day. . . .

Discussion

. . .

Civilizing the Body

The notion of the civilizing of the body through social agency owes its force to the work of Norbert Elias. Compared to the idea of socialization, which has deterministic, controlling, and individualistic connotations, civilizing the body suggests a more positive, enabling, and socially oriented enterprise. Using a historical survey, Elias (1978 [1939]: 140–1) argues that modern society (1930s), much more than earlier societies, demands a profound subjection of the instinctual life; children must rapidly acquire shame and revulsion, to meet the norms of adult behaviour. Mothers' tasks undoubtedly include teaching their children norms of social behaviour that are acceptable by current public social norms. Some of the most basic of these (establishing sleeping/waking rhythms, toilet-training, table manners, behaviour with other children and with adults) are socially assigned to mothers as tasks to be accomplished before children reach school. Pressure for mothers to meet the standards of behaviour is exerted by the wider society, through, as Foucault would put it, the activities of the disciplinary complex. Health visitors and pre-school staff see it as part of their function to instruct mothers on these points. Shilling (1993: 162) notes how this argument suggests a complementary distancing of adults from children.

Children have to traverse a long heavily controlled journey before they are socially acceptable to adults. . . .

Elias takes up issues to do with agency and structure and argues for the interdependency of people, throughout life, in a 'figuration': 'a structure of mutually oriented and dependent people'. Using the dance as metaphor, he argues that it helps us see how to eliminate the separation of individual and society: 'one can speak of a dance, but no one will imagine a dance as a structure outside the individual or as a mere abstraction' (Elias, 1978: 260–2). But it has to be added here: if children participate in the dance, they are not equal participants: adults control the dance. . . .

Regulating the Body

I distinguish here between civilizing and regulating the body. Civilizing aims at enabling the embodied person to participate in social worlds. Regulating involves controlling bodies and emotions in the interests of specific agendas: such as social, medical, and educational agendas. Thus, at home, a baby's first task is to accommodate to the social order; to eat and sleep in accordance with the 'tyranny of time' (Ennew, 1994). At school, children's bodies and feelings are managed in the interests of delivering the curriculum. . . .

The evidence suggests that children experience school as highly regulatory. What and how they learn is circumscribed by social norms. They are required to accept physical discipline within prescribed group norms. Their emotions are directly subject to regulation: they should behave in certain ways; and indirectly through the control exercised over their cognition and physical activity. Home is experienced as exercising control too, but within more negotiable frameworks.

Note

1. In the Greenstreet study, I spent over half a year with five- and nine-year-olds in one primary school in London and collected data with them and their parents (funded by Nuffield Foundation and the Institute of Education, London). The Health in Primary Schools study (funded by the Economic and Social Research Council, grant number ROOO 234476) included a random sample of 620 schools and six case-study schools in England and Wales; data were collected via questionnaires and interviews with staff and children.

References

Dunn, J. 1984. *Sisters and Brothers*. London: Fontana.

Elias, Norbert. 1978 [1939]. *The Civilizing Process*, trans. Edmund Jephcott, Oxford: Blackwell.

Ennew, J. 1994. 'Time for Children or Time for Adults', in J. Qvortrup, M. Bardy, G. Sgritta and H. Wintersberger, eds, *Childhood Matters: Social Theory, Practice and Politics*. Aldershot: Avebury Press.

Fortes, M. 1970. 'Social and Psychological Aspects of Education in Taleland', in J. Middleton, ed, *From Child to Adult: Studies in the Anthropology of Education*. Austin, TX: University of Texas Press.

James, A. 1993. *Childhood Identities: Social Relationships and the Self in Children's Experiences*. Edinburgh: Edinburgh University Press.

Mayall, B., and M.-C. Foster. 1989. *Child Health Care: Living with Children, Working for Children*. Oxford: Heinemann Educational.

Shilling, C. 1993. *The Body and Social Theory*. London: Sage.

Chapter 26

Becoming a Gendered Body: Practices of Preschools

Karin A. Martin

. . . Social science research about bodies often focuses on women's bodies, particularly the parts of women's bodies that are most explicitly different from men's—their reproductive capacities and sexuality (E. Martin, 1987; K. Martin, 1996; but see Connell, 1987, 1995). Men and women in the United States also hold and move their bodies differently (Birdwhistell, 1970; Henley, 1977; Young, 1990); these differences are sometimes related to sexuality (Haug, 1987) and sometimes not. On the whole, men and women sit, stand, gesture, walk, and throw differently. . . .

Such differences may seem trivial in the large scheme of gender inequality. However, theoretical work by social scientists and feminists suggests that these differences may be consequential. Bodies are (unfinished) resources (Shilling, 1993: 103) that must be 'trained, manipulated, cajoled, coaxed, organized, and in general disciplined' (Turner, 1992: 15). . . . [A]ccording to Foucault (1979), controlled and disciplined bodies do more than regulate the individual body. A disciplined body creates a context for social relations. Gendered (along with 'raced' and 'classed') bodies create particular contexts for social relations as they signal, manage, and negotiate information about power and status. Gender relations depend on the successful gender presentation, monitoring, and interpretation of bodies (West and Zimmerman, 1987). Bodies that clearly delineate gender status facilitate the maintenance of the gender hierarchy. . . .

Other feminist theorists (Connell, 1987, 1995; Young, 1990) argue that gender rests not only on the surface of the body, in performance and doing, but becomes *embodied*—becomes deeply part of whom we are physically and psychologically. According to Connell, gender becomes embedded in body postures, musculature, and tensions in our bodies.

> The social definition of men as holders of power is translated only into mental body-images and fantasies, but into muscle tensions, posture, the feel and texture of the body. This is one of the main ways in which the power of men becomes naturalized. . . . (Connell, 1987: 85) . . .

. . . How do adult gendered bodies become gendered, if they are not naturally so? . . . Gendering of the body in childhood is the foundation on which further gendering of the body occurs throughout the life course. The gendering of children's bodies makes gender differences feel and appear natural, which allows for such bodily differences to emerge throughout the life course.

I suggest that the hidden school curriculum of disciplining the body is gendered and contributes to the embodiment of gender in childhood, making gendered bodies appear and feel natural. Sociologists of education have demonstrated that schools have hidden curriculums (Giroux and Purpel, 1983; Jackson, 1968). Hidden curriculums are covert lessons that schools teach, and they are often a means of social control. . . . More recently, some theorists and researchers have examined the curriculum that disciplines the body

(Carere, 1987; Foucault, 1979; McLaren, 1986). This curriculum demands the practice of bodily control in congruence with the goals of the school as an institution. It reworks the students from the outside in on the presumption that to shape the body is to shape the mind (Carere, 1987). . . . [T]eachers constantly monitor kids' bodily movements, comportment, and practices. Kids begin their day running wildly about the school grounds. Then this hidden curriculum funnels the kids into line, through the hallways, quietly into the classrooms, sitting upright at their desks, focused at the front of the room, 'ready to learn' (Carere, 1987; McLaren, 1986). . . .

I suggest that this hidden curriculum that control[s] children's bodily practices serves also to turn kids who are similar in bodily comportment, movement, and practice into girls and boys, children whose bodily practices are different. Schools are not the only producers of these differences. While the process ordinarily begins in the family, the schools' hidden curriculum further facilitates and encourages the construction of bodily differences between the genders and makes these physical differences appear and feel natural. Finally, this curriculum may be more or less hidden depending on the particular preschool and particular teachers. Some schools and teachers may see teaching children to behave like 'young ladies' and 'young gentlemen' as an explicit part of their curriculums.

Data and Method

The data for this study come from extensive and detailed semistructured field observations of five preschool classrooms of three- to five-year-olds in a Midwestern city. . . .

The curriculums and routines of the two preschools were similar . . . [although] Preschool B had some explicit rules that forbade violent actions at school. Posted on the wall of the playroom was the following sign . . .

1. No wrestling.
2. No violent play, killing games, kicking, karate, etc.

3. Bikes belong on the outside of the gym.
4. No crashing bikes.
5. Houses are for playing in not climbing on.
6. Older children are off bikes when toddlers arrive.
7. Balls should be used for catching, rolling, tossing—not slamming at people.
8. Adults and children will talk with each other about problems and not shout across the room.
9. Use equipment appropriately.

Such rules were usually directed at boys, although they were not enforced consistently.

Preschool A also had some of these rules, but they were not as explicit or as clearly outlined for the teachers or the kids. . . .

We focused on the children's physicality—body movement, use of space, and the physical contact among kids or between kids and teachers. . . .

Results

. . . Children are physically active, and institutions like schools impose disciplinary controls that regulate children's bodies and prepare children for the larger social world. While this disciplinary control produces docile bodies (Foucault, 1979), it also produces gendered bodies. As these disciplinary practices operate in different contexts, some bodies become more docile than others. I examine how the following practices contribute to a gendering of children's bodies in preschool . . .

Bodily Adornment: Dressing Up

. . .

Dressing up (1). The clothes that parents send kids to preschool in shape children's experiences of their bodies in gendered ways. Clothes, particularly their colour, signify a child's gender; gender in preschool is . . . colour-coded. On average, about 61 per cent of the girls wore pink clothing each day. . . . Boys were more likely to wear primary colours, black, fluorescent green, and orange. Boys never wore pink. . . .

Fourteen per cent of three-year-old girls wore dresses each day compared to 32 per cent of five-year-old girls. . . . Wearing a dress limited girls' physicality in preschool. However, it is not only the dress itself, but [also] knowledge about how to behave in a dress that is restrictive. Many girls already knew that some behaviours were not allowed in a dress. This knowledge probably comes from the families who dress their girls in dresses.

> Vicki, wearing leggings and a dress-like shirt, is leaning over the desk to look into a 'tunnel' that some other kids have built. As she leans, her dress/skirt rides up exposing her back. Jennifer (another child) walks by Vicki and as she does she pulls Vicki's skirt back over her bare skin and gives it a pat to keep it in place. It looks very much like something one's mother might do. (Five-year-olds). . . .

Dresses are restrictive in other ways as well. They often are worn with tights that are experienced as uncomfortable and constraining. I observed girls constantly pulling at and rearranging their tights, trying to untwist them or pull them up. Because of their discomfort, girls spent much time attuned to and arranging their clothing and/or their bodies.

Dresses also can be lifted up, an embarrassing thing for five-year-olds if done purposely by another child. We witnessed this on only one occasion—a boy pulled up the hem of a girl's skirt. . . . The girl protested and the teacher told him to stop and that was the end of it. Teachers, however, lifted up girls' dresses frequently—to see if a child was dressed warmly enough, while reading a book about dresses, to see if a child was wet. Usually this was done without asking the child and was more management of the child rather than an interaction with her. Teachers were much more likely to manage girls and their clothing this way . . . Such management often put girls' bodies under the control of another and calls girls' attentions to their appearances and bodily adornments.

Dressing up (2). Kids like to *play* dress-up in preschool, and all the classrooms had a dress-up corner with a variety of clothes, shoes, pocketbooks, scarves, and hats for dressing up. Classrooms tended to have more women's clothes than men's, but there were some of both, as well as some gender-neutral clothes—capes, hats, and vests that were not clearly for men or women—and some items that were clearly costumes, such as masks of cats and dogs and clip-on tails. Girls tended to play dress-up more than boys . . . Gender differences in the amount of time spent playing dress-up seemed to increase from age three to age five. We only observed the five-year-old boys dressing up or using clothes or costumes in their play three times, whereas three-year-old boys dressed up almost weekly. Five-year-old boys also did not dress up elaborately, but used one piece of clothing to animate their play. Once Phil wore large, men's winter ski gloves when he played monster. Holding up his now large, chiselled-looking hands, he stomped around the classroom making monster sounds. . . . Children often seemed to experiment with both genders when they played dress-up. The three-year-olds tended to be more experimental in their gender dress-up than the five-year-olds, perhaps because teachers encouraged it more at this age.

> Everett and Juan are playing dress-up. Both have on 'dresses' made out of material that is wrapped around them like a toga or sarong. . . .

The five-year-old children tended to dress-up more gender normatively. Girls in particular played at being adult women.

> Frances is playing dress-up. She is walking in red shoes and carrying a pocketbook. . . . Frances and Rachel practise walking in adult women's shoes. Their body movements are not a perfect imitation of an adult women's walk in high heels, yet it does look like an attempt to imitate such a walk. . . .

. . . Children interpreted each other's bodily adornments as gendered, even when other interpretations were plausible. . . .

Kim has worn a denim skirt and tights to school today. Now she is trying to pull on a ballerina costume—pink and ruffly—over her clothes. She has a hard time getting it on. It's tight and wrinkled up and twisted when she gets it on. Her own clothes are bunched up under it. Then she puts on a mask—a woman's face. The mask material itself is a clear plastic so that skin shows through, but is sculpted to have a very Anglo nose and high cheekbones. It also has thin eyebrows, blue eyeshadow, blush, and lipstick painted on it. The mask is bigger than Kim's face and head. . . . Intermittently she picks up a plastic pumpkin since it is Halloween season and carries that around too. . . . Jason yells, 'Ugh! There's a woman!' He and the other boys playing blocks shriek and scatter about the block area. . . .

The boys' shrieks indicated that Kim was scary, and this scariness is linked in their comments about her being a woman. It seems . . . plausible that they could have interpreted her scary dress as a 'trick-o-treater', given that it was close to Halloween and she was carrying a plastic pumpkin that kids collect candy in, or that they might have labelled her a dancer or ballerina because she was wearing a tutu. Rather, her scary dress-up was coded for her by others as 'woman'.

Other types of responses to girls dressing up also seemed to gender their bodies and to constrain them. For example, on two occasions I saw a teacher tie the arms of girls' dress-up shirts together so that the girls could not move their arms. They did this in fun, of course, and untied them as soon as the girls wanted them to, but I never witnessed this constraining of boys' bodies in play. . . .

Formal and Relaxed Behaviours

. . . I identified several behaviours that were expected by the teachers, required by the institution, or that would be required in many institutional settings, as formal behaviour. . . . [R]elaxed behaviours . . . are not allowed in preschool, schools, work settings, and many institutions of the larger social world (Henley, 1977).

In the classroom in this study, boys were allowed and encouraged to pursue relaxed behaviours in a variety of ways that girls were not. Girls were more likely to be encouraged to pursue more formal behaviours. Eighty-two per cent of all formal behaviours observed in these classrooms were done by girls, and only 18 per cent by boys. However, 80 per cent of the behaviours coded as relaxed were boys' behaviours. . . .

These observations do not tell us *why* boys do more relaxed behaviours and girls do more formal behaviours. Certainly many parents and others would argue that boys are more predisposed to sloppy postures, crawling on the floor, and so on. However, my observations suggest that teachers help construct this gender difference in bodily behaviours. Teachers were more likely to reprimand girls for relaxed bodily movements and comportment. . . .

The gendering of body movements, comportment, and acquisitions of space also happens in more subtle ways. For example, often when there was 'free' time, boys spent much more time in child-structured activities than did girls. . . . Following is a list from my field notes of the most common activities boys and girls did during the child-structured activity periods of the day during two randomly picked weeks of observing:

Boys: played blocks (floor), played at the water table (standing and splashing), played superhero (running around and in playhouse), played with the car garage (floor), painted at the easel (standing).

Girls: played dolls (sitting in chairs and walking around), played dress-up (standing), colouring (sitting at tables), read stories (sitting on the couch), cut out pictures (sitting at tables).

Children sorted themselves into these activities and also were sorted (or not unsorted) by teachers. For example, teachers rarely told the three boys that always played with blocks that they had to choose a different activity that day. Teachers also encouraged girls to sit at tables by suggesting tables activities for them—in a sense giving them less 'free' time or structuring their time more. . . .

. . . [B]oys come to sit in more open positions, and to feel freer to do what they wish with their bodies, even in relatively formal settings. Henley (1977) finds that among adults men generally are more relaxed than women in their demeanour and women tend to have tenser postures. The looseness of body-focused functions (e.g., belching) is also more open to men than to women. In other words, men are more likely to engage in relaxed demeanours, postures, and behaviours. These data suggest that this gendering of bodies into more formal and more relaxed movements, postures, and comportment is (at least partially) constructed in early childhood by institutions like preschools.

Controlling Voice

. . . Voice is an aspect of bodily experience that teachers and schools are interested in disciplining. . . .

The disciplining of children's voices is gendered. I found that girls were told to be quiet or to repeat a request in a quieter, 'nicer' voice about three times more often than were boys.

Additionally, when boys were told to 'quiet down' they were told in large groups, rarely as individuals. . . .

Girls as individuals and in groups were frequently told to lower their voices. Later that same afternoon:

> During snack time the teacher asks the kids to tell her what they like best in the snack mix. Hillary says, 'Marshmallows!' loudly, vigorously, and with a swing of her arm. The teacher turns to her and says, 'I'm going to ask you to say that quietly', and Hillary repeats it in a softer voice. (Five-year-olds)

These . . . observations represent a prominent pattern in the data. . . . [B]oys playing with . . . wooden figures were allowed to express their fun and enthusiasm loudly whereas Hillary could not loudly express her love of marshmallows. Girls' voices are disciplined to be softer and in many ways less physical—toning down their voices tones down their physicality. Hillary emphasized 'marshmallows' with a large swinging gesture of her arm the first time she answered the teacher's question, but after the teacher asked her to say it quietly she made no gestures when answering. . . .

. . . The girls learn that their bodies are supposed to be quiet, small, and physically constrained. . . .

Finally, by limiting voice teachers limit one of girls' mechanisms for resisting others' mistreatment of them. Frequently, when a girl had a dispute with another child, teachers would ask the girl to quiet down and solve the problem nicely. Teachers also asked boys to solve problems by talking, but they usually did so only with intense disputes and the instructions to talk things out never carried the instruction to talk *quietly*. . . .

Bodily Instructions

Teachers give a lot of instructions to kids about what to do with their bodies. Of the explicit bodily instructions recorded 65 per cent were directed to boys, 26 per cent to girls, and the remaining 9 per cent to mixed groups. . . . These numbers suggest that boys' bodies are being disciplined more than girls. However, there is more to this story—the types of instructions that teachers give and children's responses to them are also gendered.

First, boys obeyed teachers' bodily instructions about one-half of the time (48 per cent), while girls obeyed about 80 per cent of the time. Boys may receive more instruction from teachers because they are less likely to follow instructions and thus are told repeatedly. . . . Teachers usually did not have to repeat instructions to girls—girls either stopped on their own with the first instruction, or because the teacher forced them to stop right then. . . .

Second, teachers' instructions directed to boys' bodies were less substantive than those directed to girls. That is, teachers' instructions to boys were usually to stop doing something, to end a bodily behaviour with little suggestion for other behaviour they might do. Teachers rarely told boys to change a bodily behaviour. . . . [T]eachers' instructions to boys include stop throwing, stop jumping, stop clapping, stop splashing, no pushing, don't cry, blocks are not for bopping, don't run, don't climb on that. . . . [T]eachers' instructions to girls generally were more substantive and more directive, telling girls to do a bodily behaviour rather than to stop one. Teachers' instructions to girls suggested that they alter their behaviours. . . . [I]nstructions to girls include talk to her, don't yell, sit here, pick that up, be careful, be gentle, give it to me, put it down there. Girls may have received fewer bodily instructions than did boys, but they received more directive ones. This gender difference leaves boys a larger range of possibilities of what they might choose to do with their bodies once they have stopped a behaviour, whereas girls were directed toward a defined set of options.

Physical Interaction between Teachers and Children

Teachers also physically directed kids. . . . [T]eachers often held kids to make them stop running, tapped them to make them turn around and pay attention, or turned their faces toward them so that they would listen to verbal instructions. One-fourth of all physical contacts between teachers and children was to control children's physicality in some way, and 94 per cent of such contacts were directed at boys.

Physical interaction between teachers and children was coded into three categories: positive, negative, or neutral. Physical interaction was coded as positive if it was comforting, helpful, playful, or gentle. It was coded as negative if it was disciplining, assertive (not gentle), restraining, or clearly unwanted by the child (e.g., the child pulled away). Physical interaction was coded as neutral if it seemed to have little content (e.g., shoulders touching during circle, legs touching while a teacher gave a group of kids directions for a project). About one-half of the time, when teachers touched boys or girls, it was positive. . . . For girls, the remaining physical interaction included 15 per cent that were disciplining or instructing the body and about one-

third that were neutral (e.g., leaning over the teacher's arm while looking at a book). For boys, these figures were reversed: only 4 per cent of their physical interactions with teachers were neutral in content, and 35 per cent were negative and usually included explicit disciplining and instructing of the body. . . .

This disciplining of boys' bodies took a particular form. Teachers usually attempted to restrain or remove boys who had 'gone too far' in their play or who had done something that could harm another child . . .

. . . Because boys more frequently than girls experienced interactions in which their bodies were physically restrained or disciplined by an adult who had more power and was angry, they may be more likely than girls to associate physical interaction with struggle and anger, and thus may be more likely to be aggressive or disruptive.

Physical Interaction among Children

Thorne (1993) demonstrates that children participate in the construction of gender differences among themselves. The preschool brings together large groups of children who engage in interactions in which they co-operate with the hidden curriculum and discipline each others' bodies in gendered ways, but they also engage in interactions in which they resist this curriculum.

Girls and boys teach their same-sex peers about their bodies and physicality. Children in these observations were much more likely to imitate the physical behaviour of a same-sex peer than a cross-sex peer. Children also encourage others to imitate them. . . .

The within-gender physicality of three-year-old girls and boys was more similar than it was among the five-year-olds. Among the three-year-old girls there was more rough and tumble play, more physical fighting and arguing among girls than there was among the five-year-old girls. . . .

. . . [C]ross-gender interactions were more likely to be negative than same-sex interactions. In fact, physical interactions among children were twice as likely to be a negative interaction if they were between a girl and boy than if they were among same-gender peers. Approximately 30 per cent of the interactions among girls and among boys were negative (hostile, angry, controlling, hurtful), whereas 60 per cent of mixed gender physical interactions were negative. Sixty per cent of 113 boy–girl physical interactions were initiated by boys, 39 per cent were initiated by girls, and only 1 per cent of interactions were mutually initiated. . . .

Conclusion

Children also sometimes resist their bodies being gendered. For example, three-year-old boys dressed up in women's clothes sometimes. Five-year-old girls played with a relaxed comportment that is normatively . . . masculine when they sat with their feet up on the desk and their chairs tipped backward. In one classroom when boys were at the height of their loud activity—running and throwing toys and blocks—girls took the opportunity to be loud too as the teachers were paying less attention to them and trying to get the boys to settle down. . . . These instances of resistance suggest that gendered physicalities are not natural, nor are they easily and straightforwardly acquired. This research demonstrates the many ways that practices in institutions like preschools facilitate children's acquisition of gendered physicalities.

Men and women and girls and boys fill social space with their bodies in different ways. Our everyday movements, postures, and gestures are gendered. These bodily differences enhance the seeming naturalness of sexual and reproductive differences, that then construct inequality between men and women (Butler, 1990). . . .

This research suggests one way that bodies are gendered and physical differences are constructed through social institutions and their practices. Because this gendering occurs at an early age, the seeming naturalness of such differences is further underscored. In preschool, bodies became gendered in ways that are so subtle and taken-for-granted that they come to feel and appear natural. . . .

References

Birdwhistell, Ray. 1970. *Kinesics and Contexts*. Philadelphia: University of Pennsylvania Press.

Butler, Judith. 1990. *Gender Trouble*. New York: Routledge.

Carere, Sharon. 1987. 'Lifeworld of Restricted Behaviour', *Sociological Studies of Child Development* 2: 105–38.

Connell, R.W. 1987. *Gender and Power*. Stanford, CA: Stanford University Press.

———. 1995. *Masculinities*. Berkeley, CA: University of California Press.

Foucault, Michel. 1979. *Discipline and Punish: The Birth of the Prison*. New York: Vintage Books.

Giroux, Henry, and David Purpel. 1983. *The Hidden Curriculum and Moral Education*. Berkeley, CA: McCutchan.

Haug, Frigga. 1987. *Female Sexualization: A Collective Work of Memory*. London: Verso.

Henley, Nancy. 1977. *Body Politics*. New York: Simon and Schuster.

Jackson, Philip W. 1968. *Life in Classrooms*. New York: Holt, Rinehart and Winston.

McLaren, Peter. 1986. *Schooling as a Ritual Performance: Towards a Political Economy of Educational Symbols and Gestures*. London: Routledge and Kegan Paul.

Martin, Emily. 1987. *The Woman in the Body*. Boston: Beacon Press.

Martin, Karin. 1996. *Puberty, Sexuality, and the Self: Boys and Girls at Adolescence*. New York: Routledge.

Shilling, Chris. 1993. *The Body and Social Theory*. London: Sage.

Thorne, Barrie. 1993. *Gender Play: Girls and Boys in School*. New Brunswick, NJ: Rutgers University Press.

Turner, Bryan S. 1984. *The Body and Society: Explorations in Social Theory*. New York: Basil Blackwell.

———. 1992. *Regulating Bodies: Essays in Medical Sociology*. London: Routledge.

West, Candace, and Don Zimmerman. 1987. 'Doing Gender', *Gender and Society* 1: 127–51.

Young, Iris. 1990. *Throwing Like a Girl*. Bloomington, IN: Indiana University Press.

Chapter 27

The Gaze of the Psychologist

Nikolas Rose

. . . It was once the privilege of the wealthy, the noble, and the holy to have their individuality remarked upon, described, documented, recorded for posterity in image and text. But during the nineteenth century the individualizing gaze alighted upon those at the other end of power relations—the criminal, the madman, the pauper, the defective, were to be the target of many laborious and ingenious projects to document their uniqueness, to record it and classify it, to discipline their difference.[1] Children were to become favoured objects and targets of such programs of individualization. Psychologists were to claim a particular expertise in the disciplining of the uniqueness and idiosyncrasies of childhood, individualizing children by categorizing them, calibrating their aptitudes, inscribing their peculiarities in an ordered form, managing their variability conceptually, and governing it practically.

Michel Foucault argued that the disciplines 'make' individuals by means of some rather simple technical procedures.[2] On the parade ground, in the factory, in the school, and in the hospital, people were gathered together en masse, but by this very fact they could be observed as entities both similar to and different from one another. These institutions function in certain respects like telescopes, microscopes, or other scientific instruments: they established a regime of visibility in which the observed was distributed within a single common plane of sight. Second, these institutions operated according to a regulation of detail. These regulations, and the evaluation of conduct, manners, and so forth entailed by them, estab-

lished a grid of codeability of personal attributes. They act as norms, enabling the previously aleatory and unpredictable complexities of human conduct to be charted and judged in terms of conformity and deviation, to be coded and compared, ranked and measured. . . .

Contemporaneous with the nineteenth-century transformations in the organization of asylums, prisons, hospitals, and schools, new systems were devised for documenting and recording information concerning inmates—files, records, and case histories.[3] This routine notation and accumulation of the personal details and histories of large numbers of persons identifies each individual with a dossier consisting in the facts of his or her life and character accorded pertinence by the institution and its objectives. The individual entered the field of knowledge not through any abstract leap of the philosophical imagination, but through the mundane operation of bureaucratic documentation. . . .

The first contribution of psychology to the project of individualization was the psychological test of intelligence. The psychological test was a means of visualizing, disciplining, and inscribing a difference that did not rely upon the surface of the body as the diagnostic intermediary between conduct and the psyche. The problem for which the intelligence test would be a solution arose in the early years of universal schooling in both England and France. The figure who provoked it was the feeble-minded child. . . .

. . . The feeble-minded child, and the adult that he or she would become, appeared to be a major social threat. Eugenicists saw the feeble-minded as a central element in the degeneracy or deterioration of the race.[4] The feeble-minded were kith and kin of the prostitute, the tubercular, the insane, the unemployable, the vagrant, and the libertine—all manifestations of a degenerate constitution. Feeble-mindedness was a key element in this degeneration, for not only did it clearly run in families, but the feeble-minded were unsocializable, impervious to morality and hence to the curbs that civilization imposed upon promiscuous reproduction. They were a testament to the fact that the race renewed itself most rapidly from its inferior sections, with the consequent increase in hereditary unfitness down the generations. In short, curbing their reproduction, by segregation or sterilization, was a matter of urgency, and hence their detection and ascertainment was a priority. . . .

The schoolroom provided further evidence of the problem. But it would also produce its solution. Universal schooling gathered together large numbers of children in the same physical space, and sought to discipline them according to institutional criteria and objectives. It thus established norms of conduct and performance that organized behavioural space and enabled divergences between children to be charted. Among the children unable to learn the lessons of the school were a group who were unlike the blind and deaf in that they appeared to possess the full complement of the senses. But they nonetheless did not seem to be able to benefit from instruction. These children came to be known as educational imbeciles or the feeble-minded. . . . Difference was no longer marking itself unambiguously on the surface of the individual; it was receding into the interiority of the soul. It would have to be made legible.

The intelligence test arose out of the attempts to make these invisible differences legible. . . .

From *Hereditary Genius*, which Galton published in 1869, proponents of mental measurement had sought to provide ways of grasping the variability of human mental powers in thought, so that their habitability and social consequences could be calibrated and acted upon.[5] The

statistical concept of the normal distribution was the vital cognitive mechanism that enabled Galton to visualize human variability. The simple act of comparison of the respective amount of a particular quality or attribute possessed by two members of the population enabled the mathematization of difference. This could be represented in a simple visual form once it was assumed that all qualities in the population varied according to a regular and predictable pattern, and that the characteristics of this pattern were those established by the statistical laws of large numbers. Individual difference could be made thinkable by a simple act of inscription: cumulative acts of comparison would be combined with the figure of the norm or average for the population; when represented diagramatically they would form the smooth outline of the 'normal' curve. Intellectual abilities could be construed as a single dimension, whose variation across the population was governed by precise laws. The capacity of any individual could be established in terms of their location along that curve; the variability of the intellect had been reduced to order, made graspable through its normalization into a stable, predictable, two-dimensional trace. . . .

The test that Alfred Binet devised in the French context was initially conceived as merely an administrative device for identifying children for admission to special schools for the feeble-minded.[6] In order to construct it, Binet set aside his earlier work on intelligence. In this he had concluded that intelligence could not be satisfactorily investigated by tests aiming at a diagnosis in a few hours, but required the lengthy and detailed study of particular individuals. Nevertheless, as a member of the Society for the Psychological Study of the Child, Binet sought to assist the 1904 Ministerial Commission for the Abnormal to decide on the admission of children to special schools. The Commission needed a device that would enable it to make an 'exact distribution', and to permit clinicians to 'separate subjects of inferior intelligence into categories verifiable by all'.[7] The demands of rational administration triumphed where decades of detailed scientific study had led into a cul-de-sac. . . .

The technique of the test was the most important contribution of the psychological sciences to the human technologies of the first half of the twentieth century. The test routinizes the complex ensemble of social judgment on individual variability into an automatic device that makes difference visible and notable. One no longer has to observe children for long periods of time or compare large numbers one with another in the classroom and the asylum in order to reveal their similarities and differences. The test codifies, mathematizes, and normalizes difference. It is a simple technical device, but one that can be used to realize almost any psychological schema for differentiating individuals in a brief time span, in a manageable space, at the will of the expert. It has become an indispensable part of any modern program for the government of individual differences. . . .

The work of Arnold Gesell and his colleagues provides an exemplary demonstration of the techniques for the disciplining of human difference. Gesell's work was carried out at the Yale Psycho-Clinic, which had opened in 1911 for the assessment and treatment of children having problems at school. An early photography captures the essential elements of this project. Dr Gesell is pictured in his laboratory.[8] The date is probably in the 1920s. The laboratory itself manifests in its design and equipment the characteristics of the gaze that psychologists would, from this moment on, target upon the child. It is a dome brilliantly lit within and designed for one-way vision. Outside, able to see in without being seen themselves, are observers, probably student psychologists. While one merely watches, another writes notes with pencil upon a pad. A third, probably a technician, operates a movie camera. Within the dome is the white-coated scientist. His gaze, like that of the observers within the picture, and our own, is focused upon one particular spot. At the centre of the dome, contained in a kind of playpen, sitting at a table, playing with what appears to be a small brick, is a baby. This is a photograph of Dr Arnold Gesell testing a baby. . . .

The child, no doubt, is by now an old man or woman; it left the laboratory long ago. But its traces remain in the form of records, photographs, graphs, measurements. It is these traces or inscriptions, together with those of many other similar children that have been accumulated, combined, correlated, graded, and consolidated into the object of developmental psychology.[9] For the psychologist, as for scientists elsewhere, inscriptions have a number of advantages over their subjects themselves. Some of these are immediately apparent in Gesell's own work. Children are difficult to accumulate in large numbers. Large rooms and considerable labour are required to hold them side by side, to pick out common or differentiating features. They change over time. Once dismissed from the laboratory it may be impossible to reassemble them for further examination. Only a limited number of observers can view them and thus be convinced of the value of what the psychologist has to say about them. They are unstable material for a science to work on.

Gesell solved this problem by photography. The movies were analyzed frame by frame and still photographs produced. These could be compared and contrasted, placed side by side, and examined at will, on the stable two-dimensional plane of the desk rather than in the changing, three-dimensional space of the playroom or laboratory. . . . The photographs could be assembled in various combinations in order to search out regularities. 'Representative' and 'typical' pictures could be differentiated from those that were 'odd', 'unusual', or 'atypical'. They could, that is to say, be normalized. And they could then be arranged into a visual display that summarized and condensed the multi-faceted actions of the children into a single array that could conveniently be deployed within scientific debate, in articles, textbooks, and teaching materials.

Having been thus arrayed, a further transformation could occur through work upon the inscriptions themselves. The photographs themselves 'showed' typical behaviours but they did not yet embody instructions as to how they were to be read. These instructions had to be displayed separately, in the form of captions: 'Throwing'; 'Train without chimney'; 'Tower of nine'. The captions function as directions; they serve to indicate those aspects of the photograph to which we should attend and those which are not relevant: the smile on the face, the length of hair, the 'background'. . . .

Graphic displays indivisibly weld together the concept and the trace. Thus, the line drawings produced from Gesell's work minimized the problems of reading; the perspective of developmentalism was displayed as the texture of the child itself. The object so produced had, to use Michael Lynch's term, become docile; it had internalized the norms of the scientific program in the very form of its inscription.[10] In these little drawings the child was reduced to its essential elements. Only that which was normatively pertinent was worthy of description.

The distance from the squalling, troublesome, and undisciplined infants of the laboratory to these calm, ordered, and disciplined frames is considerable. We should not, however, think of this as movement on a dimension from the concrete to the abstract. Indeed, quite the reverse. These images are far more concrete, far more real than the child itself. Children are ephemeral, shifting, elusive, changing before one's eyes, hard to perceive in any stable fashion. These images make the child stable by constructing a perceptual system, a way of rendering the mobile and confusing manifold of the sensible into a legible visual field. . . .

In Gesell's work these little line drawings exist alongside a perceptual system of another type: the table (Table 10.1). The table condensed the meaning of many pictures into a single frame. The frame provided simultaneously a means of perceiving, recording, and evaluating. It provided a summation of those features of the object-child that were developmentally significant at a particular age, together with norms—percentage figures that authoritatively announce the proportion of children who can do this or that at this age. It enabled the formulation of a series of questions through whose answers here in the form of a simple affirmative or negative, the unorthodox could be identified.

The scales, through the norms to which they were attached, introduced a new division into the lives of small children, a division between normal and abnormal in the form of the differentiation of advanced and retarded. Behavioural items that were characteristic and distinctive of different age levels were defined and organized into scales with specifications of the ages at which a given proportion of children could achieve the different levels on each scale. Non-intellectual behaviour was thus rendered into thought, disciplined, normalized, and made legible, inscribable, calculable. Norms of posture and locomotion, of vocabulary, comprehension, and conversation; of personal habits, initiative, independence, and play could now be deployed in evaluation and diagnosis. The discourse of development established a system of perception that was capable of grasping any feature of life that could be construed as changing over time. It grasped life in a form that could be effected through a few simple operations: advanced or retarded? By how many months? In the table life comes pre-digested, pre-calibrated, pre-normalized.

We should not think of these procedures of inscription as merely allowing the documentation of a familiar reality—the developing child—in a more convenient form. While children and their development, like persons and their peculiarities, have been the object of attention from philosophers, theologians, philanthropists, reformers, and savants for centuries, the devices and techniques for visualization and inscription are not merely technical aids to intellectual processes. To think this is to accord too much to a faculty of abstract thought and too little to the technical mechanisms by which thought operates. Technological changes are simultaneously revolutions in consciousness. Techniques for visualizing and inscribing individual differences transform the intellectual universe of the scientist and the practical universe of objects and relationships to which things can be done. In short, technical developments make new areas of life practicable. . . .

The scales generalized and extended some of the essential characteristics of psychometrics. But they constituted a normalizing vision of

Table 10.1   Twenty-four Month Level

(M) *MOTOR*	18 mos.	24 mos.
M-l RUNS: without falling	12	48
M-2 STAIRS: walks up and down alone		
M-9 LARGE BALL: kicks		(59)
M-17 CUBES: tower of six–seven	20	56
M-22 BOOK: turns pages singly		
(A) *ADAPTIVE*		
A-2 CUBES: tower of six–seven	20	56
A-3 CUBES: aligns two or more, train	23	62
A-20 DRAWING: imitates V stroke	47	79
A-20 DRAWING: imitates circular stroke	32	59
A-28 SENTENCES: repeats three–four syllables		
A-12 FORMBOARD: places blocks on board separately (F)(28)	(63)	
A-12 FORMBOARD: adapts in four trials	8	62
A-10 PERFORMANCE BOX: inserts square	29	70
(L) *LANGUAGE*		
L-2 SPEECH: has discarded jargon		
L-2 SPEECH: three-word sentence		73
L-2 SPEECH: uses I, me, and you		48
L-6 PICTURE CARDS: names three or more	2	57
L-6 PICTURE CARDS: identifies five or more	2	55
L-4 TEST OBJECTS: names two		(74)
L-5 BALL: 4 directions correct		51
(P-S) *PERSONAL-SOCIAL*		
FEEDING: inhibits turning of spoon		
TOILET: dry at night if taken up		
TOILET: verbalizes toilet needs fairly consistently (r)		
DRESSING: pulls on simple garment		
COMMUNICATION: verbalizes immediate experiences		
COMMUNICATION: refers to himself by his name		
COMMUNICATION: comprehends and asks for 'another'		
PLAY: hands full cup of cubes to examiner		
PLAY: plays with domestic mimicry (doll, teddy bear, etc.)		
PLAY: parallel play predominates		

Source: A. Gesell, *The First Five Years of Life*. London: Methuen, (1950: 328).

childhood that gained an even wider purchase upon reality. For these scales were not merely means of assessment. They provided new ways of thinking about childhood, new ways of seeing children that rapidly spread to teachers, health workers, and parents through the scientific and popular literature. Baby books, teacher manuals, and psychology textbooks began to incorporate 'landmarks of development' in tabular and pictorial form to enable anyone to evaluate a child. . . .[11] All who had dealt with children in their professional or personal life could now have their mind instructed through the education of their gaze. In the space between the behaviours of actual children and the ideals of the norm, new desires and expectations, and new fears and anxieties could be inspired in parents, new administrative and reformatory aspirations awakened in professionals. With the rise of a normative expertise of childhood, family life and subjectivity could be governed in a new way.

Notes

1. This chapter is based upon the argument made in my paper, 'Calculable Minds and Manageable Individuals', *History of the Human Sciences*, I (1988): 179–200.

2 M. Foucault, *Discipline and Punish* (London: Allen Lane, 1979), 191.

3 Cf. M. Donnelly, *Managing the Mind* (London: Tavistock, 1983), Ch. 7.

4. I have discussed this at length in *The Psychological Complex* (London: Routledge and Kegan Paul, 1985). For other discussions of the feeble-minded and eugenics see G.R. Searle, *Eugenics and Politics in Britain* (Edinburgh: Edinburgh University Press, 1981); C. Webster, ed, *Biology, Medicine and Society 1840–1940* (Cambridge: Cambridge University Press, 1981), esp. Chs 5–8.

5. For a discussion of the work of Galton and his followers, see R.S. Cowan, 'Francis Galton's Statistical Ideas: The Influence of Eugenics', *Isis* 63 (1972): 509–28, and R.S. Cowan, 'Nature and Nurture: The Interplay of Biology and Politics in the Work of Francis Galton', *Studies in the History of Biology* 1 (1977): 133–208. See also D. Mackenzie, *Statistics in Britain 1865–1930: The Social Construction of Scientific Knowledge* (Edinburgh: Edinburgh University Press, 1981).

6. On Binet, see T.H. Wolf, *Alfred Binet* (Chicago: University of Chicago Press, 1973).

7. For representative samples of Gesell's many works, see A. Gesell, *The Mental Growth of the School Child* (New York: Macmillan, 1925) and *Infancy and Human Growth* (New York: Macmillan, 1928).

8. I discuss these processes more theoretically in my paper, 'Calculable Minds and Manageable Individuals', op. cit. See also B. Latour, 'Visualization and Cognition: Thinking with Hands and Eyes', in H. Kushlick, ed, *Knowledge and Society*, Vol. 6 (Greenwich, CT: JAI Press, 1986) and M. Lynch, 'Discipline and the Material Form of Images: An Analysis of Scientific Visibility', *Social Studies of Science* 15 (1985): 37–66.

9. Cf. Lynch, op. cit.

10. See the reviews I.C. Buhler, 'The Social Behaviour of the Child', in C. Murchison, ed, *Handbook of Child Psychology* (Worcester, MA: Clark University Press, 1931); M. Collins, 'Modern Trends in Child Psychology', in F. C. Bartlett et al., eds, *The Study of Society* (London: Kegan Paul, Trench, Trubner, 1939); and C.J.C. Earl, 'Some Methods of Assessing Temperament and Personality', in Bartlett, *The Study of Society*, op. cit.

11. See the discussion in C. Hardyment, *Dream Babies: Child Care from Locke to Spock* (Oxford: Oxford University Press, 1984), Chapter 4.

Part X

Working Bodies

Jacqueline Low and Claudia Malacrida

Karl Marx and Friedrich Engels (1967) argue that a society's **mode of production**, the way in which goods and services are produced and delivered, quite literally shapes the bodies of workers. They first made these arguments at the time of the **Industrial Revolution**, which occurred in the late eighteenth and early nineteenth centuries and resulted in large-scale change in the economic structure of society in England from a rural agricultural economy to an urban capitalist economy based largely on factory modes of production (Perkins, 1969). **Capitalism**, in Marx's and Engels's terms, is an economic system whereby a small number of owners of the means of production (the **bourgeoisie** who own the factories) are able to make a profit (accumulate **capital**), from exploiting the wage labour of a large lowly paid workforce, the members of which are the **proletariat** who own nothing but their labour.

In writing about wage labour in this new factory system of production, they show how the worker 'becomes an appendage of the machine' or a cog in the machinery of a capitalist economy (Marx and Engels, 1967: 87). For instance, in his classic book *The Condition of the Working Class in England*, Engels (1968) provides detailed evidence demonstrating how workers' bodies become frozen in the stances they must take in the repetitive motions required by factory production. He describes how workers eventually became disabled as their legs took on the K-shape of the position that they had to maintain to work at the lathe. Marx makes plain that wage labour in such a mode of production leads 'inevit[ably to] overwork and premature death' for the worker (1964: 68). As Synnott puts it, working bodies become no more than 'disposable assets' for the capitalist (1993: 24).

Marx and Engels's analysis of early capitalism also addressed the body in its concept of the **alienation** workers experience. Under capitalism, all that workers own is their bodies, a commodity to be traded on the marketplace to the highest bidder, but the choice of what the worker will produce, and under which conditions, remains in the hands of owners. Nikolas Rose (1999) outlines the history of how owners have attempted to soften the alienation workers experience under capitalism. Prior to World War I, a handful of industrial philanthropists constructed model industrial villages where workers and their families could live in ideal conditions. Seemingly benign, these model villages in actuality operated as virtual panopticons permitting employers to constantly observe workers' bodies, family life, and moral qualities. As the war progressed, the demands on the workforce led to a focus on problems of industrial fatigue. Industrial psychology, with its focus on **ergonomics**—the design of workplace and equipment to reduce fatigue and maximize worker productivity—failed to resolve problems of worker burnout and poor productivity. Industrial psychologists thus turned their attention to the minds of workers, developing typologies of aptitude and attitude that enabled employers to separate good from bad workers and managers from labourers. The new cadre of managers, working on behalf of owners, developed and utilized disciplines like **human relations** to examine the minds of workers so as to minimize workers' dissatisfactions while maximizing their productivity. In the end, modernity's 'contented workers', while still alienated from their bodies in the classical Marxist sense, have been stripped of their potential for resistance through these seemingly humanistic disciplinary techniques.

Another approach to gaining workers' compliance was **Taylorism**, Frederic W. Taylor's version of **scientific management**, the 'attempt to apply the methods of science to the increasingly complex problems of the control of labour' and production in capitalist modes of production such as the factory (Braverman, 1974: 86). Taylor believed that by breaking down any task into its smallest component bodily actions, one could 'scientifically' determine the most productive way to complete that piece of work. In the process, workers become deskilled, and as a consequence disempowered, as they no longer have full knowledge of the task to be completed, rather they only know how to complete a single component of that task (Bahnisch, 2000).

In 'Scrubbing in Maine' Barbara Ehrenreich (2002) describes her experiences as an employee of a 'Merry Maid' type of cleaning company and an unskilled aid in a nursing home, jobs she undertook as part of her larger investigation of the social reality of low-wage work in contemporary America. You will read how the work of a maid reflects the doctrine of Taylorism in its prescribed and repetitive **time management** methods of work. For instance, Ehrenreich describes watching a training video on dusting where her boss tells her 'you know, all this was figured out with a stopwatch' (2002: 74). Echoing Marx and Engels, she goes on to write that 'we too will be vacuum cleaners' when wearing The Maid's specially designed backpack vacuum cleaners.

In her study of the working bodies of exotic dancers, Jennifer K. Wesely (2003) presents her analysis of the body technologies they must use to be successful in this type of work. By **body technologies** she means any 'techniques we engage in to change or alter our physical appearance' (2003: 644). In the same way that Marx and Engels argue that the wage worker owns nothing but his or her labour, Weseley shows how exotic dancers own nothing but their bodily performance; performances that must conform to socio-cultural expectations of femininity (see Part V). Her analysis also reveals the role played by racism in the valuing of the bodies of exotic dancers. According to Frederickson (2003), **racism** refers to the belief that some groups are more valuable than others because of assumed hereditary and corporeal differences. In this case racism means that the blonde, light-skinned body is the preferred commodity (Wesely, 2003).

References

Bahnisch, M. 2000. 'Embodied Work, Divided Labour: Subjectivity and the Scientific Management of the Body in Frederic W. Taylor's 1907 "Lecture on Management"', *Body and Society*, 6, 1: 51–68.

Braverman, H. 1974. *Labour and Monopoly Capital: The Degradation of Work in the Twentieth Century.* New York: Monthly Review Press.

Butler, J. 1990. *Gender Trouble.* New York and London: Routledge.

Ehrenreich, B. 2002. 'Scrubbing in Maine', in B. Ehrenreich, *Nickel and Dimed: On (Not) Getting By in America.* New York: Henry Holt and Company, 51–120.

Engels, F. 1968. *The Condition of the Working Class in England.* Stanford: Stanford University Press.

Frederickson, G.M. 2003. *A Brief History of Racism.* Princeton: Princeton University Press.

Marx, K. 1964. *The Economic and Philosophical Manuscripts of 1844.* New York: International Publishers.

———, and F. Engels. 1967. *The Communist Manifesto.* Introduction by A.J.P. Taylor. Harmonds-worth, UK: Penguin Books.

Rose, N. 1999. 'The Contented Worker', in N. Rose, *Governing the Soul: The Shaping of the Private Self,* 2nd edn. London and New York: Free Association Books, 61–75.

Synnott, A. 1993. *The Body Social: Symbolism, Self and Society.* London and New York: Routledge.

Wesely, J.K. 2003. 'Exotic Dancing and the Negotiation of Identity: The Multiple Uses of Body Technologies', *Journal of Contemporary Ethnography* 32, 6: 643–69.

Chapter 28

The Contented Worker

Nikolas Rose

Business efficiency and the welfare of employees
are but two sides of the same problem.[1]

E. Cadbury, 1912

Employment, in its fundamental capitalist form,
implies a purely contractual relationship between
two isolated economic actors. The worker enters
into an agreement to alienate a certain quantum
of labour power in exchange for a wage; the capitalist agrees to part with a certain quantum of
money in exchange for the right to deploy a crucial factor of production within the labour
process.[2] No doubt this stark picture captures
much of what was essential to the mode of production in early capitalism. But since the earliest
struggles over the length of the working day and
the conditions of employment, the worker has
come to be seen as something more than an
expendable and endlessly replaceable commodity.
. . .

It was in the first decades of the twentieth century that the subjectivity of the worker began to
be connected with the imperatives of economic
policy, the search for social integration, the management of industrial harmony, and the quest for
business efficiency. The majority of firms prior to
World War I had remained relatively indifferent
to the conditions of the labourer.[3] But Quaker
employers such as Rowntree at York, Cadbury at
Bournville, and Lever at Port Sunlight perceived a
fundamental relationship between the obligations
of philanthropy and the pursuit of profit. The
'industrial betterment principle' was a new rationale and technique for organizing the reciprocal

duties and obligations of employer and employee,
in which industrial labour was no longer an isolated economic exchange but was located within
relations of solidarity and ties of community. The
efficiency of production, it appeared, was directly
related to the 'welfare' of the labourers.

Industrial betterment operated on two fronts.
The first concerned relations outside the workplace, the second concerned conditions within it.
Outside the workplace, model villages, public
baths, recreation clubs, libraries, and other techniques were used to improve the culture and
standards of living of the worker. Within the
workplace, the relationships that the employee
had to the activities of work—selection, training,
working conditions, and standards of reward—
were to be organized to ensure the good health
and orderly habits of the worker. The key figures
in this new network were the 'social secretaries' or
welfare workers. Some acted as extra-mural visitors to the families and homes of the workers,
advising them on ways to conducting their affairs,
managing their budgets, and coping with sickness
or other crises. Others operated within the factories themselves, watching over health and behaviour, especially of women workers, in the light of
the possibly degrading consequences of the physical and social conditions of employment upon
their health and morals. Welfare workers thus
acted as vital go-betweens, establishing links
between the workplace, the home, and the cultural milieu, relaying advice and information,
supervising each from the perspective of the
health, hygiene, and morality of the worker.

But this unitary and embracing strategy, based upon the integration of workers and their families into bonds of social solidarity that had the workplace as their hub, was isolated and short-lived. In large part the limits on this strategy arose from the way in which, in the first 20 years of the twentieth century, 'the state' extended its scope to the government of the 'social economy'. . . .

Social insurance, from the first National Insurance Act of 1911 to the present, institutes a direct relation between the insured citizen and the state in which both parties have their rights and their duties. This new relation was intended to entail a definite reduction in the general social and political consequences of economic events—industrial conflict, unemployment, and so forth—by ensuring that, working or not, citizens became, in effect, employees of society. . . .

The principle and mechanisms of national insurance led to the decline or demise of other systems of security for the worker: Friendly Societies, community- or union-based provisions, or those, such as the Quaker schemes, based directly on the enterprise. . . .

The economic necessity for the management of the human resources of industrial life was thrown into sharp relief by the strains on production imposed by the rate of expenditure of munitions on the bloody battlefields of France. . . . Many boys and women were working up to 70 hours a week; some men worked over 100 hours. The pace and intensity of war work was having effects on the health and behaviour of munitions workers, and this in its turn was taking a toll in productivity and efficiency. It was of vital military importance to discover ways in which these effects might be minimized, and the labour process so organized to maximize efficiency and minimize fatigue, accidents, and illness. . . .

These early studies of industrial fatigue, by and large, construed the worker as a physiological apparatus whose attributes were to be analyzed, calculated, and adjusted to the design of work—lighting, rest, pauses, bench layout, and so forth—in order to minimize fatigue and maximize efficiency. But by the 1920s it became apparent that fatigue, inefficiency, and accidents were not explicable in purely physiological terms. 'The physiological factors involved in purely muscular fatigue', wrote C.S. Myers, 'are now fast becoming negligible, compared with the effects of mental and nervous fatigue, monotony, want of interest, suspicion, hostility, etc. The psychological factor must therefore be the main consideration of industry and commerce in the future.'[4] In the inter-war years these psychological factures were to become the basis of a new matrix of relations between economic regulating, management of the enterprise, and psychological expertise. The organizing institution of this matrix was the National Institute of Industrial Psychology under the direction of Charles Myers. . . .

At the National Institute of Industrial Psychology, Myers and his colleagues addressed the problems that were now becoming standard fare—fatigue, industrial accidents, 'lost time'—but they propounded a view of the nature of the productive subject, the origins of industrial discontent, and the role of industrial psychology that related the subjectivity of the worker to the demand for productivity in a new way. The worker was neither a mindless brute nor a psycho-physiological machine, but an individual with a particular psychological makeup in terms of intelligence and emotions, with fears, worries, and anxieties, whose work was hampered by boredom and worry, whose resistances to management were often founded in rational concerns, and whose productive efficiency was highly dependent upon sympathy interest, satisfaction, and contentment. If this were the case, Myers argued:

> it becomes the function of the industrial psychologist not merely to investigate methods of payment, the movements of the worker, and the length of hours of his work but also to attempt to improve the mental makeup of the worker, to study his home conditions, and to satisfy his native impulses, so far as they are satisfiable under modern industrial conditions where, despite longer education and increasing culture, industrial specialization tends to reduce him to the status of a small wheel working in a vast machine, of the nature of which he is too

often kept in complete ignorance, and towards which consequently he is apt to develop apathy or actual antagonism.[5]

The subjectivity of the worker was to be opened to knowledge and regulation in terms of two notions that were central to psychological thought and strategy in the period after World War I: individual differences and mental hygiene.[6] Firstly, workers differed among themselves, not merely in intelligence but also in emotional makeup, and these differences had important industrial consequences. Farmer and his colleagues had shown, for example, that liability to accidents could be predicted by a study of individual psychological characteristics.[7] Hence there was no 'one best way' to organize production, suitably for all tasks and workers. It was a question, rather, of fitting the job to the man and the man to the job. The worker, that is to say, was to be individualized in terms of his or her particular psychological makeup and idiosyncrasies, the job analyzed in terms of its demands upon the worker, and human resources were to be matched to occupational demands. Vocational guidance and selection would adjust recruitment to work through a psychological calculation of suitability, movement study and analysis of periods of rest and work, the design of tasks and materials, and so on, would adjust work to the psychophysiology and psychology of the worker.

Second, the human being was not to be analyzed in terms of a superficial analogy with a piece of engineering machinery, and to be degraded to a servile mechanism of management—such an attitude was not only bound to produce an entirely rational antagonism from the worker, but was also based on faulty psychology. The worker had a complex subjective life that needed to be understood if industry was to truly take account of the human factor. The terms of this understanding were derived from 'the new psychology'. The subjectivity of the worker was the outcome of the shaping of instincts by forces and constraints in early family life; the conduct of the worker was to be explained through the relationship between the personality so formed and the industrial sur-

roundings in which work took place.[8] Adjustment, that is to say, required the successful resolution of conflicting instinctual forces and their harnessing to the particular requirement of social and industrial life. . . .

In work the individual sought not merely financial returns but gratification of the particular pattern of instinctual wishes and desires that comprised their unique character or temperament. It was through the satisfaction of these instincts and the matching of work to temperament that workers would be induced to give of their best. Hence, the worker was not to be forced to work against his will, but to be encouraged by removing the obstacles and difficulties that prevented him from giving the best to his work. The worker was certainly not motivated purely by financial incentives. Men may continue to work when they are rolling in wealth; they may continue to loaf while they are well nigh starving from poverty.

At least as important, then, as methods of payment is the mental atmosphere of the works, that character of which is largely dependent on management and leadership on the one side, or loyalty and comradeship on the other, and on the satisfaction of each worker's instincts and interests, which are by no means confined to what money will buy him or her outside the factory.[9]

But not all problems could be resolved by judicious adjustment of the mental atmosphere of the workplace, or by fitting the man to the job. Some individuals had become maladapted as a consequence of the formation of their temperament in early life. Such maladapted individuals were both personally unhappy and socially inefficient. Maladaption led to social discontent, industrial inefficiency, and individual neuroses; if untreated it could even result in delinquency, crime, and full-blown insanity. At work, unconscious conflicts, unsuccessful repression of thwarted instincts, and unexpressed emotions could be found at the root of many industrial problems. Psychoneuroses, that is to say, were at least as important as rest pauses, posture, illumination, and the like. The question of industrial efficiency was, at root, one of mental hygiene—

the diagnosis and treatment of the minor mental troubles of the manager or the worker before they produced major and disabling problems; the promotion of correct habits in light of a knowledge of the nature of mental life; the organization of the factory itself so as to minimize the production of symptoms of emotional and mental instability and enhance adjustment.

Myers characterized bad managers in terms of their psychodynamics. The egotistical emotional type reacts not to situations but to the emotions that they arouse in him, is therefore apt to be unjust, lacking in balanced criticism, producing anxiety or indifference in his workers. The over-anxious manager is always grumbling and finding fault, depressing subordinates, and denying them pleasure in their work. The manager with absorbing interests or absurd prepossessions also produces a bad state of discipline, for when workers pander to his whims they tend also to pander to their own. A psychotherapeutics of management was necessary for selection and for cure.

But more crucial, perhaps, was the problem of the maladjusted worker. By 1927 Eric Farmer and others were clear that industrial inefficiency was not simply a question of individual difference, it was rooted in mild psychoneuroses. 'Telegraphist's cramp', for example, was merely one among other manifestations of such minor mental disturbances in the worker. The maladjusted worker lacked self-confidence, felt ill at ease with people, was frightened by authorities, and was anxious about unrealistic events. Under conditions of telegraphic work such a worker would develop the disorder a telegraphist's cramp, but this was only a symptom of the psychoneurosis. Not merely explanation but also prophylaxis, prevention and cure for worker inefficiency, appeared possible through the application of psychological knowledge to industrial problems.

In 'human factor' psychology, the worker was no longer conceived of as a set of psycho-physiological capacities and reactions, but as a subjective being with instincts and emotions. But while the mental hygienists talked in terms of the mental atmosphere of the factory and the emotional relations between workers and managers,

the focus of their techniques was upon the maladjusted individual, upon efficient allocation of manpower through selection and vocational guidance, upon identifying the characteristics of the normal worker in contradistinction to the neurotic, upon treatment and prophylaxis of psychoneuroses. . . .

In the United States, too, the maladjusted worker had been discovered.[10] Maladjustment, it appeared, was at the heart of dissatisfactions expressed in ways ranging from petty jealousy, through lack of cheerful co-operation, poor work performance, tiredness, irritability, distractibility, nausea, abnormal fears, and neuroses to labour agitation. It was estimated that half of the annual cost of labour turnover to industry resulted from emotional maladjustment, and that the effectiveness of about half the labour force was impaired by emotional maladjustment requiring investigation and treatment. However, this concentration on the maladjusted worker and the industrial misfit in the United States was accompanied by a rather different way of linking the subjective world of the worker with the demands of production, construed not in terms of the individual but of the group. It came to be identified with the writings of Elton Mayo and the notion of 'human relations'.[11]

Mayo had initially been concerned with the body as a psycho-physiological mechanism—the effects of rest pauses and the conditions of the workplace upon fatigue, accidents, and labour turnover. But the conclusions he drew from the long series of studies of the Hawthorne Works of the Western Electric Company conducted between 1923 and 1932 were to provide a new language for interpreting the links between the conditions of work and the efficiency of production.[12] What was now of significance was neither the objective exigencies and characteristics of the labour process—levels of light, hours of work, and so forth—nor even the maladjustments and psychoneuroses of individual workers, but the human relations of the enterprise; the informal group life that made it up, and the subjective inter-relations that comprised it.

Productivity, efficiency, and contentment were now to be understood in terms of the *attitudes* of the workers to their work, their feeling of control over their pace of work and environment, their sense of cohesion within their small working group, their *beliefs* about the concern and understanding that the bosses had for their individual worth and their personal problems. This was not simply a matter of drawing attention to a complex domain of informal organization in any plant that existed in tension with its formal organization. It was also that a range of new tasks emerged to be grasped by knowledge and managed in the factory.

On the one hand, the subjective features of group relations had to be rendered into thought and made amenable to calculation. The device used here was the non-direct interview. The Hawthorne investigations, for example, involved some 20,000 interviews whose initial purpose had been to obtain objective information. . . . The factory was a pattern of relations between those in particular organizational positions, symbolized through social distinctions, embodying certain values and expectations and requiting delicate interpretations among all involved. Problems arose, then, not only as a result of individual adjustment, but also where these values came into conflict with one another, or where the social equilibrium was disrupted by management seeking to impose changes without recognizing the sentiments and meanings attached to the old ways of doing things. Given that the management were predominantly moved by the logic of cost and efficiency, while the workers tended to operate in terms of the logic of sentiments and the inter-human relations of the plant, it was no wonder the two so often came into conflict.

But once they had been conceptualized and studied, these subjective features of work could themselves be managed to promote organizational harmony. The interviews and surveys of workers themselves had a role here, for the airing of grievances was often therapeutic in itself. But more generally, the task for management was to manage the enterprise and change within it in light of a knowledge of the values and sentiments of the work force, and to act upon these so as to make them operate for, rather than against, the interests of the firm. Personnel workers had a key

role here, not only in documenting values and sentiments, but also in working out plans in light of them, advising supervisors, and diagnosing problems of the group and individuals within it. 'Communication' became a vital instrument for realigning workers' values with management objectives, through explaining the situation, clearing up misunderstandings, and allaying fears and anxieties. Personnel workers also had a role in counselling individual workers about their difficulties to assist them in adjustment to the social organization. By such techniques management could create the internal harmony that was the condition of a happy and productive factory. The minutiae of the human soul—human interactions, feelings, and thoughts, the psychological relations of the individual to the group—had emerged as a new domain for management.[13] . . .

Before and during World War II British management thought came to accept the economic advantages of fostering the loyalty of employees through human relations styles of management: the emphasis on the need for the integration of the worker, on the social functions of group relations, on the effectiveness of participative managerial leadership.[14] . . . Management came to represent itself as an expert profession, and to claim that it was not capitalist discipline but industrial efficiency that required skilled managerial control over the process of production. The legitimacy and authority of management were to depend not only upon its basis in practical experience, but also upon a scientific knowledge that would cast this experience within the framework of technical rationality. And to manage rationally one now required a knowledge of the worker.

The language and techniques of human relations were thus one element in the managerial claim to a specific knowledge base for its expertise. They also underpinned the argument that management was independent of the simple interest the boss had in maximizing profit. Management could represent its authority as neutral, rational, and in the worker's interest. In return for the acceptance of such authority by workers and their representatives, the worker would be treated equitably, justly, honestly, fairly.

The language and techniques of human relations allowed British management to reconcile the apparently opposing realities of the bosses' imperative of efficiency with the intelligibility of the workers' resistance to it, and to claim the capacity to transform the subjectivity of the worker from an obstacle to an ally in the quest for productivity and profit. . . .

Notes

1. E. Cadbury, *Experiments in Industrial Organization* (London: Longmans, 1912), quoted in J. Child, *British Management Thought* (London: Allen & Unwin, 1969), 37. I have drawn extensively on Child's account in this section.

2. Marx's own writings on the wage form in *Capital* remain the best account of this analysis.

3. For this next section see Child, op. cit., Ch. 2, and M.M. Niven, *Personnel Management 1913–63* (London: Institute of Personnel Management, 1967).

4. C.S. Myers, cited in P. Miller, 'Psychotherapy of Work and Unemployment', in P. Miller and N. Rose, eds, *The Power of Psychiatry* (Cambridge: Polity, 1986). See also E. Farmer, 'Early Days in Industrial Psychology: An Autobiographical Note', *Occupational Psychology* 32 (1958): 264–7.

5. C.S. Myers, op. cit. For what follows I have also drawn upon P. Miller, 'Psychotherapy of Work and Unemployment', op. cit.

6. For a full discussion of the psychology of individual differences and the strategy of mental hygiene, see my *Psychological Complex*.

7. Farmer, op. cit.

8. The new psychology is discussed in detail in my *Psychological Complex,* op. cit., Chs. 7 and 8.

9. Myers, op. cit., 29–30.

10. M.S. Viteles, *Industrial Psychology* (New York: Norton, 1932), and V.E. Fisher and J.V. Hanna, *The Dissatisfied Worker* (New York: Macmillan, 1932). My discussion of the American experience is indebted to Miller, op. cit.

11. See E. Mayo, *The Human Problems of an Industrial Civilization* (New York: Macmillan, 1933). Mayo himself was not directly involved in the experiments at the Hawthorne Plant, and the claims he made for them differed in significant respects from those of the researchers themselves. For a discussion of Mayo, see M. Rose, op. cit., and P. Miller, op. cit.

12. The most detailed accounts of the actual studies are F. J. Roetblisberger and W. J. Dickson, *Management and the Worker* (Cambridge, MA: Harvard University Press, 1939), and T.N. Whitehead, *The Industrial Worker* (Oxford: Oxford University Press, 1938).

13. Roetblisberger and Dickson, op. cit., p. 151.

14. Child, op. cit.

Chapter 29

Scrubbing in Maine

Barbara Ehrenreich

. . . Now to find a job. I know from my Key West experience to apply for as many as possible, since a help-wanted ad may not mean that any help is wanted just now. Waitressing jobs aren't plentiful with the tourist season ending, and I'm looking for fresh challenges anyway. Clerical work is ruled out by wardrobe limitations. I don't have in my suitcase—or even in my closet back at home—enough office-type outfits to get me through a week. So I call about cleaning (both offices and homes), warehouse, and nursing-home work, manufacturing, and a position called 'general helper', which sounds friendly and altruistic. It's humbling, this business of applying for low-wage jobs, consisting as it does of offering yourself—your energy, your smile, your real or faked lifetime of experience—to a series of people for whom this is just not a very interesting package. At a tortilla factory, where my job would be to load dough balls onto a conveyor belt, the 'interview' is completed by a bored secretary without so much as a 'Hi, how are you?' I go to Goodwill, which I am curious about since I know from past research it has been positioning itself nationwide as the ideal employer for the postwelfare poor as well as the handicapped. I fill out an application and am told that the pay is $7 an hour and that someone will get back to me in about two weeks. During the entire transaction, which takes place in a warehouse where perhaps 30 people of both sexes are sorting through bins of used clothing, no one makes eye contact with me. Well, actually one person does. As I search for the exit, I notice a skinny, misshapen fellow standing on one foot

with the other tucked behind his knee, staring at me balefully, his hands making swimming motions above his head, whether for balance or to ward me off. . . .

. . . [A]nother $6–$7-dollar-an-hour town. . . . If the supply (of labour) is low relative to demand, the price should rise, right? That is the 'law'. At one of the maid services I apply at—Merry Maids—my potential boss keeps me for an hour and 15 minutes, most of which is spent listening to her complain about the difficulty of finding reliable help. It's easy enough to think of a solution, because she's offering '$200 to $250' a week for an average of 40 hours' work. 'Don't try to put that into dollars per hour', she warns, seeing my brow furrow as I tackle the not-very-long-division. 'We don't calculate it that way.' I do, however, and $5–$6 an hour for what this lady freely admits is heavy labour with a high risk of repetitive-stress injuries seems guaranteed to repel all mathematically able job seekers. But I am realizing that—just as in Key West, one job will never be enough. In the new version of the law of supply and demand, jobs are so cheap—as measured by the pay—that a worker is encouraged to take on as many of them as she possibly can.

After two days of sprinkling job applications throughout the greater Portland area, I force myself to sit in my room at the 6, where I am marooned until the Blue Haven will let me in on Sunday, and wait for the phone to ring. This takes more effort than you might think, because the room is too small for pacing and too dingy for daydreaming, should I have been calm enough to give that a try. Fortunately, the phone rings twice before noon, and—more out of claustrophobia than any serious economic calculation—I accept the first two jobs that are offered. A nursing home wants me on weekends for $7 an hour, starting tomorrow; The Maids is pleased to announce that I 'passed' the Accutrac test and can start on Monday at 7:30 A.M. This is the friendliest and best-paying maid service I have encountered—$6.65 an hour . . . I don't understand exactly what maid services do and how they are different from agencies, but Tammy, the office manager at The Maids, assures me that the work will be familiar and easy, since 'the work is in our blood'. I'm not so sure about the easy part after the warnings I got at Merry Maids, but I figure my back should be able to hold out for a week. We're supposed to be done at about 3:30 every day, which will leave me plenty of time for job hunting on weekday afternoons. I have my eye on a potato chip factory a 10-minute drive from the Blue Haven, for example, or I can always search out L.L. Bean and fill out catalogue orders from what I hope will be an ergonomically congenial seat. . . .

On my fourth full day in Portland, I get up at 4:45 to be sure to get to the Woodcrest Residential Facility (not its real name) for the start of my shift at 7:00. I am a dietary aide, which sounds important and technical, and at first the work seems agreeable enough. I get to wear my own clothes, meaning T-shirt and khakis or jeans, augmented only by the mandatory hairnet and apron at my own discretion. I don't even have to bring lunch, since we get to eat anything left over after the residents, as we respectfully call them, have eaten their share. Linda, my supervisor—a kindly-looking woman of about 30—even takes time out to brief me about my rights: I don't have to put up with any sexual harassment, particularly from Robert, even though he's the owner's son. Any problems and I'm to come straight to her, and I get the feeling she'd appreciate getting a Robert-related complaint now and then. . . . Today we will be working the locked Alzheimer's ward, bringing breakfast from the main kitchen downstairs to the smaller kitchen on the ward,

serving the residents, cleaning up afterward, and then readying ourselves for their lunch.

For a former waitress such as myself, this is pretty much a breeze. The residents start drifting in 40 minutes before breakfast is ready, by walker and wheelchair or just marching stiffly on their own power, and scuffle briefly over who sits where. I rush around pouring coffee—decaf only, Linda warns, otherwise things can get pretty wild. . . If someone rejects the French toast we're offering, Linda and I make toast or a peanut butter sandwich, because the idea, especially at breakfast, is to get them eating fast before they collapse into their plates from low blood sugar or escape back out into the corridor. There's a certain amount of running but no big worry about forgetting things—our 'customers' aren't strong in the memory department themselves. . . .

The ugly part is cleaning up. I hadn't realized that a dietary aide is, in large measure, a dishwasher, and there are about 40 people—counting the nurses and CNAs (Certified Nursing Assistants) who have scrounged breakfasts with the residents—to clean up after. You scrape uneaten food off the dishes and into the disposal by hand, rinse the dishes, presoak them, stack them in a rack, and load the rack into the dishwashing machine, which involves bending down almost to floor level with a full rack, which I would guess at about 15 to 20 pounds, held out in front of you. After the machine has run its course, you let the dishes cool enough to handle, unload the rack, and reload the dishwasher— all the while continuing to clear tables and fetch meals for stragglers. The trick is to always have a new rack ready to go into the machine the minute the last load is done. I've been washing dishes since I was six years old, when my mother assigned me that task so she could enjoy her postprandial cigarette in a timely fashion, and I kind of like working with water, but it's all I can do to keep up with the pace of the dishwashing machine on the one hand and the flow of dirty plates on the other. With the dishes under control, Linda has me vacuum the carpet in the dining room, which really doesn't do anything for the sticky patches, so there's a lot of climbing under tables and scratching mushed muffins off the floor with my fingernails. . . .

Surprisingly, a number of the more sentient residents seem to recognize me at the lunch service. One of them grips my arm when I bring her ham steak, whispering, 'You're a good person, you know that?' and repeats the accolade with each item I deliver. Another resident tells me I'm looking 'gorgeous', and one of the RNs actually remembers my name. This could work, I'm thinking, I will become a luminous beacon in the gathering darkness of dementia, compensating, in some cosmic system of justice, for the impersonal care my father received in a far less loving facility. I happily fill my special requests for ice cream and grilled cheese sandwiches; I laugh at the Barbara Bush joke when it comes up again, and again. The saintly mood lasts until I refill the milk glass of a tiny, scabrous old lady with wild white hair who looks like she's been folded into her wheelchair and squished. 'I want to throw you', she seems to be saying, and when I bend down to confirm this improbable aspiration, the old fiend throws the entire glass at me, soaking my khakis from groin to ankle. 'Ha ha', my erstwhile admirers cackle, 'she wet her pants!' . . .

I am rested and ready for anything when I arrive at The Maids' office suite Monday at 7:30 A.M. . . . We . . . have uniforms, ill-fitting and in an overloud combination of kelly-green pants and a blinding sunflower-yellow polo shirt. And, as is explained in writing and over the next day and a half of training, we . . . have a special code of decorum. No smoking anywhere, or at least not within 15 minutes of arrival at a house. No drinking, eating, or gum chewing in a house. No cursing in a house, even if the owner is not present, and—perhaps to keep us in practice—no obscenities even in the office. . . .

Forty minutes go by before anyone acknowledges my presence with more than a harried nod. During this time the other employees arrive, about 20 of them, already glowing in their uniforms, and breakfast on the free coffee, bagels, and doughnuts The Maids kindly provides for us. All but one of the others are female, with an average age I would guess in the late twenties, though the range seems to go from prom-fresh to well into the Medicare years. There is a pleasant sort of bustle as people get their breakfasts and fill plastic buckets with rags and bottles of cleaning fluids, but surprisingly little conversation outside of a few references to what people ate (pizza) and drank (Jell-O shots are mentioned) over the weekend. Since the room in which we gather contains only two folding chairs, both of them occupied, the other new girl and I sit cross-legged on the floor, silent and alert, while the regulars get sorted into teams of three or four and dispatched to the day's list of houses. One of the women explains to me that teams do not necessarily return to the same houses week after week, nor do you have any guarantee of being on the same team from one day to the next. This, I suppose, is one of the advantages of a corporate cleaning service to its customers: there are no sticky and possibly guilt-ridden relationships involved, because the customers communicate almost entirely with Tammy, the office manager, or with Ted, the franchise owner and our boss. . . . While I wait in the inner room, where the phone is and Tammy has her desk, to be issued a uniform, I hear her tell a potential customer on the phone that The Maids charges $25 per person-hour. The company gets $25 and we get $6.65 for each hour we work? I think I must have misheard, but a few minutes later I hear her say the same thing to another inquirer. . . .

At last, after all the employees have sped off in the company's eye-catching green-and-yellow cars, I am led into a tiny closet-sized room off the inner office to learn my trade via videotape. The manager at another maid service where I'd applied had told me she didn't like to hire people who had done cleaning before because they were resistant to learning the company's system, so I prepare to empty my mind of all prior housecleaning experience. There are four tapes—dusting, bathrooms, kitchen, and vacuuming—each starring an attractive, possibly Hispanic young woman who moves about serenely in obedience to the male voiceover: for vacuuming, begin in the master bedroom; when dusting, begin with the room directly off the kitchen. When you enter a room, mentally divide it into sections no wider than your reach. . . .

. . . When you enter a house spray a white rag with Windex and place it in the left pocket of your green apron. Another rag, sprayed with disinfectant, goes into the middle pocket, and a yellow rag bearing wood polish in the right-hand pocket. A dry rag, for buffing surfaces, occupies the right-hand pocket of your slacks. Shiny surfaces get Windexed, wood gets wood polish, and everything else is wiped dust-free. . . Every now and then Ted pops in to watch with me . . . 'You know, all this was figured out with a stopwatch', he tells me with something like pride. When the video warns against oversoaking our rags with cleaning fluids, he pauses to tell me there's a danger in undersoaking too, especially if it's going to slow me down. 'Cleaning fluids are less expensive than your time.' . . .

Vacuuming is the most disturbing video, actually a double feature beginning with an introduction to the special backpack vacuum we are to use. Yes, the vacuum cleaner actually straps onto your back, a chubby fellow who introduces himself as its inventor explains. He suits up, pulling the straps tight across and under his chest and then says proudly into the camera: 'See, I *am* the vacuum cleaner.' It weighs only 10 pounds, he claims, although, as I soon figure out, with attachments dangling from the strap around your waist, the total is probably more like 14. What about my petulant and much-pampered lower back? The inventor returns to the theme of human/machine merger: when properly strapped in, we too will be vacuum cleaners, constrained only by the cord that attaches us to an electrical outlet, and vacuum cleaners don't have backaches. . . .

After a day's training I am judged fit to go out with a team, where soon I discover that life is nothing like the movies, at least not if the movie is *Dusting*. For one thing, compared with our actual pace, the training videos were actually all in slow motion. We do not walk to the cars with our buckets full of cleaning fluids and utensils in the morning, we run, and when we pull up to a house we run with our buckets to the door. Liza, a good-natured woman in her thirties who is my first team leader, explains that we are given only

so many minutes per house, ranging from under 60 for a 1½-bathroom apartment to 200 or more for a multi-bathroom 'first timer'. I'd like to know why anyone worries about Ted's time limits if we're being paid by the hour but hesitate to display anything that might be interpreted as an attitude. As we get to each house, Liza assigns our tasks, and I cross my fingers to ward of bathrooms and vacuuming. Even dusting, though, gets aerobic under pressure, and after about an hour of it—reaching to get door tops, crawling along floors to wipe baseboards, standing on my bucket to attack the higher shelves—I wouldn't mind sitting down with a tall glass of water. But as soon as you complete one task, you report to the team leader to be assigned to help someone else. Once or twice, when the normal process of evaporation is deemed too slow, I am assigned to dry a scrubbed floor by putting rags under my feet and skating around on it. Usually, by the time I get out of the car and am dumping the dirty water used on floors and wringing out rags, the rest of the team is already in the car with the motor running. . . .

In my interview I had been promised a 30-minute lunch but this turns out to be a five-minute pitstop at a convenience store, if that. I bring my own sandwich. . . . The two older married women I'm teamed up with eat best—sandwiches and fruit. Among the younger women, lunch consists of a slice of pizza, a 'pizza pocket' (a roll of dough surrounding some pizza sauce), or a small bag of chips. Bear in mind we are not office workers, sitting around idling at the basal metabolic rate. A poster on the wall in the office cheerfully displays the number of calories burned per minute at our various tasks, ranging from about three and a half for dusting to seven for vacuuming. If you assume an average of five calories per minute in a seven-hour day (eight hours minus time for travel between houses), you need to be taking in 2100 calories in addition to the resting minimum of, say, 900 or so. I get pushy with Rosalie, who is new like me and fresh from high school in a rural northern part of the state, about the meagreness of her lunches, which consist solely of Doritos—a half bag from the day before or a freshly purchased small-sized bag. She just didn't have anything in the house, she says (though she lives with her boyfriend and his mother), and she certainly doesn't have any money to buy lunch, as I find out when I offer to fetch her a soda from the Quik Mart and she has to admit she doesn't have 89 cents. I treat her to the soda, wishing I could force her, mommylike, to take milk instead. So how does she hold up for an eight- or even nine-hour day? 'Well', she concedes, 'I get dizzy sometimes.' . . .

. . . I decide to reward myself with a sunset walk on Old Orchard Beach. . . .

. . . I edge my way through the crowd and find a seat where I can see the musicians up close—the beautiful young guitarist and the taller man playing the flute. What are they doing in this rinky-dink blue-collar resort, and what does the audience make of this surprise visit from the dark-skinned South? The melody the flute lays out over the percussion is both utterly strange and completely familiar, as if it had been imprinted in the minds of my own peasant ancestors centuries ago and forgotten until this very moment. Everyone else seems to be as transfixed as I am. The musicians wink and smile at each other as they play, and I see then that they are the secret emissaries of a worldwide lower-class conspiracy to snatch joy out of degradation and filth. When the song ends, I give them a dollar, the equivalent of about 10 minutes of sweat.

The superwoman mood does not last. For one thing, while the muscles and joints are doing just fine, the skin has decided to rebel. At first I think the itchy pink bumps on my arms and legs must be poison ivy picked up at a lockout. Sometimes an owner forgets we are coming or forgets to leave a key under the mat or changes his or her mind about the services without thinking to notify Ted. This is not, for us, an occasion for joy like a snow day for the grade-school crowd, because Ted blames us for his customers' fecklessness. When owners forget we are coming, he explains at one of our morning send-off meetings, it 'means something', like that they're dissatisfied and too passive-aggressive to tell us. . . . [B]efore we give up and declare a place a lockout, we search like

cat burglars for alternative points of entry, which can mean trampling through overgrowth to peer into windows and test all the doors. I haven't seen any poison ivy, but who knows what other members of the poison family (oak, sumac, etc.) lurk in the flora of Maine?

Or maybe the cleaning fluids are at fault, except that then the rash should have begun on my hands. After two days of minor irritation, a full-scale epidermal breakdown is under way. I cover myself with anti-itch cream from Rite Aid but can manage to sleep only for an hour and a half at a time before the torment resumes. I wake up realizing I can work but probably shouldn't, if only because I look like a leper. Ted doesn't have much sympathy for illness, though; one of our morning meetings was on the subject of 'working through it'. Somebody, and he wasn't going to name names, he told us, was out with a migraine. 'Now if I get a migraine I just pop two Excedrins and get on with my life. That's what you have to do—work through it.' So it's in the spirit of a scientific experiment that I present myself at the office, wondering if my speckled and inflamed appearance will be enough to get me sent home. Certainly I wouldn't want anyone who looks like me handling my children's toys or bars of bathroom soap. But no problem. Must be a latex allergy, is Ted's diagnosis. Just stay out of the latex gloves we use for particularly nasty work; he'll give me another kind to wear.

I should, if I were going to stay in character, find an emergency room after work and try to cop a little charitable care. But it's too much. . . .

So ours is a world of pain—managed by Excedrin and Advil, compensated for with cigarettes and, in one or two cases and then only on the weekends, with booze. Do the owners have any idea of the misery that goes into rendering their homes motel-perfect? Would they be bothered if they did know, or would they take a sadistic pride in what they have purchased—boasting to dinner guests, for example, that their floors are cleaned only with the purest of human tears? In one of my few exchanges with an owner, a pert muscular woman whose desk reveals that she works part-time as a personal trainer, I am vacuuming and she notices the sweat. 'That's a real workout, isn't it?' she observes, not unkindly, and actually offers me a glass of water, the only such relief I ever encounter. . . . 'I tell all my clients', the trainer informs me, '"If you want to be fit, just fire your cleaning lady and do it yourself."' 'Ho ho', is all I say, since we're not just chatting in the gym together and I can't explain that this type of exercise is totally asymmetrical, brutally repetitive, and as likely to destroy the musculoskeletal structure as to strengthen it. . . .

. . . On the way to the Martha Stewart-ish place, when Holly and Marge were complaining about [the owners] haughtiness in a past encounter, I had ventured to ask why so many of the owners seem hostile or contemptuous toward us. 'They think we're stupid', was Holly's answer. 'They think we have nothing better to do with our time.' Marge too looked suddenly sober. 'We're nothing to these people', she said. 'We're just maids.' . . . True, I don't look so good by the end of the day and probably smell like eau de toilet and sweat, but it's the brilliant green-and-yellow uniform that gives me away, like prison clothes on a fugitive. Maybe, it occurs to me, I'm getting a tiny glimpse of what it would be like to be black.

And look at me now, sitting on a curb at a gas station, puffing into the endless slow rain, so sweat-soaked already that it doesn't matter. . . .

Is there help for the hardworking poor? Yes, but it takes a determined and not too terribly poor person to find it. On a Thursday after work, I drive to the Mobil station across the street from The Maids and call the Prebles Street Resource Center, which is listed in the phone book as a source of free meals and all around help. I get a recorded message saying that Prebles Street closes at 3:00 P.M.—so much for the working poor!—but to try 774-HELP after that. There I wait on hold for four minutes before someone picks up. I tell him I am new to the area and employed but need some immediate food aid or cash assistance. Why do I need money if I'm employed, he wants to know—didn't I bring any money with me? It got used up on housing, I tell him, which was more expensive than I'd expected. Well, why didn't I check out the rents before I moved here,

then? I had thought of telling him about the rash too, as a mitigating circumstance, but decide that our relationship is not at a point where I want to be discussing my body. Finally, he yields and gives me another number. A sequence of four more calls ensues before I reach a helpful human, Gloria, who says I should go to the food pantry in Biddeford tomorrow between nine and five. What is this assumption that the hungry are free all day to drive around visiting 'community action centres' and charitable agencies? So Gloria sends me to Karen at another number, another voluntary agency, where I am told I am in the wrong county. Very slowly, and trying to adopt the same businesslike tone I would use if I were calling to inquire about a credit card statement, I run through my time and geography constraints once again, underscoring that I work seven days a week, at least eight hours a day, and that I happen to be in her geographic jurisdiction at the moment. Bingo! Karen relents. I can't have cash, but she'll make a call and I can pick up a food voucher at a South Portland Shop-n-Save. What would I like for dinner?

The question seems frivolous or mocking. What do I want for dinner? How about polenta-crusted salmon fillet with pesto sauce and a nice glass of J. Lohr Chardonnay? . . . My dinner choices, [Karen] explains, are limited to any two of the following: one-box spaghetti noodles, one jar spaghetti sauce, one can of vegetables, one can of baked beans, one pound of hamburger, a box of Hamburger Helper, or a box of Tuna Helper. No fresh fruit or vegetables, no chicken or cheese, and oddly, no tuna to help out with. For breakfast I can have cereal and milk or juice. Good enough. I drive to the Shop-n-Save, pick up my voucher (which again lists my meagre options) at Customer Service, and commence to shop and certainly save. I get a quart of milk, a box of cereal, a pound of chopped meat, and a can of kidney beans, figuring that the latter two will make a sort of chili or at least refried beans con carne, and fortunately the checkout woman doesn't challenge my substitution of kidney beans for baked ones. I attempt to thank her, but she is looking the other way at nothing in particular. Bottom line: $7.02 worth of food acquired in 70 minutes of calling and driving, minus $2.80 for the phone calls—which ends up being equivalent to a wage of $3.63 an hour.

Then there are weekends at the Woodcrest. I have been trying to interpret them as genuine weekends, as if, after spending the weekdays on futile and largely cosmetic labour, I had decided to volunteer to do something useful for a change. 'It must be so depressing', my sister and, of course, fellow Alzheimer's orphan writes to me, but not at all. Once you join the residents in forgetting about the functioning humans they once were, you can think of them as a band of wizened toddlers at a tea party. Then too, compared with the women at The Maids, my Woodcrest co-workers are an enthusiastic and outgoing bunch, though the faces tend to change from one weekend to the next.

Chapter 30

Exotic Dancing and the Negotiation of Identity: The Multiple Uses of Body Technologies

Jennifer K. Wesely

Body technologies are the technique we engage to change or alter our physical appearance. A continuum of body technologies might range from temporary alternations like makeup or attire on one end to more permanent or invasive changes like cosmetic surgery or drugs on the other. Although all body technologies are artificial, the technologized body passes as natural when it conforms to dominant social expectations of gendered bodies. . . .

. . . Postmodern feminist scholars, for instance, have emphasized other, less obvious meanings of body technologies through discussion of gender as performance (Butler, 1990, 1993). Drawing on her experiences of peepshow dancing, Dudash (1997) comments, 'By representing the "feminine ideal" at work we begin to see how literally *constructed* gender is, which allows us to begin *deconstructing* it' (107; emphasis in the original). . . .

. . . For instance, sex performer Annie Sprinkle blurs boundaries between performance and porn; she parodies pornographic images of her gendered body by revealing the artificiality of its technologized femininity. . . . [I]n her *Anatomy of a Pinup Photo*, Sprinkle is photographed as a porn star but labels each body technology, providing helpful statements like 'Mandatory fake beauty mark/Breasts are real but sag. Bra lifts breasts/Hemorrhoids don't show, thank goodness/Gloves cover tattoos for a more All-American girl effect, borrowed from Antionette/I can't walk and can barely hobble/Corset hides a very big belly' (Williams, 1997: 373), and so on. By sys-

tematically noting the body technologies she uses, Sprinkle unveils her performance of femininity. . . .

. . . This article addresses the idea that women are not passive recipients of or are limited to one-dimensional identity meanings, but instead engage body technologies for multiple reasons. It incorporates the realization that women's active choices about their bodies and identities might be constrained by the contexts in which they participate. . . . Ultimately, then, I investigate how dancers negotiate and grapple with these different aspects of their lived experiences in relation to their identities and bodies.

Method

The information of this study was gleaned from . . . qualitative, in-depth interviews with 20 current and former exotic dancers in a southwestern metropolitan area. . . . I also observed at two different clubs, listened to a local radio show featuring interviews with exotic dancers and club mangers in the area, and informally spoke with club personnel.

'What Can I Change about Myself to Make Me More Appealing to these Guys?'

Like all women, exotic dancers learn early on of the contemporary ideal of feminine attractiveness. This ideal is difficult, if not impossible, to attain. . . . Contemporary society is bombarded by media images of extremely thin women with large breasts, and for exotic dancers, this 'Barbie doll' body is the one that got the most attention from customers. To achieve the successful performance of this body, the stripper's outward appearance is thus carefully and often painfully (re)constructed via body technologies. . . .

One manger, Joe, discussed on a radio program how he ran a purportedly 'upscale gentleman's club'. According to several women I interviewed who worked at his establishment, he forced girls to 'weigh-in' and meet his arbitrary weight standards or risk being fired. He even directed them to do drugs to help lose weight.

> So I remember one time, Joe came in and was like, 'Ok, all you fat girls are weighing in. Including you.' And I'm like, I'm thick, I'm black, I'm supposed to be big. He's like, 'No, including you. You guys are all weighing in.' And he told you, 'Lose five, or lose 10. This is how much time you have. Lose six.' This was also his way of weeding out girls. That's how I got into crystal [metamphetamine]. I'm all, how am I supposed to lose 10 pounds in two weeks? He goes, 'Why don't you talk to so-and-so?' So I talked to so-and-so and she offered me crystal. She gave me crystal, and that's how it started. That was my weight-loss drug. (Valerie) . . .

It has been suggested that eating disorders like anorexia and bulimia may be related to the objectification of women and the conflation of thinness with ideals of female beauty (McLorg and Taub, 1987: 177). Again, this is only exacerbated in a context in which club personnel monitor the women's weight and customers financially reward them for being thin. In addition to drugs and cosmetic surgery, the women used body technologies like eating disorders, laxatives, and obsessive exercising to stay skinny enough to meet (management/customer/societal) standards. Many described starving themselves or eating in tiny amounts. . . .

. . . Harsh self-critique was often informed by reactions from customers that undermined the women's confidence or made them critical of themselves and their bodies. . . .

Self-critique was also due to the women's own evaluation of themselves in comparison to others. . . .

> When I was performing I was constantly comparing myself to other people. Constantly. 'Cause there's always somebody who looks better. There's always somebody who's got a tighter body, bigger boobs, who's got better looking abs. . . . You become very in tune with how you look and who is making money and how they look. . . .

As a result of these feelings of inadequacy, comparison, and critique, the exotic dancers employed a number of body technologies to increase their ability to make money and to feel confident and sexy in the exotic dance club; these span quite a spectrum. Even comportment and posture became ways of technologizing the physique; these technologies can be clustered on the more 'temporary' side of the continuum. Gina described,

> When you become a dancer, you learn to walk with, you know, your butt stuck out, your boobs, you learn to throw your shoulders back so your boobs are as firm looking as possible. You learn to carry yourself a certain way. . . .

A hairless pubic area is regulation in a club that, according to one woman, had a sign posted in the dressing room: 'Girls are getting too hairy!' The women shaved most, if not all, of their pubic hair. While menstruating, some described the practice of 'cut and tuck'—after inserting a tampon, the string is cut and tucked inside the vagina. . . .

According to the women, the technologies they engaged usually rewarded them financially, which upped the ante and fed into an urgency to further technologize the body. . . .

During her three years as a dancer, 21-year-old Cory had extensive cosmetic surgery, including hair implants, nose job, cheek implants, chin surgery, breast implants, tummy tuck, and liposuction. . . .

> Yeah, I didn't think I was beautiful enough to dance. But I wanted to keep on dancing. So I was like, I can make more money if I do this. And I did, but it all stared because of dancing. If I wasn't dancing, I wouldn't have done the things I did, never. . . .

'He Thought He Owned a Piece of Me'

The buying and selling of the dancers' bodies goes beyond the commodification of the image—it also occurs literally, with customers purchasing various body technologies and giving them to the dancers as 'gifts'. This happened most often through the buying of costumes and cosmetic surgery. By buying breast implants for a dancer, for instance, the customer takes control of the effort to reshape the woman's body in the fantasy image. At the same time, the women sometimes felt powerful when they convinced customers to pay for body technologies . . .

> I had this guy that used to come into the club, he was my customer, he would give me money all the time. So once I was like, I've always wanted a tummy tuck, just picture me with a tummy tuck. And he was like, yeah, you'd look so good. I was like, I need the money to do it, and he was like, you want me to get you a tummy tuck? I was like, will you, please? So he did get me a tummy tuck, which costs about $5000. (Cory) . . .

Cyclically, the sexualized, fantasy body was used to acquire the capital to afford a particular body technology, and this body technology further contributed to the objectification and instrumental use of the body. Valerie articulated this cycle: 'Dancing is like a monkey on your back. It's like a drug addiction. You dance a lot so you can get bet-

ter costumes so you can make more money so you can get better costumes. . . it's a vicious cycle.'

Sometimes the offer of cosmetic surgery was a more obvious manifestation of male coercion. . . . In this way, cultural norms that refigure women's bodies as objects of consumption for the male gaze are taken to a new and frightening level. Indeed, with the money that the customer (or pimp) pays to remake the women in his or the fantasy image, he may feel as though this re-creation belongs to him. Not just a consumer of the body with paid right to gaze, he now literally owns this body.

> So this customer asked what I wanted for Christmas, and I said, boobs! So the day after Christmas I was in surgery. He paid for it. I went to lunch with him a couple times, and I went and worked in [his town] and he let me and my daughter stay with him. But there wasn't sex between us. I don't talk to him anymore because he got possessive after the surgery. He thought he owned a piece of me. (Skye) . . .

'So I'll Ask a Guy, Do You Prefer Blondes?'

When body technologies are channelled into the reproduction of particular images of female attractiveness, they begin to erase visible difference. . . . Competition heightened as [dancers] moved closer to one standard look because there were almost always several girls who shared external attributes.

For instance, Tasha felt unique because of her hair colour. As a result of being a redhead, she was exempt from competition among other dancers. She said, 'I was the only redhead there. There was a competition between the blondes and brunettes, but I wasn't in that competition clique or anything.' Another way that women were distinguished from other dancers was on the basis of skin colour. Although some aspects of Valerie's comments below imply that skin colour is a superficial identifier, she also addressed the more complex motives of racism on the part of club management.

. . . Clubs weren't real big on hiring too many [minorities]. You didn't want six or seven black girls at a small club. You couldn't do it, because that's not what brought in the money. . . . It was better for me, 'cause if a client wanted a dark skin girl, it was me and the other girl. Not like the white girls, there was some vicious competition. . . .

When grouped together on the basis of superficial visible identifiers, the bodies of women in the club became depersonalized, dehumanized, and commodified. The commodified bodies are easily fragmented into parts and selected auction style to maximize profit.

So I'll ask a guy, do you prefer blondes, do you prefer real tits, fake tits, legs, tits, what kind of guy are you? You're like, I'm sure we have what you're looking for, we have one of everything. Tell me what you like, I'll send a couple of girls over. You like blondes, I'll send you three or four blondes and you can choose. That's what we're here for. The waitresses will do that, they'll ask them what they like. And they'll say, ok, I need four brunettes, go talk to this guy. (Rita) . . .

. . . The women often made choices about their bodies that reinforced this commodification because this proved to be most lucrative to them.

At the same time, the dancers' comments also pointed to deeper, more complex rationales inherent in the choices made about their bodies. In cruel irony, the aspects of their bodies that the women contorted, tucked, removed, implanted, and plucked so as to embody the fantasy were often also the aspects of their bodies that had originally differentiated them from other dancers. . . . Rita described technologies such as tattoos or piercings as ways of making a dancer appear— and feel—different or unusual.

There's only so many things you can do to be interesting. That's why girls get tattoos or get

pierced. You're standing there [naked] in shoes, what can you do? We all look the same. . . .

'They Only Look Good in a Strip Club'

Literature about exotic dancing has addressed the ways that dancers deal with identity problems like stigma that result from working in the sex industry (see Sweet and Tewksbury, 2000; Thompson and Harred, 1992). These works note that management of stigma and other identity issues may include the segmentation or hiding of the dancer role. Here, I suggest incorporating the ways that body technologies both hinder and assist efforts to manage identity. For instance, . . . Rita described the trouble that dancers with huge breast implants have when transitioning to life outside the club: 'In real life, when we're dressing in clothes . . . if you've got huge tits you look awful during the day. They look good only in a G-string in a strip club.' . . .

At the same time, other body technologies were used to facilitate this process. For instance, many used technologies to erase, eradicate, or separate their dancer personas before, during, and after work. Several would symbolically cleanse themselves of the dancer role after work by showering immediately. Lana said, 'I scrub myself after work. Completely. I feel like I leave the club in the shower. When I get home from work I wash the club away.' . . . While working, Jessie periodically doused herself with perfume, as if to repel odours of the club that might seep into the core of her being. . . .

Drugs and alcohol were another body technology that marked the transition into the dancer role while anesthetizing the women to the environment or instilling in them a feeling of power or bravado. In fact, drugs served multiple purposes; as mentioned above, they were often used as a technology for weight loss. . . . Samantha used alcohol for a similar purpose. She worked privately, performing at out-calls at clients' homes. But when she was hired for a bachelor party, she always got intoxicated beforehand. 'To go to a bachelor party, I have to drink, because those I cannot handle. . . .' Both as a transition into the dancer role and to numb herself, Samantha relied on alcohol. Substance like drugs and alcohol are body technologies that the women engaged to deal with the conflicts of identity they experience.

The women clarified that although drugs and alcohol were effective body technologies in the short term, in the long term, there were complications that compounded rather than alleviated identity issues. . . . [L]ater, drugs took a physical toll on them. Marie noted, 'Women stay really sickly thin with those [drugs]. Now, when I walk into the club, I actually see how sick those girls are.' Similarly, Julie said, 'That all had to do with the drugs, too. How could somebody be good-looking with those great big black bags under the eyes from five nights of not sleeping. It's like, you are ugly, bitch. Dancing and drugs, it was horrible.' . . .

Conclusion

The women in this study struggled to both be successful in the industry and have their bodies, quite literally, *mean* something to them, to help them make sense of who they are. They clearly engaged body technologies to be competitive in the industry. But they also used body technologies to mark themselves, to numb themselves, to make themselves feel, to prove something, to forget something, and a whole host of other reasons. Furthermore, the same technology may serve multiple purposes, depending on when and how it was used and with what intentions. The ways that the women used body technologies to make their bodies *mean* something to them goes beyond a dichotomy of complete resistance against or utter collusion with social expectations and norms. . . .

References

Butler, J. 1990. *Gender Trouble: Feminism and the Subversion of Identity*. New York: Routledge.

———. 1993. *Bodies that Matter*. New York: Routledge.

Dudash, T. 1997. 'Peepshow Feminism', in J. Nagel, ed, *Whores and Other Feminists*. New York: Routledge, 98–118.

McLorg, P., and D. Taub. 1987. 'Anorexia Nervosa and Bulimia: The Development of Deviant Identities', *Deviant Behavior* 8: 117–89.

Sweet, N., and R. Tewksbury. 2000. 'Entry, Maintenance, and Departure From a Career in the Sex Industry: Strippers' Experiences of Occupational Costs and Rewards', *Humanity and Society* 24: 136–61.

Thompson, W., and J. Harred. 1992. 'Topless Dancers: Managing Stigma in a Deviant Occupation', *Deviant Behavior* 13: 291–311.

Williams, L. 1997. 'A Provoking Agent: The Pornography and Performance Art of Annie Sprinkle', in K. Conboy, N. Medina, and S. Stanbury, eds, *Writing on the Body*. New York: Columbia University Press, 360–79.

Part XI

Disabled Bodies

Jacqueline Low and Claudia Malacrida

Disability studies is a relatively new sub-discipline in the humanities and social sciences. In the mid-1970s the UK-based Union of the Physically Impaired Against Segregation (UPIAS) argued for a **social model of disability**, meaning that while physical, sensory, and intellectual impairments might result in different ways of moving, communicating, and living, social factors such as inaccessibility, lack of accommodation, and prejudice are the truly disabling aspects of people's lives (Oliver, 1990). Disability activists also coined the phrase 'nothing about us without us' arguing that the traditional **medical model of disability**, which focused on curing impairments and pathologized people living with disabilities, ignored the richness of the lives of people with disabilities and the rewarding aspects of difference (Shakespeare and Watson, 2002).

Deborah Kent's (2000) article stems from this tradition. In it, she notes that although she was born blind, she has never experienced her blindness as undesirable or as an impairment, but instead feels it to be a neutral trait, like hair colour—different, but not negative. However, when Kent becomes pregnant, she learns that, even for those who know and love her, the spectre of her giving birth to a child who is blind is *not* neutral. As a result, she questions how accepting her family and friends really are. Kent's narrative is a fine example of C. Wright Mill's (2001) **sociological imagination**, which is a way of theorizing that connects personal troubles to broader social issues. In this case, Kent's personal struggle to gain acceptance ties to social issues such as the ethical dilemmas attached to genetic screening and **selective abortion** (choosing to abort a fetus because of traits like gender or disability), and the social stigmatization of difference.

The connections between the personal experience of disability, social processes, and structural forces is also illustrated in Thomas J. Gerschick and Adam S. Miller's (1995) analysis of how men living with physical disabilities cope with socio-cultural expectations about what it means to be masculine in contemporary Western society. Such expectations include the cultural stereotypes that 'real men' must be autonomous and dominant as well as physically active. These are only some of the gender traits that comprise **hegemonic**

masculinity. Gerschick and Miller argue that men with physical disabilities are **stigmatized** and thus socially devalued because their bodies prevent them from meeting the expectations of **hegemonic masculinity**. In interviewing men with physical disabilities, Gershick and Miller found that these men coped with this stigma in one of three ways that include reformulation, reliance, and rejection. Some men coped through **reformulation**, in other words by changing definitions of the different traits that make up hegemonic masculinity. In doing so they are able to see themselves as masculine despite their disability. Others practised **reliance**, by which Gershick and Miller mean that instead of questioning the validity of hegemonic masculinity, these men reinforced its dominance by refusing to engage in activities, such as wheelchair hockey, that would mark them as disabled. Finally, some of the men the authors spoke with coped via the stigma management technique of **rejection**. In other words, they rejected the limits placed upon them by hegemonic masculinity, arguing instead that they saw themselves as human beings.

Women, as well as men, have to deal with **hegemonic body norms**, and Hilde Zitzelsberger argues that women with disabilities must cope with a culture that renders them invisible due to the limited 'range of . . . acceptable bodies' that exist in contemporary Western society (2005: 393). Zitzelsberger uses the concept of **(in)visibility** to refer to the fact that while their 'disabled bodies' are highly visible in such a culture, the women she interviewed found that they were also invisible in that they are not seen as sexual, feminine beings capable of being 'spouses, partners, or mothers' (2005: 396). These women coped with (in)visibility by managing information about themselves, managing how they present themselves to others (see Part II), and, as did some of Gershick and Miller's informants, actively rejecting the tenets of hegemonic body norms.

References

Gerschick, T. J., and A.S. Miller. 1995. 'Coming to Terms: Masculinity and Physical Disability', in D. Sabo and D.F. Gordon, eds, *Men's Health and Illness: Gender, Power, and the Body*. Thousand Oaks: Sage, 183–204.

Kent, D. 2000. 'Somewhere a Mockingbird', in E. Parens and A. Asch, eds, *Prenatal Testing and Disability Rights*. Washington, DC: Georgetown University Press, 57–63.

Mills, C.W. 2001. 'The Sociological Imagination', in R. Garner, ed, *Social Theory: Continuity & Confrontation (A Reader)*. Peterborough, ON: Broadview Press, 322–30.

Oliver, M. 1990. 'The Individual and Social Models of Disability', Paper presented at Joint Workshop of the Living Options Group and the Research Unit of the Royal College of Physicians. Available at http://www.disability-archive.leeds.ac.uk/authors_list.asp?AuthorID=133&author_name=Oliver%2C+Mike. Accessed 25 January 2007.

Shakespeare, T., and N. Watson. 2002. 'The Social Model of Disability: An Outdated Ideology?', *Research in Social Science and Disability* 2: 9–28.

Zitzelsberger, H. 2005. '(In)visibility: Accounts of Embodiment of Women with Physical Disabilities and Differences', *Disability & Society* 20, 4: 389–403.

Chapter 31

Somewhere a Mockingbird[1]

Deborah Kent

When I was only a few weeks old my mother realized that I couldn't see. For the next eight months she and my father went from doctor to doctor searching for answers. At last their quest led them to one of the leading eye specialists in New York City. He confirmed everything they had already heard by that time—my blindness was complete, irreversible, and of unknown origin. He also gave them some sound advice. They should stop taking me to doctors and give up looking for a cure. Instead they should help me lead the fullest life possible. Fortunately for me, his prescription matched their best instincts.

As I was growing up people called my parents 'wonderful'. They were praised for raising me 'like a normal child'. As far as I could tell, my parents were like most of the others in my neighbourhood—sometimes wonderful and sometimes annoying. And from my point of view, I wasn't *like* a normal child—I *was* normal. From the beginning I learned to deal with the world as a blind person. I didn't long for sight any more than I yearned for a pair of wings. Blindness presented occasional complications, but it seldom kept me from anything I wanted to do.

For me blindness was part of the background music that accompanied my life. I had been hearing it since I was born and paid it little attention. But others had a way of cranking up the volume. Their discomfort, doubts, and concerns often put blindness at the top of the program. Teachers offered to lighten my assignments; Scout leaders discouraged me from going on field trips; boys shied away from asking me on dates. The message

was clear. Because I was blind, these people saw me as a liability—inadequate, incompetent, and too strange to be socially acceptable. I knew that my parents ached for me when these situations arose. It hurt them to see me being prejudged and rejected. Yet they found it hard to do battle on my behalf. Though they shared my sense of injury, they also identified with the nondisabled people who sought to exclude me. 'You have to understand how other people see things', my parents told me. 'They're trying their best. You need to be patient with them.' I struggled to show the doubters and detractors that they were wrong. Much of the time I felt that I was fighting alone.

Since one of my brothers, three years younger than I am, is also blind, it seemed more than likely that my unknown eye condition had a genetic basis. I never thought much about it until my husband, Dick, and I began to talk about having a child. Certainly, genetics was not our primary concern. We married late (I was 31, Dick 42) and were used to living unencumbered. Since we both worked as freelance writers, our income was erratic. We had to think about how we could shape our lives to make room for a child, whatever child that might be.

But somehow blindness crept into our discussions. I don't remember which of us brought up the topic first. But once it emerged, it had to be addressed. How would I feel if I passed my blindness to our son or daughter? What would it mean to Dick and to our extended families? What would it be like for us to raise a blind child together?

I premised my life on the conviction that blindness was a neutral characteristic. It created some inconveniences, such as not being able to read print or drive a car. Occasionally it locked me into conflicts with others over what I could and could not do. But in the long run, I believed that my life could not have turned out any better if I had been fully sighted. If my child were blind, I would try to ensure it every chance to become a self-fulfilled, contributing member of society. Dick said he agreed with me completely. We were deciding whether to have a child. Its visual acuity was hardly the point.

Yet if we truly believed our own words, why were we discussing blindness at all? I sensed that Dick was trying hard to say the right thing, even to believe it in his heart. But he was more troubled than he wished me to know. Once when I asked him how he would feel if he learned that our child was blind, he replied, 'I'd be devastated at first, but I'd get over it.' It was not the answer I wanted to hear.

I was blind and I was the woman Dick chose to marry, to spend his life with for better or for worse. I was his partner in all our endeavours. He accepted my blindness naturally and comfortably, as a piece of who I was. If he could accept blindness in me, why would it be devastating to him, even for a moment, if our child were blind as well? 'You know why', was all he could tell me. 'You've got to understand.'

What I understood was that Dick, like my parents, was the product of a society that views blindness, and all disability, as fundamentally undesirable. All his life he had been assailed by images of blind people who were helpless, useless, and unattractive, misfits in a sight-oriented world. I had managed to live down that image. Dick had discovered that I had something of value to offer. But I had failed to convince him that it is really okay to be blind.

Our discussions showed me a painful truth. No matter how close we grew, how much of our lives we shared, blindness would never be a neutral trait for him.

I wanted our child to be welcomed without reservation. I wanted Dick to greet its birth with joy. I did not know if I could bear his devastation if our baby turned out to be blind like me.

It was too painful to explore the implications any further. Instead I plunged into a search for information. After all, we didn't even know the real cause of my blindness. We couldn't make a decision until we gathered the facts. Surely the field of ophthalmology had learned something new over the past three decades. A series of phone calls led me to a specialist at New York University Medical Center. I was assured that if anyone could answer my questions, he was the man.

So, on a sunny morning in October, Dick and I set out for New York to learn why I am blind. We lived in a small town in central Pennsylvania at the time, and Dick wasn't used to driving in the city. He dreaded the horn-blaring, bumper-to-bumper traffic, and the desperate search for a parking space. All of his energy focused on delivering us to our destination. As we packed the car he commented, 'It's going to be a long, nervous day.' I couldn't have agreed with him more.

Parking on the streets of Manhattan was as difficult as Dick had feared. Finally we squeezed into a spot a dozen blocks from the hospital and set out on foot. The city engulfed us with its fumes and bustle and grinding noise. We didn't try to talk above the traffic. Really, there was nothing new to say.

We had walked several blocks when I was dimly aware of a strange sound. It was remarkably like the song of a bird, the clear, warbling notes ringing out against the concrete walls around us. At first I assumed it was a recording turned full blast, or some mechanical toy worked by a child. But as we drew nearer Dick remarked, 'There's a crowd of people standing by a tree. They're all looking at something. Oh hey, there's a bird up there!'

I've been an avid birder most of my life, and the song was unmistakable. It was a mockingbird. The mockingbird thrives in fields and gardens. It gathers scraps and snippets from the songs of other birds and braids them into a pattern all its own. The mockingbird sings exuberantly from April to June, but by late summer it usually falls silent. Yet this one poured forth its song on East 23rd Street in mid-October, out of place and out of season. It seemed utterly fearless and confident, staking a claim for itself in that inhospitable city landscape. It had something to say, and it was determined to be heard.

New Yorkers are used to almost anything, but the extraordinary song of this tiny creature brought them to a standstill. For a little while Dick and I paused too. We stood on the pavement, listening and marvelling. Then we pushed through the revolving door and into the antiseptic halls of the medical centre.

I expected a battery of tests, maybe a referral to yet another expert. But the doctor dilated my pupils, gazed into my eyes, and announced, 'I'll tell you what you have, and I'm 100 per cent certain. You've got Leber's congenital amaurosis.' Leber's is a genetic condition, he explained, autosomal recessive in nature. Both of my parents carried the recessive gene, and each of their children had a one-in-four chance of inheriting the eye condition.

What were my chances of passing Leber's on to my own children, I asked. The doctor explained that I would inevitably give one recessive gene for Leber's to my child. But unless my partner happened to carry the same recessive gene, there was no possibility that our child would be affected. The chances were slight that Dick would prove to be another carrier.

The discussion could have ended with that simple exchange of information. But the doctor had more to say. 'You have a good life, don't you?' he asked. 'If you have a child with Leber's, it can have a good life, too. Go home and have a dozen kids if you want to!'

Even from a total stranger, those were wonderful words. They affirmed that I was not a liability to the world. I was a worthwhile human being with a variety of traits to pass on to future generations. To this New York physician my Leber's genes were not a curse. They need not be extinguished, any more than my genes for dark brown hair. I was valued for who I was. My child, sighted or blind, could be valued in the same way. I floated out of the doctor's office and found Dick

in the packed waiting room. 'Hey, guess what!' I cried in triumph. 'I've got Leber's congenital amaurosis!'

The trip to New York cemented our decision to have a child. We left the city with a new certainty, a sense that we were ready for whatever came our way. Yet I knew Dick was comforted by the fact that Leber's is relatively rare, and that probably he did not carry the recessive gene. I wished that he didn't need that comfort.

Within the year we were parents-to-be. We awaited the birth of our child with the eagerness, wonder, and anxiety common to expectant parents everywhere. We seldom mentioned the possibility that our baby might be blind. Leber's congenital amaurosis seemed safely remote, a flash of lightning that wouldn't strike again. But it could reappear, I knew. I lived with the small unspoken fear that, if our child were blind, Dick would feel betrayed—by medical science, by fate, by me.

Dick had his doubts about coaching me through labour and viewing the birth. To support us both his sister came along to our Lamaze classes. She even stayed with us in the birthing room to help out in case Dick should faint dead away. But nobody fainted. When our daughter Janna arrived, we greeted her with greater joy than I could have imagined. Her welcome was boundless and wholly unreserved.

My parents flew out to visit us when we brought Janna home from the hospital. Mom helped with the cooking and housecleaning and insisted that I get as much rest as I could. I spent every conscious moment nursing, rocking, diapering, and marvelling at the extraordinary new being who had entered our lives. I was too happy and excited to feel exhaustion.

I wasn't worried about Janna's vision or anything else. But one day my mother confided that my father had told her, 'We've still got to find out if the baby's blind.' I was stunned by his concern and by her sense that it was justified. My parents raised all three of their children, including my blind brother and me, with sensitivity and unwavering love. In all of us they tried to nurture confidence, ambition, and self-respect. Yet they felt apprehensive about the prospect that their granddaughter might also be blind. Blindness had never become neutral for them, any more than it had for Dick.

It was almost time for Mom and Dad to go home when Dick said to my mother, 'You've raised two blind children. What do you think—can this kid see or not?' My mother said she really couldn't be sure. Janna was barely a week old; it was too soon to tell. The day after my parents left, Dick found the answer on his own. As Janna lay in his arms, awake and alert, he moved his hand back and forth above her face. Distinctly he saw her turn her head to track the motion. She saw his hand. She followed it with her eyes.

'She can see!' Dick exulted. He rushed to the phone and called my parents with the news. I listened quietly to their celebrations. I don't know if anyone noticed that I had very little to say.

How do I myself feel about the fact that Janna can see? I am glad that her world is enriched by colour as well as texture and sound. When she snaps a picture with her new camera or poses before the mirror in her favourite dress, I draw pleasure from her delight. As her mother I want her to have every advantage, and I know that some aspects of her life are easier because she has sight. She can play video games with her friends; she can thumb through magazines and note the latest fashions. All too soon now she will be learning to drive a car.

Beyond that, I am glad Janna will never be dismissed as incompetent and unworthy simply because she is blind. I am grateful that she will not face the discrimination that threads its way through my life and the lives of most people with disabilities. But I know her vision will not spare her from heartbreak. She will still meet disappointment, rejection, and self-doubt, as all of us must.

I will always believe that blindness is a neutral trait, neither to be prized nor shunned. Very few people, including those dearest to me, share that conviction. My husband, my parents, and so many others who are central to my life cannot fully relinquish their negative assumptions. I feel that I have failed when I run into jarring reminders that I have not changed their perspective. In those crushing moments I fear that I am not truly accepted after all.

But in recent years a new insight has gradually come to me. Yes, my own loved ones hold the unshakeable belief that blindness is and always will be a problem. Nevertheless, these same people have made me welcome. Though they dread blindness as a fate to be avoided at almost any cost, they give me their trust and respect. I don't understand how they live without discomfort amid such contradictions. But I recognize that people can and do reach out, past centuries of prejudice and fear, to forge bonds of love. It is a truth to marvel at, and a cause for hope and perhaps some small rejoicing.

Sometimes Dick reminisces about the day Janna turned her head to watch his moving fingers. In his voice I hear an echo of the excitement and relief that were so vivid for him on that long-ago morning. Each time I hear the story I feel a twinge of the old pain, and for a few moments I am very much alone again.

But I have my own favourite stories to recall. I remember our long, nervous day in New York, and the doctor who told me to go home and have a dozen kids. And somehow I have never forgotten the mockingbird that sang so boldly in a place where no one thought it belonged, making a crowd of busy people stand still to listen.

Note

1. Previously published in Michele Wates and Rowen Jade, eds, *Bigger Than the Sky: Disabled Women on Parenting* (London: Women's Press, 1999).

Chapter 32

Coming to Terms: Masculinity and Physical Disability

Thomas J. Gerschick and Adam S. Miller

Men with physical disabilities are marginalized and stigmatized in American society. The image and reality of men with disabilities undermine cultural beliefs about men's bodies and physicality. The body is a central foundation of how men define themselves and how they are defined by others. Bodies are vehicles for determining . . . status and prestige. Men's bodies allow them to demonstrate the socially valuable characteristics of toughness, competitiveness, and ability (Messner, 1992). . . . The bodies of men with disabilities serve as a continual reminder that they are at odds with the expectations of the dominant culture. . . .

. . . We examine two sets of social dynamics that converge and clash in the lives of men with physical disabilities. On the one side, these men must deal with the presence and pressures of hegemonic masculinity, which demand strength. On the other side, societal members perceive people with disabilities to be weak.

For the present study, we conducted in-depth interviews with 10 men with physical disabilities to gain insights into the psychosocial aspects of men's ability to come to terms with their physical and social condition. We wanted to know how men with physical disabilities respond to the demands of hegemonic masculinity and their marginalization. . . .

Hegemonic Masculinity and Physical Disability

. . . Murphy (1990) observes that men with physical disabilities experience 'embattled identities'

because of the conflicting expectations placed upon them as men and as people with disabilities. On the one side, contemporary masculinity privileges men who are strong, courageous, aggressive, independent, and self-reliant (Connell, 1987). On the other side, people with disabilities are perceived to be, and are treated as, weak, pitiful, passive, and dependent (Murphy, 1990). . . .

Disability, Masculinity, and Coming to Terms

Although no two men constructed their sense of masculinity in exactly the same way, there appeared to be three dominant frameworks our informants used to cope with their situations. These patterns can be conceived of in relation to the standards inherent in dominant masculinity. We call them the three Rs: *reformulation*, which entailed men's redefinition of hegemonic characteristics on their own terms; *reliance*, reflected by sensitive or hypersensitive adoptions of particular predominant attributes; and *rejection*, characterized by the renunciation of these standards and either the creation of one's own principles and practices or the denial of masculinity's importance in one's life. . . . [O]ne should note that none of our interviewees entirely followed any one of these frameworks in defining his sense of self. . . . For example, some of our informants relied on dominant standards in their view of sexuality and occupation, but also reformulated the prevailing ideal of independence.

Gerschick and Miller:

PART XI: D...

248

second patter...
nalization ...
nant ma...
athletic...
Just ...
m...

Therefore, we discuss the primary way in which these men with disabilities related to hegemonic masculinity's standards, while recognizing that their coping mechanisms reflected a more complex combination of strategies. . . .

Reformulation

Some of our informants responded to idealized masculinity by reformulating it, shaping it along the lines of their own abilities, perceptions, and strengths, thus defining their manhood along these new lines. These men tended not to overtly contest these standards but—either consciously or unconsciously—recognized in their own condition an inability to meet these ideals as they were culturally conceived. An example of this came from Damon, a 72-year-old quadriplegic who survived a spinal-cord injury in an automobile accident 10 years earlier. Damon said that he had always desired, and had, control of his life. Although Damon required round-the-clock personal care assistants (PCAs), he asserted that he was still a very independent person:

> I direct all of my activities around my home where people have to help me to maintain my apartment, my transportation which I own, and direction in where I go. I direct people how to get there and I tell them what my needs will be when I am going and coming and when to get where I am going. . . .

Hegemonic masculinity's definition of independence privileges self-reliance and autonomy. Damon required substantial assistance: indeed, some might term him *dependent*. However, Damon's reformulation of the independence ideal, accomplished in part through a cognitive shift, allowed him to think otherwise. Harold, a 46-year-old polio survivor, described a belief and practice akin to Damon's. . . . 'When I say independence can be achieved by acting through other people, I actually mean getting through life, liberty, and the pursuit of happiness while utilizing high quality and dependable attendant care services.' . . .

Social class pla[y]... Damon and Harol[d]... afford round-the-c[lock]... of our informan[t]... ship, many peop[le]... welfare system ... quality of assistance un[e]... much more difficult to conceive... independent. . . .

Perhaps the area in which men who reformulate most closely paralleled dominant masculinity was the emphasis they placed on their occupation. Our sample was atypical in that most of our informants were professionally employed on a full-time basis and could therefore draw on class-based resources, whereas unemployment among people with disabilities is very high. Just as societal members privilege men who are accomplished in their occupation, Harold said he finds both purpose, and success, in his career: 'No one is going to go through life without some kind of purpose. Everyone decides. I wanted to be a writer. So I became a writer and an observer, a trained observer.'

Brent said that he drew much of his sense of self, his sense of self-esteem, and his sense of manhood from his occupational accomplishments. . . . Brent denied the importance of the prevailing ideal that a man's occupational worth was derived from his 'breadwinner' status:

> It is not so important to be the breadwinner as it is to be competent in the world, you know, to have a career, to have my name on the door. That is what is most important. It is that recognition that is very important to me. . . .

Reliance

However, not all of the men with physical disabilities we interviewed depended on a reformulative approach. We found that many of our informants were concerned with others' views of their masculinity and with meeting the demands of hegemonic masculinity. They primarily used the

n, reliance, which involved the inter-
 many more of the ideals of predomi-
culinity, including physical strength,
sm, independence, and sexual prowess.
s some men depended on reformulation for
ch of their masculine definition, others, despite
heir inability to meet many of these ideals, relied
on them heavily. . . . [T]heir inability to meet society's standards bothered them very much.

This subset of our informants found themselves in a double bind that left them conflicted.
They embraced dominant conceptions of
masculinity as a way to gain acceptance from
themselves and from others. Yet they were continuously reminded in their interactions with others
that they were 'incomplete'. As a result, the identity behind the facade suffered; there were, then,
major costs associated with this strategy.

The tension between societal expectations and
the reality of men with physical disabilities was
most clearly demonstrated by Jerry, a 16-year-old
who had juvenile rheumatoid arthritis. . . .

The significance of appearance and external
perception of manliness is symptomatic of the
difficulty men with physical disabilities have in
developing an identity and masculinity free of
others' perceptions and expectations. Jerry said:

I think [others' conception of what defines a
man] is very important because if they don't
think of you as one, it is hard to think of yourself as one or it doesn't really matter if you think
of yourself as one if no one else does. . . .

. . . Jerry said that he faced a . . . persistent
threat to his autonomy—his independence and his
sense of control—from others being uncomfortable around him, and persisting in offering him
assistance he often did not need. This made him
angry, though he usually did not refuse the help
out of politeness. Thus, with members of his social
group, he participated in a 'bargain': they would
socialize with him as long as he remained in a
dependent position where they could 'help' him.

This forced, situational passivity led Jerry to
emphasize his autonomy in other areas. For
instance, Jerry avoided asking for help in nearly

all situations. This was directly tied to reinforcing
his embattled manhood by displaying outward
strength and independence: 'If I ever have to ask
someone for help, it really makes me like feel like
less of a man'. . . .

Jerry internalized the prevailing masculine
ideal that a man should be independent; he relied
on that ideal for his definition of manhood. His
inability to meet this ideal—partly through his
physical condition, and partly from how others
treated him—threatened his identity and his
sense of manhood, which had to be reinforced
even at the expense of self-alienation. . . .

Michael, a 33-year-old manager we interviewed, . . . also internalized many of the standards of hegemonic masculinity. A paraplegic
from an auto accident in 1977, Michael struggled
for many years after his accident to come to terms
with his condition. . . .

His reliance on dominant masculinity . . .
started with his predisability past, and continued
during his recovery as a coping mechanism to
deal with his fears. The hegemonic standard
Michael strove most to achieve was that of independence. It was central to his sense of masculinity before, and at the time of our interview.
Indeed, it was so important that it frustrated him
greatly when he needed assistance. . . .

I feel that I should be able to do everything for
myself and I don't like . . . I don't mind asking
for things that I absolutely can't do, like hang-
ing pictures or moving furniture or having my
oil changed in my car, but there are things that
I'm capable of doing in my chair like jumping
up one step. That I feel like I should be able to
do and I find it frustrating when I can't do this
sometimes . . .

Scott acquired a poliolike virus when he was 25
years old that left him permanently paraplegic, a
situation that he did not initially accept. In an
aggressive attempt to regain his physical ability, . . .
Scott obsessively attacked his rehabilitation . . .

. . . However, he did not return to hockey, the
sport he loved as a youngster; in fact, he refused
to even try the sled-based equivalent.

Here was Scott's frustration. His spirit of athleticism was alive, but he lamented the fact that he could not compete exactly as before:

[I miss] the things that I had. I played hockey, that was my primary sport for so many years. Pretty much I did all the sports. See, it would be like the equivalent to wheelchair hockey. Some friends of mine have talked to me about it, [but] I'm not really interested in that. Because it wouldn't be real hockey. And it would make me feel worse, rather that better.

In this respect, Scott had not completely come to terms with his limitations. He still wanted to be a 'real' athlete, competing in the same sports, in the same ways, with the same rules, with others who shared his desire for competition. Wheelchair hockey, which he derogatorily referred to as 'gimp hockey', represented the antithesis of this for him. . . .

. . . Constructing hegemonic masculinity from a subordinated position is almost always a sisyphean task. One's ability to do so is undermined continuously by physical, social, and cultural weakness. 'Understandably, in an effort to cope with this stress [balancing the demands for strength and the societal perception of weakness]', writes political scientist Harlan Hahn, 'many disabled men have tended to identify personally and politically with the supposed strength of prevalent concepts of masculinity rather than with their disability' (1989: 3). To relinquish masculinity under these circumstances is to court gender annihilation, which is untenable to some men. Consequently, relying on hegemonic masculinity becomes more understandable (Connell, 1990: 471).

Rejection

Despite the difficulties it presents, hegemony, including that related to gender, is never complete (Janeway, 1980; Scott, 1985). For some of our informants, resistance took the form of creating alternative masculine identities and sub-cultures that provided them with a supportive environment. These men were reflected in the final pattern: rejection. Informants who followed this pattern did not so much share a common ideology or set of practices, rather they believed that the dominant conception of masculinity was wrong, either in its individual emphases or as a practice. One of these men developed new standards of masculinity in place of the ones he had rejected. Another, seemingly, chose to deny masculinity's importance, though he was neither effeminate nor androgynous. Instead, they both emphasized their status as *persons*, under the motto of 'people first'. This philosophy reflected a key tenet of the disability rights movement.

Alex, a 23-year-old, first-year law student, survived an accident that left him an incomplete quadriplegic when he was 14. Before that time, he felt he was an outsider at his private school because he eschewed the superficial, athletically oriented, and materialistic atmosphere. Further, he said the timing of the accident, when many of his peers were defining their social roles, added to this outsider perspective in that it made him unable to participate in the highly social, role-forming process. 'I didn't learn about the traditional roles of sexuality and whatever the rules are for such behaviour in our society until later', he said. 'Because of my physical characteristics, I had to learn a different set of rules.'

Alex described himself as a 'nonconformist'. This simple moniker appeared to be central to his conception of selfhood and masculinity. Alex, unlike men who primarily reformulate these tenets, rejected the attitudinal and behavioural prescriptions of hegemonic masculinity. He maintained that his standards were his own—not society's—and he scoffed at commonly held views of masculinity.

For example, Alex blamed the media for the idea that men must be strong and attractive . . .

As for the importance of virility and sexual prowess, Alex said 'there is a part of me that, you know, has been conditioned and acculturated and knows those [dominant] values', but he sarcastically laughed at the notion of a man's sexual prowess being reflected in 'making her pass out' and summed up his feelings on the subject by adding 'you have to be willing to do things in a nontraditional way'.

Alex's most profound rejection of a dominant ideal involved the importance of fathering, in its strictest sense of the man as impregnator:

> There's no reason why we [his fiancée and himself] couldn't use artificial insemination or adoption. Parenting doesn't necessarily involve being the male sire. It involves being a good parent . . . That's, that's not the sole definition of, parenting doesn't mean that it's your physical child. It involves responsibility and an emotional role as well. I don't think the link between parenthood is the primary link with sexuality. Maybe in terms of evolutionary purposes, but not in terms of a relationship.

Thus, Alex rejected the procreation imperative encouraged in hegemonic masculinity. However, although Alex took pride at overtly rejecting prevailing masculinity as superficial and silly, even he relied on it at times. Alex said he needed to support himself financially, and would not ever want to be an emotional or economic burden in a relationship. On one level, this is a common concern for most people, disabled or not. But on another level, Alex admitted that it tied into his sense of masculinity:

> If I was in a relationship and I wasn't working, and my spouse was, what could be the possible reasons for my not working? I could have just been fired. I could be laid off. Who knows what happened? I guess, I can see an element of, but that's definitely an element of masculinity and I guess I am just as influenced by that as, oh, as I guess as other people, or as within my definition of masculinity. What do you know? I have been caught. . . .

Thus, men with disabilities who rejected or renounced masculinity . . . realized that it was societal conceptions of masculinity, rather than themselves, that were problematic. In doing so,

they were able to create alternative gender practices. . . .

Conclusion

. . . Based on our interviews, . . . men with physical disabilities depend on at least three patterns in their adjustment to the double bind associated with the demands of hegemonic masculinity and the stigmatization of being disabled. Although each of our informants used one pattern more than the others, none of them depended entirely on any one of the three. . . .

The reliance pattern is reflected by an emphasis on control, independence, strength, and concern for appearances. Men who rely on dominant conceptions of masculinity are much more likely to internalize their feelings of inadequacy and seek to compensate or overcompensate for them. Because the problem is perceived to be located within oneself, rather than within the social structure, this model does not challenge, but rather perpetuates, the current gender order.

A certain distancing from dominant ideals occurs in the reformulation pattern. But reformulation tends to be an independent project, and class-based resources play an important role. As such, it doesn't present a formidable challenge to the gender order. . . .

The rejection model, the least well represented in this chapter, offers the most hope for change. Linked closely to a sociopolitical approach that defines disability as a product of interactions between individuals and their environment, disability (and masculinity) is understood as socially constructed.

Members of the disability rights movement, as a result, seek to reconstruct masculinity through a three-prong strategy. First, they focus on changing the frame of reference regarding who defines disability and masculinity, thereby changing the dynamics of social construction of both. Second, they endeavour to help people with disabilities be more self-referent when defining their identities. To do that, a third component must be implemented: support structures, such as alternative subcultures, must exist. If the disability rights movement is successful in elevating this struggle to the level of collective practice, it will challenge the legitimacy of the institutional arrangements of the current gender order. . . .

References

Connell, R.W. 1987. *Gender and Power: Society, the Person, and Sexual Politics*. Stanford, CA: Stanford University Press.

———. 1990. 'A Whole New World: Remaking Masculinity in the Context of the Environmental Movement', *Gender & Society* 4, 4: 452–78.

Hahn, H. 1989. 'Masculinity and Disability', *Disability Studies Quarterly* 9, 3: 1–3.

Janeway, E. 1980. *Powers of the Weak*. New York: Knopf.

Messner, M. 1992. *Power at Play: Sports and the Problem of Masculinity*. Boston: Beacon.

Murphy, R.F. 1990. *The Body Silent*. New York: Norton.

Scott, J.C. 1985. *Weapons of the Weak: Everyday Forms of Peasant Resistance*. New Haven, CT: Yale University Press.

Chapter 33

(In)visibility: Accounts of Embodiment of Women with Physical Disabilities and Differences

Hilde Zitzelsberger

. . .

Introduction

Relationships between cultural representations of bodies and people's experiences are fundamental to understanding the conditions that shape the lives of people with physical disabilities and differences in Western societies. Within discursive fields, subjects are produced and placed 'within a hierarchy of bodily traits that determines the distribution of privilege, status, and power' (Garland Thomson, 1997: 6). Consequently, meanings attached to bodies and their lived effects occur in interactions with social and built environments in everyday life. . . .

An exploratory, descriptive study was conducted to elicit how women born with physical disabilities and differences experienced their embodied selves in relation to the ways that bodies are represented in contemporary Western cultural discourses and practices. Some participating women did not refer to themselves as disabled, but preferred the term 'difference'. Given growing discourses about diversity, identities, and social justice, various terms are taken up by individuals and groups. In this article, I use both the terms 'disabilities' and 'differences' to reflect the language of the study group, and refer to individual women as 'disabled' or 'different' according to how they specifically identified themselves. . . .

Methods

Using qualitative methods, the focus of the study was to explore the experiences of embodiment of women born with physical disabilities and differences. . . . The primary research questions were: 'In what ways do women with physical disabilities and differences experience their bodies in their everyday lives?'; 'In what ways do discourses and practices related to disability, difference, and gender shape women's experiences of their bodies?'; and 'In what contexts or ways do women conform to, question, counter, or resist these discourses and practices?' . . .

Introducing the Participants

The study group consisted of 14 women who have lived with physical disabilities and differences since birth. . . .

. . . All participants, to varying degrees, were committed to social and political issues of disability and difference, and many have been involved in education, advocacy, and activism. Pseudonyms are used for all participants. . . .

Findings

The participants' experiences of visibility and invisibility are consequences of a narrow range of normative standards of 'acceptable' bodies that inscribe cultural meanings and values upon their embodiments. . . . Participants also came to see differently by resisting imposed perceptions and transforming their ways of seeing themselves. The findings are described through three processes: imposing in/visibility; negotiating in/visibility; and seeing differently: transforming. Women's stories indicated that lived dimensions of in/visibility were not separate or sequential, but occurred simultaneously throughout their lives.

Imposing (In)visibility

Impositions of others' perceptions of their embodiments were significant in the women's accounts and occurred in everyday social encounters. Hope explained her experience of being paradoxically both invisible and visible in social spaces:

> We talked a bit about me feeling exposed walking down the street in the village, people staring at me and I thought that I was visible there but visible as someone different, someone that has a disability that walked down the street with crutches. So the focus was on physically being visible. Not emotionally being visible because a person could stare at me and see my crutches, but they would not go any further than that. They would not go and think that I could be visible in many different ways. I could be visible as a woman that could have a relationship, as a woman that could be a friend to someone, as a woman that could be seen in a workplace, as a woman that could be a mother one day.

Women's bodies may be highly noticed, yet their capacities, lives, and desires unseen. . . . For example, Angela explained knowing her body as less disabled with the use of her scooter but experiencing a heightened visibility and categorization as a person with a disability. She remarked:

> I felt less disabled because I wasn't as limited . . . but other people started to view me as more disabled. . . . All of a sudden I saw myself as a person with a disability . . . Just having that piece of equipment really identified myself.

Frequently, hypervisibility of the women's disability or difference was described as accompanied by being ignored or shunned. However, some women . . . described highly intrusive and hostile gazes and reactions, which made them feel unwelcome in places that assume 'abled bodies' or preferred ideals of female bodies. . . . For example, Katlin remarked:

> A lot of stuff around the body and disability can be very conflicting at times because society tells you that you should look a certain way. . . . Not that I would even want to look like Cindy Crawford, but you can't always make that, especially if you're a person with a disability. . . . It's sort of interesting because I think . . . if I let myself go, then this is what people expect of a person with a disability. . . . Like I mean anybody could go a little longer than they should between haircuts or maybe waxes or whatever, but you think if I walk around like this . . . then they are going to think, well this is obvious this is a person with a disability and look how they look. . . .

When they could not be securely placed within the narrow range of stereotypical images of women or people with disabilities, the women found that they garnered confused attention from others. Discourses of women with disabilities as non-gendered, non-sexual, childlike, and dependent extend to assumptions regarding of women being unable to be sexual, spouses, partners, or mothers. Noticeable body differences caused confusion and comment. Angela continued to explain:

> When people see me or even get to know me and they know that I'm married and have a family, I think I tend to break that stereotype. And they're really surprised and they'll say that. They'll say, 'Oh, how do you manage?' . . . Or they'll say, 'That's great.' Well you wouldn't go up to somebody and say, 'That's great you have children.' . . .

Negotiating (In)visibility

. . . The women's strategies took multiple and diverse forms . . . Generally, the ways they presented themselves supported how they wanted to be seen and were motivated by the need/desire to lessen social visibility and stigmatization, have a legitimized embodied presence, and a sense of belonging and participation. For example, Inoad stated, 'It's important for me to be able to present myself in a way that will make society accept me . . . I don't want to be excluded and I want to be an equal participant.' She described her actions to subvert other's gazes and responses to her facial difference:

> The projection that I put out is that I love myself, I love the way I look. . . . I need to know that they see what I want them to see. . . . My body language, which is friendly, upbeat, energetic, [laugh] a little in your face, a little pushy. But you know, what kind of makes people not see the other stuff, is my smile, my eyes, eye contact, how I touch people. Of course the way I move my body, like I move in a way I think that says I want to include you so that makes people feel good about who they are, a little, hopefully. I'm open to them.

Women's bodies often are a focal point in interactions with others. Through pulling others into her sphere of her positive self-regard and energy, this woman attempted to thwart negative perceptions and enter into more reciprocal relationships with others. Attempts to put others at ease so that they do not have to confront or accommodate their physical difference are common strategies many participants . . . employed in social environments to minimize social, economic, and personal penalties to themselves.

Throughout the lives of all the participants, intentional strategies have been undertaken to minimize their disabilities or difference, including avoiding social places and gatherings, moving their bodies infrequently or tactically, and/or concealing parts of their bodies. Highlighting her hypervigilance about the visibility of her disability, Jacqueline observed: 'To this day when I look at myself in the mirror, like in a change room, the first thing I think is—does this emphasize the curvature of my spine?' In order to moderate her social in/visibility, Grace remarked on her use of concealing clothing, hair colouring, and makeup so that she can perceive herself as more positively present:

> I cover up as much of me as possible. . . . It covers up the disability side, the side that I think most people don't understand. [pause] Like I feel more visible and more a part of when I do that. . . .

Negotiating disclosures includes complexities beyond 'do I or don't I tell you' such as if, when, and how. In negotiating social ideals of attractive, autonomous, controlled bodies, some women . . . at times chose not to reveal their bodily needs and limits, or minimized their needs for accommodation. . . . Yet, in purposefully negotiating ways to participate, women also transgressed social perceptions that disallow their participation in work and other social places.

. . . All participants, in various ways, sought to undercut inaccurate or distorted assumptions of their personhood and lives, and sometimes to be seen and acknowledged regardless of the response. Despite Hope's desire 'that we should all be who we are' and striving to be more fully present as a disabled lesbian, she discussed the need to navigate disclosures and silences in the context of physical and emotional safety:

> I also try to assess the situation see if it's safe. . . . And in an environment like [accessible transportation], for example, it sometimes can feel very unsafe, because you're trapped. It's just you and the driver and the doors are locked, so there's no escape if the situation were to get a little more confrontational. . . . I feel again invisible . . . I then am silent really. Aspects of my being are not able to come out at times, to come to the surface and be more exposed and because by having someone automatically assume that I'm something else that I'm not. . . .

Seeing Differently: Transforming
Through their lived knowledge of imposed and negotiated (in)visibility, participants moved

towards transforming the value and meanings of their bodies for themselves. This process occurred after periods of questioning and reflecting on their experiences of (in)visibility in many social contexts. In various ways and times, all the women have rejected the ways they are seen through hegemonic cultural discourses about disability and difference. . . . Sunshie, who has struggled with acceptance in her family and ethnic community remarked, 'I'd rather not be around my family because if they can see something bad in me, I can see something bad in them and that's not good.' Through rejecting the 'gaze' of dominant cultures, many women . . . also constructed their own views of their bodies as different from but not an inferior form of what is generally socially constituted as a normative body. Of the value of difference, Villanell remarked: 'Difference can be seen as good thing and you do learn to . . . view difference as a source of power instead of looking at it as a negative thing. I feel a lot of power in that.' . . . Most women described being better able to resist imposed subject positions after exposure to alternative discourses, such as those offered by feminist, disability . . . culture, and activism.

Reconstructing and manifesting alternative definitions, a number of the women . . . exposed, destabilized, and expanded the imposed narrow range of cultural representations of female 'beauty'. For example, Inoad spoke about possibilities of redefining the meaning of her facial difference for herself:

> I think I'm decorated, I think I'm colourful. . . . It's almost like somebody who has a really cool tattoo, like it's art! And I really see myself as a walking piece of art. And it's so strange how other people don't see that.

At times, some women's sense of their beauty and uniqueness resulted from their difference, rather than from similarity to normative ideals. Yet, we live in an extremely visually oriented culture that embraces the dominant idealized aesthetics and demands that we construct and present ourselves in accordance with a narrow range of accepted female physicality. Inoad described this continual conflict:

> Some days it feels like I just want to be like everybody else which would be without a facial difference . . . being like everybody else would be not having a major difference that stands out. Just kind of being average. Just kind of blending in, you know you don't look like a supermodel, you just look like an average person of a specific race and that you can belong in that culture or race. . . . But, most days I am very happy to be different and I thrive on being different. . . .

Discussion

The women's experiences of (in)visibility are consequences of representations of bodies that impose cultural meanings and values that delimit and distance their embodiments from normative standards of 'acceptable' bodies. . . . Significantly, the women's accounts demonstrated, as one participant put it, disability as 'a way of being seen'. Mitchell has suggested 'hypervisibility, and the invisibility that derives from it, are crucial to the experience of disability' (2001: 394). The women's experiences of invisibility and hypervisibility are recursively connected and must be understood in relationship to the other. Given the narrow range of normative appearances and capacities of 'acceptable' bodies, the participants were subject to heightened visibility and invalidation of their bodies in conjunction with invisibility of their selves and lives, as persons and as women. The women's identities and capacities—as citizens, as workers, as lovers, as mothers—often were denied, invalidated, and unnoticed by others. Yet, processes and effects of being seen by others are reciprocal as women's own perceptual experiences informed their ways of knowing their bodies and situations.

As the women incorporated, negotiated, and resisted normative discourses of disability and difference throughout their lives, there was variability in the ways they experienced their bodies and their motivations of action. . . . Participants' stories reflected how being perceived foremost as physically disabled or different by others rendered invisible and/or marginalized their identities and experiences of gender and associated sexual and erotic choices. However, participants were also subjected to social perceptions of what is desirable in terms of women's embodiments. Thus, living within and often interiorizing cultural notions of femaleness or femininity, many women often felt themselves ambiguously positioned both within and outside of the category of 'woman' (Garland Thomson, 1997). With regard to the women who more closely approximated normative gendered conventions of female bodies, heightened visibility of their 'feminine' appearance was linked to visibility of their disability. Similarly, gendered identities and roles of women are built on assumptions of heterosexual sexuality and women's caring work, particularly in the family and home (Fine and Asch, 1988; Morris, 1992; Asch and Fine, 1992, 1997). Categorized and excluded as disabled or different, many women's identities as sexual, spouse, and mother were also unseen or questioned. In acknowledging both disability and gender as discursive constructs with lived effects, the women were engaged in interlocking effects of multiple and conflicting discourses of gender, disability, and difference. . . .

References

Asch, A., and M. Fine. 1992. 'Beyond Pedestals: Revisiting the Lives of Women with Disabilities', in M. Fine, ed, *Disruptive Voices: The Possibilities of Feminist Research*. Ann Arbor, MI: University of Michigan Press, 139–71.

———. 1997. 'Nurturance, Sexuality, and Women with Disabilities: An Example of Women and Literature' in L.J. Davis, ed, *The Disability Studies Reader*. New York: Routledge, 241–59.

Fine, M., and A. Asch. 1988. 'Introduction: Beyond Pedestals', in M. Fine and A. Asch, eds, *Women with Disabilities: Essays in Psychology, Culture, and Politics*. Philadelphia: Temple University Press, 1–40.

Garland Thomson, R. 1997. *Extraordinary Bodies: Figuring Physical Disability in American Culture and Literature*. New York: Columbia University Press.

Mitchell, W. J.T. 2001. 'Seeing Disability', *Public Culture* 13: 391–97.

Morris, J. 1992. 'Personal and Political: A Feminist Perspective on Researching Physical Disability', *Disability, Handicap, and Society* 7, 2: 157–66.

Part XII

Sporting Bodies

Claudia Malacrida and Jacqueline Low

Gendered analyses of sport have tied athleticism to **hegemonic masculinity**, the culturally dominant and normative attributes of masculinity that include competitiveness, instrumental thinking, emotional control, and physical power. Historically, organized sports have been the domain of males, symbolizing their strength, autonomy, and even godliness (Synnott, 1993). In contemporary times, masculinity is virtually synonymous with strength, skill, and power in sport, and athletics defines masculinity in opposition to femininity, which is characterized as soft, gentle, and non-competitive (Connell, 1983, 1995). Feminists in the 1970s recognized the importance of women's access to sports in terms of attaining gender equality and lobbied to gain funding and recognition for women's athletic prowess (Woodward, Green, and Hebron, 1989). The selections by Shari L. Dworkin (2001) and Gay Mason (1992) build on these ideas.

Dworkin argues that, although women have entered into the world of competitive sport in ways that challenge normative femininity as weak or passive, barriers remain to women's competitiveness, particularly in highly stereotyped arenas like strength training and body-building. Reminiscent of Bartky's (1988; see also the introductory chapter of this volume) theory about women policing themselves and their bodies to comply with dominant ideals of femininity, Dworkin notes that women who work out engage in strategies to limit their bodies' strength and mass. Ironically, although lifting weights may offer women the opportunity to experience their bodies as strong and powerful, women's gendered socialization causes them to create their own limits. These women's strategies reflect the broader struggle of professional female weightlifters for recognition in the public realm. During the 1980s, women's bodybuilding appeared to be moving toward increasing power and mass. However, the male bodybuilding establishment has been very resistant to rewarding extreme female bodybuilders, instead promoting women who maintain a **'feminine apologetic'** by keeping their body mass smaller, wearing ultra-feminine hair and makeup, and having breast augmentation to maintain a hyperfeminine appearance (Heywood, 1998).

Mason also discusses gendered tensions related to bodybuilding. Drawing on Foucault

(1977), she notes that **the gaze** is a means of expressing gendered power relations, where typically men observe and women act as passive objects. Male bodybuilding presents contradictions to this use of the gaze, since the muscled male body is highly scrutinized and gazed upon. Thus, media representations of male bodybuilders stress the effort, power, and agency of the men, as a way to counteract objectification. This is not always successful, however, and male bodybuilders remain a subject of derision because of their assumed **narcissism** (self-absorption, particularly in relation to one's own appearance, which is a stereotype that is highly associated with femininity) and their purported impotence due to steroid use (Mason, 1992: 30). Mason also notes that, although women bodybuilders comply with feminine norms through being objects of the gaze, they challenge those norms in terms of their bodily shape and size. Media portrayals of these women thus actively counteract this challenge by trivializing the women's accomplishments and focusing on their tender emotions, their gentle expressions, and their 'seductive looks' (33).

Race, as well as gender, is a significant issue in the study of the body and sport (St Louis, 2003). Over 40 years ago a group of prominent biological and social scientists met in Moscow to discuss the concept of **race**, a concept that presumes that there are 'real' physical and behvioural differences between racially defined groups (Frederickson, 2003). At the end of their deliberations they issued what they called the **Moscow Declaration** in which they concluded that 'genetic diversity within groups is probably as great as that between groups', meaning that the concept of race has no validity (Lashley and Hylton, 1997: 206). However, Brett St Louis (2003) argues that this has not stopped people from making racist assumptions about the supposed 'natural' superiority of the black athlete. In this reading St Louis shows how these stereotypical beliefs about black athletic ability have been **reified** (constructed as real) based on **phenotypical** aspects (observable characteristics like skin colour) of the person and become part of the **ontology** (truth) interwoven into explanations of 'African American athletic prowess' (2003: 76). Such explanations rest on the assumptions that underpin **sociobiology**, a discipline where it is assumed that there are biological determinants for social behaviour, and St Louis argues that they serve to perpetuate racism in the form of 'embodied racial pathologies' (2003: 76).

References

Bartky, S.L. 1988. 'Foucault, Femininity, and the Modernization of Patriarchal Power', in L. Diamond and L. Quinby, eds, *Feminism & Foucault: Reflections on Resistance*. Boston: Northeastern University Press, 61–85.

Connell, R.W. 1983. 'Men's Bodies', *Australian Society*, 33–39.

———. 1995. 'Men's Bodies', in *Masculinities*. Cambridge: Polity Press.

Dworkin, S.L. 2001. 'Holding Back: Negotiating a Glass Ceiling on Women's Muscular Strength', *Sociological Perspectives* 44, 3: 333–50.

Foucault, M. 1977. *Discipline & Punish: The Birth of the Prison*. New York: Pantheon.

Frederickson, G.M. 2003. *A Brief History of Racism*. Princeton: Princeton University Press.

Heywood, L. 1998. *Bodymakers: A Cultural Anatomy of Women's Bodybuilding*. New Brunswick, NJ: Rutgers University Press.

Lashley, H., and K. Hylton. 1997. Guest editorial, *Leisure Studies* 16: 205–09.

Mason, G. 1992. 'Looking into Masculinity: Sport, Media, and the Construction of the Male Body Beautiful', *Social Alternatives* 11, 1: 27–32.

St Louis, B. 2003. 'Sport, Genetics and the 'Natural' Athlete: The Resurgence of Racial Science', *Body & Society* 9, 2: 75–95.

Synnot, A. 1993. 'Tomb, Temple, Machine, and Self', in *The Body Social: Symbolism, Self and Society*. New York and London: Routledge, 7–37.

Woodward, D., E. Green, and S. Hebron. 1989. 'The Sociology of Women's Leisure and Physical Recreation: Constraints and Opportunities', *International Review for the Sociology of Sport* 24, 2: 121–36.

Chapter 34

'Holding Back': Negotiating a Glass Ceiling on Women's Muscular Strength

Shari L. Dworkin

. . .

Fitness, Gender, Bodies

An analysis of women's participation in sport and fitness reveals a highly politicized terrain of gender relations. Contemporary US culture tends increasingly to applaud and embrace athletic, powerfully strong women. The 1996 'Year of the Woman' Olympics, the 1997 premiere season of the WNBA, the 1999 Women's World Cup, and an ever-increasing number of women participating in high-school and college athletics are just a few indicators of this trend. Corporate ad campaigns have hopped aboard the athletic empowerment wave to target women as a demographic, offering powerful messages about female fitness fanatics who 'just do it'. In the worlds of both sport and fitness, muscular ideals have pushed the previous cultural ideals of the tiny, slim body to include 'allowances for substantial weight and bulk' (Bordo, 1993: 191). Thus, many view today's fit woman as embodying power and agency in a manner that challenges definitions of women as weak, passive, or docile (Guthrie and Castel-nuovo, 1998; Heywood, 1998; Kane, 1995; MacKinnon, 1987).

There is some question, however, about the extent to which this bodily agency poses resistance to the gender order. For instance, some ask if the more muscular bodily ideal is merely the most recent form of docile bodily self-surveillance (Foucault, 1979) that aids patriarchal capitalism through the suggestion that bodies need to be increasingly industrious (Bartky, 1988). Further-

more, cheering women on to 'Just Do It' ignores the fact that numerous Third World women stitch Nike sneakers for low wages so that American women may more inexpensively 'just do' their privileged leisure time (Cole and Hribar, 1995; Dworkin and Messner, 1999). While certain women disproportionately benefit from being physically powerful and healthy, an individualized fit bodily politics may be criticized as being removed from collective forms of empowerment that can challenge oppressive institutions and practices (Dworkin and Messner, 1999).

Despite these limitations, many women have experienced sport and fitness as sites of power and agency where they have rejected narrow constructions of femininity and where they can embrace physical power and independence (Bolin, 1992b; Cahn, 1994; Hargreaves, 1994; Heywood, 1998; Kane, 1995). . . .

However, while men's participation in many sport and fitness activities has historically been consistent with dominant conceptions of masculinity as well as heterosexuality, women's participation has tended to bring their femininity and heterosexuality into question (Blinde and Taub, 1992; Cahn, 1994; Griffin, 1998; Kane, 1995; Lenskyj, 1987; Nelson, 1994). Thus, not only do women challenge narrow constructs of masculinity and femininity through being active, fit agents, but they are also subject to narrow conceptions of womanhood that often become conflated with heterosexual attractiveness. Connell's (1987) concepts of hegemonic masculinity and emphasized femininity shed light on this discussion.

'Hegemonic masculinity' is defined as the dominant form of masculinity in a given historical period—usually based on a white, heterosexual, and middle-class norm. 'Emphasized femininity' refers to the most privileged forms of femininity that shift over time in ways that correspond to changes in hegemonic masculinity (Connell 1987, 1995).

Since female bodybuilders have musculature and size that challenge norms of emphasized femininity, women's bodybuilding has been an intriguing realm in which to examine gendered bodily negotiations. Bolin (1992a, 1992b) demonstrates that women's bodybuilding both challenges and reproduces ideals of emphasized femininity because the increasing size of the female bodybuilder is only acceptable once 'tamed' by beauty. It is for this reason that judges of bodybuilding contests have been found to institutionally reward women for various 'feminine' physical markers (e.g., breast implants, painted nails, dyed hair) even when the goal of the sport is to display muscle mass, size, symmetry, and density. And, of course, commercialization is integrally linked to the kinds of femininity that are displayed and rewarded by and in the media. Research on media, women, and sport and fitness has shown that women are not presented solely as resistant and powerful athletes but rather are framed ambivalently through sexualizing and trivializing their athletic performances (Duncan and Hasbrook, 1988; Duncan and Messner, 2000; Kane and Greendorfer, 1994). . . .

The Study

I employed participant observation over the course of two years, four days a week, for two to six hours a day in several local gyms on the West Side of Los Angeles from 1996 to 1998. . . .

In addition to participant observation at the two sites, I also carried out 33 in-depth interviews with women and hundreds more informal interviews with women who attended fitness centres during the course of my ethnographic work. . . .

The Glass Ceiling on Women's Strength

. . . Researchers have highlighted how women in male-dominated fields and professional occupations such as law, science, the military, and business reach a glass ceiling (Reskin and Phipps, 1988). Such a ceiling might be defined as a limit on professional success wherein women attempt to venture upward and are stopped. I argue that . . . the concept is also useful for understanding many women in fitness. That is, women in fitness—particularly those who seek muscular strength—may find their bodily agency and empowerment limited not by biology but by ideologies of emphasized femininity (Connell, 1987) that structure the upper limit on women's bodily strength and musculature. Approximately three-fourths of the women I interviewed at fitness sites expressed awareness of a glass ceiling, which they described as an upper limit on the quest for seeking more muscular strength. This was expressed through a shared explicit fear of and repulsion to female bodybuilders' bodies, a fear of becoming too big or bulky themselves, and narratives that focused on how to structure fitness practices so as to ensure (new definitions of) emphasized femininity. While there was a shared understanding of the limits that women would allow regarding their muscular size, the three groups of women (non-, moderate, and heavy lifters) consciously negotiated a glass ceiling on strength in unique ways. As so much recent work has been carried out regarding heavy weightlifters, I centre here on non- and moderate lifters so as to analyze the largest groups of day-to-day women in fitness.[1]

Non-lifters

It was common for everyday women at fitness sites to express fears that with the 'wrong' kind of exercise, their bodies might develop 'excessive' bodybuilders' musculature. . . . One expression of this fear emerged from non-lifters, who constituted approximately 25 per cent of the women at the two fitness sites. Non-lifters focused on weight work and bulk as 'masculine' bodily villains and cardiovascular work as a 'feminine' bodily saviour. An example of this was Alyssa, a 32-year-old white woman at Elite Gym, who had a small to medium build, wore a tight brown one-piece bodysuit, and agreed to an interview while her legs spun steadily on the pedals of a recline bike, saying it would 'be great to pass the time'. She explained that she was a former drug addict who felt that she was 'fat' at one time but that 'changed one day' when her boyfriend told her she was fat. She said, '[His telling me that was] the best thing that ever happened to me. It totally motivated me to work out.' Alyssa did a cardiovascular workout five to seven days a week for at least one hour a day, with no weightlifting, and explained,

> [I do this to] be more toned, and to burn fat, and to not get bigger . . . of course. I don't want to be buff, but lean. . . . I don't want to look like a female bodybuilder . . . I don't ever want to be nonfeminine. Women should have curves and be soft to some extent, you know?

Alyssa said first that she was once larger because of excess body fat and then expressed fears about increasing in size from weightlifting. For Alyssa and some others, it appears to be *size*—muscle or fat—that is the powerfully feared transgression against femininity (Dworkin, forthcoming; Haravon, 1995; Lamm, 2000). . . .

Other non-lifters agreed that cardiovascular work somehow contributed to the feminine while weights detracted from it. Several non-lifters in fact had lifted weights in the past but stopped because of tension between what they thought their bodies *should* do and knowledge of what their bodies *actually* do. . . . Unlike Alyssa, who had never lifted, Joelle had lifted in the past and knew that her muscles responded to weights in a way that defied what she felt women's bodies 'should' do. Not only did she describe gaining muscle as a masculinized look that she disliked, but she did not even see gains of muscle mass as appropriate to or in the realm of the fathomable for womanhood: 'I should have been a man!!' Last, when Joelle told me that lifting light weights and doing lots of repetitions would prevent her from gaining mass, she reflected a common pattern of discourse I found in gyms. 'They say lift light' was a commonsense solution offered by trainers to female clients' concerns about acquiring big muscles. Rather than cheer women on to simply 'just do it' women were told to not do 'too much of it' and to 'just hold back' on weightlifting. The widespread use of avoiding weights or 'lifting lightly' on the two sites so as to 'ensure' femininity revealed a conscious struggle with what constitutes an acceptable upper limit on women's strength and size. . . .

While numerous non-lifters told me they stayed away from the weight room so as to avoid bulk and to maintain their femininity, a handful of other non-lifters assigned an economy of value to cardiovascular work while stating that weight work wasn't 'necessary'. During the course of fieldwork, some non-lifters did not express an overt disgust or fear of muscle but used expressions such as 'I don't need muscle', 'I don't want muscle', or 'I don't see the need for it.' Looking at the depth of these narratives made more clear the underlying meanings of these frequently offered statements. Cardiovascular work was indeed referred to as the much more valuable activity. For instance, Mimi, a 24-year-old Latina from Mid-Gym, stated that she did not lift weights and instead chose only cardiovascular work because she had 'limited time': 'The goal is to maximize the amount of calories burned and cardio gives me the greatest bang for the buck.' . . .

Moderate Lifters

Moderate lifters, who constituted approximately 65 per cent of the women at the two fitness sites, shared complex and contradictory views of the pleasures and dangers of weights. . . .

Moderate lifters uniquely mediated the perceived pleasures and 'evils' of weightlifting not by avoiding weights altogether but by seeking strength and pushing upward on a glass ceiling on strength. . . . Moderate lifters carefully negotiated this upper limit, watched their bodies for signs of 'excess' musculature, and consciously adjusted or stopped their weight workouts accordingly. So as to mediate an expressed fear of bulk with a simultaneous desire to seek strength, several distinct strategies were used that pushed upward on a glass ceiling on strength yet bumped up against it and then 'held back'. These strategic practices were to 'keep the weight the same' across weight sets instead of increasing weights, to 'stop lifting' weights for a period of time, to 'back off' in terms of the number of days or time spent in the weight room, and to 'hold back' on the amount of weight lifted.

'Keep the Weight the Same'

Lucia, a 35-year-old African-American woman from Mid-Gym, had beads of sweat forming on her temples as she lifted herself up and down off of an incline sit-up bench. One afternoon in the weight room, at the end of her workout, she agreed to an interview off to one side of the weight room where stretching mats were available. She stated that she did cardiovascular work three or four times a week for 45 minutes combined with numerous sets of light weights for 15 to 30 minutes. When I asked her if she could explain why she did her workout this way, she said: 'Well, cardiovascular work helps me to lose weight . . . and I do many sets of the same weight and don't increase it because I don't want to be like some women who are losing their femininity, you know, their curves. I don't want to be like a female bodybuilder.'

Repeatedly, the icon of the female bodybuilder is drawn on to structure women's fitness choices and to make clear where the upper limit on women's size and strength lay. Like many non-lifters, moderate lifters often described a desire to retain their curves and viewed weights as the transgressive activity that could contribute to a 'loss' of femininity. Lucia constructed and was constructed by current definitions of emphasized femininity in which slender is no longer adequate, while toned, firm, curvy, and muscled (but not too much) is (Bordo, 1993).[2] Despite fears about weights and masculinization and a loss of femininity, she did not resolve this tension by avoiding weights altogether (as did non-lifters). In fact, she routinely did many sets of the same weight, strategically working with knowledge of an upper limit on strength, and soothed fears of masculinization by not *increasing* the weight across several sets. . . .

'Backing Off'

Annette, a 33-year-old Asian-American woman from Elite Gym, moved through the weight room with confidence and athleticism. Her movements lacked the hesitation, fear, or uncertainty that many other women's body postures showed. When we spoke, she explained that she 'spun' (took a stationary bike class) six days a week for an hour and lifted weights twice a week for 30 to 45 minutes. She stressed that she used to lift five days a week, 'religiously', for nearly an hour but that she had decided to 'back off' to two days a week. When I asked her if she could help me understand why, she said:

> I like strength, and I like maintaining my physical structure with muscles, but I don't like the look of being too buff. I liked it *then*, but *now* I like lean, fit, a little buff, feminine. I don't wanna look like Cory Everson. I want to lean out more.

Annette pointed to historically arbitrary and changeable notions of 'feminine' bodies. 'The look' she described certainly extended beyond historical definitions of women's bodies as voluptuous (1950s) or very slim (1960s–1970s) to include current ideals defined as 'lean, fit, a little buff, feminine'. Yet she also highlighted other functional uses for strength. Seeking strength and desiring longevity were part of why she lifted weights, while not wanting to 'look too buff' limited her time in the weight room. . . .

'Holding Back'

Kit, a 19-year-old African-American woman at Mid-Gym, had one of the most muscular frames among moderate lifters, and she frequently dared to venture into free weight spaces that were often largely male dominated. During our interview, she stated that her workout included one hour of cardiovascular work once a week and 30 minutes two days a week and weightlifting three days a week for 15 minutes across three exercises (bench press, rowing, and squats). She discussed how she was taught to lift weights in high school when she was on the track team, how she used to play basketball in high school, and how she still loved to 'shoot hoops'. She said that she wanted to 'touch the rim' when she shot baskets and added, 'That's why I do those crazy squats.' When I asked her about her sets and repetitions, she informed me that she carried out three sets on each exercise and that she started with a weight that 'is comfortable' and increased the weight over two other sets. In this way she departed from several moderate lifters who kept the weight the same across sets and instead shared this practice with nearly all of the heavy lifters. After describing how she increased the weight over three sets, she laughed, shook her head, and added: 'My mother says to not lift too much, that I'll get too big . . . so I'm always worried about that.' When I asked her if she ever responded to her mom, she replied: 'Yeah, I tell her not to worry, that women don't have to fear getting big because they don't have a lot of testosterone.' Acknowledging the tensions between bodily common sense and actual bodily knowledge and experience, I then asked her why she was always worried about her mom's warning. She replied: 'Well, I am worried about getting bigger. That's why I keep the reps low and I don't do too many.'

Like Annette, Kit described a functional use for weightlifting. She wanted improved sports performance, and 'crazy squats' moved her toward that goal. At the same time, despite commonsense beliefs that women can't get big, she was concerned about the cultural dictates that women should not get too big. To solve the ironic tension between what women are told they *can't* do and yet *shouldn't* do, she sought improved sports experience but was careful not to increase her size. In this way functional reasons led women to push upward on an upper limit on size and strength, yet at the same time fears of bulk consistently led many to bump up against a culturally produced upper limit on strength and size. . . .

Discussion and Conclusions

. . . When using the naked eye, it appears that absolute, biological difference between women and men is the sole culprit in explaining the bodies we see. What is left out of this equation is women's conscious negotiation with a historically produced upper limit on strength and size. In opposition to quick commonsense claims that women are biologically different from men and therefore cannot gain much muscle, my ethnographic and interview work revealed that muscle *is* something that women can and do gain. In fact, based on tensions between what bodies *should* do, what bodies *actually* do, and culturally shifting standards of emphasized femininity, approximately three-fourths of the women at the fitness sites expressed an awareness of an upper limit on the quest for muscular size and strength. Non- and moderate lifters in fact used very specific weightlifting and cardiovascular strategies in fitness settings to mediate these tensions. . . .

The glass ceiling on muscular size is not simply imposed on women. Rather, they actively define it, wrestle with it, nudge it up and down, and shape its current and future placement. Women in fitness sites are immersed in an arena of continual negotiation as to the placement of the ceiling, which is in part influenced by historically shifting definitions of emphasized femininity. . . .

Despite the message that women should 'just do it', ideals of emphasized femininity lead many women in the weight room to 'just hold back'.

Notes

1. However, it should be noted that while heavy lifters might be assumed to 'break through' a glass ceiling, they also shared intriguing negotiations in narratives regarding an upper limit on strength and size with non- and moderate lifters. Heavy lifters' narratives and practices are analyzed in another project.

2. African-American women and Latinas in the moderate lifting category offered some strands of thought that revealed that ideals of thinness were not embraced. This was particularly evident when transcribing portions of interviews that included discussions of media images from fitness

magazines. However, describing the icon of the female bodybuilder as despised and undesirable was consistent across race for women in the moderate lifting category, as was an expressed cautiousness about musculature and weightlifting practices.

References

Bartky, Sandra L. 1988. 'Foucault, Femininity, and the Modernization of Patriarchal Power', in I. Diamond and L. Quinby, eds, *Feminism and Foucault: Reflections on Resistance*. Boston: Northeastern University Press, 61–86.

Blinde, Elaine M., and Diane E. Taub. 1992. 'Women Athletes as Falsely Accused Deviants: Managing the Lesbian Stigma', *Sociological Quarterly* 4: 521–33.

Bolin, Anne. 1992a. 'Flex Appeal, Food, and Fat: Competitive Bodybuilding, Gender, and Diet', *Play and Culture* 5: 378–400.

———. 1992b. 'Vandalized Vanity: Feminine Physique Betrayed and Portrayed', in F. E. Mascia-Less and P. Sharpe, eds, *Tattoo, Torture, Mutilation, and Adornment: The Denaturalization of the Body in Culture and Text*. Albany: State University of New York Press.

Bordo, Susan. 1993. *Unbearable Weight: Feminism, Western Culture, and the Body*. Berkeley: University of California Press.

Cahn, Susan K. 1994. *Coming On Strong: Gender and Sexuality in Twentieth-Century Women's Sport*. New York: Free Press.

Cole, Cheryl L., and Amy Hribar. 1995. 'Celebrity Feminism: Nike Style Post-Fordism, Transcendence, and Consumer Power', *Sociology of Sport Journal* 12: 347–69.

Connell, Raewyn. 1987. *Gender and Power*. Stanford: Stanford University Press.

———. 1995. *Masculinities*. Berkeley: University of California Press.

Duncan, Margaret Carlisle, and Cynthia A. Hasbrook. 1988. 'Denial of Power in Televised Women's Sports', *Sociology of Sport Journal* 5: 1–21.

———, and Michael A. Messner. 2000. *Gender in Televised Sports: 1989, 1993, and 1999*. Los Angeles: Amateur Athletic Foundation.

Dworkin, Shari L. Forthcoming. 'A Woman's Place is in the . . . Cardiovascular Room? Gender Relations, the Body, and the Gym', in A. Bolin and J. Granskog, eds, *Bodies in Motion: Women, Culture, and Exercise/Sport*. New York: State University of New York Press.

———, and Michael A. Messner. 1999. 'Just Do . . . What? Sport, Bodies, Gender', in J. Lorber, B. Hess, and M. Marx Ferree, *Revisioning Gender*. Thousand Oaks, CA: Sage, 341–61.

Foucault, Michel. 1979. *Discipline and Punish: The Birth of the Prison*. New York: Vintage Books.

Griffin, Pat. 1998. *Strong Women, Deep Closets: Lesbians and Homophobia in Sport*. Champaign, IL: Human Kinetics.

Guthrie, Sharon, and Shirley Castelnuovo. 1998. *Feminism and the Female Body: Liberating the Amazon Within*. Boulder, CO: Lynne Rienner.

Haravon, Lea. 1995. 'Fat Bodies and Foucault, or Inside Every Fat Woman Is a Subjugated Knowledge Trying to Get Out', Paper presented at the annual meeting of the North American Society for Sociologists in Sport.

Hargreaves, Jennifer. 1994. *Sporting Females: Critical Issues in the History and Sociology of Women's Sport*. New York: Routledge.

Heywood, Leslie. 1996. *Dedication to Hunger: The Anorexic Aesthetic in Modern Culture*. Berkeley: University of California Press.

———. 1998. *Bodymakers: A Cultural Anatomy of Women's Bodybuilding*. New Brunswick, NJ: Rutgers University Press.

Kane, Mary Jo. 1995. 'Resistance/Transformation of the Oppositional Binary: Exposing Sport as a Continuum', *Journal of Sport and Social Issues* 19, 2: 191–218.

———, and Susan Greendorfer. 1994. 'The Media's Role in Accommodating and Resisting Stereotyped Images of Women in Sport', in P. Creedon, ed, *Women, Media and Sport: Challenging Gender Values*. Thousand Oaks, CA: Sage, 28–44

Lamm, Normy. 2000. 'It's a Big Fat Revolution', in M.B. Zinn, P. Hondagneu-Sotelo, and M.A. Messney, *Gender through the Prism of Difference*. Boston: Allyn & Bacon, 104–08.

Lenskyj, Helen. 1987. 'Female Sexuality and Women's Sport', *Women's Studies International Forum* 4: 381–6.

Mackinnon, Catherine A. 1987. *Feminism Unmodified: Discourses on Life and Law*. Cambridge, MA: Harvard University Press.

Nelson, Mariah Burton. 1994. *The Stronger Women Get, the More Men Love Football: Sexism and the American Culture of Sport*. New York: Avon Books.

Reskin, Barbara, and P. Phipps. 1998. 'Women in Male Dominated Professional and Managerial Occupations', in A.H. Stromberg and S. Harkess, *Women Working*. Mountainview, CA: Mayfield Publishing, 190–205.

Chapter 35

Looking into Masculinity: Sport, Media, and the Construction of the Male Body Beautiful

Gay Mason

Dillon considered the human body a shrine. His 6-foot, 250-pound frame attested to his disciplined worship of the bench press, the squat, and injectable testosterone cypionate. Dillon loved to oil his delts, flex his pecs, and pump iron. He looked forward to the day he could command $3000 for a three-minute 'guest pose' of his thighs.

At an initial glance the description of Dillon could be an opener for a 'day in the life' story of a bodybuilder. A closer reading, however, might argue that it describes a state of narcissism/auto-eroticism, an adulation of physical power/success/achievement, and a view of the body as subject in the exchange of money, i.e., a commodification of the person.

Sporting activity is a generator of cultural meanings. One of the most important of these is the ideology of masculinity. Some critics argue that the sporting discourse provides a prime site for the construction of 'maleness', offering as it does the learning of a specific combination of force and skill. Connell, for example, maintains that it is the central experience of school life for most boys. Thus, to be an adult male means the ability to occupy space, to have a 'physical presence in the world'.[1] These are visually expressed in sharply-defined outlines, rough textures, and angular planes. Their real significance, however, lies in the ease with which they can be translated into statements of social power. To quote Connell:

> Force and competence are . . . translations into the language of the body of the social relations

which define men as holders of power, women as subordinate. They become statements embedded in the body, not just in a mental body-image, but in the very feel and texture of the body, its attitudes, its muscular tension, its surfaces.

This is important as it is one of the main ways in which the superiority of men become 'naturalized', i.e., seen as part of the order of nature. . . . And it is especially important in allowing this belief and the attendant practices to be sustained by men who in other social relations are personally powerless, who cannot sustain any claim to potency.

Anthony Easthope supports Connell's views. He also claims that the dominant masculine ideology or hegemonic masculinity requires males to suppress the feminine within them, leading to a gross distortion of masculine characteristics. An extension of his argument is that it is only on the playing field or the battleground that it is socially permissible for males to express the feminine since these contexts are so obviously male that there is no doubt as to one's membership of the dominant sex.[2] . . .

The Spectator as an Active Element in the Construction of Gendered Images

Foucault, in his discourse on power, draws attention to the relations of empowerment involved in the act of looking. The relationship between the power of . . . 'the gaze' and gender constructs has featured in more recent analyses.[3] It is generally argued that the act of looking is 'a means of transfixing, possessing, taking control', and it is men who are able to exert this power. To quote Berger:

> Men act and women appear. Men look at women. Women watch themselves being looked at. This determines not only most relations between men and women but also the relationship of women to themselves. The surveyor of woman in herself is male; the surveyed female. Thus, she turns herself into an object— and most particularly an object of vision; a sight.

Most media advertising addresses the 'looked-at-ness' and passivity of women, that is, of women waiting for men to observe them, in this way functioning as an ideological apparatus for the reproduction of gender relations. . . .

. . . [W]hen men do feature in photographs as stars and celebrities they are positioned within the masculine mystique. As Dyer notes, they are usually depicted looking up and out of the picture frame as if expressing spirituality—certainly not suggesting an interest in the viewer. If male models do look at the viewer, the gaze seems to reach beyond the boundary of the frame, (often described as a 'penetrating look'), and is accompanied by a set-expression of the mouth.[4]

Images of men have great difficulty in coming to terms with the contradiction of being looked at and attempting to deny it. One way around this problem is to position the model within the symbols of the masculine mystique. That is, the model may suggest readiness for action, be engaged in some sort of masculine activity, or be surrounded with sporting symbols. . . .

Associated with this are other signs of male power such as muscularity and a hardness of body. Media techniques of lighting and camerawork may be used to exacerbate these qualities. Both Waltes and Dyer claim that this 'hardness' of the body derives from phallic symbolism, and may be emphasized by postures of hardened fists

and sinews, clenched jaws, and bulging muscles. In short, the male subject always strives to be empowering.

Images of men founded on these instabilities are strained, but it is, according to Dyer, precisely this straining that is valued as being the definition of masculinity. Thus,

> [l]ooked at but pretending not to be, still yet asserting movement, phallic but weedy—there is seldom anything easy about such imagery . . . Whether head held high, reaching up for an impossible transcendence or penis jerking up in a hopeless assertion of phallic mastery, men and women alike are asked to value the very things that make masculinity such an unsatisfactory definition of being human.

It needs to be pointed out that since media representations largely construct a masculine spectator, problems are created for the female viewer. For example, in a Hollywood film the spectator identifies with the male hero and with the objectification of the female. Female viewers are forced into assuming a position of masochism if they identify with the female subject, or of distancing themselves from the objectified female and identifying with the male hero. Thus, femininity as spectacle is structured into mainstream cinema. Mulvey, who has written extensively on this topic, asserts that the pleasure of women must involve a 'type of psychic transvestism' or temporary masculinization.

There are occasions, however, when the male hero becomes a spectacle or an object of voyeuristic pleasure in narrative, and an anxiety is created within the text culminating in the body being punished or wounded. Devices used to restore phallic mastery to images of men presented as passive include clenched fists, bulging muscles, the hardened jaws, and a proliferation of phallic symbols.[5] Stallone films, for example, are brimming with masculine signifiers in every frame.

Despite this, it does now seem possible to represent the male body as a pleasurable object on condition that 'this pleasure can be contained within a narcissistic/auto-erotic discourse'. Moore cites representations of George Michael from the pop group Wham, which actively invite the female gaze. She argues that these new images of men seem to leave a gap for the female spectator since they do not present the male as all-powerful, but as an object of pleasure and desire. Thus, it can be argued that as these new 'representations of male homosexual desire' become incorporated into the mainstream they offer the possibility of disturbing 'the suffocating dualism of the theory that provides little pleasure for women'.[6] [W]hat they certainly permit is a 'coming' of a long repressed male narcissism.[7] Male bodies are now being legitimated as an object of desire, though the display of genitals is still forbidden and the phallus, hidden from animation, is still shrouded in mystery.

What is apparent from the material discussed above is the fact that the communication process is a complex one; the media are not merely conveyers of messages, but require, and in fact, are constructors who bring a network of social concepts and ideological conceptions to bear in their reading of media texts.

Media Constructions, Bodybuilding, and Ideology

At this juncture it is appropriate to examine media constructions of bodybuilding texts and their relationship to ideology. A number of generalizations evolving around notions of the gaze, the manufacture of gender difference, and trivialization can be made.

The Paradox of 'The Gaze': Who Has the Power to Look?

It has been argued that political statements are frequently sited in the body. In the case of bodybuilding, these statements are assertions of male dominance expressed as exaggerations of the male physique. Thus, the assertion of muscular power, mastery, and skill are expressions of masculine hegemony in physical terms. A key signifier here in the appraisal of male bodies is muscularity, which, in popular mythology, is a sign of

power. As Dyer describes the process, muscles are biological and therefore 'natural'. Since Nature is inevitable and unchallengeable and women generally cannot rival male muscularity, the naturalness of muscles legitimates male power and dominance.

A paradox exists in representations of male bodybuilders, however, since the roles of looking are reversed and the male becomes the object of the gaze. As Walters outlines the problem:

> The bodybuilder's goal is appearance not action. He is less like the sportsman trying to improve on his time or performance than he is like the woman, who sees her body as raw material to be pummelled, pounded, starved, and even cut into better shape.[8]

This narcissistic admiration of the body offers an explanation as to why bodybuilders, despite their muscularity, are often on the receiving end of derogatory statements as to their sexual prowess and their authenticity as 'real men'.[9] Consequently there is an attempt in bodybuilding magazines to disavow or deflect the subjectification of the male image by a preoccupation with 'bigness' and power, together with statistical details of musculature, size, strength, and achievement,[10] that is, with an excessive display of male signifiers. Frequently this is supported by an emphasis on goal setting and lengthy descriptions of disciplined training programs. Thus, the photograph of Ralf Moller, which reveals what might be referred to as a 'bodybuilding cheesecake' subject, almost 'feminine' in its address to the viewer, is offset by statements as to his size ('the world's biggest bodybuilder') and statistics. 'Bigness' is a concept that dominates media constructions of the bodybuilding industry, although frequently articles will concentrate on parts of the anatomy together with training recipes. Here the actions become a means of deflecting the voyeuristic gaze away from the male subject.

Another example of the paradox of the male subject is provided in the Cyergenics advertisement. The male subject draws on connotations typically used in soft porn. Typically 'feminine' in its construction and photographed with a soft lens, it depicts the body of a young man apparently caught in the act of contemplation, his face turned away from the camera and his body wide open to, even inviting, the gaze of the viewer. However, the written text provides the spectator with the necessary clues for interpreting the visuals viz. he is muscular and strong and commanding; women are entranced by his masculinity:

> She walked with an almost feline grace, calculatingly and hungrily towards me. As she approached me, her eyes seemed to devour me with an almost insatiable desire. It was then that I knew what was going to happen. She reached out to my bare chest and gently caressed my left pectoral, over a stream of sweat and oil. Her eyes left mine and darted to my legs, and then slowly upwards. When our eyes again met, she purred, 'I'm impressed'. Before I could think of something cool to say, she grabbed my tricep and said with total confidence, 'Now, how about a real workout?'[11]

A re-reading of the visual text clearly associates muscularity and physical power with sexual conquest. Despite this, there are tensions between the visual and written texts, and the male as object of the gaze, which are not completely resolved.

The difficulties raised by the subjectification of the male image also problematize the position of the female spectator. Schwartzenegger, who likens his body to living sculpture, argues that since half his audiences are women, women are now looking at men. This implies that women are now taking voyeuristic pleasure in the objectification of the male body and that there is some reversal of roles in who has the 'power of the look'.

Given the usual conditions in which looking takes place in pornography, it would appear, however, that role reversal does not constitute a sufficient explanation for this phenomena, if, in fact, it is true. A number of key elements are still lacking viz. the male subject still controls the look (i.e., he is still depicted as empowering), and there is a lack of sadism and submission built into

the images of men while these features are invariably present with female pinups. It is more likely that rather than a reversal of power relations we are witnessing an occurrence that acts as a support of the male ego system. That is, the male bodybuilder may be more concerned with auto-eroticism than he is with a female audience. In fact, women could be totally dispensed with, since the greatest thrill of working out, in Schwarzenegger's words, is 'the pump':

> . . . [B]lood is rushing into your muscles . . . like your skin is going to explode any minute . . . It feels fantastic . . . [like] having sex with a woman and coming . . . I am getting the feeling . . . of coming day and night . . . I think it's fantastic . . . I'm in heaven all the time.[12]

Perhaps this association of eroticism and bodybuilding is why the video jacket of *Pumping Iron* describes the film as 'A movie with heart, soul, blood, guts, perspiration, and plenty of muscle, a throbbing, mesmerizing, even erotic film adventure.'[13]

The Manufacture of Gender Difference

The preoccupation with control, mastery of the body by the mind, aggression, self-discipline, straining, striving, and sexual potency, and the dominance of women, all sit very comfortably within the masculine mystique. Not surprisingly, visual images of both men and women presented in the bodybuilding industry magazines tend to support this ideology and to follow the conventions dictated for representations of gender. The advertisements for Joe Weider's BIG weight gaining powder are excellent examples. Typically, the males in both these advertisements do not acknowledge the viewer—being absorbed in more spiritual matters; the women are positioned to reveal buttocks, bosoms, arched backs, and most importantly, evince the traditional 'come-on' look in their address to the viewer. While the depiction of successful female bodybuilders is not as blatantly 'feminine', they still tend to be governed by this style of presentation.

This manufacture of gender difference is also expressed in the more literary content of bodybuilding magazines that are designed to cater for men and women. While a survey of magazines reveals a constant diet of articles on sexual potency, hair, achievement, goal setting, food, exercises, etc., the address is primarily to the male reader. For example, an article on skin begins by asking the question 'Are you Mr. Sensitive?'[14] while another on sexual aging states that as 'you get older you may even lose your erection during sex'. Indeed, this article reads more like a *Playboy* copy. Accompanying visuals connote masculine fantasies of dominance and group sex.

The magazine *Muscle and Fitness* does attempt to acknowledge its female readers because it uses non-sexist language in its editorials and usually carries one or two articles specifically addressed to women, as a regular feature in each issue. One wonders, however, whether some of these are also included for purposes of male titillation, e.g., articles on breasts. However, given the general content, the female reader is constantly confronted with a problem of identification that can only be resolved by 'psychic transvestism' or temporary masculinization.[15]

Trivialization

The general bias of sport in favour of men places women bodybuilders in something of a conundrum. If they adhere to the goals of bodybuilding and succeed too well in developing muscle size, they will be penalized in competition. That is, they must not threaten the traditional concepts of gender difference and male domination of physical strength. As one of the judges at the 1983 Women's World Cup in which Bev Francis came eighth, confessed:

> As a bodybuilder you are the best, but in a women's bodybuilding competition I just felt that I couldn't vote for you.[16]

The rules for judging women's bodybuilding contests specifically require that priority be given to femininity rather than to musculature. This standard of difference is enshrined in the rules set out by the International Federation of Bodybuilding, viz.:

> First and foremost, the judge must bear in mind that he or she is judging a woman's bodybuilding competition and is looking for the ideal feminine physique. Therefore, the most important aspect is shape, a feminine shape. The other aspects are similar to those described for assessing men, but in regard to muscular development, it must not be carried to excess where it resembles the massive muscularity of the male physique.[17]

It is therefore not surprising that the media response to female sporting achievement is trivialization, positioning women within a gendered discourse. *The Melbourne Herald's* description of Glynis Nunn's victory at the Los Angeles Olympics is worthy of attention as a paradigm of this type of journalism, viz.:

> Tears flowed like spring rain as the elfin Australian realized she had become her country's first track and field gold medalist for 16 years . . . There were women athletes at the Olympics who were distinguished by moustaches and physiques that would alarm Dean Lukin, and it is enough to say Glynis Nunn was not one of these . . . Here was an athlete of undiminished femininity, who smiled warmly and spoke softly, who ran lightly and jumped and threw with grace, who triumphed with modesty, and who accepted her hour of happiness in the time-honoured woman's way. She cried. That's why the World applauded.[18]

Similar processes are also at work in media descriptions of female bodybuilders. One of the contestants in the United Bodybuilder's Australian Titles was hailed by the *Weekend Australian* in the following terms. 'Michelle's certainly got a great smile . . . She is a lithe, personable, blue-eyed blonde, who would not be out of place in a Farrah Fawcett [sic] look-alike contest.'[19]

The trivialization and gender bias of the media towards representations of women's sport has been well documented. MacNeill, in her comparison between television representations of bodybuilding (The Women's World Bodybuilding

Championships) and aerobics (*Orion Entertainment's 20 Minute Workout*) suggests that ideological politics are a major influence in the program presentations. Analyzing in some detail camera angles, framing of images, and camera techniques, she concluded that these media portrayals were coloured by an apparent desire to ensure the sex typing of the subjects. This was further enhanced by judging criteria and posing. She cites, for example, the use of sexually oriented gestures like bodywaves, arched backs, hand movements, and constant wiggling [20]; women smile, kiss the camera, and create seductive looks contrary to male performances that are presented in a more serious manner [21]; female bodybuilding poses are borrowed from the male competitions carrying with them masculine connotations, but females must also include a dance transition between poses that tend to blur muscular definition. Indeed, posing routine and music are an important factor influencing a female contest's overall placing. Cory Everson, a recent Ms Olympia title holder who is noted for her free posing technique and dramatic music routines, argues that more exciting experimentation in this area can aid ticket sales by making women's bodybuilding competitions more distinctive to men's. It can also keep 'the judges happy'.

Music and verbal commentaries are important media devices for signifying hegemonic ideology. In MacNeill's study of televised women's bodybuilding, the commentary was shared between a female expert and a male commentator whose questions were designed to focus attention on the concerns thought to be foremost in the minds of the audience, viz. 'Are these women feminine?' Ultimately the audience is confirmed in the belief that 'X' woman is feminine since she is a mother and 'Y', despite her muscularity, is basically like any other woman because she has a boyfriend.

We can therefore conclude that while there are tensions for the subjectivity of the male image in bodybuilding, on balance, media representations work to confirm hegemonic masculinity.

***

It has been argued in the foregoing analysis that, contrary to popular belief, sport is an area of human activity loaded with political meanings. Grounded in a 'politics of the body', sport is a prime area for the construction of hegemonic masculinity and gender difference. It fosters force, skill, strength, physical competence, and even violence as masculine prerogatives; it provides an environment for empathic communication[22] and bonding between males. To the extent that it carries out these functions it works to provide men with a monopoly of the means of physical force and to exclude women from exposure to activities that will encourage physical competence. The media in their representational constructions are important agencies in supporting and reinforcing this ideological hegemony, rendering it 'natural', 'normal', and therefore invisible.

Much of the social power of masculinity is dependent upon a belief in the natural physical superiority possessed by males as exemplified and developed in sporting activity. It would seem, therefore, that any real challenge to masculine hegemony must be accompanied by breaking down psychological barriers to the physical competence of women and of challenging the 'naturalness' of muscular development. Women's bodybuilding, because it challenges the notion of physical strength as an exclusive male terrain, has the potential to be counter-hegemonic. This potential is negated by media coverage that continues to trivialize the achievements of women in this area and to depict the muscularity of males as 'natural'. An important liberating factor, then, is a media that assumes a more neutral position in the negotiation of new forms of power.

Notes

1. R.W. Connell, *Which Way is Up? Essays on Class, Sex and Culture*. (Allen and Unwin: Sydney, 1983), 18.

2. Ibid., 28. Anthony Easthope, *What a Man's Gotta Do: The Masculine Myth in Popular Culture* (Paladin: London, 1986), 66.

3. Mulvey, Dyer, Walters, Kuhn, Moore, Gamman, and Marshmerit to cite a few.

4. Richard Dyer, 'Don't Look Now—the Male Pin-Up', *Screen*, Vol. 23. 1983: 66.

5. See J. McKay, 'No Pain, No Gain?', *Sport and Australian Culture*. (Prentice Hall: Sydney, 1991).

6. Moore, ibid., 53.

7. This narcissism is not to be confused with an accompanying change in male attitudes, since if both men and women are looking at each other narcissistically then no advances have been made towards a genuine understanding of gender.

8. Walters, op. cit.

9. Before the availability of gay magazines, bodybuilding magazines were the only accessible representation of the male body.

10. See Margaret Morse, 'Sport on Television: Replay and Display', in E. Ann Kaplan, *Regarding Television*, American Film Institute, Los Angeles, 1983. Morse discusses the use of slow motion techniques and the disavowal of male voyeurism.

11. *Muscle and Fitness*, December 1986: 176–7.

12. Arnold Schwartzenegger et al., *Pumping Iron*.

13. Ibid. Schwartzenegger, the star of *Pumping Iron*, who has stood with a Colossus-like stride over the international bodybuilding scene for many years, displays some very interesting personality parallels with the masculine hegemony. In the film he admits to an obsession with heroes:

(As a child) I was always dreaming about very powerful people, dictators and things like that . . . I was always impressed by people who could be remembered for hundreds of years.

14. *Muscle and Fitness*, August 1988: 25, 38. *Muscle and Fitness*, September 1988: 84.

15. Refer back to Mulvey, op. cit.

16. Susan Mitchell and Ken Dyer, *Winning Women: Challenging the Norms in Australian Sport*. (Hammondsworth, UK: Penguin, 1985), 97.

17. Quoted in Margaret MacNeill, 'Active Women, Media Representations and Ideology', in Jean Harvey and Hart Cantelon, *Not Just a Game: Essays in Canadian Sport Sociology* (Ottawa: University of Ottawa Press, 1988), 206.

18. C. Williams et al., 'Patriarchy, Media, and Sport', in Lawrence and Rowe, *Power Play: Essays in the Sociology of Sport* (Sydney: Hale and Iremonger, 1986), 221.

19. *The Weekend Australian*. August 1986, 24–5.

20. The routines of some contestants at the 1988 Queensland Women's Body Building Championships would have been more appropriate for a King's Cross Strip Show. Erotic gestures elicited the anticipated audience response of remarks like 'look at the bum', etc.

21. MacNeill, op. cit., 201.

22. Refer to Umberto Eco, 'Sports Chatter', *Travels in Hyperreality* (Picador: London, 1986).

Chapter 36

Sport, Genetics, and the 'Natural Athlete': The Resurgence of Racial Science

Brett St Louis

. . . The body, specifically through the interpretation of phenotypical appearances, has long been an important resource for the formation of racist inferences. Placing this centrality of the body to racist ideals alongside the contemporary emergence of more implicit and subtle forms of racism based on the idea of insurmountable cultural difference, sport is now more than ever a valuable and acceptable site for the representation and demonstration of embodied racial difference. . . . The signification of racial group characteristics within modern sports continues to reflect the embodied formation of race evident within much Enlightenment and post-Enlightenment social thought and nineteenth-century racial science that mobilized notions of phenotypical difference as a means to reinforce European civilizational, cultural, and national superiority. Whether it is the reification of a fundamental African-American athletic prowess (Hoberman, 1997), the archetypal tactical ingenuity of white athletes (Burfoot, 1999), or the naturalistic mythology attached to Kenyan distance runners (Bale, 1999; Maguire, 1999), sport can be used to . . . reinforce embodied racial pathologies.

It is worth noting that such reified, archetypal and mythologized representations are not simply benign pathologies that confirm, and remain at, commonsense levels of social explanation. . . . [T]he visual image of sporting performance is both its symbol and its meaning . . . Therefore, an *image* of an athlete running *means* that an athlete is running and, situated within a guiding racial ontological matrix, the success or failure of their individual performance might be extended to symbolize the character and ability of the particular racial group to which they belong. Surpassing the limited salience of popular racial pathologies as scientific forms of explanation, this conflation of image and meaning has been reworked as a symbolic representation of visual and biological truth that forms the basis for many discussions of the causal link between racial genetic inheritance and athletic achievement. . . .

. . . I argue that the notion of the racial basis of athletic ability strategically employs genetic science in order to support erroneous understandings of racial physicality and dismiss the irrational 'politically correct' dogmas of social constructionism. The significance of scientific truth claims within the racial athleticism paradigm and the social authority of science that restricts ethical debate by limiting the scope of critiques within a correct/incorrect science problematic. This article suggests that formal scientific analysis and its 'biocultural' concession to the significant social and cultural formative aspects of racial athletic ability are respectively 'scientific representations' of enduring racial myths . . . As a corrective I argue that such objective scientific analyses of the racial distribution of athletic ability depend on the continual reification of racial distribution of athletic ability depend on the continual reification of racial biological heredity within a social and cultural hierarchy that is analogous with the standard ideas expressed in the longer tradition of racial science.

Sport, Genetics, and Racial Taxonomy

The publication of Richard Herrnstein and Charles Murray's *The Bell Curve* (1996) signalled an important public moment in the race and IQ debate; similarly, recent discussions of the links between race and athletic ability over the past 10 years exemplify new forms of racism that combine scientific and cultural frameworks. These debates, largely prevalent in North America as a result of a longer concern with the relationship between race and sport (Dyreson, 1989), have been conducted within special issues of journals and magazines, as well as significant contributions in single-authored books (Kohn, 1995; Hoberman, 1997). While opinion is sharply divided, Amby Burfoot's 1992 article 'White Men Can't Run' publicly advanced a controversial biological explanation for the 'obvious' and 'incontrovertible fact: black-skinned athletes are winning most races' (Burfoot, 1999: 62). This hypothesis is arguably most vigorously and extensively articulated in Jon Entine's provocatively entitled and controversial book, *Taboo: Why Black Athletes Dominate Sports and Why We're Afraid to Talk About It* (2000).

Broadly put, the arguments for naturalized racial athletic aptitudes might be summarized as based upon an observable and measurable physical and physiological genetic advantage among black athletes. The suggestion is that physical specificities of body size and proportion, namely skeletal structure and musculature, and the physiological facts of subcutaneous differences in the muscles, enzymes, and cell structures, form the basis for black athletic advantage. However, it is crucial to note that these typologies are seen to emerge from a more fundamental *genetic* basis: 'Preliminary research suggests that different *phenotypes* are at least partially encoded in the genes—conferring *genotypic* differences, which may result in an advantage in some sports' (Entine, 2000: 18). . . .

These radicalized genotypes are posited as generating physiological characteristics that, in turn, facilitate specific physical capacities that emerge within sporting practices. . . .

. . . Burfoot and Entine combine the universality of race and the particularities of athletic performance within an evolutionary history of Africa. The disparate physical and physiological attributes required for speed and endurance are understood to have evolved throughout West and East Africa genotype. Therefore, genetic basis of the capacity for speed and endurance within contemporary black sporting performance is intermediately traceable to respective West or East African racial ancestry which, in turn, emerges from an originary 'African' gene pool. . .

The recognition that 'elite black athletes have a phenotypic advantage—a distinctive skeletal system and musculature, metabolic structures, and other characteristics forged over tens of thousands of years of evolution' (Entine, 2000: 18) is not simply a disinterested scientific observation of sporting performance. It is explicitly attached to a political position and the controversy surrounding scientific debates on race has sometimes been understood as a result of an atmosphere charged with direct racism and 'unconscious' racist attitudes (Bouchard, 1988). . . .

Race and the Limits of Science, or, The Science of Limits

The vocational will to truth within the natural and physical sciences has been strenuously scrutinized and notable critiques have regarded the scientific process as one of verification and falsification (Popper, 1963: 215–50), which, instead of producing conclusive proof, acts as paradigmatic knowledge situated within and relative to distinct historical contexts (Kuhn, 1970). The broader limitations of absolute scientific truth claims are conspicuous in the consistent use of disclaimers stipulating that the connection between race, genetics, and sporting ability and performance are *virtually* or *generally* recognizable and that the data used *might suggest* certain conclusions or *indicate* a particular *tendency* (Bouchard, 1988; Boulay et al., 1988; Malina, 1988; Samson and Yerlès, 1988; Burfoot, 1999; Entine, 2000). . . .

The problematical reduction of sporting ability and performance to racial genotype is transparent . . . For example, the enthusiastic belief that the Human Genome Project 'will decipher all 100,000 human genes . . . and tell us more about ourselves than we are prepared to know, including, in all likelihood, why some people run faster than others' (Burfoot, 1999: 54) bases its argument on one strand of *contested* scientific *opinion* on the total number of genes within the human genome and their *purported* functions. . . . [T]he point is that scientific information on, and knowledge about, the function of genes is neither definitive nor conclusive.

Analyses of black sporting success through racial taxonomies and the genetic heredity of athletic ability are further problematized by gender. If the scientific hypothesis of black sporting supremacy is able to assert the existence of hereditary genetic traits as accountable for the racial distribution of sporting ability, then we might easily expect to witness the dominance of black women as well as men. But, regarding women's athletic performance within the same 'perfect laboratory', why is this patently not the case? Why are women's Olympic 100 metres finals not all-black events? Why are we unable to trace the 'racial ancestry' of all the holders of women's world track running records to Africa? . . .

The 'taboo' is thus recast as a mirage, and the well-documented sporting dominance of the 'black race' is reified through the narrow constituency of black *men*. However, the significant problems regarding the particular subject of black men and the general object of race are especially evident when we turn to the term 'black'. The terminological imprecision and confusion over the concept of race presents a major theoretical and political problem within discussions of the racial distribution of inherited genetic athletic ability. The numerous assertions of race as socially and culturally constructed not only profoundly disrupt notions of its biological essence (Benedict, 1935; Miles, 1989; Guillaumin, 1995), but also problematize the validity of its critical and common usage. Even Burfoot and Entine account for the question mark over the organic salience of

race in qualifying the retention of their commitment to scientism. Burfoot concedes that 'the word "black" provides little information about any one person or any group. . . . West Africans and East Africans, are both blacks, but in many physical ways they *are more unlike each other* than they are *different from most whites*' (1999: 59, emphasis in original). . . .

. . . Craig Venter . . . asserted that 'serious' genomic scholarship does not understand race as a scientific concept (2001: 6). Accepting Barbara Culliton's assertion that race 'has no basis in science. The biologic concept of race is now believed to be untenable' the adherents of genetically determined and distinct races might be regarded as outside the orthodoxy of the very scientific community that they draw on for legitimization and authority (2001).

Scientific Representations and Racial Mythology

. . . In the context of sport, when considering the signification of the (racialized) body the simple fact is that disinterested corporeal matter is fundamentally uninteresting. Bone density and structure and the aerobic or anaerobic capacities of muscle fibres, are intrinsically meaningless until they are ascribed particular social values or become a receptacle for embodied experience and knowledge. Therefore, the ability to run is meaningless outside a particular socialized experience and function that is further enhanced by the value attached to being able to run quickly over a specified distance. The perception of sport as a set of universalized physical activities endows it with intrinsic and naturalized properties that ignore the given and interested social contexts that the specific technical, aesthetic, temporal, and spatial structures of sports as well as their particular rules and regulations emerged within (Blake, 1996). This contests the notion of sport as innocent 'play' and recasts it as developing specific bodily regimes that are charged with symbolic significance that animate a series of discourses including race. . . .

These theoretical insights are instructive for understanding the scientific analysis of the radicalized sporting body and allow us to recognize the scientific analyses outlined above as scientific *representations*. . . . The methodological errors of these residual representational and qualitative factors are astutely recognized by Ben Carrington and Ian McDonald: 'It seems that one of the basics of scientific statistical methodology—that all first-year undergraduates know only too well——namely that correlation does not prove causation, is lost on many of those working within university sport science departments' (2001: 6). The production of sports scientists' research hypotheses and subjects, the chosen experimental and observational techniques, and methods of data analysis are inextricably linked to and informed by their subjective and qualitative prior understanding of race (Fleming, 2001). This suggests that the correlation between race and athletic ability is not observed by a value-free scientific eye, but that preexisting ideas about racial, physical, and moral capacities frame the very question and investigation of innate athleticism and athletic propensity. . . .

. . . [Burfoot] begins by noting that when 'pure explosive power—that is, sprinting and jumping—is required for excellence in a sport, blacks of West African heritage excel' (1999: 62). However, understanding the varied requirements of different sports, he notes that as a sport moves away from speed and toward technique and other prerequisites, like eye–hand coordination, the more other racial groups find themselves on a level playing field' (1999: 62–3). Burfoot's conceptualization of the practical and symbolic formations of sport creates a critical distinction between the expression of the 'pure' body and bodily performance mediated by the mind. This distinction does not simply point to different modes of play, but produces racially ascribed ontological characteristics and cognitive abilities. . . . [T]his separation of 'explosive power' and 'technique' isolates the former as a primal physicality (synonymous with 'African ancestry') at least to some degree separated from the cognitive skills crucial for the understanding and execution of technique prevalent within other racial groups.

This distinction between the physical and cognitive realms of embodiment returns us to the familiar scenario of the racialized mind/body split that provided the basis for nineteenth-century racial science that grew out of earlier speculative racial geographies and anthropologies. The discourse of black hyper-physicality that Burfoot alludes to draws on the racial taxonomies that contrast the primal physicality and sensuality of black bodies, and their infantile minds, with the cultured sociability of white Europeans. This is evident in wide-ranging examples that include Hegel's (1975) conception of 'World History' and Locke's (1960) recognition of the 'spontaneous hand of nature' that distinguish between those Europeans who exercised reason to develop and improve their physical and social environment and the barbaric and uncultivated Others who, living as beasts in a state of nature, were unable to master their surroundings and merely collected from the land. . . .

This racially ascribed paradigm where one is *either* physically capable or cognitively endowed is not simply a historical anomaly of philosophical and scientific knowledge but demonstrates particular racialized narratives that have mutated within our contemporary cultural vocabulary. . . . These folkloric narratives that constructed black slaves as automatons and informed the representation of the 'buck' drew on the psychological ideas of black sensuality, exuberance, and instinctive impassivity allied to the physiological notions of significant anatomical difference and hardiness. These popular representations assumed a sporting resonance, drawing on perceptions of a black racial propensity to endure pain, display quick reflexes and maintain a state of relaxation as well as extensive conjectures on physique including limb length, bone density, enhanced musculature, hyperextensibility, projecting heel bones, and durable Achilles tendons. These physical, physiological, and psychological stereotypes are clearly unified in the summation of Dean Cromwell, the head coach of the US Olympic team in the 1936 Berlin Olympics that included Jesse Owens:

> . . . the Negro excels in the events he does because he is closer to the primitive than the

white man. It was not long ago that his ability to sprint and jump was a life-and-death matter to him in the jungle. His muscles are pliable, and his easy-going disposition is a valuable aid to the mental and physical relaxation that a runner and jumper must have. (cited in Hoberman, 1997: 199)

As much as we might like to think that such crude pathologies are now simply historical incongruities, they are continually recycled in a range of examples including Roger Bannister's self-consciously ignorant curiosity over long-defunct notions of racial skeletal differences and climatic adaptation, and Burfoot's equation of Asians' lack of sporting success with 'their' diminished physical stature. . . .

The Biocultural Third Way, or, The Naturalization of Culture

It has long been argued that the participatory over-representation of certain racial groups within particular sports is the result of a socially constructed tradition whereby individuals gravitate towards certain sports and athletic events because of a desire to emulate role models within their ethnic group (Edwards, 1973; Cashmore, 1982). However, while accepting the social viability of this perspective many commentators remain unconvinced of its singular explanatory salience in that it neither identifies nor explains the supposed intrinsic physical ability required for success. Therefore, . . . some revisit the sociobiology paradigm and argue for a 'biocultural approach' as the only feasible alternative to the unproductive polarities of sociological and anthropological constructionism and unrestrained biologism. Indeed, both Burfoot and Entine subscribe to this position and gesture towards the significance of social roles and processes of socialization within racial group sporting achievement as a crucial intangible that undiluted scientism cannot account for. Accepting that '[n]ature (the overall cultural environment) is just as important as biology (genetics)' (1999: 54), Burfoot acknowledges

the efficacy of a biocultural approach that articulates biological and cultural factors. Similarly, Entine suggests that '[b]lack athletic success *reflects* biocultural factors' inasmuch as 'cultural conditions exaggerate the small but meaningful differences that led to the athletic edge' (2000: 279, emphasis added). . . .

The retention of a basic notion of intrinsic biological differences between different racial groups creates a series of problems that prevent this biocultural third way from offering a progressive resolution of the constructionism/biologism impasse. The statement that black athleticism *reflects* biocultural factors and *exaggerates* small biological differences foregrounds the biological factors and minimizes contributory cultural factors. Despite gesturing towards the significance of culture, the stubborn primacy of physical and physiological factors implicitly undermines the salience of an articulated biological–cultural approach. . . .

. . . The very notion that biology and culture are separate entities that might be objectively articulated (and then tacitly disconnected) within a biocultural perspective on race ignores the extent and meaning of their intimate historical and conceptual entanglement. . . .

. . . The blurred line between nature and culture suggests that the ideas and practices of biology are themselves social in formation and application. . . .

'The Subordination of Ethics to Science'

. . . Arguments for the racial basis of athletic propensity are presented as examples of scientific truth that are misunderstood and distorted by ideological dogmas of politically correct notions of social justice.

The caricaturing and dismissal of opposing voices as impassioned and irrational sociological and anthropological metapolitical positions diminish debate and polarize opinion around a fundamental distinction between the scientific objectification of the concrete and the subjective abstraction of social values. This foreclosure is enhanced by the application of methodological exemptions that allow Entine to dismiss critiques that raise the problems arising from extrapolating particular observations into general propositions as demanding an indisputable certainty that create virtually impossible scientific standards. Nevertheless, if, as Entine argues, many major scientific theories would remain unproven if they required validation by 'observable evidence or laboratory experiments', we are left to contemplate how necessarily incomplete and disputable scientific knowledge can be mobilized to definitively dismiss valid social questions derived from ethical premises and humanistic concerns.

The hegemonic authority of scientific expertise can also restrict ethical debate through its implicit regulatory aspects. This is evident in the temptation to position Entine and his fellow travellers within scare quotes as 'scientists' involved in 'pseudo-science', or what Hoberman (1997) refers to as 'tabloid science'. As 'scientists' they are opposed to 'proper' scientists/science and their errors can be explained as the mistakes of 'bad' and 'incorrect' science. Scott Fleming's (2001) excellent critique of the thread of racial science within the history of sports science debates on race and sporting performance points out how many such analyses have been unscientific, illogical, and biased. However, this position implies the possibility of a truly scientific, logical, and impartial analysis of the relationship between genetics, race, and athletic ability without specifying the social and ethical responsibilities of such a redemptive project. Therefore, the unregulated disciplinary and social power of science remains; the dismissal of biological determinism as 'bad science' does not eradicate the ethical dangers of a conjectural scientific objectivity that is disseminated and understood within a subjective social world subject to abstract ethical values. . . .

New Genetics, Old and New Racisms, and the Enduring Fascination with Racial Difference

. . . If, as Marek Kohn notes, '[n]o sport can be assumed to be the sort of culture-free system a scientist would ideally like' (1995: 80), and the genetic codification of racial sporting ability is subject to varied exceptions and inexplicable phenomena, a critical question key to the refutation of racial science remains: why does the notion of inherited genetic racial characteristics remain viable and compelling? Crucially, the frontiers opened by the new genetics have engendered moral and ethical debate on ownership, property rights, and profit attached to medical research, and foregrounded the relationship between the public and the private spheres, and commercial and individual rights. Similarly, scientific analyses of sport cannot gesture towards its social implications without being committed to engage them fully. It is also perhaps most important to note that a belief in the impartial, concrete truths of objective science does not buy immunity from the subsequent ethical ramifications and responsibilities entailed in pursuing a fundamental fascination with naturalized racial differences. Therefore, even though the notion that social behaviour such as criminality might be phenotypically measurable and medicalized as criminal congeniality through the practices of phrenology might appear ludicrous to us now, the articulation of race, genetics, and sporting ability and performance retraces much of the same path. In this sense nineteenth-century racial science does not merely signal naive historical mistakes, but serves as a rehearsal of the articulate racisms of the present that use the simplicity of the common-sense world of sports to animate a reinvigorated scientific racism.

References

Bale, John. 1999. 'Kenyan Runners in a Global System', in R.R. Sands, ed, *Anthropology, Sport, and Culture*. Westport, CT: Bergin and Garvey, 73–95.

Benedict, Ruth. 1935. *Patterns of Culture*. London:

Routledge and Kegan Paul.

Blake, Andrew. 1996. *The Body Language: The Meaning of Modern Sport*. London: Lawrence and Wishart.

Bouchard, Claude. 1988. 'Genetic Basis of Racial

Differences', *Canadian Journal of Sport Sciences* 13, 2: 104–8.

Boulay, Marcel R., Pierre F.M. Ama, and Claude Bouchard. 1988. 'Racial Variation In Work Capacities and Powers', *Canadian Journal of Sport Sciences* 13, 2: 121–35.

Burfoot, Amby. 1992. 'White Men Can't Run', *Runner's World* August: 89–95.

———. 1999. 'African Speed, African Endurance', in R.R. Sands, ed, *Anthropology, Sport, and Culture*. Westport, CT: Bergin and Garvey, 53–63.

Carrington, Ben, and Ian McDonald. 2001. 'Introduction: "Race", Sport, and British Society', in B. Carrington and I. McDonald, eds, *'Race', Sport and British Society*. London: Routledge, 1–26.

Cashmore, Ellis E. 1982. *Black Sportsmen and Society*. London: Routledge and Kegan Paul.

Culliton, Barbara. 2001. http://www.celera.com/genomics/news/articles/02_01/Whose_genome.cfm: 29 March.

Dyreson, Mark. 1989. 'Melting-pot Victories: Racial Ideas and the Olympic Games in American Culture during the Progressive Era', *International Journal of the History of Sport* 6, 1: 49–61.

Edwards, Harry. 1973. *The Sociology of Sport*. Homewood, IL: Dorsey Press.

Entine, Jon. 2000. *Taboo: Why Black Athletes Dominate Sports and Why We're Afraid to Talk About It*. New York: Public Affairs.

Fleming, Scott. 2001. 'Racial Science and South Asian and Black Physicality', in B. Carrington and I. McDonald, eds, *'Race', Sport and British Society*. London: Routledge, 105–20.

Guillaumin, Collette. 1995. *Racism, Sexism, Power and Ideology*. London: Routledge.

Hegel, G.W. F. 1975. *Lectures on the Philosophy of World History: Introduction, Reason in History*. Cambridge: Cambridge University Press.

Herrnstein, Richard J., and Charles Murray. 1996. *The Bell Curve: Intelligence and Class Structure in American Life*. London: Simon and Schuster.

Hoberman, John. 1997. *Darwin's Athletes: How Sport has Damaged Black America and Preserved the Myth of Race*. New York: Houghton Mifflin.

Kohn, Marek. 1995. *The Race Gallery: The Return of Racial Science*. London: Jonathan Cape.

Kuhn, Thomas. 1970. *The Structure of Scientific Revolutions*, 2nd edn. Chicago: University of Chicago Press.

Locke, John. 1960. *Two Treatises of Government*. Cambridge: Cambridge University Press.

Maguire, Joseph. 1999. *Global Sport: Identities, Societies, Civilizations*. Cambridge: Cambridge University Press.

Malina, Robert M. 1988. 'Racial/Ethnic Variation in the Motor Development and Performance of American Children', *Canadian Journal of Sports Sciences* 13, 2: 136–43.

Miles, Robert. 1989. *Racism*. London: Routledge.

Popper, Karl. 1963. *Conjectures and Refutations: The Growth of Scientific Knowledge*. London: Routledge and Kegan Paul.

Samson, Jacques, and Magdeleine Yerlès. 1988. 'Racial Differences in Sports Performance', *Canadian Journal of Sport Sciences* 13, 2: 109–16.

Venter, Craig. 2001. 'Door Opens on Deeper Mysteries', *The Guardian*, 12 February: 6.

Part XIII

Racialized Bodies

Jacqueline Low and Claudia Malacrida

hris Shilling (1993) argues that the notion of a **naturalistic body**, a body that was believed to be knowable through biological facts, emerged during the eighteenth century and has since been used as a justification for the subordination of women, non-whites, and other marginalized groups in society. For example, under the Colonial Period (seventeenth–nineteenth centuries) the success of the slave trade required that blacks be constructed as somehow not fully human in order to enable people to accept them as commodities to be sold and/or held as private property (Shilling, 1993). Among the **cultural myths** (false beliefs) used for these purposes were the beliefs that the African male is 'naturally' driven by unrestrained and rampant sexuality, the bodily evidence for which was said to be an abnormally large penis and the belief that sexual relations took place between Africans and apes (Shilling, 1993: 56). These beliefs helped to construct the black male as dangerous and threatening in his non-humanness. Such myths about racial difference persist to the present day despite the fact that biological and social science research shows that genetic diversity within groups is probably as great as that between groups (Lashley and Hylton, 1997: 206). However invalid the naturalistic concept of race, **racism**, the devaluing of certain groups based on what are assumed to be behavioural traits resulting from physical characteristics, persists (Lashley and Hylton, 1997; Frederickson 2003).

In 'Feared and Revered: Media Representations of Racialized and Gendered Bodies', Sarah Neal (2000) addresses contemporary depictions of black males as dangerous and demonstrates how racial and gender **stereotypes** (assumptions about groups of people based in part on truth and in part on cultural myths), contained in **cultural discourses** (commonly shared ways of thinking and talking about things) of race and gender, shape how certain bodies are represented in mainstream print media. In her analysis of newspaper coverage of the fatal stabbing of Jonathan Zito, a white man, by Christopher Clunis, a black man diagnosed with schizophrenia, she found that the published photographs of Zito and Clunis are both reflective of and also reinforce 'post-colonial notions of race and gender' (Neal, 2000: 103). Neal shows how these notions framed public understanding of the case, fuelling racism and turning attention away from the problems inherent in the British Government's 1990 Community Care Act, in which people with mental illnesses were deinstitutionalized without adequate support in the community.

Dorothy E. Roberts (1990) offers a historical overview of the ways that women's reproductive bodies have been differentially treated, depending on women's raced and classed positions. She begins her analysis with slavery in the American South, noting that black women's bodies and reproductive capacities were not their own, but were instead characterized as economic and sexual resources for white male owners. She continues her analysis with the tensions poor women face between protecting their unborn children from workplaces that are dangerous or toxic and keeping their jobs so they can provide for their families. Taking the question of reproductive choice beyond abortion issues, Roberts develops a **reproductive continuum** that includes everything from the right to become pregnant and the ability to experience a healthy pregnancy, to the capacity to provide care for a child. At each level of this reproductive continuum, poor women and women of colour experience barriers that are systemic, racist, and potentially harmful. Roberts notes that, without reproductive control, all women will face obstacles in achieving equality and autonomy, but for poor women and women of colour, the challenges are much higher and the costs are more personally burdensome.

In analyzing the case of the murder of Pamela George, an Aboriginal woman, by two young white males, Sherene H. Razack (2000) also foregrounds how racism, inspired by the colonial dehumanizing of 'Indian' bodies and sexist representations of Native women within white, **patriarchal** (male-dominated) Canadian society, is inextricably linked to Pamela George's murder. She concludes that this is because such violence towards Aboriginal women is commonplace and that 'men who buy the services of an Aboriginal woman in prostitution, and who then beat her to death, are enacting a quite specific violence perpetrated on Aboriginal bodies throughout Canada's history' (2000: 96). Further, because Aboriginal women have been historically constructed as both less than human and unproblematically available to satisfy white men's sexual needs, the courts found it impossible to imagine that the body of a woman like Pamela George could be considered rapeable or worthy of the same justice that might be afforded to a non-Native woman. As a consequence, the issues of racism and sexism were conspicuously not referred to during the trail and sentencing of her assailants. In essence, Pamela George became **racialized**, meaning that her humanness was erased by socially constructed stereotypes that serve the interests of dominant, white society.

References

Frederickson, G.M. 2003. *A Brief History of Racism*. Princeton: Princeton University Press.

Lashley, H., and K. Hylton. 1997. Guest editorial, *Leisure Studies* 16: 205–09.

Neal, S. 2000. 'Feared and Revered: Media Representations of Racialized and Gendered Bodies—A Case Study', in L. McKie and N. Watson, eds, *Organizing Bodies: Policy, Institutions, and Work*. New York: Palgrave, 102–116.

Razack, S.H. 2000. 'Gendered Racial Violence and Spacialized Justice: The Murder of Pamela George', *Canadian Journal of Law and Society* 15, 2: 91–130.

Roberts, D.E. 1990. 'The Future of Reproductive Choice for Poor Women and Women of Colour', *Women's Rights Law Reporter* 12, 2: 59–67.

Shilling, C. 1993. *The Body and Social Theory*. London: Sage.

Chapter 37

Feared and Revered: Media Representations of Racialized and Gendered Bodies—A Case Study

Sarah Neal

Introduction

This chapter examines how the newspaper media chose to represent two individuals who were involved, in very different ways, in a particularly tragic event in the early 1990s. Central to the chapter is a concern as to what extent certain notions of race and gender shaped those representations. In November 1992 Christopher Clunis, a young man severely mentally ill with schizophrenia, walked onto the platform at Finsbury Park tube station in North London and approached Jonathan Zito, a young man, completely unknown to him, who was waiting for a train with his brother. Christopher Clunis fatally stabbed Jonathan Zito three times in the face piercing his eye. Christopher Clunis, who made no attempt to leave the scene of the killing, was immediately arrested. Jonathan Zito's death and the circumstances that led to it were to dominate populist and policy debates around mental health care provision throughout the early and mid-1990s. During this period a six-month NHS inquiry into the care and treatment of Christopher Clunis was set up and the published report of the inquiry appeared in 1994. This chapter argues that a number of reasons can be identified as contributing to placing Jonathan Zito's death at the heart of public concern. First, and most obviously, was Jonathan Zito himself, an innocent victim who was killed in a horrific manner both in terms of the actual injuries and because the attack took place in the daytime in the 'every day' urban location of a tube station platform. Second, Jonathan Zito's widow, Jayne

Zito, a beautiful and articulate young white woman who had been married to Jonathan Zito for just three months, became an increasingly public figure. (Importantly, Jayne Zito was knowledgeable and experienced in the field of mental health care.) Third, Christopher Clunis was a young African/Caribbean who was also of 'considerable height and powerful build' (Ritchie et al., 1994: 8). Finally, widespread public anxiety as a response to an individual tragedy does not usually occur in a social vacuum and the extent of concern over Jonathan Zito's death can be linked to broader issues of mental health care systems. The passing of the 1990 NHS and Community Care Act has signalled a significant shift in public policy on mental health care. This shift saw the move away from the old and established strategy of containing mentally ill people in institutions towards the practice of care in the community. . . . [T]he care in the community policy heightened populist concern as to what extent the public could be protected from madness. The events of December 1992 powerfully symbolized the apparent inability of the new system of care in the community to protect the public.

Clearly the body in a variety of interpretations underpins these variables. The gendered, feminized body of Jayne Zito; the ultimately vulnerable body of Jonathan Zito; the racialized, dangerous body of Christopher Clunis, and the sane/healthy (public) body ever threatened by mad/diseased (Other) body. The cogency of the combination of these themes, packaged by the media, resulted in an NHS inquiry and, seven years later, it retains a highly evocative place in populist and policy agendas. . . . The media's coverage of the Zito/Clunis story involved the articulation of a range of anxieties that, drawing on post-colonial notions of race and gender, came together to offer particular frameworks for public understanding. . . .

Media, Representation, and Methodology

The relationship between the media, race, representations, cultural myths, and common-sense stereotypes has been extensively commented on elsewhere (Hartmann and Husbands, 1974; . . . Fiske, 1994; Campbell, 1995; Fergason, 1998; Gabriel, 1998) and there is insufficient space to rehearse these debates in depth here. However, it is important to refer briefly to some of the key themes that have occupied the literature. Perhaps the most obvious of these is the way in which the media and the representations that it offers are heavily anchored to the wider socio/economic/political contexts in which it operates. . . .

The media coverage of the death of Jonathan Zito and the circumstances of the tragedy linked directly into a particular set of public anxieties over a changed mental health care system that were being expressed during the early 1990s. The media representations of the individual bodies involved further nourished these anxieties by tapping into the broader 'discursive reserves' (Fergason, 1998) of race and gender. This is not to argue that race or gender were openly named issues in the media reporting of the events surrounding Jonathan Zito's death, but rather to argue that within the visual and written media text it is possible to track a systematic, but coded, *invitation* to make a raced and gendered sense of the Clunis/Zito incident, an invitation to make what Hall (1990) has called 'a racist chain of meaning'. Pictorial images, headlines, and captions are crucial elements of this invitation process as these act as 'cueing devices' that are able to invoke certain discursive reserves (Fergason, 1998: 130). . . .

Transported into the public (populist) gaze via the media it is the coverage of the three interconnected events of Jonathan Zito's death, Christopher Clunis's trial, Jayne Zito, and the campaign for a public inquiry that provides the focus for the primary data collection and analysis of this chapter. . . . [M]y task is to interpret the media interpretations of these events that took place between December 1992 and July 1993 and examine the 'cultural meaning-making' (Campbell, 1995) that the media reporting gave these events. . . .

Racialized and Gendered Bodies

Black Dangerousness

Within racialized and gendered discourses the black[1] (male and female) body represents a number of fantasies that ambiguously veer between fascination and fear, desire and danger, attraction and repulsion (Gilman, 1985; Young, 1994; Pieterse, 1997; Nwekto-Simmonds, 1997). However, the historically constructed link between the black male body and the notions of threat and danger has more overtly dominated white imaginations. One of the most recent and bizarre examples of this domination has been the 1992 acquittal of the Los Angeles Police Department Officers in the Rodney King verdict in which a member of the jury claimed that King 'was in complete control' and 'directing all the action' . . .

. . . Winston Rose was a young African/Caribbean who was suffering from mental crisis. The family doctor decided a period of compulsory hospitalization was needed and called in Social Services, psychiatrists, and the police for the sectioning. Winston Rose, who had no history of violent behaviour and who was not displaying any violent tendencies, was actually sitting in his garden shed reading when, executing the Section Order, the police officers jumped on him and restrained him in an illegal neck-hold that choked him to death. Explaining the reasons for the type of extreme action used, one of officers stated: 'all I knew was that he was big and coloured' (cited in Francis, 1993: 192). The apparent simplicity of the racism of this statement is significant in itself because it obscures the complexity of the connections between physicality and race. Both the death of Winston Rose and the Rodney King verdict demonstrate the extent to which the black male body, irrespective of its actions, occupies a consistent place as a signifier of danger (requiring pre-emptive violent containment) within white racial phobias (Hawkins and Thomas, 1991).

Winston Rose is also important here as he raises the spectre of madness. While the rapist and the mugger are racialized folk devils who continue to stalk contemporary urban landscapes, more recently these have been joined by another folk devil—the violent schizophrenic. In the 1990s the potent fusion of insanity and blackness has secured a place within populist racialized discourses and the practices of various state-sponsored agencies such as the police and the psychiatric systems. For example, African-Caribbean people are diagnosed with a major psychotic illness at five times the rate of the general population, and 60 per cent of those black people who do enter the psychiatric system do so via Section 136 of the 1983 Mental Health Act. Yet only 10–15 per cent of the general population enter psychiatric care through this compulsory route (Sashidaran, 1994: 3).[2] As a result, Francis argues that in the late twentieth century 'madness has become synonymous with blackness' (1993: 179), which echoes Gilman's assertion that 'the mad black is the nexus at which all [white] fears coalesce' (1985: 136). This process has meant that discourses surrounding mental illness and dangerous/violent behaviour, as with discourses around immigration and law and order, evoke notions of race without directly identifying race as an issue . . . Media coverage and interpretations of Christopher Clunis and his killing of Jonathan Zito occurred very much within this *racialized* process, effectively evoking race rather than explicitly naming race as the basis of an explanatory framework of the event. . . .

In foregrounding the question of the freedom of Christopher Clunis rather than, or as well as, the question of the care and treatment he was receiving it is possible to identify an agenda that is actually questioning how a situation had arisen in which a large, young, black, madman had not been contained within either the mental health care or the criminal justice systems. In other words, there is a certain degree of incredulity that is expressed in the media coverage that is not only about the failings of a psychiatric system to treat a severely mentally ill person, but also about the failings of a psychiatric system to detain/contain an individual who appeared to be the very embodiment of a *visible* and *traditional* source of danger and menace in white imaginations.

The media used the concepts of size, blackness, and madness to evoke the obviousness of Clunis as a social danger. It was this obviousness that fed directly into the expressions of incredulity as to Christopher Clunis's 'freedom' and his being cared for in the community. For example, the *Independent* devoted a whole inside page detailing its own in-depth investigations of 'events that led to a random killing' (19 July 1993). . . .

Importantly, Christopher Clunis's body is drawn for the reader at a very early stage of the article (second paragraph). Describing the scene at Finsbury Park tube station minutes before Jonathan Zito was attacked, the article notes that 'several passengers became alarmed by his size [he was more than 6 ft tall and weighed 18 stone], sloppy appearance, and erratic, unnerving behaviour'. Race is the unspoken variable here, but a small head-and-shoulders picture of Clunis is located directly to the side of this information. Through a working of written and visual text the article immediately foregrounds the *obviousness* of Clunis as a figure of danger and menace: large, black, disturbed. There is a colonial undertow within the language used to describe why Clunis alarmed passengers on the tube station platform—his physicality ('size', 'sloppy appearance') and his demeanour ('erratic, unnerving behaviour') evoke notions of primitiveness, wildness, and, ultimately, of the uncivilized. Similar themes are evident in the *Mail's* reporting of Christopher Clunis's trial. The *Mail* tells the reader how '18 stone Clunis, from North London, had been discharged from at least nine mental units over five years despite deteriorating psychosis and a long

history of violence involving a fascination for knifes'. Again it is possible to see here a fusion of physicality, insanity, and danger that is connected to, and framed by, the notions of race. The suggestion or evocation of racially embodied black madness and danger is made via the incorporation, as in the *Independent*, of the visual text. Placed significantly *between* photographs of Jayne Zito on one side and Jonathan and Jayne Zito on their wedding day on the other, a head-and-shoulders picture of Christopher Clunis stares solemnly out, directly above the sub-headline that identifies him as the 'psychotic knifeman'.[3]
. . .

. . . For the media Christopher Clunis was much more than a severely mentally ill person in need of appropriate care that was not made available to him with ensuing terrible and tragic consequences. Placed within the public gaze Christopher Clunis operated within a racialized landscape in which he embodied, at both a literal and a symbolic level, post-colonial anxieties about blackness and madness. . . .

[S]houlders shots of Christopher Clunis, Jonathan Zito, and Jayne Zito form the background to superimposed roughly torn newspaper clippings that scream a variety of headlines relating to mental illness, violence (rape, attacks, killings) and failures in mental health care policy. The seeming chaos of the illustration belies a coherent fusion of populist anxieties that blend concepts of race, gender, mental illness, and safety. However, the extent to which Christopher Clunis, in himself, symbolized the mythologized nexus of western anxieties involved the representation of his antithetical cultural construction—white feminine vulnerability. It is on the racialized body of Jayne Zito that I now focus.

White Feminine Vulnerability

The academic focus on whiteness has emerged as a relatively new area of analysis and although the analysis of whiteness has tended to come from the areas of gender (Ware, 1993; Frankenburg, 1993), class (Roediger, 1991, 1994) cultural, and lesbian and gay studies (Morrison, 1992; . . . Dyer, 1997), the unifying notion behind such a

focus is an interrogation of the meaning of whiteness and the place of whiteness within ideas of race and racialized discourses. As Frankenburg crucially notes: 'any system of differentiation shapes those on whom it bestow privilege as those whom it oppresses . . .' (1993: 1). . . .

Looking at the ways in which the media selected to represent Jayne Zito it is possible to see a process in which racialized bodies are placed (in visual and written text) so as to emphasize not simply the horror of what happened on Finsbury Park tube station, but also to relate that horror to an historical and cultural hegemonic discourse whereby constructions of black masculine violent insanity/danger depend on and revolve around white feminine vulnerability (Ware, 1993). However, looking at the representations of Jayne Zito it is also possible to see a process in which whiteness is able to reproduce itself as whiteness *without* being '*explicitly* set against non-white' (Dyer, 1997: 13; my emphasis). For example, when the *Evening Standard* (19 July 1993) covered the story of the failures of the mental health care and criminal justice systems to detain Christopher Clunis—'A Catalogue of Blunders'—the accompanying visual is simply a single large picture of Jayne Zito, although the actual report has very little direct relevance to her.

In examining the configurations of both these processes what I became aware of as I read and re-read the media coverage in the six months following Jonathan Zito's death was, in many ways, the peripheral position that Jonathan Zito was allocated. . . . For example, on the front page of the *Independent* (19 July 1993) that bore the headline 'The Tragic Scandal of a Schizophrenic Killer that Nobody Stopped' the written text is 'bookended' by two head-and-shoulders pictures: on the left Jayne Zito and on the right Christopher Clunis. Not only is Jonathan Zito visually absent, but what the visual text emphasizes is the juxtapositioning, the antithetical positioning of the white subject and the black/non-white subject. This absence is again apparent in the same issue on the full-page investigation *Independent* journalists conducted into the events surrounding Jonathan Zito's death. The written text is completely dominated by a head-and-shoulders photograph of Jayne Zito that covers at least a quarter of the page. While there are photographs of both Christopher Clunis and Jonathan Zito, these are very small and buried within the text. Similarly, in its full-page coverage of the trial of Christopher Clunis, the *Daily Mail* (29 June 1993) uses three pictures to accompany the text, the largest of these is a photograph of Jonathan and Jayne Zito, on their wedding day, next to this is a picture of Christopher Clunis, and next to this is the third picture that is not of Jonathan Zito, but of Jayne Zito. It is then the image of Jayne Zito that is repeated and thereby emphasized at a visual level. As Jonathan Zito is allocated a decentred position then, Jayne Zito comes to occupy an increasingly centred location within the public gaze. This centred location is set explicitly against Christopher Clunis and inhabits its own place as a site in which the racialized gendered body is reproduced. . . . The reader is told early on in the article of how 'Jayne, whose courage has touched the nation, is beautiful, tanned, and with long blonde hair'. In this way the text provides an immediate connection between moral quality (courage) and a specific and idealized white beauty (tanned and blonde). . . . [F]urther this specific form of femi-

nized, idealized beauty. It is within these arenas that Jayne Zito, as a public body, worked perfectly: she effectively operated at the intersection between a specific, idealized beauty, moral superiority, and tragedy. Just as Christopher Clunis symbolized the racialized and gendered figure of fear in the white pschye so too Jayne Zito symbolized the raced and gendered figure of femininized vulnerability and dignity that also inhabits that same white pschye. Lurking at the heart of the media's use of these symbols are the older notions of the civilized and the uncivilized. These notions have been deracialized and coded in order to operate in more contemporary discursive contexts. For example, the media's emphasis on Jayne Zito's compassion for Christopher Clunis and her knowledge of mental health care served to centre the notion of forgiveness in the face of savagery and thereby mined a neo-colonial theme of civilization. So while Jayne Zito is the 'dignified widow who bears no hatred' (*Independent*, 19 July 1993), Christopher Clunis is the 'psychotic knifeman' (*Evening Standard*, 30 June 1993; *Mail*, 28 June 1993), the 'freed schizophrenic' (*Mail*, 22 July 1993), and the 'schizophrenic killer' (*Independent*, 19 July 1993; *Evening Standard*, 19 July 1993). . . .

Notes

1. The term black is being used in this chapter to refer to people of African and African/Caribbean/American descent.
2. Section 136 of the 1983 Mental Health Act grants the police powers to arrest anyone in a public place whom they deem to be a threat to themselves or others and compulsorily remove that person to psychiatric care.
3. This image is reminiscent of the media coverage of Winston Silcott after his (subsequently quashed) conviction for the murder of PC Blakelock in the mid-1980s. For example, the *Sun* (20 March 1987) used a head-and-shoulders picture of Winston Silcott with the caption 'Face of Monster'. . . .

References

Campbell, C. 1995. *Race, Myth and the News*. London: Sage.

Dyer, R. 1997. *White*. London: Routledge.

Fergason, R. 1998. *Representing 'Race', Ideology, Identity and the Media*. London: Arnold.

Fiske, J. 1994. *Media Matters: Everyday Culture and Political Change*. Minneapolis: University of Minnesota.

Francis, E. 1993. 'Psychiatric Racism and Social Police: Black People and the Psychiatric Services', in W. Harris and C. James, eds, *Inside Babylon: The Caribbean Diaspora in Britain*. London: Verso.

Frankenburg, R. 1993. *The Social Construction of Whiteness*. London: Routledge.

Gabriel, J. 1998. *Whitewash: Racialized Politics and the Media*. London: Routledge.

Gilman, S. L. 1985. *Difference and Pathology: Stereotypes of Sexuality, Race and Madness*. London: Cornell University Press.

Hall, S. 1990. 'The Whites of Their Eyes: Racist Ideologies and the Media', in M. Alvarado and J. Thompson, eds, *The Media Reader*. London: British Film Institute.

Hartmann, P., and C. Husbands. 1974. *Racism and the Mass Media*. London: Davis Poytner.

Hawkins, H., and R. Thomas. 1991. 'White Policing of Black Populations: A History of Race and Social Control in America', in E. Cashmore and E. McLaughlin, eds, *Out of Order? Policing and Black People*. London: Routledge.

Morrison, T. 1992. *Playing in the Dark: Whiteness and the Literary Imagination*. Cambridge, MA: Harvard University Press.

Nkweto-Simmonds, F. 1997. 'My Body, Myself: How Does a Black Woman Do Sociology?', in H. Mirza, ed, *Black British Feminism: A Reader*. London: Routledge.

Pieterse, J.N. 1992. *White on Black: Images of Africa and Blacks in Western Popular Culture*. London: Yale University Press.

Ritchie, J.H., D. Dick, and R. Lingham. 1994. *The Report into the Care and Treatment of Christopher Clunis*. HMSO.

Roediger, D. 1991. *The Wages of Whiteness: Race and the Making of the American Working Class*. London: Verso.

Sashidaran, S., and Francis, E. 1993. 'Epidemiology, Ethnicity and Schizophrenia', in W. Ahmed, ed, *Race and Health in Contemporary Britain*. Buckingham: Open University Press.

Ware, V. 1993. *Beyond the Pale, White Women, Racism and History*. London: Verso.

Young, R. 1995. *Colonial Desire: Hybridity in Theory, Culture and Race*. London: Routledge.

Chapter 38

The Future of Reproductive Choice for Poor Women and Women of Colour

Dorothy E. Roberts

. . . Throughout American history the subordination of women has been tied to their reproductive capacity.[1] . . . Women have been denied autonomy over their bodies and over fundamental life decisions by restricting their reproductive choices.[2] Without the ability to determine their reproductive destinies, women will never achieve an equal role in social, economic, and political life and will continue to be politically subordinate to and economically dependent on men.[3]

We cannot understand, for example, the danger of a company's policy of excluding all fertile women from employment unless we understand the connection between reproductive freedom and equality. . . .

This connection between denying reproductive choice and oppression will necessarily be the sharpest for poor women and women of colour.[4] Because of poverty, these women have fewer real options and are dependent on government funds to realize the decisions they make. Because the government is more involved in their lives, through their use of public facilities and bureaucracies, they are more susceptible to government monitoring and supervision.[5] Because it is harder for them to meet the ideal middle-class standard of what a woman or mother should be,[6] society is more likely to approve of, or overlook, punishing them for making reproductive decisions.[7] Because they have less access to lawyers, the media, and advocacy organizations, and because society has convinced many that they are powerless,[8] they are less likely to challenge government restrictions of their rights. Reproductive freedom is a right that belongs to all women; but, its denial is felt the hardest by poor and minority women.

What are the limitations on poor women's reproductive freedom? To answer that question we must first come to an understanding of what reproductive choice means. . . .

. . . It involves a broader concept of both the words 'reproductive' and 'choice'. A woman's reproductive life is clearly implicated in more than just the decision to use contraceptives and to have an abortion. Reproduction encompasses a range of events and conditions from the ability to bear children, to conception, to carrying a fetus, to abortion, to delivering a baby, to caring for a child. Each stage in turn involves myriad decisions that the woman must make; her decisions at each stage may be affected by numerous factors— economic, environmental, legal, political, emotional, ethical.[9] Reproductive freedom then must extend, for example, to decisions about sterilization and medical treatment during pregnancy; it must include access to fertilization technologies and to prenatal and perinatal care.[10] . . .

A choice—at least where fundamental rights are concerned—means more than the abstract ability to reach a decision in one's mind. A true choice means an uncoerced selection of one course of action over another and the ability to follow one's chosen course.[11] An indigent woman may have the legal option to decide that she wants to terminate her pregnancy. She may even feel that an abortion is essential to her economic, physical, and emotional survival. But if the government will pay for her childbirth expenses and not for an abortion, and she has no money for either option, she does not have a choice.[12]

I do not have the time today to discuss in detail all of the ways that the reproductive choices (in the sense I just described) of poor women are limited. Let me instead use the example of a hypothetical young woman in the inner city—Mary—who finds that she is pregnant. What are the conditions that limit her choice?

Perhaps she became pregnant because she lacked information about birth control or contraceptives were not readily available to her.[13] Or the intercourse that caused her pregnancy may have been unwanted in the first place, either because of abuse or pressure from her partner.[14] Maybe she is a crack addict and had sex in exchange for drugs.[15] Or perhaps she felt pressure to become pregnant from a more subtle source: lack of any hope for employment or other personal fulfillment may have led her to seek self-worth in motherhood.[16] If she did receive birth control counselling, she may have been directly advised to be sterilized,[17] or forced, by lack of alternatives to make sure she has no further pregnancies.[18]

Once pregnant, Mary may have wanted to terminate her pregnancy, but didn't know where to get information about abortion[19] and couldn't afford one anyway.[20] Perhaps she really wanted a baby, but knows she would be solely responsible for its care and can't afford to raise a child on her own.[21]

If Mary decides to keep the baby, it is likely that poor nutrition, indecent housing, and stress have already put her pregnancy at risk.[22] She cannot afford to go to a private doctor for prenatal care and there may be no public prenatal clinic in her community.[23] If she is a drug addict, she has virtually no chance of getting treatment for her drug problem or health care for her pregnancy.[24] If she lives in a jurisdiction where the district attorney has announced a policy to prosecute pregnant drug addicts,[25] she may stay away from any available care to avoid detection.[26] Faced with the threat of jail, she may try to abort the fetus in any way possible. Once the baby is born, she may be tempted to abandon it.

Can we say that Mary has reproductive freedom in any meaningful sense? . . .

. . . [W]hen it comes down to the knife and drugs and taxpayers' money, women don't matter much and poor women of colour don't matter at all.

. . . In *Maher v. Roe*,[27] the court already permitted states to deny welfare payments for nontherapeutic abortions even though they pay for medical expenses related to childbirth. . . .

Of course, the reality for poor women is that these decisions do deny them the choice to terminate their pregnancy. The Court has allowed states to make it impossible for an indigent woman to obtain an abortion (at least a safe one) by foreclosing both government reimbursement for private abortions and the use of public hospitals. And by approving a policy of 'encouraging childbirth'[28] by providing funds for that option alone, the Court has permitted the government to use financial coercion to influence women's reproductive decisions.[29]

Forced medical procedures—typically caesarean sections and blood transfusions[30]—are one manifestation of a rights theory advanced by some legal scholars and enforced by judges. The argument goes: if a woman chooses to exercise her right to have a baby, rather than have an abortion, she forfeits her right to bodily autonomy.[31] The state's interest in protecting the fetus may therefore outweigh the woman's interest in making decisions about her physical health and lifestyle. This is the only area of the law where a competent adult has been required to compromise her own health and bodily integrity for the sake of another.[32] The trend towards increased state control of pregnant women's decisions will have the greatest effect on poor women of colour. This disparate impact has already been demonstrated by empirical evidence. A study of 15 court-ordered caesarean published in 1987 found that 81 per cent involved black, Hispanic, and Asian women; 24 per cent were not native English speakers.[33]

Finally, I want to address what the prosecution of pregnant drug addicts means for the future of reproductive choice for poor women. Across the country, district attorneys have instituted a policy of prosecuting women who use drugs during pregnancy on charges of child abuse and distributing drugs to a minor.[34] Again, the rationale for this decision is protecting the rights of the fetus. The barbarity of this policy can only be comprehended in light of the deplorable status of prenatal care for these women. The lack of adequate prenatal care for poor women already results in a disproportionate number of low birthweight babies and high infant mortality rates.[35] The virtual non-existence of centres for pregnant drug addicts exacerbates the problem for the women being punished.[36] This policy means that not only does our society tell poor inner-city women that we will not recognize your right to choose to have an abortion, we will not recognize your right to have a healthy pregnancy, but if you are a drug addict, we will punish you for having a baby.

It does not take an expert to figure out that these prosecutions will not result in healthier pregnancies. They will have just the opposite effect: they will deter pregnant drug addicts from seeking help in order to avoid jail.[37] This policy will also divert attention from the critical need for universal prenatal care and drug counselling on demand by convincing some that incarceration is the solution to the problem of unhealthy babies in poor communities. . . .

Shouldn't every woman be able to walk down the street in her community at night without the fear of being attacked? (I include rape as a denial of reproductive choice.)[38]

Shouldn't every woman be able to make an uncoerced decision whether to carry a pregnancy to term and have the means to carry out her choice?

Shouldn't every woman have access to prenatal care so that she can give birth to a healthy baby?

Shouldn't every woman who is a drug addict and wants to have a healthy baby have a place to go for help without fear she will be prosecuted for a crime?

Shouldn't every woman have the right to decide what medical procedures a doctor may perform on her body, even if she is pregnant?

I realize that these questions can only be answered affirmatively as broader problems of poverty, racism, and sexism are solved. But I think we can begin by expanding our concept of reproductive choice, understanding its connection to women's status in our society, and recognizing the fundamental, inalienable human right of every woman to control her life by controlling her reproductive destiny.

Notes

1. C. MacKinnon, *Feminism Unmodified* 7, 97 (1987); Law, *Rethinking Sex and the Constitution,* 132. *University of Pennsylvania Law Review* 955, 957–62 (1984).

2. Law, op. cit., 960–2. For a discussion of laws restricting access to contraception and abortion, see *Roe v. Wade*, 410 US 113, 138–44 (1973); *Griswold v. Connecticut*, 381 US 479 (1965).

3. K. Kolbert, 'Developing A Reproductive Rights Agenda', in *Reproductive Laws for the 1990s: A Briefing Handbook 8* (N. Taub and S. Cohen, eds, 1988); R. Petchesky, *Abortion and Woman's Choice 5* (1984) ('Reproduction affects women as women; it transcends class divisions and penetrates everything— work, political, and community involvements, sexuality, creativity, dreams'); *Webster v. Reproductive Health Services*, 109 S. Ct. 3040,

3077, (1989) (Blackmun, J., concurring in part and dissenting in part) ('. . . millions of women and their families have ordered their lives around the right to reproductive choice, and . . . this right has become vital to the full participation of women in the economic and political walks of American life').

4. L. Nsiah-Jefferson, 'Reproductive Laws: Women of Colour and Low-Income Women', in *Reproductive Laws for the 1990s*, 18–19 (see note 3).

5. McNulty, *Pregnancy Police: The Health Policy and Legal Implications of Punishing Pregnant Women for Harm to Their Fetuses*, 16 N.Y.U. REV. L. & Soc. CHANGE 277, 319 (1988).

6. For example, many poor women of colour cannot afford proper prenatal care. In 1986, half of all black women did not receive adequate prenatal

care. Children's Defense Fund, *The Health of America's Children: Maternal and Child Health Data Book* 4, Table 1.1, 51–3 (1989). It appears that in recent years access to prenatal care has actually declined among poor and black women, resulting in high rates of infant mortality and low birth weight. McNulty, op. cit., 293–4; Fossett and Perloff, 'The Poor Need Access to Prenatal Care', *New York Times*, 12 August 1989: 22, col. 1; Hughes, Johnson, Rosenbaum, and Simons, 'The Health of America's Mothers and Children: Trends in Access to Care', 20 *Clearinghouse Review* 472, 473–4 (1986). See also D. Binsacca et al., 'Factors Associated with Low Birthweight in an Inner City Population: The Role of Financial Problems', 77 *American Journal of Public Health* 505 (1987). (Lack of prenatal care is largely responsible for infant mortality and morbidity in the United States). In 1986, the mortality rate for black infants was more than twice that of white infants. Children's Defense Fund, op. cit. Other factors that contribute to the poor reproductive outcomes of poor women and women of colour include general ill health, broken families, lack of social supports, and exposure to environmental hazards. Nsiah-Jefferson, op. cit., 35

7. I view the prosecution of pregnant drug addicts, for example, as punishing these women for having babies. . . . One reason for the recent proliferation of these prosecutions may be society's belief that the defendants, mostly poor and black, do not deserve to be mothers.

   Another example of poor minority women who are penalized for departing from middle-class norms of motherhood are single mothers, especially teenagers. See, for example, *Toomey v. Clark*, 876 F.2d 1433 (9th Cir. 1989) (held state juvenile court's consideration of 16-year-old girl's pregnancy in deciding to bind her over for trial in adult court did not violate her right to equal protection); *Chambers v. Omaha Girls Club*, 834 F.2d 697 (8th Cir. 1987), *reh'g denied*, 840 F.2d 583 (1988) (affirmed dismissal of Title VII action brought by unmarried black staff member of private social club for girls who was fired because she became pregnant). In her article 'Sapphire Bound!', 3 WIS. L. REV. 539 (1989), Professor Regina Austin chal-

lenges misconceptions about black teenage pregnancy and single motherhood. She suggests that 'young, single, sexually active, fertile, and nurturing black women are being viewed ominously because they have the temerity to attempt to break out of the rigid economic, social, and political categories that a racist, sexist, and class-stratified society would impose upon them', Ibid., 555.

8. For a discussion of the political powerlessness of black women, see Scales-Trent, 'Black Women and the Constitution: Finding Our Place, Asserting Our Rights', 24 *Harvard Civil Rights–Civil Liberties Law Review* 9, 26 (1989): 30–4. Black women had to struggle both as blacks and as women to gain the right to vote. Ibid., 30. Black women are under-represented among elected officials and over-represented among the poor. The poverty rate for black mothers is about three times that of white mothers; it is also higher than that of black men. Ibid., 33. Studies of political alienation demonstrate that black women also feel powerless. Ibid., 33. Professor Scales-Trent notes that '[i]n a society which sees as powerful both whiteness and maleness, black women possess no characteristic which is associated with power'. Ibid., 13. She points out, however, that society's view of black women as powerless does not negate black women's strengths and contributions. Ibid, 13, n. 17. See Austin, op. cit., 341 ('Minority women do amazing things with limited resources, are powerful in their own communities, and . . . can mount scathing critiques of the sources of their oppression'). For examples of black women who have wielded political power, see generally A. Garland, *Women Activists: Challenging the Abuse of Power* 119–31 (1988); L.D. Hutchinson, *Anna J. Cooper: A Voice from the South* (1981) (describing the work of feminist, human rights activist and scholar Anna Julia Cooper); J. Robinson, *The Montgomery Bus Boycott and the Women Who Started It: The Memoir of Jo Ann Gibson Robinson* (1987); P. Giddings, *When and Where I Enter: The Impact of Black Women on Race and Sex in America* 46 (1984); D. Sterling, ed, *We Are Your Sisters: Black Women in the Nineteenth Century* (1984): 104–80; G. Lerner, ed, *Black Women in White America: A Documentary History* (1973): 196–215, 319–57, 435–56,

497–520. See also M.H. Washington, *Invented Lives: Narratives of Black Women 1860–1960* (1988).

9. N. Gertner, 'Interference with Reproductive Choice', in *Reproductive Laws for the 1990s: A Briefing Handbook*: 237; R. Petchesky, op. cit., 5.

10. Gertner, op. cit., 243.

11. Binion, 'Reproductive Freedom and the Constitution: The Limits on Choice', *Berkeley Women's L.J.*: 16 n. 23; Tribe, 'The Abortion Funding Conundrum: Inalienable Rights, Affirmative Duties, and the Dilemma of Dependence', 99 *Harvard Law Review* 330: 333–5 (1985).

12. Binion, op. cit., 19j; Tribe, op. cit., 336–7.

13. See Smits, 'Women, Health, and Development: An American Perspective', 104 *Annals of Internal Medicine* 263 (1986).

14. The profile of the most frequent rape victim in this country is a young, poor black woman. A. Karmen, 'Introduction to Part II, Women Victims of Crime', in *The Criminal Justice System and Women*, 185, 188 (B.R. Price and N.J. Sokoloff, eds, 1982). Black women are between two and three times more likely to be raped than white women. Women with incomes of $3000 or less are raped four times as often as middle-income and affluent women. Ibid. One study shows that the rate of rape for black women is 50 per cent—four times as high as that for white women. M. Amir, *Forcible Rape*, table 3.7 (1971).

Police and judges have disbelieved black rape complainants more often than white victims. Robin, 'Forcible Rape: Institutionalized Sexism in the Criminal Justice System', in Price and Sokoloff, 1982; Note, 'Police Discretion and the Judgment that a Crime Has been Committed—Rape in Philadelphia', 117 *University of Pennsylvania Law Review* 277 (1968). For a discussion of the refusal of the criminal justice system to take the rape of black women seriously, see Omolade, *Black Women, Black Men and Tawana Brawley: The Shared Condition*, 12 *Harvard Women's Law Journal* 12, 12 (1989): 16.

Black women workers are also frequent victims of sexual harassment on the job. See R. Austin, 'Employer Abuse, Worker Resistance, and the Tort of Intentional Infliction of Emotional Distress', 41 *Stanford Law Review*: I (1988); Gruber and Bjorn, 'Blue Collar Blues: The Sexual Harassment of Women Autoworkers', 9 *Work and Occupation* 271 284–5 (1982); see Omolade, op. cit., 14; G. Lerner, ed, *Black Women in White America: A Documentary History*, 165; J. Jones, *Labor of Love, Labor of Sorrow: Black Women, Work and the Family, From Slavery to the Present*, 149–50.

The sexual exploitation of black women has historically been reinforced by the view of black women as sexually available and less virtuous than white women. Austin, op. cit., at S70 (describing 'Jezebel', the ideological construct of the black female slave whose licentious ways excused white men's sexual abuse); P. Giddings, op. cit., 82–8; Lerner, op. cit., 149–63.

15. The crack epidemic in this country has had a terrible toll on women. There are indications that in several urban areas in the United States more women than men now use crack. According to a Justice Department report, for example, crack related arrests of women exceed those of men in New York, Washington, Kansas City, Missouri, and Portland, Oregon. Kolata, 'On Streets Ruled By Crack, Families Die', *New York Times*, 11 August 1989: A1, col. I. Some inner-city women who are addicted to crack trade sex for drugs or turn to prostitution to support their addiction. Ibid.

16. Teenage pregnancy is a response to economic and political powerlessness caused by a failing educational system, unemployment, and inadequate health-care services. Austin, op. cit., 558–9. Black teenagers may use pregnancy as a means within their control to attempt to improve their lives. Becoming a mother is a way to secure intimacy, love, attention, identity, and the father's financial assistance. Ibid. 560 ('Teenage pregnancy is a product of the teens' contradictory pursuit of romance, security, status, freedom, and responsibility within the confines of their immediate surroundings'); D. Frank, *Deep Blue Funk & Other Stories: Portraits of Teenage Parents* 11 (1983); E. Anderson, 'Sex Codes and Family Life Among Poor Inner-City Youths', 501, *Annals of the American Academy of Political and Social Science* Jan. 1989: 59, 61–76.

17. Poor women of colour have been subjected to sterilization abuse for decades. This abuse may take

the form of blatant coercion and trickery or more subtle influences on women's decisions to be sterilized. Nsiah-Jefferson, op. cit., 44–5; Levin and Taub, 'Reproductive Rights', in C. Lefcourt, ed, *Women and the Law*: 10A-27-28 (1987); Clarke, 'Subtle Forms of Sterilization Abuse: A Reproductive Rights Analysis', in R. Arditti, R.D. Klein, and S. Minden, eds, *Test-Tube Women* (1984). In the 1970s, for example, doctors conditioned delivering babies and performing abortions on consent to sterilization. Physicians and other health-care providers still urge minority women to consent to sterilization because they view their family size as excessive or believe these women are incapable of effectively using other methods of birth control. Nsiah-Jefferson, op. cit., 44–5.

18. Sterilization services are provided by states under the Medicaid program, while information about and access to other contraceptive techniques may not be available. Ibid., 45–6.

19. Federal regulations prohibit abortion counselling and referral by family planning clinics that receive funds under Title X of the Public Health Service Act. See *New York v. Sullivan*, 889 F.2d 401 (2d. Cir. 1989) (holding that these regulations do not violate the constitutional rights of pregnant women); *Massachusetts v. HHS*, 58 U.S.L.W. 2564 (1st Cir. 1989) (holding that the regulations are unconstitutional). These regulations mean that poor women who use Title X-funded clinics are unable to obtain information about abortions at the clinic or even learn where such information can be obtained.

20. The limits on federal and state Medicaid funding for abortion make it impossible for many indigent women to obtain abortions. See generally, V. O'Hair, 'A Brief History of Abortion in the United States', 262 *Journal of the American Medical Association* 1875 (1989). The Supreme Court has upheld the denial of funding for abortions that are not necessary to save the life of the mother. *Harris v. McRae*, 448 US 297 (1980). See discussion at 18–19, *infra*. Even where state Medicaid funding is available, poor women may not be able to obtain abortions due to misinformation. Women are not always informed of their right to obtain Medicaid-funded abortions because abortion providers are either unaware that reimbursement is available or are unwilling to accept Medicaid. Nsiah-Jefferson, op. cit., 20–1.

Another obstacle to obtaining an abortion is the increasing difficulty in finding doctors who will perform them. Access to abortion services is especially limited for women living in rural areas. Eighty-two per cent of the 3116 counties in the United States have no abortion services at all. Ibid., 21; Belkin, 'Women in Rural Areas Face Many Barriers to Abortions', *New York Times*, 11 July 1989: AI, col. 3. In northern Minnesota, for example, one clinic in Duluth is the only source of abortions for 24 neighbouring counties. The doctor who performs these abortions flies in from Minneapolis once a week because local doctors refuse to perform the procedure. Belkin, op. cit, A1. Native American women who live on reservations are among the most restricted. Not only are they denied federal funding for abortions, but Indian Health Services facilities (which may be the only available health care within hundreds of miles) are prohibited from performing abortions even if private funds are available. Nsiah-Jefferson, op. cit., 21–2.

There have been recent reports that fewer doctors throughout the country are willing to perform abortions because of the stigma and harassment they experience. See Kolata, 'Under Pressures and Stigma, More Doctors Shun Abortion', *New York Times*, 8 January 1990: A1, col. 1; Letters, 'Harassment Makes Doctors Fear Abortion', *New York Times*, 22 January 1990: A.14, col. 3. This growing shortage of abortion services has the greatest impact on poor women who cannot afford the cost of travelling to available facilities.

21. In 1984, 52 per cent of black female-headed families lived in poverty. G. Jaynes and R. Williams, eds, *A Common Destiny: Blacks and American Society* 279 (1989).

22. Nsaiah-Jefferson, op. cit., 35; Institute of Medicine, *Preventing Low Birthweight* 52–72 (1985).

23. See note 6.

24. The needs of pregnant addicts have been virtually ignored by drug treatment programs. Treatment centres either overtly refuse to treat pregnant women or are effectively closed to them because of

lengthy waiting lists or lack of child care. R. Brotman, D. Hutson, and F. Suffet, eds, *Pregnant Addicts and Their Children: A Comprehensive Care Approach* 21 (1984); McNulty, op. cit., 301–02. A recent survey of 78 drug treatment programs in New York City conducted by Dr Wendy Chavkin revealed that 54 per cent denied treatment to pregnant women; 67 per cent refused to treat pregnant addicts on Medicaid; and 87 per cent excluded pregnant women on Medicaid addicted specifically to crack. Less than half of those programs that did accept pregnant addicts provided prenatal care and only two provided child care. Chavkin, 'Help, Don't Jail, Addicted Mothers', *New York Times*, 18 July 1989: A21, cot. 2. See also Marriott, 'Treatment for Addicts Is as Elusive as Ever', *New York Times*, 9 July 1989: E5, col. 4 (New York State offers fewer than 50,000 drug treatment slots, compared to an estimated 879,800 heavy drug users).

25. There has been a growing trend across the country to prosecute women who give birth to drug-exposed babies. At least 50 so-called 'fetal abuse' cases have been brought nationwide. Paltrow, Fox, and Goetz, 'State by State Case Summary of Criminal Prosecutions Against Pregnant Women and Appendix of Public Health and Public Interest Groups Opposed to These Prosecutions', 20 April 1990 (unpublished memorandum to ACLU Affiliates and Interested parties on file with *The Women's Rights Law Reporter*; Lewin, 'Drug Use in Pregnancy: New Issue for the Courts', *New York Times*, 5 February 1990: A14, col. 1. See generally, 'Jail For Crack Moms?' *Christian Science Monitor*, 25 October, 1989: 20, col. 1; Sherman, *Keeping Babies Free of Drugs,* The National Law Journal, 16 October 1989, at 1, col. 4; McNamara, 'Fetal Endangerment Cases on the Rise', *Boston Globe*, 3 October 1989: 1, col. 1. In July 1989, a black crack addict named Jennifer Johnson was convicted in Florida on two counts of delivering a controlled substance to a minor based on traces of a cocaine metabolite found in the urine of her newborn children. *State v. Johnson*, No. E89-890-CFA, slip op. (Fla. Cir. Ct. 13 July 1989). The prosecution's theory was that Ms Johnson delivered the cocaine metabolite to her children during the 60-second period that blood was still pumped through the umbilical cord after the babies were delivered.

In addition, judges have sentenced pregnant drug addicts charged with unrelated crimes to prison sentences in order to protect the fetus. Cohen, 'When a Fetus Has More Rights Than the Mother', *Washington Post*, 28 July 1988: A21, col. I; Lewin, 'When Courts Take Charge of the Unborn', *New York Times*, 9 January 1989: AI, col. 1; Davidson, 'Pregnant Addicts: Drug Babies Push Issue of Fetal Rights', *L.A. Times*, 25 April 1989: pt. 1, p. l, col. 1. See *United States v. Vaughn*, Crim. No. F 2172-88 B (DC Super. Ct. 1988). State lawmakers have introduced legislation designed to facilitate the prosecution of women who use drugs during pregnancy. Marcotte, 'Crime and Pregnancy', A.B.A.J. Aug. 1989: 14.

The most common penalty imposed on women who use drugs during pregnancy is the immediate removal of their newborns. Some child protection agencies automatically institute neglect proceedings to obtain custody of babies with positive toxicologies. Sherman, op. cit.; Davidson, op. cit; Besharov, 'Crack Babies: The Worst Threat Is Mom Herself', *The Washington Post* 6 August 1989: Bl, col. 1.

26. See Paltrow, '"Fetal Abuse": Should We Recognize It as A Crime?', A.B.A.J. Aug. 1989: 39; McNulty, op. cit., 308 and n. 207; G. Annas, 'Protecting the Liberty of Pregnant Patients', 316 *New England Journal of Medicine*: 1213, 1214 (1987).

27. 432 U.S. 464 (1977).

28. The Supreme Court has held that states may 'make a value judgment favouring childbirth over abortion'. Maher, 432 US: 474. They may also implement that judgment by 'encouraging childbirth' through the allocation of public funds. Ibid.; Webster, 109 S. Ct. at 3052.

29. See note 12.

30. See generally Gallagher, 'Medical Choices During Pregnancy: Whose Decision Is It Anyway?', 41 *Rutgers Law Review* 591 (1989); Kolder, Gallagher, and Parsons, 'Court-Ordered Obstetrical Interventions', 316 *New England Journal of Medicine* 1192 (1987); Rhoden, 'The Judge in the Delivery Room: The Emergence of Court-Ordered Caesareans,' 74

California Law Review 1951 (1986).

31. Robertson, 'Procreative Liberty and the Control of Conception, Pregnancy, and Childbirth', 69 *Virginia Law Review* 405, 437–8 (1983); Robertson, 'The Right to Procreate and in Utero Fetal Therapy', 3 *Journal of Legal Medicine* 333, 359 (1982). Other commentators have proposed a balancing approach weighing the mother's rights against those of the fetus—to justify overriding a woman's right to bodily autonomy in favor of fetal protection. See, for example, Note, 'Developing Maternal Liability Standards for Prenatal Injury', 61 *St John's Law Review* 592, 610–12 (1987); Mathieu, 'Respecting Liberty and Preventing Harm: Limits of State Intervention in Prenatal Choice', 8 *Harvard Journal of Law and Public Policy* 19, 45–54 (1985); Myers, 'Abuse and Neglect of the Unborn: Can the State Intervene?', 23 *DUG Law Review*. 1, 62–5 (1984); Note, 'Parental Liability for Prenatal Injury', 14 *Columbia Journal of Law and Social Problems*. 47, 77–80 (1978).

32. Goldberg, op. cit., 594–5 and n. 24 (1989); Rhoden, op. cit., 1975–82.

33. Kolder, Gallagher, and Parsons, op. cit., 1192–96. See Gallagher, 'Fetus as Patient', in *Reproductive Laws for the 1990s: A Briefing Handbook* 157, 183–4.

34. See note 25.

35. See note 6.

36. See note 26.

37. See note 26 and accompanying text.

38. See Stefan, 'Whose Egg Is It Anyway?: Reproductive Rights of Incarcerated, Institutionalized, and Incompetent Women', 13 *NOVA Law Review*. 405, 427 (1989).

Chapter 39

Gendered Racial Violence and Spatialized Justice: The Murder of Pamela George

Sherene H. Razack

. . .

Introduction

On Easter weekend, 17 April 1995, Pamela George, a woman of the Saulteaux (Ojibway) nation and a mother of two young children, was brutally murdered in Regina, a small Canadian prairie city. Beyond the fact that Pamela George came from the Sakimay reserve on the outskirts of the city, and that she occasionally worked as a prostitute, . . . court records of the trial of the two white men accused of her murder and media coverage of the event reveal few details of her life or the life of her community. More is known about her two murderers, young, white, middle-class men. . . . Nineteen-year-old university athletes Steven Kummerfield and Alex Ternowetsky set out to celebrate the end of term. They went out drinking in isolated areas . . . and then cruised 'the Stroll', the city's streets of prostitution. Eventually, after failing to persuade one Aboriginal woman working as a prostitute to join them in the car, . . . they finally succeeded in persuading another Aboriginal woman, Pamela George, who was working as a prostitute that night, to enter the car. The two men drove George to an isolated area outside the city, a place littered with bullet casings and condoms. Following oral sex, they took turns brutally beating her and left her lying with her face in the mud. . . . The next morning, . . . they heard a radio report describing a body found outside the city. After both first confided their involvement in the murder to a number of friends and to one of their parents, one man left town to take up his summer job planting trees in the northern forests of British Columbia. The other man flew to the mountain resort of Banff, Alberta . . . In early May, nearly one month after the murder, after following a tip and having exhausted the list of suspects who were mostly Aboriginal and/or of the 'streets' of the Stroll, the Royal Canadian Mounted Police (RCMP) arrested both men for the murder of Pamela George. The arrest of two young, white, middle-class men for the murder of an Aboriginal woman working as a prostitute sent shock waves through the white population of this small prairie city.

At the trial two years later, the Defence at first tried to argue that Pamela George managed to walk away from the isolated field and was killed by someone else, an Aboriginal man. They also argued that since both men were highly intoxicated, they bore diminished responsibility for the beating. . . . Both the Crown and the Defence maintained that the fact that Pamela George was a prostitute was something to be considered in the case.[1] The judge sparked a public furor when he instructed the jury to bear this in mind in their deliberations. The men were convicted of manslaughter and sentenced to six and a half years in prison . . . The objections of the Native community and some members of the white community stemmed from their belief that the crime was at the very least one of second-degree murder and that the judge acted improperly in directing the jury to a finding of manslaughter.[2] . . .

I propose to show that a number of factors contributed to masking the violence of the two accused and thus diminishing their culpability and legal responsibility for the death of Pamela George. Primarily, I claim that because Pamela George was considered to belong to a space in which violence routinely occurs, and to have a body that is routinely violated, while her killers were presumed to be far removed from this zone, the enormity of what was done to her remained largely unacknowledged. . . .While it is certainly patriarchy that produces men whose sense of identity is achieved through the brutalizing of a woman, the men's and the court's capacity to dehumanize Pamela George derived from their understanding of her as the (gendered) racial Other whose degradation confirmed their own identities as white—that is, as men entitled to the land and the full benefits of citizenship. . . . I reject the view that the spatialized justice I describe, the values that deem certain bodies and subjects in specific spaces as undeserving of full personhood, has more to do with class than it does with race. . . . I emphasize here that race overdetermined in bringing Pamela George *and her murderers* to this brutal encounter, and bringing the court to the position where the men's culpability for their actions was diminished.

To bring the racial or colonial aspects of this encounter more prominently in view, I trace two inextricably linked collective histories: the histories of the murderers, two middle-class white men, and those of Pamela George, a Saulteaux woman. . . .

Space, Gendered Racial Violence, and the Making of White Settler Societies

. . . Two white men who buy the services of an Aboriginal woman in prostitution, and who then beat her to death, are enacting a quite specific violence perpetrated on Aboriginal bodies throughout Canada's history . . .

Dispossession, Spatial Containment, and Sexual Violence

. . . [T]he slum administration replaces colonial administration. The city belongs to the settlers and the sullying of civilized society through the presence of the racial other in white space gives rise to a careful management of boundaries within urban space. . . . The inner city is racialized space, the zone in which all that is not respectable is contained.[3] Canada's colonial geographies exhibit this same pattern of violent expulsions and the spatial containment of Aboriginal peoples to marginalized areas of the city . . . Here, however, both colonial and slum administration persist. Reserves remain lands administered by the Indian Act, while city slums are regulated through a variety of municipal laws. . . .

Sexual violence towards Aboriginal women was an integral part of nineteenth-century settler technologies of domination. . . . Sarah Carter documents the important role that stereotypical representations of Aboriginal women played in maintaining the spatial and symbolic boundaries between settlers and natives. . . . The negative images of these women, portrayed as licentious and bloodthirsty, help to justify the increasing legal regulation of Aboriginal women's movement and their confinement to reserves. . . . White men in positions of authority often beat Aboriginal women, sometimes fatally.[4] Oral narratives of Lakota women living at the end of the nineteenth century suggest that the NWMP had easy sexual access to Aboriginal women whose families were starving.[5]

Newspaper records of the nineteenth century indicate that there was a near universal conflation of Aboriginal woman and prostitutes and an accompanying belief that when they encountered violence, Aboriginal women simply got what they deserved. . . .

The nineteenth-century spatial containment of Aboriginal peoples to reserves largely remained in place until the 1950s. . . . By the 1960s, however, a steady stream of Aboriginal peoples flowed from the reserves to the city. With a high birth rate, Aboriginal peoples left reserves in increasing numbers, impoverished among other things, by a series of federal government cutbacks for housing. In 1971, the census indicated only 2860 Aboriginal peoples in Regina but unofficial estimates placed the number closer to 30,000 by mid-decade.[6] . . .

. . . Women form the majority of these migrants (58 per cent), relocating to the city for a variety of reasons, including a loss of tribal status, violence, lack of housing, and employment. Once in the city, however, the majority of urban Aboriginal peoples are left in a 'jurisdictional limbo' between the city and the reserve.[7] . . . [T]he urban Aboriginal population remains more marginal than their reserve counterparts, without access to social services and networks.[8]

Although there is no systematic study of the sexual violence Aboriginal women endure today on the streets at the hands of white men, the cases that do surface suggest that the nineteenth century perception of the Aboriginal woman as licentious and dehumanized squaw . . . continues to prevail. The Aboriginal Justice Inquiry's discussion of the 1971 murder of Helen Betty Osborne in The Pas, Manitoba, elaborates on its prevalence. Brutally murdered by two white men, Osborne, an Aboriginal student who was walking down a downtown street, was picked up in town and driven to a more secluded spot where she was assaulted and killed. As the Commissioners of the Aboriginal Justice Inquiry concluded, Osborne's attackers 'seemed to be operating on the assumption that Aboriginal women were promiscuous and open to enticement through alcohol or violence. It is evident that the men who abducted Osborne believed that young Aboriginal women were objects . . .'[9]

The Making of White Men: The Two Accused

. . . Alex Ternowetsky and Steven Kummerfield's histories begin in the colonial practices described above. In their everyday life, they would have had almost no chance of encountering an Aboriginal person. Absent from the university, the ordered suburbs of their families, the chalets and cottages, spaces that come into existence through the violent dispossession of Aboriginal peoples, Aboriginal bodies must be sought out in those marginal spaces of the city. Why would white men seek out these bodies? Why would they leave their own spaces of privilege? . . . How do young white men such as Alex Ternowetsky and Steven Kummerfield come to know themselves as beings for whom the definition of a good time is to travel to the parts of the city inhabited by poor and mostly Aboriginal peoples and there to purchase sexual services from an Aboriginal woman? . . . [T]he subject who must cross the line between respectability and degeneracy and, significantly, return unscathed, is first and foremost a colonial subject seeking to establish that he is indeed in control and lives in a world where a solid line marks the boundary between himself and racial/gendered others. . . . [V]iolence establishes the boundary between who he is and who he is not. It is the surest indicator that he is a subject in control. . . .

. . . [T]he spatial boundaries and transgressions that enable the white, middle-class male to gain mastery . . . are generally evident in a man's use of a woman in prostitution. When they purchase the right of access to the body of a prostitute, men, whether white and middle-class or not, have an opportunity to assert mastery and control, achieving in the process a subjectivity that is intrinsically colonial as well as patriarchal. Naturalized as necessary for men with excess sexual energy, prostitution is seldom considered to be a practice of domination that enables men to experience themselves as colonizers and patriarchs, that is, as men with the unquestioned right to go anywhere and to do anything to the bodies of women and subject populations they have conquered (or purchased). . . .

How did the two men enact their colonial histories? Race is not at first glance as evident as gender although neither exists independently. . . .

Kummerfield and Ternowetsky inhabited a world in which the homo-social bonding, drinking, and aggression. . . were important features.

. . . On the weekend of the murder, both men indulged in extensive drinking with their friends. . . .

Of the dozen or so male friends of the accused who testified, all were white male athletes attending university. In this remarkably homogeneous shared world of young, white, athletic, middle-class men (some of whom even had the same first Christian names), drinking and socializing occurred in isolated spaces mainly outside of their respectable homes. . . .

The sense of identity that both accused gained from their activities with other men was premised on a shared whiteness. . . . [E]vidence of their shared whiteness is most apparent in their own and their friends' and families' responses to Pamela George and to the Stroll. The men told several of their friends about the events the night of the murder and received considerable support and advice. . . . Steven Kummerfield confided to his best friend Tyler Stuart, with whom he had once gone to the area of prostitution, that 'we beat the shit out of "an Indian hooker"'.[10] In Tyler Stuart's account, Kummerfield also elaborated that he said to Pamela George 'If you don't give us head, we're going to kill you.'[11] Stuart, apparently mostly concerned about the transmission of disease to Kummerfield's white girlfriend, advised his friend to break up with her if he hadn't worn a condom the night of the murder.[12] In none of these conversations was there any indication that the men acknowledged that a woman had been brutally murdered; her death seemed almost incidental. . . The men seemed to possess a collective understanding of Pamela George as a thing, an objectification that their exclusively white worlds would have given them little opportunity to disrupt. . . .

In addition to their own isolated spaces, the men also inhabited those of middle-class respectability. They inhabited the spaces of the university, which Carol Schick demonstrates to be so clearly white space on the Canadian prairies,[13] and sports arenas, again white space as Laura Robinson demonstrates with respect to hockey.[14] The suburban households out of which they came enabled them to wear expensive clothing including the labels of Club Monaco, Nike, and Timberland[15]. . .

In this all-white masculine world of privilege, the Stroll, the area of prostitution described in the trial . . . represented the dangerous world of racial Others, a frontier on the edge of civilization. Police described the Stroll as a world of drugs and prostitution, and most of all, as a space of Aboriginality. . . .

On the night of the murder . . . Kummerfield and Ternowetsky drove to a place where they could buy liquor and then headed to the streets of the Stroll. They encountered Charlene Rosebluff, an Aboriginal woman working as a prostitute. In her account, they offered her $60, which neither of them had. Rosebluff refused to get in the car because there were two men and both were drunk. When she refused, the two men yelled at her using a string of racial slurs. At the trial, they acknowledged that this was possible and that they were likely to have used racial epithets.[16] One man then got into the trunk of the car while the other drove around and tried to persuade Rosebluff twice again. . . . She again refused. The men switched positions and tried one more time. This time, when Pamela George agreed to get into the car, they drove her to a country field two miles outside the city.

When young white men enter racialized urban spaces their skin-privilege clearly marks them as out of place. They are immediately read as johns, and as rich white men who have come 'slumming'. In this respect, they experience an unfamiliar racial marking. . . .

It is difficult to avoid both the historical and contemporary racial and spatial parallels between the murders of Helen Betty Osborne and Pamela George. Equally, newspaper reports in 1999 calling attention to cases of Aboriginal men found frozen to death after Saskatoon police apparently dropped them outside the city limits in the dead of winter outline the tremendous violence of the eviction of Aboriginal peoples from urban space. In each instance, white men forcibly and fatally removed Aboriginal bodies from the city space, a literal cleansing of the white zone. The violence is itself cleansing, enabling white men to triumph over their own internal fears that they may not be men in control. . . .

During the trial, the murder scene and the Stroll were described as spaces somehow innately given to illicit and sexual activity. The bodies of Charlene Rosebluff, Pamela George, and a number of Aboriginal men were represented variously as bodies that naturally belonged to these spaces of prostitution, crime, sex, and violence. This degenerate space, into which Kummerfield and Ternowetsky ventured temporarily, was juxtaposed to the spaces of respectability. Each space required a different legal response. In racialized space, . . . violence may occur with impunity. Bodies from respectable spaces may also violate with impunity, particularly if the violence takes place in the spaces of prostitution, racial spaces.

Unmapping Law: Gendered Racial Violence in Anomalous Zones

. . . The inhabitants of such zones were invariably racialized,[17] evacuated from the category human, and denied the equality so fundamental to liberal states. . . .

. . . [D]uring the trial, Pamela George came to be seen as a rightful target of the gendered violence inflicted by Kummerfield and Ternowetsky. . . . [H]er murder was characterized as a natural by-product of the space and thus of the social context in which it occurred, an event that is routine when the bodies in question are Aboriginal. . . . Pamela George remained simply 'the prostitute' or the 'Indian'. In the absence of details about George's life and critical scrutiny of the details of the lives of the accused, a number of subject positions remained uninterrogated. Thus, not only did George remain the 'hooker' but Ternowetsky and Kummerfield remained boys who 'did pretty darn stupid things'; their respective spaces, the places of white respectability, and the Stroll simply stood in opposition to each other, dehistoricized and decontextualized. . . .

The Stroll and the Street

The perception that the Stroll and Aboriginal bodies are spaces of violence, while the university and white suburbs are spaces of civility, is first demonstrated by the candid responses of the police when questioned as to who[m] they initially pursued and why. The boundary between the streets and the university and suburbs was so firmly entrenched in the minds of the police that they spent the first three weeks after the murder 'rounding up the usual suspects'. . . .

The suspects all speculated that George was murdered by a 'bad Trick'[18] but this made little impression on the police and they continued looking for Aboriginal men or men from the 'streets'. The police had to overcome a number of obstacles in order to keep their focus on suspects from the streets, obstacles that ultimately defeated them. For one thing, the shoe marks at the murder scene indicated that the murderer likely wore Caldera Nike hiking boots, expensive shoes that no suspect from the streets possessed. . . .

. . . When details of her life emerged, such as the fact that Pamela George had a cousin in prison, and her father had himself been falsely accused of a crime,[19] they only confirmed the equation of Aboriginality with violence, a state of affairs that remained unconnected to the violence of the colonizers. In place of details that might have given her personhood, there were a myriad of other details that instead reassured the Court of her belonging to spaces of violence. The needle marks on her arm,[20] the tattoos on her body with the words 'Ed' and 'I love mom',[21] the stories of her ripping off clients (stories the police report they heard from Lenny Hall),[22] the mention of her sister who was also a prostitute,[23] and the detailed descriptions of how prostitutes conducted their business (but not how clients participate) leave a powerful image of degeneracy. This degeneracy was clearly racial. She was described as a member of the Mongoloid or Mongolian race[24] when a strand of her hair was classified in evidence. Stephen Kummerfield described her as 'shuffling' away from him in fear when she saw Alex Ternowetsky jump out of the trunk.[25] . . .

Ultimately, it was Pamela George's status as a prostitute hence not as a human being, and her belonging to spaces beyond universal justice, that limited the extent to which the violence done to her body could be recognized and the accused made accountable for it. . . . The social meaning of place and bodies must all be studiously ignored even as the law depends on these meanings to evaluate the violence. . . .

. . . While Pamela George remained stuck in the racial space of prostitution where violence is innate, the men were considered to be far removed from the spaces of violence. She was of the space where murders happen; they were not. . . .

It is no small irony that racism, so rarely named during the trial, only emerged explicitly during sentencing. . . . Racelessness was pursued to the bitter end, however. When there were complaints made against him after the trial, Mr Justice Malone confirmed (in a letter to Chief Justice Allan McEachern) that race over-determined the trial, but noted that only a strategy of racelessness (ignoring everyone's race) countered it:

> I suspect the real basis for most of the complaints, including the two that I have dealt with, is the underlying feeling that because the two accused were white and the victim was a First Nations person they received special treatment and the jury's verdict [of manslaughter and not murder] was based on racism. This was certainly the reaction of several First Nations spokesmen and extensive media coverage was given in their remarks in this regard. Furthermore, both accused came from financially secure homes and enjoyed the material benefits associated therewith. Their position in life was in striking contrast to the position of the victim. Every effort was made during the trial by counsel and

myself to deal with the case strictly on the basis of relevant evidence and not on the financial and social positions of the accused and their victim or their race.[26]

Here, colour-blindness as a legal approach, the belief that justice can only be achieved by treating all individuals as though they were the same, held full sway.

Race, social position, and, I would add, gender, were indeed made to disappear during the trial and in sentencing. The social meaning of spaces and bodies was deliberately excluded as evidence. . . It was not then possible to interrogate what white men thought they were doing in journeying to the Stroll to buy the services of an Aboriginal prostitute. It was also not possible to interrogate the meaning of consent and violence in the space of prostitution and between white and Aboriginal bodies. Since bodies had no race, class, or gender, the constructs that ruled the day, heavily inflected with these social relations, coded rather than revealed them explicitly. Thus, 'prostitute', and people of 'the street' came to signify the racial Other and the spaces of violence. In contrast, the university, the chalet, the cottage, the suburban home, the isolated spaces in which the men socialized, were unmarked. . . .

Notes

1. R. v. *Kummerfield & Ternowetsky*, 'Transcript of 12–15, 18–22, 25–28 November, and 2–5, 9–12, and 17–20 December 1996 [1997] (Regina, Sask. Prov. Ct. [Crim. Div.]: 4755 (hereinafter 'Transcript').

2. B. Pacholik. 'Relief, and Anger. Aboriginal Spokesman Demands Appeal', *Regina Leader Post* (21 December 1996): A1.

3. D. Goldberg, *Racist Culture, Philosophy and the Politics of Meaning* (Cambridge, MA: Blackwell Publishers, 1993), 185–205.

4. S. Carter, *Capturing Women: The Manipulation of Cultural Imagery in Canada's Prairie West* (Montréal and Kingston: McGill-Queen's University Press, 1997), 179.

5. Ibid., 180.

6. J.W. Brennan, *Regina: An Illustrated History* (Toronto: Lorimer & Canadian Museum of Civilization with the Secretary of State, 1989), 165.

7. Canada, *Report of the Royal Commission on Aboriginal Peoples: Perspectives and Realities*, vol. 4 (Ottawa: Supply and Services Canada, 1996), 543.

8. D. Anaquod and V. Khaladkar, 'Case Study: The First Nations Economy in the City of Regina', CD-ROM: *For Seven Generations: An Information Legacy of The Royal Commission on Aboriginal Peoples* (Ottawa: Libraxus, 1997), 1–2.

9. Manitoba, *Report of the Aboriginal Justice Inquiry of Manitoba: The Deaths of Helen Betty Osborne and John Joseph Harper*, vol. 2 (Winnipeg: Queen's Printer, 1991), 52.

10. 'Transcript', 858.

11. Ibid., 846–910.

12. Ibid., 871.

13. . . . C. Schick, 'Keeping the Ivory Tower White: Discourses of Racial Domination', *Canadian Journal of Law and Society* 15, 2: 2000.

14. J. Robinson, *Crossing the Line: Violence and Sexual Abuse in Canada's National Sport* (Toronto: McClelland & Stewart, 1998), 226.

15. 'Transcript', 3843.

16. Ibid., 3933.

17. For example, Sander Gilman shows how prostitutes in nineteenth-century Europe were depicted with African features even though they were nearly all white. S. Gilman, 'Black Bodies, White Bodies: Toward an Iconography of Female Sexuality in Late Nineteenth-Century Art, Medicine, and Literature', in J. Donald and A. Rattansi, eds, *'Race' Culture and Difference* (London: The Open University, 1992), 171. . .

18. 'Transcript', 2922.

19. T. Sutter, 'She Was My Baby', *Regina Leader Post* (13 May 1995, Saturday Magazine): 1.

20. 'Transcript', 1113.

21. Ibid., 33, 132.

22. Ibid., 4248.

23. Ibid., 2993.

24. Ibid., 2619.

25. Ibid., 3562.

26. Justice Malone, 'Response to the Honourable Chief Justice Allan McEachern to Complaints by Ms Sharon Ferguson-Hood and Ms Ailsa Watkinson and Others, February 6, 1997' [1997] (Regina, Sask. Prov. Ct. [Crim. Div.]).

Part XIV

Consumer Bodies

Claudia Malacrida and Jacqueline Low

Social theorist Anthony Giddens (1991) argues that late modernity has meant a loss of traditions and shared meanings, forcing us to constantly engage in working on our personal identity and conveying it to others. Chris Shilling (1993) further argues that the body has become a *project* and is now the means through which we achieve this identity. **Body modification**, the manipulation of the body through activities such as tattooing, piercing, cosmetic surgeries, cosmetic dental work, and dieting, is a consumer activity engaged in by many of us as a way to construct our identity. In his section, Christian Klesse (1999) discusses extreme forms of body modification used by 'modern primitives' that are often connected to attempts by practitioners to disassociate themselves from modern consumer culture. The images Klesse discusses in his article are available on-line, so that readers can see the imagery and practices of 'modern primitives' for themselves on the website of *Body Play* magazine, an e-zine published by Fakir Musafar, a key figure in the movement. The web address is http://www.bodyplay.com/.

Klesse notes that many of these extreme body modifications, just as those that are mainstream, have become **commodified** (commodification takes place when economic value is assigned to something that traditionally would not be considered in economic terms) through the proliferation of tattoo and piercing establishments. These body modifications are also problematic in terms of **cultural appropriation** (the adoption of some specific elements of one culture by a different, often more privileged, cultural group) and **othering**, the projection of racial, cultural, and sexual judgments onto a social group not of one's own, as a way to define and secure one's own positive identity through the stigmatization of an 'other'. Modern Primitives claim that they copy the rituals and body modification practices used by 'primitive' people as a way to connect with them and to refuse late modernity's alienating lifestyle. However, critics note that these privileged, Western groups are engaging in a fantasy that ignores the reasons for these bodily manipulations in their cultures of origin. More importantly, 'modern primitivism' engages in the consumption of Third World practices while ignoring racial, economic, and globalized power relations between the Developed World (primarily Western, European countries) and the Developing World.

The power relations embedded in body modification are also the focus of Rose Weitz's (2003) analysis of women's hair styles. Weitz interviews women about their choices concerning hair colour, length, and style and finds that many women engage in 'traditional' bodily manipulations, making calculated choices in terms of gender stereotypes about their hair. Thus, women chose to become blonde in hopes that it will improve their social and sexual lives, or they chose so-called serious hairstyles believing this would benefit them in the corporate world. These 'traditional' choices indicate that the women were very aware of Bourdieu's notion of **physical capital**, where physical attributes can be worked on, improved, and leveraged for economic capital. These women's choices also indicate an understanding that hair and appearance are heavily tied to women's sexual success—for heterosexual women, conventionally attractive hair means attracting a desirable mate, while for lesbians, conventionally attractive hair can mean passing as straight and avoiding stigmatization.

Weitz questions, however, the amount of power attached to these women's traditional bodily manipulations. She notes that the 'choices' that women make in terms of their hair are severely constrained, and that complying to norms of hegemonic femininity can actually reduce women's power because they are seen as pretty, but 'less than competent' (142). On the other hand, women who adopt 'non-traditional' hair strategies are also limited in their ability to resist dominant norms of femininity. For example, women who chose to wear non-traditional hairstyles described losing jobs, encountering homophobia, and being the targets of racism. Consequently, Weitz finds that, in general, the women's strategic body manipulations were characterized more often by **accommodation** (complying with dominant norms) than **resistance** (challenging dominant norms) to common standards of femininity and appearance.

A **consumer culture** is one in which the mass production of goods and services associated with capitalist social structure necessitates the mass consumption of those goods and services by members of that society (Featherstone, 1999). Consequently, within consumerist culture the body becomes subject to regimes of maintenance via consumption of a variety of marketed goods such as diet and exercise books, gym memberships, and cosmetic surgery (Featherstone, 1999). In her analysis of men's use of cosmetic surgery, Kathy Davis starts from the premise that the use of cosmetic surgery 'can not be understood as a matter of individual choice' nor as a practice peculiar to consumerist culture where men and women are equally obliged to consume products with the goal of perfecting their bodies (2002: 74). Rather, she argues that men's consumption of cosmetic surgery is different from women's use of the same practices within consumerist society. She points out that among the core components of **hegemonic masculinity**, the dominant cultural construct of what it means to be a man, is the notion of a **rational** (reason, thinking) and **instrumental** (doing, acting) male where the truly masculine body is one 'that "does", but is never, never "done to"' (Bordo, 1994: 288). Thus, men who engage in cosmetic enhancement of their bodies and the surgeons who perform those surgeries are subject to **stigma**, the devaluing of their selves and bodies that results from engagement in practices that conflict with attributes of hegemonic masculinity (see also Parts IV and V).

References

Bordo, S. 1994. *Unbearable Weight*. Berkeley: University of California Press.

Davis, K. 2002. '"A Dubious Equality": Men, Women, and Cosmetic Surgery', *Body and Society* 8, 1: 49–65.

Featherstone, M. 1999. 'The Body in Consumer Culture', in M. Featherstone, M. Hepworth, and B.S. Turner, eds, *The Body: Social Process and Cultural Theory*. London: Sage, 170–96.

Giddens, A. 1991. *Modernity and Self-Identity*. London: Sage.

Klesse, C. 1999. '"Modern Primitivism": Non-mainstream Body Modification and Racialized Representation', *Body and Society* 5: 15–38.

Shilling, C. 1993. *The Body and Social Theory*. London: Sage.

Weitz, R. 2003. 'Women and Their Hair: Seeking Power through Resistance and Accommodation', in R. Weitz, ed, *The Politics of Women's Bodies: Sexuality, Appearance, and Behavior*. New York and Oxford: Oxford University Press, 135–51.

Chapter 40

'Modern Primitivism': Non-mainstream Body Modification and Racialized Representation

Christian Klesse

I make a statement, I've chosen myself. I am a part of this culture but I don't believe in it. My body modifications are my way to say that. (Idexa, in *BP & MPQ* 2, 2: 11)

Introduction: Marking the Body and Marking the Problem

. . . 'Modern Primitives' are a subcultural movement in the intersection of the tattoo, piercing, and sado-masochism scenes. The movement originated in the 1970s in California, USA, growing in numbers and significance in the following decades.

The term 'Modern Primitives' applies to people, who 'respond to primal urges' to do '*something*' with their bodies (Fakir Musafar, in Vale and Juno, 1989: 13). Fakir Musafar, the most prominent body modifier within the Modern Primitives movement, who also claims to be its founder, has created the term 'Body Play' for this kind of practice. In his magazine *Body Play and Modern Primitives Quarterly* (*BP & MPQ*), whose analysis has provided the basis for many of the claims made in this article,[1] he defines 'Body Play' as 'the deliberate, ritualized modification of the human body. It is a deep rooted, universal urge that seemingly transcends time and cultural boundaries' (*BP & MPQ* 1, 1: 3). . . .

The reasons individual Modern Primitives give for engaging in these activities, however, are highly diverse. Personal motives put forward include spirituality, rites of passage, fun, sexual enhancement,

the importance of pain, aesthetics, group affiliation, shock value, etc. (see Myers, 1992: 287–96). Modern Primitives, thus, may best be described as being 'composed of multiple communities' (Torgovnick, 1995), of different (sexual) orientations and persuasions. However, the ethnic background of most of the people involved in Modern Primitive practices is white (Eubanks, 1996; Myers, 1992). Modern Primitives seem to be quite popular within the non-mainstream body modification scene(s) (Myers, 1992), their elaborated philosophies, however, are not shared on a large-scale basis (Sweetman, 1997; Torgovnick, 1995).

One of the most significant characteristics of the Modern Primitives movement is their appropriation of 'primitive rituals'. In their search for radical corporal, psychic, and spiritual experiences and their performance of sexual events and encounters, Modern Primitives seek inspiration by so-called 'primitive societies' through the adoption of their communal rites and body modification techniques. . . .

. . . According to Eubanks, Modern Primitives' adoption of ritual forms of body modification displays 'a blatant disregard for the history and the context of the symbols and practices involved' (Eubanks, 1996: 74). Modern Primitives' rejection of modern society presents itself as a commitment to sexual freedom and bodily expression, coded in a naive longing for the 'authentic primitive', a profoundly essentialist concept. This involves a variety of problems, such as the reinforcement of the traditional dualism of Western thought (self/other; male/female; nature/culture) and, most important-ly: the *denial of cultural difference* in a universalist humanist vision of a 'primal urge'. . . .

Modernity, Identity, and the Body

Theorists of modernity have emphasized the profound effects of social and economic change, resulting in shifts and breaks within personal processes of identification. Zygmunt Bauman states: 'Though all too often hypothesized as an attribute of a material identity, identity has the ontological status of a project and a postulate' (Bauman, 1996: 19). The experience of fracture has always been at the heart of identity, and identity building has always remained an indi-vidual task. Economic and social developments in late modernity have made this task even more difficult. The postmodern condition to a certain degree universalized experiences of alienation, distinctiveness, and strangeness (Bauman, 1993).

Anthony Giddens (1990, 1991), too, claims that the maintenance of self-identity has become a particular problem. According to him, late modernity has dissolved most traditional systems of meaning and social order in an unprecedented fashion. As a result individuals are forced to engage in a heightened reflexivity about life and its meaning. In this context of 'ontological inse-curity' self-identity has become deliberative. It does not emerge automatically from one's social position. Thus, people are engaged in a perma-nent re-ordering of identity narratives in which a concern with the body is central.

The Body as an Individual Project

In . . . 'late modernity . . . we have become responsible for the design of our own bodies', says Anthony Giddens (1991: 102). There has been an unprecedented individualization of the body. Technological developments, among oth-ers, allow for the alteration of the body. Shilling (1993) has theorized this development with the concept of '*body projects*'.

In the affluent West there is a tendency for the body to be seen as an entity which is in the process of becoming; a project which should be worked at and accomplished as part of an individual's self-identity. (Shilling, 1993: 5) . . .

The theory of *body projects* contains a . . . prob-lem of generalization. Although Shilling (1993) acknowledges that these projects have to be theo-rized as a gendered, ethnicized, and class-bound phenomenon, this, in my opinion, is insufficiently elaborated. As a result, the dimensions of choice . . . is circumscribed by the complex articulations of gender, ethnicity, ability, and class, not to forget location/space. This perspective should be *central* to any theory of the body and identity. . . .

The Display of the Body as a Source of Identity in Consumer Capitalism

. . . People nowadays, Mike Featherstone (1991) claims, are more concerned with their bodies. In particular the *presentation of the body*, emphasiz-ing style, 'looks', and appearance, has been charged with new identity functions. This strong concern with the body is linked to the consump-tion of commodities or services. Furthermore, in consumer culture the 'display' and the 'perform-ance' of bodily properties and styles has not only become an option, it is *increasingly expected*. In this context the new body images of consumer culture imply a *strong sexualization of the body*. Consumer culture reinforces 'the notion that the body is a vehicle of pleasure and self-expression' (Featherstone, 1991: 170). Self-realization and the self-conscious cultivation of style thus appear as a normative demand of modernism.

Although Modern Primitives rigorously reject the materialism of Western consumer culture, tattooing and piercing, for example, do not escape commodification. In the meantime, small-scale businesses of professional piercers and tat-too artists have been established in all larger cities and definitely establish a profitable mar-ket. *Body Play and Modern Primitives Quarterly* is full of adverts for these mushrooming business-es. . . .

Modernity, Community, Sociality, and the Body

As a distinctive subcultural style, Modern Primitivism raises questions of community, too. The application of Shilling's theory of body projects has put a strong emphasis on individualism as a specific feature of the late modern condition in Western societies. . . .

The intense individual act of getting tattooed or pierced, however, for Modern Primitives has also the meaning of *creating collectivity*. Princess Cruise states in *BP & MPQ*:

> Among the people I love and respect, whose world views I share in fundamental ways, so many have cut, coloured, stretched, compressed, decorated, and otherwise modified their bodies that I even want to do it too. I want to be like them: I want them to know when they see me across a crowded room that I associate myself with them; . . . that we are . . . family. (*BP & MPQ* 2, 3: 5) . . .

. . . Within the Modern Primitives movement the spiritual leather and s/m scene groups of friends refer to themselves as a tribe (Thompson, 1991). The kinship-based social model that has been associated with 'primitive' culture seems to offer a stronger promise of belonging than any other form of social association practised in Western industrialized societies. 'Primitivism' offers a broad range of inspiration and possibilities of identification to people, who feel alienated in their contemporary societies.

Alienation, the Crisis of Identity, and Primitivism as Identity Space

. . . The subjective feeling of alienation within and from contemporary Western societies is an important reason for the romanticizing turn of this mainly white subculture to the 'primitive' world. Fakir Musafar, for example, states that he has felt 'like an alien in this culture' since his early childhood (Vale and Juno, 1989: 6). . . .

. . . According to Friedman (1994), the vanishing of the modern identity space and the resulting 'identity crisis consists in the surging to the surface of what is peripherized within us, a closing in of what is peripherized outside of us, a search for meaning and "roots" in the widest sense' (Friedman, 1994: 85).

In particular 'free' sexuality and an 'unconstrained' body have been projected into the 'realm of the Other'. . . .

. . . It was in the gendered and sexualized images of the 'sensual oriental', or the 'natural' and 'primitive African', that the ambiguities of the situation of Western men and women were worked through. The colonial imaginary and the colonial context provided the space where uninhibited sexual relationships, based on the idea of an unproblematic and free body, could be fantasized. The Romantic movement, as a response to the Enlightenment rationalism, created the notion of the 'noble savage', an imaginary figure that can clearly be identified in the work of writers such as Rousseau and Diderot (Bloch and Bloch, 1980). The subtleties of sexualization, objectification, and subordination are disguised in these *extremely positive depictions and evaluations* of 'primitivism'.

Shifts towards 'primitivism', thus, are no singular phenomenon in history; the ambivalences of the Enlightenment and the naturalism and anti-rationalism of Romanticism were the precedents of contemporary Modern Primitivism. Sexuality and the body have been very significant issues within all these primitivist discourses and they are the predominant features of Modern Primitivism. 'Within Western culture, the idiom "going primitive" is in fact congruent in many ways to the idiom "getting physical"' (Torgovnick, 1990: 228). 'Primitivism' thus has had a long history within the repertoire of colonial fantasy and imagination.

The Ambivalence of Colonial Discourses, Mimicry, and the Illusion of Sameness

. . . Many Modern Primitives talk about being strongly impressed by early ethnographic material.

Old films, photographs, for example from the volumes of the *National Geographic*, a huge range of material is used for inspiration and stimulation (*BP & MPQ* 2, 4: 22; Thompson, 1991: 294; Vale and Juno, 1989: 7). Many Modern Primitives privately collect these products. Moreover, such images have repeatedly been reproduced in an uncritical manner within *BP & MPQ*. . . .

. . . In particular Fakir Musafar, but also other Modern Primitives, like to juxtapose photographs of themselves with temporary body modifications with older ethnographic material that shows their 'primitive' models in the same position. . . .

Modern Primitives and the Primitivist Discourse

Modern Primitives are enthusiastically committed to 'primitivism'. This is expressed in their positive reference to 'primitive people', 'primitive societies', and in their adoption of 'primitive' body modification techniques and 'primitive rituals'. . . .

The 'primitive' in the discourse of Modern Primitivism is a catch-all without any geographical and historical specificity, a homogenizing fantasy. Modern Primitives seem to be more interested in the bodily practices of the 'primitive models' than in a thorough exploration of other societies' philosophies. For them, what is interesting of the 'primitive' is his or her body (modification), and 'marking the body' is seen as the most 'primitive' act (Levi Straus, 1989: 158).

However, Modern Primitives commonly claim to have further goals and interests. They reject the cultural assumptions of modern Western societies and the associated notion of progress. According to them, the terrible state in which we find our world can only be superseded by a return to the 'primitive', or at least by the integration of 'primitive' knowledges, techniques, or lifestyles into modern life. . . . Their notion of the 'primitive' in general is shaped by an absolute idealization and romanticization. For example, Fakir Musafar says, in pure, 'primitive' societies there is no cruelty, ugliness, no possessive attitudes, no sexual violence,

and no transgression (Vale and Juno, 1989: 21; *BP & MPQ* 1, 2: 4).

Eubanks (1996) argues that although Modern Primitives claim to work on changing their contemporary societies, they simply adore an idealized 'primitive' past. . . .

'Primitivism' and Anthropology

The word 'primitive' appeared for the first time in the fifteenth century to signify the meaning 'original' or 'ancestor', referring to animals, occasionally even men. . . .

As a 'scientific' idea it crystallized in the philosophical anthropological discussion in the 1860s and 1870s. Modernity has been obsessed with the study of 'primitive lifestyles', 'primitive societies', etc. Ethnography and anthropology have been the scientific disciplines in the forefront of the study of the 'primitive'. Early anthropological writers developed the evolutionist theory of a 'primitive society', drawing on a variety of assumptions that basically constructed 'primitive society' as the *antithesis* or mirror image of modern Western societies. Although this theory was not based on any historical evidence and early criticism was available, it has not been dropped from anthropological discussion. The 'persistence of this illusion' has to be seen in the ideological suitability of the concept for the West's political claims of superiority (Kuper, 1988). The notion of 'primitivism' has been and still is used as an ideological means for legitimizing colonial and imperial politics. . . .

Evolutionism as Enlightenment Thought and Common-sense Persuasion

. . . The imagining of a 'primitive society' as a primal and original form of human association was easily translatable into a simple hierarchy, because of its strong evolutionist connotations. Evolutionist ideas emerged on the discursive agenda from the sixteenth and seventeenth centuries. The Renaissance produced the 'temporalization of the great chain of being'. Enlightenment thought developed evolutionism as a coherent and hegemonic world view.

The increasingly *racialized* construction of an epistemology around the binaries modern/

primitive, developed/non-developed, civilized/savage, rational/irrational, enlightened/magic, culture/nature (and so on) strengthened the conviction that Western identity is superior to that of all non-Western peoples and cultures (Young, 1995). Originating in anthropological discourses, the notion of 'primitivism' has spread into other disciplines (such as literature, art history, psychology) and into popular culture (advertising, fashions, and new media productions). The notions of both 'primitivism' and 'evolutionism' today foundationally inform hegemonic world views within Western societies (Lutz and Collins, 1993: 240). . . .

Modern Primitivism as Legacy of Colonialism in Late Imperial Culture

Modern Primitives' celebration of 'primitive societies', in my view, is just another extreme version of this primitivist discourse. Despite its enthusiasm for 'the primitive', this discourse deploys similar assumptions. With a blatant disregard for history and societal and geographic contexts, groups and societies are lumped together in the category of 'primitives'. The dualism between the 'primitive' societies and the 'West' is maintained. . . .

Note

. . .

1. My main sources are the magazine *Body Play and Modern Primitives Quarterly* (vols 1–3, 1992–5), and the book *Re/Search #12. Modern Primitives* (Vale and Juno, 1989).

References

Bauman, Zygmunt. 1993. *Modernity and Ambivalence*. Cambridge: Polity Press.

———. 1996. 'From Pilgrim to Tourist—or a Short History of Identity', in S. Hall and P. du Gay, eds, *Questions of Cultural Identity*. London: Sage, 18–36.

Block, Maurice, and Jean H. Bloch. 1980. 'Women and the Dialectics of Nature, in Eighteenth–Century French Thought', in P. MacCormack and M. Strathern, eds, *Nature, Culture, and Gender*. Cambridge: Cambridge University Press, 25–41.

Body Play and Modern Primitives Quarterly vols. 1–3, 1992–5.

Eubanks, Virginia. 1996. 'Zones of Dither: Writing the Postmodern Body', *Body & Society* 2, 3: 73–88.

Featherstone, Mike. 1991. 'The Body in Consumer Culture', in M. Featherstone, M. Hepworth, and B.S. Turner, eds, *The Body: Social Process and Cultural Theory*. London: Sage, 170–96.

Friedman, Jonathan. 1994. *Cultural Identity and Global Process*. London: Sage.

Giddens, Anthony. 1990. *The Consequences of Modernity*. Cambridge: Polity Press.

———. 1991. *Modernity and Self-Identity*. Cambridge: Polity Press.

Kuper, Adam. 1988. *The Invention of Primitive Society: Transformations of an Illusion*. London and New York: Routledge.

Lutz, Catherine A., and Jane L. Collins. 1993. *Reading National Geographic*. Chicago and London: University of Chicago Press.

Myers, James. 1992. 'Nonmainstream Body Modification: Genital Piercing, Branding, Burning, and Cutting', *Journal of Contemporary Ethnography* 21, 3: 276–306.

Shilling, Chris. 1993. *The Body and Social Theory*. London: Sage.

Straus, Davie Levi. 1989. 'Modern Primitives', in V. Vale and A. Juno, eds, *Re/Search # 12: Modern Primitives. An Investigation of Contemporary Adornment and Ritual*. San Francisco: Re/Search Publications, 157–8.

Sweetman, Paul. 1997. 'Marked Bodies, Oppositional Identities? Tattooing, Piercing, and the Ambiguity of Resistance', Paper presented at the *Body & Society* Day Conference on Body Modification, Nottingham Trent University, 16 June.

Thompson, Mark, ed. 1991. *Leatherfolk: Radical Sex, People, Politics and Practice*. Boston: Alyson Publications.

Torgovnick, Marianna. 1990. *Gone Primitive: Savage Intellects, Modern Lives*. Chicago and London: University of California Press.

———. 1995. 'Piercings', in R. De La Campa, E.A. Kaplan, and M. Sprinker, eds, *Late Imperial Culture*. London and New York: Verso, 197–210.

Vale, V., and A. Juno, eds. 1989. *Re/Search # 12: Modern Primitives. An Investigation of Contemporary Adorn-ment and Ritual*. San Francisco: Re/Search Publications.

Young, Robert J.C. 1994. 'Egypt in America: Black Athena, Racism, and Colonial Discourse', in A. Rattansi and S. Westwood, eds, *Racism, Modernity, Identity: On the Western Front*. Cambridge: Polity Press, 150–70.

Chapter 41

Women and Their Hair: Seeking Power through Resistance and Accommodation

Rose Weitz

Hairstyles serve as important cultural artifacts, because they are simultaneously public (visible to everyone), personal (biologically linked to the body), and highly malleable to suit cultural and personal preferences (Firth, 1973; Synnott, 1987). In this article, I argue that women's hair is central to their social position.[1] I explore how women use their hair to try to gain some power and analyze the benefits and limitations of their strategies. More broadly, I use these data to explore how accommodation and resistance lie buried in everyday activities, how they are often interwoven, and why resistance strategies based on the body have limited utility (Dellinger and Williams, 1997; Elowe MacLeod, 1991). . . .

Introduction

Power refers to the ability to obtain desired goals through controlling or influencing others. . . . The body is [an important] site for struggles over power . . . As Michel Foucault (1979, 1980) described, to carry out the tasks of modern economic and social life, societies require 'docile bodies', such as regimented soldiers, factory workers who perform their tasks mechanically, and students who sit quietly. To create such bodies, 'disciplinary practices' have evolved through which individuals both internalize and act on the ideologies that underlie their own subordination. In turn, these disciplinary practices have made the body a site for power struggles, and, potentially, for resistance, as individual choices about the body become laden with political meanings. . . .

Defining Resistance and Accommodation

To date, the term *resistance* remains loosely defined, allowing some scholars to see it almost everywhere and others, almost nowhere. One way that the latter group limits their vision of resistance is by defining actions as resistance only if they are effective. Such a definition seems far too narrow, however, for even failed revolutions would not qualify. Moreover, as Stombler and Padavic (1997) suggest, even small acts with no obvious effects on the broader system may affect individuals and pave the way for later social change. . . .

Another possibility is to define an action as resistance if its intent is to reject subordination, regardless of either its effectiveness or the extent to which it also supports subordination (Stombler and Padavic, 1997). . . .

. . . In this article, I use examples from women's hair management strategies to suggest that we need to more narrowly define resistance as actions that not only reject subordination but do so *by challenging the ideologies that support that subordination*. For example, factory workers' collective efforts to raise wages through union activity challenge the ideological basis of class subordination by arguing that factory workers have as much right as factory managers and owners to a decent wage. Similarly, and as I will show, some women consciously adopt hairstyles (such as short 'butch' cuts or dreadlocks) in part to challenge the ideology that women's worth depends on their attractiveness to men and that women's attractiveness depends on looking as

Euro-American as possible. Like slaves' rebellious songs, women's rebellious hairstyles can allow them to distance themselves from the system that would subordinate them, to express their dissatisfaction, to identify like-minded others, and to challenge others to think about their own actions and beliefs. Thus, these everyday, apparently trivial, individual acts of resistance offer the potential to spark social change and, in the long run, to shift the balance of power between social groups. . . . By extension, *accommodation* refers to actions that accept subordination, by either adopting or simply not challenging the ideologies that support subordination. . . .

Methods

This paper is based on interviews collected between 1998 and 2001 with 44 women, all but five of whom live in Arizona. Respondents were obtained primarily through word of mouth. To avoid biasing the sample toward women who were unusually invested in their hair, I asked for referrals to women who 'like to talk in general and are willing to talk about their hair'. . . .

Although nonrandom, the sample is highly diverse. Respondents ranged in age from 22 to 83. Twenty-nine were Anglo, eight Mexican-American, four African-American, two Asian, and one half-Chicana and half-Anglo. . . .

Findings

In this section, I will describe the ways women use their hair to seek power in both their personal and professional lives. Analysis of the data revealed two strategies women used to accomplish this task: traditional strategies that emphasize accommodation to mainstream norms for female attractiveness and nontraditional strategies that emphasize resistance to those norms. . . .

Seeking Power through Traditional Strategies

The most common way women use their hair to

seek power is through strategies that de-emphasize resistance and instead emphasize accommodation to mainstream ideas about attractiveness. . . . For purposes of convenience, I will refer to those who meet these norms as 'conventionally attractive'.

There is widespread agreement that conventionally attractive hair gives women power, or at least makes them feel powerful—a point made by many women in this study.[2] . . . Results from numerous research studies (summarized in Jackson, 1992, and Sullivan, 2001) suggest that conventional attractiveness is in fact a realistic route to power for women, in both intimate relationships and careers. Attractive women are less lonely, more popular, and more sexually experienced, both more likely to marry and more likely to marry men of higher socio-economic status. Compared to similarly qualified unattractive women, conventionally attractive women are more often hired, more often promoted, and paid higher salaries.

The following story, told by Cecilia, a 20-something student, demonstrates the conscious and rational decision-making process women may use to get power through conventional attractiveness:

> I can think of an occasion where I changed my hair while I was dating this guy. I had this feeling that he was losing attraction for me and I'd just been feeling the need to do something to my appearance. And my hair is always the easiest way to go. It's too expensive to buy a new wardrobe. There's nothing you can do about your face. So your hair, you can go and have something radically done to it and you'll look like a different person. At least that's the way I see it.
>
> So I remember I was dating this guy, and I was away at school when I was dating him, and I went home for the weekend, and he was going to come down that weekend. . . . So I went home and I got my hair cut off. I cut off about seven or eight inches, and it was kind of a radical haircut, you know shaved, kind of asymmetrical again, and I put a red tint on it. . . .

And when he saw me, when he walked into my house, it was like, 'Whoa!' You know? And he said, 'Oh, my God, look at it!' And he just couldn't stop talking about it. He made a comment saying that he felt differently about me. He said, 'I don't know, there's just something about you. I don't know. I really want to be with you.'

When I asked Cecilia how she felt about his rekindled interest in her, she replied: 'I was pretty pleased with myself.'

Although this may seem like a limited form of power compared to, say, winning election to a government office, this power embedded in doing femininity well (Bordo, 1989) is power nonetheless: with a minimum investment of money and time, this woman obtained a desired goal and influenced the behaviour and emotions of another person. . . .

Even women who are uninterested in male attention may find that meeting norms for conventional attractiveness works to their benefit: for example, Erica, a young lesbian, explained that her long hair allows her to pass as heterosexual and thus has helped her get and keep jobs (in the same way that using makeup benefitted the lesbians interviewed by Dellinger and Williams [1997]). Similarly, and regardless of sexual orientation, female athletes often wear their hair long, curled, and dyed blonde as part of a 'feminine apologetic' that enhances their attractiveness to men and protects them from being stigmatized as lesbian (Hilliard, 1984; Lowe, 1998). . . .

In sum, the women described in this section are neither blindly seeking male approval nor unconsciously making decisions based on an internalized ideology of femininity. Instead, like women who use cosmetic surgery (Davis, 1995) or makeup (Dellinger and Williams, 1997), they are actively and rationally making choices based on a realistic assessment of how they can best obtain their goals, given both their personal resources and the cultural and social constraints they face. Yet can these strategies be considered resistance? On the one hand, each of these strategies is an intentional course of action designed to

resist subordination by helping members of a subordinate group increase their power—or at least sense of power—relative to the dominant group. On the other hand, most of these strategies pose little if any challenge to cultural ideas about women or to the broader distribution of power by gender, for they implicitly support the ideology that defines a woman's body as her most important attribute and that therefore conflates changes in a woman's appearance with changes to her identity. Because these strategies do not challenge the cultural ideologies supporting subordination, at best they can improve the position of an individual woman, but not of women as a group. . . .

The Limits of Power Obtained through Traditional Strategies

Not surprisingly, given the accommodations embedded in traditional strategies, women often find that power obtained through these strategies is circumscribed, fragile, bittersweet, and limiting. The power to attract a man, after all, is not the same as the power to earn a living independently . . .

Power based on conventional attractiveness is also fragile, achieved one day at a time through concentrated effort and expenditures of time and money. Linda, a 40-year-old Asian-American woman, pays to have her hair permed every few months because she thinks otherwise it looks 'too Asian'. Because her hair straightens out when it gets wet, she always carries an umbrella, never swims with friends, and dries her hair after showering before letting anyone see her. Her concern proved justified the one time a lover (of four years) saw her with wet straight hair, and told her never to wear her hair straight.

Even those who look attractive on most days still face the occasional 'bad hair day'—a true catastrophe for those who consider their hair a significant source of power. Felicia, a Chicana in her twenties, remarked, 'If I'm having a bad hair day, I'm having a bad day in general. . . . My day is just shot.' Moreover, conventional attractiveness must decline with age (although it can be fought with facelifts, hair dyeing, and the like.)

This power is bittersweet, too, for it is only partly under the individual's control: a woman who seeks attention and power through her appearance cannot control who will respond, when, or how. As explained to me by LaDonna, a young African-American woman whose long and wavy hair attracts considerable male attention: 'It's kind of funny because I know [my hair] will get me attention, and I do things to make it look nice that I know will get me attention, but sometimes I don't wear my hair down because I *don't* want the attention.' Nor can she control which men will be attracted to her (will it be her handsome neighbour or her married boss?) or for what reasons (will he think she is pretty because he simply likes long hair or because he thinks anything that looks 'white' is superior?). . . .

Finally, power obtained through traditional strategies is not only circumscribed, fragile, and bittersweet, but also limiting, since increasing one's power in these ways may *reduce* one's power in traditionally male realms. Most basically, the same hairstyles that identify a woman as conventionally attractive and increase her power in intimate relationships highlight femininity. Yet our culture links femininity with incompetence (Valian, 1998; Wiley and Crittenden, 1992). Thus, although men can only benefit from attractiveness, women can also be harmed by attractiveness if it leads others to regard them as less competent. . . .

Seeking Power through Nontraditional Strategies

The problems inherent in traditional strategies lead some women, either additionally or instead, to seek power through nontraditional strategies in which elements of resistance to mainstream ideas of attractiveness outweigh any elements of accommodation.

The meanings and implications of the strategies described in this section vary considerably depending on women's ethnicity. Reflecting the broader tendency for individuals to change hairstyles as a way of marking status transitions (McAlexander and Schouten, 1989), white women often choose new hairstyles that highlight professionalism and downplay femininity as a first step toward entering professional training or work. For example, Tina, a young graduate student described how, after college, she cut her hair as

> sort of like the completion of transition to adulthood. . . . I felt like I needed to make some sort of definitive statement about if I was going to get through life . . . this was the way I was going to do it. . . . I'm not going to get through life by being girly. I don't want to live that way . . ., relying on the attention, specifically of men, but also relying on people's responses to your appearance. And, particularly, [on] an appearance that is feminine by stereotypical social convention.

She now has a short, spiky haircut that, she said, 'makes me feel more powerful because it's like I've beat the system, you know? . . . The system's trying to take [my power] away and I've succeeded in not letting them.' . . .

Once in the world of work, other haircuts often follow, as white women learn to believe—or learn that others believe—that femininity and professional competence are antithetical. In such situations, women may consciously use their hair to defeminize themselves. Stacy, a bicultural (Anglo/Chicana) graduate assistant who typically pulls her long hair back into a ponytail when she teaches explained:

> If you have really long hair people tend to see you as more womanly. . . . Particularly when I teach, I don't want people to look at me as more womanly. That's why I wear my hair back: to be taken more seriously, to look more professional, to just be seen as a person as opposed to like a woman. . . .

African-American women, on the other hand, are far less likely to adopt any strategy that might downplay their femininity. Faced with a dominant culture that already defines them as less attractive and feminine than other women (Hill Collins, 1991: 67–90; Weitz and Gordon, 1993), they are more likely to seek out a style that looks 'professional' but still meets mainstream norms of femininity. They thus typically rely on wigs or on expensive formulations for changing the natural texture of their hair, and avoid both hairstyles that others might associate with radical political stances (such as dreadlocks or Afros) and the elaborate hairstyles often favoured by working-class African-American women (Fernandez Kelly, 1995). . . .

Other women remain interested in attracting men, but not based on the traditional norms of submissive femininity that underlie mainstream attractiveness norms. Stacy provided a dramatic example:

> My boyfriend . . . used to say that . . . what made me attractive was my hair was so pretty. So I deliberately kind of cut it off, a little bit spitefully, but kind of just to say I'm more than my hair. I felt powerful when I cut my hair off. Like maybe in the sense that I feel that [men] prefer long hair, that I wasn't ruled by that and I could like set my own standards. And sort of like, it's being in control of your hair gives you somewhat of a power.

Still other women find a sense of power not through rejecting attractiveness per se but through broadening the definition of attractiveness to include appearances that occur more naturally within their own ethnic group (Banks, 1997; Craig, 1995). These new definitions explicitly challenge the ideology that defines minority women's appearances as inferior and that encourages minority women to engage in time-consuming and painful disciplines to conform to dominant appearance norms. Thus, three of the four African-American women I interviewed described their past decisions to wear an Afro, braids, or dreadlocks as explicitly political statements about their identities. . . .

In sum, like the traditional strategies described previously, the strategies described in this section are intentional actions designed to resist subordination and increase the power of members of a subordinate group. Unlike most of the traditional strategies, however, each of these strategies challenges the ideology that underlies subordination, even though only some of the women frame their actions in ideological terms. Thus, all these strategies contain elements of resistance.

At the same time, however, these strategies contain elements of accommodation. . . .

The Limits of Obtaining Power through Nontraditional Strategies

Given these problems, it is not surprising that, like traditional strategies, nontraditional strategies also offer only limited effectiveness. Whereas those who emphasize conventional attractiveness and femininity risk unwanted male sexual attention, those who defeminize their appearance and/or adopt more professional hairstyles risk desexualization (Bartky, 1988) and the loss of desired male attention. After all, just because a woman wants a professional job doesn't mean she doesn't want a boyfriend or husband. . . .

Moreover, if a woman adopts a look that others consider not only less feminine but frankly unattractive, she may find that professional success also eludes her, for, as described earlier, conventionally attractive women receive more job offers, higher salaries, and more promotions than unattractive women. And regardless of a woman's sexual orientation, she risks discrimination if her hairstyle leads others to label her a lesbian—experiences shared by several short-haired respondents.

The stories told by African-American women, meanwhile, emphasize the very real consequences paid by those who reject mainstream ideas about attractiveness—even if they still strive to look attractive by their own definitions (Banks, 1997). As Norma described:

> I remember I went to interview for a job and the guy wouldn't hire me because I had an Afro. A white guy. He said, 'It's your hair. I don't like your hairstyle. You've got to do something about your hair.' I didn't change my hairstyle of course, I just walked out. I figured I didn't need that job that much. . . .

These comments were seconded by the other African-American women I interviewed. Similar remarks were made by a woman with wildly curling 'Jewish' hair and by an immigrant who viewed long braided hair as a valued sign of her Pakistani identity but incompatible with American professional norms. For all these women, any aspect of their appearance that called attention to their minority status reduced their perceived competence and their social acceptability in the workplace. . . .

Conclusions

Findings from this study suggest that, far from being 'docile bodies', women are often acutely aware of cultural expectations regarding their hair. Yet rather than simply acquiescing to those expectations, women can consciously seek power by accommodating to those expectations, resisting them, or combining these two strategies. Nevertheless, we must not overstate women's agency in this matter, for their options are significantly constrained by both cultural expectations and social structure. Consequently, the hair management strategies women adopt to increase their power in some realms often decrease it in others. As a result, women do not so much choose between the available strategies as balance and alternate them, using whichever seems most useful at a given time.

The inherent limitations on the power available to women through their hairstyles raise the question of why women continue to seek power in this way (or, more generally, through their appearance). As we have seen, women consciously use culturally mandated appearance norms to achieve their personal ends. To say that women consciously use these norms, however, does not mean that they are free to ignore them. No matter what a woman does or doesn't do with her hair—dyeing or not dyeing, curling or not curling, covering with a bandana or leaving uncovered—her hair will affect how others respond to her, and her power will increase or decrease accordingly. Consequently, women use their hair to improve their position because they recognize that not doing so can imperil their position. Of course, the power and any other gains achieved through hair or other aspects of appearance are circumscribed, fragile, bittersweet, and limiting. Yet the power achieved in this way is no less real. Moreover, for many women, appearance remains a more accessible route to power than does career success, financial independence, political achievement, and so on.

The same constraints on women's options and agency that make seeking power through appearance a reasonable choice also explain why, although some of the strategies women use to gain power through their hair contain elements of resistance, *all* contain elements of accommodation (cf. Elowe MacLeod, 1991). Compared to resistance, accommodation offers women (and any other subordinate group) a far more reliable and safer route to power, even if that power is limited. As a result, the strategies women typically use can help individual women gain power, or at least a sense of power, in some arenas, but do little to improve the situation of women as a group. Rather, these strategies unintentionally lend support to those who equate women's bodies with their identities, consider women's bodies more important than their minds, assume that women use their bodies to manipulate men, or assume that femininity and competence are antithetical (thus handicapping visibly 'feminine' women socially). . . .

Notes

. . .

1. Hair and appearance also affect men's social position, but to a much lesser extent (Jackson, 1992; Sullivan, 2001). In addition, because the parameters for acceptable male appearance are both narrower (allowing less experimentation and less pressure to adapt to fashion) and broader (allowing much more natural variation), most men can

obtain a socially acceptable haircut with little time, energy, or cost. The exceptions are, truly, exceptional: actors and models, gay men whose communities emphasize appearance, middle-aged middle managers whose companies are downsizing, the recently divorced, and so on.

2. I do not distinguish in this [article] between actual power and a sense of power because all the data are based on women's perceptions, and the distinction between a woman feeling that she has power or feeling a sense of power is slight at best.

References

Banks, Ingrid. 1997. *Social and Personal Constructions of Hair: Cultural Practices and Belief Systems among African American Women.* Ph.D. Diss., University of California, Berkeley.

Bartky, Sandra Lee. 1988. 'Foucault, Femininity, and the Modernization of Patriarchal Power', in Irene Diamond and Lee Quinby, eds, *Feminism and Foucault: Reflections on Resistance.* Boston: Northeastern University Press.

Bordo, Susan R. 1989. 'The Body and the Reproduction of Femininity: A Feminist Appropriation of Foucault', in Alison M. Jaggar and Susan R. Bordo, eds, *Gender/body/knowledge.* New Brunswick, NJ: Rutgers University Press.

Craig, Maxine. 1995. *Black is Beautiful: Personal Transformation and Political Change.* Ph.D. diss., University of California, Berkeley.

Davis, Kathy. 1991. 'Remaking the She-Devil: A Critical Look at Feminist Approaches to Beauty', *Hypatia* 6, 2: 21–42.

———. 1995. *Reshaping the Female Body: The Dilemma of Cosmetic Surgery.* New York: Routledge.

Dellinger, Kirsten, and Christine L. Williams. 1997. 'Makeup at Work: Negotiating Appearance Rules in the Workplace', *Gender & Society* 11: 151–77.

Fernandez Kelly, M. Patricia. 1995. 'Social and Cultural Capital in the Urban Ghetto, in Alejandro Portes, ed, *The Economic Sociology of Immigration: Essays on Networks, Ethnicity, and Entrepreneurship.* New York: Russell Sage.

Firth, Raymond. 1973. *Symbols: Public and Private.* Ithaca, NY: Cornell University Press.

Foucault, Michel. 1979. *Discipline and Punish: The Birth of the Prison.* New York: Vintage.

———. 1980. *History of Sexuality.* New York: Pantheon.

Hill, Patricia Collins. 1991. *Black Feminist Thought: Knowledge, Consciousness, and the Politics of Empowerment.* London: Routledge.

Hilliard, Dan C. 1984. 'Media Images of Male and Female Professional Athletes: An Interpretive Analysis of Magazine Articles', *Sociology of Sport Journal* 1: 251–62.

Jackson, Linda. 1992. *Physical Appearance and Gender: Sociobiological and Sociocultural Perspectives.* Albany: State University of New York Press.

Lowe, Maria R. 1998. *Women of Steel: Female Body Builders and the Struggle for Self-Definition.* New Brunswick, NJ: Rutgers University Press.

McAlexander, James H., and John W. Schouten. 1989. 'Hair Style Changes as Transition Markers', *Sociology and Social Research* 74: 58–62.

MacLeod, Arlene Elowe. 1991. *Accommodating Protest: Working Women, the New Veiling, and Change in Cairo.* New York: Columbia University Press.

Stombler, Mindy, and Irene Padavic. 1997. 'Sister Acts: Resisting Men's Domination in Black and White Fraternity Little Sister Programs', *Social Problems* 44: 257–75.

Sullivan, Deborah A. 2001. *Cosmetic Surgery: The Cutting Edge of Commercial Medicine in America.* New Brunswick, NJ: Rutgers University Press.

Synnott, Anthony. 1987. 'Shame and Glory: A Sociology of Hair', *British Journal of Sociology* 38: 381–413.

Valian, Virginia. 1998. *Why So Slow?: The Advancement of Women.* Cambridge, MA: MIT Press.

Weitz, Rose, and Leonard Gordon. 1993. 'Images of Black Women among Anglo College Students', *Sex Roles* 28: 19–45.

Wiley, Mary Glenn, and Kathleen S. Crittenden. 1992. 'By Your Attributions You Shall Be Known: Consequences of Attributional Accounts for Professional and Gender Identities', *Sex Roles* 27: 259–76.

Chapter 42

'A Dubious Equality': Men, Women, and Cosmetic Surgery

Kathy Davis

Several years ago, I wrote *Reshaping the Female Body* (Davis, 1995) . . . My central argument was that cosmetic surgery cannot be understood as a matter of individual choice; nor is it an artifact of consumer culture which, in principle, affects us all. On the contrary, cosmetic surgery has to be situated in the context of how gender/power is exercised in late modern Western culture. Cosmetic surgery belongs to a broad regime of technologies, practices, and discourses, which define the female body as deficient and in need of constant transformation.

Since the book was published, I have had the opportunity to talk to many different audiences—students, social scientists, philosophers, medical practitioners, consumer advocates, and feminist activists—and I invariably get the same response. They say: 'What you have told us about women is very interesting. But what about men? Don't men worry about their appearance and want to look younger, thinner, and more attractive? Don't men have cosmetic surgery, too?'

My standard response and simultaneous defence of my 'selective' approach to cosmetic surgery up until now has been to point out that, statistically, women are the primary targets of cosmetic surgery. Both numerically and ideologically, men as recipients of cosmetic surgery are the exception rather than the rule. They comprise such a small group that their importance for understanding the phenomenon of cosmetic surgery is negligible and, therefore, all but irrelevant.

However, in the past few years, . . . there has been a small, but steady increase in the number of men having cosmetic surgery. As of 1998, about 10 per cent of the 2.8 million cosmetic surgery procedures in the United States were performed on men . . .

The media in the United States and Europe abound with stories of how men, like women, suffer doubts about their appearance, agonize over their baldness, worry about their 'beer bellies' and underdeveloped pecs, bemoan their sagging eyelids and worry lines, and dissolve into panic about the size of their penis . . . Reports indicate that men are currently spending billions of dollars on beauty products, gym memberships and exercise equipment, hair-colour treatments and transplants, and, of course, cosmetic surgery. . . .

. . . Mike Featherstone (1991) . . . views men's involvement in cosmetic surgery as part of the universal capitulation to the seductions of consumer capitalism. Margaret Gullette (1994) worries that men are falling into the same cultural traps that have been laid for women and that feminists need to form alliances with men on this issue. . . . Gender differences in bodily experience, body practices, and cultural discourses on beauty and body alteration are converging in the direction of sexual equality. . . .

I must admit that my feelings are mixed about this assumption of parity between the sexes in the realm of physical appearance. I find it difficult to see men as the new victims of the 'beauty myth'. I am doubtful that cosmetic surgeons—most of whom are men—will ever enthusiastically promote, let alone perform, surgery on members of their own sex. But, most importantly, I am uneasy about this discourse of equality. It seems to erase women's long and painful history of altering their bodies to conform with the cultural dictates of femininity, while, at the same time, it denies men's specific experiences with their bodies and the cultural meanings of masculinity in relation to cosmetic surgery. . . .

In my view, the new equality discourse on cosmetic surgery resonates with the process of homogenization and the neutralization of differences based on structured forms of inequality that Bordo (1993) describes as integral to late modern, Western culture. When men and women are treated as generic individuals with the same desire for physical attractiveness, it is assumed that they are both equally subject to the pressures of cultural ideals of beauty. And, consequently, cosmetic surgery can be presented as a *similarly* desirable (or undesirable) and socially acceptable (or unacceptable) way for both sexes to change their bodies, their identities, and their lives. . . .

Media Representations

In the early 1990s, a British program called *Plastic Fantastic* was aired . . .

The makers of *Plastic Fantastic* emphasized at the outset of the program that cosmetic surgery was of interest to both sexes. To illustrate this claim, they devoted three of the programs to men and cosmetic surgery . . . In the first, the focus is on a baby-boomer generation of men in search of perennial youth and anxious to maintain its position in the work world. . . . In the program on pectoral implants . . . the recipients are male go-go dancers, bartenders, and fitness fanatics who want to take the 'easy way'. Experts remark that implants are a sign of 'gym culture with a vengeance', and that men are frequently more 'vain' than women. Many protest that they couldn't imagine having implants themselves and they are scarcely able to disguise their disapproval at such 'frivolous' interventions. The surgeons aren't enthusiastic, either, but, as they put it, 'If we don't do them, someone else will.' . . .

While their reasons for wanting the surgery resonate with the reasons women give for wanting cosmetic surgery—feeling different, lack of self-confidence, being teased about their appearance—these men's presentation is so full of hesitation and shame, that the viewer feels more pity than understanding. While the male 'experts' describe the operation as 'appalling', the female 'experts' can't contain their laughter.

They make jokes about 'shrunken willies'. . . The surgeons are almost unanimously negative about the surgery, exclaiming that it's 'nonsense' . . . The emphasis is on side effects, risks, and lack of adequate knowledge, and they are much more negative about penis augmentations than they were about breast augmentations. . . .

The augmentation candidates are white women of different age groups and social backgrounds. They are introduced by name and they are shown full-face . . . Their reasons seem plausible and their enthusiasm for the operation is so convincing that it is hard for the viewer not to take their point of view. Although some of the 'experts' are a bit ambivalent . . ., they remain basically non-judgmental . . .

Having watched and analyzed many similar television programs about cosmetic surgery, I believe that *Plastic Fantastic* is a typical example of the way in which the media portrays the new trend of cosmetic surgery for men. On the one hand, cosmetic surgery is presented as just as relevant for men as it is for women. The viewer is warned not to believe that only women care about their appearances and try to do something about it. However, scratch the surface of this rhetoric of sexual equality and one immediately finds an unmistakable ambivalence about men and cosmetic surgery. In their ambiguity, the reactions of the patients, experts, and surgeons on *Plastic Fantastic* suggest that cosmetic surgery is not quite the same kind of undertaking for men and women, after all. While the patients and experts seem to find it understandable and even 'natural' for women to have their bodies altered surgically, a man who has cosmetic surgery seems uncomfortable or—in the case of penile surgery—deeply ashamed. Experts clearly regard him as, at best, ridiculous and, at worst, an aberration, someone who is different, deviant, or even pathological. The surgeons appear to embrace cosmetic surgery for women with enthusiasm—as essentially beneficial and unproblematic. Cosmetic surgery for men, however, is treated as a potentially dangerous and risky endeavour. . . .

A case in point is the response of the medical profession in the Netherlands to penile augmentation surgery. It was heralded in the early 1990s as a revolutionary solution to the problem of 'locker-room anxiety'. However, just two years later, it was discontinued. . . . In the United States, penile surgery has also become controversial as practitioners increasingly face criticisms from their colleagues and costly malpractice suits from disappointed patients. . . .

Medical Texts

In recent years, plastic surgery has begun to address the specific needs and problems of the male patient. . . . *Clinics in Plastic Surgery* (Connell, 1991) devoted an entire issue to male aesthetic surgery. . . . From a medical point of view, cosmetic surgery was depicted as the same for men and women. However, while the procedures and technologies were treated as similar, men and women as patients definitely were not.

Most surgical texts represent female patients as struggling with bodies that do not meet the cultural norms of feminine beauty. . . . Surgeons expect women to have 'self-esteem issues' when it comes to their appearance. Since medicine has historically defined the female body as deficient and in need of repair, cosmetic surgery is easily legitimated as a 'natural' and, therefore, acceptable therapy for women's problems with their appearance.

In contrast, surgeons describe men as having cosmetic surgery for different reasons than women do. Men seek out surgery for 'functional reasons' or 'clear-cut physical complaints' rather than the 'purely aesthetic reasons' put forth by women (Flowers, 1991: 689). . . .

Although the 'cultural barriers' to men having cosmetic surgery may have been crumbling since the 1960s, men who desire cosmetic surgery still tend to be regarded with some suspicion (Haiken, 1997: 155–61). In the medical literature, they are referred to as 'overly-narcissistic' and 'effeminate'. . . .

Terms like 'delusional psychotic', 'grandiose ambitions', 'latent schizophrenic', and 'suicidal' abound in medical texts about the male cosmetic surgery patient. . . . In 1991, one author noted that probably 15 per cent of all men seeking rhinoplasties were the victims of 'severe psychological obsession' and should be screened out immediately (Daniel, 1991).

The assumption seems to be that 'normal' men don't care about their appearance and, if they do, there must be something wrong with them. . . .

Male patients also have more unrealistic ideas about what surgery can accomplish than women (Mladick, 1991: 797), and they are notoriously less satisfied with the results of the operations. In the well-known and widely cited textbook *The Unfavourable Result in Cosmetic Surgery* (1972 [1984]), women are described as generally willing to accept even the most negative outcome, while male patients tend to display 'emotionally malignant reactions' to surgical failures. . . .

As if this weren't enough to make surgeons feel ambivalent about their male patients, they also worry about the dissatisfied male patient's tendency toward paranoia and aggression against the surgeon in the form of litigations, threatening postcards, or midnight visits to the surgeon's home. Disgruntled male patients have been known to become violent with, in at least one case, fatal results. . . .

Masculinity

. . . Formerly hidden from sight, men's bodies are currently on display in magazines, television, and films . . ., provid[ing] powerful models for how the male body should look: bulging biceps, well-defined pecs, washboard stomachs . . .

While such representations of muscle-bound masculinity do seem to provide the impetus for many of the newer cosmetic technologies for men

. . ., and may, indeed, shape some men's desire for cosmetic surgery, it seems to me that this is only part of the story. Masculinity takes many forms and certain forms are more dominant or, as Connell (1995) would say, 'hegemonic', than others. In Western culture, it is not the muscular bodybuilder or the provocative male centerfold who are 'hegemonic' and at the top of the hierarchy; it is Rational Man who embodies real power (Morgan, 1993; Seidler, 1994). High-level executives in the corporate world, financiers, Pentagon military strategists, professors at Ivy League universities, or professional men in the upper echelons of medicine and law all inhabit positions of wealth and power that enable them to legitimate and reproduce the social relationships that, in turn, generate their dominance. The dominance of these men rests on the repudiation of all telltale signs of femininity and gayness in themselves, and the capacity to represent themselves as universal norm—the unquestioned and unquestionable standard against which all others are measured and fail to measure up. It is the fiction of a unified masculinity, which generates a deep-seated fear of the inferior 'other' (i.e., women, but also men who are less deserving due to their class, sexual preference, ethnicity, 'race', or nationality) (Connell, 1995; Frosh, 1994; Segal, 1990; Young, 1990a). Indeed, controlling other men may be at least as, if not more, important than controlling women. Homophobia and a keen sense of 'competitiveness', combined with a 'combination of the calculative and the combative' interaction with other men, seem to be the central features of masculine power of the 'Rational Man' variety (Donaldson, 1993: 654–5).

The male body sits on uneasy footing with the discourses and practices of this particular brand of 'hegemonic masculinity'. For masculinity, which is guided by the dictates of rationality ('mind over matter'), the body is, at best, irrelevant, and, at worst, an intrusive obstacle to the more important activities of the mind. The body is something to be ignored, denied, or, at least, kept firmly out of sight. If the male body comes into play at all, it is as the performing body: the body that has everything under control, the body

that 'does', but is never, never, 'done to' (Bordo, 1994: 288).

This raises the question whether cosmetic surgery can be a way for men to meet the cultural requirements of masculinity. . . . Given the meanings associated with hegemonic masculinity in Western culture, I would argue cosmetic surgery cannot 'enhance' masculinity for men in the same way it 'enhances' femininity for women for the simple reason that the very act of having surgery signifies a symbolic transgression of the dominant norms of masculinity.

First, men who desire cosmetic surgery distance themselves from the norm of rational masculinity as disembodied. . . . [T]his norm implicitly requires that the body and all its material or emotional vulnerabilities be denied, hidden, or transcended. The male cosmetic surgery patient is preoccupied with his body, however. His body—its appearance and the suffering it entails—is a central rather than a peripheral concern. . . .

Second, men who admit suffering because of how they look, display behaviour that, in our culture, is coded as feminine. . . .

Third, men who place their bodies under the surgeon's knife lose control—at least temporarily—of their bodies. . . . In a culture where agency, power, and control are linked to masculinity, by becoming a patient, a man takes on attributes that are at odds with hegemonic notions of masculine power. . . .

In this context, it is hardly surprising that many male surgeons are reluctant to perform operations on male patients, or are inclined to find reasons why cosmetic surgery is inappropriate for men in general. It also makes sense that surgeons attempt to alleviate their uneasiness by distancing themselves from their male patients and relegating them to the position of 'other'—that is, different, deviant, disturbed, and dangerous. . . .

The Genderedness of Cosmetic Surgery

The current media hype on men as the latest objects of the 'surgical fix' is not simply a case of mistaken thinking. On the contrary, it follows from a discourse of equality that currently pervades late modern Western culture and, as such, has far-reaching and systematic ideological implication. Equality discourse neutralizes the salience of gender (and other categories of difference) for understanding how men and women experience their bodies, as well as the specific cultural modes of embodiment that are available to them. Under the banner of the new sexual equality in the realm of beauty practices, it becomes impossible to grasp why cosmetic surgery seems like such a 'natural' and unproblematic step for a woman to take, while it is a shameful and humiliating operation for a man, only to be undertaken at great cost to his sense of self and how others perceive him. And, last but not least, equality discourse erases the long-standing feminist critique of the gendered underpinnings of the contemporary cultural obsession with beauty. Cultural discourses and practices, which render certain bodies 'drab, ugly, loathsome, or fearful' (Young, 1990b: 123) become obsolete and therefore irrelevant. . . .

Note

The quotation in the title is taken from Mike Featherstone (1991: 179).

References

Bordo, Susan. 1993. *Unbearable Weight*. Berkeley, Los Angeles, and London: University of California Press.

———. 1994. 'Reading the Male Body', in L. Goldstein, ed, *The Male Body*. Ann Arbor: Michigan University Press, 265–306.

Connell, Bruce, ed. 1991. 'Male Aesthetic Surgery', *Clinics in Plastic Surgery* 18, 4: 653–890.

Connell, R.W. 1995. *Masculinities*. Berkeley, and Los Angeles: University of California Press.

Daniel, Rollin K. 1991. 'Rhinoplasty and the Male Patient', *Clinics in Plastic Surgery* 18, 4: 751–61.

Davis, Kathy. 1995. *Reshaping the Female Body*. New York and London: Routledge.

Donaldson, Mike. 1993. 'What is Hegemonic Masculinity?', *Theory and Society* 22: 643–57.

Featherstone, Mike. 1991. 'The Body in Consumer Culture', in M. Featherstone, M. Hepworth, and B.S. Turner, eds, *The Body*. London: Sage, 170–96.

Flowers, Robert S. 1991. 'Periorbital Aesthetic Surgery for Men', *Clinics in Plastic Surgery* 18, 4: 689–729.

Frosh, Stephen. 1994. *Sexual Difference, Masculinity and Psychoanalysis*. London and New York: Routledge.

Gullette, Margaret Morganroth. 1994. 'All Together Now: The New Sexual Politic of Midlife Bodies', in L. Goldstein, ed, *The Male Body*. Ann Arbor: Michigan University Press, 221–47.

Haiken, Elizabeth. 1997. *Venus Envy: A History of Cosmetic Surgery*. Baltimore, MD, and London: Johns Hopkins University Press.

Mladick, Richard A. 1991. 'Male Body Contouring', *Clinics in Plastic Surgery* 18, 4: 797–822.

Morgan, David. 1993. 'You Too Can Have a Body Like Mine: Reflections on the Male Body and Masculinities', in S. Scott and D. Morgan, eds, *Body Matters*. London and Washington, DC: The Falmer Press, 69–88.

Segal, Lynn. 1990. *Slow Motion: Changing Men, Changing Masculinities*. London: Virago.

Seidler, Victor J. 1994. *Unreasonable Men: Masculinity and Social Theory*. New York and London: Routledge.

Young, Iris Marion. 1990a. *Justice and the Politics of Difference*. Princeton, NJ: Princeton University Press.

———. 1990b. *Throwing Like a Girl and Other Essays in Feminist Philosophy and Social Theory*. Bloomington and Indianapolis: Indiana University Press.

Part XV

Aging Bodies

Jacqueline Low and Claudia Malacrida

Recent research showing the potential health dangers of hormone replacement therapy (HRT) has changed medical thinking in terms of its safety and **efficacy** (effectiveness). Medical directives have changed from a position where such drugs were advocated as a necessary intervention in the lives of all menopausal women to a 'medical tool that is appropriate only for some women' (Picard, 2007). As a result, almost half of Canadian women using HRT have stopped taking these drugs. However, HRT was for decades medical science's, and the pharmaceutical industry's, answer to the socially constructed female problem of menopause. For example, over 40 years ago Dr Robert A. Wilson (1966) extolled the virtues of being forever young and forever feminine through the use of HRT in his best-selling book, *Feminine Forever*. In this book he emphasized the positive effects of using HRT and paid scant attention to the serious iatrogenic effects of these drugs. **Iatrogenesis** is a concept that refers to the side effects, complications, and other health problems a person acquires when he or she undergoes medical therapy (Illich, 1975). In the case of HRT the iatrogenic effects include increased risk of cervical and breast cancers.

In her chapter, Joy Webster Barbre (1993) compares social constructions of women and women's menopausal bodies in the Victorian era (1840–1900) with contemporary constructions and concludes that while women today differ in many ways from Victorian women; in both cases menopause is seen as a crisis that robs a woman of her youth, femininity, and ability to reproduce. Loss of these attributes then becomes understood as a literal loss of womanhood, turning menopause into a crisis that must be medically managed through HRT.

In their article on male sexual function, Barbara L. Marshall and Stephen Katz (2002) note that, since the nineteenth century, a tendency toward medicalization and an increased negativity towards aging has led to an increasingly 'corrective' approach to men's natural aging processes. The discipline of **gerontology**, the study of aging, has contributed to the understanding of male aging as pathological, and as something that may appear to occur with old age, but that actually begins much earlier. More recently, the focus on 'healthy aging' turned to male sexual function, in part because of the rise of another discipline, **sexology** (the study of sexual behaviour, which became established in the mid-twentieth century through the work of influential figures such as Kinsey [2007], Masters and Johnson [1966], and Hite [2003]). These two disciplines—gerontology and sexology—together constructed a psychological explanation for male impotence. However, in the mid-1980s, the discipline of **urology** (the field of medicine that focuses on the urinary tracts of males and females, and on the reproductive system of males) finally and emphatically situated the 'problem' as physiological rather than psychological. Since then, erectile dysfunction has been medicalized, and like many medicalized phenomena, this has resulted in increasingly broad definitions of pathology, an increasingly wide range of people who may be affected by the 'disease', and an increasingly strident discourse about the risks that individuals must avoid in order to prevent potential decline. Thus, the shift from a psychological to a medical model of impotence has operated as a disciplinary force for men who are exhorted to engage in a wide range of preventative bodily strategies in order to age 'successfully'.

In 'Aging, Alzheimer's, and the Uncivilized Body', Chris Gilleard and Paul Higgs (2000) describe how bodies that are rendered mindless and unable to care for themselves through dementia or senility have become the **de-civilized body**, the antithesis of the **civilized body**, the person who in response to the cultural imperative for control of the body has acquired the capacity for self-control in the absence of external control of the body (Elias, 1978; see also Part II). Throughout their reading they trace how the process of the de-civilizing of the body has become, almost exclusively, one that is conceptualized as symptoms of Alzheimer's disease, a process they call the **alzheimerization of aging**. Gilleard and Higgs demonstrate how this process owes much to the activities of the pharmaceutical industry in their zeal to develop new drugs to treat Alzheimer's disease. Moreover, they show how by conceptualizing the symptoms of aging as a disease, the de-civilizing of the body has been transformed from a natural part of human aging into something that affects risk groups, the members of which need to adopt health promotion lifestyles. A significant consequence of this change is that the care of de-civilized bodies becomes an individual rather than a collective and social responsibility.

References

Adelman, R.C. 1995. 'The Alzheimerization of Aging', *The Gerontologist* 35, 4: 526–32.

Barbre, J.W. 2003. 'Meno-boomers and Moral Guardians: An Exploration of the Cultural Construction of Menopause', in J.C. Callahan, ed, *Menopause: A Midlife Passage*. Bloomington, IN: Indiana University Press, 23–35.

Elias, N. 1978. *The Civilizing Process: The History of Manners*. Oxford: Basil Blackwell Publishers.

Gilleard, C., and P. Higgs. 2000. 'Aging, Alzheimer's, and the Uncivilized Body, in *Cultures of Aging: Self, Citizen and the Body*. Harlow, England: Prentice Hall, 168–192.

Hite, S. 2003. *The Hite Report: A Nationwide Study of Female Sexuality*. Edinburgh: AK Press, Seven Stories Publishing.

Illich, I. 1975. *Medical Nemesis: The Expropriation of Health*. Toronto: McClelland and Stewart.

Kinsey, A. 2007. The Kinsey Institute for Research in Sex, Gender, and Reproduction. http://www.kinseyinstitute.org/research/ak-data.html.

Marshall, B.L., and S. Katz. 2002. 'Forever Functional: Sexual Fitness and the Aging Male Body', *Body and Society* 8, 4: 43–70.

Masters, W.H., and V.E. Johnson. 1966. *Human Sexual Response*. New York: Bantam Books.

Picard, A. 2007. '44% of Canadian women abandon HRT', *The Globe and Mail Online* 8 February. Available at: http://www.theglobeandmail.com. Accessed 8 February 2007.

Wilson, R.A. 1966. *Feminine Forever*. London: W. H. Allen.

Chapter 43

Meno-boomers and Moral Guardians: An Exploration of the Cultural Construction of Menopause

Joy Webster Barbre

In a recent issue of the *Los Angeles Times,* staff writer Linda Roach Monroe asserted that the United States is about to experience a 'meno-boom'. According to Monroe, with the aging of more than 30 million baby boom generation women, the number of women affected by menopause in the United States will increase by more than 33 per cent over the next two decades. As the baby boomers turn into meno-boomers, menopause is likely to receive more and more of this kind of coverage in mainstream American culture. Authenticated by scientific studies and medial evidence, the information presented will probably, like Monroe's article, relate that the difficulties associated with menopause and poor health in old age may be substantially reduced when healthy living, proper medical management, and, according to some, hormone replacement therapy, begin early in the premenopausal years. . . .

Menopause is a biological phenomenon with a set of physiological imperatives that do not change over time. All women who live long enough will experience or have experienced menopause. Therefore, menopause would seem to be a natural biological occurrence, over which culture has little influence. However, menopause does not occur in a vacuum. It, like other events resulting from women's reproductive biology, menstruation and childbirth for instance, is given meaning and value by the culture within which it occurs. . . .

. . . In order to begin to . . . bring into focus how the contemporary model of menopause can be seen as a cultural construct, . . . I explore the cultural construction of menopause in Victorian America. . . .

Victorian Womanhood in America

In nineteenth-century America, the Victorian world view was one that centred around notions of rationality, individualism, 'scientific' thought, and moral authority. For the burgeoning middle class, centres of production had moved from the home to the industrial realm, and concepts of a separation between the public and private spheres were emerging. The ideal Victorian woman was perceived to be inherently intuitive, passive, delicate, affectionate, nurturing, and domestic, attributes that afforded her a dimension of moral superiority. These 'innate' qualities made women unfit for the harsh and competitive realities of industrialized society (the public sphere). . . . [T]hey were qualities that were best expressed in marriage and motherhood, thereby making women particularly suited to the home (private sphere). The private sphere was thus perceived as women's domain, the place where they, with their moral superiority, created an atmosphere in which men could revitalize their moral sensibilities after their exposure to corrupting immoral influences in the public sphere. The home was also the place where women's 'innate' qualities could be utilized to ensure that children would be reared to responsibly fulfill their moral obligations as adults. In this manner, Victorian women came to be seen as guardians of Victorian morality.

Science, rapidly replacing religion as the realm of discourse that could best explain the universe and guide people's lives, played an important role in the rationalization and justification of these separate sphere conceptions. Though perceived as objective, and therefore the conveyor of 'truth', science was in fact a part of the broader culture in which it existed. As such, it reflected and reinforced the broader culture's assumptions about how a well-ordered society should work. Medical and moral realms became intertwined as 'scientific' evidence emerged that rationalized the broader culture's moral convictions, and an elaborate body of medical and biological theory explained and justified the culture's conceptions about women's inherent nature and hence their role as moral guardians (Martin, 1987; . . . Wood, 1984; Banner, 1983; Evans, 1989; Gordon, 1977; May, 1980).

Nineteenth-century Medical Theory and Women's Bodies

Mid-nineteenth-century medical theory postulated that the ganglionic nervous system served as a storage for the 'vital force' and was the source of all energy. This nervous system was directly connected to the reproductive system and the central nervous system, including the brain. This physiology was not peculiar to women, but because of women's more complex reproductive physiology—puberty, menstruation, childbirth, lactation, menopause—their reproductive organs drew more energy from the ganglionic system, and hence, their storage of 'vital force' was always in danger of depletion. Any breakdown in a woman's reproductive organs could cause trauma to her nervous system and through it to other parts of her body. In a like manner, any shock to her nervous system could damage her reproductive organs. In any of these cases, extra demands were placed on her 'vital forces', which were already in short supply because of her reproductive biology (Tilt, 1882). In effect, this theory rationalized what was already suspected, namely, that women and men were suited to different societal realms because of their reproductive organs.

A woman's reproductive organs governed her entire being; they dictated her personality, her abilities and limitations, and hence her social role. . . . Perhaps M.L. Holbrook put it most succinctly when he noted that it seemed, 'as if the Almighty, in creating the female sex, has taken the Uterus and built up a woman around it' (Wood, 1984: 223). . . .

. . . [E]ducation presented particular peril because it diverted the 'vital force' away from the uterus, and to the brain. As one respected doctor reported,

> I have known many to lose their catamenia [menstruation] by severe application of the mind to studies . . . to rack her brain learning Latin is nonsense. She can't learn it, in the first place. She can only try till it makes her sick . . . they [women] cannot . . . participate in the affairs of nations or municipalities; because by the very nature of their moral and physical constitution, they are bound to the horns of the family altar. . . (Meigs, 1848: 352–64)

Clearly, nineteenth-century conceptions about women's biology were tightly bound to the ideology surrounding women's social roles and promoted woman's position as moral guardian. And when Victorian assumptions about women's aging are also explored, we can begin to see how the era's construction of womanhood shaped the meanings and values ascribed to menopause during this period.

Definitions of Female Old Age in Victorian America

During the nineteenth century, when the uterus was the primary definer of womanhood and menopause signalled the end of the very core of woman's existence, menopause heralded the onset of female old age . . . . By mid-nineteenth century, many women were living well into old age. . . . Thus, while large numbers of nineteenth-century women had many years of life left after menopause, the culture considered them years of old age.

In Victorian culture female old age was often presented as a pleasurable stage of life. . . .

. . . Dixon wrote, 'The crowning glory of a healthy woman, is a large family . . . when faithfully carried out . . . she is adding to her length of years, and the happiness of her old age' (1857: 315).

Ideally, for the post-menopausal Victorian woman life was to be a continuation of the nurturing, domestic, and moral aspects of her younger days, but with the added dimensions of improved health and beauty and veneration and respect for her example of right living. Women could enjoy the promise of old age, but not until they had passed through menopause, a period of danger laden with physical risks and hidden cultural significance.

Victorian Perceptions of Menopause

Menopause was the point at which the system that had regulated women's entire lives failed, and the crisis it presented was not to be taken lightly. Doctors asserted that because of the integral connection between women's reproductive organs and their central nervous systems, menopause, when the reproductive organs were in a disturbed state, '. . . is universally admitted to be a critical and dangerous time for her' (Tilt, 1882: 15). Chronic ill health, chronic debility, consumption, rheumatism, ulcerated legs, diabetes, urinary tract problems, hemorrhoids, gout, tooth decay, heart disease, shingles, chronic diarrhea and constipation, deafness, and cancer are just a few of the conditions doctors warned could be brought on by menopause (Tilt, 1882: 106–224).

Reflecting the culture's emphasis on women's moral superiority, one of the most serious conditions associated with menopause was 'moral insanity'. . . . Tilt explained . . .

During the change of life the nervous system is so unhinged that the management of the mental and moral faculties often taxes the ingenuity of the medical confidant . . . [the disturbance]

can cause normally moral women to act without principle . . . be untruthful . . . be peevish . . . even have fits of temper . . . steal . . . leave their families . . . brood in melancholy self absorption. (1882, 101)

The perceived association between menopause and moral insanity was so pervasive that Victorian era court records indicate moral insanity due to menopause was often accepted as a defence in cases of shoplifting (Abelson, 1989: 184–7). While the ailments listed above were perceived to be the result of menopause, prescriptions for surviving this dangerous period of life indicate that a woman's behaviour determined whether she would have the kind of menopause that caused these conditions.

Packaged as medical advice, the counsel about menopause given to Victorian women . . . conveyed a warning that the hazards of menopause could be avoided if women held fast to their 'innate' nurturing, delicate, and moral nature. . . . [W]omen were advised to retire from the world, devote themselves to domesticity . . .

For the nineteenth-century woman, it was not only her behaviour during menopause that determined the kind of old age she would have; the accumulated experiences of her past life were also a contributing factor. Indiscretions in earlier life, as one doctor noted, '. . . will find this period [menopause] a veritable Pandora's box of ills' (Haller, 1972: 65). . . . Charles Meigs asserted that '. . . a badly passed youth will show up in a disastrous menopause', and related the example of a young woman who attempted to delay the onset of her monthly menses by cold baths so that she might attend a dance. Meigs reported that her efforts were successful, but at the change of life she suffered diseases of the womb that were directly related to this one incident (1848: 349–55). . . .

Women, Culture, and Menopause in Contemporary America

Today's model of womanhood appears to bear little resemblance to the nineteenth-century model described above. Reproduction is still a core element in our culture's definition of woman, but giving birth and rearing children comprise only one option in a woman's life, not the very reason for her existence. . . . No matter what the choices, or age, today's woman is competent and capable in all areas. She is able to succeed in her chosen career, raise perfect children, create the perfect home, and juggle the numerous demands of all three. She is sexually responsive, youthfully attractive, intellectually stimulated, and thus a perfect companion for the man in her life. She keeps up on current affairs, supports the right causes, and knows what foods and behaviours are scientifically proven to be best for the human body. In her busy schedule she finds time to take care of herself in order to assure that she will be attractive, energetic, physically fit, and healthy well into old age. On this model of womanhood the menopausal woman differs little from her younger sister. . . .

However, like our Victorian sisters a century ago, we, the women of today, are also warned that menopause is a crisis. As Dr Wulf H. Utian recently wrote,

Many women perceive menopause—like menses and pregnancy—as just another physiologic event in the course of female reproduction, and do not seek medical help. . . . We now know that menopausal symptoms must not be ignored. Even 'asymptomatic menopause' may initiate silent, progressive, and ultimately lethal sequelae.

The definition of 'sequelae' is 'a pathological condition resulting from a disease' (*American Heritage Dictionary*, 1982). The disease in question here is estrogen deficiency disease, a disease which, we are warned, causes pathological conditions. The cause of this disease is reported to be menopause.

According to numerous medical and scientific experts and commercial drug companies, hormone replacement therapy (HRT) is an important treatment for this disease, and many advise that women begin a program of HRT at or before menopause and continue therapy for the rest of their lives. . . .

The assertion that HRT is a reasonable course of treatment for all women is not new. Roughly 30 years ago, when our mothers were being told that the 'empty nest syndrome' could cause psychological problems at menopause, Dr Robert Wilson wrote his best seller, *Feminine Forever*, in which he asserted that, with HRT, 'Menopause is curable . . . Menopause is completely preventable . . . Instead of being condemned to witness the death of their own womanhood . . . [women] will remain fully feminine—physically and emotionally—for as long as they live' (1966, 15–19). In the 1990s, Wilson's rationale for advocating HRT seems chauvinistic and even anachronistic. Few of us view menopause as the death of womanhood. And yet, at that time, on the prevailing model of womanhood as represented by June Cleaver, Donna Reed, and Margaret Anderson, femininity was virtually synonymous with motherhood. Wilson's medical advice was shaped and formed by the culture's assumption that menopause presented a psychological crisis in women's lives and, like the Victorian doctors before him, his underlying message reflected and reinforced the era's cultural assumptions about women's social roles and women's biology. . . .

. . . Today the scientific evidence once again suggests that menopause is a physiological crisis; but as in the 1960s and the nineteenth century, the unspoken message reinforces and reflects our current model of ideal womanhood. For instance, . . . today's ideal woman, whatever her age, is youthfully attractive and physically fit. Robert G. Wells recently wrote, 'HRT may not be the elusive "fountain of youth", but it surely qualifies as one of its "springs"' (1989: 70). This claim for the benefits of HRT may provide us with a starting point in our search for the ways in which current advice on menopause constructs a model of menopause that is consistent with contemporary cultural assumptions about women's biology, women's social roles, and women's aging.

Definitions of what it means to be a woman have been constructed in different ways at different times throughout America's history. These changing definitions have emerged from changing broader cultural assumptions about how the world works. However, one essential element in all of these definitions has remained constant—woman's physiological ability to reproduce. And yet, the natural biological process of menopause—the end of those reproductive abilities—is an unavoidable experience for most women. It is an event that all definitions of womanhood must somehow accommodate in ways that are consistent with broader definitions of womanhood. Just as the models presented to women in the past must be questioned for the ways in which they were constructed to accomplish this accommodation, we, the women of today, must also question the model we are receiving. We must ask if the current rush to save us from menopause is the result of new 'objective' medical and scientific knowledge—a breakthrough in human's ability to correct nature's mistakes. Or is the perceived need to save women influenced by something more complex—specifically, by current assumptions about women's biology, women's social roles, and women's aging, as well as the broader cultural values that prevail in America today?

References

Abelson, Elaine S. 1989. *When Ladies Go A-Thieving: Middle-Class Shoplifters in the Victorian Department Store*. New York: Oxford University Press.

American Heritage Dictionary, 2nd College edn. 1982. Boston: Houghton Mifflin.

Banner, Lois W. 1983. *American Beauty*. Chicago: University of Chicago Press.

Dixon, Edward Henry, MD. 1857. *Woman and Her Diseases, from the Cradle to the Grave*. New York: A. Ranney.

Evans, Sara M. 1989. *Born for Liberty: A History of Women in America*. New York: The Free Press.

Gordon, Linda. 1977. *Woman's Body, Woman's Right*. New York: Penguin.

Haller, John S., Jr. 1972. 'From Maidenhood to Menopause: Sex Education for Women in Victoria-America', *Journal of Popular Culture* 6, 1: 49–70.

Martin, Emily. 1987. *The Woman in the Body: A Cultural Analysis of Reproduction*. Boston: Beacon.

May, Elaine Tyler. 1980. *Great Expectations: Marriage & Divorce in Post-Victorian America*. Chicago: University of Chicago Press.

Meigs, Charles. 1848. *Females and Their Diseases*. Philadelphia: Lea and Blanchard.

Tilt, Edward John, MD. 1882. *The Change of Life in Health and Disease. A Clinical Treatise on the Diseases of the Ganglionic Nervous System Incidental to Women at the Decline of Life*, 4th edn. New York: Bermingham.

Utian, Wulf H., MD. 1989. 'Renewing Our Commitment to the Remaining 85%'. *Menopause Management* 2, 1: 2.

Wells, Robert G., MD. 1989. 'Should All Postmenopausal Women Receive Hormone Replacement Therapy?' *Senior Patient* 6, 1: 65–70.

Wood, Ann Douglas. 1984. 'The Fashionable Diseases: Women's Complaints and Their Treatment in Nineteenth Century America', in Judith Walzer Leavitt, ed, *Women and Health in America*. Madison: University of Wisconsin Press.

Chapter 44

Forever Functional: Sexual Fitness and the Aging Male Body

Barbara L. Marshall and Stephen Katz

. . .

Sexual Decline and the Aging Male Body

Before modern medicine fashioned age as a special problem in the nineteenth century, and applied its biological and experimental know ledges to 'discovering' and coding it, there was a long and amusing history of writers who praised the arts of living long lives. Their treatises offered a potpourri of commonsensical, mystical, scientific, and philosophical advice, most of which counselled moderation in diet, drink, exercise, and sexual activity itself (see Cole, 1992; Gruman, 1966; Troyansky, 1989). For example, Renaissance Italian writers warned that male sexual virility could be affected by diet, behaviour, herbal remedies, heat and humidity conditions, stimulants, excessive sexual activity, and diabolical influences (Bell, 1999). . . .

Further, Menghi reported that male impotence could be caused by the devil mischievously imposing himself between a man and woman during sexual intercourse, a situation only remedied by the couple turning to ritual, pilgrimage, and prayer. Thus, sexual function can wane due to a universe of forces aside from aging—behavioural, dietary, climatic, natural and supernatural, real and imaginary.[1] . . .

The Climacteric

Sir Henry Halford, once physician to King George III of England, is credited with producing the first medical treatise on the male climacteric, 'On the Climacteric Disease' (1813). Carole Haber notes that Halford's influential notion of the climacteric as a disease marked by the *abrupt* onset of symptoms, only became popular some decades later when aging began to attract wider medical attention (1983: 69–70). In his republished paper Halford states:

> The period of the occurrence of this change in men, in general, is so very irregular, that it may be occasionally remarked at any time between 50 and 75 years of age; and I will venture to question, whether it not, in truth, a disease, rather than a mere declension of strength and decay of the natural powers. (1831: 4)

As a disease, the symptoms involved a 'falling away of the flesh in the decline of life, without any obvious source of exhaustion' (1831: 5). Added to this vague diagnosis was the problem of exact determination, since the climacteric was assumed to disguise itself within other diseases and complaints. In the end Halford admits that there is no cure. 'I have nothing to offer with confidence in that view beyond a caution that the symptoms of the disease be not met by too active a treatment' (1831: 13). Nevertheless, the climacteric disease marked the onset of old age and became a widening reference point for behavioural, emotional, and physiological changes associated with it. It also legitimized medical intervention into the lives of aging individuals by problematizing male, mid-life aging.

Later George Day, a foremost translator of French and German literature on old age (Haber, 1983: 64), supported Halford's contentions about the overwhelming yet mysterious power of the climacteric, noting that it is less common in women because men lead more exhausting and active lives (Day, 1849: 62–3). It is also untreatable, but manageable through diet, rest, and the avoidance of excitement (1849: 63). Other geriatric research followed (e.g., MacLachlan, 1863; Skae, 1865), expanding the symptomatology of the climacteric to include sexual decline, not as a physical problem of functionality but as a moral problem requiring adjustment to the passage of time in the body. After all, in the nineteenth-century male sexual potency was linked to the idea of semen supply and its procreative power (Gullette, 1994). Reserving one's semen was advisable in order to ensure better sexual capabilities, and for those who lived intensively and lasciviously, the consequences could only be negative—dissipation and pathology. . . .

. . . As the forerunner to the male midlife crisis or 'viropause' in the later twentieth century, the climacteric also made it possible for the aging process to be shaped by modern expertise in ways that articulated it with the moral and technical ideologies of the time. Above all, the idea of the climacteric was a popular crisis furnishing the public with a decline schematic of male life base on age, useful not only for registering a host of new 'age-based' problems, including sexual ones, but also for promoting a culture of rejuvenation and anti-aging technology.

Rejuvenation and Positive Gerontologic Aging

In the early twentieth century the widespread hostility towards aging and old age, fostered by climacteric science, new hormonal research, pension reform debates, the idealization of youthfulness, and the industrial era's expectations of mechanic bodies, renewed the imaginative appeal of life-extension possibilities. . . . The most famous example in the late nineteenth century was French-American neurologist, Dr Charles E. Brown-Sequard, who experimented with animal gland extracts and promoted the idea that especially sex-glandular injections had remarkable revitalizing powers. In 1889, at age 72 and citing his own rejuvenation as proof, Brown-Sequard inspired a public sensation about his 'method' and 'formula', which a drug company marketed in an elixir called 'Pohl's Spermine Preparations'. In the early twentieth century, doctors such as French-Russian Serge Veronoff, Austrian Eugen Steinach, and American Harry Benjamin (1959), stepped up research into animal gland grafts and surgical rejuvenation in the battle against aging. Surgical rejuvenation most famously involved the 'Steinach operation'—cutting and tying of the vas deferens to redirect the testicular ejaculation of sperm into the body. . . .

. . . While inevitably failing to comprehend the aging process in any lasting way, the advocates above and many others in the rejuvenation movement created a vast archive of sensationalistic, pseudo-scientific experimentation in the first half of the twentieth century. . . .

The term *gerontology* was coined by Elie Metchnikoff (1845–1916), the celebrated Nobel-prize winning scientist who worked at the Pasteur Institute in Paris from 1888 until his death in 1916. . . . While Metchnikoff saw aging as a process of cellular involution, where cell decay outbalances cell growth, he speculated that defence against senile decay could be mustered with the use of animal organ injections and a diet rich in sterilized or sour milk to control harmful bacterial flora.[2]

Thus, Metchnikoff helped to launch gerontology not only as a science of aging, but one inspired by a discourse of optimism; in particular, an optimism eliminated once the body was understood as a site of ongoing struggle between vital forces within tissues and cells. . . .

By the early to mid-twentieth century we have three predominant ideas about men, sexual function, aging, and the life course. First, aging was characterized by a pathological, climacteric-induced process, whose crisis points emerge not only in old-old age but in young-old age or middle age as well. In fact the medical and cultural anxieties about the male decline moved 'down' into middle age as rejuvenation therapies and early gerontology alighted on this time of life as an opportunity for effective intervention (see Gullette, 1994). . . .

Second, there was the emergent status and problematization of sexual function as an indicator of successful aging. Since impotence and related sexual dysfunctions were seen as biologically derived, the choice was either to accept and adjust to them—although deferral and management could be achieved through a prudent lifestyle—or indulge in the increasingly discredited rejuvenating nostrums of Steinach, or Brown-Sequard in an attempt to restore sexual function. . . .

Third, there was the powerful allure of science. Despite its codifying the aging body within an expansive pathologizing discourse of senescence, science was also seen as the solution to the worst manifestations of aging. Beginning with Metchnikoff and continuing in the present, professional gerontologists embraced the positive as an ethical and intellectual resource with which to sustain the optimistic promise of their field. As such, gerontological practices have been saturated with positive agendas around ideals of vitality, activity, autonomy, mobility, choice, and well-being. . . .

However, in the middle of the twentieth century, this positive development was stymied when confronted with sexual decline, especially since scientific gerontology and sexology had made sexual decline an element of a climactericized middle-aging. . . .

The Psychology of Impotence

While remnants of nineteenth-century conceptions of the 'spermatic economy' (Haller, 1989) persisted into the new century,[3] new configurations of physiological and psychological factors were beginning to form in understanding impotence, and psychological explanations rapidly became favoured. . . . Hirsch (1947), for example, clearly distinguished between the primarily psychic impotence of those aged 20 to 45, and the more physically derived impotence of these older than 45. While the prognosis for psychotherapy to successfully treat the former was good, 'normal' sexual aging was still viewed as an adjustment to physical decline. However, the psychotherapy to successfully treat the former was good, 'normal' sexual aging was still viewed as an adjustment to physical decline. However, the psychological paradigm quickly expanded to include aging men as well, who were increasingly told that it was their anxiety over their supposedly inevitable loss of sexual function, their *fear* of loss to potency that was causing their *premature* sexual decline. . . . Overall, two axioms characterized the advice given to men from the 1960s through the 1980s: first, that psychological factors were primarily responsible for loss of sexual function, and second, that to cease having sex would hasten aging in itself. . . . Gerontology and sexology shared common ground in asserting that both physiological and psychological factors were fundamental in making sexual activity, particularly sexual intercourse, a healthy and necessary component of successful aging. Indeed, the passive acceptance of age-related changes in sexual capacity that had characterized the professional advice of the past, now became viewed as a pathological adaptive strategy rooted in ignorance or fear. . . . Hence, psychological and couple counselling are as important as remedies as are the more tricky (and unreliable) hormone therapies, penile prostheses, and vitamin-mineral supplements. . . .

From 'Impotence' to 'Erectile Dysfunction'

While sex therapy (for both young and old) seemed confident in its assumption of a primarily psychological basis for impotence, a different turn was being taken in urological research. In 1983, Dr Giles Brindley astounded an audience of his colleagues at a conference by injecting his penis with phenoxybenzamine and displaying, for all to see, an erection obtained by purely chemical means.[4] While this led to the development of new therapies for impotence, such as intracavernosal injection and transurethral thera- pies, the more revolutionary import was to visibly sever the mechanism of penile erection from any sort of psychological or emotional arousal, or even tactile stimulation, and to reconceptualize it as a primarily physiological event. . . .

Significant as well as a reversal of the assump- tion that fear, depression, anxiety, or other psy- chological factors could act on the body to produce impotence. Instead, 'as the physical causes of impotence have become better appreci- ated, emphasis has shifted to the potentially very serious emotional consequences of impotence' (Morganstern and Abrahams, 1988: 6). This has been a pivotal move in the construction of impo- tence—now reconceptualized as 'erectile dys- function'—as a threat to both the physical and psychological well-being of an aging population, and hence as matter for public concern. . . .

The new focus on 'erectile dysfunction' epito- mizes the manner in which truth-claims about the sexual body have become increasingly med- icalized. Such truth claims rest on the privileged access of science to the natural body, and increas- ingly on the ability to visualize and objectively record both the 'normal' and 'pathological' opera- tions of the sexual body. . . .

Constructing the Epidemic

While Kinsey's 1948 report on male sexuality took a 'glass half full' approach, stressing that impotence was a 'relatively rare phenomenon' with only 27 per cent of men becoming impotent by 70 years of age, it has been widely criticized for its non-representativeness and small number of older men surveyed. Most widely cited is the Massachusetts Male Aging Survey (MMAS), which was a probability sample of 1700 men aged 40 to 70 conducted in the Boston area between 1987 and 1989 (Feldman et al., 1994; McKinlay and Feldman, 1994).[5] The MMAS found consistent age- related decline in 'erectile function' (defined here as the ability to 'get and keep an erection good enough for sexual intercourse') . . . Significant in the MMAS was the 'grading' of degrees of erectile

dysfunction by age (mild, moderate, complete), but foregrounded in subsequent reporting of the date were overall prevalence rates of 'some degree of erectile dysfunction' at 52 per cent. Here, the glass is half empty:

> Once a man enters the [40 to 70] age group his odds of developing erectile dysfunction are at least as high as his odds of avoiding it. If this doesn't constitute an epidemic, I don't know what would! (Melchiode and Sloan, 1999: 9)

Reported prevalence rates in articles citing the MMAS tend to adopt the broadest definition of erectile dysfunction. Not surprisingly, given the advantages of defining the largest market possible for potential treatment, the tendency in both sci- entific and popular reports is to include all of those suffering from 'some degree' of difficulty. This puts reported rates from the USA at 39 per cent of 40-year-olds, and 67 per cent of 70-year- olds. These prevalence rates are then applied against demographic projections of age changes in the population to predict incidence rates, future increases, and policy consequences (see Aytac et al., 1999; Keith, 2000). . . .

Risky Business

A large and growing body of literature had sug- gested that the project of the self in late moderni- ty is largely a body-project (Featherstone, 1991; Shilling, 1993; Williams and Bendelow, 1998). It is characterized, on the one hand, by an increas- ing individualization of risk, but on the other, an increasing reliance on expert advice and con- sumer goods (Giddens, 1991; Rose, 1996; Slater, 1997). Both commercial and public health pro- motion discourses about 'positive aging' (Hepworth, 1995) have actively incorporated the fear of erectile failure into more general models of 'healthy living'.

Men's Health, a popular men's magazine that emphasizes health, fitness, and sexual performance, has a regular feature called 'the game show' where profiles of three men are presented and the reader is invited to discern, from the information given, which one will first manifest the phenomenon of the month (Who will go bald first? Who will look old first?). The October 2000 issue focused on 'Who will be impotent first?' (McDonald, 2000). Each of the three men profiled presented a different set of 'risk factors'. George is 31, overweight with a family history of high blood pressure and diabetes. Joe, while only 25, is a competitive cyclist. Carlos is 63—age is his sole risk factor. Each profile also included what they're doing right—George had sex nearly every day, Joe is in excellent physical shape and has sex five times per week, Carlos leads a 'health-obsessed' lifestyle and has sex three to five times per week. When we turn the page to find out who wins (loser?), a detailed 'scorecard' is provided that assigns a points value to an array of 12 'impotence factors' (age, health, stress, diet, exercise, alcohol, smoking, temper, depression, sexual activity, performance anxiety, saddle sports). Scores could range from a low of -23 to a maximum of +10. George came in at the low score (and hence highest risk) of -4, Carlos, despite his age, got a positive 5, and Joe a very positive 7. Of course, the reader is invited to fill out the scorecard for himself, and if a score of -3 or less is obtained, they are exhorted that 'You are high-risk and need to change your lifestyle immediately'. Those with a score of +3 are obviously doing something right, but still there is the warning to continue doing it ('Continue what you're doing and enjoy a long, hard life'). That the high-risk individual identified in this feature (George) is only 31 years old and currently reports having sex every day is significant, as is the fact that the 'point value' available for scoring are, with the exception of a total of four negative points for age and family history factors, all related to matters that are seen to be manipulable by lifestyle. George, for example, is told that while he doesn't have problems yet, 'his poor diet, sedentary lifestyle, and family history will eventually catch up with him', but that 'fortunately, his fate isn't inevitable'. He needs to exercise and eat right, which will cause him to 'lose weight, control his blood pressure, and increase his sex-life expectancy'. If not, the experts predict he has 'about 10 years left'. The message here is not only one of constant vigilance, even in the absence of any percepti-ble sense of bodily decline, but also one of equating the loss of erection with the end of life itself.

Age, then, is a 'risk factor' among many. While there is an acknowledged link between age and the prevalence of erectile dysfunction, a simple causal link is now severed. . . .

While medical practitioners have long prescribed various regimes of bodily hygiene as a means of prolonging or restoring one's vital powers, the intensified medicalization of sexuality mandates compulsory tumescence. . . . Maintaining penile erectility is not just a benefit of a healthy lifestyle, it is a compelling reason for that lifestyle, and stands as a signal indicator of 'ageless aging'. The erect penis becomes a visible index (almost in a Durkheimian sense) of masculinity, emotional health, and physical health, and one that is no longer tied to bodily age. Whether through preventative bodily discipline or remedial therapy, the onus is on the responsibly aging individual to remain 'forever functional'. If one event can be singled out as securing this view of male sexual fitness, then it would have to be the introduction of Viagra, which hit the North American market in the spring of 1998.

The Pharmaceutical 'Fix'

. . . Within months of its release, Viagra attained iconic status. Not only were millions of prescriptions written, but a slew of mass-market paperbacks hit the stands, extensive coverage appeared in every mainstream media outlet, it was the subject of countless comedy monologues, cartoons and jokes, and hundreds of Internet sites emerged which offered on-line prescriptions and home delivery. Viagra was heralded by both the popular media and the medical therapeutic community as 'revolutionary'. Far more than a pharmaceutical product, the little blue diamond-shaped pill has become a cultural signifier of virility, bioperfection, potentially unlimited sexual performance, and a new era in sexuality (Marshall, 2002).

Viagra-sildenafil citrate is a pharmacological compound that suppresses an enzyme that allows blood to flow out of the penis, thus facilitating the achievement and maintenance of an erection. While biotechnical remedies for rehabilitating erections have been common practice for many years,[6] what sets Viagra apart is its relationship to the development of a molecular science of sexuality, its locating by the medial and therapeutic communities within the 'natural' sexual response cycle, and its cultural take-up as the 'magic bullet' that will usher in a whole new era of both sexual medicine and sexual relations (Marshall, 2002).

While the initial justification of the 'disease model' of erectile dysfunction was clearly framed in terms of a discernible physiological basis, and its relationship to potentially serious health problems such as diabetes, hypertension, and arterial sclerosis, the efficacy of Viagra in producing erections *regardless* of the etiology, not to mention the huge profitability of expanding the market, has considerably broadened the clinical framing of erectile dysfunction.[7] In fact, it is asserted that the existence of a highly successful and well-tolerated treatment reveals the 'true incidence of erectile dysfunction' (Broderick, 1998: 205), which has hitherto been clearly 'underdiagnosed' (Seiden, 1998: 3). The user is now configured not just as the man who, for whatever reason, is unable to get or keep an erection much of the time, but includes all those whose erections could be 'improved'. Both the popular literature and recent advertising suggest that you might have ED and *not even known it!*[8] One doctor sums it up well:

> Should a man take the pill to improve erections if he doesn't think he has ED? The issue can be side-stepped by saying that if a man takes the pill and his erections improve, then he had ED after all. (Lamm and Couzens, 1998: 82)

Originally marketed to a 'mature' audience as a treatment for an identifiably age-related condition within the context of stable heterosexual relationships (with Bob Dole as its most memorable spokesman), Viagra is now being pitched to an ever younger, and potentially single, market. . . .

Along with the lifestyle discipline required to maintain erectile function, pharmaceutical and other biotechnical advances figure prominently in the expanding horizon of sexual fitness, with its emphasis on prevention and the refusal of bodily limits.[9]

> In sports, what were once considered insurmountable barriers—the four-minute mile, the seven-foot high jump, and so forth—are now accomplished routinely. Furthermore, the peak years of an athlete have been dramatically extended by conditioning procedures, nutritional knowledge, and medical breakthroughs. I can see no reason why the years of active sexuality cannot be expanded, and with it the penis of aging men. (Danoff, 1993: 158)

Viagra (or Viagra-like drugs) may also have prophylactic potential, similar to that of aspirin in warding off heart disease: 'Some experts are predicting that, in the near future, the drug will be taken two or three times a week, even when the man is not engaging in sex, to ensure erectile health' (Lamm and Couzens, 1998: 137). . . .

Conclusions

. . . Even after the late twentieth-century reassertion of an overwhelmingly physiological basis for impotence, the assumption that to remain sexually active is to remain young seems unquestioned: 'The strenuous use of your penis will sharpen your mind, exalt your soul, and keep you feeling vigorous. In short, you don't stop having sex because you get old, *you get old because you stop having sex*' (Danoff, 1993: 155–6, emphasis in the original). . . .

Notes

. . .

1. One of the most popular Renaissance treatises on prolongevity was *How to Live for a Hundred Years and Avoid Disease* (1558), written by Louis Cornaro, a sixteenth-century Venetian nobleman. While Cornaru explains the success of his health

regimes for living into his centenarian years, which focus obsessively on diet, hygiene, temperance, and living 'a sober and orderly' life ([1558] 1935: 33), he hardly considers sexual function, desire, or decline as part of them.

2. Throughout his career Metchnikoff maintained that lactic bacteria in soured milk and fermented foods were essential to balancing and detoxifying the effects of harmful intestinal phagocytes, an idea that also inspired a sour milk craze in Paris in 1902 (Cole, 1992: 189).

3. Bernard McFadden, for example, warned men of the danger of oversexed women who would sap their 'vital economy':

> If your wife is abnormally sexed and seems to enjoy these relations at all times, then you have a problem before you which is not by any means easy to solve. A very plain talk is absolutely essential under such circumstances, if you wish to avoid serious inroads upon your vital economy. (1923: 54)

4. This incident is widely recounted in both the scientific and popular literatures as a watershed in the shift from psychological to physiological aetiologies of impotence. See Broderick (1998) and Whitehead and Malloy (1999).

5. The other major study cited is the National Health Life Survey of 1992, which was a probability sample of men and women aged 18 to 59. Rates of erectile dysfunction were determined by a yes/no answer to the question: 'During the last 12 months, had there ever been a period of several months or more when you . . . had trouble achieving or maintaining an erection?' The NHSLS researchers suggest that a 'yes' answer to this question would be comparable to the MMAS definition of moderate to complete impotence (22 per cent) in the 50- to 55-year-old group, declining to 10 per cent in the 55- to 59-year-old group (Laumann et al., 1999).

6. These run the gamut from early forms of splints and supports, hormonal and glandular therapies, rejuvenation 'tonics', herbal remedies and penile 'exercises', to more recently standardized treatments including penile implants and prostheses, vacuum cylinders, penile injections, urethral suppositories, and oral medications. Historically, this is an arena of treatment in which struggles for legitimacy and authority over diagnosis and prescription have figured prominently.

7. Numerous clinical trials have demonstrated that Viagra is most effective in cases of erectile dysfunction for which *no* organic origin has been identified (classified as 'psychologenic') (Shabsigh, 1999; Steers, 1999). That it so effectively 'works' in these cases acts to reinforce the conviction that the dysfunction must have been a physiological matter after all.

8. Nor, indeed, might your partner: 'Erectial dysfunction can range widely in severity from men who are completely "impotent" in every negative and absolute sense of the word to men whose problems are so slight that not even their partners are aware they have it' (Katzenstein, 1998: 5).

9. Zygmunt Bauman (1998) has usefully distinguished between 'health' and 'fitness': while the former has some criteria of fulfillment, the latter has no boundaries.

References

Aytac, I.A., J.B. McKinlay, and R.J. Krane. 1999. 'The Likely Worldwide Increase in Erectile Dysfunction Between 1995 and 2025 and Some Possible Policy Consequences', *British Journal of Urology International* 84: 50–6.

Bell, R.M. 1999. *How to Do it: Guides to Good Living for Renaissance Italians*. Chicago: University of Chicago Press.

Benjamin, H. 1959. 'Impotence and Aging', *Sexology* November: 238–43.

Broderick, G.A. 1998. 'Impotence and Penile Vascular Testing: Who Are These Men and How Do We Evaluate the Etiology and Severity of their Complaints?', *Journal of Sex Education and Therapy* 23, 3: 197–206.

Cole, T.R. 1992. *The Journey of Life: A Cultural History of Aging in America*. New York: Cambridge University Press.

Danoff, D.S. 1993. *Superpotency: How to Get It, Use It and Maintain It for a Lifetime*. New York: Warner Books.

Day, G.E. 1849. *A Practical Treatise on the Domestic Management of Most Important Diseases of Advanced Life*. Philadelphia: Lea and Blanchard.

Featherstone, M. 1991. 'The Body in Consumer Culture', in M. Featherstone, M. Hepworth, and B. Turner, eds, *The Body: Social Process and Cultural Theory*. London: Sage, 170–96.

Feldman, H.A., I. Goldstein, D.G. Hatzichristou, R.J. Krance, and J.B. McKinlay. 1994. 'Impotence and its Medical and Psychosocial Correlates: Results of the Massachusetts Male Aging Study', *Journal of Urology* 151: 54–61.

Giddens, A. 1991. *Modernity and Self-Identity*. Cambridge: Polity Press.

Gruman, G.J. 1966. *A History of Ideas about the Prolongation of Life: The Evolution of Prolongevity Hypotheses to 1800*. (Transactions of the American Philosophical Society, vol. 56, pt. 9.) Philadelphia: American Philosophical Society.

Gullette, M.M. 1994. 'Male Midlife Sexuality in a Gerontocratic Economy: The Privileged Stage of the Long Midlife in Nineteenth-Century Age-Ideology', *Journal of the History of Sexuality* 5, 1: 58–89.

Haber, C. 1983. *Beyond Sixty-Five: The Dilemma of Old Age in America's Past*. New York: Cambridge University Press.

Halford, Sir Henry. 1831. *Essays and Orations*. London: John Murray.

Haller, J.S. 1989. 'Spermatic Economy: A Nineteenth-Century View of Male Impotence', *Southern Medical Journal* 82, 8: 1010–16.

Hepworth, M. 1995. 'Positive Aging: What is the Message?', in R Bunton, S. Nettleton, and R. Burrows, eds, *The Sociology of Health Promotion: Critical Analysis of Consumption, Lifestyle and Risk*. London: Routledge, 176–90.

Hirsch, E. 1947. *Sex Power in Marriage*. Chicago: Research Publications.

Keith, A. 2000. 'The Economics of Viagra', *Health Affairs* 19, 2: 147–57.

Lamm, S., and G.S. Couzens. 1998. *The Virility Solution: Everything You Need to Know About Viagra, the Potency Pill that Can Restore and Enhance Male Sexuality*. New York: Fireside Books (Simon and Schuster).

McDonald, K. 2000. 'Who Will Be Impotent First?', *Men's Health* October: 70–2.

McFadden, B. 1923. *Manhood and Marriage*. New York: McFadden Publications.

McKinlay, J.B., and H.A. Feldman. 1994. 'Age-Related Variation in Sexual Activity and Interest in Normal Men: Results from the Massachusetts Male Aging Study', in A.S. Rossi, ed, *Sexuality Across the Life Course*. Chicago: University of Chicago Press, 261–85.

MacLachlan, D. 1863. *Practical Treatise on the Diseases of and Infirmities of Advanced Life*. London: John Churchill and Sons.

Marshall, B. L. 2002. 'Hard Science: Gendered Constructions of Sexual Dysfunction in the Viagra Age', *Sexualities* 5, 2: 131–58.

Melchoide, G., and B. Sloan. 1999. *Beyond Viagra: A Commonsense Guide to Building a Healthy Sexual Relationship for Both Men and Women*. New York: Owl Books (Henry Holt and Co.).

Morganstern, S., and A. Abrahams. 1988. *Love Again, Live Again*. Englewood Cliffs, NJ: Prentice Hall.

Rose, N. 1996. *Inventing Ourselves: Psychology, Power and Personhood*. Cambridge: Cambridge University Press.

Seiden, O.J. 1998. *Viagra: The Virility Breakthrough*. Rocklin, CA: Prima Publishing.

Shilling, C. 1993. *The Body in Social Theory*. London: Sage.

Skae, F. 1865. 'Climacteric Insanity in the Male', *Edinburgh Medical Journal* 11: 232–44.

Slater, D. 1997. *Consumer Culture and Modernity*. Cambridge: Polity Press.

Troyansky, D. 1989. *Old Age in the Old Regime: Image and Experience in Eighteenth-Century France*. Ithaca, NY: Cornell University Press.

Williams, S.J., and G. Bendelow. 1998. *The Lived Body: Sociological Themes, Embodied Issues*. London: Routledge.

Chapter 45

Aging, Alzheimer's, and the Uncivilized Body

Chris Gilleard and Paul Higgs

. . . While most people become resigned to the 'inevitability' of some aspects of bodily aging, of changes in appearance and changes in the efficiency of bodily functioning, few can contemplate with equanimity that the mind too is mortal. More than the 'unconscious' irrationalities of physical need and desire, the embodied irrationality of dementia challenges the notion of a disembodied rationality that has been such a central tenet of classical social theory. In this sense 'senility', to revert to the use of this premodern term, represents the ultimate failure of the modernist project, the failure of what Elias terms 'the civilized body'. The body rendered mindless by senility can no longer sustain its claim to an identity based on personal and social agency. Those behaviours most associated with self-care—looking after oneself, keeping oneself clean, controlling bodily functions, and modulating the expression of emotions, controls that Elias described as central to the civilizing process, become eroded. A body the mind has lost control of becomes instead the *de-civilized* body.[1]

Elias and the Civilized Body

Shilling identifies three key aspects to the civilizing process as described by Elias: socialization, rationalization, and individualization of the body.[2] Bringing bodily functions under social control, emphasizing the importance of poise and self-discipline, and locating identity specifically within the body were, for Elias, key develop-

ments in the emergence of modern ideas about people's relationships with each other and the development of separate public and private selves. The public failure of the individual to exercise control and the evident inability to effectively exercise such control exclude the person from participation as an agent within the civilized (social) world.

The process of civilization, in this formulation, is the slow but steady extension that the modern state has made over the regulation and control of social life. Increasing state control, in turn, demands greater 'self-control' on the part of the individual in public. . . .

Dementia, in this sense, is the public failure of an individual's claim to self-mastery and self-control. It is, however, an unwitting failure, for it is not the case that the person with dementia has chosen to transgress or that he or she has deliberately sought to exclude him- or herself from the civilizing processes of society. The progressive loss of agency, of socialized intent, in dementia is represented culturally as an 'internal' failure, a failure of control that presupposes a bodily not a social or personal failing. Traditionally the inability to look after oneself has been accepted as a not uncommon way through which old age begins, or ends.

For many centuries, the term 'dementia' was used as a way of acknowledging that some individuals cannot comport themselves in a civilized fashion. Society rather than the individual was expected to do something about such public manifestations of personal loss of self-control, however meagre that response might be. Aside from the steady centralization of the response, this continued to be the dominant model of welfare provision throughout much of the twentieth century. Civilization could best be measured by the improvements of the comprehensiveness, regularity, and reliability of that response as well as the number of hospital beds provided. In recent times this model of civilized charity has come under increasing criticism. The new paradigm seeks to represent all forms of disability as a particular demand for services. Such demand is considered best met by allowing the free play of market forces to determine the appropriate supply of services. The former recipients of a universal welfare system are redefined. They have become 'active' participants in market-like relationships: clients, consumers, customers, or, rather more ambiguously, 'users'. By so continuing to support a discourse of social agency for disabled people, the 'liberal' argument goes, the unhealthy dependency that is structured by state administered charity is avoided. . . . To enshrine the legitimacy of this position, such 'liberal' discourse has had to be applied to all disabled groups. Exceptions made for one group weaken the coherence of the argument as a universal principle of government. . . .

Tracing the reconstruction of dementia from its representation as a natural if tragic fate befalling those reaching 'old age' to its reframing as a distinct neurological condition affecting certain 'at-risk' individuals, we aim to show how the 'progressive' developments in the area of dementia care mirror this wider shift in social policy. But this *re-civilizing* of 'senility' is not solely the result of changing social policy and the associated commodification of welfare. It reflects . . . particularly the changing way that modern medicine is beginning to approach and interpret 'old age'.

Over the course of the last century modern medicine has undergone three distinct shifts in its approach to aging and old age. It began with the studious avoidance of old age that was enshrined in the practice of late-nineteenth-century hospital medicine.[3] The next phase coincided with the mid-century professionalization of medicine, when hospital doctors offered 'benign' support

for and surveillance of 'old people' through the emergence in post-war Britain of 'geriatric medicine'. Now, at the turn of the century, a new approach is jostling for position, one that can best be described as 'anti-aging medicine'. . . .[4] [O]ld age is reconstructed more as a compendium of risky but potentially avoidable medical conditions. Aging and Alzheimer's are treated as understandable, remediable, and preventable.

To understand more clearly the significance of the civilized body in the cultural representation of aging we must look first at how medicine, psychiatry, and psychology began to separate *civilized* normal aging from *uncivilized* abnormal aging. The distinction between these two processes played a central role in the new scientific gerontology of the mid-century. . . .

. . . Moreover, behind many . . . attempts to re-civilize the uncivilized body lie other more material goals, not least to shift the public cost of a fourth-age identity towards the private choices of less costly third-age ones. This re-appraisal of senility, this particular program of re-civilizing the fourth age, involves three key elements. First and probably the easiest to chart is the conversion of the post-war problem of senility into the . . . problem of Alzheimer's disease. Second, and consequentially related to the former, is the transformation of the public health focus upon dementia from one that was based on an epidemiology of need to one that is based on an epidemiology of risk. The third element is the wider shift in social policy referred to above, namely the reframing of health and welfare from a social right given to needy but helpless citizens to a choice of goods and services offered to individual citizen-clients, who have acquired this new status through the concomitant re-inscription of their 'personhood' within the discourses servicing Alzheimer's disease.

The Post-war Transformation of Senility

Age-related mental decline was one of the central topics in the newly founded gerontological research programs of the 1940s and 1950s. Much of that research effort sought to establish what constituted normal mental decline and how if at all it contrasted with abnormal deterioration. . . .

. . . [I]n Britain the integration of mental hospitals, local authority infirmaries, and the regional acute hospital system achieved by the 1948 National Health Service Act provided the most important impetus for the gradual 'medicalization' of dementia—the precursor to the later 'Alzheimerization' of aging.

This process began with the work of the British psychiatrist Martin Roth in the 1950s and 1960s. Roth's pioneering work laid the foundations for a new subdiscipline, 'psychogeriatrics', and he continued to influence much of British mental health care policy for older people for the next two decades. . . .

. . . The late 1960s and early 1970s saw the further consolidation and institutionalization of psychogeriatrics within the British health-care system. New psychogeriatric units opened . . . Rehabilitation units were set up, often by the simple act of renaming a couple of wards in the local mental hospital. Discharge of psychogeriatric patients into newly built local authority homes for the elderly mentally inform demonstrated that rehabilitation was indeed taking place. Senility was derided as a term and fragmented as a concept. In its place came senile dementia and arteriosclerotic dementia, illnesses to be carefully distinguished from conditions that merely masqueraded as senility, such as 'acute confessional states', depression', and 'paraphrenia'. This 'modern' approach toward senile dementia was celebrated in a review article published in 1972 and entitled 'Senile Dementia: A Changing Perspective'.[5]

This 'new perspective' was to last little more than a decade. By the 1980s another new agenda has begun to take over . . . [S]enility was finally abandoned, first transformed into senile dementia, and then, when the very remnants of senility were cast aside, re-emerging as a new public health hazard—Alzheimer's disease. It was at this junction that US interest resurfaced in this 'new' disease.

The Branding of Alzheimer's and the Scientific Approach

. . . By the 1980s, senility had been almost completely set aside as both a lay and a medical term. Consigned to history, its place was being taken over by Alzheimer's, scourge of the third age. . . . The uncivilized body remained, but it was to be located in a more carefully delineated set of illnesses that were to be called 'Alzheimer's disease' or 'related disorders'.

Why did the rebranding and copyrighting of Alzheimer's disease prove so singularly successful? Up until the 1960s, neuropathological investigations into the aging brain had been a research backwater . . . Alzheimer's disease had been considered a rare condition affecting a small minority of people in late middle age, modelled upon the original account of the eponymous disease published at the beginning of the twentieth century. In the original paper, Alzheimer described neuropathological changes in the brain of a middle-aged woman who had become progressively more forgetful, confused, and 'senile' . . . [M]any neuropathologists observed similar pathology in a wide variety of 'clinical' conditions. They were not seen as having major diagnostic significance, being considered common features of neuropathology observed in the brains of many older people who showed no signs of senility.[6] The real 'cause' of senile dementia was sought elsewhere and there was little interest in linking up the 'rare' pre-senile dementias that affected the middle-aged with the mental infirmity commonly associated with senility. . . .

A key change took place in 1979. At that point, a Conservative government came to power in Britain, favourably disposed to the 'new right' economics that had a distaste for central planning, seeking to promote individual choice and individual responsibility.[7] Coincidentally, reports began to emerge outlining a potential treatment strategy based on evidence[8] of a specific deficiency in the cholinergic system of the brain in patients with dementia.[9] Studies of the cholinergic system conducted on the brains of people variously described as suffering from 'Alzheimer's disease', 'senile dementia', 'senile dementia and other abiotrophies', or simply 'elderly people' suggested a selective loss of those nerve cells that used acetylcholine as the chemical transmitter of impulses in the brain—but with no apparent loss of the receptor sites to which the acetylcholine molecules would bind. This latter finding was important because it meant that if one could somehow increase the production of acetylcholine, receptor sites still existed in the brain to 'receive' the neurotransmitter and thus restore mental functioning. . . .

The impact of the 'cholinergic hypothesis',[10] the flurry of drug trials and the concomitant interest in 'reframing' senility as 'Alzheimer's disease' led to a mushrooming of Alzheimer's disease societies in Europe, America, and Australia. From 1980 on all references to senility began to fade. A new terminology appeared, variously senile dementia—Alzheimer's type (SDAT); dementia, Alzheimer's type (DAT); and primary degenerative dementia (PDD). Spurred on by the pharmaceutical industry's desire to conduct treatment studies of dementia, national bodies were set up to rationalize and legitimize the diagnosis of Alzheimer's dementia, placing an official stamp on the term and finally and completely severing any remaining connection with senility. The initiative moved from Britain to the United States, home of the giant pharmaceutical companies. . . .

Subsequent drug research pursued the cholinergic hypothesis with considerable determination through a heavily financed program of research and development and lobbying. . . . National and international regulatory processes have integrated the operationalized definitions of Alzheimer's with the systematization of drug research paradigms. Reinforced by these very material pay-offs, Alzeimer's has now acquired a virtual monopoly on the 'problem of senility'.[11]

Alzheimer's and the State

The reframing of dementia as a neurological disorder, the introduction of the cholinergic hypothesis, the widespread growth in drug trials, and the proliferation of Alzheimer's disease societies have helped reconstitute dementia as a 'third-age' issue. Those who had once been excluded from the processes of normal 'civilized' aging, under the category 'the demented elderly', are being reintroduced and re-civilized as the victims of Alzheimer's disease. However, the retired people who are entering anti-dementia drug trials are recruited from populations that are comparatively young, rich, healthy, socially integrated, male, and ethnically very white—attributes that characterize the successfully retired. . . .[12]

But senility has not vanished. It survives and indeed grows in the midst of other debates concerning a very fourth-age issue—the provision of long-term care. Despite the arrival of FDA- and CSM-approved anti-dementia drugs, the fate of large numbers of people suffering from dementia is to spend some part of their lives within an institution. In contrast to the participants in Alzheimer treatment trials, the residents of these nursing homes are typically old, widowed, female, poor, and most notably senile.[13] With the demise of the asylum, the state hospital, and other vestiges of public charity, the provision of long-term care has moved increasingly into private hands. But despite the privatization of provision, the financing of long-term care remains predominantly in the hands of the state—via Medicaid and Medicare in the Unites States, via local government departments of social security in Britain—. . . anxieties over escalating costs have led governments around the world to seek ways of providing less expensive supportive services that might keep the needy and the frail at home, via the policies of community care. Increased rationing and targeting of services have been employed so the state can more tightly define those who amongst the retired population might form the core of a fourth-age, state-dependent constituency—a constituency, as it were, of *uncivilized* bodies, unable to care for their selves. Those who are so targeted are at the same time those whose aging most alienates them from others. Their 'uncivilized' loss of control makes social relationships difficult and social action impossible. Though the family has long been seen as the source of shelter and support for failed identities, families are increasingly ill-equipped to want or be able to sustain such dependency. . . .

As long as it was believed that this fate was confined to an identifiable minority of the retired population, and as long as it was believed appropriate to redistribute some of the economic growth of a society to improving the welfare of those unable to contribute to that growth, it was possible for the state to conceive of long-term care as a necessary and containable cost. As dementia became increasingly acknowledged as an age-dependent state, as the epidemiological evidence clearly predicted an exponential growth in its future prevalence as a direct function of population aging, and as the fiscal crisis of the mid-1970s reoriented the politics of welfare in the subsequent decade, governments began to view long-term care as an escalating claim on public expenditure.

By redefining senility as Alzheimer's, it seemed as if the problem could be more precisely pinned down and rendered more manageable. The Alzheimerization of 'uncivilized' aging ought then to free up the third age to concentrate upon smart drugs and 'staying young' mental activity programs. But the copyrighting of Alzheimer's effectively excluded, through its scientistic criteria, a large number of 'uncivilized' bodies who remained recalcitrantly senile, to whom no anti-dementia drug prescription could or would be offered. In response, another new paradigm began to emerge—one that frames the problem of Alzheimer's not as an inevitable responsibility for the state but as an avoidable risk for the individual. . . .

Alzheimer's—From Need to Risk

The early epidemiological research into dementia was conducted . . . to obtain reasonable estimated of need for services. . . . [A] number of . . . epidemiological surveys were carried out during the 1960s and 1970s in countries influenced by this social democratic tradition of matching needs with resources through central planning.[14] The results of these studies showed a clear consensus. Every prevalence study showed that the longer people live the more likely they are to experience

failing intellectual powers and a growing inability to manage themselves. The consequence seemed to be an inevitable need for greater and greater 'long-term care' provision as the population aged.

In the Regan–Thatcher years of the 1980s the emerging Alzheimerization of aging research[15] led to dissatisfaction with these 'old' studies. The committee-based operationalization of Alzheimer's required that surveys more clearly delineate 'Alzheimer's disease' from 'dementia'. Dementia was treated as an unsatisfactory category, undifferentiated and redolent of the earlier term 'senility'. It had to be subordinated to the more precise delineation attributed to . . . Alzheimer's disease. As a result a number of studies were conducted in the 1980s that provided separate prevalence estimates of dementia and of Alzheimer's. Unsurprisingly, both sets of figures closely paralleled each other. . . . [D]ementia/Alzheimer's was rare amongst 60- and 70-year-olds. It was, however, commonly and usually observed amongst 90-year-olds.

By the mid-1980s, an interest in identifying the 'risk' factors associated with Alzheimer's disease appeared. . . . The most significant outcome of these studies was to identify the raised prevalence of Alzheimer's amongst first-degree relatives—i.e., indicating that Alzheimer's had a familial component. This provided the beginnings of a notion that there were indeed people 'at risk' of developing Alzheimer's (and by implication many others not at risk). . . .

. . . [G]rowing evidence that genetic factors were involved in 'disease expression' strengthened support for a specific biological aetiology.[16] From this point, epidemiological research changed track and by the late 1980s it had began to focus almost exclusively on the question of individual risk. . . .

. . . The cumulative impact of such risk factor research suggests that a primary prevention strategy for Alzheimer's disease is realizable—one that offers a role for individual lifestyle management as well as one that means opportunities for clinical trials.[17]

Of course incidence studies do more than simply suggest risk factors—they also indicate something about our lifetime chances of developing Alzheimer's/dementia. Although not always made salient, what incidence studies indicate most clearly is that the greatest risk that can be conferred arises from living a very long life. Thus, the risk of developing dementia rises inexorably with each passing year and shows no sign of 'plateauing' even at the very oldest ages.[18] As a result of nothing but the passage of time, a condition initially representing a very small risk for 'third-agers' becomes a very large risk for the majority of 'fourth-agers'. . . . [R]isk factors . . . may help determine when but they do not determine whether a person develops Alzheimer's.[19]

Alzheimer's is remarkably democratic, affecting people in developed countries as much as those in the Third World, affecting men and women, white-collar and blue-collar workers, rich and poor with apparent total disregard for status. Despite the ubiquitous finitude that Alzheimer's seems to express, research continues to seek potential 'risk groups' who may need special treatment or who may need to adapt a 'health-promoting' lifestyle. Even when the 'inevitability' factor of senility is recognized, the aspirational Alzheimer's scientists merely shift the argument towards an emphasis on a reduced period of 'dementia-related disability' . . .

Given the likelihood that most people will reach their 85th birthday neither senile nor needing to be placed in an institution, acting upon a concern to keep one's mind active is unlikely to make much difference. But by making Alzheimer's something that you might develop rather than a matter of fate and the length of life, it becomes possible to present it not as an uncivilized status deserving pity and charity but as a risk against which to be insured. The significance of the shift in epidemiological research from need to risk lies in its underlying relationship to the rise of 'governmentality' more generally and 'governmentality' of old age in particular. . . .

Alzheimer's and Sustainable Aging

In the 1970s few people had ever heard of Alzheimer's disease. At the end of the twentieth century it is probably one of the most widely known medical conditions in the developed world. It continues to spawn a vast research and clinical literature. People of a certain age now joke about developing Alzheimer's when embarrassed by a lapse of memory or attention. Regular Alzheimer's Disease Society 'awareness' weeks ensure that the subject does not get forgotten. Although research continues to refer to dementia as a broad umbrella term, studies of dementia and studies of Alzheimer's overlap to such an extent that dementia seems likely soon to be completely subsumed under the term 'Alzheimer's disease and related disorders'. . . .

But if Alzheimer's disease is something that sustains an important and significance that gives it potential cultural capital within the context of inspirational medicine, and provides a name that helps dignify the disabilities of dementia in ways that senility and dementia do not, it is an achievement of 'civilization' that comes with a cost. That cost involves shunting dementia into a residual social category, a kind of antechamber where social death precedes biological death. Those excluded from the scientific civilizing category of Alzheimer's remain a potential or actual public burden. Other attempts at re-civilizing dementia have equally costly consequences. Whether the circumstances of those who become mentally frail are treated as the result of a personal flaw, arising from the individual's inappropriate or ineffective management of risk, or whether they are represented as the reproduction of a malignant social psychology embedded within the practices and institutions to which they are consigned, the consequence remains. The 'cost' of mental frailty in old age is transformed from a responsibility to be planned for and borne by any 'aging' state to one that resides primarily with individuals—whether as victims or as carers.

Within late modern society, where lifestyle consumerism and the search for personal fulfillment and recognition play such an important role in the dynamic of social life, failure to embody the culture resulting from a loss in the capacity for self-care represents one of the most serious of identity flaws. Indeed, it challenges the sustainability of any 'culture of aging'. If there should be limits to human aging, the morality of the mind may prove the most instrumental in setting those limits and . . . the most unyielding to any attempt to blur or redefine them. Redistributive policies do not guard against the impoverishment of dementia whilst gender politics address those who care, not those who suffer from dementia. Consumer choice and the technologies of the self seem of little account in preventing the occurrence of dementia or in transforming its meaning. Yet, despite all the contradictions, the modernist project remains undaunted. Over 100 anti-dementia preparations are or have reached the stage of clinical testing. Not one of them is hemlock.

Notes

1. N. Elias, *The History of Manners. The Civilizing Process*, vol. I. (New York: Urizen Books, 1978).
2. C. Shilling, *The Body and Social Theory*. (London: Sage, 1996), 163–7.
3. See R. Jones, 'The Varieties of Dementia and the Question of Dementia in Relation to Responsibility', *Journal of Mental Science* 58 (1912): 411–24.
4. For an account of those excluded from admission to the hospitals that opened during the course of the nineteenth century, see F. B. Smith, *The People's Health, 1830–1910* (London, Weidenfeld and Nicolson, 1990). They included significantly 'the dirty and unrespectable, the very poor, women burdened with small children, and the aged' (254).
5. See the introduction in R.M. Klatz, ed, *Advances in Anti-Aging Medicine* (Mary Ann Liebert, Inc., New York, 1996).
6. See, for example, E. Grunthal, 'Uber die Alzheimersche Krankheit', *Zeitschrift fur die Gesellschaft Neurologie und Psychiatrie*, 101 (1926): 128–46; N. Gellerstedt, 'Zur keuntius altersinvolution', *Uppsala Lakareforenings Forhandlingar*, 38 (1992): 1–193; D. Rothschild, 'Pathologic Changes in Senile Psychoses and Their Psychobiologic Significance', *American Journal of Psychiatry*, 93 (1937): 757–84; D. Rothschild and M.L. Sharp, 'The Origin of Senile Psychoses: Neuropathologic Factors and Factors of a More Personal Nature', *Diseases of the Nervous System*, 2: (1941): 49–54.
7. . . . See, for example, M. Friedman and R. Friedman, *Free to Choose* (Harmondsworth: Penguin, 1980); F.A. Hayek, *The Road to Serfdom* (London: Routledge and Kegan Paul, 1944).
8. Evidence of a specific deficiency in those enzyme systems involved in the metabolic pathway to the neurotransmitter acetylcholine was reported in three key papers; P. Davies and A.J.F. Maloney, 'Selective Loss of Central Cholinergic Neurones in Alzheimer's disease', *The Lancet* ii (1976): 1403; E. K. Perry, P. H. Gibson, G. Blessed, R.H. Perry, and B. Tomlinson, 'Neurotransmitter Enzyme Abnormalities in Senile Dementia', *Journal of Neurological Sciences*, 334 (1977): 247–65; P. White, 'Neocortical Cholinergic Neurons in Elderly People', *The Lancet* ii (1977): 680–1.
9. P. Etienne, S. Gauthier, and G. Johnson, 'Clinical Effects of Choline in Alzheimer's Disease', *The Lancet* I (1978): 508–9; B.H. Peters and H. Levin, 'Effects of Physostigmine and Lecithin on Memory in Alzheimer's Disease', *Annals of Neurology* 6 (1979): 219–21.
10. The 'cholinergic hypothesis' became a shorthand way of describing those models of Alzheimer's dementia that saw the loss of cholinergic neurons as the core aetiological foundation of the mental decline in dementia and the restoration of that cholinergic deficit as the means of remedying Alzheimer/dementia. See E. K. Perry, 'The Cholinergic Hypothesis—Ten Years On', *British Medical Bulletin* 42 (1986): 63–9.
11. Since the NINCDS and ADRDA criteria were established they soon became linked to the FDA's requirements for anti-dementia drug trials, so that all anti-dementia drug trials conducted since the late 1980s have become driven by the Alzheimer terminology. Studies using drug compounds that originated prior to the 'cholinergic hypothesis'— variously though of as improving cerebral circulation or cerebral activiation—have tended to stick to more old-fashioned terms, but these studies

invariably appear in non-mainstream publications (typically Francophone research) and clearly exist outside the contemporary Alzheimer canon (e.g., J.Y. Dartenue, T. Belloussof, M. Meriaud, M. Clavel, and H. Chousasat, 'Etude en double-aveugle du Praxiline dans l'insuffisance circulatoire du veillard', *Geriatrie* 6: 325–7.

12. See L.S. Schneider, J.T. Olin, S.A. Lyness, and H. C. Chui, 'Eligibility of Alzheimer's Disease Clinic Patients for Clinical Trials', *Journal of the American Geriatric Society* 445 (1997): 923–8.

13. See K. Rockwood, P. Stolec, and I. McDowell, 'Factors Associated with Institutionalization of Older People in Canada: Testing a Multifactorial Definition of Frailty', *Journal of the American Geriatrics Society* 44 (1996): 578–82.

14. . . . The rationale for such studies was stated clearly in Roth's 1980 account of priorities for psychiatric research in later life: 'Epidemiological and sociological investigations are needed to define the character and size of the problem that are . . . emerging and so make possible the planning of future health and social services for the aged' (M. Roth, in M. Lader, ed, *Priorities in Psychiatric Research*, [Chichester: Wiley & Sons, 1980]: 92).

15. The term 'Alzheimerization of aging' was coined by Richard Adelman, professor of biological chemistry at the University of Michigan, in a critical editorial published in 1995 (R.C. Adelman, 'The Alzheimerization of Aging', *The Gerontologist* 35 [1995]: 526–32).

16. See for example J.C.S. Breitner, 'Genetic Factors', in A. Burns and R. Levy, eds, *Dementia* (London: Chapman and Hall, 1994), 281–93.

17. L.J. Thal, A. Carta, R. Doody, et al., 'Prevention Protocol for Alzheimer Disease', Position paper from the International Working Group on Harmonization of Dementia Drugs Guidelines, *Alzheimer's Disease and Associated Disorders*, 11 (Supplement 3, 1997): 6–7.

18. For illustrative incidence studies, see G. Letenneur, D. Commenges, J.F., and P. Barbergcr-Gateau, 'Incidence of Dementia and Alzheimer's Disease in Elderly Community Residents of South-Western France', *International Journal of Epidemiology* 23 (1994): 1256–64; A. Ott, M.M.B. Breteler, F. van Harskamp, T. Stijnen, and A. Hofman, 'Incidence and Risk of Dementia: The Rotterdam Study', *American Journal of Epidemiology* 147 (1998): 574–80; W.A. Rocca, R.H. Cha, S.C. Waring, and E. Kokmen, 'Incidence of Dementia and Alzheimer's Disease: A Reanalysis of Data From Rochester, Minnesota, 1975–1984', *American Journal of Epidemiology* 148 (1998): 51–62.

19. M.R. Meyer, J.T. Tschanz, M.C. Norton, K.A. Welsh-Bohmer, D.C. Steffens, B.W. Wyse, and J.C.S. Breitner, (1998) 'APOE Genotype Predicts When—Not Whether—One is Predisposed to Develop Alzheimer Disease', *Nature Genetics* 19 (1998): 321–2.

Part XVI

Postmodern Bodies

Claudia Malacrida

Postmodernism, as Marxist theorist Frederic Jameson defines it, heralds the end of modernity's thrust towards perfection and progress, and the movement from industrial capitalism to high consumerism; it also signifies the demise of distinctions between high culture and popular culture, purity and eclecticism, and tradition and innovation (2001). In addition, postmodern culture is characterized by cultural forms in which the possibilities for innovation and freedom are facilitated by eclectic use of multiple cultural styles, norms, and ideas. In turn, this cultural pastiche potentially erodes traditional forms of authority and normativity. Postmodernism is thus positioned as acting in contradistinction to modernity, with its belief in biological determinism, liberal humanism, and rationalism. But how does postmodernism relate to body theories? In this final section, we are exposed to the writings of three postmodern theorists who explain that, for them, the body is no longer limited by its physical, 'natural' components, but is instead both postmodern and ultimately posthuman.

In speaking about a **posthuman** future, theorists speculate that cyberspace and science will eventually create a world in which future beings will no longer be tied to their physical bodies (often derisively spoken of as 'wetware' or simply 'meat'); instead, posthuman entities will comprise an evolved self that incorporates artificial intelligence and uploaded consciousness, transcending current human forms (Sullins, 2000). Another envisioned possibility is that the posthuman entity will not be completely disconnected from the body, but could instead be 'a completely augmented biological human created through a combination of advanced technologies such as genetic engineering and therapies, psychopharmacology, neural interfaces, and wearables, with the unlimited capability to shape himself, as well as his [sic] environment' (Miller, 2004: 62).

Theorists seem to agree that the posthuman body remains in the future; however, they argue that we are currently living in a transitional moment where the **transhuman** body is not the stuff of science fiction, but is in fact already with us. Technologies such as therapeutic cloning, stem cell treatments, germline engineering, cybernetic implants, and pharmaceutical enhancements have resulted in bodies that are foundationally different from those of even 20 years ago, and raise ethical and legal questions that have already been outstripped by technological advancements (Miller, 2004). The three articles included in this section offer insights into some of the dilemmas and possibilities attached to these new, transhuman bodies, addressing both moral and political aspects of this brave new world.

Donna J. Haraway's chapter, 'A Cyborg Manifesto: Science, Technology, and Socialist-Feminism in the Late Twentieth Century' (1991) can be read as a postmodernist, transhuman response to some of the more modernist concerns of second wave feminism. As we may recall, Chris Shilling has argued that many of our contemporary theories of the body are founded on feminist concerns about female reproduction, female sexual exploitation, violence against female bodies, and problems relating to the representation and objectification of women's bodies. Second wave feminism drew heavily on modernist notions of reality: 'women' were seen as 'naturally' sharing the same embodied experiences and oppressions as a result of their shared biology. To Haraway, this **essentialist** idea that women's bodies necessarily and naturally share core, biologically based, and determinative qualities, is limiting. Instead, Haraway offers us the vision of the **cyborg**, 'a cybernetic organism, a hybrid of machine and organism' (149) that offers us a way to transcend the bounds of history and materiality and that provides us with a way out of problematic gender and possibly class relations. For Haraway, this is particularly important in considering the tensions between the public and private spheres. Traditional feminists have argued that women's roles in the private spheres have been naturalized and politicized as a means of keeping women oppressed. They have also argued that women's connections to reproduction and home care have culturally allied them to 'nature' and 'animal', while men's work has been culturally cemented as 'rational' and 'machine'. Haraway argues that, with cyborg technologies, traditional distinctions between the private (women's) sphere and the public (men's) sphere and between nature and machine break down. In addition, traditional bodily dualism such as self/other, culture/nature, god/human, and male/female can be potentially bridged. When reading Haraway's chapter, it is clear that, to her, cybernetics offers a politics of the body that is both revolutionary and liberatory; in her manifesto, the cyborg offers us a way out of problematic gender, race, sexuality, and class relations.

Victoria L. Pitts's reading provides insight into the culture and politics of transhuman bodies in the fields of art, music, and literature in cyberpunk communities (2003). In a case of life imitating art, **cyberpunks** have experimented with interfaces of body and machine as a means of expression, and as a way to denaturalize the body. Not surprisingly, cyberpunks make broad use of the Internet as a forum for body play. For an example of cyberpunk, you may want to visit http://www.psymbiote.org/. Like Haraway, Pitts discusses the potential of cyborg bodies to transcend the limits of race, gender, and biology, but she also cautions against optimism, noting that cyberculture as it currently sits has failed to transcend gender norms and gender roles, even when the body is absent. In the end, for Pitts, the question of transhuman liberation remains open; to her, it remains unclear whether body modification and cybernetics will free us from embodied regimentation, or whether the racialized, gendered, and classed power relations that have traditionally underpinned the body will simply be replicated in posthuman bodies.

The possibilities of transhuman interventions have been explored publicly by writers, scientists, and particularly artists such as Stelarc, an Australian performance artist who explores the body's relation to machines, prosthetics, virtual reality, and robotics (see http://www.stelarc.va.com.au/). Orlan, another transhuman performance artist, has been engaged in a series of projects in which she performs body modifying surgeries, which are filmed while she is awake and during which she speaks about the politics of medical technologies, consumption, fashion, art, body image, and beauty (Clarke, 1999). According to Julie Clarke's 'The Sacrificial Body of Orlan' (1999), Orlan's exposure of the inner surfaces of her face during her surgeries, and her production of a self that she both conceives and constructs acts to destabilize ideals about feminine beauty, since it exposes the efforts to which women must and do go to achieve 'beauty', and because it exposes the artificiality of beauty standards. Orlan maintains an interesting website at http://www.orlan.net/. In addition to taking on beauty and the beauty industry, Orlan's work also takes on 'Religion and Science: two major paradigms that have mediated and defined the human body' (195). Through creating and recreating herself, she challenges the idea of God-as-creator, and by controlling the process of her body's medical reconstruction, she challenges the belief that medical science is the only discipline with the legitimacy to control and manipulate bodies. Thus, using her own cyborg body, Orlan engages in a similar political challenge to that envisioned by Donna Haraway, deconstructing dualisms of god/human, science/consumption, and nature/culture.

References

Clarke, J. 1999. 'The Sacrificial Body of Orlan', *Body & Society* 5: 185–207.

Haraway, D.J. 1991. 'A Cyborg Manifesto: Science, Technology, and Socialist-Feminism in the Late Twentieth Century', in *Simians, Cyborgs, and Women: The Reinvention of Nature*. New York: Routledge, 148–81.

Jameson, F. 2001. *Postmodernism, or, The Cultural Logic of Late Capitalism*. Durham, NC: Duke University Press.

Miller, S. 2004. 'Human, Transhuman, Posthuman: What's the Difference and Who Cares?' *Futures Research Quarterly* 20: 61–7.

Pitts, V.L. 2003. *In the Flesh: The Cultural Politics of Body Modification*. New York: Palgrave MacMillan.

Sullins, J. 2000. 'Transcending the Meat: Immersive Technologies and Computer Mediated Bodies', *Journal of Experimental & Theoretical Artificial Intelligence* 12: 13–22.

Chapter 46

A Cyborg Manifesto: Science, Technology, and Socialist-Feminism in the Late Twentieth Century

Donna J. Haraway

An Ironic Dream of a Common Language for Women in the Integrated Circuit

. . . A cyborg is a cybernetic organism, a hybrid of machine and organism, a creature of social reality as well as a creature of fiction. Social reality is lived social relations, our most important political construction, a world-changing fiction. The international women's movements have constructed 'women's experience', as well as uncovered or discovered this crucial collective object. This experience is a fiction and fact of the most crucial, political kind. Liberation rests on the construction of the consciousness, the imaginative apprehension, of oppression, and so of possibility. The cyborg is a matter of fiction and lived experience that changes what counts as women's experience in the late twentieth century. This is a struggle over life and death, but the boundary between science fiction and social reality is an optical illusion.

Contemporary science fiction is full of cyborgs—creatures simultaneously animal and machine, who populate worlds ambiguously natural and crafted. Modern medicine is also full of cyborgs, of couplings between organism and machine, each conceived as coded devices, in an intimacy and with a power that was not generated in the history of sexuality. . . .

By the late twentieth century, our time, a mythic time, we are all chimeras, theorized and fabricated hybrids of machine and organism; in short, we are cyborgs. The cyborg is our ontology; it gives us our politics. The cyborg is a condensed image of both imagination and material reality, the two joined centres structuring any possibility of historical transformation. In the traditions of 'Western' science and politics—the tradition of racist, male-dominant capitalism; the tradition of progress; the tradition of the appropriation of nature as resource for the productions of culture; the tradition of reproduction of the self from the reflections of the other—the relation between organism and machine has been a border war. The stakes in the border war have been the territories of production, reproduction, and imagination. This chapter is an argument for *pleasure* in the confusion of boundaries and for *responsibility* in their construction. It is also an effort to contribute to socialist–feminist culture and theory in a postmodernist, non-naturalist mode and in the utopian tradition of imagining a world without gender, which is perhaps a world without genesis, but maybe also a world without end. The cyborg incarnation is outside salvation history. . . .

The cyborg is resolutely committed to partiality, irony, intimacy, and perversity. It is oppositional, utopian, and completely without innocence. No longer structured by the polarity of public and private, the cyborg defines a technological polis based partly on a revolution of social relations in the *oikos*, the household. Nature and culture are reworked; the one can no longer be the resource for appropriation or incorporation by the other. The relationships for forming wholes from parts, including those of polarity and hierarchical domination, are at issue in the cyborg world. . . .

. . . I want to signal three crucial boundary breakdowns that make the following political–fictional (political–scientific) analysis possible. By the late twentieth century in US scientific culture, the boundary between human and animal is thoroughly breached. . . .

Biological–determinist ideology is only one position opened up in scientific culture for arguing the meanings of human animality. . . . The cyborg appears in myth precisely where the boundary between human and animal is transgressed. Far from signalling a walling off of people from other living beings, cyborgs signal disturbingly and pleasurably tight coupling. . . .

The second leaky distinction is between animal–human (organism) and machine. . . . Late twentieth-century machines have made thoroughly ambiguous the difference between natural and artificial, mind and body, self-developing and extremely designed, and many other distinctions that used to apply to organisms and machines. Our machines are disturbingly lively, and we ourselves frighteningly inert.

Technological determination is only one ideological space opened up by the reconceptions of machine and organism as coded texts through which we engage in the play of writing and reading the world.[1] 'Textualization' of everything in poststructuralist, postmodernist theory has been damned by Marxists and socialist feminists for its utopian disregard for the lived relations of domination that ground the 'play' of arbitrary reading.[2] It is certainly true that postmodernist strategies, like my cyborg myth, subvert myriad organic wholes (for example, the poem, the primitive culture, the biological organism). In short, the certainty of what counts as nature—a source of insight and promise of innocence—is undermined, probably fatally. The transcendent authorization of interpretation is lost, and with it the ontology grounding 'Western' epistemology. But the alternative is not cynicism or faithlessness, that is, some version of abstract existence, like the accounts of technological determinism destroying 'man' by the 'machine' or 'meaningful political action' by the 'text'. Who cyborgs will be is a radical question; the answers are a matter of survival. . . .

The third distinction is a subset of the second: the boundary between physical and non-physical is very imprecise for us. . . . Modern machines are quintessentially microelectronic devices: they are everywhere and they are invisible. Modern machinery is an irreverent upstart god, mocking the Father's ubiquity and spirituality. The silicon chip is a surface for writing; it is etched in molecular scales disturbed only by atomic noise, the ultimate interference for nuclear scores. Writing, power, and technology are old partners in Western stories of the origin of civilization, but miniaturization has changed our experience of mechanism. Miniaturization has turned out to be about power; small is not so much beautiful as pre-eminently dangerous, as in cruise missiles. Contrast the TV sets of the 1950s or the news cameras of the 1970s with the TV wrist bands or hand-sized video cameras now advertised. Our best machines are made of sunshine; they are all light and clean because they are nothing but signals, electromagnetic waves, a section of a spectrum, and these machines are eminently portable, mobile—a matter of immense human pain in Detroit and Singapore. People are nowhere near so fluid, being both material and opaque. Cyborgs are ether, quintessence.

The ubiquity and invisibility of cyborgs is precisely why these sunshine-belt machines are so deadly. They are as hard to see politically as materially. They are about consciousness—or its simulation.[3] . . .

So my cyborg myth is about transgressed boundaries, potent fusions, and dangerous possibilities that progressive people might explore, as one part of needed political work. One of my premises is that most American socialists and feminists see deepened dualisms of mind and body, animal and machine, idealism and materialism in the social practices, symbolic formulations, and physical artifacts associated with 'high technology' and scientific culture. From *One-Dimensional Man* (Marcuse, 1964) to *The Death of Nature* (Merchant, 1980), the analytic resources developed by progressives have insisted on the necessary domination of technics and recalled us to an imagined organic body to integrate our resistance. Another of my premises is that the need for unity of people trying to resist worldwide intensification of domination has never been more acute. But a slightly perverse shift of perspective might better enable us to contest for meanings, as well as for other forms of power and pleasure in technologically mediated societies.

From one perspective, a cyborg world is about the final imposition of a grid of control on the planet, about the final abstraction embodied in a Star Wars apocalypse waged in the name of defence, about the final appropriation of women's bodies in a masculinist orgy of war (Sofia, 1984). From another perspective, a cyborg world might be about lived social and bodily realities in which people are not afraid of their joint kinship with animals and machines, not afraid of permanently partial identities and contradictory standpoints. The political struggle is to see from both perspectives at once because each reveals both dominations and possibilities unimaginable from the other vantage point. . . .

Fractured Identities

It has become difficult to name one's feminism by a single adjective—or even to insist in every circumstance upon the noun. Consciousness of exclusion through naming is acute. Identities seem contradictory, partial, and strategic. With the hard-won recognition of their social and historical constitution, gender, race, and class cannot provide the basis for belief in 'essential' unity. There is nothing about being 'female' that naturally binds women. There is not even such a state as 'being' female, itself a highly complex category constructed in contested sexual scientific discourses and other social practices. Gender, race, or class consciousness is an achievement forced on us by the terrible historical experience of the contradictory social realities of patriarchy, colonialism, and capitalism. And who counts as 'us' in my own rhetoric? Which identities are available to ground such a potent political myth called 'us', and what could motivate enlistment in this collectivity? Painful fragmentation among feminists

(not to mention among women) along every possible fault line has made the concept of *woman* elusive, an excuse for the matrix of women's dominations of each other. For me—and for many who share a similar historical location in white, professional middle-class, female, radical, North American, mid-adult bodies—the sources of a crisis in political identity are legion. The recent history for much of the US left and US feminism has been a response to this kind of crisis by endless splitting and searches for a new essential unity. But there has also been a growing recognition of another response through coalition—affinity, not identity.[4] . . .

I do not know of any other time in history when there was greater need for political unity to confront effectively the dominations of 'race', 'gender', 'sexuality', and 'class'. I also do not know of any other time when the kind of unity we might help build could have been possible. None of 'us' have any longer the symbolic or material capability of dictating the shape of reality to any of 'them'. Or at least 'we' cannot claim innocence from practising such dominations. White women, including socialist feminists, discovered (that is, were forced kicking and screaming to notice) the non-innocence of the category 'woman'. . . .

Cyborgs: A Myth of Political Identity

. . . To recapitulate, certain dualisms have been persistent in Western traditions; they have all been systemic to the logics and practices of domination of women, people of colour, nature, workers, animals—in short, domination of all constituted as others, whose task is to mirror the self. Chief among these troubling dualisms are self/other, mind/body, culture/nature, male/female, civilized/primitive, reality/appearance, whole/part, agent/resource, maker/made, active/passive, right/wrong, truth/illusion, total/partial, God/man. . . .

High-tech culture challenges these dualisms in intriguing ways. It is not clear who makes and who is made in the relation between human and machine. It is not clear what is mind and what body in machines that resolve into coding practices. In so far as we know ourselves in both formal discourse (for example, biology) and in daily practice (for example, the homework economy in the integrated circuit), we find ourselves to be cyborgs, hybrids, mosaics, chimeras. Biological organisms have become biotic systems, communications devices like others. There is no fundamental, ontological separation in our formal knowledge of machine and organism, of technical and organic. . . .

There are several consequences to taking seriously the imagery of cyborgs as other than our enemies. Our bodies, ourselves; bodies are maps of power and identity. Cyborgs are no exception. A cyborg body is not innocent; it was not born in a garden; it does not seek unitary identity and so generate antagonistic dualisms without end (or until the world ends); it takes irony for granted. One is too few, and two is only one possibility. Intense pleasure in skill, machine skill, ceases to be a sin, but an aspect of embodiment. The machine is not an *it* to be animated, worshipped, and dominated. The machine is us, our processes, an aspect of our embodiment. We can be responsible for machines; *they* do not dominate or threaten us. We are responsible for boundaries; we are they. Up till now (once upon a time), female embodiment seemed to be given, organic, necessary; and female embodiment seemed to mean skill in mothering and its metaphoric extensions. Only by being out of place could we take intense pleasure in machines, and then with excuses that this was organic activity after all, appropriate to females. Cyborgs might consider more seriously the partial, fluid, sometimes aspect of sex and sexual embodiment. Gender might not be global identity after all, even if it has profound historical breadth and depth.

The ideologically charged question of what counts as daily activity, as experience, can be approached by exploiting the cyborg image. Feminists have recently claimed that women are given to dailiness, that women more than men somehow sustain daily life, and so have a privileged epistemological position potentially. There is a compelling aspect to this claim, one that makes visible unvalued female activity and names it as the ground of life. But *the* ground of life? What about all the ignorance of women, all the exclusions and failures of knowledge and skill? What about men's access to daily competence, to knowing how to build things, to take them apart, to play? What about other embodiments? Cyborg gender is a local possibility taking a global vengeance. Race, gender, and capital require a cyborg theory of wholes and parts. There is no drive in cyborgs to produce total theory, but there is an intimate experience of boundaries, their construction and deconstruction. There is a myth system waiting to become a political language to ground one way of looking at science and technology and challenging the informatics of domination—in order to act potently.

One last image: organisms and organismic, holistic politics depend on metaphors of rebirth and invariably call on the resources of reproductive sex. I would suggest that cyborgs have more to do with regeneration and are suspicious of the reproductive matrix and of most birthing. For salamanders, regeneration after injury, such as the loss of a limb, involves regrowth of structure and restoration of function with the constant possibility of twinning or other odd topographical productions at the site of former injury. The regrown limb can be monstrous, duplicated, potent. We have all been injured, profoundly. We require regeneration, not rebirth, and the possibilities for our reconstitution include the utopian dream of the hope for a monstrous world without gender.

Cyborg imagery can help express two crucial arguments in this essay: first, the production of universal, totalizing theory is a major mistake that misses most of reality, probably always, but certainly now; and second, taking responsibility for the social relations of science and technology means refusing an anti-science metaphysics, a demonology of technology, and so means embracing the skilful task of reconstructing the boundaries of daily life, in partial connection with others, in communication with all of our parts. It is not just that science and technology are possible means of great human satisfaction, as well as a matrix of complex dominations. Cyborg imagery can suggest a way out of the maze of dualisms in which we have explained our bodies and our tools to ourselves. This is a dream not of a common language, but of a powerful infidel heteroglossia. It is an imagination of a feminist speaking in tongues to strike fear into the circuits of the supersavers of the new right. It means both building and destroying machines, identities, categories, relationships, space stories. Though both are bound in the spiral dance, I would rather be a cyborg than a goddess.

Notes

1. Starting points for left and/or feminist approaches to technology and politics include Cowan (1983), Rothschild (1983), Traweek (1988), Young and Levidow (1981, 1985), Weizenbaum (1976), Winner (1977, 1986), Zimmerman (1983), Athanasiou (1987), Cohn (1987a, 1987b), Winograd and Flores (1986), Edwards (1985); *Global Electronics Newsletter*, 867 West Dana St, #204, Mountain View, CA 94041; *Processed World*, 55 Sutter St, San Francisco, CA 94104; ISIS, Women's International Information and Communication Service, PO Box 50 (Cornavin), 1211 Geneva 2, Switzerland, and Via Santa maria Dell'Anima 30, 00186 Rome Italy. Fundamental approaches to modern social studies of science that do not continue the liberal mystification that it all started with Thomas Juhn, include Knorr-Cetina (1981), nor-Cetina and Mulkay (1983), Latour and Woolgar (1979), Young (1979). The 1984 Dictionary of the Network for the Ethnographic Study of Science, Technology, and Organizations lists a wide range of people and projects crucial to better radical analysis; available from NESSTO PO Box 11442, Stanford, CT 94305.

2. A provocative, comprehensive argument about the politics and theories of 'postmodernism' is made by Fredric Jameson (1984), who argues that postmodernism is not an option, a style among others, but a cultural dominant requiring radical reinvention of left politics from within; there is no longer any place from without that gives meaning to the comforting fiction of critical distance. Jameson also makes clear why one cannot be for or against postmodernism, an essentially moralist move. My position is that feminists (and others) need continuous cultural reinvention, postmodernist critique, and historical materialism; only a cyborg would have a chance. The old dominations of white capitalist patriarchy seem nostalgically innocent now: they normalized heterogeneity, into man and woman, white and black, for example. 'Advanced capitalism' and postmodernism release heterogeneity without a norm, and we are flattened, without subjectivity, which requires depth, even unfriendly and drowning depths. It is time to write *The Death of the Clinic*. The clinic's methods required bodies and works; we have texts and surfaces. Our dominations don't work by medicalization and normalization any more; they work by networking, communications redesign, stress management. Normalization gives way to automation, utter redundancy. Michel Foucault's *Birth of the Clinic* (1963), *History of Sexuality* (1976), and *Discipline and Punish* (1975) name a form of power at its moment of implosion. The discourse of biopolitics gives way to technobabble, the language of the spliced substantive; no noun is left whole by the multinationals. These are their names, listed from one issue of *Science*: Tech-Knowledge, Genentech, Allergen, Hybritech, Compupro, Genen-cor, Syntex, Allelix, Agrigenetics Corp., Syntro, Codon, Repligen, Micro-Angelo from Scion Corp., Percom Data, Inter Systems, Cyborg Corp., Statcom Corp., Intertec. If we are imprisoned by language, then escape from that prison-house requires language poets, a kind of cultural restriction enzyme to cut the code; cyborg heteroglossia is one form of radical cultural politics. For cyborg poetry, see Perloff (1984); Fraser (1984). For feminist modernist/postmodernist 'cyborg' writing, see HOW(ever), 871 Corbett Ave, San Francisco, CA 94131.

3. Baudrillard (1983). Jameson (1984: 66) points out that Plato's definition of the simulacrum is the copy for which there is no original, i.e., the world of advanced capitalism, of pure exchange. See

Discourse 9 (Spring/Summer 1987) for a special issue on technology (cybernetics, ecology, and the postmodern imagination).

4. Powerful developments of coalition politics emerge from 'Third World' speakers, speaking from nowhere, the displaced centre of the universe, earth: 'We live on the third planet from the sun'—*Sun Poem* by Jamaican writer Edward Kamau Braithwaite, review by Mackey (1984). Contributors to Smith (1983) ironically subvert naturalized identities precisely while constructing a place from which to speak called home. See especially Reagon (in Smith, 1983: 356–68). Trinh T. Minh-ha (1986–87).

References

Athanasiou, Tom. 1987. 'High-tech Politics: The Case of Artificial Intelligence', *Socialist Review* 92: 7–35.

Cohn, Carol. 1987a. 'Nuclear Language and How We Learned to Pat the Bomb', *Bulletin of Atomic Scientists*: 17–24.

———. 1987b. 'Sex and Death in the Rational World of Defence Intellectuals', *Signs* 12, 4: 687–718.

Cowan, Ruth Schwartz. 1983. *More Work for Mother: The Ironies of Household Technology from the Open Hearth to the Microwave*. New York: Basic.

Edwards, Paul. 1985. 'Border Wars: The Science and Politics of Artificial Intelligence', *Radical America* 19, 6: 39–52.

Knorr-Cetina, Karin. 1981. *The Manufacture of Knowledge*. Oxford: Pergamon.

———, and Michael Mulkay, eds. 1983. *Science Observed: Perspectives on the Social Study of Science*. Beverly Hills: Sage.

Latour, Bruno, and Steve Woolgar. 1979. *Laboratory Life: The Social Construction of Scientific Facts*. Beverly Hills: Sage.

Rothschild, Joan, ed. 1983. *Machina ex Dea: Feminist Perspectives on Technology*. New York: Pergamon.

Traweek, Sharon. 1988. *Beamtimes and Lifetimes: The World of High Energy Physics*. Cambridge, MA: Harvard University Press.

Weizenbaum, Joseph. 1976. *Computer Power and Human Reason*. San Francisco: Freeman.

Winner, Langdon. 1977. *Autonomous Technology: Technics Out of Control As a Theme in Political Thought*. Cambridge, MA: MIT Press.

Winograd, Terry, and Fernando Flores. 1986. *Understanding Computers and Cognition: A New Foundation for Design*. Norwood, NJ: Ablex.

Young, Robert M. 1979. 'Interpreting the Production of Science', *New Scientist* 29 (March): 1026–8.

———, and Les Levidow, eds. 1981, 1985. *Science, Technology and the Labour Process*, 2 vols. London: CSE and Free Association Books.

Zimmerman, Jan, ed. 1983. *The Technological Woman: Interfacing with Tomorrow*. New York: Praeger.

Chapter 47

Cyberpunk, Biomedicine, and the High-tech Body

Victoria L. Pitts

Molly Millions of William Gibson's cyberpunk novels *Neuromancer* and *Mona Lisa Overdrive* has artificially enhanced vision, a modified nervous system, and electro-prosthetic razor blade fingertips. For her, body modification is an endless process of customizing and upgrading. As she warns another character in *Neuromancer*, one can't let others 'generation-gap you', or surpass your own body modifications with the newest gadgets and technologies, lest you lose the competitive edge.[1] Millions is a samuri, a hired gun whose modifications are more than helpful. In Millions's universe, body modification technologies are not controlled by the dictates of biomedicine nor guided by cosmetic surgery experts. Customizing the body is rather a quotidian and populist project of survival and success. Millions' existence is structured by the demands of a high-tech, post-industrial cyber-universe, and her fate depends upon constant adaptations.

The development of cyberpunk as an iconic futurology began with the science fiction of the 1980s—most importantly the work of Gibson—that narrated imaginaries of post-humanism. Because of their status as human-machine hybrids and the ontological implications of always being under construction, Molly Millons and other Gibson cyborgs have become tropes for post-human subjectivity. . . .

. . . The past 15 years have seen the advance of 'actual' post-human bodies in the expansion of biomedicine and cosmetic surgery, the development of hacker and game-player cultures on the Internet, new forms of performance art, and the explosion of body mod communities. Body modification cultures, where the body's status as a work in progress is celebrated, are particularly salient places to investigate the cyborgian body. In a sense, the body modification movement as a whole is a post-human experiment. All facets of the body modification community identify the body as a space of self-writing, including those linking their bodies to those of indigenous peoples, rebelling against traditional gender norms, eroticizing the body, or embracing cutting-edge fashions. . . .

Cyberpunk body modification is distinct, though, in its futuristic aims to exploit the denaturalization of the body and escalate the literal deconstruction of the body's limits. Cyberpunk is an aesthetic that pursues futuristic, high-tech body projects beyond the limits of fashion, history, and culture. Cyberpunk body artists are distinguished by their use of biomedical, information, and virtual technologies; by their interest in body experiments and inventions; and by discursively positioning the body as a limitless frontier of exploration. In cyberpunk fashion, they unblinkingly assume the technologized body and champion its possibilities.

Having emerged in the 1990s out of body modification, punk, performance art, and cyber-subcultures, cyberpunk body artists are often called 'extreme', even from within body mod communities. The modifications in Gibson's novels—tooth reshaping, subdermal implants, neural extensions, body/Internet hook-ups, among others—have been actualized by cyberpunk-inspired body artists in the performance art and body modification communities. Among these is Stelarc, an Australian performance artist who earned early renown for his 'suspensions', in which his body hung from wires and hooks in a number of seemingly impossible poses. In other instances, he made himself a neurally connected 'Third Hand' that he could write with, and turned himself into an Internet-wired robot. Cyberpunk body modifiers also include the performance artist Orlan, as well as other body modifiers such as those who participate in creating a cyber-subcultural community on the Internet. Here and elsewhere in the body modification communities, cyberpunk has begun to materialize in the flesh, radically extending the denaturing of the body that already characterizes post-modern body projects. . . .

Imagining Cyborgs: From Technoindividualism to Feminism

High-tech body modification has been hailed in cyber discourse—in science fiction, theory, and cyber subcultures—as freeing the body-subject from the constraints of biology, language, and history. The cyberpunk model rejects the Enlightenment understanding of the body as biologically fixed, presenting the body rather as always already shaped by human technologies. It also eschews bodily conventions and norms, pursuing instead technological inventions and interventions to expand or transform the body's performance, appearance, longevity, and purpose. Its futurism envisions high-tech hardware and software as tools for change and customization, and it assumes and sometimes champions the breakdown of traditional categories of subjectivity that are seen to be located in the body, such as sex and race.

Beginning with this celebration of technology's denaturing of the body, cyberpunk for some approaches a highly individualist, post-ideological fantasy of limitless (virtual) space and technological transformation. In place of the natural body or the socially constructed body over which the indi-

vidual has no control, the cyberpunk aesthetic often hails the modified body as a harbinger of, and vehicle for, individual freedoms. . . .

For instance, the Extropians, a cyber subculture, have articulated a utopian and libertarian version of the post-human body. Terranova has examined the Extropians' Internet discourse of post-humanism. The Extropian Manifesto, published on-line by the Extropy Institute in California, describes post-humans as 'persons of unprecedented physic, intellectual, and psychological ability, self-programming and self-defining, potentially immortal, unlimited individuals'.[2] Rather than fearing technology as taking over the human, Extropians celebrate the potential of a human-machine hybrid, which they see as the next stage in human evolution. Terranova writes:

> The story-line underlying . . . [post-humanism] can be summarized in this way: there has been a huge ontological shift not only in the nature of human society, but in that of our very bodies. The 'invasion' of the human body and psyche by the machine is destined to increase over the years (it is already doing so spectacularly) and give rise to a potentially new race of human beings whose symbiosis with the machine will be total.[3]

Extropians argue in their manifestos that those who seek to become post-human are already *trans*-human, to the extent that they envision human life beyond the biologically given. Post-humanism would embrace science and technology to 'seek the continuation and acceleration of the evolution of intelligent life beyond its currently human form'.[4] Extropians suggest that evolution through science and technology will be a matter of individual choice and individual planning. Evolution, in other words, will be personally customized. . . .

These visions of the high-tech body raise questions about how trans- or post-human individuals are located in social relations, and whether technology can be used to free individual bodies from social inscription. Will we all have the ability to choose our own bodies? How will we use our enhanced abilities? To what extent is body modification a personal matter, and to what extent is it a social and political one? For their part, Extropians assert that this will be a post-ideological age. They presume that heightened intelligence, reason, and self-customization will disengage the body from politics and render questions of power irrelevant. For instance, they define their 'extropia' not as utopian, but as an 'open, evolving framework allowing individuals and voluntary groupings to form the institutions and social forms they prefer'.[5] These presumptions rely on libertarian ideas of individual rationality, choice, and voluntarism.

In contrast to this techno-individualism, there are also critical discourses that embrace high-tech bodies. For instance, the denaturing of identity implied in the high-tech body is also a point of departure for cyberfeminism, which emphasizes the presence of power relations in embodiment and is concerned with deconstructing them.[6] Cyberfeminist enthusiasm for technology centres around the possibilities of reworking embodied roles such as gender and sexuality, although it does not assume these outcomes as inevitable. Cyborg technologies, for instance, might free women from biologically based roles such as pregnancy. They also can denaturalize other gendered roles. Transsexual surgery, for example, a twentieth-century cyborg technology, has already challenged the fixity of nature-based sex and revealed the ways in which femininity and masculinity are scripts that can be learned. (Transgenderism, a much older body project, more radically disturbs the taken-for-grantedness of the dominant sex/gender formula. Transgenderism implies that gender does not automatically follow from biological sex, and so unfixes the meanings of biological differences.) Theoretically, cyberspace also offers opportunities beyond traditional limits of the body to denaturalize gender and explore new forms of embodiment. . . .

Yet the enthusiasm surrounding cyberculture has been tempered with acknowledgements that cyberculture has not achieved freedom from normative gender constraints, or from racism and other oppressions related to identity.[7] As Caroline Bassett suggests in her study of a virtual 'city' in which participants can choose their own on-line genders, *actual* on-line gender performance involves *both* gender play and 'rigid adherence to gender norms'.[8] For instance, homophobia has not disappeared from the gender-experimental on-line universe, and Bassett finds 'extreme conformity' in some of the body images employed.[9] Neither does race disappear in cyber culture. Among many other examples, the expansion of neo-Nazi and other reactionary cybercultures on the Internet suggest that cybersubjects can simply map their notions of the body and identity onto virtual spaces, and use information technology to circulate racist, patriarchal, and heteronormative discourses. . . .

BME and 'Extreme' Body Art

The interface between high technology and the body is also pursued by body modifiers who gather in cyberspace, for example in *Body Modification Ezine* (*BME*), an on-line body modification community and electronic magazine. Not only do readers post photos and stories of their own body modifications, but they also participate in on-line chat to debate, discuss, and create ongoing discourse about the personal and social meanings of body modification. Diverse factions of the body modification community meet at *BME*—male and female, gay and straight, tribalist and fetishist, as well as those interested in high-tech and surgical forms of body modification.

Shannon Larratt, the founder and editor of *BME*, began the site in 1994 and saw it thrive in the late 1990s. Through his promotion of *BME* (which is now recognized as the leading body mod site on the Web), his display of his own 'extreme' body modifications on the site, and his editorial writing, he is recognized by insiders as part of the vanguard in the body modification movement. Shannon credits *BME*, and other sites on the web, with the spread of body modification as a sub-cultural movement. He describes the purpose of *BME* as building a community of body modifiers that may be geographically dispersed but share a common sense of alienation from mainstream society. As he puts it, *BME* 'lets people know that what they're doing is OK, that it might just not be insanity'.[10]

In keeping with its aim to provide support to body modifiers who elsewhere might be highly stigmatized, body modifiers who use *BME* find there a high level of tolerance for the most radical body modification practices. *BME* publishes photos and stories of all kinds of body modifications, including what it calls 'extreme' body modifications.[11] These include high-tech practices such as subdermal implants in which metal, bone, and plastic items are surgically inserted into the face, arms, head, and elsewhere, and Western, high-tech versions of indigenous practices, such as aboriginal subincisions, or surgeries of the genitals. Shannon's own modifications include not only the subincision, but also multiple body piercings, tribal tattoos, stretched earlobes, brandings, and a tongue splitting. Shannon's description of the latter reveals a highly deviant appropriation of medical technology. Shannon describes multiple techniques for tongue splitting. One involves the assistance of a willing dentist (he describes, for instance, an Italian dentist who has performed this surgery). The dentist uses a scalpel to create small (5 mm) cuts, and then uses a cautery agent to stop the bleeding. After healing, this procedure is repeated again and again until the tongue is split down the middle to the desired length. Another process involves using tongue piercings and fishing line. A third technique, the one he used for himself, involves the assistance of an oral surgeon and a laser. Shannon reports that after his surgery, his tongue still has its original sense of taste, and that the tongue remains at least as agile: 'In most cases', he writes, 'separate control of the two halves [of the tongue] can be achieved.'[12]

Shannon's vision of body modification embraces the cyberpunk attitude of bodies without limits, provocatively asking, 'do we really need bodies? What kind of bodies could we create?'[13] In his essays and editorials, he focuses on the techniques of body modification and, like Ste-

larc, on what is technically possible. He embraces the denaturalized body and, in post-humanist fashion, resolutely denies any moral or ethical limits to body modification, arguing that 'all of us' are modern primitives.[14] His argument is that the worldwide, diverse use of body modifications across cultures means that it is 'normal' for us to modify ourselves. He argues for diversity and 'would like to see more extreme visible modifications happening', which, as he puts it, 'makes the world interesting'.[15]

The discourse of *BME* denaturalizes the body and endorses an ethic of individualism: we should neither be forced to conform to the dictates of our own culture nor be limited to body modifications that have already been invented. Echoing others' embrace of choice through technology, there is a liberal emphasis on customization, individuality, and personal freedom. At the same time, it is clear that *BME* members need to address the body's sociality. . . . For many members of *BME*, extreme body modification carries social and material consequences with which they have to cope. Shannon warns that being heavily modified will significantly affect one's job marketability and social acceptability, and describes implants, stretched earlobes, and facial tattoos as 'a permanent stigmatization to most'.[16] The highly individualistic discourse of *BME* is tempered with these acknowledgments that members of subculture face social and material consequences for what they do with their bodies. Although the aim of customization is often articulated as the expression of personal freedom and individuality, body modifiers are measured against social norms that provide ideal and proper models of embodiment.

Meanwhile, *BME* addresses another social pressure for body modifiers: commercialization. Subcultural style is often commodified by the fashion and culture industries as not only acceptable, but self-consciously hip forms of fashion. . . .

Tattoo culture is already 'rapidly losing its deviant status', as Angus Vail puts it, and some of the newest cyberpunk inventions and neotribal appropriations are readily consumed in the popular culture marketplace.[17] Even Orlan's modifications have found commercial appeal, having been mimicked by fashion designers on the catwalk.[18] While Orlan appears flattered by this 'tribute', she also expresses disdain for the popularization of her body modifications, and she isn't as happy to be the inspiration for subcultures:

> I wasn't surprised to be imitated by people who have body piercing and tattoos. I'm not against these things, but it's quite obvious that the majority of people who are into those things believe that they're liberating themselves from the dictates of a certain society, but in fact it all boils down to the same thing because they are conforming to the dictates of a smaller, mini-society . . . someone told me they had recently seen a San Francisco group on TV who have bolts and plaques on their heads, as well as needles. They were just punks, or they might as well [have] been.[19]

Orlan's disdain for punks seems to reflect, to my mind, a surprising lack of appreciation for the creative aspects of subcultural fashion. Certainly, her dislike of subcultural body art reveals her reverence for individualism: although cyberpunks might be rebellious, the collective nature of their rebellion is, for her, unacceptable. For their part, subcultures draw the line at fashion; they have long been concerned about commercialization and often attempt to distance themselves from it. (In his well-known work on subcultures, Howard Becker described such a process in 1963.[20]) As Shannon puts it in a *BME* editorial called 'Rejection of Current Trends in Pop Culture', there has been what he terms a 'ridiculous surge' in the popularity, newsworthiness, and marketability of body modifications.[21] Opposed to conformity, *BME*'s anti-fashion discourse applauds a willingness to provoke disdain, accept risk, and push the envelope of body aesthetics.[22] In this vein, Shannon asserts that of all body modifications, his favourites are 'facial implants, because I admire people who are willing to make that kind of *pioneering social sacrifice*'.[23]

Among those who make such 'sacrifices' is Andrew, a well-known body piercer in his mid-

twenties who has been celebrated on *BME* and other sites for his extreme approach to body modification. Like other body modifiers, Andrew links the body and technology to personal agency, and envisions that both natural and social constraints can be surpassed through body modification. Andrew argues that through technology, 'we can take control of what we otherwise could not'. While his body modifications are aimed at self-empowerment and individual customization, he acknowledges that this vision is threatened by fashionalization: 'when you can go into JC Penneys', he argues, 'and get a body piercing'. Through experimentation and invention, Andrew has pursued self-customization far beyond the limits of fashion. He has appropriated biomedical technologies, endured physical risk, and provoked stigma in the project to customize his body . . .

Andrew's aesthetic of body modification combines a modern primitivist interest in cultural appropriation with a cyberpunk fascination for high technology and biomedical knowledge. Among his other self-surgeries, Andrew conducted a subincision on himself. The slicing of the penis was modelled after a traditional Aboriginal practice. However, he fused his understanding of traditional uses of the practice (beginning with *National Geographic)* with knowledge gained from studying the anatomy textbooks ordinarily used by medical students, and he used a topical anesthetic, sutures, and scalpels.

> I had a working knowledge of anesthetics both topical and injectible. I had everything down, done all my homework, tested [the topical anesthetic] on different areas of the body. I tested on genital tissues, no problems—it's standard in the [medical] industry to be used for this.

This kind of experimentation involves physical risks as well as fears of stigma. Andrew's subincision, a procedure he has successfully performed on others, did not proceed without incident. Alarmingly, he experienced a reaction to the anesthetic and had internal bleeding. Yet given the highly stigmatized nature of this practice, he found himself unable to seek medical attention. He explains,

> I'm not going to go [to the hospital] because I'm not an Australian aborigine am I? You can't take the chance to explain yourself. You have to weigh [the situation]. . . . I had a second degree chemical burn in reaction to an anesthetic that ended up burning some of my urethra . . . had an allergic reaction, and coupled with the fact that the vessels that had been sealed off had become uncauterized, I had large blood vessels draining inside subcutaneous tissues. I blew up and that's a real bad scene. So either go there [to the hospital] with an inch and a half split among the underside of the phallus, and explain that, or try to surgically [fix it myself].
> VP: *So you didn't go to the hospital?*
> ANDREW: I didn't go to the hospital . . . I've had to do about 25 small surgeries [to fix it] . . . Now it's fine. Your body can do anything . . . I'm doing fine.

Andrew's cyberpunk attitude toward body modification is reflected in his highly deviant appropriation of medical procedures to create implants and conduct self-surgeries, as well as his insistence on the body that can 'do anything' a remarkable point of view given his experience with subincision. . . .

Customizing Bodies

The high-tech body modifiers described here share an enthusiasm for technology's capacity to facilitate self-customization. Stelarc, Shannon, and Andrew employ radically individualist language to describe the meaning of their body projects. . .

This individualism is partly predicated on the disappearance, shrinkage, or obsolescence of the material body through technological intervention. . . .

The disappearing body is often equated with freedom from the effects of power. For instance, Stelarc's notion of customization as a matter of individualizing evolution, or making each individual 'a species unto him or herself', suggests that technology is a vehicle for liberating the self from the social, a view also endorsed by cybercultures like the Extropians. In his words, the body is 'no longer the site of collapsing the personal and political if it's no longer there'.[24] He implies not only that technology itself is a neutral instrument of individual agency, but also that the socially marked body is increasingly irrelevant. He suggests that embodied categories of power such as race, gender, sexuality, and class are both uncoupled with the body-subject and denied by technology. . . . Stelarc envisions a world of postmodern relativism, in which all identities and bodies are denatured, liberated from any inevitable effects of power. To my mind, although Stelarc describes some of the radical possibilities of techno-ontology, this relativism problematically denies his own social situatedness. . . .

I agree with MacKendrick that these practices, so personally risky for participants, can create important critical effects. . . .

However, high-tech body modifiers do not wholly eschew dominant ideologies in their body projects. For instance, both cyberpunk and cosmetic medicine link the denatured body to the liberal subject who can personally choose her identity. The vision articulated by cyberpunks that a person can 'be who you want to be' is also the mantra of high-tech cosmetic culture. As Anne Balsamo describes, the cosmetic industries are served well by this liberal sense of identity freedom:

> [These industries] have capitalized on the role of the body in the process of 'identity semiosis'—where identities becomes signs and signs become commodities. The consequence is the technological production of identities for sale and rent. Material bodies shop the global marketplace for cultural identities that come in different forms, the least permanent as clothes and accessories worn once and discarded with each new fashion season, the most dramatic as the physical transformation of the corporeal body accomplished through surgical methods.[25]

Cyberpunk surgeries have a lot in common with their culturally legitimized counterparts. They are informed by a sense of identity as ontologically freed by the breakdown of the body's limits.

Cyberpunk subjectivity, like that of the cosmetic surgery consumer, is seen as the product of individual choice to shop, invent, and create bodies and identities through technological means. . . .

Notes

1. William Gibson, *Neuromancer* (New York: Ace Books, 1984): 59. David Brande's article first directed me to this passage. See David Brande, 'The Business of Cyberpunk: Symbolic Economy and Ideology in William Gibson', *Configurations* 2, 3 (1994): 511.
2. *Extropian Manifesto,* cited in Terranova, 2000: 273.
3. Ibid., 270.
4. *Extropian FAQ,* cited in Terranova, 2000: 273.
5. 'EP3.0', http://www.extropy.org.
6. For Donna Haraway, technology, power, and consciousness are interconnected, and the advancement of a more pluralist culture depends not only upon the former but also the latter.
7. See, for instance, Mary Flanagan and Austin Booth, eds, *Reload: Rethinking Women + Cyberculture* (Cambridge, MA: MIT Press, 2002).
8. Caroline Bassett, 'Virtually Gendered: Life in an On-Line World', in *The Subcultures Reader*, ed. Gelder and Thorton, 1997: 549.
9. Ibid. See also Howard Rheingold, *The Virtual Community: Finding Connection in a Computerized World* (London: Seeker and Warburg, 1994).
10. 'Interview with Shannon Larratt', by Raven, *Body Modification Ezine* (*BME*), http://BME/FreeQ.com/culture/wb/wb/wb000.html-wbo14.htm.
11. Although the body modifiers on *BME* are highly tolerant, these are usually the focus of the hate mail that *BME* receives from outsiders.
12. 'Interview with Shannon Larratt', *BME*.
13. Personal correspondence between the author and Shannon Larratt, September 1998.
14. 'Interview with Shannon Larratt', *BME*.
15. Shannon Larratt, 'Editorial: Extreme Modifications: Why?,' *BME*.
16. Ibid.
17. Vail, 1999: 271.
18. As Orlan says in an interview: 'The fashion industry has now caught up with me. My work appeals to many fashion designers. One in particular uses it in a very literal way—perhaps you saw it in his catalogues?—and there is one who pays tribute to my work by making up his models with the same bumps as me' (interview in Ayers, 2000: 180).
19. Ibid., 182. She also argues here that she is 'not in favour of fashion and its dictates'.
20. In body modification's subcultural discourse, 'real' body modifiers are contrasted to kids, rock stars, and supermodels. Although it is clear by now that there *isn't* a clear line between fashion and subcultural style, that practices might carry symbolic weight either as authentic subcultural practices or as inauthentic commercial knock-offs might reveal how members 'classify themselves' in relation to 'how much they give in to outsiders'. Howard Becker, 'The Culture of a Deviant Group: The Jazz Musician', in *The Subcultures Reader*, 57.
21. Shannon Larratt, 'Rejection of Current Trends in "Pop Culture"', *BME*.
22. The visibility, risk, and quantity of body modifications in cyberpunk is not universally embraced among all subcultural body modifiers, of course, but has subcultural capital among those whom Raelyn Gallina, in her interview with the author, identified as a 'certain subset . . . taking this to the farthest extreme, to the edges . . . It's already an edge thing, as now they're taking it even further. . . . There are those edges that are going so extreme that it's . . . like the image is breaking up.'
23. 'Interview with Shannon Larratt', *BME* (emphasis mine).
24. Stelarc, interview in Farnell, 2000: 131.
25. Balsamo, 1995: 225.

References

Ayers, Robert. 2000. 'Serene and Happy and Distance: An Interview with Orlan', in Mike Featherstone, ed, *Body Modification*. London: Sage.

Bailey, David, and Stuart Hall. 1992. 'The Vertigo of Displacement', *Ten.8* 2, 3: 15.

Balsamo, Anne. 1995. 'Forms of Technological Embodiment: Reading the Body in Contemporary Culture', in Mike Featherstone and Roger Burrows, eds, *Cyberspace/Cyberbodies/Cyberpunk: Cultures of Technological Embodiment*. London: Sage.

Bassett, Caroline. 1997. 'Virtually Gendered: Life in an On-Line World', in Ken Gelder and Sarah Thorton, eds, *The Subcultures Reader*. London: Routledge.

Becker, Howard. 1997 [1963]. 'The Culture of a Deviant Group: The "Jazz" Musician', in Gelder and Thorton, eds, *The Subculture Reader*.

Body Modification Ezine, http://www.BME.FreeQ.com.

Brande, David. 1994. 'The Business of Cyberpunk: Symbolic Economy and Ideology in William Gibson', *Configurations* 2, 3: 509–36.

Clough, Patricia. 1998. *The End(s) of Ethnography: From Realism to Social Criticism*, 2nd edn. New York: Peter Lang.

Davis, Kathy. 1997. 'My Body is My Art: Cosmetic Surgery as Feminist Utopia?', *European Journal of Women's Studies* 4: 23–37.

Dery, Mark. 2000. 'Ritual Mechanics: Cybernetic Body Art', in David Bell and Barbara M. Kennedy, eds, *The Cybercultures Reader*. London: Routledge.

Farnell, Ross. 2000. 'In Dialogue with "PostHuman" Bodies: Interview with Stelarc', in Mike Featherstone, ed, *Body Modification*.

Featherstone, Mike. 1995. *Undoing Culture: Globalization, Postmodernism and Identity*. London: Sage.

Flanagan, Mary, and Austin Booth, eds. 2002. *Reload: Rethinking Women + Cyberculture*. Cambridge MA: MIT Press.

Foucault, Michel. 1978. *The History of Sexuality, Volume I, An Introduction*, trans. Robert Hurley. New York: Pantheon.

———. 1979. *Discipline and Punish*, trans. Alan Sheridan. New York: Vintage.

Gelder, Ken. 1997. 'The Birmingham Tradition and Cultural Studies', in Gelder and Thorton, eds, *The Subcultures Reader*.

Gibson, William. 1984. *Neuromancer*. New York: Ace Books.

Goodall, Jane. 2000. 'An Order of Pure Decision: Un-Natural Selection in the Work of Stelarc and Orlan', in Featherstone, ed, *Body Modification*.

Gordon, Isa. n.d. 'The Psymbiote Speaks: On Generating a Cyborg Body'. Available at http://www.isa@psymbiote.org.

Haraway, Donna. 2000 [1991]. 'A Cyborg Manifesto: Science, Technology and Socialist-Feminism in the Late Twentieth Century', in Bell and Kennedy, eds, *The Cybercultures Reader*.

Larratt, Shannon. n.d. 'Editorial: Extreme Modifications: Why?', *Body Modification Ezine (BME)*, http://BME.FreeQ.com.

———. n.d. 'Rejection of Current Trends in "Pop Culture"', *BME*.

Leary, Timothy. 2000. 'The Cyberpunk: The Individual as Reality Pilot', in Bell and Kennedy, eds, *The Cybercultures Reader*.

MacKendrick, Karmen. 1998. 'Technoflesh, or Didn't That Hurt?' *Fashion Theory* 2, 1: 3–24.

Melluci, Alberto. 1996. *Challenging Codes*. Cambridge: Cambridge University Press.

Muniz, Jose Esteban. 1997. 'The White to be Angry: Vaginal Davis's Terrorist Drag', *Social Text* 52/53, 15 (3–4): 81–90.

Oxford English Dictionary. 1978. Oxford: Oxford University Press.

Rheingold, Howard. 1994. *The Virtual Community: Finding Connection in a Computerized World*. London: Secker and Warburg.

Ross, Andrew. 2000. 'Hacking Away at the Counter-Culture', in Bell and Kennedy, eds, *The Cybercultures Reader*.

Sandoval, Chela. 2000. 'New Sciences: Cyborg Feminism and the Methodology of the Oppressed', in Bell and Kennedy, *The Cybercultures Reader*.

Shelton, Anthony. 1996. 'Fetishism's Culture', in Nicolas Sinclair, ed, *The Chameleon Body*. London: Lund Humphries.

Terranova, Tiziana. 2000. 'Post-Human Unbounded: Artificial Revolution and High-Tech Subcultures', in Bell and Kennedy, eds, *The Cybercultures Reader*.

Thacker, Eugene. 2001. 'The Science Fiction of Technoscience: The Politics of Simulation and a Challenge for New Media Art', *Leonardo* 34, 2: 155–8.

Vail, D. Angus. 1999. 'Slinging Ink or Scratching Skin? Producing Culture and Claiming Legitimacy among Fine Art Tattooists', *Current Research on Occupations and Professions* 11.

Webster's New Collegiate Dictionary. 1959. Springfield, MA: G & C Merriam Co.

Zurbrugg, Nicholas. 2000. 'Marinetti, Chopin, Stelarc and the Auratic Intensities of the Postmodern Techno-Body', in Featherstone, ed, *Body Modification.*

Chapter 48

The Sacrificial Body of Orlan

Julie Clarke

The Body Electric

As we approach the twenty-first century, there appears to be a general consensus among critics of new technologies that the human body is being distanced from its material and visceral nature, particularly through the use of computer imaging programs that posit the human body as digital information that may be enhanced, manipulated, and altered. . . .

We are living at a time in which the perceived boundaries between genders, the self and its image, real and virtual, synthetic and organic, interior and exterior, public and private space, past and future have been all but erased. In this technological culture body images appear to be infinitely mutable, yet still linked to existing iconographic and ideological systems.

More and more our identity is linked to image, and that image is inherently linked with technology. In this environment we are forced to ask ourselves such questions as: how does an individual operate within an environment that on one hand makes image important, but simultaneously determines body status based on what is unseen? To what extent is our present state of being determined by current computer technologies? Are we our image?

In the midst of the polemics surrounding the status of the body in technology, the French performance artist Orlan began a project in 1990 called *The Reincarnation of Saint Orlan*.[1] The project is a series of nine operation/performances to redesign her face and body with cosmetic surgery.[2] Using the facial features of women from Renaissance art, she created a prototype with the aid of computer technology.[3]

Superficially, it seemed that Orlan was intent on becoming the epitome of all beautiful women throughout Art History, and on displaying in a very public way the process of plastic surgery and the construction of women. I intend to show that Orlan's project is about self-image and identity within technological culture, and one which challenges white Western notions of homogeneity by engaging with aberrant body forms and the abject. She performs this by appropriating Judeo-Christian iconography, including blood and its associative notions of sacrifice and transformation, Greek mythology, with its emphasis on marvellous and grotesque beings, and French literature. . . .

Aesthetic

Orlan's more recent performance aesthetic is dissection, recalling the spectacle of autopsy theatres in Europe during the Renaissance. She is *echorcée*, reminiscent of Enlightenment anatomical studies, in which the flayed body, looking very much alive, displays the splendour of internal body viscera. Jonathan Sawday argues that 'as a theatrical performance indeed, the anatomy demonstration rivalled the stage for the hold it exerted. . .' (1995: 269). This is true today, for to witness an operation on a human body is an experience like no other. No dramatization of war or horror can surpass the knowledge that what is being observed in the operating theatre is a body that while simultaneously alive, expresses the stasis and bodily mutilation associated with traumatic death. Orlan's facial surgery displays a different theatre of spectacle, one which is linked not only with autopsy and the medical technologies of surveillance but also with the greedy consumption of fashion. . . . According to Glenda Nalder, a 'characteristic of recent feminist work in performance and machine art has been its use of the viscera to rupture and to seep through the boundaries at the human/machine interface' (1993: 22). Orlan does this to reveal the media's reliance on surface images and to inject the dry virtual space of computer imaging with images of wet body material. Orlan's photographs of the inside of her face show that even the sinews and muscles of the face are surfaces that fix the eye and seduce us into the realm of the abject. She reveals that all bodily images no matter how beautiful or horrific are reduced to pure surface by technological imaging.

Image

While our self is more than our face, it is our face that greets the world. To change our face is to change our identity and the way that we communicate in society. When Orlan consciously decided to transform her facial features, she sacrificed the old self in favour of a new one that had been evolving since the 1970s, and one which questioned the status of the body. . . .

Orlan's 'reincarnation' highlights corporeality at a time when body status is defined by electronic imaging. There is a stress on DNA code; the face, retina, and fingerprints may be scanned in electronic transactions to authenticate identity. As such, Orlan's operation/performances could be seen as an extreme example of body inscription, in which she uses the surface of her flesh as an indicator of a culture disintegrating into its images. However, Orlan does not just reveal the surface of her face and body creating more images to be consumed; she shows the abject, bloodied subcutaneous layers beneath the skin that signify the organic and the imminence of death.

> The body interior speaks directly of our mortality. Hence the sight of these hidden contours has traditionally been denied us since they are

usually encountered only at the risk of enduring great pain and quite possible death. (Sawday, 1995: 12)

The gaping, fleshy wounds of surgery on Orlan's face challenge media images of beautiful body forms, which are more attractive to a viewing audience, because they are linked concepts of transcendence. . . .

. . . Through her performance Orlan asks that the audience interrogate the image of her reconstructed face and the way it relates to notions of identity in a technological culture. In a spectacular representation she offers her body as meat and pre-packages her photographic image for consumption by the art community. Her face prior to surgery is marked up with black lines, like a carcass ready for the butcher's cut. These raw images of her surgery are continually played out against images of her intact and healing face, and the organic body is revealed as remodelled and reincarnated by technological intervention. Orlan consistently contrasts the 'natural' women, untouched by cosmetic surgery, with the cultural impact of technological and medical intervention.

Orlan is not against plastic surgery, but 'against the standards of beauty, against the dictates of dominant ideology that impress themselves more and more on feminine and masculine flesh' (Armstrong, 1995b: 13). . . .

Orlan has said: 'My work and its ideas incarnated in my flesh pose questions about the status of the body in our society and its evolution in future generations via new technologies and upcoming genetic manipulations' (Armstrong, 1996b: 9). . . .

Style

Mary Russo, in her discussion of carnival and theory states that:

> The grotesque body is the open, protruding, extended, secreting body, the body of becoming, process, and change. The grotesque body is opposed to the classical body, which is

monumental, static, closed, and sleek, corresponding to the aspirations of bourgeois individualism; the grotesque body is connected to the rest of the world. (1997: 325)

When we look at Orlan's face, the constructed portrait reveals a self colonized by technological invasion, and a physical body being displaced by image. Her deviant face, with high forehead and small horns is the mutant offspring of surgical intervention, enabling Orlan to embrace images of the carnival and of the grotesque. As Russo asserts:

Making a spectacle out of oneself seemed a specifically feminine danger. . . . For a women, making a spectacle out of herself had more to do with a kind of inadvertency and loss of boundaries: the possessors of large, aging, and dimpled things displayed at the public beach, of overly roughed cheeks, of a voice shrill in laughter, or of a sliding bra strap—a loose, dingy bra strap especially—were at once caught out by fate and blameworthy. (1997: 318)

Although women scrutinize themselves in the mirror before they go into public, what they see is their double. What they don't see is the image of the self as seen by others. Self-portraiture in some ways deals with the nuances of the inner notion of self-identity represented by the mirror.

By restructuring her face, Orlan creates a woman that is obtainable only by technological intervention, and one who is continually constructed through media images. By assaulting the vision of the spectator through the abject, she not only shocks the viewer, but also challenges their perceptions of beauty, for she is not beautiful; her new face is too smooth, controlled, and expressionless. By engaging with and embracing notions of the grotesque, she transgresses standards set by the beauty industry.

The Sacrificial Body

Orlan uses Judeo-Christian symbolism to speak about the history of body fragmentation and relics, and posits the body as sacrificial. The body has to be sacrificed in order for it to be transcended. According to Georges Bataille:

It is the common business of sacrifice to bring life and death into harmony, to give death the upsurge of life, life the momentousness and the vertigo of death opening on to the unknown. Here life is mingled with death, but simultaneously death is a sign of life, a way into the infinite. Nowadays sacrifice is outside the field of our experience and imagination must do duty for the real thing. (1987: 91)

Orlan speaks about sacrifice, through her use of Judeo-Christian iconography and Greek mythology. Grapes, blood, crosses, skulls, horns, pitchforks, music, text, and costume are used as essential elements in her operation/performances. . . .

In [one] photograph Orlan's lips, exposed and wet, are like purple grapes with their thin membrane peeled. Blood from the wound, which trickles slowly down her cheek renders the mouth passive. In this way she draws attention to preconceived notions of femininity. The mouth need not speak; the lips only need to be perfectly shaped, reiterating perhaps that women who are beautiful are not expected to be articulate. The blood-cut on Orlan's mouth hints not only of childbirth and the episiotomy (a small incision made by the surgeon, so that the vagina will not tear), but also the lips and mouth as areas of eroticism, may be related to the mouth of the newborn child (a new identity), who cannot yet articulate desire through language.[4] Orlan, who has not paid her 'tribute to nature, in experiencing the pains of childbirth' (1996: 92), gives birth to her new self via the opened, bleeding wound. Ash explains that '[t]he agonizing pain of the crucifixion, the suffering of Christ in his passion, was the suffering, the "passion" of a woman giving birth' (1990: 86).

Reincarnation

. . . *This is My Body* . . . *This is My Software* is the title of Orlan's first exhibition in the United

Kingdom in 1996, which highlighted photographic images of Orlan's seventh operation/performance, *Omnipresence*. The title reveals two things, first, that Orlan views the body as 'software'—information that can be modified, and, second, that she is playing on the words of Christ at the Last Supper.

In 1971 when she named herself Saint Orlan, it was a cynical attack on Christianity, and her pseudo-canonization was a strategy to align herself and her actions with the heroic aspects ascribed to sainthood.[5] She draped robes around her body (*Saint Orlan*, 1971) and (*Drapery—The Baroque*, 1979), defiled, slashed, and remade them into collage (*A Documentary Study: The Head of the Medusa*, 1978; *1001 Reasons Not to Sleep*, 1979). Robes are significant as clothing that establishes identity or status within culture, and in the *Reincarnation of Saint Orlan*, skin is the literal costume of the body and face. The soft fabric, as outer surface of her head is cut, reconfigured, and sewn into a new garment for her identity. Like Buffalo Bill, the transvestite serial killer in *The Silence of the Lambs*, whose fantasy was to wear the body of a female, Orlan's metamorphosis also involves the notion of becoming other through the reconfiguration of flesh.[6] . . .

Orlan said 'The body is Obsolete. I fight against God and DNA' (Armstrong, 1995b: xiv). . . .

. . . [T]o 'fight against God and DNA' is to fight against Religion and Science: two major paradigms that have mediated and defined the human body. They are also entities that are unseen and outside of our usual realm of experience. To deny DNA is to deny that bodies can be reduced to code, a strategy to escape from the biological, destined-to-die body, to the post-biological, technologically enhanced body, in which life may be extended.

Reliquaries

Emile Durkheim remarked: 'there is no religious ceremony where blood does not have a part to play'. Some of these ways were 'the anointing of men with the blood of others, sacred images being drawn in blood soaked ground, and steams of blood being poured upon rock, and entry into and with the sacred' (1915: 137). For Orlan, blood is a link with the sacrificial; a way to speak about life, death, and transformation, no longer enabled by religion, but by science and technology.

As Orlan remarks:

> The vision of my body being opened painlessly was extremely seductive aesthetically . . . I found it similar to the light coming through the windows of a church illuminating the religious imagery inside. (in Gale, 1995: 31) . . .

. . . At the Sydney Biennale in Australia in December 1992, Orlan included phials containing samples of her liquefied flesh and blood drained off during the 'body sculpting' part of the operations and at the Sandra Deering Gallery in New York other relics, blood, and fat procured via liposuction were exhibited (Rose, 1993: 85).

Aligning herself with Catholicism and Saints through the use of robbing and veiling her exhibition of reliquaries further positions this part of Orlan's project within the cult of relics and within a discourse that invests power in the body, even in fragmentation. Orlan offers not only the supposed link with transformation of matter that the relic provides, but also the commodification of body parts, linked in this culture with the female body. . . .

In the display and sale of her relics[7] Orlan raises important issues in regard to the commodification of the human body, particularly in relation to genetic engineering, donor organs, and fetal experimentation. However, it is more importantly a remnant of her former self, a casting off of the old, which is transformed into the new self-identity. Current ideas about virtual bodies and virtual selves spilling out into the mediascape continue the debate about original or compensatory bodies; and with new technologies such as the Internet, personas may be created that have nothing to do with an original physical body.

The relationship between the body and its double, real and virtual bodies, and technological body images is addressed by Orlan in her reliquary *Blood and Phototransfer on Gauze*. The original relic from her *Omnipresence* performance (1993) shows Orlan's bloodied facial imprint impregnated into the cloth; the trace of her lips and the marks of incision are clearly seen as the surgeon removes it from her face.[8] The image is a bloody trace of her skeletal facial structure. However, the image reproduced in *Art and Text* (Moos, 1996) has a phototransfer of Orlan's face fused into the final relic. In this image produced by surgical intervention and imaging technologies, she meshes past with future, blurring foreground and background together in a total immersion of surface and texture. The imprint, like a psychological blot test, spills upwards revealing the head of a goat, with small horns protruding from the forehead. The image is of the satyr, or devil; imagery that is echoed in the triptych of the operation in which Orlan brandishes a pitchfork and a human skull is depicted with horns.[9] In this depiction Orlan plays with distinct binaries: human/animal, sacred/profane, normal/pathological, perfection/abjection, life and death. . . .

This particular reliquary is reminiscent of the facial section of the Shroud of Turin, which is posited as holding the image of Christ, after the crucifixion.[10] Housed in Turin, France, since 1532, the shroud is historically linked with the Mandylion cloth, 'a picture of Christ not made by human hands' (Kersten and Gruber, 1994: 110). Originally located in Edessa, the Mandylion cloth had been highly revered since the sixth century; it was 'so important that many copies were prepared, and all were claimed to be the original' (Kersten and Gruber, 1994: 110). The Shroud of Turin is believed to be either the original or copy of this cloth. . . .

When cloth is wrapped around a corpse, various substances are expelled into the material, leaving traces of corporeal matter. In some ways the cloth becomes a body of evidence that attests to Christ's death and resurrection, but more importantly that Christ has risen unified and intact. Orlan's relic survives as testament that she has sacrificed her self-identity to Art and the tech-

nologies that enable body modification. And this is what incites negative criticism, for society in general is not opposed to cosmetic surgery, it is however opposed to deliberate body mutilation. . . .

By constructing this phototransfer on gauze, Orlan asks us to question the authenticity surrounding the relic; the original and simulacrum. She provokes us with the question 'Is self identity our body or our image?'—a potent question in light of the current rhetoric that surrounds the body in cyberspace interactions. Questions also arise about the sacrificial body posited through Christ's crucifixion and suffering—he who give his earthly body for his father, and Orlan, who has 'given her body to Art'. 'J'ai donné mon corps à l'art' is the text that accompanies a photography of Orlan after her *Omnipresence* operation. In the postcard she looks like a woman who has been bashed, her hair is dishevelled and her eyes are bloodshot.[11] . . .

Nature/Culture

In recent photo-documentation Orlan has either one or both breasts exposed. Barbara Rose suggests that Orlan's exposure of one breast aligns her with the Virgin Mary, who is often represented exposing only one breast and 'to differentiate Saint Orlan from a topless pin-up' (1993: 84). As the identity of Saint Orlan developed during Orlan's performances in the 1980s 'her trademark became this single exposed breast jutting out irreverently through virginal fabrics' (Lovelace, 1995: 23). According to Jennifer Ash, 'the bleeding body of Christ crucified can be recognized as maternal in function, the bleeding wound in Christ's side functions as a lactating breast' (1990: 86), a statement supported by Sawday when he said that 'there also existed a tradition of Christ represented as a nurturing female body' (1995: 217).

While Orlan's exposed breast may refer to breast-feeding, it is more likely that the reference is to Christ's wound that was assimilated as 'the later bleeding of the Cross to the earlier bleeding of the circumcised infant' (Bynum, 1992: 87). . . . It may be that Orlan also refers to the Renaissance '*Anatomia*', which sought to uncover the mysteries of the female body through dissection of the uterus, and to more recent surgical intervention into the female body, such as breast reduction, silicon implants, reconstructive surgery, and the commodification of the female breast in the media. . . .

Orlan, although seduced by the rhetoric of technology, has turned to excess as a strategy against the benign and controlled nature of the screen, and the homogenization of body images. Her new identity, although not extreme, is a site of resistance in a society bent on eliminating forms that threaten the status quo. By linking her performances with Judeo-Christian iconography she established her work as sacrificial. More importantly she is involved with what may be called trans-human aesthetics that circulates around experimentation and investigation of the human form as a strategy to uncover what is human. The aesthetic is a crossover from the idea that the body is contained, immutable, bounded, restrained by natural forces, and sacred. Its philosophy denies that the human has any fixed nature, and instead looks to mutation and differentiation to expand the repertoire of human interaction and invention. . . .

Notes

1. 30 May 1990, in Newcastle, England.
2. She has undergone seven operations, beginning on 27 July 1990, when she had a chin prosthesis inserted by Dr Cherif Sahar. The September and 8 December 1990 operation—*The Lips of Europa*—was performed by Dr Bernard Cornette de Saint-Cyr. *The Mouth of Europa and the Figure of Venus* operation was performed in July 1991. The February 1992 operation/performance was carried out at the Performance Festival in Liege. In February 1993 the *Omnipresence* performance occurred. In November 1993 she had implants inserted in her temples by Dr Marjorie Cramer. 'There have also been three attempts to put a cleft in her chin' (Norris, 1996: 40).
3. The prototype was made from the chin of Botticelli's *Venus*, the nose of Gerome's *Psyche*, a Fontainbleau *Diana's* eyes, the lips of Gustave Moreau's *Europa*, and the brow of Leonardo's *Mona Lisa*.
4. Gina Pane, a French performance artist of the 1960s also dealt with issues surrounding the commodification of the female face, the relationship of the mouth to language, and the taboos related to blood and other bodily fluids.
5. Orlan was born Mireilla Porte in 1947 (Lovelace, 1995: 15).
6. *The Silence of the Lambs*, 1991, Dir. Jonathan Demme, Orion. He intended to construct the garment from pieces of flesh cut from his victims.
7. The relic, through history, has been a source of hope and spiritual peace and a material link to [the] idea of immortality. More than this, it is a potent sign of transformation from this life to an afterlife, as promoted by Catholicism.
8. See photographs of the cloth in Armstrong (1995a: 61) and in Orlan, *This is My Body . . . This is My Software* (1996: 77).
9. *Triptyque opéation—opéra 5ème à la tête mort* (1993) in Orlan, *This is My Body . . .* (1996: 44).
10. In 1988, at the order of the Vatican, three groups of experts, using the so-called radiocarbon method, dated the linen cloth to the fourteenth century. See preface to Kersten and Gruber (1994).
11. Parisian postcard, CARTed 14, Pasca Pithois, 16 ave. de Normandie, 50130 Octeville France (1995).

References

Armstrong, Rachel. 1995. 'Orlan, Mute', *Digital Art Critique* 1 (Spring): xiv.

———. 1996. 'Cut Along the Dotted Line', *Dazed and Confused* 17.

Ash, Jennifer. 1990. 'The Discursive Construction of Christ's Body in the Later Middle Ages: Resistance and Autonomy', in T. Threadgold and A. Cranny-Francis, eds, *Feminine, Masculine and Representation*. Sydney: Allen and Unwin.

Bataille, Georges. 1987. *Eroticism: Death and Sensuality*, trans. Mary Dalwood. London: Marion Bayars.

Bynum, Caroline W. 1992. *Fragmentation and Redemption—Essays on Gender and the Human Body in Medieval Religion*. New York: Zone.

Durkheim, Emile. 1915. *The Elementary Forms of the Religious Life*, trans. Joseph Ward Dwain. London: George Allen and Unwin Limited.

Gale, David. 1995. 'Knife Work', *Gentlemen's Quarterly* (London) February: 31.

Kersten, Holger and Elmar R. Gruber. 1994. *The Jesus Conspiracy: The Turin Shroud and the Truth about the Resurrection*. Shaftesbury, Dorset; Rockport, MA; Brisbane, Queensland: Element Books.

Lovelace, Carey. 1995. 'Orlan: Offensive Acts', *Performing Arts Journal* (Johns Hopkins University Press), 17, 1: 13–25.

Moos, Michel. 1996. 'Memories of Being', *Art and Text* 54 (May): 69.

Nalder, Glenda. 1993. 'Under the VR Spell', *Eyeline 21* (Australia) Autumn.

Orlan. 1996. *Orlan: Ceci est mon corps . . . Ceci est mon logiciel. . . /This is My Body . . . This is My Software*, ed. D. McConquodlae. London: Black Dog Publishing Limited and the Authors.

Rose, Barbara. 1993. 'Is It Art?', *Art in America* February 82–7, 105

Russo, Mary. 1997. 'Female Grotesques: Carnival and Theory', in K. Conboy, M. Medine and S. Stanbury, eds, *Writing on the Body*. New York: Columbia University Press, 318–36. (Orig. 1986 in *Feminist Issues/Critical Issues*, 1986.)

Sawday, Jonathan. 1995. *The Body Emblazoned: Dissection and the Human Body in Renaissance Culture*. London: Routledge.

Index

abnormal bodies, xi, 30, 47, 129–30, 133, 139–40, 190–1, 281, 340, 348

abortion, x, 9, 17, 42, 174, 180, 186–7, 239, 282, 290–2, 294–6

accommodation, 11, 239, 254, 306–07, 314–19, 333

aesthetic body, 28, 39–41; *see also* aestheticism

aestheticism, 4, 19, 23–4, 26, 28, 38–43, 46–7, 52, 61, 65–6, 71, 112, 255, 276, 308, 323, 360–1, 364, 369, 372, 374; *see also* aesthetic body

agency, 8, 121, 127, 137, 162, 203–04, 232, 258, 260–1, 319, 324, 342–3, 364–5

aging, x, xiv, 11, 19, 23, 26, 59, 61, 118, 122, 271, 326–30, 332–49, 371; *see also* aging body; aging populations

aging body, xiv, 26, 59, 61, 176, 326, 334, 342, 371; *see also* aging; aging populations

aging populations, 11, 336; *see also* aging; aging body

agoraphobia, 3, 113–15

AIDS, 13, 15, 17, 19, 122

alienation, xiii, 2, 27, 69, 71, 101, 218–19, 221, 248, 293, 305, 309–10, 345, 363

alzheimerization of aging, xiv, 327, 344, 346, 349

Alzheimer's, 228, 233, 327–8, 342–9

anatomically based rules, 124, 128

anorexia, 5, 17, 19, 22, 26, 65, 101–02, 110–15, 144, 235, 238, 265

Anti-Semitism, 75, 92

Aristotle, 38, 44

baby savers, 104; *see also* maternalists

back stage performance, 196; *see also* bodily performance; expressions given; expressions given off; face work; front stage performance; impression management; personal fronts; presentation of self

Barbre, Joy Webster, xiv, 326

Bartky, Sandra Lee, xii, 4, 5, 257, 258, 260, 265, 318, 320

beauty norms, 5

Becker, Anne E., xii, 52

binary model of gender, 125–6, 133, 141–2, 144–6; *see also* dualism; gender

Binet, Alfred, 213, 217

biodeterminism, 29, 74, 84, 117

biomedical model, 28, 42, 44, 57–8, 149, 360

biopower, xi, xiii, 5, 73, 78–80, 82, 148

bisexuality, xi, 13, 64

black dangerousness, xiv, 285; *see also* blackness

blackness, xiv, 45–6, 48–50, 59–60, 104, 108, 119, 128, 131–2, 184, 232, 235, 237, 258, 275–8, 280–2, 285–9, 291–6, 304, 313, 320, 358; *see also* black dangerousness

blindness, 127, 128, 131, 213, 239, 242–5, 303; *see also* disability; disabled body

blood, 13, 43, 75, 89, 92, 93, 120, 150, 166–8, 185, 228, 270, 291, 296, 299, 338, 365, 369–74; *see also* Blood Protection Law

Blood Protection Law, 92

Blum, Linda M., xiii, 100–01

bodies out of time, xi, 174, 189–93; *see also* cultural anomalies

bodily adornment, 65, 206–07, 265, 312, 313

bodily capital, 52, 57; *see also* cultural capital; physical capital

bodily cultivation, 65–8, 71, 111–21, 124; *see also* body alteration; body modification; body technologies; cosmetic surgery; plastic surgery

bodily instructions, 71, 209–10, 214

bodily performance, xii, 22, 23, 119, 121–2, 220,

234–5, 261, 264, 272, 274–7, 279, 309, 361; *see also* backstage performance; expressions given; expressions given off; front stage performance; impression management; personal fronts; presentation of self

bodily practices, xiv, 4, 14, 18, 28, 77, 78, 80, 100, 195, 206, 311

bodily regulation, xii, 3, 14, 128, 148, 195, 198, 204, 212, 295, 298

bodily representation, xii, 100

body alteration, 234; *see also* bodily cultivation; body modification; body technologies; cosmetic surgery; plastic surgery

body as absent presence, xii, 2, 7

body as commodity, 10, 14, 19, 218, 220–1, 236–7, 267, 305, 309, 343, 363, 372, 374

body as machine, 11–12, 28, 41–3, 117, 224, 337; *see also* Cartesian mechanism; mechanistic body

bodybuilding, xiv, 257–9, 261, 265, 269–73, 320

body discipline, 4, 24; *see also* self-discipline; self-policing; self-surveillance; technologies of the self

body image, 10, 11, 26, 63, 112, 138, 267, 309, 352, 362, 369, 373–4

bodyism, 52, 57, 61

body maintenance, 4, 18

body modification, xii, 52, 62, 305–08, 311–12, 352, 353, 360–8, 373; *see also* bodily cultivation; body alteration; body technologies; cosmetic surgery; piercings; plastic surgery

body morphology, 52, 67–71, 133

body play, 305, 308–09, 312, 351

body-reflexive practice, 102, 120–2

body stories, 125–6, 141–2, 144–6; *see also* erasing body stories; migrating body stories; oscillating body stories; transcending body stories

body technologies, 219–20, 234–8, 309; *see also* bodily cultivation; body alteration; body modification; cosmetic surgery; plastic surgery

bonding craze, 100–04

Bordo, Susan, xiii, 26, 58, 62, 64, 101–02, 260, 263, 265, 307, 316, 320, 322, 324, 325

Boston Women's Health Collective, 9, 63

Bourdieu, Pierre, xi, 1, 2, 11, 13, 18–19, 100, 306

bourgeoisie, 34, 170, 218

Bowlby, John, 104

breast, xiii, 2, 70–1, 100–01, 103, 105–09, 112, 117, 125, 133, 141–5, 234–7, 257, 261, 271, 322, 326, 373–4; *see also* breast-feeding

breast-feeding, 100–09, 154, 185, 373

Butler, Judith, 102, 211, 220, 234, 238

caesarean, 158, 162, 183–4, 296

cancer, 15, 18, 20, 92, 93, 106, 165–9, 183, 187, 326, 331

capital, ix, xi, 1–2, 6, 18, 52, 57, 100, 218, 220, 226, 236, 306, 320, 347, 357, 366; *see also* bodily capital; cultural capital; economic capital; physical capital

capitalism, ix, xii, 2, 8, 9, 11–13, 15, 25, 51, 71, 102, 118, 139, 154, 218, 219, 221, 225, 260, 306, 309, 321, 350, 352, 354, 356, 358

caregiving, 67

carnival, 61–2, 370–1, 375

Cartesian dualism, 28, 42; *see also* dualism

Cartesian mechanism, 42; *see also* body as machine

central tendency, 196; *see also* normal distribution

Chase, Cheryl, xiii, 124–5, 129, 132

Christ, 39–40, 371–3, 375

civilized body, xiv, 13, 28, 30–1, 33, 35, 37, 40, 170–1, 195, 197, 203–04, 327–8, 342–3, 348; *see also* civilizing process; de-civilized body; uncivilized body

civilizing process, x, xv, 13, 28, 40, 170–1, 197, 203–04, 342; *see also* civilized body; de-civilized body; uncivilized body

Civilizing Process, The, ix, 28

Clarke, Julie, xiv, 352

climacteric, 334–5, 341

clitoris, 133–6, 138

colonialization, xi, xiv, 29, 103, 109, 281, 282, 285–9, 299–300, 310, 311, 313

commodification, 10, 14, 19, 236, 237, 267, 305, 309, 343, 372, 374; *see also* body as commodity

conjoined twins, 124, 126–7, 129–30, 138

Connell, Raewyn, xiii, 10, 101–02, 173–4, 205, 211, 249, 251, 257–8, 260–1, 265, 267, 325, 272, 323–4

constructed bodies, 199, 201, 361

constructionism, 14, 101, 274, 278

constructionist relativism, 3, 14

consumer culture, 4, 9, 11–13, 18–19, 305–07, 309, 312, 321, 325, 341; *see also* consumerism; consumption

consumerism, xiv, 2, 155, 347, 350; *see also* consumer culture; consumption

consumption, xii, 9, 11, 25, 104, 112, 185, 201–02, 236, 305–06, 309, 331, 341, 352, 370; *see also* consumer culture; consumerism

control axis of anorexia, 111

controlling voice, 209

conventional attractiveness, 315–16, 318

corporeality, x, 4, 9–10, 39, 44, 52, 57–8, 60–1, 101–02, 169, 171, 190, 220, 276, 365, 370, 373

cosmetics, 23–4, 65, 365; *see also* makeup

cosmetic surgery, x, 4, 18, 117, 135, 234–6, 305–07, 316, 320–5, 360, 365–6, 369, 370, 373; *see also* plastic surgery

crack babies, 184, 186, 296

crack epidemic, 294

criminal biology, 88, 95, 99

criminology, 29, 74, 84, 87, 90

cross-dresser, 24, 141; *see also* transvestite

cultural anomalies, 174, 189, 191–2; *see also* bodies out of time; dirt as matter out of place; matter out of place

cultural appropriation, 305, 364

cultural capital, xi, 2, 320, 347, 366; *see also* bodily capital; physical capital

cultural discourse, 252, 255, 281, 321, 325; *see also* discourse

cultural myths, 281, 285

cybergenics, 269

cybernetics, 2, 120, 179–80, 350–2, 354, 359, 367

cyberpunk, 351, 360–1, 363–6

cyborg, xiv, 60, 351–2, 354–62

Darwin, Charles, 46, 47, 49, 74, 88–91, 180

Davis, Kathy, xiv, 306, 316

de-civilized body, 327, 342; *see also* civilized body; civilizing process; uncivilized body

definition of the situation, 51, 54–6

dehumanization, 79–82

dementia, 93, 209, 327, 342–9

demographic changes, xiv, 2, 9, 11–12, 93, 337

demography, xi, 2; *see also* demographic changes

diet, xi, 4, 11–13, 17–19, 20, 22, 63, 65–6, 68–9, 106, 110–11, 128, 152, 161, 265, 271, 305–06, 334–5, 338, 340

dirt as matter out of place, x, xiii, 170, 189; *see also* cultural anomalies; matter out of place

dirty dying, 149; *see also* messy deaths

disability, xi, xiii–xiv, 3, 74–7, 119, 131–2, 149, 239–41, 243, 245–56, 343, 347; *see also* blindness; disabled body; medical model of disability; physical disability; social model of disability

disability rights movement, 131, 249–51; *see also* disability; disabled body; medical model of disability; physical disability; social model of disability

disabled body, xiii, 239–40; *see also* blindness; disability; medical model of disability; physical disability; social model of disability

disciplinary gaze, 4, 79; *see also* gaze

disciplinary practices, 21–3, 77, 81, 117, 206, 314

disciplinary society, 21; *see also* disciplined body; disciplinary gaze; disciplinary practices

disciplined body, ix, xi, xiv, 1, 3–5, 7–9, 12, 14–15, 17–18, 20–7, 43, 61, 65, 73–83, 117, 121, 174, 195–7, 202, 204–05, 209–15, 217, 219, 224–5, 239, 258–9, 265, 267, 269, 270, 311–12, 318, 320, 338–9, 342, 352, 358, 367; *see also* disciplinary gaze; disciplinary practices; disciplinary society

discourse, xi, xiii, 14, 23, 26, 28, 44–5, 58, 62, 66–7, 71, 76, 100–02, 107, 118, 122, 125, 137, 146, 149, 158–9, 162, 173, 190, 202, 215, 252–3, 255–6, 262, 266–8, 271, 276–7, 281, 285–7, 304, 310–13, 321–2, 324–5, 327, 330, 335–7, 343, 356–9, 361–4, 366, 372; *see also* cultural discourse

discreditable stigma, 51, 57; *see also* discrediting stigma; spoiled identities; stigma; stigma management

discrediting stigma, 51; *see also* discreditable stigma; spoiled identities; stigma; stigma management

disembodied mothering, 101; *see also* disembodiment; embodiment

disembodiment, ix, x, 7, 18, 101, 106, 324, 342; *see also* embodiment; disembodied mothering

docile bodies, xi, xiii, 5, 21, 22, 73, 206, 314, 319

doctor–patient relationship, 98

dominant masculinity, 246–7, 267; *see also* hegemonic body norms; hegemonic masculinity; masculine body; masculinity

Douglas, Mary, ix, x, xiii, 132, 149–50, 158–9, 163, 169–71, 174, 189, 190–1, 193–4

dramaturgy, x

dreadlocks, 314, 318

Dreger, Alice Domurat, xiii, 124, 138–9

drug use, 120, 183, 184–5, 291, 296

dualism, 1, 8, 22, 28, 38–40, 42, 43, 60, 101, 110, 269, 309, 312, 351, 352, 355–8; animal/human, 131, 373; Cartesian dualism, 28, 42; male/female,

133, 137, 138, 141, 145, 176, 196, 309, 351, 356;
nature/culture, 10, 15, 309, 352, 373;
primitive/civilized, 312, 356
dual status of the body, 7–8; *see also* dualism
DuBois, W.E.B., 131–2
Durkheim, Emile, 1, 8–9, 13–14, 338, 372, 375
Dworkin, Shari L., xiv, 257, 262, 265

economic capital, xi, 1, 306; *see also* capital; capitalism
Ehrenreich, Barbara, xiii, 11, 13, 115, 219
Ekins, Richard, xiii, 125–6, 141, 143
Elias, Norbert, ix, x–xii, xiv–xv, 8, 12, 28, 30–1,
170–1, 195, 197, 203–04, 327–8, 342, 348
Ellis, Havelock, 46, 49, 85, 91
embodiment, x, xi, 1–2, 4, 7–10, 16, 18–19, 26, 46,
52, 57–8, 60–3, 65–6, 71, 77, 100, 111, 119, 122,
124, 136, 142, 187, 196–8, 204–05, 220, 252,
254, 258, 274, 276, 286–7, 325, 341–2, 351–2,
356–7, 362–3, 365; *see also* disembodied mothering;
disembodiment
emotion work, xiii, 19
emphasized femininity, 260–1, 263, 264; *see also* femininity;
hegemonic femininity
Engels, Friedrich, ix, 9, 41, 44, 218, 220
Enlightenment, 1, 4, 14, 81, 128, 131, 162, 274,
310–11, 361, 369
Epicureans, 38
Epidemiologist, 152–3
episiotomy, 157–8, 160, 193, 371
epistemology, 181, 311, 355
erasing body stories, 125, 141, 144; *see also* body stories;
migrating body stories; oscillating body stories;
transcending body stories
erectile dysfunction, 327, 336–40
ergonomics, 219, 228
essentialism, 35, 84, 136, 308
eugenics, xiii, xiv, 74–7, 79–80, 83, 85, 87–91, 95, 98,
187, 213, 217
euthanasia, 75, 96–8, 168
exclusive motherhood, 100, 107
exercise, xi, 4, 10–11, 18, 23, 25, 66, 111, 117,
201–03, 232, 261, 263–4, 271, 306, 321, 334,
338; *see also* sport
expressions given, 51; *see also* back stage performance;
bodily performance; expressions given off; front
stage performance; impression management; presentation
of self; signifiers; sign vehicles

expressions given off, 51; *see also* back stage performance;
bodily performance; expressions given; front
stage performance; impression management; presentation
of self; signifiers; sign vehicles
extropian, 361, 362, 365, 366

face work, 52, 60; *see also* bodily performance; expressions
given; expressions given off; impression management;
personal fronts; presentation of self
Fausto-Sterling, Anne, 138, 140, 146–7
Featherstone, Mike, xii, xiv, 11, 13, 18–20, 64, 306–
09, 313, 321, 325, 337, 341, 367–8
feeble-minded/feeble-mindedness, 77, 83, 93, 97–8,
196, 212–13, 217
feminine apologetic, 257, 316
feminine body, 5, 22, 24, 26; *see also* emphasized femininity;
feminine ideal; femininity; hegemonic femininity
Feminine Forever, 326, 328, 332
feminine ideal, 234; *see also* emphasized femininity;
hegemonic femininity
femininity, xi, 1, 5, 10, 17, 24–6, 61, 108, 114–17,
125, 173, 175–7, 220, 234, 240, 256–8, 260–5,
267, 268–9, 271–2, 287, 306, 316–20, 322–4,
326–8, 332, 352, 362, 370–1, 375; *see also* emphasized
femininity; hegemonic femininity
feminism, x–xiv, 2, 5, 9–12, 14, 17, 63, 100–02, 105,
107–10, 113–15, 118, 120, 123, 132, 136, 138,
147, 173, 175, 181–2, 189, 205, 234, 255–8, 265–
6, 289, 292–3, 320–1, 325, 351–2, 354–9, 361–2,
367, 370, 375; *see also* patriarchy
femme fatale, 179–80
fetal alcohol syndrome (FAS), 174, 184, 186
fetal rights, xiii, 173, 183–5, 187, 188, 296
fistula, 166–8
food, 12, 18, 22, 41, 60, 62, 66–71, 77, 94, 103–04,
111, 113, 168, 172, 184, 189, 199, 201–03, 228,
232–3, 265, 270, 332, 340
Foucault, Michel, xi–xiii, 3–5, 14, 17, 19, 21–2, 25–7,
73, 75, 77–83, 102, 148, 150, 173–4, 196–7, 203,
205–6, 211–12, 217, 257–60, 265, 267, 314, 320,
358, 367
Frank, Arthur W., ix, xii, 2–5
Fredrickson, George Marsh, 220, 258–9, 281, 283
front stage performance, 196

Galton, Francis, 74, 213, 217

gay, xi, xiv, 11, 59–64, 113, 115, 126–7, 136–7, 144, 273, 287, 320, 362; *see also* homosexuality; lesbianism

gaze, 4–5, 25, 73–4, 77– 82, 105, 173, 197, 212, 214–15, 217, 236, 244, 253–5, 258, 268–70, 285, 287–8; *see also* disciplinary gaze; individualizing gaze

gender, xii–xiv, 2, 4, 10, 16, 22, 24, 43, 51, 74, 101, 112–13, 115–19, 121–3, 125–6, 133, 136–47, 176, 178–9, 195–7, 205–08, 210–11, 220, 234, 238–9, 249–52, 256–8, 260, 265, 268–73, 276, 281, 284–5, 287, 300, 303, 306, 309, 312, 316, 320–1, 325, 328, 348, 351–2, 354, 356–7, 360, 362, 365, 375; *see also* binary model of gender; gendered bodies; gender hierarchy; gender/power axis

gendered bodies, xiii, 12, 63, 143, 197, 205, 207, 209, 211, 234, 288; *see also* gender; gender hierarchy; gender/power axis

gender hierarchy, 116, 196, 205, 252, 324; *see also* gender; gendered bodies; gender/power axis

gender/power axis, 101, 112–13; *see also* gender; gendered bodies; gender hierarchy

genetics, 48, 74, 77, 83, 92–3, 95–6, 116–17, 131, 180, 187, 239, 242, 244, 258–9, 274–9, 281, 349–50, 358, 370, 372; *see also* genetic science; genotypes

genetic science, 274; *see also* genetics; genotypes

genocide, 75, 93

genotypes, 276, 349

gerontology, 326–7, 335–6, 343

Gerschick, Thomas, xiv, 239–40

Gilleard, Chris, xiv, 327–8

Gilman, Sander L., xii, 29–30, 57, 63, 285, 289, 304

Goffman, Erving, ix, x, xii, 4, 6–7, 11, 13, 16, 43–4, 51–3, 55, 57–8, 60, 63, 73, 75, 78, 80, 82–3, 132, 196–7

governmentality, xi, xv, 150, 347

Graham, Elizabeth, xiii, 174, 189, 194

Greenpeace, 10

grotesque, 46, 48, 62, 369–71, 375

habitus, xi

Haraway, Donna J., xiv, 60, 63, 181, 351–2, 366–7

health insurance, 186

health maintenance, 199, 201–03

health promotion, 104, 148, 151–4, 327–8, 341

hedonism, 18–38

hegemonic body norms, 240; *see also* dominant masculinity; emphasized femininity; feminine ideal; femininity; hegemonic femininity; hegemonic masculinity

hegemonic femininity, 173, 306; *see also* emphasized femininity; feminine ideal; femininity; hegemonic body norms

hegemonic masculinity, xiii, 101–02, 121–2, 173, 240, 246–50, 257, 260–1, 267, 272, 307, 324–5; *see also* dominant masculinity; hegemonic body norms; masculine body; masculinity

hermaphrodism, 123–4, 126–7, 133, 135–9, 146

heteronormativity, 133, 362

heterosexuality, 10, 25, 260

hidden curriculum, 196–7, 205–06

Higgs, Paul, xiv, 327–8

historical materialism, 2, 358

Hitler, Adolf, 92–3, 96

homophobia, 265, 306, 324, 362

homosexuality, 10, 13, 62, 92, 98, 116–17, 136, 139, 146, 269; *see also* gay

hormone replacement therapy, 326, 329, 332–3

hospice, 150, 165–72, 175

human relations, 32, 56, 219, 224–6

hyper-physicality, 277

hypervisibility, 253, 255; *see also* (in)visibility

iatrogenesis, 152–4, 157, 326

immunization, xiii, 148–56

impotence, 118, 258, 327, 334, 336–41

impression management, 51–72, 361, 240; *see also* back stage performance; expressions given; expressions given off; face work; front stage performance; personal fronts; presentation of self; signifiers; sign vehicles

individualism, 22, 170, 310, 329, 361–5, 371

individualization, x, 87, 148–9, 157, 174, 195–6, 212, 309, 337, 342

individualization of risk, x, 148–9, 157, 337; *see also* risk assessment; risk culture; risk society

individualizing gaze, 212; *see also* gaze

individuation, 28

industrial fatigue, 219, 222

Industrial Revolution, ix, 9, 29, 218

institutionalization, 76–7, 82, 132, 344, 349

intelligence test, 212–13

Intersex Society of North America, 137; *see also* intersexuality

intersexuality, xiii, 124–5, 133–9; *see also* Intersex Society of North America

(in)visibility, 240–1, 252–5; *see also* hypervisibility

Johns Hopkins University, 133–5, 139, 174, 178–9, 181, 325, 375

Katz, Stephen, xiv, 326
Kent, Deborah, xiv, 239–40
King, Dave, xiii, 124–6, 143, 147
Kinsey, Alfred, 327–8, 337
Klesse, Christian, xiv, 305

lactation, 70, 71, 103, 330, 373
Lane, Karen, xiii, 148–50, 161, 164, 173, 175
Lawton, Julia, xiii, 149–50, 174–5
lesbianism, xi, 24, 26, 47, 64, 105, 126–7, 131, 136–7, 143–5, 254, 265, 287, 306, 316, 318; *see also* gay
Lombroso, Cesare, 29, 47–8, 50, 74, 84–91, 95
Low, Jacqueline, xiii

Maids, The, 227–9, 232–3; *see also* Merry Maids
makeup, xiii, 5, 11, 23, 24, 26, 234, 254, 257, 316; *see also* cosmetics
Malacrida, Claudia, xii
Marshall, Barbara L., xiv, 326, 328
Martin, Emily, xiii, 10, 12–13, 173, 175, 211, 330, 333
Martin, Karin A., xiii, 196–7, 211
Marx, Karl, ix, xi, 1–2, 8–9, 14, 41, 44, 218–20, 226, 265
masculine body, 307; *see also* dominant masculinity; hegemonic masculinity; masculinity
masculinity, xiii, xiv, 1, 10, 13, 22, 47, 57–8, 59, 61, 63, 90, 101–02, 108, 114, 116–23, 125, 134–5, 143, 145, 173–5, 177, 211, 239–40, 246–51, 257–61, 265, 267–73, 287, 301, 307, 322–4, 362, 370, 375; *see also* dominant masculinity; hegemonic body norms; hegemonic masculinity; masculine body
Mason, Gay, xiv, 257–9
material objectivism, 3, 14
maternalists, 14, 43, 84, 249; *see also* baby savers
matter out of place, x, xiii, 149, 170, 174, 189, 190; *see also* bodies out of time; cultural anomalies; dirt as matter out of place

Mauss, Marcel, xi, 7, 13
Mayall, Berry, xiii, 195, 197, 204
McFadden, Bernard, 340–1
mechanistic body, 28, 42–3; *see also* body as machine; Cartesian mechanism
Medicaid, 184, 186, 295–6, 345
medical model, 28, 46, 48, 57, 107, 148–50, 157–9, 161, 163, 175, 239, 327
medical model of disability, 239; *see also* disability; disabled body; physical disability; social model of disability
medicalization, x, xiii, xiv, 3, 15–16, 75, 92, 101–02, 104, 131, 137–8, 147, 160, 173, 194, 279, 326–7, 337–8, 344, 358; *see also* medicalization of anti-Semitism; medicalized body
medicalization of anti-Semitism, 92; *see also* medicalization; medicalized body
medicalized body, 3, 15; *see also* medicalization
menopause, 12, 174, 176, 180, 190, 192–4, 326–7, 329–33
men's studies, 10, 114, 266
menstruation, 12–13, 112, 136, 145, 174, 176, 180, 190–4, 329–30
mental health, 72, 284, 285–8, 344
Merry Maids, 227–8; *see also* Maids, The
messy deaths, xiii; *see also* dirty dying
migrating body stories, 125, 141–4, 146; *see also* body stories; erasing body stories; oscillating body stories; transcending body stories
Miller, Adam S., xiv, 239–40
Mills, C. Wright, 240
misogyny, 29
mode of production, 218, 221
modernity, xi, 2–3, 8, 12–14, 19–20, 22, 81, 101, 104, 148, 150, 155, 157, 160, 194, 219, 305, 307, 309–13, 337, 341, 350
modern primitivism, xiv, 305, 307–13
Monaghan, Lee F., xii, 51–2
Money, John, 134, 139
moral insanity, 331
moral panics, 29, 196
mortification, 4, 17, 28, 41
Moscow Declaration, 258; *see also* race
Murray, Charles, 275, 280
muscular backlash, 11

naked body/naked bodies, 34–5, 77–8, 135, 189, 237

narcissism, 24, 27, 111, 121, 258, 267–9, 273, 323

natural athlete, 259, 274–5, 277, 279

naturalism, 310

naturalistic body, 281

naturalization, 265, 278, 360

Nazis, xiii, 74–5, 83, 92–6, 98–9

Neal, Sarah, xiv, 281, 283

neo-Nazi, 362

non-normant bodies, xiii

non-whites, 74, 100 107, 184, 287

normal distribution, 196, 213; *see also* central tendency

normalization, 122, 124, 128–30, 134–5, 196, 213, 358

normalizing discourse, 23, 58; *see also* cultural discourse; discourse

nose, 32–4, 40, 45–7, 68, 167, 208, 236, 374

Oliver, Michael, 239–40

ontology, 9–10, 258, 274, 277, 309, 354–5, 357, 360–1, 365–6

Orlan, xiii, xiv, 352, 361, 363–4, 366–7, 369–75

Orphism, 38, 118

oscillating body stories, 125, 141, 144; *see also* body stories; erasing body stories; migrating body stories; transcending body stories

other-centredness, 67

othering, 30, 48, 305

panopticon, 4, 19, 21, 25–6, 73, 78–9, 173, 219

pathologize, xiii, 100, 239

patriarchy, xiii, 4–5, 10, 16–17, 19, 21, 23, 25–27, 100–01, 118, 258, 260, 265, 273, 282, 299–300, 320, 356, 358, 362; *see also* feminism

penis, 17, 108, 119, 134–5, 137, 141–4, 268, 281, 321–2, 336, 338–9, 364; *see also* phallus

per, 125, 145–6

performance, x, xii, xiv, 12, 22–3, 81, 101, 118–19, 121–2, 205, 211, 213, 216, 220, 224, 234–5, 238, 264, 269, 274–7, 279–80, 308–09, 337–8, 352, 360–2, 369–70, 372–4; *see also* back stage performance; bodily performance; front stage performance

personal fronts, 52, 60; *see also* expressions given; expressions given off; face work; impression management; presentation of self

phallus, 135–6, 138, 269, 365; *see also* penis

phenotypes, 258, 274–5, 279

photography, 29, 74, 197, 214, 373

physical capital, xi, 2, 6, 18, 52, 100, 306; *see also* bodily capital; cultural capital

physical disability, 119, 132, 239–41, 246–8, 252–3, 256; *see also* disability; disabled body

piercings, xii, xiv, 146, 237, 305, 308–09, 312–13; *see also* body modification

Pilgrim, David, xiv, 148, 150, 153, 155

Pitts, Victoria L., xiv, 351–3

pity, 129, 132, 322, 347

plastic surgery, 12, 43, 138, 140, 323, 325, 369–70; *see also* cosmetic surgery

play, 120, 123, 128, 200–02, 206–11, 214–15, 249, 251, 263, 265, 267, 273, 276–7, 289

politeness, 32, 248

Pollitt, Katha, xiii, 173–5

pollution, 10, 15, 149, 169–70, 172, 174, 187, 189, 190

pollution behaviour, 149, 169–70, 174; *see also* pollution rituals

pollution rituals, 149, 169; *see also* pollution behaviour

pornography, 234, 238, 270

post-human, 350, 352–3, 360–1, 367–8

postmodernism, 16, 20, 350–2, 354–5, 358, 367

poststructuralism, xi, xiv, 355

posture, xi, 22, 118, 134, 205, 208–09, 211, 215, 223, 235, 263, 268

pregnancy, 9–10, 12, 69–71, 106, 174, 180, 183–7, 190–4, 282, 290–4, 296–7, 332, 362

presentation of self, 11; *see also* bodily performance; expressions given; expressions given off; face work; impression management; personal fronts

Presentation of Self in Everyday Life, The, 51

preventative discipline, 174

Proctor, Robert N., xiii, 74–5, 77, 83

proletariat, 218

prostitute, 30, 45–50, 98, 144, 187, 213, 298–304; *see also* prostitution

prostitution, 10, 29, 46–7, 49–50, 282, 294, 298–303; *see also* prostitute

psychometrics, 215

quarantine, 42, 93–95

race, xiii, xiv, 2, 29–30, 38, 45–6, 48, 74–5, 83, 85, 92–9, 104, 107, 132, 173, 213, 255, 258–9, 265,

274–89, 292, 294, 296, 298–305, 307–08, 311, 324, 351–2, 356–7, 361, 362, 365; *see also* black dangerousness; blackness; Moscow Declaration; race degeneration; racial hygiene; racial hygienist; racialization; racialized body; racial mythology; racial pathology; racial violence; racism; whiteness

race degeneration, 74; *see also* race; racial hygiene; racial hygienist; racialization; racialized body; racial mythology; racial pathology; racial violence; racism

racial hygiene, 75, 93, 95, 98; *see also* race; race degeneration; racial hygienist; racialization; racialized body; racial mythology; racial pathology; racial violence; racism

racial hygienist, 95, 98; *see also* race; race degeneration; racial hygiene; racialization; racialized body; racial mythology; racial pathology; racial violence; racism

racialization, 45–6; *see also* race; race degeneration; racial hygiene; racial hygienist; racialized body; racial mythology; racial pathology; racial violence; racism

racialized body, xiv, 276–8, 281–8, 292; *see also* race; race degeneration; racial hygiene; racial hygienist; racialization; racial mythology; racial pathology; racial violence; racism

racial mythology, 274, 276; *see also* race; racial hygiene; racial hygienist; racialization; racialized body; racial pathology; racial violence; racism

racial pathology, 98, 258, 274; *see also* race; race degeneration; racism; racial hygiene; racial hygienist; racialization; racialized body; racial mythology; racial violence

racial violence, 283, 298–9, 301–03; *see also* race; race degeneration; racial hygiene; racial hygienist; racialization; racialized body; racial mythology; racial pathology; racism

racism, xii, xiv, 29, 50, 74, 83, 119, 131, 173, 220, 237, 258–9, 274–5, 279–83, 285, 288–9, 292–3, 303, 306, 313, 354, 362; *see also* race; race degeneration; racial hygiene; racial hygienist; racialization; racialized body; racial mythology; racial pathology; racial violence

Rafter, Nicole Hahn, xiii, 74

rape, 4, 16–17, 116–17, 282, 287, 292, 294; *see also* sexual violence

rationality, 1, 19–20, 79, 162, 225, 324, 329, 342, 362

rationalization, xiii, 2, 8, 12, 20, 56, 330, 342

rational man, 324

Razack, Sherene H., xiv, 282–3

reconstructing bodies, 199, 201

reflective, 14, 26, 281; *see also* reflexivity

reflexive modernity, 148

reflexivity, x, 309; *see also* reflective

reformulation, 240, 246–8, 250; *see also* rejection; reliance

reification, xiv, 9, 12, 258, 274, 276

rejection, 240, 245–6, 249, 250; *see also* reformulation; reliance

reliance, 107, 190, 240, 246–8, 250, 337, 370; *see also* reformulation; rejection

Renaissance, ix, xi, 13, 17, 28, 40–1, 311, 334, 339–40, 369, 374–5

reproductive choice, 282–3, 290–5, 297

reproductive continuum, 282

reproductive firsts, 174, 189

reproductive freedom, 290–1, 294

resistance, 5, 15, 17, 22, 24–6, 63, 77, 102, 125, 134, 138, 150–1, 153, 155, 162, 211, 219, 222, 226, 238, 249, 251, 258, 260, 265, 294, 306–07, 312, 314–20, 356, 374, 375

risk, x, xiii, 9–10, 16, 55, 69–71, 77, 125, 127, 148–59, 161–3, 173–5, 186–7, 227, 235, 291, 318, 326–7, 337–8, 341, 343, 346–7, 349, 364, 366, 370

risk assessment, 148, 152, 154–5, 157, 159, 162; *see also* individualization of risk; risk; risk culture; risk society

risk culture, 148; *see also* individualization of risk; risk; risk assessment; risk society

risk society, 148, 150, 162–3; *see also* individualization of risk; risk; risk assessment; risk culture

Roberts, Dorothy E., xiv, 282–3

Rogers, Anne, vi, xiv, 148, 150–1, 153, 155

Rose, Nikolas, xiii, xiv, 196–7, 212

Russell, Susan, 196–7

sado-masochism, 308

scientific management, 43, 219–20; *see also* Taylor, Frederic W.; Taylorism

secularization, 25, 40

self-care, 195, 199, 201–02, 342, 347

self-discipline, 5, 61, 73, 81, 270, 342; *see also* body discipline; self-policing; self-surveillance; technologies of the self

self-policing 4, 5, 25, 26, 73, 173; *see also* body discipline; self-discipline; self-surveillance; technologies of the self

self-surgery, 364–365; *see also* surgery

self-surveillance 21, 26, 260; *see also* self-discipline; self-policing; technologies of the self

senility, 327, 342–7

sex, xi, xiii, 2–4, 10, 13, 15, 16, 19, 24–5, 29, 36, 38, 40, 42, 44–9, 52, 59–62, 91–2, 98, 103, 107, 111–14, 116–22, 124–5, 127, 129, 133–6, 139–41, 143, 144–6, 147, 172, 175, 183, 210–11, 228, 234, 236–8, 240, 248–51, 253–6, 267, 269–72, 281–2, 291–4, 298–301, 304–06, 308, 310–11, 312, 316, 318, 320–2, 324–8, 330, 333–41, 351, 356–7, 359, 361, 362; *see also* sexism; sexology; sexuality; sexualized body; sexual violence

sexism, xii, 52, 282, 292, 294; *see also* sex; sexology; sexuality; sexualized body; sexual violence

sexology, 85, 327, 336; *see also* sex; sexism; sexuality; sexualized body; sexual violence

sexuality, xii–xiv, 3–4, 10, 13, 16–17, 20, 25, 29–30, 39, 45–6, 48–50, 60, 83, 107, 109–11, 113, 116–17, 124–5, 128, 133–9, 141, 144, 146, 205, 211, 246, 249–50, 256, 260, 265–6, 281, 289, 292, 304, 307, 310, 337–9, 341, 351, 354, 356, 358, 362, 365, 367; *see also* sex; sexism; sexology; sexualized body; sexual violence

sexualized body, 4, 15–16, 236–7; *see also* sex; sexism; sexology; sexuality; sexual violence

sexual violence 114, 299–300, 311; *see also* rape

Shilling, Chris, ix, xii, 1–2, 29, 203–05, 211, 281, 283, 305, 307, 309–10, 312, 337, 341–2, 348, 351

Shroud of Turin, 373

sick role, 3, 16

signifiers, 49, 268–9, 286, 338; *see also* expressions given; expressions given off; impression management; presentation of self; sign vehicles

sign vehicles, 51, 53; *see also* expressions given; expressions given off; impression management; presentation of self; signifiers

social capital, xi, 2

social construction, xiv, 10, 13, 15, 24, 57, 125, 217, 250, 288, 326, 359

social control, x–xii, 4–5, 7–8, 28, 30, 40, 73–5, 77–82, 86, 88, 90, 94, 96, 98, 124, 137, 157–8, 162, 173, 180, 189, 205, 289, 342

social death, 347

social facts, 9, 117

social figuration, ix, x, 28

socialization, xiii, 10, 36, 118, 122, 153, 195–6, 202–03, 213, 248, 257, 276, 278, 300, 303, 342

social model of disability, xiii, 239–41; *see also* disability; disabled body; medical model of disability; physical disability

social space, xi, xii, 14, 173, 211, 253

sociobiology, 116–18, 181, 258, 278

sociological imagination, 7, 239–40

Socrates, 38

somatic illness, 42

somatic sensation, 69

spatial appropriation, 22–3, 205, 208

spoiled identities, 6, 52, 57, 63, 75, 132; *see also* discreditable stigma; discrediting stigma; stigma; stigma management

sport, 12–13, 18–19, 22, 117, 119–23, 249, 257–61, 265–7, 271–7, 279–80, 304, 320; *see also* exercise

Stelarc, 352, 361, 363, 365–8

St Louis, Brett, xiv, 258–9

stereotypes, 11, 171, 179, 253, 258

sterilization, 42, 77, 83, 88, 96, 98, 100, 213, 290, 294–5

stigma, xiii, 4, 6, 16, 44, 51–2, 57, 60, 62, 74–5, 81–2, 132, 137, 237–8, 240, 265, 295, 307, 364; *see also* discrediting stigma; discreditable stigma; spoiled identities; stigma management; stigmata

stigma management, 52, 240; *see also* discrediting stigma; discreditable stigma; spoiled identities; stigma

stigmata, 47–8, 85–6; *see also* stigma

Stoicism, 39

surgery, x, 4, 12, 18, 43, 117, 130, 133–5, 137–43, 145–6, 153, 166, 180, 233, 235–6, 306, 316, 320–5, 360, 362, 366–7, 369, 370, 373–4; *see also* self-surgery

surveillance, 2, 4, 12, 21, 25–6, 42, 69, 73, 78–9, 153, 157, 159, 173, 195, 343, 370; *see also* self-policing; self-surveillance

symbolic capital, xi, 2

symbolic interactionism, x

Synnott, Anthony, xii, 28, 30, 44, 171, 218, 220, 314, 320

talking body, 4, 15

tattoo, xii, xiv, 42, 86, 128, 146, 234, 236, 255, 265, 302, 305, 308–10, 312, 363–4, 368

Taylor, Frederic W., 43, 219–20; *see also* scientific management; Taylorism

Taylorism, 219; *see also* scientific management; Taylor, Frederic W.

techno-individualism, 362

technologies of the self, 78, 81, 83, 348; *see also* disciplined body; self-discipline; self-policing; self-surveillance

time management, 219

time-out rooms, xiii, 75–82

tongue splitting, 363

total institutions, xiii, 73, 75–6, 78–80, 82

transcending body stories, 141–2, 145–6; *see also* body stories; erasing body stories; migrating body stories; oscillating body stories

transgender, xi, xiii, 125–6, 137, 141–7, 362

transgressive bodies, xiii, 124–47, 263

transhuman, 350–3

transsexual, xi, 126, 137, 141–3, 145–7, 362

transvestite, 141, 144, 372; *see also* cross-dresser

Turner, Bryan S., xii, 3, 6, 8–9, 11, 13–15, 19–20, 61, 64–5, 72, 205, 211, 307, 312, 325, 341

unbounded bodies, 150, 165, 167–71, 175

uncivilized bodies, 242, 247, 327–8; *see also* civilized body; civilizing process; de-civilized body

urbanization, 29

urology, 138, 140, 327

Viagra, xiv, 338–341

Virgin Mary, 373

virtual body/virtual bodies, 26, 52, 57–8, 61, 65, 142, 352, 360–1, 366–7, 369, 372

Weber, Max, xi, 1–2, 8–9, 13–14, 19–20

Weitz, Rose, x, xiv, 306–307, 317, 320

Wesely, Jennifer K., xiv, 219, 220

white feminine vulnerability, 287

whiteness, xiv, 30, 44, 46, 48–9, 58, 74, 100, 104, 107–08, 119, 128, 131, 184, 237, 261–2, 274–7, 280–2, 284–9, 293–4, 298–304, 308, 310, 317–18, 320, 345, 356, 358, 367, 369; *see also* race

Wilson, Robert, 326, 328, 332

workers' bodies, ix, xiii, 2, 5, 9, 12, 14, 23, 26, 41–3, 73, 80, 83, 119, 218–39, 244, 255, 294, 314, 256

Zitzelsberger, Hilde, xiv, 240–1